Fodor's Pacific North Coast

Tenth New Edition

D1015200

Fodor's Travel Publications, Inc.
New York • Toronto • London • Sydney • Auckland

Fodor's Pacific North Coast

Editor: Larry Peterson
Contributors: Steven K. Amsterdam, Tom Barr, Robert Brown, Susan Brown, Ray Chatelin, John Doerper, Mary Engel, Tom Gaunt, Alison Hoffman, Eve Johnson, Jeff Kuechle, Mike Miller, Glenn W. Sheehan, Loralee Wenger, Terri Wershler, Adam Woog
Creative Director: Fabrizio La Rocca
Cartographer: David Lindroth
Illustrator: Karl Tanner
Cover Photograph: D. Carriere/H. Armstrong Roberts

Design: Vignelli Associates

Special Sales

Contents

Foreword   *vi*

Highlights   *ix*

Fodor's Choice   *xii*

Introduction   *xxii*

1 Essential Information   *1*

Before You Go *2*

Visitor Information *2*
Tours and Packages *2*
When to Go *4*
Festivals and Seasonal Events *5*
What to Pack *8*
Taking Money Abroad *9*
Getting Money from Home *9*
Currency *10*
What It Will Cost *10*
Passports and Visas *11*
Customs *12*
Traveling with Cameras, Camcorders, and Laptops *12*
Language *13*
Insurance *13*
Car Rentals *15*
Rail Passes *16*
Student and Youth Travel *16*
Traveling with Children *17*
Hints for Travelers with Disabilities *18*
Hints for Older Travelers *20*
Further Reading *21*

Arriving and Departing *21*

From the North America by Plane *21*
From the U.S. by Car *24*
From the U.S. by Train *24*
From the U.S. by Bus *25*
From the U.K. by Plane *25*

Staying in the Pacific North Coast *25*

Getting Around *25*
Telephones *30*
Radio Stations *30*
Mail *30*
Tipping *31*
Opening and Closing Times *31*
Shopping *31*
Participant Sports and Outdoor Activities *32*
Spectator Sports *36*

Beaches *36*
Dining *37*
Lodging *38*
Credit Cards *40*

Great Itineraries *40*

2 Portraits of the Pacific North Coast 47

"Pacific Northwest Microbrews: Good for What Ales You,"
by Jeff Kuechle *48*
"In the Footsteps of the First Settlers,"
by Glenn W. Sheehan *54*

3 Portland 60

4 Western Oregon 105

5 Seattle 151

6 Washington State 216

7 Vancouver 262

8 British Columbia 325

9 Southeast Alaska 359

Index 406

Maps

Pacific North Coast *xvi–xvii*
The United States *xviii–xix*
World Time Zones *xx–xxi*
Downtown Portland *65*
Portland Outside City Center *71*
Portland Dining *80–81*
Portland Lodging *86–87*
Eastern Oregon *96*
Oregon *108–109*
The Oregon Coast and Willamette Valley/Wine Country *112*
Salem *124*
Downtown Seattle *158–159*
Metropolitan Seattle *162*
Downtown Seattle Dining *174–175*
Metropolitan Seattle Dining *176*
Seattle Lodging *182–183*
Puget Sound *199*
Washington *218–219*
Bellingham/Whatcom and Skagit Counties *224*

Tacoma *228*
Olympic Peninsula *232*
Long Beach Peninsula *237*
Yakima Valley *241*
Vancouver Exploring *264–265*
Tour 1: Downtown Vancouver *271*
Tour 2: Stanley Park *276*
Tour 3: Granville Island *279*
Downtown Vancouver Dining *290*
Greater Vancouver Dining *291*
Vancouver Lodging *299*
Downtown Victoria *310*
Vancouver Island *331*
British Columbia *338–339*
Southeast Alaska *366*
Ketchikan *368*
Wrangell *371*
Petersburg *373*
Sitka *375*
Juneau *379*
Haines *381*
Skagway *385*

Foreword

We wish to express our gratitude to those who have helped with this guide, including Portland/Oregon Visitors Association; Oregon Historical Society; Seattle/King County News Bureau, especially Barry Anderson and David Blandford; Elvira Quarin at Tourism Vancouver; The Whistler Resort Association; Robert Brown with the Canadian Consulate General; and Hinda Simon.

While every care has been taken to ensure the accuracy of the information in this guide, the passage of time will always bring change, and consequently, the publisher cannot accept responsibility for errors that may occur.

All prices and opening times quoted here are based on information supplied to us at press time. Hours and admission fees may change, however, and the prudent traveler will avoid inconvenience by calling ahead.

Fodor's wants to hear about your travel experiences, both pleasant and unpleasant. When a hotel or restaurant fails to live up to its billing, let us know and we will investigate the complaint and revise our entries where the facts warrant it.

Send your letters to the editors of Fodor's Travel Publications, 201 E. 50th Street, New York, NY 10022.

Highlights and Fodor's Choice

Highlights

Oregon The world's largest airplane, **Howard Hughes's *Spruce Goose,*** was bought by an Oregon aviation company in 1992 and moved from its former home in Long Beach, California. It is now the centerpiece of a new tourist attraction, the **Evergreen AirVenture Museum** in McMinnville, Oregon (40 miles south of Portland), that is scheduled to open in late 1995. AirVenture's collection includes such World War II–era planes as a B-17 Flying Fortress, a Spitfire XVI, P-51 Mustang, an ME-109 Messerschmidt, P-38 Lightning, along with an E-75 Steerman, among many others. What makes this aviation museum unique is that all of its exhibits can and do fly—the facility adjoins McMinnville Municipal Airport, which will be used for daily demonstration flights. The museum grounds will also include an aircraft restoration facility, a youth aviation camp, and a weekend farmer's market showcasing Willamette Valley produce.

One of the jewels of the National Park system, **Crater Lake Lodge** is scheduled to reopen in May 1995 after an exhaustive three-year renovation. Crafted from native stone and timber in 1914, the lodge perches on the crater's rim some 1,000-feet above the lake's sapphire-colored surface. Views from the hotel's 75 guest rooms, and from the soaring, fire-lit Great Hall and formal lakeside dining room, are among the most spectacular in the region. Rugged-looking Mission-style hickory bark and peeled log furnishings were carefully chosen to re-create the lodge's original romantic, western rustic grandeur.

Washington Although Seattle may not be quite as "hot" a destination as it was over the past few years, it still ranks way up there among U.S. cities to visit. A recent survey of 30,000 *Conde Nast Traveler* magazine readers pegged Seattle as the **fourth-favorite metropolitan destination** in the country. Although some locals say that greater Seattle has sprawled itself right out of its charm, there are still plenty of reasons to visit, and some of the most appealing are everyday local phenomena rather than official tourist sites—sidewalk espresso stands, microbrews, micropubs, and a lively nightlife scene that ranges from opera to grunge rock, Shakespeare to improvisation.

A must-see in town is Woodland Park Zoo's **tropical rain forest exhibit,** which opened in 1992. The exhibit, which takes visitors through the complex layers of a rain forest, was named the best in the country in 1993 by the American Association of Zoological Parks and Aquariums.

In the fall of 1993, the **Seattle Children's Theatre** opened the **Charlotte Martin Theatre,** a $10 million facility adjacent to the Pacific Science Center at the Seattle Center. SCT is the second-largest professional resident children's theater company in the country, and has commissioned more than 55 new plays, adaptations, and musicals, many of which have gone on to be produced by theater companies across the United States.

Elsewhere in the state, interpretive centers are wowing the crowds with up-close-and-personal views of the natural world. Visitors to the **Mount St. Helens National Volcanic Monument** taking Exit 49 from I–5 and proceeding 5 miles east on Route 504 can see a video and slide show of the mountain's volcanic eruption in May of 1980 at the (original) Mount St. Helens Visitor Center at Silver Lake. Another 38 miles to the east—and nearer the exploded mountain— is the new **Coldwater Ridge Visitor Center,** which opened in May 1993 after the connecting highway was completed. There are slide shows, interpretive displays, and hands-on exhibits on the return of plant and animal life to this area that was so devastated by the volcanic blast. There are trails, and the glass-domed center provides spectacular panoramic views of the crater, which is some 7 miles away; Coldwater Lake; and the mud flows in the Toutle River Valley. The center also has a bookstore, gift shop, and cafeteria.

A new $10.5 million **Columbia Gorge Interpretive Center** is set to open at Stevenson in May 1995, replacing the Skamania County Historical Museum in the lower level of the courthouse annex. The center, across the street from the Skamania Lodge and Conference Center, is designed to resemble the sawmill that once stood on the site, which overlooks the Columbia River and Rock Creek Cove. An interpretation of the walls of the Columbia River Gorge will wind through the facility, and a series of tableaux and dioramas will depict the area's natural and cultural heritage. Exhibits will remain on display in the museum until the new center opens.

Alaska   **CampAlaska Tours,** a popular tour operator offering outdoor vacations throughout the state, has added a sister company, **Alaska Travel Alternatives,** that emphasizes even more challenging adventure vacations, such as river running. Indeed, the popularity of this kind of special-interest travel continues to increase here, and Alaskan tour operators are rising to the challenge by offering more and more kayaking, backpacking, bird-watching, and other intriguing trips. The adventure traveler has many options here.

The **White Pass & Yukon Route** (WP & YR) in Skagway, Southeast Alaska, keeps chugging along. Dating from the turn-of-the-century Klondike gold rush, the revived narrow-gauge railroad offers scenic excursions between Skagway and the 2,865-foot summit of the gold trail called White Pass—20 miles each way. The WP & YR has extended the trip 8 miles to Fraser, British Columbia, and has provided connections for motorcoach passengers traveling between

Whitehorse, capital of Canada's Yukon Territory, and Skagway.

The rail line also offers a rail-motorcar service for hikers crossing the famed Chilkoot Pass, a main route to the Klondike gold fields in 1897–98. Motorcars (small work cars on rails) depart Lake Bennett, British Columbia, for the 41-mile trip to Skagway each morning from mid-June to mid-September.

British Columbia The high-speed ferry service **Sealink Express,** carrying passengers only, continues to effortlessly transport visitors from downtown Vancouver to downtown Victoria, allowing visitors to take in both towns without the long trip to and from the regular car-ferry terminals. Another ferry company, Sea Containers, Ltd., is currently refurbishing its *Princess Marguerite* ferry with possible plans to put it to work on the Vancouver–Prince Rupert route along the Inside Passage. The plans for a new car ferry linking Victoria with Seattle, Washington, are still in the making.

Local Vancouver sightseeing has been improved, too, thanks to the **Vancouver Trolleys,** like old-fashioned streetcars, that take you on a guided tour of all the major attractions (Stanley Park, English Bay, Gastown, Robson Street, Granville Island, the Vancouver Museum, Queen Elizabeth Park, Chinatown, and Science World) for an all-day unlimited-stop ticket.

Fodor's Choice

No two people will agree on what makes a perfect vacation, but it's fun and helpful to know what others think. We hope you'll have a chance to experience some of Fodor's Choices yourself in the Pacific Northwest. For detailed information about each entry, refer to the appropriate chapter.

Portland

Attractions Oregon Museum of Science and Industry

Pioneer Square Courthouse

Portland Building

Salmon Street Plaza fountain

Special Moments Celebrations at The Rheinlander Restaurant

Saturday and Sunday Market

Restaurants Atwater's (*Very Expensive*)

Zefiro (*Expensive*)

Patzzo Ristorante (*Moderate*)

Dan and Louis's Oyster Bar and Restaurant (*Inexpensive*)

Hotels Heathman (*Very Expensive*)

Red Lion/Lloyd Center (*Expensive*)

Ramada Inn Airport (*Moderate*)

Best Western/Fortniter Motel (*Inexpensive*)

Western Oregon

Sights View of the Columbia River Gorge from Crown Point

Multnomah Falls from U.S. 30 and I–84
(Columbia River Gorge)

View of Haystack Rock from the beach (Cannon Beach)

Crater Lake from the rim

Attractions Oregon Coast Aquarium, Newport

Shakespeare Festival Exhibit Center, Ashland

Wildlife Safari, Roseburg

Restaurants The Bistro, Cannon Beach (*Expensive*)

Nick's Italian Cafe, McMinnville (*Expensive*)

Chateaulin, Ashland (*Moderate–Expensive*)

The Chetco River Inn, Brookings (*Moderate*)

La Serre, Yachats (*Moderate*)

The Whale Cove, Port Orford (*Moderate*)

Kum-Yon's, Coos Bay (*Inexpensive*)

Hotels Timberline Lodge, Timberline (*Expensive*)

The Steamboat Inn, Steamboat (*Moderate–Expensive*)

Franklin Street Station Bed & Breakfast, Astoria (*Moderate*)

This Olde House B&B, Coos Bay (*Moderate*)

The Sylvia Beach Hotel, Newport (*Moderate*)

Seattle

Attractions International District

Pike Place Market

Seattle Aquarium

Space Needle

Woodland Park Zoo

Special Moments Sitting in on the "Out to Lunch" concert series at one of Seattle's parks

Seeing Seattle at night from the Space Needle's observation deck

Reading the hundreds of name tiles on the floor of the Pike Place Market

Seeing Mt. Rainier looming above Puget Sound on a clear day when "the mountain comes out"

Hotels Alexis (*Very Expensive*)

Four Seasons Olympic Hotels (*Very Expensive*)

Edgewater (*Expensive*)

Sorrento (*Expensive*)

Inn at the Market (*Moderate–Expensive*)

Meany Tower Hotel (*Inexpensive*)

Restaurants Fuller's (*Expensive*)

The Painted Table (*Expensive*)

Wild Ginger (*Moderate*)

Saigon Gourmet (*Inexpensive*)

Washington

Scenic Travels The 23-mile loop on Highway 11, along Chuckanut Bay

A ferry ride through the San Juan Islands

Highway 101 north from Hoquiam to Quinault Lake and west to Queets and Kalaloch

Attractions	Hoodsport Winery, Hoodsport
	Hovander Homestead Park, Ferndale
	Northwest Trek Wildlife Park, Eatonville
	Point Defiance Park, Tacoma
Hotels	Inn at Langley, Langley (*Expensive*)
	James House, Port Townsend (*Moderate–Expensive*)
	Olde Glencove Hotel, Gig Harbor (*Moderate*)
Restaurants	Il Fiasco, Bellingham (*Expensive–Very Expensive*)
	C'est Si Bon, Port Angeles (*Expensive*)
	The Shoalwater Restaurant, Seaview (*Moderate–Expensive*)
	Alice's Restaurant (*Moderate*)
	Fountain Café, Port Townsend (*Moderate*)
	Tides Tavern, Gig Harbor (*Inexpensive*)

Vancouver

Attractions	Butchart Gardens, Victoria
	Dr. Sun-yat Sen Classical Garden, Stanley Park
	Granville Public Market, Granville Island
	Vancouver Aquarium
Shopping	Fourth Avenue (between Burrard and Balsam streets)
	Government Street, Victoria
	Market Square, Victoria
	Robson Street
Restaurants	Les Deux Gros, Whistler (*Expensive*)
	Tojo's (*Expensive*)
	English Bay Café (*Moderate*)
	The Raintree (*Moderate*)
	Six Mile House, Victoria (*Inexpensive*)
	Phnom Penh (*Inexpensive*)
Hotels	Le Chamois, Whistler (*Very Expensive*)
	Hotel Grand Pacific, Victoria (*Very Expensive*)
	Le Meridien (*Very Expensive*)
	Wedgewood Hotel (*Expensive*)
	Hotel Georgia (*Moderate*)
	Craigmyle Guest House, Victoria (*Inexpensive–Moderate*)
	Sylvia Hotel (*Inexpensive*)

British Columbia

Attractions	O'Keefe Historic Ranch, Okanagan Valley
	Museum of Northern British Columbia, Prince Rupert
	Native Heritage Center, Duncan
Great Outdoors	Adams River Salmon Run, Okanagan Valley
	Inside Passage
	Pacific Rim National Park, Vancouver Island
Restaurants	Sooke Harbour House, Sooke (*Very Expensive*)
	The Aerie, Malahat (*Expensive*)
	The Mahle House, Nanaimo (*Moderate*)
Hotels	The Aerie, Malahat (*Very Expensive*)
	Lake Okanagan Resort, Kelowna (*Very Expensive*)
	The Kingfisher Inn, Courtenay (*Moderate*)
	Lac le Jeune Resort, Kamloops (*Moderate*)

Southeast Alaska

Special Moments	The howl of a train whistle near Skagway
	The roll of a humpback whale in Glacier Bay
	A misty morning in Sitka with bald eagles on high
	The scream of a salmon reel near Ketchikan
	Helicopter flightseeing over Juneau's glaciers
Activities	Rafting through an eagle sanctuary near Haines
	Watching Indian totem carvers at Ketchikan
	Hiking the route of the gold rush on the Chilkoot trail near Skagway
	Stopping in to the Red Dog Saloon in Juneau
Hotels	Glacier Bay Lodge, Glacier Bay National Park (*Expensive*)
	Captain's Choice Motel, Haines (*Moderate–Expensive*)
	Ingersoll Hotel, Ketchikan (*Moderate*)
	The Prospector, Juneau (*Moderate*)
	Golden North Hotel, Skagway (*Moderate*)
Restaurants	The Channel Club, Sitka (*Moderate–Expensive*)
	The Summit, Juneau (*Moderate–Expensive*)
	Glacier Bay Country Inn, Glacier Bay (*Moderate*)
	Salmon Falls Resort, Ketchikan (*Moderate*)
	The Beachcomber Inn, Petersburg (*Inexpensive*)
	The Fiddlehead, Juneau (*Inexpensive–Moderate*)

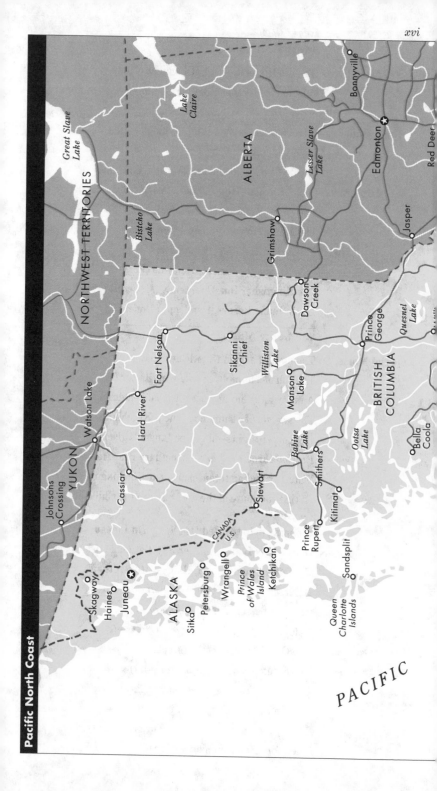

Pacific North Coast

PACIFIC

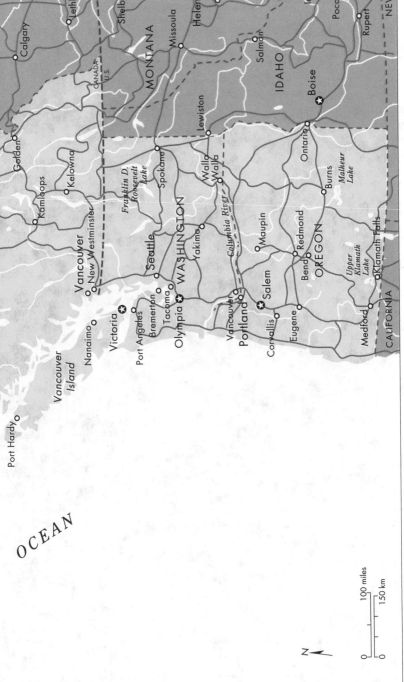

The United States

CANADA

BRITISH COLUMBIA
Vancouver
Calgary
ALBERTA
SASKATCHEWAN
MANITOBA
Regina
Trans-Canada Hwy.
Winnipeg

Seattle
Olympia
WASHINGTON
Columbia
Spokane
Great Falls
Missouri R.
NORTH DAKOTA
Fargo
Portland
Salem
OREGON
IDAHO
Boise
Snake R.
MONTANA
Helena
Billings
Bismarck
SOUTH DAKOTA
Pierre
Missouri R.

WYOMING
Cheyenne
NEBRASKA
Lincoln

Carson City
Sacramento
San Francisco
NEVADA
Salt Lake City
UTAH
Denver
COLORADO
Colorado Springs
KANSAS

Fresno
Las Vegas
Colorado R.
CALIFORNIA
Santa Barbara
Los Angeles
San Diego

ARIZONA
Flagstaff
Phoenix
Tucson
Santa Fe
Albuquerque
NEW MEXICO
El Paso

OKLAHOMA
Oklahoma City
Amarillo

PACIFIC OCEAN

BAJA CALIFORNIA
SONORA
CHIHUAHUA
Rio Grande
MEXICO
COAHUILA

TEXAS
Austin
San Antonio

RUSSIA
ARCTIC OCEAN
Bering Strait
Nome
Bering Sea
ALASKA
Fairbanks
CANADA
Anchorage
ALEUTIAN ISLANDS
Juneau
PACIFIC OCEAN

NUEVO LEON
TAMAULIPAS

Honolulu
Oahu
Maui
HAWAII
Hawaii
PACIFIC OCEAN

0   400 miles
0   400 km

N

World Time Zones

+12 +13

MONDAY
SUNDAY

-9

-10

International Date Line

-11

-10

+11

+12

-3

-4

7

-5   -4

14 15

-3:30

13

5   -8   8   -6   9

16

17

6   10

11

18

12   -4

22

19

-5

20   -4   -3

-3

23

-3

21   24

2

+11   +12 -   -11   -10   -9   -8   -7   -6   -5   -4   -3   -2

Numbers below vertical bands relate each zone to Greenwich Mean Time (0 hrs.).
Local times frequently differ from these general indications,
as indicated by light-face numbers on map.

Algiers, **29**   Berlin, **34**   Delhi, **48**   Istanbul, **40**
Anchorage, **3**   Bogotá, **19**   Denver, **8**   Jerusalem, **42**
Athens, **41**   Budapest, **37**   Djakarta, **53**   Johannesburg, **44**
Auckland, **1**   Buenos Aires, **24**   Dublin, **26**   Lima, **20**
Baghdad, **46**   Caracas, **22**   Edmonton, **7**   Lisbon, **28**
Bangkok, **50**   Chicago, **9**   Hong Kong, **56**   London (Greenwich), **27**
Beijing, **54**   Copenhagen, **33**   Honolulu, **2**   Los Angeles, **6**
                         Dallas, **10**   Madrid, **38**
                                                                              Manila, **57**

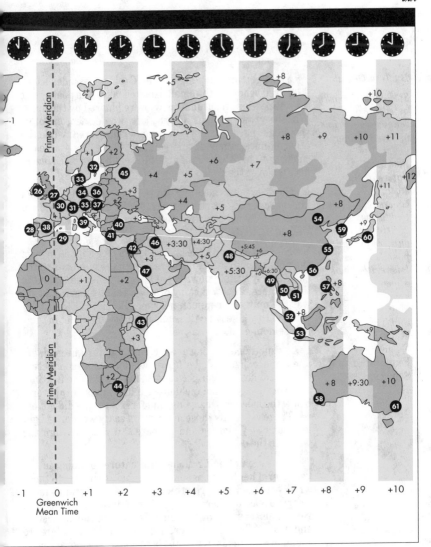

Mecca, **47**

Mexico City, **12**

Miami, **18**

Montréal, **15**

Moscow, **45**

Nairobi, **43**

New Orleans, **11**

New York City, **16**

Ottawa, **14**

Paris, **30**

Perth, **58**

Reykjavík, **25**

Rio de Janeiro, **23**

Rome, **39**

Saigon (Ho Chi Minh City), **51**

San Francisco, **5**

Santiago, **21**

Seoul, **59**

Shanghai, **55**

Singapore, **52**

Stockholm, **32**

Sydney, **61**

Tokyo, **60**

Toronto, **13**

Vancouver, **4**

Vienna, **35**

Warsaw, **36**

Washington, D.C., **17**

Yangon, **49**

Zürich, **31**

Introduction

By Tom Gaunt

Tom Gaunt works as editor of the magazine section of The Business Journal of Portland. *A native of the state, Tom has covered Northwest politics and culture for the past 12 years. His writing has appeared in* Pacific Northwest Magazine, OMNI, *and* The Oregon Magazine of Nature, Exploration and Science.

It was getting dark high in the Oregon Cascades as we rowed ashore at the small, isolated lake. The peaks, just wrapped in an autumn snow, were blurred by the dusk. With less than an hour of light left, we decided one of us should get back to camp quickly, unencumbered, while the other deflated the raft and carried it back the 4 miles to camp, with little chance of making it out before pitch blackness fell over the dense forest.

Maybe it was because my brother is older and has bad knees, or perhaps it was just because I was soaking wet and needed to change anyway. But I elected to be the one who walked in the dark.

Soon I was alone with the lake as a wispy fog slipped in from the upper basin; the tall firs creaked in the wind and to the east, barely visible now, three rugged peaks shrugged in the distance. I knew that my brother, rapidly moving away, was the only other human near me. Behind me were hundreds of tiny lakes like this one, all empty and quiet in their own seldom-explored basins.

I was very alone, feeling at once joyous and frightened, exalted and exhausted, both overwhelmed and completely free. I had not just *connected* with nature in some fleeting, superficial way; I had melded with it. Things of the world below the meadows, canyons, and forests simply did not exist. There were only those moments of scary wonder as I got into some dry clothes and prepared to walk through the woods in the dark.

The sensation of being alone with nature, of being in the very cup of her hands, is something that is familiar to those who live in the Pacific Northwest. There are certainly more remote areas, but here nature can be enjoyed for what it is. Here man seems to have found his niche in the ecosystem and, more or less, stays there as pleased with his failures to conquer nature as with his occasional, temporary successes.

To understand the people of the Pacific Northwest—and there are roughly 10 million of us in an area about the size of Western Europe—one has to understand the land and the climate and how the two combine to cast their spell. For even in the cities of the Pacific Northwest, nature is never far away. In Seattle, Mount Rainier and the Olympics entrance commuters stuck in traffic; in Vancouver, British Columbia, the Coast Range juts out over downtown, keeping the metropolis in line; and in Portland, city fathers have kept 4,700 acres of primitive forestlands that harbor deer, elk, and the odd bear and cougar in the hills just north of the city center. It's not a zoo, it's just there, a piece of primeval forest that serves as a constant reminder of nature's endur-ing presence here. No matter how many planes Seattle's Boeing Corporation churns out, or how many chips come out of Oregon's high-tech Silicon Forest, or how many shares of stock change hands in the volatile Vancouver Stock Exchange, the relationship with nature and the wilds is not altered. There is always this mixture of respect and love, fear and admiration, topped off with simple awe.

These feelings come naturally when you survey the land-scape—an array of shapes, colors, textures—but still there are the simultaneous sensations of solitude and inclusion. To understand, look at the far corners of this land: southern Alaska and southeastern Oregon.

Swathed in Sitka spruce, the islands scattered below the Alaskan mountains are like small individual worlds. Roads and people are few. The intrepid can kayak through the in-lets and fjords for days on end, catching salmon or watching the glaciers peel majestically off into the sea, sheet by sheet. Roughly in the middle of this region is Juneau, the only state capital that is inaccessible by road. Here it is common for legislative aides to live in makeshift camps in the hills above town and ski to the state's modest capitol building. Behind the coast ranges are deep, remote river canyons and lakes that stretch all the way east to where the mighty Rockies dribble off into a few bumps on the tundra. Moving south along Coastal British Columbia, the terrain is no less steep, but the glaciers shrink back into the hang-ing valleys, leaving only a few waterfalls. Other than fish-ing vessels and the occasional cruise ship, this is lonely country, beautiful, but often pelted with wild rain storms and blizzards that blast straight across the north Pacific.

L ikewise, southeast Oregon is solitary country. It is a land of extremes, a high desert where it is not at all uncommon, especially in the spring or fall, to find the highest and lowest temperature reading in the lower 48 states in the same county. A 100-mile drive across the de-sert and scrub land is not likely to turn up another soul. What people there are—many of them descendants of Basque settlers a century ago—tend to their stock on the arid plains. The land is dominated by Steens' Mountain, a 60-mile-long slab of desert floor that over the millennia gradually tilted upward. From the west, the gain in eleva-tion is barely noticeable at first, just a steppe rolling into the distance. But after 30 miles of bad road, the mountain simply breaks off into space, the Alvord Desert a gasping 5,000 feet below. And beyond, the gray horizon fades into Nevada and Idaho.

Whether it is the cathedrallike island forests of southern Alaska or the sagebrush-covered frontier of southeastern Oregon, the awe is there—subtle yet omnipresent. In many ways, the land here shapes us, mellowing and hypnotizing us until other ways of life seem improbably complicated. I

don't know how many people I've known who come back
from visiting New York or San Francisco or some other fa-
mously bustling place and say something along the lines of,
"It was very exciting, but I don't know why anyone would
go to the trouble of living there."

Go to the trouble . . . A key phrase. In the Pacific Northwest, going to the trouble is more likely to be the conse-
quence of some recreational choice. You go to the trouble of
rafting a river just for the hell of it; you go to the trouble of
hiking to the top of a butte you've never climbed before; or
you go to the trouble of taking a road in the baking deserts
of eastern Oregon and Washington just to see the mirages
disappear as you approach them.

Okay, so Pacific Northwesterners may seem a bit
flaky—carefree, perhaps—but some say this con-
tagious attitude simply comes with the land. The
Native Americans of the Pacific Northwest had it pretty
easy compared with their brethren on the Great Plains.
Whereas a family of Sioux might need to scour 100 square
miles of land to get enough food to live on, West Coast Indians only needed to dip into the river for fish or take a few
steps out of the village for game. Sure, the weather was
damp, but wood for shelter and warmth was plentiful and
the time saved gathering food went toward monumental
projects of art such as the totems of Coastal British Columbia.

Even today this plenty is obvious. While Pacific Northwest
cuisine has become popular on some menus, picking a single
cuisine here is a difficult task. Most distinctive cuisines of
the world have developed because of shortages, not bounty;
folks had only a few basic items, and they had to be creative
in cooking them up in different ways. But in the Pacific
Northwest, food is seldom a problem. The ocean and rivers
teem with scallops, crab, salmon, crayfish, sturgeon, and
everything in between. The region abounds with fresh water. Wineries and breweries are liberally scattered
throughout the area. The Hood River and Yakima, Okanagan, and Rogue valleys are famous for their orchards. Dair-
ies dot the western areas and cattle graze the eastern
expanses on ranches the size of Delaware.

In the Pacific Northwest, rich is defined as living a clean
life; nature deals the bonuses. What people here compro-
mise in salaries, they are compensated for by having the opportunity to hike, fish, hunt, or just wake up every morning
with a view of a forest. Some might call this simple living,
others just call it wacky. Some examples: Portland has
twice elected as mayor a local tavern owner who bikes
around the city in lederhosen and calls out "Whoop, whoop"
at the drop of a photo opportunity. And a few years ago,
there was a strong effort (serious does not seem to be the
right word) to make the rock-and-roll classic "Louie,
Louie" the state song of Washington.

Is there some sort of pattern here? Perhaps all the rain twists great and creative minds? When Lewis and Clark arrived almost 200 years ago, the rain almost drove them crazy, and that was after only one winter! Imagine a lifetime of gray winters; you look out of your window in October at a line of dark clouds rolling in from the west and know there will be only a handful of clear days (probably below freezing) until mid-March. Northwest author Ken Kesey has blamed everything from impotence to union problems on this drizzly season. True, residents of the Pacific Northwest drink more and are more likely to commit suicide than others in the country, but it may be that the weather helps us keep a sense of the absurd and the macabre; for example, in Portland's new Oregon Convention Center the men's rooms have etchings of Oregon waterfalls perched above the urinals.

So we're a little eccentric. But remember, when an impulse sends you ripping down an untracked ski run or landing a thrashing steelhead in a river at flood stage, the humdrum details of daily life become pretty ridiculous, like some sort of cosmic joke, and you fade back to a private place, to *your* lake beneath the peaks. Just before dark.

1 Essential Information

Before You Go

Visitor Information

For free travel information, contact the following tourism offices:

In the U.S. **Alaska Division of Tourism** (Dept. 909, Box 110801, Juneau, AK 99811–0801, tel. 907/465–2010).
Oregon Tourism Division (775 Summer St. NE, Salem, OR 97310, tel. 800/543–8838 in OR or 800/547–7842 out of state).
Washington Tourism Development Division (Box 45213, Olympia, WA 98504, tel. 206/586–2088, 206/586–2102, or 800/544–1800).

In Canada **Tourism British Columbia** (1117 Wharf St., Victoria, B.C. V8W 2Z2, tel. 800/663–6000).

In the U.K. For touring tips and brochures, contact the **United States Travel and Tourism Administration** (Box 1EN, London WIA 1EN, tel. 071/495–4466), **Canadian High Commission, Tourism Division** (Canada House, Trafalgar Sq., London SW1Y 5BJ, tel. 071/930–6857), or **Tourism British Columbia** (1 Regent St., London SW1Y 4NS, tel. 071/930–6857).

Tours and Packages

Should you buy your travel arrangements to the Pacific North Coast packaged or do it yourself? There are advantages either way. Buying packaged arrangements saves you money, particularly if you can find a program that includes exactly the features you want. You also get a pretty good idea of what your trip will cost from the outset. Generally, you have two options: fully escorted tours and independent packages. Escorted tours are most often via motorcoach, with a tour director in charge. They're ideal if you don't mind having limited free time and traveling with strangers. Your baggage is handled, your time rigorously scheduled, and most meals planned. Such tours are therefore the most hassle-free way to see a destination, as well as generally the least expensive. Independent packages allow plenty of flexibility. They generally include airline travel and hotels, with certain options available, such as sightseeing, car rental, and excursions. Such packages are usually more expensive than escorted tours, but your time is your own.

While you can book directly through tour operators, you will pay no more to go through a travel agent, who will be able to tell you about tours and packages from a number of operators. Whatever program you ultimately choose, be sure to find out exactly what is included: taxes, tips, transfers, meals, baggage handling, ground transportation, entertainment, excursions, sports or recreation (and rental equipment if necessary). Ask about the level of hotel used, its location, the size of its rooms, the kind of beds, and its amenities, such as pool, room service, or programs for children, if they're important to you. Find out the operator's cancellation penalties. Nearly everyone charges them, and the only way to avoid them is to buy trip-cancellation insurance (*see* Trip Insurance, *below*). Also ask about the single supplement, a surcharge assessed to solo travelers. Some operators do not make you pay it if you agree to be matched up with a roommate of the same sex, even if one is not found by departure time. Remember that a program that has features you won't use may not be the most cost-wise choice for you.

Fully Escorted Tours Escorted tours are usually sold in three categories: deluxe, first-class, and tourist or budget class. The most important differences are the price, of course, and the level of accommodations. Some operators specialize in one category, while others offer a range.

Contact **Maupintour** (Box 807, Lawrence, KS 66044, tel. 913/843–1211 or 800/255–4266) and **Tauck Tours** (11 Wilton Rd., Westport, CT 06881, tel. 203/226–6911 or 800/468–2825) in the deluxe category; **Brendan Tours** (15137 Califa St., Van Nuys, CA 91411, tel. 818/985–9696 pr 800/421–8446), **Brennan Tours** (1402 3rd Ave., Suite 717, Seattle, WA 98101, tel. 206/622–9155 or 800/237–7249), **Caravan Tours** (401 N. Michigan Ave., Chicago, IL 60611, tel. 312/321–9800 or 800/227–2826), **Gadabout Tours** (700 E. Tahquitz Way, Palm Springs, CA 92262, tel. 619/325–5556 or 800/952–5068), **Globus** (150 S. Los Robles Ave., Pasadena, CA 91101, tel. 818/449–0919 or 800/556–5454), **Holland American Westours** (300 Elliott Ave. W., Seattle, WA 98119, tel. 206/281–3535 or 800/426–0327), and **Princess Tours** (2815 2nd Ave., Suite 400, Seattle, WA 98121, tel. 206/728–4202) in the first-class category; and **Cosmos,** a division of Globus (at the same number), and **Gray Line of Seattle** (720 S. Forest St., Seattle, WA 98134, tel. 206/624–5813) in the budget category.

Most itineraries are jam-packed with sightseeing, so you see a lot in a short amount of time (usually one place per day). To judge just how fast-paced the tour is, review the itinerary carefully. If you are in a different hotel each night, you will be getting up early each day to head out, travel to your next destination, do some sightseeing, have dinner, and go to bed; then you'll start all over again. If you want some free time, make sure it's mentioned in the tour brochure; if you want to be escorted to every meal, confirm that any tour you consider does that. Also, when comparing programs, be sure to find out if the motorcoach is air-conditioned and has a rest room on board. Make your selection based on price and stops on the itinerary.

Independent Packages Independent packages are usually offered by airlines, tour operators who may also do escorted programs, and any number of other companies from large, established firms to small, new entrepreneurs. Most packages to the Pacific North Coast are through the major airlines that service the area.

Contact **American Airlines Fly AAway Vacations** (tel. 800/321–2121) and **United Airlines' Vacation Planning Center** (tel. 800/328–6877).

Programs come in a wide range of prices based on levels of luxury and options—in addition to hotel and airfare, sightseeing, car rental, transfers, admission to local attractions, and other extras. Note that when pricing different packages, it sometimes pays to purchase the same arrangements separately, as when a rock-bottom promotional airfare is being offered, for example. Again, base your choice on what's available in your budget for the destinations you want to visit.

Special-Interest Travel Special-interest programs may be fully escorted or independent. Some require a certain amount of expertise, but most are for the average traveler with an interest and are usually hosted by experts in the subject matter. When the program is escorted, it enjoys the advantages and disadvantages of all escorted programs; because your fellow travelers are apt to be passionate or knowledgeable about the subject, they can prove as enjoyable a part of your travel experience as the destination itself. The price range is wide, but the cost is usually higher—sometimes a lot higher—than for ordinary escorted tours and packages, because of the expert guiding and special activities.

Biking **Backroads** (1516 5th St., Suite Q333, Berkely, CA 94710, tel. 510/527–1555 or 800/245–3874) offers a variety of biking programs throughout the Northwest, including Washington, Oregon, Vancouver, and Alaska.

Nature **Oceanic Society Expeditions** (Fort Mason Center, Bldg. E, San Francisco, CA 94123, tel. 415/441–1106 or 800/326–7491) offers a "Killer Whales" expedition off Vancouver Island, with accommodations aboard its 68-foot boat.

Camping and **AmeriCan Adventures** (6762 Cenpinela Ave., Culver City, CA
Wilderness 90230, tel. 310/390–7945 or 800/864–0335) offers individual and group camping trips throughout the West Coast, including Alaska and the Yukon.

The Resource Institute (Box 139, 2319 N. 45th St., Seattle, WA 98103, tel. 206/784–0762) offers cultural and environmental educational tours through Alaska and the Inside Passage.

When to Go

The Pacific North Coast's mild, pleasant climate is best from June through September. Hotels in the major tourist destinations are often filled in July and August, so it's important to book reservations in advance. Summer temperatures generally range in the 70s, and rainfall is usually minimal. Nights, however, can be cool, so if you're going to enjoy the nightlife, take along a sweater or jacket.

Spring and fall are also excellent times to visit. The weather usually remains quite good, and the prices for accommodations, transportation, and tours can be lower (and the crowds much smaller!) in the most popular destinations.

In winter, the coastal rain turns to snow in the nearby mountains, making the region a skier's dream. World-class ski resorts such as British Columbia's Whistler Village are luring a growing number of winter visitors from around the world.

Climate Tempered by a warm Japan current and protected by the mountains from the extreme weather conditions found inland, the coastal regions of Oregon, Washington, British Columbia, and Southeast Alaska experience a uniformly mild climate.

Average daytime summer highs are in the 70s; winter temperatures are generally in the 40s. Snow is uncommon in the lowland areas. If it does snow (usually in December or January), everything grinds to a halt—but children love it!

The area's reputation for rain is somewhat misleading, as the amount of rainfall in the Pacific North Coast varies greatly from one locale to another. In the coastal mountains, for example, 160 inches of rain falls annually, creating temperate rain forests. In eastern Oregon, Washington, and British Columbia, near-desert conditions prevail, with rainfall as low as six inches per year.

Seattle has an average of only 36 inches of rainfall a year—less than New York, Chicago, or Miami. The wetness, however, is concentrated during the winter months, when cloudy skies and drizzly weather persist. More than 75% of Seattle's annual precipitation occurs from October through March.

The following are average daily maximum and minimum temperatures for major cities in the Pacific North Coast region.

Portland	**Jan.**	44F 33	7C 1	**May**	67F 46	19C 8	**Sept.**	74F 51	23C 10
	Feb.	50F 36	10C 2	**June**	72F 52	22C 11	**Oct.**	63F 45	17C 7
	Mar.	54F 37	12C 3	**July**	79F 55	26C 13	**Nov.**	52F 39	11C 4
	Apr.	60F 41	15C 5	**Aug.**	78F 55	25C 13	**Dec.**	46F 35	8C 2

Seattle	**Jan.**	45F 35	7C 2	**May**	66F 47	19C 8	**Sept.**	69F 52	20C 11
	Feb.	50F 37	10C 3	**June**	70F 52	21C 11	**Oct.**	62F 47	16C 8
	Mar.	53F 38	12C 3	**July**	76F 56	24C 13	**Nov.**	51F 40	10C 4
	Apr.	59F 42	13C 5	**Aug.**	75F 55	24C 13	**Dec.**	47F 37	8C 3

Vancouver	**Jan.**	41F 32	5C 0	**May**	63F 46	17C 8	**Sept.**	64F 50	18C 10
	Feb.	46F 34	8C 1	**June**	66F 52	19C 11	**Oct.**	57F 43	14C 6
	Mar.	48F 36	9C 2	**July**	72F 55	22C 13	**Nov.**	48F 37	9C 3
	Apr.	55F 41	13C 5	**Aug.**	72F 55	22C 13	**Dec.**	45F 34	7C 1

Juneau	**Jan.**	29F 18	-2C -8	**May**	55F 38	13C 3	**Sept.**	56F 42	13C 6
	Feb.	34F 22	1C -6	**June**	62F 44	16C 7	**Oct.**	47F 36	8C 2
	Mar.	38F 26	3C -4	**July**	64F 48	18C 9	**Nov.**	37F 28	3C -2
	Apr.	47F 31	8C -1	**Aug.**	62F 46	17C 8	**Dec.**	32F 23	0C -5

Information Sources For current weather conditions for cities in the United States and abroad, plus the local time and helpful travel tips, call the **Weather Channel Connection** (tel. 900/932–8437; 95¢ per minute) from a touch-tone phone.

Festivals and Seasonal Events

The Pacific North Coast comes alive each year in a burst of colorful festivities. The following is a sample of noteworthy seasonal events. For dates and more details, contact the local state or provincial tourism department.

British Columbia **Mid-May. Vancouver Children's Festival,** the largest event of its kind in the world, presents dozens of performances in mime, puppetry, music, and theater. Tel. 604/687–7697.

Late May. Swiftsure Race Weekend draws more than 300 competitors to Victoria's harbor for an international yachting event. Tel. 604/592–2441.

Late May. Victoria Day, a national holiday, is usually celebrated throughout Canada on the penultimate weekend in May.

Late June. Canadian International Dragon Boat Festival, Vancouver is a multicultural festival featuring dragon boat races based on Chinese legend. Community and children's activities, dance, and visual arts are featured. Tel. 604/684–5151.

Late June. Du Maurier International Jazz Festival celebrates a broad spectrum of jazz, blues, and related improvised music, with more than 200 performances in 20 locations in Vancouver. Tel. 604/682–0706.

July 1. Canada Day inspires celebrations around the country in honor of Canada's birthday.

Mid-July. Harrison Festival of the Arts, in Harrison Hot Springs, offers a spectrum of artistic expression with a unique blend of international, national, and regional artists and performers. Tel. 604/796–3664.

Mid-July. Vancouver Sea Festival features water-related activities, such as a wooden- and heritage-boat festival, plus a parade, fireworks, entertainment, and a carnival. Tel. 604/684–3378.

Late July. International Bathtub Race takes to the high seas, from Nanaimo to Vancouver. Tel. 604/754–8474.

Late July–early Aug. Squamish Days is the largest logging sport show in the world, featuring sports events, a chair-carving contest, and a parade. Tel. 604/892–9244.

Early Aug. Abbotsford International Air Show takes off with a three-day extravaganza of military and civilian flight performances and presents a large aircraft display. Tel. 604/852–8511.

Mid-Aug.–early Sept. Pacific National Exhibition, western Canada's biggest annual fair, brings top-name entertainment and a variety of displays to Vancouver. Tel. 604/253–2311.

Washington **Early–mid-Apr. Skagit Valley Tulip Festival** showcases millions of colorful tulips and daffodils in bloom. Tel. 206/428–8547.

Mid-May. Viking Fest celebrates the Norwegian community of Poulsbo's proud heritage. Tel. 206/779–4848.

Late May. Northwest Folklife Festival lures musicians and artists to Seattle for one of the largest folkfests in the United States. Tel. 206/684–7300.

Late June–early July. Fort Vancouver Days in Vancouver is a citywide celebration with rodeo, a bluegrass festival, a chili cook-off, and the largest fireworks display west of the Mississippi. Tel. 206/693–1313.

Mid-July. Bite of Seattle serves up sumptuous specialties from the city's finest restaurants. Tel. 206/232–2982.

Mid-July–early Aug. Seafair, Seattle's biggest event of the year, kicks off with a torchlight parade through downtown and culminates in the Blue Angels air show and hydroplane races on Lake Washington. Tel. 206/728–0123.

Late July. Pacific Northwest Arts and Crafts Fair in Bellevue highlights some of the best work of Northwest artists and craftspeople. Tel. 206/454–4900.

Late Aug. Washington State International Kite Festival sends kites of all shapes and sizes flying above Long Beach. Tel. 206/451–2542.

Late Aug.–early Sept. Bumbershoot, a Seattle festival of the arts, presents more than 400 performers in music, dance, theater, comedy, and the visual and literary arts. Tel. 206/684–7200.

Early–mid-Sept. Western Washington Fair brings top entertainment, animals, food, exhibits, and rides to the town of Puyallup. Tel. 206/841–5045.

Mid-Sept. Wooden Boat Festival has historic boat displays, demonstrations, and a street fair in Port Townsend. Tel. 206/385–3628.

Oregon **Mid-Feb.–late Oct. Oregon Shakespearean Festival,** held in Ashland annually since 1935, presents a repertoire of classic and contemporary plays. Tel. 800/533–1311 in OR or 800/547–8052 outside OR.

Mid-May. Sandcastle Day transforms Cannon Beach into a sculpted fantasyland of fanciful castles and creatures. Tel. 503/436–2623.

Late May. Fleet of Flowers Memorial Service, which begins at Depoe Bay, scatters a mass of flowers into the ocean to commemorate those lost at sea. Tel. 503/765–2889.

Late May–mid-June. Portland Rose Festival features 24 days of diverse events, such as ski racing on nearby Mt. Hood, an air show, a hot-air-balloon classic, the Grand Floral parade, and auto racing. Tel. 503/227–2681.

Mid-June–early Sept. Peter Britt Gardens Music and Arts Festival features folk, country, bluegrass, and jazz music, as well as musical theater and dance, on the stages of Jacksonville. Tel. 800/332–7488 in OR or 800/882–7488 outside OR.

Late June–early July. Oregon Bach Festival, sponsored by the University of Oregon School of Music, brings the works of the great composer to Eugene. Tel. 503/346–5666.

Early Aug. Mt. Hood Festival of Jazz brings nationally acclaimed jazz musicians to Gresham for performances in an outdoor setting. Tel. 503/666–3810.

Late Aug.–early Sept. Oregon State Fair, which is held in Salem for 11 days prior to Labor Day, hosts concerts, flea markets, horse and livestock shows, and sporting events. Tel. 503/378–3247.

Alaska **Late Mar. Seward's Day** is celebrated around the state on the last Monday in March and commemorates the signing of the 1867 treaty purchasing Alaska from Russia.

Mid-May. Little Norway Festival, a three-day event, honors the town of Petersburg's Scandinavian heritage. Tel. 907/772–3646.

Mid-May. Southeast Alaska State Fair, which takes place in Haines, features entertainment; a timber show; workshops; contests; and agriculture, home-arts, fine-arts, and crafts exhibits. Tel. 907/766–2478.

June. Sitka Summer Music Festival presents internationally known musicians ranging from classical to pop in the Centennial Building. Tel. 907/747–6774.

Oct. 18. Alaska Day commemorates the formal transfer of Alaska from Russia to the United States.

What to Pack

Clothing Residents of the Pacific North Coast are generally informal by nature and wear clothing that reflects their disposition. Summer days are warm but evenings can cool off substantially. Layered clothing is the local preference—sweatshirts, sweaters, and jackets are removed or put on as the day progresses. If you plan to explore the region's cities on foot, or if you choose to hike along mountain trails or beaches, bring comfortable walking shoes.

Dining out is usually an informal affair, although some restaurants require a jacket and tie for men and dresses for women. Residents tend to dress conservatively when going to the theater or symphony, but it's not uncommon to see some patrons wearing jeans. In other words, almost anything is acceptable for most occasions.

Passengers aboard cruise ships bound for Alaska should check with their travel agents about the dress code on board. Some vessels expect formal attire for dinner, while others do not. In all cases, you will need a waterproof coat and warm clothes if you plan to spend time on deck.

Miscellaneous If you plan on hiking or camping during the summer, insect repellent is a must. Bring an extra pair of eyeglasses or contact lenses. If you have a health problem that may require you to purchase a prescription drug, pack enough to last the duration of the trip, or have your doctor write a prescription using the drug's generic name, since brand names vary from country to country. And don't forget to pack a list of the addresses of offices that supply refunds for lost or stolen traveler's checks.

Luggage Free baggage allowances on an airline depend on the airline,
Regulations the route, and the class of your ticket. In general, on domestic flights you are entitled to check two bags—neither exceeding 62 inches, or 158 centimeters (length + width + height), or weighing more than 70 pounds (32 kilograms). A third piece may be brought aboard as a carryon; its total dimensions are generally limited to less than 45 inches (114 centimeters), so it will fit easily under the seat in front of you or in the overhead compartment. There are variations, so ask in advance. The single rule, a Federal Aviation Administration safety regulation that pertains to carry-on baggage on U.S. airlines, requires that carryons be properly stowed and allows the airline to limit allowances and tailor them to different aircraft and operational conditions. Charges for excess, oversize, or overweight pieces vary, so inquire before you pack.

Safeguarding Your Before leaving home, itemize your bags' contents and their
Luggage worth; this list will help you estimate the extent of your loss if your bags go astray. To minimize that risk, tag them inside and out with your name, address, and phone number. (If you use your home address, cover it so that potential thieves can't see it.) At check-in, make sure that the tag attached by baggage handlers bears the correct three-letter code for your destination. If your bags do not arrive with you, or if you detect damage, do not leave the airport until you've filed a written report with the airline.

Taking Money Abroad

Traveler's Checks Although you will want plenty of cash when visiting small cities or rural areas, traveler's checks are usually preferable. The most widely recognized are **American Express, Citicorp, Thomas Cook,** and **Visa,** which are sold by major commercial banks. American Express also issues *Traveler's Cheques for Two,* which can be countersigned and used by you or your traveling companion. Some checks are free; usually the issuing company or the bank at which you make your purchase charges 1%–2% of the checks' face value as a fee. Be sure to buy a few checks in small denominations to cash toward the end of your trip, when you don't want to be left with more foreign currency than you can spend. Always record the numbers of checks as you spend them, and keep this list separate from the checks.

Currency Exchange American money is readily accepted in much of Canada (especially in communities near the border), but it is advisable to convert U.S. dollars to Canadian dollars at a bank or foreign-exchange office in order to get the most favorable rate. Traveler's checks and major U.S. credit cards are accepted in larger cities and resorts, but in smaller towns and rural areas, you may need cash.

Getting Money from Home

Cash Machines Automated-teller machines (ATMs) are proliferating; many are tied to international networks such as **Cirrus** and **Plus.** You can use your bank card at ATMs away from home to withdraw money from an account and get cash advances on a credit-card account (providing your card has been programmed with a personal identification number, or PIN). Check in advance on limits on withdrawals and cash advances within specified periods. Remember that on cash advances you are charged interest from the day you get the money from ATMs as well as from tellers. And note that transaction fees for ATM withdrawals outside your home turf will probably be higher than for withdrawals at home.

For specific Cirrus locations in the United States and Canada, call 800/424–7787 (for U.S. Plus locations, 800/843–7587), and press the area code and first three digits of the number you're calling from (or the calling area where you want an ATM).

American Express Cardholder Services The company's **Express Cash** system lets you withdraw cash and/or traveler's checks from a worldwide network of 57,000 American Express dispensers and participating bank ATMs. You must *enroll first* (call 800/227–4669 for a form and allow two weeks for processing). Withdrawals are charged not to your card but to a designated bank account. You can withdraw up to $1,000 per seven-day period on the basic card, more if your card is gold or platinum. There is a 2% fee (minimum $2.50, maximum $10) for each cash transaction, and a 1% fee for traveler's checks (except for the platinum card), which are available only from American Express dispensers.

At AmEx offices, cardholders can also cash personal checks for up to $1,000 in any seven-day period; of this, $200 can be in cash, more if available, with the balance paid in traveler's checks, for which all but platinum cardholders pay a 1% fee. Higher limits apply to the gold and platinum cards.

Wiring Money   You don't have to be a cardholder to send or receive an **American Express MoneyGram** for up to $10,000. To send one, go to an American Express MoneyGram agent, pay up to $1,000 with a credit card and anything over that in cash, and phone a transaction reference number to your intended recipient, who needs only present identification and the reference number to the nearest MoneyGram agent to pick up the cash. There are MoneyGram agents in more than 60 countries (call 800/543–4080 for locations). Fees range from 5%–10%, depending on the amount and how you pay. You can't use American Express, which is really a convenience card—only Discover, Master-Card, and Visa credit cards.

You can also use **Western Union.** To wire money, take either cash or a check to the nearest office. (Or you can call and use a credit card.) Fees are roughly 5%–10%. Money sent from the United States or Canada will be available for pick up at agent locations within minutes. (Note that once the money is in the system it can be picked up at *any* location. You don't have to miss your train waiting for it to arrive in City A, because if there's an agent in City B, where you're headed, you can pick it up there, too.) There are approximately 20,000 agents worldwide (call 800/325–6000 for locations).

Currency

The United States and Canada both use the same currency denominations—dollars and cents—although each currency has a different value on the world market. In the United States, the most common paper currency comes in $1, $5, $10, and $20 bills. Common notes in Canada include the $2, $5, $10, and $20 bills. (Canada recently phased out its $1 bill, replacing it with a $1 gold-colored coin nicknamed the "loonie" by Canadians because it contains a picture of a loon on one side.) Coins in both countries come in denominations of 1¢ (penny), 5¢ (nickel), 10¢ (dime), 25¢ (quarter), and 50¢.

What It Will Cost

Prices for meals and accommodations in the Pacific North Coast are generally lower than in other major North American regions. Prices for first-class hotel rooms in major cities (Seattle, Portland, Vancouver, and Victoria) range from $100 to $200 a night, although you can still find some "value" hotel rooms for $65 to $90 a night. Most hotels offer weekend packages that offer discounts of up to 50%. Don't look for these special deals during the peak summer season, however, when hotels are nearly filled to capacity.

As a rule, costs outside the major cities are lower, but prices for rooms and meals at some of the major deluxe resorts can rival those at the best big-city hotels.

In Alaska, food costs are higher because the state has to import virtually all of its produce, as well as its manufactured goods, from the "lower" 48 states.

Compared with many other parts of the world, the Pacific Northwest is a travel bargain. The region is becoming increasingly popular with Japanese visitors, for example, who find prices for hotels, meals, and commodities to be quite a steal.

Prices in Canada are always quoted in Canadian dollars. When comparing prices with those in the United States, costs should be calculated via the current rate of exchange. At press time (fall 1993), the Canadian dollar was worth US$.75, but this exchange rate can vary considerably. Check with a bank or other financial institution for the current rate. A good way to be sure you're getting the best exchange rate is by using your credit card. The issuing bank will convert your bill at the current rate.

Sales tax varies among areas. Oregon and Alaska have no sales tax, although some cities levy a tax on hotel rooms. Portland, for example, has a 9% room tax. The sales tax in Washington is 7.9%. Seattle adds 5% to the rate for hotel rooms. Canada's 7% Goods & Services Tax (GST) is added to hotel bills but will be rebated to foreign visitors. (*See* Shopping in Staying in the Pacific North Coast, *below*). In British Columbia, consumers pay an 8%–10% provincial and municipal tax. The percentage varies from one municipality to another.

Passports and Visas

U.S. and Canadian Citizens
Citizens and permanent residents of the United States and Canada are not required to have passports or visas to visit each other's country. However, native-born citizens should carry identification showing proof of citizenship, such as a birth certificate, a voter-registration card, or a valid passport. Naturalized citizens should carry a naturalization certificate or some other proof of citizenship. Individuals under the age of 18 who are not accompanied by their parents should bring a letter from a parent or guardian giving them permission to travel in another country. Permanent residents of the United States who are not U.S. citizens should carry their Alien Registration Receipt Cards. U.S. citizens interested in visiting Canada for more than 90 days may apply for a visa that allows them to stay for six months. For more information, contact the Canadian Embassy (501 Pennsylvania Ave. NW, Washington, DC 20001, tel. 202/682–1740).

U.K Citizens
To enter the United States or Canada, you will need a valid, 10-year British passport (£15 for a standard 32-page passport, £30 for a 94-page passport). Note that a one-year British passport is not acceptable for entry under any circumstances. You can obtain passport application forms from most travel agents and major post offices, or from the **Passport Office** (Clive House, 70 Petty France, London SW1H 9HD, tel. 071/279–3434 or 071/279–4000).

You will not need a visa if you are staying in the United States for 90 days or less, have a return or onward ticket on a major airline, and complete a visa waiver form and an arrival/departure card. There are some exceptions to this, so check with your travel agent or with the Visa Unit of the **United States Embassy** (Visa and Immigration Dept., 5 Upper Grosvenor St., London W1A 2JB, tel. 071/499–3443 for recorded information or 071/499–7010). Visa applications must be made by mail. If you will be entering from Canada, you can complete the visa waiver form at the port of entry.

British visitors are not required to have a visa to enter Canada. Their stay in Canada, however, cannot exceed six months without authorization from Canadian immigration.

Customs

Americans may bring home from Canada $400 in foreign goods, as long as you've been out of the United States for at least 48 hours and you haven't made an international trip in 30 days. Each member of the family is entitled to the same exemption regardless of age, and exemptions may be pooled. Visitors to Canada who meet the minimum-age requirements of the province of entry (19 years in British Columbia) may take in either 1.1 liters (40 ounces) of liquor or wine or 24 12-ounce cans or bottles of beer. Visitors over 16 may take in 50 cigars, 200 cigarettes, and 400 grams (14 ounces) of manufactured tobacco. Gifts valued at less than $40 each can also be brought into Canada, providing they do not contain tobacco or alcohol. Gifts valued at more than $40 are subject to regular import duty on the excess amount.

Visitors age 21 or over can take into the United States 200 cigarettes or 50 cigars, or two kilograms of tobacco; one liter of alcohol; and duty-free gifts to a value of $100. For further information on United States customs regulations consult the brochure "Know Before You Go," which carefully outlines what returning U.S. residents may and may not bring back into the country, and at what cost. Contact U.S. Customs Service (1301 Constitution Ave., Washington, DC 20229).

British citizens may import from countries outside the EC such as the United States and Canada 200 cigarettes, 100 cigarillos, 50 cigars or 250 grams of tobacco; 1 liter of spirits or 2 liters of fortified or sparkling wine; 2 liters of still table wine; 60 milliliters of perfume; 250 milliliters of toilet water; plus £36 worth of other goods, including gifts and souvenirs. For further information or a copy of "A Guide for Travellers," which details standard customs procedures as well as what you may bring into the United Kingdom from abroad, contact **HM Customs and Excise** (New King's Beam House, 22 Upper Ground, London SE1 9PJ, tel. 071/620–1313).

Canada has very strict gun-control laws. Firearms with no legitimate sporting or recreational use are not allowed into the country. This includes all handguns, automatic weapons, and any rifle or shotgun that has been modified. For further information on Canadian customs regulations, write to **Revenue Canada** (Customs and Excise, Ottawa, Ont. K1A 0L5, tel. 613/993–6220).

Traveling with Cameras, Camcorders, and Laptops

About Film and Cameras If your camera is new or if you haven't used it for a while, shoot and develop a few rolls of film before leaving home. Pack some lens tissue and an extra battery for your built-in light meter and invest in an inexpensive skylight filter, to both protect your lens and provide some definition in hazy shots. Store film in a cool, dry place—never in the car's glove compartment or on the shelf under the rear window.

Films above ISO 400 are more sensitive to damage from airport security X-rays than others; very high speed films, ISO 1000 and above, are exceedingly vulnerable. To protect your film, don't put it in checked luggage; carry it with you in a plastic bag and ask for a hand inspection. Such requests are honored at American airports. Don't depend on a lead-lined bag to protect film in checked luggage—the airline may very well turn up the dosage of radiation to see what you've got in there. Airport metal detectors do not harm film, although you'll set off the alarm if you walk through one with a roll in your pocket. Call the Kodak Information Center (tel. 800/242–2424) for details.

About Camcorders Before your trip, put new or long-unused camcorders through their paces, and practice panning and zooming. Invest in a skylight filter to protect the lens, and check the lithium battery that lights up the LCD (liquid crystal display) modes. Take along an extra pair of the rechargeable nickel-cadmium batteries that are the camera's power source, so while you're using your camcorder you'll have one battery ready and another recharging.

About Videotape Unlike still-camera film, videotape is not damaged by X-rays. However, it may well be harmed by the magnetic field of a walk-through metal detector. Airport security personnel may want you to turn the camcorder on to prove that it is a camera, so make sure the battery is charged when you get to the airport.

About Laptops Security X-rays do not harm hard-disk or floppy-disk storage. Most airlines allow you to use your laptop aloft but request that you turn it off during takeoff and landing so as not to interfere with navigation equipment. Make sure the battery is charged when you arrive at the airport, because you may be asked to turn on the computer at security checkpoints to prove that it is what it appears to be. If you're a heavy computer user, consider traveling with a backup battery.

Language

Canada is officially a bilingual country (English and French). You will see many signs and services offered in both languages; however, little French is spoken on Canada's west coast.

Insurance

For U.S. Residents Most tour operators, travel agents, and insurance agents sell specialized health-and-accident, flight, trip-cancellation, and luggage insurance as well as comprehensive policies with some or all of these features. Before you make any purchase, review your existing health and homeowner policies to find out whether they cover expenses incurred while traveling.

Health-and-Accident Insurance Supplemental health-and-accident insurance for travelers is usually a part of comprehensive policies. Specific policy provisions vary, but they tend to address three general areas, beginning with reimbursement for medical expenses caused by illness or an accident during a trip. Such policies may reimburse anywhere from $1,000 to $150,000 worth of medical expenses; dental benefits may also be included. A second common feature is the personal-accident, or death-and-dismemberment, provision, which pays a lump sum to your beneficiaries if you die or to you if you lose one or both limbs or your eyesight. This is similar to the flight insurance described below, although it is not necessarily limited to accidents involving airplanes or even other "common carriers" (buses, trains, and ships) and can be in effect 24 hours a day. The lump sum awarded can range from $15,000 to $500,000. A third area generally addressed by these policies is medical assistance (referrals, evacuation, or repatriation and other services). Some policies reimburse travelers for the cost of such services; others may automatically enroll you as a member of a particular medical-assistance company.

Flight Insurance This insurance, often bought as a last-minute impulse at the airport, pays a lump sum to a beneficiary when a plane crashes and the insured dies (and sometimes to a surviving passenger who loses eyesight or a limb); thus it supplements the airlines' own coverage as described in the limits-of-liability paragraphs on your ticket (up to $75,000 on international flights, $20,000 on domestic ones—and that is generally subject to litigation). Charging an airline ticket to a major credit card often automatically signs you up for flight insurance; in this case, the coverage may also embrace travel by bus, train, and ship.

Baggage Insurance In the event of loss, damage, or theft on international flights, airlines limit their liability to $20 per kilogram for checked baggage (roughly about $640 per 70-pound bag) and $400 per passenger for unchecked baggage. On domestic flights, the ceiling is $1,250 per passenger. Excess-valuation insurance can be bought directly from the airline at check-in but leaves your bags vulnerable on the ground.

Trip Insurance There are two sides to this coin. **Trip-cancellation-and-interruption insurance** protects you in the event you are unable to undertake or finish your trip. **Default** or **bankruptcy insurance** protects you against a supplier's failure to deliver. Consider the former if your airline ticket, cruise, or package tour does not allow changes or cancellations. The amount of coverage to buy should equal the cost of your trip should you, a traveling companion, or a family member get sick, forcing you to stay home, plus the nondiscounted one-way airline ticket you would need to buy if you had to return home early. Read the fine print carefully; pay attention to sections defining "family member" and "preexisting medical conditions." A characteristic quirk of default policies is that they often do not cover default by travel agencies or default by a tour operator, airline, or cruise line if you bought your tour and the coverage directly from the firm in question. To reduce your need for default insurance, give preference to tours packaged by members of the United States Tour Operators Association (USTOA), which maintains a fund to reimburse clients in the event of member defaults. Even better, pay for travel arrangements with a major credit card, so you can refuse to pay the bill if services have not been rendered—and let the card company fight your battles.

Comprehensive Policies Companies supplying comprehensive policies with some or all of the above features include **Access America, Inc.,** underwritten by BCS Insurance Company (Box 11188, Richmond, VA 23230, tel. 800/284–8300); **Carefree Travel Insurance,** underwritten by The Hartford (Box 310, 120 Mineola Blvd., Mineola, NY 11501, tel. 516/294–0220 or 800/323–3149); **Tele-Trip** (Mutual of Omaha Plaza, Box 31762, Omaha, NE 68131, tel. 800/228–9792), a subsidiary of Mutual of Omaha; **The Travelers Companies** (1 Tower Sq., Hartford, CT 06183, tel. 203/277–0111 or 800/243–3174); **Travel Guard International,** underwritten by Transamerica Occidental Life Companies (1145 Clark St., Stevens Point, WI 54481, tel. 715/345–0505 or 800/782–5151); and **Wallach and Company, Inc.** (107 W. Federal St., Box 480, Middleburg, VA 22117, tel. 703/687–3166 or 800/237–6615).

These companies may also offer the above types of insurance separately.

U.K. Residents Most tour operators, travel agents, and insurance agents sell specialized policies covering accident, medical expenses, personal liability, trip cancellation, and loss or theft of personal property. Some policies include coverage for delayed departure and legal expenses, winter sports, accidents, or motoring abroad. You can also purchase an annual travel-insurance policy valid for every trip you make during the year in which it's purchased (usually only trips of less than 90 days). Before you leave, make sure you will be covered if you have a preexisting medical condition or are pregnant; your insurers may not pay for routine or continuing treatment, or may require a note from your doctor certifying your fitness to travel.

The **Association of British Insurers,** a trade association representing 450 insurance companies, advises extra medical coverage for visitors to the United States.

For advice by phone or a free booklet, "Holiday Insurance," that sets out what to expect from a holiday-insurance policy and gives price guidelines, contact the Association of British Insurers (51 Gresham St., London EC2V 7HQ, tel. 071/600–3333; 30 Gordon St., Glasgow G1 3PU, tel. 041/226–3905; Scottish Provincial Bldg., Donegall Sq. W, Belfast BT1 6JE, tel. 0232/249176; call for other locations).

Car Rentals

All major car-rental companies are represented in the Pacific Northwest, including **Avis** (tel. 800/331–1212 or 800/879–2847 in Canada); **Budget** (tel. 800/527–0700); **Dollar** (tel. 800/800–4000); **Hertz** (tel. 800/654–3131 or 800/263-0600 in Canada); and **National** (tel. 800/227–7368). In cities, unlimited-mileage rates range from about $26 per day for an economy car to $50 for a large car; weekly unlimited-mileage rates range from $105 to $230. Rates are higher in Alaska and in some rural areas.

Requirements Your own U.S., Canadian, or U.K. driver's license is acceptable. If you are taking a rental car across the United States–Canada border, keep a copy of the rental contract with you. It should bear an endorsement stating that the vehicle is permitted entry into the other country.

Extra Charges Picking up the car in one city or country and leaving it in another may entail drop-off charges or one-way service fees, which can be substantial. The cost of a collision or loss-damage waiver (*see below*) may also be high.

Cutting Costs If you know you will want a car for more than a day or two, you can save by planning ahead. Major international companies have programs that discount their standard rates by 15%–30% if you make the reservation before departure (anywhere from two to 14 days), rent for a minimum number of days (typically three or four), and prepay the rental. Ask about these advance-purchase schemes when you call for information. More economical rentals are those that come as part of fly/drive or other packages, even those as bare-bones as the rental plus an airline ticket (*see* Tours and Packages, *above*).

Other sources of savings are the companies that operate as wholesalers—companies that do not own their own fleets but rent in bulk from those that do and offer advantageous rates to their customers. Rentals through such companies must be arranged and paid for in advance. Among them are **Auto Europe** (Box 1097, Camden, ME 04843, tel. 207/236–8235, 800/223–5555, or 800/458–9503 in Canada), **Connex International** (23 N. Division St., Peekskill, NY 10566, tel. 914/739–0066, 800/333–3949, or 800/843–5416 in Canada), and **Europe by Car** (mailing address: 1 Rockefeller Plaza, New York, NY 10020; walk-in address: 14 W. 49th St., New York, NY 10020, tel. 212/581–3040 or 212/245–1713; 9000 Sunset Blvd., Los Angeles, CA 90069, tel. 213/252–9401 or 800/223–1516 in CA). You won't see these wholesalers' deals advertised; they're even better in summer, when business travel is down. Always ask whether unlimited mileage is available. Find out about any required deposits, cancellation penalties, and drop-off charges, and confirm the cost of the collision damage waiver (CDW).

One last tip: Remember to fill the tank when you turn in the vehicle, to avoid being charged for refueling at what you'll swear is the most expensive pump in town.

Insurance and Collision Damage Waiver The standard rental contract includes liability coverage (for damage to public property, injury to pedestrians, etc.) and coverage for the car against fire, theft (not included in certain countries), and collision damage with a deductible—most commonly $2,000–$3,000, occasionally more. In the case of an accident, you are responsible for the deductible amount unless you've purchased the CDW, which costs an average $12 a day, although this varies depending on what you've rented, where, and from whom.

Because this adds up quickly, you may be inclined to say "no thanks"—and that's certainly your option, although the rental agent may not tell you so. Note before you decline that deductibles are occasionally high enough that totaling a car would make you responsible for its full value. Planning ahead will help you make the right decision. By all means, find out if your own insurance covers damage to a rental car while traveling (not simply a car to drive when yours is in for repairs). And check whether charging car rentals to any of your credit cards will get you a CDW at no charge. In many states, laws mandate that renters be told what the CDW costs, that it's optional, and that their own auto insurance may provide the same protection.

Rail Passes

VIA Rail Canada (tel. 800/665–0200) offers a **Canrailpass** that is good for 30 days. System-wide passes cost $282 (Jan. 6–June 6 and Oct. 1–Dec. 14) and $420 (June 7–Sept. 30). Youth passes (age 24 and under) are $377 in peak season and $257 during the off-season. Prices are quoted in U.S. dollars. Tickets can be purchased in the United States or the United Kingdom from a travel agent, from **Long Haul Leisurail** (Box 113, Peterborough PE1 1LE, tel. 0733/51780), or upon arrival in Canada. This offer does not apply to Canadian citizens.

Student and Youth Travel

Travel Agencies The foremost U.S. student travel agency is **Council Travel,** a subsidiary of the nonprofit Council on International Educational Exchange. It specializes in low-cost travel arrangements, is the exclusive U.S. agent for several discount cards, and, with its sister CIEE subsidiary, **Council Charter,** is a source of airfare bargains. The Council Charter brochure and CIEE's twice-yearly *Student Travels* magazine, which details its programs, are available at the Council Travel office at CIEE headquarters (205 E. 42nd St., New York, NY 10017, tel. 212/661–1450) and at 37 branches in college towns nationwide (free in person, $1 by mail). The **Educational Travel Center** (ETC, 438 N. Francis St., Madison, WI 53703, tel. 608/256–5551) also offers low-cost rail passes, domestic and international airline tickets (mostly for flights departing from Chicago), and other budgetwise travel arrangements. Other travel agencies catering to students include **Travel Management International** (TMI, 18 Prescott St., Suite 4, Cambridge, MA 02138, tel. 617/661–8187) and **Travel Cuts** (187 College St., Toronto, Ont. M5T 1P7, tel. 416/979–2406).

Discount Cards For discounts on transportation and on museum and attractions admissions, buy the **International Student Identity Card** (ISIC) if you're a bona fide student, or the **International Youth Card** (IYC) if you're under 26. In the United States, the ISIC and IYC cards cost $15 each and include basic travel accident and sickness coverage. Apply to **CIEE** (*see* address *above*, tel. 212/661–1414; the application is in *Student Travels*). In Canada, the cards are available for $15 each from **Travel Cuts** (*see above*). In the United Kingdom, the cards cost £5 and £4 respectively at student unions and student travel companies, including Council Travel's London office (28A Poland St., London W1V 3DB, tel. 071/437–7767).

Hosteling An **International Youth Hostel Federation** (IYHF) membership card is the key to more than 5,300 hostel locations in 59 countries; the sex-segregated, dormitory-style sleeping quarters, including some for families, go for $7–$20 a night per person. Membership is available in the United States through **American Youth Hostels** (AYH, 733 15th St. NW, Washington, DC 20005, tel. 202/783–6161), the American link in the worldwide chain, and costs $25 for adults 18–54, $10 for those under 18, $15 for those 55 and over, and $35 for families. Volume 2 of the two-volume *Guide to Budget Accommodation* lists hostels in Asia and Australasia as well as in Canada and the United States ($13.95 including postage). IYHF membership is available in Canada through the **Canadian Hosteling Association** (1600 James Naismith Dr., Suite 608, Gloucester, Ont. K1B 5N4, tel. 613/748–5638) for $26.75, and in the United Kingdom through the **Youth Hostel Association of England and Wales** (8 St. Stephen's Hill, St. Albans, Herts. AL1 2DY, tel. 0727/55215) for £9.

Traveling with Children

Many local organizations, such as public libraries, museums, parks and recreation departments, and YMCA/YWCAs, have special events throughout the year for children of all ages. Check local newspaper listings for such activities as plays, storytelling, sporting events, and so forth.

Publications *Family Travel Times,* published 10 times a year by **Travel With**
Newsletter **Your Children** (TWYCH, 45 W. 18th St., 7th Floor Tower, New York, NY 10011, tel. 212/206–0688; annual subscription $55), covers destinations, types of vacations, and modes of travel.

Books *Traveling with Children—And Enjoying It*, by Arlene K. But-
ler ($11.95 plus $3 shipping per book; Globe Pequot Press, Box
833, Old Saybrook, CT 06475, tel. 800/243–0495 or 800/962–
0973 in CT) helps plan your trip with children, from toddlers to
teens. From the same publisher is *Recommended Family Resorts in the United States, Canada, and the Caribbean*, by Jane
Wilford with Janet Tice ($12.95).

Tour Operators **GrandTravel** (6900 Wisconsin Ave., Suite 706, Chevy Chase,
MD 20815, tel. 301/986–0790 or 800/247–7651) offers international and domestic tours for grandparents traveling with their
grandchildren. The catalogue, as charmingly written and illustrated as a children's book, positively invites armchair traveling with lap-sitters aboard. **Rascals in Paradise** (650 5th St.,
Suite 505, San Francisco, CA 94107, tel. 415/978–9800, or 800/
872–7225) specializes in programs for families.

Getting There
Airfares On domestic flights, children under 2 not occupying a seat travel free, and older children currently travel on the "lowest applicable" adult fare.

Baggage The adult baggage allowance applies for children paying half or
more of the adult fare. Check with the airline for particulars.

Safety Seats The FAA recommends the use of safety seats aloft and details
approved models in the free leaflet ""**Child/Infant Safety Seats
Recommended for Use in Aircraft**" (available from the Federal
Aviation Administration, APA–200, 800 Independence Ave.
SW, Washington, DC 20591, tel. 202/267–3479). Airline policy
varies. U.S. carriers must allow FAA-approved models, but
because these seats are strapped into a regular passenger seat,
they may require that parents buy a ticket even for an infant
under 2 who would otherwise ride free.

Facilities Aloft Airlines provide other facilities and services for children, such
as children's meals and freestanding bassinets (to those sitting
in seats on the bulkhead, where there's enough legroom to accommodate them). Make your request when reserving. The annual February/March issue of *Family Travel Times* gives
details of the children's services of dozens of airlines ($10; *see
above*). "Kids and Teens in Flight" (free from the U.S. Department of Transportation, tel. 202/366–2220) offers tips for children flying alone.

Baby-sitting Most large hotels offer licensed baby-sitters or referrals. Re-
Services sorts are more likely to provide children's services than are
downtown hotels, which are geared to business travelers. Contact individual hotels for specifics, as facilities vary widely.

Hints for Travelers with Disabilities

Organizations **Barrier Free Alaska** (7233 Madelynne Dr., Anchorage, AK
99504–4656, tel. 907/337–6315) gives disabled travelers information about accessible facilities throughout the state.

Shared Outdoor Adventure Recreation (SOAR, tel. 503/238–
1613), a Portland organization, provides local listings of recreational activities for individuals with disabilities.

Several organizations provide travel information for people
with disabilities, usually for a membership fee, and some pub-
lish newsletters and bulletins. Among them are the **Information Center for Individuals with Disabilities** (Fort Point Pl., 27–
43 Wormwood St., Boston, MA 02210, tel. 617/727–5540 or 800/

462–5015 in MA between 11 and 4, or leave message; TDD/TTY tel. 617/345–9743); **Mobility International USA** (Box 3551, Eugene, OR 97403, voice and TDD tel. 503/343–1284), the U.S. branch of an international organization based in Britain (*see below*) and present in 30 countries; **MossRehab Hospital Travel Information Service** (1200 W. Tabor Rd., Philadelphia, PA 19141, tel. 215/456–9603, TDD tel. 215/456–9602); the **Society for the Advancement of Travel for the Handicapped** (SATH, 347 5th Ave., Suite 610, New York, NY 10016, tel. 212/447–7284, fax 212/725–8253); the **Travel Industry and Disabled Exchange** (TIDE, 5435 Donna Ave., Tarzana, CA 91356, tel. 818/368–5648); and **Travelin' Talk** (Box 3534, Clarksville, TN 37043, tel. 615/552–6670).

In Canada The **Canadian Paraplegic Association** (780 S.W. Marine Dr., Vancouver, BC V6P 5Y7, tel. 604/324–3611) provides information on touring British Columbia for travelers with disabilities. Information for the hearing-impaired is available from the **Western Institute for the Deaf** (2125 W. 7th Ave., Vancouver, BC V6K 1X9, tel. 604/736–7391, TDD 604/736–2527). The annual *British Columbia Accommodation Guide* (tel. 800/663–6000) includes a list of hotel facilities for individuals who are disabled.

In the United Main information sources include the **Royal Association for Dis-**
Kingdom **ability and Rehabilitation** (RADAR, 25 Mortimer St., London W1N 8AB, tel. 071/637–5400), which publishes travel information for the disabled in Britain, and **Mobility International** (228 Borough High St., London SE1 1JX, tel. 071/403–5688), the headquarters of an international membership organization that serves as a clearinghouse of travel information for people with disabilities.

Travel Agencies **Access Alaska** (3710 Woodland Dr., Suite 900, Anchorage, AK
and Tour Operators 99517, tel. 907/248–4777) provides information and referral to disabled visitors to Alaska. **Challenge Alaska** (Box 110065, Anchorage, AK 99511–0065, tel. 907/563–2658) provides recreational opportunities for people with disabilities. Activities include downhill and cross-country skiing, sea kayaking, canoeing, camping, fishing, swimming, dogsledding, and backpacking.

Directions Unlimited (720 N. Bedford Rd., Bedford Hills, NY 10507, tel. 914/241–1700), a travel agency, has expertise in tours and cruises for the disabled. **Evergreen Travel Service** (4114 198th St. SW, Suite 13, Lynnwood, WA 98036, tel. 206/776–1184 or 800/435–2288) operates Wings on Wheels Tours for those in wheelchairs, White Cane Tours for the blind, and tours for the deaf and makes group and independent arrangements for travelers with any disability. **Flying Wheels Travel** (143 W. Bridge St., Box 382, Owatonna, MN 55060, tel. 800/535–6790 or 800/722–9351 in MN), a tour operator and travel agency, arranges international tours, cruises, and independent travel itineraries for people with mobility disabilities. **Nautilus,** at the same address as TIDE (*see above*), packages tours for the disabled internationally.

Publications The Easter Seal Society (521 2nd Ave. W, Seattle, WA 98119, tel. 206/281–5700) publishes *Access Seattle,* a free guide to the city's services for the disabled.

Circling the City—A Guide to the Accessibility of Public Places in and Near Portland, Oregon , a 144-page book, is available from the Junior League (4838 S.W. Scholls Ferry Rd., Portland, OR 97225, tel. 503/297–6364).

In addition to the fact sheets, newsletters, and books mentioned above are several free publications available from the Consumer Information Center (Pueblo, CO 81009): "New Horizons for the Air Traveler with a Disability," a U.S. Department of Transportation booklet describing changes resulting from the 1986 Air Carrier Access Act and those still to come from the 1990 Americans with Disabilities Act (include Department 608Y in the address), and the Airport Operators Council's *Access Travel: Airports* (Dept. 5804), which describes facilities and services for the disabled at more than 500 airports worldwide.

Twin Peaks Press (Box 129, Vancouver, WA 98666, tel. 206/694–2462 or 800/637–2256) publishes the *Directory of Travel Agencies for the Disabled* ($19.95), listing more than 370 agencies worldwide; *Travel for the Disabled* ($19.95), listing some 500 access guides and accessible places worldwide; the *Directory of Accessible Van Rentals* ($9.95) for campers and RV travelers worldwide; and *Wheelchair Vagabond* ($14.95), a collection of personal travel tips. Add $2 per book for shipping. The Sierra Club publishes *Easy Access to National Parks* ($16 plus $3 shipping; 730 Polk St., San Francisco, CA 94109, tel. 415/776–2211).

Hints for Older Travelers

Organizations The **American Association of Retired Persons** (AARP, 601 E St. NW, Washington, DC 20049, tel. 202/434–2277) provides independent travelers the Purchase Privilege Program, which offers discounts on hotels, car rentals, and sightseeing, and the AARP Motoring Plan, provided by Amoco, which furnishes domestic trip-routing information and emergency road-service aid for an annual fee of $39.95 per person or couple ($59.95 for a premium version). AARP also arranges group tours, cruises, and apartment living through AARP Travel Experience from American Express (400 Pinnacle Way, Suite 450, Norcross, GA 30071, tel. 800/927–0111); these can be booked through travel agents, except for the cruises, which must be booked directly (tel. 800/745–4567). AARP membership is open to those 50 and over; annual dues are $8 per person or couple.

Two other membership organizations offer discounts on lodgings, car rentals, and other travel products, along with such nontravel perks as magazines and newsletters. The **National Council of Senior Citizens** (1331 F St. NW, Washington, DC 20004, tel. 202/347–8800) is a nonprofit advocacy group with some 5,000 local clubs across the United States; membership costs $12 per person or couple annually. **Mature Outlook** (6001 N. Clark St., Chicago, IL 60660, tel. 800/336–6330), a Sears Roebuck & Co. subsidiary with 800,000 members, charges $9.95 for an annual membership.

Note: When using any senior-citizen identification card for reduced hotel rates, mention it when booking, not when checking out. At restaurants, show your card before you're seated; discounts may be limited to certain menus, days, or hours. If you are renting a car, ask about promotional rates that might improve on your senior-citizen discount.

Educational Travel **Elderhostel** (75 Federal St., 3rd floor, Boston, MA 02110, tel. 617/426–7788) is a nonprofit organization that has offered inexpensive study programs for people 60 and older since 1975. Programs are held at more than 1,800 educational institutions in the United States, Canada, and 45 other countries; courses cover everything from marine science to Greek myths and cowboy poetry. Participants generally attend lectures in the morning and spend the afternoon sightseeing or on field trips; they live in dorms on the host campuses. Fees for programs in the United States and Canada, which usually last one week, run about $300, not including transportation.

Tour Operators **Saga International Holidays** (222 Berkeley St., Boston, MA 02116, tel. 800/343–0273), which specializes in group travel for people over 60, offers a selection of variously priced tours and cruises covering five continents. If you want to take your grandchildren, look into **GrandTravel** (*see* Traveling with Children, *above*).

Further Reading

History The late Bill Spiedel, one of Seattle's most colorful characters, wrote about the early history of the city in books replete with lively anecdotes and legends; *Sons of the Profits* and *Doc Maynard* are two of his best. *Washingtonians, A Biographical Portrait of the State,* edited by David Brewster and David M. Buerge, is a series of essays on well-known and influential residents who have left their mark on the state. *Skookum,* by Shannon Applegate, is the history of an Oregon pioneer family.

At the Field's End, by Nicolas O'Connell, features interviews with 20 leading writers who are all closely connected to the Pacific Northwest and reflect the character of the region. *Whistlepunks and Geoducks—Oral Histories from the Pacific Northwest,* by Ron Strickland, is a collection of stories told by old-timers from all walks of life in Washington State. Gloria Snively's *Exploring the Seashore* offers a guide to shorebirds and intertidal plants and animals in Washington, Oregon, and British Columbia. The *Northwest Sportsman Almanac,* edited by Terry W. Sheely, provides an in-depth guide to fishing and hunting in the Pacific North Coast.

Fiction Well-known fiction writers of the region include Raymond Carver, Ursula LeGuin, Jean Auel, Aaron Elkin, Frank Herbert, J. A. Jance, Ken Kesey, W. P. Kinsella, Jack Hodgin, Tom Robbins, Willo Davis Roberts, William Stafford, Walt Morey, and Norman Maclean.

Arriving and Departing

From North America by Plane

Flights are either nonstop, direct, or connecting. A **nonstop** flight requires no change of plane and makes no stops. A **direct** flight stops at least once and can involve a change of plane, although the flight number remains the same; if the first leg is late, the second waits. This is not the case with a **connecting** flight, which involves a different plane and a different flight number.

Airports and Airlines The Pacific North Coast has three major airports: Seattle, Portland, and Vancouver. All major U.S. carriers—**Alaska** (tel. 800/426–0333), **American** (tel. 800/433–7300), **Continental** (tel. 800/525–0280), **Delta** (tel. 800/221–1212), **Northwest** (tel. 800/225–2525), **TWA** (tel. 800/221–2000), **United** (tel. 800/241–6522), and **USAir** (tel. 800/428–4322)—offer regular flights into Seattle and Portland from points throughout the United States. **American Airlines, Delta,** and **United** fly direct to Vancouver from various points in the United States. **Air Canada** (tel. 800/663–8868) and **Canadian Airlines International** (tel. 800/426–7000) offer frequent service from all major Canadian cities to Vancouver.

Most Alaska-bound flights touch down in Anchorage. Nonstop service is also available to Fairbanks, Juneau, and Ketchikan. Southeastern Alaska cities are connected through Seattle, while northern locations are reached through Anchorage or Fairbanks. **Alaska, Continental, Delta, MarkAir** (tel. 907/243–1414 or 800/478–0800), **Northwest,** and **United** are the major U.S. carriers serving Alaska.

Flying Time Nonstop flying time from New York to Seattle or Portland is approximately 5 hours; flights from Chicago are about 4–4½ hours; flights between Los Angeles and Seattle take 2½ hours. Flights from New York to Vancouver take about 8 hours with connections; from Chicago, about 4½ hours nonstop; and from Los Angeles, about 3 hours nonstop.

Cutting Flight Costs The Sunday travel section of most newspapers is a good source of deals. When booking, particularly through an unfamiliar company, call the Better Business Bureau to find out whether any complaints have been registered against the company, pay with a credit card if you can, and consider trip-cancellation and default insurance.

Promotional Airfares All the less expensive fares, called promotional or discount fares, are round-trip and involve restrictions. The exact nature of the restrictions depends on the airline, the route, and the season and on whether travel is domestic or international, but you must usually buy the ticket—commonly called an APEX (advance purchase excursion) when it's for international travel—in advance (seven, 14, or 21 days are usual). You must also respect certain minimum- and maximum-stay requirements (for instance, over a Saturday night or at least seven and no more than 30, 45, or 90 days), and you must be willing to pay penalties for changes. Airlines generally allow some changes for a fee. But the cheaper the fare, the more likely the ticket is to be nonrefundable; it would take a death in the family for the airline to give you any of your money back if you had to cancel. The lowest fares are also subject to availability; because only a certain percentage of the plane's total seats will be sold at that price, they may go quickly.

Consolidators Consolidators or bulk-fare operators—also known as bucket shops—buy blocks of seats on scheduled flights that airlines anticipate they won't be able to sell. They pay wholesale prices, add a markup, and resell the seats to travel agents or directly to the public at prices that still undercut the airline's promotional or discount fares. You pay more than on a charter but ordinarily less than for an APEX ticket, and, even when there is not much of a price difference, the ticket usually comes without the advance-purchase restriction. Moreover, although tickets are marked nonrefundable so you can't turn them in to the airline for a full-fare refund, some consolidators sometimes give you your money back. Carefully read the fine print detailing penalties for changes and cancellations. If you doubt the reliability of a company, call the airline once you've made your booking and confirm that you do, indeed, have a reservation on the flight.

The biggest U.S. consolidator, C.L. Thomson Express, sells only to travel agents. Well-established consolidators selling to the public include **Council Charter** (205 E. 42nd St., New York, NY 10017, tel. 212/661–0311 or 800/800–8222), a division of the Council on International Educational Exchange and a longtime charter operator now functioning more as a consolidator; **Travac** (989 6th Ave., New York, NY 10018, tel. 212/563–3303 or 800/872–8800), also a former charterer; and **UniTravel** (Box 12485, St. Louis, MO 63132, tel. 314/569–0900 or 800/325–2222).

Charter Flights Charters usually have the lowest fares and the most restrictions. Departures are limited and seldom on time, and you can lose all or most of your money if you cancel. (Generally, the closer to departure you cancel, the more you lose, although sometimes you will be charged only a small fee if you supply a substitute passenger.) The charterer, on the other hand, may legally cancel the flight for any reason up to 10 days before departure; within 10 days of departure, the flight may be canceled only if it becomes physically impossible to operate it. The charterer may also revise the itinerary or increase the price after you have bought the ticket, but if the new arrangement constitutes a "major change," you have the right to a refund. Before buying a charter ticket, read the fine print for the company's refund policy and details on major changes. Money for charter flights is usually paid into a bank escrow account, the name of which should be on the contract. If you don't pay by credit card, make your check payable to the escrow account (unless you're dealing with a travel agent, in which case, his or her check should be payable to the escrow account). The Department of Transportation's Consumer Affairs Office (I–25, Washington, DC 20590, tel. 202/366–2220) can answer questions on charters and send you its "Plane Talk: Public Charter Flights" information sheet.

Charter operators may offer flights alone or with ground arrangements that constitute a charter package. Well-established charter operators include **Council Charter** (205 E. 42nd St., New York, NY 10017, tel. 212/661–0311 or 800/800–8222), now largely a consolidator, despite its name, and **Travel Charter** (1120 E. Long Lake Rd., Troy, MI 48098, tel. 313/528–3500 or 800/521–5267), with Midwestern departures. **DER Tours** (Box 1606, Des Plains, IL 60017, tel. 800/782–2424), a charterer and consolidator, sells through travel agents.

Discount Travel Travel clubs offer their members unsold space on airplanes,
Clubs cruise ships, and package tours at nearly the last minute and at well below the original cost. Suppliers thus receive some revenue for their "leftovers," and members get a bargain. Membership generally includes a regular bulletin or access to a toll-free telephone hot line giving details of available trips departing anywhere from three or four days to several months in the future. Packages tend to be more common than flights alone, so if airfares are your only interest, read the literature before join-

ing. Reductions on hotels are also available. Clubs include **Discount Travel International** (114 Forrest Ave., Suite 203, Narberth, PA 19072, tel. 215/668–7184; $45 annually, single or family), **Moment's Notice** (425 Madison Ave., New York, NY 10017, tel. 212/486–0503; $45 annually, single or family), **Travelers Advantage** (CUC Travel Service, 49 Music Sq. W, Nashville, TN 37203, tel. 800/548–1116; $49 annually, single or family), and **Worldwide Discount Travel Club** (1674 Meridian Ave., Miami Beach, FL 33139, tel. 305/534–2082; $50 annually for family, $40 single).

Smoking   Smoking is now banned on all domestic flights of less than six hours' duration in the United States, and on all Canadian flights, including flights to and from Europe and the Far East.

From the U.S. by Car

The U.S. interstate highway network provides quick and easy access to the Pacific North Coast in spite of imposing mountain barriers. From the south, I–5 runs from the U.S.–Mexican border through California, into Oregon and Washington, and ends at the U.S.–Canadian border. Most of the population is clustered along this corridor. From the east, I–90 stretches from Boston to Seattle. I–84 runs from the midwestern states to Portland.

The main entry point into Canada by car is on I–5 at Blaine, Washington, 30 miles south of Vancouver. Two major highways enter British Columbia from the east: the Trans-Canada Highway (the longest highway in the world, running more than 5,000 miles from St. John's, Newfoundland, to Victoria, British Columbia) and the Yellowhead Highway, which runs through northern British Columbia from the Rocky Mountains to Prince Rupert.

Border-crossing procedures are usually quick and simple (*see* Passports and Visas *and* Customs, *above*). The I–5 border crossing at Blaine, WA, is open 24 hours a day and is one of the busiest border crossings anywhere between the United States and Canada. Peak traffic times at the border northbound into Canada are daily at 4 PM. Southbound, delays can be expected evenings and weekend mornings. Try to plan on reaching the border at off-peak times. There are smaller highway border stations at various other points between Washington and British Columbia but they may be closed at night.

From the U.S. by Train

Amtrak (tel. 800/872–7245), the U.S. passenger rail system, has daily service to the Pacific North Coast from the midwestern United States and California. The *Empire Builder* takes a northern route from Chicago to Seattle. The *Pioneer* travels from Chicago to Portland via Denver and Salt Lake City. The *Coast Starlight* begins in Los Angeles, makes stops throughout western Oregon and Washington, and terminates its route in Seattle. At present, there are no trains that cross the border from Seattle into Canada.

Canada's passenger service, **VIA Rail Canada** (tel. 800/665–0200), operates transcontinental routes on the *Canadian* three times weekly between eastern Canada and Vancouver. A second train, the *Skeena*, runs three times weekly between Jasper, Alberta, to the British Columbia port city of Prince Rupert.

From the U.S. by Bus

Greyhound Lines (tel. 800/231–2222) operates bus service to Washington, Oregon, and British Columbia from various points in the United States and Canada. Bus service in North America—though fairly economical—has not been a first-class means of travel in recent years. But Greyhound and other bus companies are taking great pains to improve service. New amenities may include an on-board host/hostess, meals, and VCRs.

From the U.K. by Plane

Airlines and Airfares British travelers reach the Pacific North Coast via the main international gateways of Seattle and Vancouver. Southeast Alaska is served by regular, connecting flights to Anchorage from the United Kingdom.

British Airways (tel. 081/897–4000) services Seattle, Vancouver, and Anchorage from Heathrow. **KLM** (tel. 081/751–9000; in U.S. tel. 800/777–5553) travels to Vancouver from 25 U.K. and Irish airports via Amsterdam. **Air Canada** (tel. 081/759–2636) flies from Heathrow to Vancouver; **Canadian Airlines International** (tel. 081/667–0666 or 0345/616767 outside London) services Vancouver from Gatwick. **Japan Air Lines** (tel. 071/408–1000) provides service to Anchorage from Heathrow.

Fares on scheduled flights vary considerably. January to March are the cheapest months to fly, and midweek flights nearly always offer some reductions.

Charters With weekly flights to Vancouver, **Globespan Ltd.** (tel. 0293/562690), **ASAT** (tel. 0737/778560), and **Unijet** (tel. 0444/459100) offer sizable reductions on fares. At press time, prices began at £425 round-trip. You can also find good deals through specialized ticket agencies such as **Travel Cuts** (tel. 071/637–3161).

Staying in the Pacific North Coast

Getting Around

By Plane Regional air travel has changed considerably in the past few years. National carriers have given up many of their shorter routes to secondary cities, but smaller, regional companies have taken up the slack. These companies are often owned by, or have joint marketing and reservation systems with, larger airlines. Instead of operating jets, they often fly turboprop planes that hold 10–50 passengers.

Leading regional carriers in the Pacific North Coast are **Horizon Air** (tel. 800/547–9308) and **United Express** (tel. 800/241–6522). The two airlines provide frequent service between cities in Washington and Oregon. Horizon Air also flies internationally from Seattle to Vancouver and Victoria.

The two major regional carriers in Canada are **Air BC** (tel. 800/663–8868 or 800/776–3000) and **Canadian Partner** (tel. 800/426–7000). They serve communities throughout western Canada and have daily flights from Vancouver and Victoria into Seattle. **Air BC** also has several daily flights between Vancouver and Portland. **Helijet Airways** (tel. 604/273–1414) provides jet helicopter service from Vancouver to Victoria as well as Whistler ski resort.

There is frequent jet service from Seattle to Juneau on **Alaska Airlines** (tel. 800/426–0333) and **Delta Air Lines** (tel. 800/221–1212). Alaska Airlines also serves the smaller cities of Ketchikan, Wrangell, Sitka, Petersburg, and Yakutat from Juneau. Another regional air carrier, **Markair** (tel. 800/426–6784), now flies from Seattle to Juneau as well as serving 130 points in Alaska.

With all the water surrounding the Pacific North Coast, float planes are a common and convenient means of transportation. Accommodating 5–15 passengers, the planes fly at fairly low elevations and provide a great way to see the scenery.

In addition to its regular airport service, Air BC has float-plane service between Vancouver and Victoria harbors. **Kenmore Air** (tel. 800/543–9595) has scheduled flights from Seattle's Lake Union to Victoria and points in the San Juan Islands. Along with several other float-plane companies, Kenmore provides fly-in service to remote fishing resorts along the coast of British Columbia.

In Alaska, float planes (or air taxis) are an essential means of air transportation, connecting many small communities and fishing lodges.

By Train The Pacific North Coast has a number of scenic train routes in addition to those operated by Amtrak and VIA Rail Canada. The **Rocky Mountaineer** (Great Canadian Railtour Co., Ltd., 340 Brooksbank Ave., Suite 104, North Vancouver, BC V7J 2C1, tel. 800/665–7245) is a two-day rail cruise between Vancouver and the Canadian Rockies, May–October. There are two routes—one to Banff/Calgary and the other to Jasper—through landscapes considered to be the most spectacular in the world. An overnight hotel stop is made in Kamloops.

On Vancouver Island, VIA Rail (tel. 604/383–4324) runs the *E&N Railway* daily from Victoria north to Nanaimo. **BC Rail** (Box 8770, Vancouver, B.C. V6B 4X6, tel. 604/631–3500) operates daily service from its North Vancouver terminal to the town of Prince George. At Prince George, it is possible to connect with VIA Rail's *Skeena* service east to Jasper and Alberta or west to Prince Rupert. BC Rail also operates a summertime excursion steam train, the *Royal Hudson*, between North Vancouver and Squamish, at the head of Howe Sound.

A dramatic and scenic excursion in southeastern Alaska is **The White Pass and Yukon Route** (Box 435, Skagway, AK 99840, tel. 800/343–7373). The narrow-gauge railroad carried passengers and ore from the Klondike gold mines of the Yukon to Skagway until it was closed down in the early 1980s. In 1988, the line was reopened as far as Fraser, British Columbia. Bus service is available from Fraser to Whitehorse in the Yukon Territory.

Both **Princess Cruises/Tours** (tel. 206/728–4202) and **Holland America Line/Westours** (tel. 206/281–3535) offer rail tours on the Alaska Railroad into the interior of Alaska as a postcruise option.

By Bus
Scheduled Service
Greyhound Lines (tel. 800/231–2222) operates regular intercity bus routes to points throughout the region. **Gray Line of Seattle** (tel. 206/624–5077) has daily bus service between Seattle and Victoria via the Washington State ferry at Anacortes. Smaller bus companies provide service within local areas. One such service, **Pacific Coach Lines** (tel. 800/661–1725), runs from downtown Vancouver to Victoria (via the British Columbia ferry system). Bus service to Alaska from the lower 48 states is possible via Greyhound, with connections to other bus companies via Whitehorse in the Yukon Territory. **Quick Coach Lines** (tel. 604/244–3744; 800/665–2122 in the U.S.) provides bus service between Seattle's Sea-Tac Airport and Vancouver's major hotels and cruise terminal.

Charters
Several companies operate charter bus service and scheduled sightseeing tours that last f om a few hours to several days. Most tours can be booked locally and provide a good way for visitors to see the sights comfortably within a short period of time. **Gray Line** companies in Portland (tel. 503/226–6755), Seattle (tel. 206/624–5077), Vancouver (tel. 604/681–8687), and Victoria (tel. 604/388–5248) run such sightseeing trips.

By Car
Except for a short distance north of Vancouver, there are no roads along the rugged mainland coast of British Columbia and southeast Alaska.

Alaskan cities such as Juneau have no direct access by road; cars must be brought in by ferry. Skagway and Haines are the only towns in southeast Alaska accessible directly by road. The trip—a grueling 1,650 miles from Seattle—passes through British Columbia and the Yukon Territory.

Speed Limits
The speed limit on U.S. interstate highways is 65 miles per hour in rural areas and 55 miles per hour in urban zones and on secondary highways. In Canada (where the metric system is used), the speed limit is usually 100 kilometers per hour on expressways and 80 kilometers per hour on secondary roads.

Insurance
Vehicle insurance is compulsory in the United States and Canada. Motorists are required to produce evidence of insurance if they become involved in an accident. Upon arrival, visitors from foreign countries should contact an insurance agent or broker to obtain the necessary insurance for North America.

Winter Driving
Winter driving in the Pacific North Coast can sometimes present some real challenges. In coastal areas, the mild, damp climate contributes to roadways that are frequently wet. Winter snowfalls are not common (generally only once or twice a year), but when snow does fall, traffic grinds to a halt and the roadways become treacherous and stay that way until the snow melts.

Tire chains, studs, or snow tires are essential equipment for winter travel in mountain areas. If you're planning to drive into high elevations, be sure to check the weather forecast beforehand. Even the main-highway mountain passes can be forced to close because of snow conditions. During the winter months, state and provincial highway departments operate snow advisory telephone lines that give pass conditions.

Auto Clubs The **American Automobile Association** (AAA) and the **Canadian Automobile Association** (CAA) provide full services to members of any of the Commonwealth Motoring Conference (CMC) clubs, including the Automobile Association, the Royal Automobile Club, and the Royal Scottish Automobile Club. Services are also available to members of the Alliance Internationale de l'Automobile (AIT), the Federation Internationale de l'Automobile (FIA), and the Federation of Interamerican Touring and Automobile Clubs (FITAC). Members receive travel information, itineraries, maps, tour books, information about road and weather conditions, emergency road services, and travel-agency services.

By Ferry Ferries play an important part in the transportation network of the Pacific North Coast. In some areas, ferries provide the only form of access into and out of communities. In other places, ferries transport thousands of commuters a day to and from work in the cities. For visitors, ferries are one of the best ways to get a feel for the region and its ties to the sea.

British Columbia The **British Columbia Ferry Corporation** (1112 Fort St., Victoria, B.C. V8V 4V2, tel. 604/386–3431 in Victoria or 604/669–1211 in Vancouver; for recorded schedule information, tel. 604/656–0757 in Victoria or 604/685–1021 in Vancouver) operates one of the largest and most modern ferry fleets in the world, with 38 ships serving 42 ports of call along the coast of British Columbia. More than 15 million passengers ride this fleet each year.

The busiest ferries operate between the mainland and Vancouver Island, carrying passengers, cars, campers, RVs, trucks, and buses. Peak traffic times are Friday afternoons, Saturday mornings, and Sunday afternoons, especially during summer months and holiday weekends. The company also provides scheduled service on the *Queen of the North* between Port Hardy at the northern end of Vancouver Island and the port city of Prince Rupert. From there, connections can be made to Alaskan ferries that travel still farther north, or to a VIA Rail train heading east through the Canadian Rockies. Connections to the Queen Charlotte Islands (reservations strongly recommended) can also be made via another British Columbia ferry.

The *Queen of the North* sails every two days during the summer and once a week during the winter. Summer cruises (June–Sept.) take 15 hours (all in daylight), so passengers can enjoy every bit of the spectacular coastal scenery. Reservations are strongly recommended. For reservations, contact British Columbia Ferry Corporation (*see above*).

Clipper Navigation (2701 Alaskan Way, Pier 69, Seattle, WA 98121, tel. 800/888–2535) operates three passenger-only jet catamarans between Seattle and Victoria; the largest holds 300 people, the smallest 250. Each boat makes the scenic crossing in just under three hours. A longer run (five hours) that includes stops in Friday Harbor and Port Townsend has recently been added.

Black Ball Transport's (430 Belleville St., Victoria, B.C. V8V 1W9, tel. 604/386–2202 in Victoria or 206/457–4491 in Port Angeles) MV *Coho* makes daily crossings year-round, from Port Angeles to Victoria. The *Coho* can carry 800 passengers and 100 cars across the Strait of Juan de Fuca in 1½ hours. Advance reservations are not accepted.

Gray Line Cruises (tel. 206/738–8099) operates the 200 passenger-only *Victoria Star,* which provides boat service between Bellingham and Victoria from mid-May to mid-October.

Victoria Rapid Transit operates the passenger-only *Victoria Express* (Box 1928, Port Angeles, WA 98362, tel. 206/452–8088 or 800/633–1589 for reservations in Washington) and offers a one-hour crossing of the Strait of Juan de Fuca between Port Angeles and Victoria from the end of May through the end of October.

Washington The **Washington State Ferry System** (Colman Dock, Seattle, WA 98104, tel. 206/464–6400 or 800/843–3779 in WA) has 25 ferries in its fleet, which carries more than 23 million passengers a year between points on Puget Sound and the San Juan Islands. Reservations are not available on any domestic routes.

If you are planning to take a ferry, try to avoid peak commuter hours. The heaviest traffic flows are eastbound in the mornings and on Sunday evenings, and westbound on Saturday mornings and weekday afternoons. The best times for travel are 9–3 and after 7 PM on weekdays. In July and August, you may have to wait up to two hours to take a car aboard one of the popular San Juan Islands ferries. Walk-on space is always available; if possible, leave your car behind.

Alaska The transportation lifeblood of southeastern Alaska is the **Alaska Marine Highway System** (Box R, Juneau, AK 99811, tel. 907/465–3941, 907/465–3942, or 800/642–0066 from the lower 48 states). From their southern terminus in Bellingham, Washington, the Alaska ferries carry passengers and vehicles through the Inside Passage year-round, with stops at Prince Rupert, Skagway, Haines, Ketchikan, Sitka, Wrangell, Petersburg, Stewart, and Juneau. Smaller car ferries serve several other towns and villages in southeast Alaska. The boats take the same route as the luxury cruise ships, but at a fraction of the cost.

Staterooms are available, but cabin space is always booked months in advance. Reservations for staterooms usually become available in early December for the following year. Space is always sold out quickly, but passengers without staterooms are welcome to sleep in public lounges or on deck.

During the summer, U.S. forest rangers ride the larger ferries, offering interpretive programs along the route. Short local land tours, coinciding with ferry stopovers, are available in many communities. During the fall, winter, and spring, ferry rates are lower and senior citizens are entitled to free passage between ports in Alaska.

The **AlaskaPass Travelpass** (Box 351 Vashon Island, WA 98070, tel. 800/248–7598) provides transportation aboard any Alaska or British Columbia ferry as well as many connecting bus and train services. Passes of varying lengths enable the independent traveler to exercise a high degree of flexibility in choosing an itinerary.

By Cruise Ship Cruise ships travel British Columbia's Inside Passage to Alaska from mid-May through early October. Most ships start or end their seven-day journeys in Vancouver, making stops at several Alaskan ports along the way. A few companies provide land tours in conjunction with their week-long cruises into the Yukon Territory and other parts of Alaska.

More than 25 ships offer cruises to Alaska, including those operated by **Admiral Cruises, Alaska Sightseeing, Clipper Cruises, Crystal Cruises, Cunard Line, Costa Cruises, Holland America, Kloster Cruise Line, Princess Cruises, Regency Cruise Line, Royal Caribbean Cruise Line, Royal Cruise Line, Special Expeditions,** and **World Explorer Cruises.** For more information, contact your travel agent or the Cruise Lines International Association (CLIA, 17 Battery Pl., Suite 631, New York, NY 10004, tel. 212/425–7400).

Telephones

The telephone area codes in the Pacific North Coast are 503 for Oregon; 206 for western Washington, including Seattle; 509 for eastern Washington, including Spokane; 604 for British Columbia; and 907 for Alaska, except for the town of Hyder in southeast Alaska, which uses the 604 area code.

Pay telephones cost 25¢ for local calls. Charge phones are also found in many locations. These phones can be used to charge a call to a telephone-company credit card, your home phone, or the party you are calling: You do not need to deposit 25¢. For directory assistance, dial 1, the area code, and 555–1212. For local directory assistance, dial 1 followed by 555–1212. You can dial most international calls direct. Dial "0" to reach an operator.

Many hotels place a surcharge on local calls made from your room and include a service charge on long-distance calls. It may be cheaper for you to make your calls from a pay phone in the hotel lobby rather than from your room.

Radio Stations

The air waves are packed in Seattle, Portland, and Vancouver, but the following are the top stations.

Seattle **KBSG-AM (1210)/FM (97.3)**, '50s, '60s, and '70s music; **KING-FM (98.1)**, classical; **KIRO-AM (710)**, news, sports, and features; **KMPS-AM (1300)/FM (94.1)**, country music; **KUOW-FM (94.9)**, National Public Radio—news, classical music, and features; and **KUBE-FM (93.3)**, contemporary rock.

Portland **KEX-AM (1190)**, news and features; **KINK-FM (101.9)**, contemporary rock; **KKGR-AM (1230)**, contemporary country music and news; **KOPB-FM (91.5)**, National Public Radio—classical, music, news, and features; **KXYQ-FM (105.1)**, contemporary hard rock; **KXL-AM (750)**, news and talk; and **KYL-FM (95.5)**, easy listening.

Vancouver **CFOX-FM (99.3)**, contemporary rock; **CFUN-AM (1410)/FM (100.1)**, oldies and hits; **CBU-AM (1370)**, CBC Radio—news and features; and **CJJR-FM (93.7)**, country music.

Mail

Postal Rates Postage rates vary for different classes of mail and destinations. Check with the local post office for rates before mailing a letter or parcel. At press time, it cost 29¢ to mail a standard letter anywhere within the United States. Mail to Canada cost 40¢ per first ounce, and 23¢ for each additional ounce; mail to Great Britain and other foreign countries cost 50¢ per half-ounce.

First-class rates in Canada are 46¢ for up to 30 grams of mail delivered within Canada, 52¢ for up to 30 grams delivered to the United States, 70¢ for up to 50 grams. International mail and postcards run 92¢ for up to 20 grams, $1.26 for 20–50 grams.

Receiving Mail Visitors can have letters or parcels sent to them while they are traveling by using the following address: Name of addressee, c/o General Delivery, Main Post Office, City and State/Province, U.S./Canada, Zip Code (U.S.) or Postal Code (Canada). Contact the nearest post office for further details. Any item mailed to "General Delivery" must be picked up by the addressee in person within 15 days or it will be returned to the sender.

Tipping

Tips and service charges are usually not automatically added to a bill in the United States or Canada. If service is satisfactory, customers generally give waiters, waitresses, taxi drivers, barbers, hairdressers, and so forth, a tip of 15%–20% of the total bill. Bellhops, doormen, and porters at airports and railway stations are generally tipped $1 for each item of luggage.

Opening and Closing Times

Washington and Oregon Most retail stores in Washington and Oregon are open 9:30–6 seven days a week in downtown locations and later at suburban shopping malls. Downtown stores sometimes stay open late Thursday and Friday nights. Normal banking hours are weekdays 9–6; some branches are also open on Saturday morning.

Alaska In Alaska, most city retail outlets open Monday–Saturday 10–6 or 10–7. Shopping malls stay open until 8 or 9. Most banks operate 10–3.

British Columbia In British Columbia, many stores close on Sunday. Outlets that cater to tourists are the notable exception. Normal banking hours in Canada are 10–3 on weekdays, with extended hours in many locations. Some banks in major cities are now open on Saturday morning.

Shopping

What to Buy The Pacific North Coast offers shoppers quite a selection of locally made crafts and souvenirs. Some of the most distinctive items are produced by Native American artists, who manufacture prints, wood carvings, boxes, masks, and other items. Shops in Seattle, Portland, and Vancouver carry a wide variety of these objects, but collectors can find the best selection and prices in the small communities located on Vancouver Island.

Another popular "souvenir" for visitors is freshly caught salmon. Fish vendors can pack a recent catch in a special airlines-approved box that will keep the fish fresh for a couple of days. A package of smoked salmon—which will keep even longer—is another alternative.

Public markets are among the best places to purchase salmon and other gifts. Seattle's historic Pike Place Market and Vancouver's Granville Island Market offer a wonderful array of fish stalls, fresh fruit and vegetable stands, arts and crafts vendors, and small shops that sell practically everything.

Shoppers in Alaska will find good buys on gold-nugget jewelry, woven baskets, items made from jade, and specialty foods, including salmon and wild-berry products. Also available and unique to Alaska are carvings made from fossilized walrus ivory that are produced only by indigenous native carvers. Look for the "Made in Alaska" logo, which indicates an item that was genuinely manufactured in Alaska.

Because residents of the Pacific North Coast have such an active lifestyle, many leading manufacturers and retailers of outdoor equipment and apparel have their headquarters there. Recreation Equipment Inc. (REI) has several stores in the Seattle area that sell everything from high-quality sleeping bags and backpacks to freeze-dried food and mountain-climbing equipment. Eddie Bauer, the famous recreational clothing and equipment catalog distributor and retailer, was founded in Seattle and still has outlets there. One of the world's leading athletic shoe manufacturers, Nike, is based in Oregon and has retail shops in Portland. Its space-age store in downtown Portland is worth a visit.

Taxes Oregon and Alaska charge no sales tax; Washington's tax is 7%–8.2%, depending on municipality; provincial sales tax in British Columbia is 6%. Canada's Goods and Services Tax (GST) is 7%, applicable on virtually every purchase except basic groceries and a small number of other items. Visitors to Canada may claim a full rebate of the GST on any goods taken out of the country as well as on short-term accommodations. Rebates can be claimed either immediately on departure from Canada at participating duty-free shops or by mail. Rebate forms can be obtained at most stores and hotels in Canada or by writing to **Revenue Canada** (Visitor's Rebate Program, Ottawa, Ontario, Canada K1A 1J5, tel. 613/991–3346 or 800/668–4748 in Canada). Claims must be for a minimum of $7 worth of tax and can be submitted up to a year from the date of purchase. Purchases made during multiple visits to Canada can be grouped together for rebate purposes.

Participant Sports and Outdoor Activities

Bicycling Bicycling is a popular sport in the Pacific North Coast, appealing to both families out for a leisurely ride and avid cyclists seeking a challenge on rugged mountain trails.

Several cycling organizations sponsor trips of various lengths and degrees of difficulty, both on- and off-road. For further information, contact **Portland Wheelmen Touring Club** (Box 40753, Portland, OR 97240, tel. 503/282–7982), **Washington State Bicycle Association** (tel. 206/329–2453), **Cascade Bicycle Club** (tel. 206/522–2453), and **Bicycling Association of British Columbia** (1200 Hornby St., Vancouver, B.C. V6Z 2E2, tel. 604/669–2453).

Rentals are available from bicycle shops in most cities.

Boating The sheltered waters of Puget Sound and the Inside Passage, plus the area's many freshwater lakes, make boating one of the most popular outdoor activities in the Pacific North Coast. On sunny days, a virtual fleet of boats dots the waterways; in fact, some experts say that there are more boats per capita in the Puget Sound area than anywhere else in the world. For charters, outfitters, and information, see the boating section in each chapter.

Because of the region's mild climate, it is possible to enjoy boating throughout the year. Charters, which are available with or without a skipper and crew, can be rented for a period of a few hours to several days. The calm waterways are also rated among the best in the world for sea kayaking, an appealing way to explore the intertidal regions. **The Trade Association of Sea Kayaking (TASK)** (Box 84144, Seattle, WA 98124, tel. 206/621–1018) provides information on outfitters, rentals, seminars, and safety.

Cruising and particularly deep-sea-fishing charters are available from many ports throughout the Pacific North Coast. Campbell River on British Columbia's Vancouver Island, Neah Bay and Port Angeles on Washington's Olympic Peninsula, Westport on the Long Beach Peninsula in southern Washington, and Depoe Bay in Oregon are leading fishing and charter ports.

The area's swift rivers also provide challenges to avid canoers and kayakers. A word of warning, however: Many of these rivers should be attempted only by experienced boaters. Check with local residents or outfitters to find out what dangers may lie downstream before taking to the waterways.

Climbing/ Mountaineering The mountains of the Pacific North Coast have given many an adventurer quite a challenge. It is no coincidence that many members of the U.S. expedition teams to Mt. Everest have come from this region.

With expert training and advanced equipment, mountaineering can be a safe sport, but you should never go climbing without an experienced guide. Classes are available from qualified instructors. For more information, contact **Mazama Club** (909 N.W. 19th Ave., Portland, OR 97209, tel. 503/227–2345), **The Mountaineers** (300 3rd Ave. W, Seattle, WA 98119, tel. 206/284–8484), and **Rainier Mountaineering Inc.** (Paradise, WA 98397, tel. 206/569–2227).

Fishing The coastal regions and inland lakes and rivers of the Pacific Northwest are known for their excellent fishing opportunities. Fishing lodges, many of which are accessible only by float plane, cater to anglers in search of the ultimate fishing experience.

Visiting sportsmen must possess a nonresident license for the state or province in which they plan to fish. Licenses are easily obtainable at sporting-goods stores, bait shops, and other outlets in popular fishing areas.

For information on fishing regulations, contact **Washington Department of Fisheries** (Administration Bldg., Room 115, Olympia, WA 98504, tel. 206/586–1425 for Washington salmon fishing or marine licenses), **Washington State Department of Wildlife** (600 Capitol Way N, Olympia, WA 98501, tel. 206/753–5700 for freshwater fishing), **Oregon Department of Fish and Wildlife** (506 S.W. Mill St., Portland, OR 97208, tel. 503/229–5403), or **Alaska Department of Fish and Game** (Box 3-2000, Juneau, AK 99802, tel. 907/465–4112). In British Columbia, separate licenses are required for saltwater and freshwater fishing. Information and licenses for saltwater fishing can be obtained from the **Department of Fisheries and Oceans** (555 W. Hastings

St., Suite 400, Vancouver, BC V6B 5G3, tel. 604/666–0384). For freshwater fishing, contact the **Ministry of Environment, Fish and Wildlife Information** (Parliament Bldgs., Victoria, BC V8V 1X5, tel. 604/387–9740).

Most coastal towns have charter boats and crews that are available for deep-sea fishing. State and provincial tourism departments can provide further information on charters.

Golf The Pacific North Coast has many excellent golf courses, but not all of them are open to the public. Consequently, visitors may find it difficult to arrange a tee time at a popular course. If you are a member of a golf club at home, check to see if your club has a reciprocal playing arrangement with any of the private clubs in the areas that you will be visiting.

Hiking There are many trails in the Pacific North Coast that are geared to both beginning and experienced hikers. The **National Parks and Forests Outdoor Recreation Information Center** (915 2nd Ave., Room 442, Seattle, WA 98174, tel. 206/220–7450) can provide maps of trails that are well marked and well maintained. Guidebooks that describe the best trails in the area are readily available in local bookstores. The *Footsore* series of books, published by The Mountaineers (306 2nd Ave. W, Seattle, WA 98119, tel. 206/285–2665), are among the best.

Hunting An autumn visit to the Pacific North Coast yields opportunities for hunting deer and waterfowl in the coastal areas and around inland lakes. Big-game hunters, who are on the trail for elk, moose, and bear, should go to British Columbia or Alaska, where outfitters are available to act as guides.

For more information on hunting facilities and licenses, contact **Washington State Department of Wildlife** (600 Capitol Way N, Olympia, WA 98501, tel. 206/753–5700), **Oregon Department of Fish and Wildlife** (506 S.W. Mill St., Portland, OR 97208, tel. 503/229–5403), **British Columbia Ministry of Environment, Wildlife Branch** (810 Blanshard St., Victoria, BC V8W 2H1, tel. 604/387–9740), or **Alaska Department of Fish and Game** (Box 3-200, Juneau, AK 99802, tel. 907/465–4112).

Sailboarding The Columbia River, particularly at Hood River, Oregon, is known as the best spot in the world for windsurfing. Puget Sound and some of the inland lakes are also popular venues for the sport. Sailboard rentals and lessons are available from local specialty shops. In British Columbia, the town of Squamish is quickly becoming another major windsurfing destination.

Scuba Diving The crystal-clear waters of Puget Sound and the Inside Passage—with their diversity of marine life—present excellent opportunities for scuba diving and underwater photography. For information on dive shops, equipment rentals, and charter boats in British Columbia, contact **Dive B.C.** (707 Westminster Ave., Powell River, B.C. V8A 1C5, tel. 604/485–6267).

Skiing Skiing is by far the most popular winter activity in the area. *Downhill* Moist air off the Pacific Ocean dumps snow on the coastal mountains, providing excellent skiing from November through the end of March and sometimes into April. Local newspapers regularly list snow conditions for ski areas throughout the region during the winter season. Resort and lift-ticket prices tend to be less expensive here than at the internationally known ski destinations. Most Washington ski resorts cater to those who've come for a day of skiing rather than a longer stay.

The Whistler and Blackcomb mountains, north of Vancouver, comprise the biggest ski area in the region. Whistler Village resort boasts the longest and second-longest vertical drops (more than a mile each) of any ski area in North America. Aside from Whistler/Blackcomb, British Columbia has many other excellent ski resorts scattered throughout the province, including several that are only minutes from downtown Vancouver.

Washington has 20 ski areas, several of which are located just east of Seattle in the Cascade Mountains. Snoqualmie Pass, the ski area closest to Seattle—about 45 minutes east—contains three ski areas: Snoqualmie, Ski Acres, and Alpental. Other major ski resorts nearby include Mt. Baker, Crystal Mountain, Stevens Pass, and Mission Ridge.

Oregon's primary ski facility, Mt. Bachelor, in central Oregon, is rated one of the best ski areas in North America. Located 50 miles east of Portland, Mt. Hood's five ski areas offer skiing (on glaciers!) well into the summer months.

Cross-country Cross-country skiing is a popular and less expensive way to enjoy the winter wilderness. Many downhill ski resorts also have well-marked and well-groomed cross-country trails. Washington operates a system of more than 40 **SnoParks** (Office of Winter Recreation, Parks and Recreation Commission, 7150 Cleanwater La., KY-11, Olympia, WA 98504, tel. 206/586–0185) that are a series of groomed cross-country trails within state parks in which, for the price of a one-day ($7), three-day ($10), or seasonal ($20) pass, skiers have access to trails in 70 locations statewide.

Swimming Despite all the water surrounding the region, there is not as much swimming as one might expect along the Pacific North Coast. While the sandy ocean beaches attract throngs of people during the summer, most sun worshipers spend little time in the water—it's just too cold!

Similarly, the waters of Puget Sound are generally too cold for swimming, and the beaches are mostly rocky. The best swimming beaches can be found around the Parksville area of Vancouver Island, where the combination of low tide, sandy beaches, and shallow water creates fairly warm swimming conditions.

Wildlife Viewing The Pacific North Coast offers ample opportunities for viewing wildlife, both on land and on water. Bald eagles, sea lions, dolphins, and whales are just a few of the animals that can be observed in the region. The best way to identify native creatures is with a pair of binoculars and a good nature guide at hand. Books on regional wildlife can be found in local bookstores.

Northwest Interpretive Association (83 S. King St., Suite 212, Seattle, WA 98104, tel. 206/553–2636), in cooperation with the **National Park and Forest Services,** operates *Pacific Northwest Field Seminars*. This nonprofit program offers outdoor courses from April through October covering topics such as nature writing and photography, wildlife, ecology, birding, geology, volcanology, and backpacking. Fees average about $35 per day for one- to four-day seminars.

Spectator Sports

Baseball The **Seattle Mariners** (tel. 206/628–0888 for tickets) of the American League play in the 60,000-seat indoor Kingdome. Tickets are almost always available. The baseball season runs from April to early October.

Several minor league teams play in smaller outdoor stadiums, including the **Vancouver Canadians** (tel. 604/872–5232), the **Tacoma Tigers** (tel. 206/752–7707), and the **Everett Giants** (tel. 206/258–3673).

Basketball The region fields two big-league basketball teams: the **Seattle SuperSonics** (tel. 206/281–5850) at the Seattle Coliseum and the **Portland Trail Blazers** (tel. 503/234–9291) at the Memorial Coliseum.

Dog Racing Greyhounds race at the **Multnomah Kennel Club Dog Race Track** in Portland (tel. 503/243–2706) from May to September.

Football The **Seattle Seahawks** (tel. 206/827–9766 for tickets) of the National Football League play in the Kingdome during the fall, but games are almost always sold out. Tickets are usually available for the **British Columbia Lions** (tel. 604/685–4344) of the Canadian Football League, who play in the indoor British Columbia Place Stadium in Vancouver. One of the most consistently successful university football teams in the United States is the **University of Washington Huskies** (tel. 206/543–2200). They take to the gridiron at 73,000-seat Husky Stadium, which overlooks Lake Washington.

Hockey The **Vancouver Canucks** (tel. 604/254–5141) of the National Hockey League hit the ice at the Pacific Coliseum. Minor-league "junior" hockey has a strong following in both Seattle and Portland.

Horse Racing Thoroughbred horse racing takes place at **Portland Meadows** (tel. 503/285–9144) in Portland and **Exhibition Park** (tel. 604/254–1631) in Vancouver from April to October. Harness racing occurs from April to October at the **Cloverdale Raceway** (tel. 604/576–9141), located south of Vancouver near the U.S. border.

Powerboating Each year thousands of spectators watch unlimited-class hydroplanes, or "thunder boats," race on Seattle's Lake Washington in early August as the grand finale of **Seafair** (*see* Festivals and Seasonal events in Before You Go, *above*).

Beaches

The Pacific coasts of Oregon, Washington, and British Columbia have long, sandy beaches that run for miles at a stretch. But the waters are often too cold or treacherous for swimming. Even in summertime, beach goers must be prepared to dress warmly.

The most accessible—and warmest—ocean beaches in the region are in Oregon, where a number of resort communities are established. Most of the Oregon coastline has been protected as public land, so it can be enjoyed by everyone.

The beaches of Washington are more remote from the major centers of population. Seattle is a two- to three-hour drive from the nearest ocean beaches. Even in summer, the beaches are never crowded.

Most of the west coast of Vancouver Island is totally isolated. Pacific Rim National Park is one of the few places where ocean beaches are accessible. On the eastern coast of Vancouver Island, there are a number of good swimming beaches around the town of Parksville.

The gravel beaches of Washington's Puget Sound and British Columbia's Inside Passage attract few swimmers or sunbathers, but the beaches are popular for beachcombing and viewing abundant marine life.

Dining

Many restaurants in the Pacific North Coast serve local specialties such as salmon, crab, oysters, and other seafood delicacies. Seattle's Pike Place Market and Vancouver's Granville Island Market display bountiful supplies of local seafood and produce, and these are good places to scan what you might find on restaurant menus. Ethnic foods are also becoming increasingly popular, especially Asian cuisines such as Japanese, Korean, and Thai.

There is tremendous emphasis on and enjoyment of the hearty and savory fare available in this area. Chefs of all stripes key their menus to the seasonal availability of local produce. In June strawberries are in season, July brings in Walla Walla Sweets (a softball-size mild onion and a local delicacy), blackberries (which grow wild, and can be picked from the roadside) take the forefront in August, and the Washington apple crop comes in in the fall.

Portions of Washington, Oregon, and British Columbia are major wine-producing regions. Local wines are often featured in the best restaurants. Beer, too, is a popular local product, and microbreweries have enjoyed increasing popularity throughout the Northwest. Often located in or connected with a local pub, some of these breweries produce only enough specialty beers (called microbrews) for their own establishments. Some, however, such as Red Hook Ale, Ballard Bitter, and Anchor Ale, are also available from regular beer outlets. Some wineries and microbreweries offer tours and tastings.

Coffee has become a passion in Seattle. Lattés (the local version of cafe au lait), cappuccinos, and espressos are the beverages of choice in the finer—and even not so fine—restaurants around town (you can get a latte at the downtown McDonald's). Espresso stands do a brisk business on almost every other downtown corner. The latest phenomenon are drive-through espresso stands that are popping up in suburban areas. The coffee craze is also spreading to Portland and Vancouver. Enjoy!

As a general rule, restaurants in metropolitan areas are more expensive than those outside the city. But many city establishments, especially those that feature foreign cuisines, are surprisingly inexpensive. Because of space limitations, we have listed only restaurants recommended as the best within each price range.

Lodging

Rates Although the names of the various hotel and motel price categories are standard, the prices listed under each may vary from
one area to another. This variation reflects local price standards: For example, a Moderate price in a large urban area
might be considered Expensive in a rural region. In all cases,
price ranges for each category are clearly stated before each
listing.

Hotels Most big-city hotels cater primarily to business travelers, with
such facilities as restaurants, cocktail lounges, swimming
pools, exercise equipment, and meeting rooms. Room rates often reflect the range of amenities offered. Most cities also have
less expensive hotels, which are clean and comfortable but have
fewer upscale facilities. A new accommodations trend is all-
suite hotels, which offer more intimate facilities and are gaining popularity with business travelers. Examples are **Courtyard By Marriott** (tel. 800/321–2211) and **Embassy Suites Hotels**
(tel. 800/362–2779).

Many properties offer special weekend rates, sometimes up to
50% off regular prices. However, these deals are usually not extended during peak summer months, when hotels are normally
full.

Vancouver, Seattle, and Portland have all experienced major
hotel building booms during the past 10 years. Most of the major chains have properties in one or all of these cities. For more
information, contact **Canadian Pacific** (tel. 800/828–7447),
Delta (tel. 800/877–1133), **Doubletree** (tel. 800/528–0444), **Four
Seasons** (tel. 800/332–3442), **Hilton** (tel. 800/445–8667), **Holiday Inn** (tel. 800/465–4329), **Hyatt** (tel. 800/233–1234), **Marriott**
(tel. 800/228–9290), **Ramada** (tel. 800/228–2828), **Red Lion Hotels and Inns** (tel. 800/547–8010), **Sheraton** (tel. 800/325–3535),
Stouffer (tel. 800/468–3571), **West Coast Hotels/Coast Hotels**
(tel. 800/426–0670), and **Westin** (tel. 800/228–3000).

Motels/Motor Inns The familiar roadside motel of the past is fast disappearing
from the landscape. In its place are economical chain-run motor
inns that are strategically located at highway intersections.
Some of these establishments offer very basic facilities; others
provide restaurants, swimming pools, and other amenities.

Nationally recognized chains include **Best Western** (tel. 800/
528–1234), **Days Inn** (tel. 800/325–2525), **La Quinta Inns** (tel.
800/531–5900), **Motel 6** (tel. 800/437–7486), **Quality Inns** (tel.
800/228–5151), **Super 8 Motels** (tel. 800/848–8888), and
Travelodge (tel. 800/255–3050). **Nendel's** (tel. 800/547–0106)
and **Shilo Inns** (tel. 800/222–2244) are regional chains.

Inns These establishments generally are located outside cities and
have anywhere from 8 to 20 rooms. Lodging is often in an old
restored building with some historical or architectural significance. Inns are sometimes confused with bed-and-breakfasts
because they may include breakfast in their basic rate.

Bed-and-Breakfasts Bed-and-breakfasts are private homes that reflect the personalities and tastes of their owners. Generally, B&Bs have 2–10
rooms, some with private baths and others with shared facilities. Breakfast is always included in the price of the room.

B&Bs have flourished in recent years. Some homes advertise to the public, while others maintain a low profile. Most belong to a reservation system through which you can book a room.

Reservation services in the Pacific North Coast include **Best Canadian Bed & Breakfast Network** (1090 W. King Edward Ave., Vancouver, B.C. V6H 1Z4, tel. 604/738–7207), **Hometours International, Inc.** (1170 Broadway, Suite 614, New York, NY 10001, tel. 212/689–0851 or 800/367–4668), **Northwest Bed & Breakfast Travel Unlimited** (610 S.W. Broadway, Portland, OR 97205, tel. 503/243–7616), and **Traveller's Bed & Breakfast** (Box 492, Mercer Island, WA 98040, tel. 206/232–2345). The **Oregon Bed and Breakfast Guild** (Box 3187, Ashland, OR 97520) publishes a directory of establishments within the state. Before leaving the United Kingdom, you can book a B&B through **American Bed & Breakfast, Inter-Bed Network** (31 Ernest Rd., Colchester, Essex CO7 9LQ, tel. 0206/223162).

Resorts The Pacific North Coast has quite a variety of resorts—from rural fishing lodges to luxury destination showpieces.

Dozens of small fishing resorts nestle along the coast and within the interior of British Columbia and southeast Alaska. Most are rustic lodges, providing basic accommodations for sports enthusiasts, but others offer such deluxe comforts as gourmet meals and hot tubs in a wilderness setting.

The Whistler Village resort in British Columbia is best known for its world-class skiing. But Whistler is equally impressive as a year-round destination with golf, tennis, swimming, mountain biking, and horseback riding.

Locals and visitors alike favor the grand settings at the Inn at Semi-Ah-Moo in Blaine, Washington, and the Rosario Resort in the San Juan Islands for getaway trips. A new resort on the Washington side of the Columbia River, Skamania Lodge, is now open. Most of the Oregon coast is resort country; one of the state's most famous resorts, Salishan Lodge at Gleneden Beach, is located there.

Camping Camping is a popular and inexpensive way to tour the Pacific Northwest. Oregon, Washington, Alaska, and British Columbia all have networks of excellent government-run parks that offer camping and organized activities. A few state and provincial parks will accept advance camping reservations, but most do not. Privately operated campgrounds sometimes have extra amenities such as laundry rooms and swimming pools. For more information, contact the local state or provincial tourism department.

YMCAs/YWCAs YMCAs or YWCAs are usually a good bet for clean, no-frills, reliable lodging in large towns and cities. These buildings are often centrally located, and their rates are significantly lower than those at city hotels. Nonmembers are welcome, but they may pay slightly more than members. A few very large Ys have accommodations for couples, but sleeping arrangements are usually segregated.

Home Exchange This is obviously an inexpensive solution to the lodging problem, because house-swapping means living rent-free. You find a house, apartment, or other vacation property to exchange for your own by becoming a member of a home-exchange organization, which then sends you its annual directories listing available exchanges and includes your own listing in at least one of them. Arrangements for the actual exchange are made by the two parties to it, not by the organization. Principal clearinghouses include **Intervac U.S./International Home Exchange** (Box 590504, San Francisco, CA 94159, tel. 415/435–3497), the oldest, with thousands of foreign and domestic homes for exchange in its three annual directories; membership is $62, or $72 if you want to receive the directories but remain unlisted. The **Vacation Exchange Club** (Box 650, Key West, FL 33041, tel. 800/638–3841), also with thousands of foreign and domestic listings, publishes four annual directories plus updates; the $50 membership includes your listing in one book. **Loan-a-Home** (2 Park La., Apt. 6E, Mount Vernon, NY 10552, tel. 914/664–7640) specializes in long-term exchanges; there is no charge to list your home, but the directories cost $35 or $45 depending on the number you receive.

Apartment and Villa Rentals If you want a home base that's roomy enough for a family and comes with cooking facilities, a furnished rental may be the solution. It's generally cost-wise, too, although not always—some rentals are luxury properties (economical only when your party is large). Home-exchange directories do list rentals—often second homes owned by prospective house swappers—and there are services that can not only look for a house or apartment for you (even a castle if that's your fancy) but also handle the paperwork. Some send an illustrated catalogue and others send photographs of specific properties, sometimes at a charge; up-front registration fees may apply.

Among the companies is **Rent a Home International** (7200 34th Ave. NW, Seattle, WA 98117, tel. 206/789–9377 or 800/488–7368). **Hideaways International** (767 Islington St., Box 4433, Portsmouth, NH 03802, tel. 603/430–4433 or 800/843–4433) functions as a travel club. Membership ($79 yearly per person or family at the same address) includes two annual guides plus quarterly newsletters; rentals are arranged directly between members, not by the club staff.

Credit Cards

The following credit card abbreviations have been used in this book: AE, American Express; D, Discover; DC, Diners Club; MC, MasterCard; and V, Visa.

Great Itineraries

Native Culture of the Pacific North Coast

Hundreds of years before the first white explorers reached the region, scores of Native American nations were comfortably settled in the Pacific North Coast. These "First People" profoundly influenced the development of the region, and many art forms and artifacts are displayed in museums up and down the coast.

It should be noted that this is an ambitious agenda, requiring extensive use of both the British Columbia and the Alaska Marine Highway ferry systems. Distances between points of interest in this part of North America can be great, and it is necessary to spend considerable time in transit. Because of the time involved, you may want to travel only as far as the B.C.

ferries go, instead of continuing your journey into Alaska. If you do continue on, and for any of the longer legs, it is advisable to book a stateroom when reserving passage. Nevertheless, seeing this heritage in combination with breathtaking displays of nature more than offsets any inconveniences that may be encountered.

Length of Trip 17–19 days

Getting Around From Vancouver, take the B.C. Ferry from Tsawwassen to Victoria, on Vancouver Island; Route 14 West from Victoria will take you to Sooke. All stops between Victoria and Port Hardy can be reached from Route 19, traveling northwest. The B.C. Ferry takes you from Port Hardy to Prince Rupert, on the mainland, where you can pick up Route 16 east to Hazelton. The Alaska Ferry System supplies transportation to all destinations north of Prince Rupert.

The Main Route 2 Nights: Vancouver

A great starting point, Vancouver offers much background on what you will see and experience in the tour to follow. Visit the **Vancouver Museum** and the **Museum of Anthropology** to acquaint yourself with the various tribes that have inhabited the regions you'll be exploring. You can see the first of many totem poles in **Stanley Park,** and stop by the **Wickaninnish Gallery** on Granville Island, where temporary exhibits of Native American crafts can be seen. A meal at **Quilicum** and a shopping stop at **Images for a Canadian Heritage** should be part of your downtown Vancouver agenda.

1 Night: Victoria

Take the ferry from Tsawwassen to Victoria, capital of British Columbia, and spend some time at the **Royal British Columbia Museum,** where you'll find—among many other fascinating exhibits—the Kwakiutl Indian Bighouse. In nearby Sooke, visit the **Sooke Regional Museum,** which offers extensive historical background on the Salish tribe that once flourished in this region. Call ahead for the schedule of weaving demonstrations held at the museum periodically.

1 Night: Duncan

The main draw here is the **Native Heritage Centre,** a sprawling complex devoted entirely to the culture of the tribes that have populated Vancouver Island. You can spend at least a day studying the many facets of Indian life addressed here, from interpretive dance and storytelling, to carving, weaving, and native cuisine. Authentic Native American items may be purchased at **Big Foot, Modeste Mill,** and **Hills Indian Crafts.** Visit the nearby town of Chemainus. In 1983, the town was dying after the closure of the local sawmill. The town turned to tourism for survival by inviting artists to paint murals on buildings. Today, 32 murals depict the early settlement and industry of the area. Shops and galleries feature local crafts and art.

1 Night: Nanaimo

Petroglyph Provincial Park is named for the many distinctive rock carvings found in this area. A visit to the **Nanaimo Centennial Museum** will explain the significance of these curiosities. While you're there, you can take a look at the dioramas representing various aspects of Native American life.

1 Night: Campbell River

A 15-minute ferry ride from Campbell River takes you to the **Kwagiulth Museum and Cultural Centre** in the Cape Mudge Reserve on Quadra Island. The Kwagiulth tribe has recently opened **Tsa-Kwa-Luten Lodge** where you can dine on authentic native food and experience tribal ceremonies in the resort's Big House. Here you will find masks and costumes used in the Potlatch ceremonies (an event in which gifts are exchanged), spiritual gatherings convened to honor rites of passage such as birth, marriage, and death. In addition to the Potlatch regalia, the center offers tours (phone ahead), videos, dancing, and crafts demonstrations.

1 Night: Port McNeill

The B.C. Ferry takes you from Port McNeill to Alert Bay in about 40 minutes. There you'll find the **U'mista Cultural Center** (tel. 604/974–5403), which features its own collection of Potlatch masks and tribal dress, as well as jewelry, artifacts, a burial box, and videos on the prohibition of the Potlatch (which documents what happened to the native peoples) and on Spirit Lodge (a tape combining video presentations and live performers), which was previously seen at Expo '86 in Vancouver. The center focuses on the Kwakwaka'wakw, a group of 16 tribes in the area who shared the same language, Kwak'wala.

1 Night: Port Hardy–Prince Rupert (16½-hour ferry)

1 Night: Prince Rupert

While in Prince Rupert, plan to visit the **Museum of Northern British Columbia,** which has an excellent collection of coastal Indian art as well as demonstrations of wood carving and other crafts. A boat tour of the Metlakatla Indian Village is also available through the museum.

1 Night: Hazelton

'Ksan Village, about 120 miles east of Prince Rupert on Route 16, is a side trip well worth taking. The village offers just about everything you could ask for in one location: Guided tours, native dancing, pre-European artifacts, and Potlatch entertainment can be experienced in a truly authentic setting framed by the majestic Skeena Mountains.

1–2 Nights: Prince Rupert–Ketchikan (6-hour ferry)

Your first port in Alaska, **Ketchikan,** is the fourth-largest city in the state, with the added distinction of having more totem poles than any other city in the world. Recommended stops here include the **Tongass Historical Museum, Totem Bight State Historical Park,** and **Saxman Indian Village.** Also try to get a look at the mural on the campus of the University of Alaska, Southeast, titled *Return of the Eagle.*

1 Night: Ketchikan–Wrangell (5-hour ferry)

Some of the most interesting totem poles in Alaska can be found in this timber and fishing community. Visit **KikSadi Indian Park, Shakes Island,** and **Chief Shakes gravesite** for some prime examples. **Wrangell City Museum** houses an eclectic collection that includes Indian artifacts and petroglyphs. For more of the latter, walk along **Petroglyph Beach** at low tide.

1 Night: Wrangell–Sitka (17-hour ferry)

Evidence of native cultures abound in Sitka, and two attractions in particular should not be missed: the **Sheldon Jackson Museum,** which has a variety of pieces representing the full spectrum of Alaska's Native American life, and **Sitka National Historical Park,** which offers audiovisual presentations that provide interesting and informative background on native cultures.

1–2 Nights: Sitka–Juneau (8½-hour ferry)

The Alaska State Museum, located in Juneau—the state's capital and its third-largest city—has one of the finest Native American exhibits in the Pacific North Coast, and you should plan to spend as much time here as your schedule will allow. **Wickersham House** offers a more personal collection of photographs, carvings, basketry, and other artifacts.

For those whose appetites are *still* not sated, the Alaska ferry continues from Juneau to Haines, where the **Sheldon Museum and Cultural Center** and the **Chilkat Center for the Arts** offer extensive exhibits as well as native dancing and demonstrations of various crafts, such as carving and weaving. For more information, *see* Off the Beaten Track, in Chapter 9, for excursions to Kake, Angoon, and/or Hoonah.

Further Information Although schedules, fares, and hours of operation are listed in appropriate chapters, it is always advisable to confirm these by calling ahead; they often change seasonally, sometimes for reasons that seem almost arbitrary. For ferry information, *see* Getting Around by Ferry in Staying in the Pacific North Coast, *above.* If you wish to book staterooms, and it is advised for some of the longer legs, do so well in advance because they go quickly, especially during peak season. For details on specific attractions, consult Chapter 7, Vancouver; Chapter 8, British Columbia; and Chapter 9, Southeast Alaska.

Sampling the Wines of the Northwest

Whether you're an experienced oenophile or just making the leap from simply ordering a glass of house red, you will find much to delight and instruct you among the vineyards and wineries of the Pacific North Coast. Only California produces more domestic wine than does Washington State, and Oregon boasts many gold-medal winners among its varietals. This itinerary takes you through the Yakima and Willamette valleys, two major wine-producing regions of the United States. In addition to enhancing your appreciation of the grape, your route will take you through some of the most magnificent countryside in an area that is known for its scenery.

Length of Trip 12 days

Getting Around By car from Seattle, take I–90 east to Ellensburg and I–82 south to Yakima; 97 south takes you into Oregon. Go west on I–84 toward Hood River and pick up 35 south to 26 west; from there head west on 212 to I–205 south and 213 south into Salem. From Salem, take 22 west to 99 west, where you can go south to Corvallis or north into Portland. From Portland, take 8 west to Forest Grove.

The Main Route **2 Nights: Seattle**

Take the Winslow ferry from the Seattle terminal to the **Bainbridge Island Vineyard and Winery,** or visit the **Ste. Michelle**

Winery in Woodinville, 15 miles northeast of Seattle. Be sure to stop by some of the city's wine merchants who carry a wide selection of local products.

1 Night: Ellensburg

On the way to this former trading post, make a stop at the **Snoqualmie Winery,** about 30 minutes from downtown Seattle. While in Ellensburg, spend an hour or two exploring the town's historical district, or visit Olmstead Park, before heading on to Yakima.

2 Nights: Yakima

You're in the heart of Washington's wine country now, with literally dozens of operations to visit. Pick up the brochure offered by the Yakima Valley Wine Growers Association; it will help you choose three or four good stops.

1 Night: Hood River

Route 97 south takes you through the **Yakima Indian Reservation** to this lovely town at the junction of the Hood and Columbia rivers. If your interests include sailboarding, you'll want to spend more time here, because Hood River is rapidly becoming this sport's most popular destination. The surrounding area is covered with orchards, and several wineries await your inspection.

2 Nights: Salem

Route 35 south from Hood River loops through some magnificent orchard country and around Mt. Hood before becoming Route 26 west. Pick up Route 212 west to Route 205 south; a few miles farther takes you to Route 213 south, which you'll follow right into Salem. Along this stretch you might want to stop at the **Mt. Angel Abbey,** a century-old Benedictine seminary whose architecture alone warrants attention.

You could spend weeks exploring the **Willamette Valley Wineries** that border Route 99W (driving south) from Salem, but the concentration of establishments is so great that you'll be able to get a representative survey within a couple of days. Before leaving Salem, climb to the top of the **capitol dome** for a panoramic view of the city, valley, and mountains.

1 Night: McMinnville

Take Route 99W north to the home of **Oregon's International Pinot Noir Celebration,** which is held in August. What was true of the southern leg of this highway is even more so as you head north; use the brochure published by the Oregon Wine Center to distinguish among wineries.

2 Nights: Portland

Continuing north on 99W will take you through the wine towns of **Lafayette, Dundee, Newberg,** and **Tualatin,** each of which has at least one site you'll want to explore. **Beaverton, Hillsboro,** and **Forest Grove**—west of Portland on Route 8—have several noteworthy establishments.

Further Information Phone ahead to the places you plan to visit; changes in season, weather, or management that might affect your itinerary can occur at any time. *See* the Exploring sections in Chapter 3, Portland; Chapter 4, Western Oregon; Chapter 5, Seattle; and

Chapter 6, Washington State, for phone numbers and addresses.

Formal and Informal Florals: The Gardens of British Columbia and Washington State

British Columbia and Washington State share many things; among these are a moist climate, relatively moderate temperatures, and fertile soil. As a result, the Pacific North Coast is area rich in varied vegetation, and residents have capitalized on this desirable condition by fashioning numerous formal gardens, shrubbery mazes, parks, and commercial flower farms throughout the area.

This excursion through Vancouver, Victoria, and Seattle and its vicinity offers you an opportunity to experience the pastoral charms of many diverse arrangements and species of vegetation, as well as a close look at many types of birds and animals, both native and exotic.

Length of Trip 7 days

Getting Around From Vancouver, take the B.C. Ferry from Tsawwassen to Victoria. From Victoria, take one of the Victoria Clippers to Seattle. From Seattle, take Route 90 east to Route 405 north to Route 522 east to Route 202 into Woodinville. From Seattle, take Route 5 north to Mount Vernon, or south to Tacoma.

The Main Route **2 Nights: Vancouver**

The **Dr. Sun Yat-Sen Gardens,** which re-create design elements found in several authentic Chinese arrangements, were constructed by native artisans using traditional methods and tools. You can appreciate the difference between the Chinese and the Japanese styles with a visit to the **Nitobe Garden,** considered to be the most authentic of its kind outside of Japan. **Queen Elizabeth Park** is the site of the Bloedel Conservatory, in which you can see free-flying tropical birds among the botanical displays. Plan to spend some time at the **Van Dusen Botanical Garden,** which contains one of the largest collections of ornamental plants in the country. Two hours east of Vancouver, just off the Trans-Canada Highway near the resort town of Harrison Hot Springs, is **Minter Gardens,** a beautifully designed oasis of color.

1 Night: Victoria

Crystal Gardens offers a dazzling array of flowers, tropical birds, and monkeys in a glass-roofed structure that was once a swimming pool. **Butchart Gardens** boasts Italian, Japanese, and English rose gardens on its 25-acre site. Also worth a look is the **Fable Cottage Estate,** 3½ acres of brightly colored blooms.

3 Nights: Seattle

Stop by the visitor center at the north end of Washington Park for information on the **Washington Park Arboretum,** where the walkways are named after flowers. In nearby Woodinville is the **Chateau Ste. Michelle Winery,** where you can stroll through formal gardens, picnic on the grounds (designed by the Olmsted family, architects of New York City's Central Park), and enjoy complimentary tastings at the winery.

About one hour north of Seattle on Route 5 is the town of Mount Vernon, home to the commercial farms of **La Conner Flats** and **Roozengaarde,** which are open to the public. The heady fragrance, dazzling flowers, and sheer expanse of color are well worth the trip. In April, the Skagit Valley is carpeted with thousands of tulips and daffodils in an extraordinary display of color.

Tacoma, less than an hour south of Seattle on Route 5, has two noteworthy attractions. The **Seymour Botanical Conservatory,** located in Wright Park, features an extensive selection of exotic plant life inside an imposing Victorian-style greenhouse. After admiring the flower gardens and waterfront views in 700-acre **Point Defiance Park,** check out the world-class zoo and aquarium exhibits.

Further Information Obviously, the time of year you choose to visit the gardens will have much to do with the kinds of flowers you'll see; hours of operation and admission charges may change throughout the year as well. Telephone ahead for information for the season. Address and telephone listings can be found in Chapter 5, Seattle; Chapter 6, Washington State; Chapter 7, Vancouver; and Chapter 8, British Columbia.

2 Portraits of the Pacific North Coast

Pacific Northwest Microbrews: Good for What Ales You

By Jeff Kuechle

Portland-based writer Jeff Kuechle does his best to support the Northwest's burgeoning microbrewery industry. His contributions have appeared in Pacific Northwest, Ford Times, Emmy, *and* L.A. Times.

Freshly poured ale sparkles a rich amber in the light of a sun-dappled May afternoon on the loading-dock beer garden of the Bridgeport Brewpub in Portland, Oregon. To the south rise the office towers of downtown Portland, which supply not a few of Bridgeport's customers. To the north is the graceful span of the Fremont Bridge, from which the tiny brewery takes its name.

The customer tips back his glass and takes a long, thirsty swallow. The ale cascades along his tongue, tweaking taste buds that for years have known only pale, flavorless industrial lagers. A blast of sweet malt explodes at the back of his mouth, counterpointing the citrusy sting of the hops. *This* is flavor, something missing from American beer for far too long.

Sip by sip, beer connoisseurs from all over the world are learning that the Pacific Northwest—particularly Portland and Seattle—has become the best place in the world outside the European continent to imbibe their favorite brew. Microbreweries (companies producing fewer than 20,000 kegs per year) can now be found in Manhattan, Minneapolis, and Maui, from Boulder, Colorado, to the Outer Banks of Cape Hatteras, but it all started in the Pacific Northwest. On any given evening, there are at least 40 locally brewed beers and ales available for tasting in pubs in Portland and Seattle, and no fewer than 30 of North America's 150-odd "cottage breweries" are located within 400 miles of Portland, the dynamic center of this brewing storm. There are more brew pubs per capita in Portland and Seattle than in any other U.S. city.

And while most East Coast entries in the microbrewing sweepstakes produce German-style lagers—the most familiar brewing style to American palates—the microbrewers of the Pacific Northwest go for wildly adventuresome bitters, stouts, and porters. "We're used to gutsy beers," says Fred Eckhardt, publisher of the Portland-based newsletter "Listen to Your Beer." "When you get grabbed by a new beer in Portland, you know you've been grabbed."

Perhaps the best place to sample hand-crafted ale is a well-run brew pub, which stimulates the human spirit with conviviality, pleasant warmth, intelligent conversation, the scent of malt, and hearty food. Combatting the chilly, damp, British-style climate of the Northwest, brew pubs become places of refuge where you can shake the tears of a hostile world from your umbrella, order a pint of cask-conditioned bitter, and savor a complex substance that caresses the senses.

These are beers, it should be noted, that would make a megabrewery marketing consultant blanch. Take Grant's Imperial Stout. So dark that even a blazing summer sun, viewed through a pint glass of the pitch-black stuff, yields not a glimmer, Imperial Stout is heavy with choice whole barley malt, citrusy Cascade hops, and honey; it contains twice the alcohol, four times the calories, and a hundred times the flavor of a Bud Light. At a time when everyone supposedly wants to stay skinny and sober, who in his right mind would brew such a beer?

Back in 1982, when Paul Shipman of the Red Hook Brewery in Seattle and Bert Grant of Grant's Ales in Yakima trundled out the first kegs of microbrewery ale tapped in America since Prohibition, they little dreamed that they were ushering in an era of modest revolutionary ferment. Not that these tiny breweries exactly have the Clydesdales quaking in their traces: Anheuser-Busch annually *spills* a thousand times more beer than Bridgeport—one of the most successful microbreweries in America—produces in a year. Still, as America's megabrewers respond to a growing demand for variety by dressing up their beers with labels like "extra gold" and "dry," then actually make their lack of flavor a selling point ("No aftertaste!"), the Northwest's thriving microbrewery industry provides a real alternative for those of us who like beer to taste like *beer*.

There's something inherently noble about a well-crafted pint, something ancient and universal. Anthropologists now theorize that agriculture and brewing may have provided the stimulus for the very foundation of human civilization. Certainly there is nothing new in the idea of a city or region being served by a number of small, distinctive breweries. More than 5,000 years ago, in Egypt, the many breweries of ancient Pelusium were as famous as the city's university. (Even then, books, beer, and scholarly contemplation went hand in hand.) Even the ancient Greeks and Romans, though more partial to wine than grain beverages, drank beer; evidence shows that there were more than 900 public houses in Herculaneum before Mt. Vesuvius sounded its fateful "last call" in AD 79.

Brewing wasn't perfected, however, until it was introduced to northern climes. Teutonic ancestors could imagine no greater paradise than Valhalla, a banquet-hall with 540 doors and an unquenchable supply of ale. For the Tudor English, ale was far more than an amusement—it was a staple of life, "liquid bread," a source of national strength, and brewers who cut corners and overcharged for an inferior product were fined heavily, imprisoned, or both. It may be a coincidence that during the 1970s Britain's Campaign for

Real Ale movement—credited with single-handedly re-
storing fine ale to United Kingdom pubs—paralleled the
resurgence in the British economy and national pride. It
may also be a coincidence that the return of the
microbrewery ale to the Northwest signaled the end of a
bitter recession here, and the beginning of a rapid climb
into prosperity. Then again, it may not. Who knows how often the Boeing engineer or the Nike designer has, while
trading pleasantries with a new acquaintance over a glass
of hell-black stout, gotten just the idea he needed for that
important project?

"We don't want to take over the beer market," says the
most exuberant practitioner of the trade, Oregon brewpub
owner Mike McMenamin. "We just want to have our own
identity. It adds a lot of fun, and there's so little fun in the
business world today." McMenamin stands in what he calls
his "Captain Neon Fermentation Chamber." Tucked away
in Portland's West Hills, in the kitchen of a former fast-food
restaurant, McMenamin watches the yeast clouds billow
across his open fermentation tanks. A weird twisting of
neon light—blue, purple, ale-amber—casts a surrealistic
pallor over the nascent ale.

"We just love beer—we're experimenting all the time,"
says the tall, bearded McMenamin. "We want to keep on the
cutting edge of what's happening in American brewing.
When someone says 'You can't do that,' we know that's a
good place to start." Though brewing purists insist that
"real beer" should contain only four ingredients—water,
malted barley, hops, and yeast—the McMenamins reject
such notions out of hand, producing a variety of wildly distinctive brews such as raspberry stout; Java Ale, made
with fresh-ground coffee in the mash; and Wisdom Ale,
which included a collection of carefully researched ingredients designed, Mike McMenamin says, "to make you smart-
er." And whether or not the purists approve, the public
seems to, for McMenamin's seven tiny breweries—three in
Portland, one in suburban Hillsboro, one in Lincoln City at
the coast, one in Salem, and one in Eugene—can't keep up
with the demand for his products, which are sold only at his
network of 21 pubs.

Five years ago, the typical McMenamin pub was an
amalgam of fresh local microbrewery beers, cheerfully psychedelic art, wild neon sculptures, classic rock
on the jukebox, and sandwiches with names like the
Engroovenator and the Captain Neon Burger. At the most
recent additions to the McMenamin empire, you can still
find the Grateful Dead on the stereo, and fresh microbrewery beer still flows in copious draughts—only now
most of it is produced in-house. At outlets such as the
brand-new McMenamin's on Broadway and the Thompson
Brewery in Salem, a subtle shift in focus is apparent. For
one thing, they occupy a brand-new office/retail building

and a meticulously restored Victorian house, respectively, rather than the more modest addresses of the earlier pubs. The artwork has also been reined in a bit, at least in the public areas. The McMenamins employ two house artists, Joe Cotter and Lyle Hehn, who roam from pub to pub late at night adding hand-painted scenes and details as the spirit moves them. Though much of their finest work has now been relegated to back-of-the-house areas (for example, the brewery mural at the Salem location that turns the Capitol Building into a turbo-powered spaceship, with Uncle Sam tipping his hat astride the dome), there is still ample evidence of their work: the grinning imp-face, for example, that's visible only in one of the mirrors at McMenamin's Broadway.

Each of Portland's microbreweries has its own distinctive style, its own array of products, and its own army of followers, ready on the instant to debate the relative merits of Portland Ale versus Widmer Weizen. "The variety does make us work harder," says Art Larrance, one of the founders of Portland Brewing, located in an old creamery just off the railroad tracks. In this ornate pub, the brew kettle shines behind a two-story-high window beneath a skylight, and a music loft provides a view of the after-work crowd bellying up to a brass-railed bar for a pint of Grant's or the popular Portland and Timberline ales. Hot jazz swings out of the music loft every Thursday night for a live radio show sponsored by the brewery.

Inside a historic gray building just across the river from the Portland Brewing Company, Widmer Brewing co-owner and brewmaster Kurt Widmer dons a well-worn pair of Wellington boots and scampers around the wet concrete floor of his brewery preparing to pump the burbling "wort," or raw beer, in his brew-kettle to the stainless-steel fermenting tank a few feet away. The air is thick with steam and the rich fragrance of malt. Widmer tests a bit of the liquid for specific gravity—a measurement of eventual alcohol content—then, satisfied, throws a lever to begin the pumping process.

The redwood-sheathed brew kettle was custom-made to Widmer's specifications at a local metal fabrication company. Until a recent move to ritzier digs, other pieces of his equipment had more checkered pasts. The whirlpool tank, used to clarify the wort before it is fermented, began its days as a shrimp cooker in a coastal processing plant. Other vats were scavenged from area creameries. And his fermenting tanks? "Those came from the [never-completed] Pebble Springs nuclear power plant," Widmer smiles. "I picked them up for a real good price—and they're built to the highest standards in the land."

Widmer, a former Internal Revenue Service employee and homebrewer, is the Portland area's only German-style brewer. While he, like most Northwest brewers, loves the fine local hops, his products tend to emphasize malt flavors and a pleasant yeasty spiciness over the refreshing bitterness of the Northwest's English-style ales. Though one of the most recent micros to come on-line, Widmer has had no difficulty developing a following. After just four years in the marketplace, Widmer is the best-selling microbrew in the state, thanks to an extremely active marketing and distribution team. Production has climbed an average of 30%–40% every year; now that Widmer's dream brewery, located in a historic warehouse just across the Willamette River from his present location, is on-line, the company will soon exceed the legal production for a microbrewery of 20,000 kegs per annum.

"We've already vastly exceeded our projections," Widmer says. "We threw our business plan away a year ago, because it was hopelessly outdated."

From a standpoint of both business and brewing, no Portland micro is more respected than Bridgeport, the oldest. Founded in 1984 by local winemakers Dick and Nancy Ponzi, Bridgeport now combines expertly brewed English-style ales with one of the city's most popular pub operations. As originally conceived by the Ponzis and brewmaster Karl Ockert, the pub was little more than a tasting room, located in the same 1880s-vintage former rope factory as the brewery, with only a single tap, a few tables, and a dart board.

As anyone who has attempted to fight through the crush at the pub's bar on a recent Friday night can tell you, a slightly different attitude prevails at Bridgeport today. Though the atmosphere is still casual, the pub's highly regarded selection of light and dark ales, handmade pizza with a sourdough beer wort crust, and the opportunity to watch the brewers at work through steamy windows behind the bar, pack the place every night of the week.

One of the things that sets Bridgeport apart from other Portland-area breweries is the pub's skill with true cask-conditioned ales, available nowhere else in the city. Made in the traditional English style, these ales are pumped unfiltered directly into the keg at the end of fermentation, to lie undisturbed in a cool cellar for several weeks. There is no added carbon dioxide; cask-conditioned ales contain only the natural carbonation produced during the fermentation process. The result, drawn from one of the antique "beer-engine" hand-pumps at the end of the bar, is a smoother, noticeably less fizzy pint, with all the rich flavors of malt and hops allowed to shine through.

In Seattle, gems such as the Trolleyman Pub keep the Emerald City in the running with other Northwest Coast brewpubs. Tucked away in a corner of Red Hook's state-of-the-art facility in Fremont—just north of downtown Seattle—The Trolleyman poured its inaugural pint in 1988. The popular, low-key pub's five taps dispense brewery-fresh Red Hook ESB, golden Ballard Bitter, coffee-hued Black Hook porter, spicy Wheat Hook, and seasonal brews such as Winter Hook strong ale. There is one cask-conditioned tap, pouring a rotating selection of real ales.

The firelit pub, filled with long trestle tables, comfortable overstuffed furniture, and the sweet, malty aromas of new-brewed ale, is warm and inviting. From the competent kitchen flows a steady stream of hearty pub fare: black bean chili, puff pies crammed with chicken and beef, and a mean lasagne. Of particular interest to those visiting the pub will be the story of the former brewer who invited a young lady for a midnight hot-tub in the mash ton, with results worthy of a segment of the TV show "Cheers." It's a Northwest legend!

So with all these beers to choose from, where do you begin? What should you look for in a microbrewery ale? First and foremost, variety. At any given time in Portland and Seattle, there are 30–40 fresh, locally made brews on tap. They range in color from pale straw to ebony-black, in strength from a standard 3½% alcohol to an ominous 8½%.

And the flavor? Well, you'll just have to taste for yourself. There is the rich sweetness of malt, counterbalanced by good bitter hops. There are the mocha java overtones of roasted barley, used in stouts and porters, and the spiciness of malted wheat. There are sweet ales and tart ales, mild inconsequential ales, and ales so charged with flavor they linger on the palate like a fine Bordeaux.

Above all else, you should look for an ale you can savor, an ale you can taste without wanting to swallow too quickly. The dearest emotion to a brewer's heart is the beer drinker's feeling of regret that the last swig is gone.

In the Footsteps of the First Settlers

By Glenn W. Sheehan

A principal investigator at SJS Archaeological Services, Inc., in Bridgeport, PA, Glenn W. Sheehan has worked extensively in the Pacific Northwest and Arctic regions.

There's a sort of primeval mystery about the majestic landscapes of the Pacific Northwest Coast, something elemental and ancient that can give you a strange sense of being dislocated in time. Drive along the coastal roads of Washington's Olympic Peninsula, for example, and you'll pass magnificent rain forest, pounding surf, and partially submerged chunks of headland stranded at sea. Every bridge you cross takes you over an ancient fishing stream where prehistoric Indians harvested salmon. The oldest trees along the road bear scars where these Indians pulled off bark strips dozens of feet long, which they used for clothing, construction work, and rope making. Stop to look out over the water, and you feel the presence of ancient whale hunters scanning the horizon for spouts among the waves.

It isn't just a question of landscape, either. Elders in the Eskimo (Inuit is the preferred term in Canada) and Indian communities along the coast still pass on stories told to them by their ancestors, stories that can sometimes be traced as far back as 1,000 years, and their tribal art is a living expression of cultures whose origins are lost in the mists of prehistory.

Despite a lack of hard evidence, many archaeologists believe the first people to inhabit the New World arrived by way of the Pacific North Coast. Unlike Columbus and the seafaring Vikings, Polynesians, Chinese, and Japanese, all of whom crossed oceans to arrive at different points in North and South America, it is believed that the first Americans came on foot. If these pioneers had boats at all, they were small ones, not designed for long-distance travel across oceans. They came via Alaska and traveled through Canada into the western United States.

Although these assertions sound feasible, there aren't any known archaeological sites to support them. The oldest documented sites in the New World are believed to be 20,000–13,000 years old; the oldest known sites in the Pacific Northwest are Indian settlements that fall at the younger end of this range, at about 13,000 years old. Why then is the Pacific Northwest Coast believed to be the point of entry for the earliest settlers? Because it's the only place where people could have walked into the New World or used their small boats to travel along the coast without excessive danger. The last Ice Age tied up so much water that ocean levels probably dropped by hundreds of feet around the world. On certain winter days today, a person can walk between Alaska and the Soviet Union on ice when the oceans freeze over. But during the Ice Age the oceans were so reduced that the seabed was temporarily exposed as dry land, supporting vegetation and game, with fish in the rivers and sea mammals on the coast. So much ground was exposed, in fact, that the Old World and the New were connected by dry land. And though their languages and blood types differ, evidence strongly suggests that both the Eskimos and Indians have their roots somewhere in Asia. As one Eskimo friend of mine once said, "You know, those Chinese look an awful lot like us. They must be descended from Eskimos."

Why then aren't there any sites to prove this migration theory? All human activity may have been confined to lower ground levels now hidden under the ocean, reason the archaeologists. Or people may have traveled in small numbers, so their remains aren't easily detected. Or we may have already found these sites without recognizing them as such. Even though the two American continents were not inhabited with people at the outset, they did have abundant herds of large game, animals that had no fear of humans. Hunters with such easy prey wouldn't stay in one place for long; as they killed off their local supply of meat, or as the animals learned how to avoid people, the hunters moved on. So it is possible that the settlers arrived in the Pacific Northwest, lived a nomadic life there for a while, and then roamed on to other parts of North America and into South America.

The first Americans came to a land we wouldn't recognize today. Most of Canada, Alaska, and the northern United States were still under ice. Arctic weather and the forests, animals, and plants that are found in today's far north were prevalent halfway down the lower 48 states. Then the weather changed: The ice sheets melted and the ice receded north. The animal and plant distributions we see today started to become established about 10,000 years ago. Rivers and streams that were previously frozen started to run fast and clear at low temperatures. Conditions for pioneering salmon became so ideal that by 5,000 or so years ago, there were huge runs extending hundreds of miles inland.

For hunters it was a revolutionary time. Herds of large animals started to diminish or disappear, and the big-game hunters were increasingly confronted with more work and less to show for their efforts. Many hunters in the Pacific Northwest Coast, particularly those in Washington, British Columbia, and southeastern Alaska, turned to fishing instead. Their nomadic life following the herds became a more settled one as they switched to fishing. And as they started to settle down, they were able to accumulate more material things.

The first Americans moved north to south, from Alaska to Canada and then to the lower 48 states and finally into Central America and South America. The more recent inhabitants who made their living from salmon fishing, however, headed in the opposite direction, from the lower Pacific Northwest up into Canada and Alaska. The art and culture of these people spread and flourished in the Pacific Northwest and continued to do so in the centuries preceding their contact with European explorers. Archaeological sites of these fishing peoples date back 2,500 years and more.

Native Americans often moved when they felt their villages had grown too big. According to stories told by Indian elders, entire clans would depart and make new settlements along the Pacific Coast. Battles between Indian tribes, and warfare between the Eskimos and Indians, also prompted the relocation of some villages. And eventually, as the native and Euro-American economies became entwined, some Indians and Eskimos abandoned their villages. Many of these villages can still be seen today: Houses may have fallen, totem poles may have been reduced by museum acquisitions, and the forest is once again dense, but the villages are there. Not only can archaeologists find and excavate the abandoned sites of these people, they also can talk to their descendants. When an archaeologist is puzzled by an object he digs out of the ground, he can consult the elders of various Indian and Eskimo groups, who can often identify it and describe its use. And when the elders can't identify an object, they can often point researchers in the right direction.

During this prehistoric fishing era, the most prosperous natives were those of Washington, British Columbia, and southern Alaska. They had the good life, and they flaunted it. Their art was larger than life, while their potlatches (celebratory feasts) gave new meaning to the words conspicuous consumption. The success of the fishing peoples led to imitation. The natives of Kodiak Island were Eskimo, for example, and their ancestors came to the New World to fish and hunt sea mammals along the coast, rather than hunt the big land-bound game as the Indians' ancestors did. Surprising enough, however, the Kodiak people achieved a society in many ways remarkably similar to that of Indian tribes living to the east and south. Their art, archaeology, and legends demonstrate the connections.

Indian groups were open to the ways of others too. In the far north of Alaska, where trees don't grow and fish runs can be counted in dozens instead of millions, Eskimo hunters had great success in capturing large whales. Indian groups of the lower Pacific Northwest did the same, using many of the whale-hunting techniques and rituals employed by people as far away as Point Barrow on the Arctic Coast.

Although the native groups along the Pacific Northwest Coast were lucky enough to avoid outright war with the European and American settlers, they did suffer some adversity. The natives of Kodiak, for example, were viciously attacked by Russians, and many natives eventually lost land in Canada and the United States. All the natives suffered when commercial fishing and river dams reduced salmon runs, and again when Yankee whalers destroyed whales in huge numbers. Despite these setbacks, however, both the Indians and Eskimos have retained much of their culture and way of life into the present.

One of the best-known archaeological sites of these settlers is Ozette, located on the Makah Reservation in Washington's Olympic Peninsula. The finds of the site can be viewed by the public, and visitors can request permission to visit the site itself. Call the Makah Reservation (tel. 206/645–2711) for information. The village of Ozette was partially covered by a mud slide several hundred years ago. This apparent catastrophe ironically turned out to preserve the village, however, for the wet mud provided an anaerobic environment hostile to most decay-causing organisms. As a result, the mud-covered section of Ozette was preserved in its entirety, a kind of New World Pompeii.

Archaeologists usually excavate with masons' trowels because they generally dig up stone and ceramics, objects that a skillfully handled trowel won't harm. But at Ozette in the 1970s, there was a delightful obstacle to overcome. Basketry, cordage, clothing, and all kinds of soft materials had been preserved, but since they were preserved wet, they were particularly soft, and the trowels cut through them like mud. Even experienced excavators couldn't feel the damage they were doing to the objects.

A whole new excavation approach was undertaken, called "wet site" archaeology. Using water hoses to excavate the village, the archaeologists discovered that mud and debris could be washed away, leaving artifacts intact. During the handlers' first clumsy attempts at hosing down the mud, artifacts could be seen tumbling downhill with the water, but after some trial and error, the workers were able to keep even small finds in place.

One of the most exciting aspects of the Ozette excavation was the support archaeologists received from Indians living in the region. The Makah tribe encouraged archaeologists to excavate Ozette and assisted in the fieldwork; tribal members provided logistical support and helped interpret finds. And the tribe even built a museum based on the artifacts on its grounds at Neah Bay.

The Indians also helped prepare artifacts for public display, which turned out to be quite a challenge. Generally, archaeological finds of stone and ceramic pieces are preserved simply by being cleaned first in water and then glued together. But Ozette produced all kinds of perishable artifacts, objects that quickly started to deteriorate once they were removed from their muddy entombment. So the Makah Tribe provided laboratory space and helped the archaeologists preserve and stabilize the finds.

These descendants of the ancient Indians went one step further and created a living experiment on the site. The Makah people worked outside to build a plank house, like those in Ozette, and then attempted to use the interior in the same ways their ancestors did. Life in the house was set up based upon the directions of tribal elders, historic accounts, and archaeological interpretations. In the end, the house looked as if one good mud slide would turn it into another ruined Ozette home. After this experimental period, the tribe dismantled the house and rebuilt it inside the Makah museum.

A large dugout canoe was also built for the museum. The art of making canoes had almost died out, but it was revived to capture an important part of life in Ozette. Young and old worked together to build the boat and to pass on these ancient skills.

Other archaeological sites in the area require a bit more effort to explore. From southern Alaska to Oregon, you can find hundreds of petroglyphs (rock carvings) and pictographs (rock paintings). Only a handful of them can be dated, however, so they can't be attributed to any particular group of people. Some are easily accessible, and seen by the public every day. Others are so hidden you can only find them if you happen to stumble upon them. Still other carvings are positioned at the tidal zone and consequently are under water at high tide. One worthwhile guide to the many accessible rock carvings is Beth and Ray Hill's *Indian Petroglyphs of the Pacific Northwest.*

Prehistoric Indians also carved petroglyphs on land, although mostly facing the ocean, or else overlooking a river or waterway. Pictographs, on the other hand, can be seen throughout the Northwest Coast. Some of these detailed rocks have been jackhammered from their embedded frames and carted away; others have eroded, and still others lie beneath reservoirs. But the vast majority are right where they were created, and with permission from native or nonnative landowners, or government agencies, visitors can examine them. More than 500 sites are known. One protected site open to the public is Petroglyph Park in the town of Nanaimo, on Vancouver Island. Petroglyphs at Wrangell, Alaska, are also open to the public.

The ancient craft of carving giant totem poles out of trees has survived as a living art form, with plenty of demand for new poles. Carvers today often work in public throughout the Pacific Northwest, at museums or on the grounds of institutions that have commissioned their artwork. Young workers aspire to apprentice with master carvers, and gift shops all over the region offer miniature reproductions.

The totem pole is the best-known example of current Northwest Coast tribal art, but masks, tools, and a variety of paintings and prints also continue the artistic tradition of the area. Artwork can be purchased at local galleries, many of which are located on Indian lands and are run by Indians. The choices are broader and the prices lower here than they are in the native art galleries of New York and California. The Dukuah Gallery (1971 Peninsula Rd., Ocluelet, B.C., V0R 3A0, tel. 604/726–7223) is run by native Lillian Mac and her husband, Bert Mac, the hereditary Chief of the Toquant tribe. Native artists visit and work in the gallery year-round.

The British Columbia Provincial Museum in Victoria, with its unique collection of prehistoric fish bones, is an outstanding research center, with representation from all five species of salmon and almost every other fish that might have been harvested by prehistoric natives. Each fish skeleton has been mounted on wires, with all the bones together in proper anatomical order. While this is a scientific collection, it verges on being a work of art in itself, with skeletal fish elongating and compressing into fantastic shapes.

In Vancouver, at the University of British Columbia's Museum of Anthropology, there's an excellent archaeological collection that's very accessible to the public. Visitors can open any of the Plexiglass-covered drawers to examine even the most delicate artifacts. Other artifacts can be seen at the Thomas Burke Memorial Washington State Museum at the University of Washington in Seattle, and at the Alaska State Museum in Juneau, where they also have a first-rate collection of historic baleen (fibrous plates that hang from the roof of the whale's mouth) baskets. Only native hunters and artisans are legally permitted to own unprocessed baleen.

Any overview of Northwest Coast archaeology inevitably leaves out more than it includes. Paleo-Indian sites, Russian fur-hunting activities, cave sites in Washington's channeled scablands, mastodons and mammoths, and cairns dug up 100 years ago can all be found along the Pacific Northwest Coast. And if you visit the area searching for a glimpse of the past, native people will share their stories, researchers may invite you to observe their work, artisans will explain their ancient crafts, and the museums will let you view even the most fragile artifacts. For here, one thing remains constant: the people's eagerness to document and understand the past.

3 Portland

By Tom Barr

Updated by
Jeff Kuechle

Portland is a big city with small-town charm. In its unparalleled natural setting the city contains striking examples of up-to-the-minute postmodern architecture, an effective and intelligent transit system, clean air and water, an extensive system of colorful parks and gardens, and a lively arts scene. If this is the city of the future (and many think so), it is one that retains a human scale, and one in which the quality of life of its citizens is a high and constant priority.

Since the 1970s, the arts, environmental issues, and history have been as important to Portlanders as economic development. This focus has brought about successful neighborhood revitalization and preservation projects as well as ambitious cultural programs, such as the establishment of a resident professional Shakespeare company and innovative neighborhood theaters. The benefits for the residents and visitors alike is an attractive city in which there's much to do day or night, rain or shine.

As far back as 1852, with the establishment of the Boulevard, Portland began setting aside city land as parks, leaving a legacy of an urban setting in which one can enjoy nature, as in 4,700-acre Forest Park, which contains the last ancient forest left in any U.S. city. The recreational system has grown to 250 parks, public gardens, and greenways, and within Portland's city limits are the world's smallest park (officially recognized in *The Guiness Book of World Records*), the nation's largest urban wilderness, and the only extinct volcano within city limits in the continental United States.

The arts in Portland flourish in unexpected places: You'll find creations in police stations, office towers, banks, playgrounds, and on the sides of buildings. Downtown, the brick-paved transit mall is a veritable outdoor gallery of elaborate fountains and sculptures, although, like most artistic endeavors, it elicits some ambivalence; since the mall is restricted to bus and pedestrian traffic, many motorists would gladly trade a statue and fountain or two for a few extra parking spaces.

Known as the City of Roses, Portland takes full advantage of its temperate climate. Since 1907 it has celebrated its award-winning flowers, and today the Portland Rose Festival is a multiweek extravaganza with auto and boat races, visiting navy ships, and a grand floral parade second in size only to Pasadena's. Other annual events are a citywide Neighborhood Fair and an Art Quake featuring everything from painting and sculpture to mime, rock and blues, symphony orchestras, and dance.

The city, which began as a 1-square-mile Indian clearing, has become a metropolis of 485,000 people; the 132 square miles now include 90 diverse and distinct neighborhoods. A center for sports and sportswear, as well, Portland and its surroundings are home to headquarters and factories for Jantzen, Nike, and Pendleton. A variety of high-tech, shipbuilding, furniture, fabricated-metals, and other manufacturers has helped to give it a broad economic base. The city's prime geographic location, at the confluence of the Columbia and Willamette rivers, has helped it achieve its rank as the third-largest port on the West Coast. Five main terminals export automobiles, steel, livestock, grain, and timber. Shipyards repair tankers and tugboats, cruise ships, and navy vessels.

For all its emphasis on looking forward, Portland has not forgotten its past. Preserving the city's architecture is of major importance; in such areas as the Skidmore–Old Town, Yamhill, and Glazed Terra-Cotta National Historic Districts, 1860s brick buildings with cast-iron columns and 1890s ornate terra-cotta designs uphold the legacy of Portland's origins.

Along with historic structures, today's visitor can enjoy Portland's innovative art, architecture, theater, fine dining, and a healthy, clean environment that this city has created for an enviably livable present without neglecting its past or mortgaging its future.

Essential Information

Arriving and Departing by Plane

Airports **Portland International Airport** (tel. 503/335–1234) is located in northeast Portland, approximately 12 miles from the city center. It is served by Alaska (tel. 503/224–2547 or 800/426–0333), Air Canada (tel. 800/776–3000), American (tel. 800/433–7300), America West (tel. 800/247–5692), Continental (tel. 503/224–4560 or 800/525–0280), Delta (tel. 800/221–1212), Horizon (tel. 800/547–9308), Morris Air (tel. 503/280–8800 or 800/466–7747), Northwest (tel. 800/447–4747 or 800/225–2525), Reno Air (tel. 800/736–6247), TWA (tel.503/282–1111 or 800/221–2000), and United (tel. 800/241–6522).

Between the Airport and City Center
By Car From the airport, take I–84 (Banfield Freeway) west to the City Center exit. Going to the airport, take I–84 east to I–205N; follow I–205N to the airport exit.

By Bus **Raz Tranz** (tel. 503/246–3301) operates buses to specified downtown Portland hotels, to the Best Western Inn at the Convention Center, and to Amtrak and Greyhound depots. Departures are approximately every 30 minutes between 5:30 AM and 12:05 AM. The fare is $7 adults one way, $1 children 6–12, children under 6 free. **Tri-Met** (tel. 503/238–7433) runs about every 15 minutes to and from the airport, making regular stops every two blocks. Service begins daily at 5 AM and ends at about 11:50 PM. Exact times vary depending on the direction in which you're headed. Call for specific schedules: 95¢ for one- and two-zone trips; $1.25 for three zones.

By Taxi The trip to or from the airport by taxi takes about 30 minutes. The fare is approximately $20.

Arriving and Departing

By Car I–5 enters from north and south; I–84 is the major east-side corridor, while U.S. 26 and U.S. 30 are primary east–west thoroughfares. Bypass routes are I–205, which loops through east Portland, and I–405, which arcs around western downtown.

By Train **Amtrak** service departs from Union Station (800 N.W. 6th Ave., tel. 800/872–7245), with destinations throughout the country.

By Bus **Greyhound/Trailways** (550 N.W. 6th Ave., tel. 503/243–2310) travels to points across the country.

Getting Around

By Car Most city-center streets are one-way only, and S.W. 5th and 6th avenues, between Burnside Street and S.W. Madison, are limited to bus traffic. Unless posted, it is legal to turn right on a red light. Left turns from a one-way street onto another one-way street on a red light are also legal. While most parking meters run 8 AM–6 PM, many streets have special posted rush-hour regulations. Sunday parking is free.

By Light Rail **Metropolitan Area Express** (tel. 503/22–TRAIN), or MAX, transports passengers from S.W. 11th Avenue and Morrison Street in the city center to Lloyd Center and to the eastern suburban community of Gresham. There are 27 stations along the 15-mile route. Transportation operates daily, 5:30 AM–1 AM, with a fare of 95¢ for one- and two-zone trips, $1.25 for three zones, and $3.25 day tickets and monthly passes. Senior citizens and disabled persons pay 45¢.

By Bus **Tri-Met** (tel. 503/238–7433) operates bus service throughout the greater Portland area. Fares are the same for both Tri-Met and MAX, and tickets can be used on either system. There is a Tri-Met information office at Pioneer Square (6th and Morrison Sts. downtown; open weekdays 9–5).

By Taxi Taxi fare is $2 at flag drop plus $1.50 per mile. The first person pays by meter; each additional passenger pays 50¢. Cabs cruise the city streets but it's a safer bet to phone for one. Major companies are **Broadway Deluxe Cab** (tel. 503/227–1234), **New Rose City Cab** (tel. 503/282–7707), **Portland Taxi Company** (tel. 503/256–5400), and **Radio Cab** (tel. 503/227–1212).

Important Addresses and Numbers

Tourist Information The **Portland/Oregon Visitors Association** (26 S.W. Salmon St., at World Trade Ct. 3, tel. 503/222–2223) is open weekdays 8:30–5, Saturday 9–3.

Emergencies Dial 911 for fire, police, or medical assistance.

Hospitals **Eastmoreland Hospital** (2900 S.E. Steele St., tel. 503/231–3490); **Emanuel Hospital and Health Center** (2801 N. Gantenbein Ave., tel. 503/280–4128); **Providence Medical Center** (4805 N.E. Glisan St., tel. 503/230–6000); **St. Vincent Hospital** (9205 S.W. Barnes Rd., tel. 503/297–4411).

Dentists **Willamette Dental Group PC** (1933 S.W. Jefferson St., tel. 503/644-3200) has seven offices throughout the metro area and is open Saturdays.

Late-night Pharmacies *Near downtown:* Fred Meyer (100 NW 20th, tel. 503/226–7179) is open until 10 PM.

Near Lloyd Center: Fred Meyer (3030 NE Weidler, tel. 503/280–1333) is open until 10 PM.

Guided Tours

Orientation **Gray Line Sightseeing** (tel. 503/285–9845) operates city tours April 18–October 31; call for departure times. **Willamette Riverboat Cruises** (tel. 503/234–6665) has scheduled dinner cruises, Sunday brunches, Portland harbor excursions, and Oregon City Falls tours. The cruises are seasonal, so call ahead.

Walking Tours The **Portland/Oregon Visitors Association** (tel. 503/222–2223) has self-guiding tour brochures plus maps and guides to art galleries and select neighborhoods. Walking tours range from a 6-block jaunt in the Yamhill Historic District to a 7-mile marathon through several historic areas.

Highlights for First-time Visitors

The Grotto (*see* Tour 2)
Pioneer Courthouse Square (*see* Tour 1)
Portland Saturday Market (*see* Tour 1)
Washington Park (*see* Tour 2)
Yamhill National Historic District (*see* Tour 1)

Exploring Portland

Tour 1: Downtown Portland

Numbers in the margin correspond to points of interest on the Downtown Portland map.

The Willamette River is the east–west dividing line, and Burnside Street separates north from south. While Portland's 200-foot-long blocks make them easy walking for most visitors, others may wish to explore the core by either MAX light rail or Tri-Met bus (*see* Getting Around, *above*).

❶ Start at **Pioneer Courthouse Square** (S.W. Broadway and S.W. Morrison St., tel. 503/223–1613), a broad, art-filled brick piazza that is downtown Portland's heart and soul. The square's design echoes the classic central plazas of European cities, and it is a frequently the scene of special events. It's also Portland's premier people-watching venue, where the neatly dressed office crowd mingles harmoniously with some of the city's stranger elements. As you make your way through the square, look down at the 64,000 bricks—each engraved with the name of someone who bought it to help pay for the square. The best time to be here is noon, when a goofy weather machine blasts a fanfare, and a shining sun, stormy dragon, or blue heron rises out of a misty cloud to confirm the day's weather.

If you walk west to Broadway and Salmon streets, you'll encounter **The Heathman Hotel** (tel. 503/241–4100), an imposing pink-brick edifice favored by visiting actors and opera stars. The sumptuous lobby features a collection of 10 prints of endangered species by Andy Warhol, among other artworks. The hotel welcomes visitors who come in just to admire the art.

From the square, walk south on 6th Avenue for two blocks.
❷ Here, at the corner of 6th Avenue and Salmon Street, is **Nike Town,** a sort of F.A.O. Schwarz for the athletically inclined. The international athletic-ware giant is headquartered in Beaverton, just outside Portland. This futuristic, almost surreal-looking factory outlet is a showplace for the mind-bogglingly broad Nike line. A life-size plaster cast of Michael Jordan captured in mid-jump dangles from the ceiling near the basketball shoes. Waterproof sandals, for joggers who fancy mountain streambeds, are displayed floating in a tank of exotic tropical fish. Autographed sports memorabilia, video monitors, and statuary compete for your attention with the many products for sale. The children's department upstairs offers

Downtown Portland

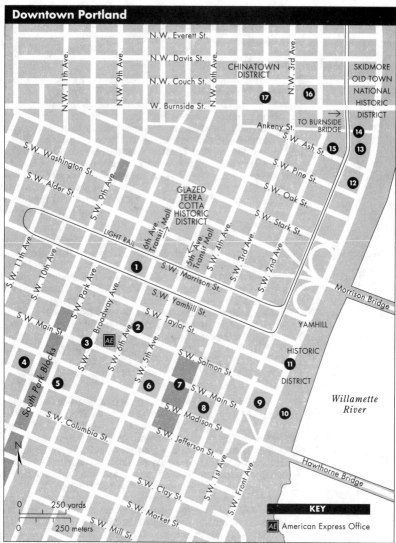

American Advertising Museum, **16**

Central Fire Station, **13**

Chapman and Lownsdale Squares, **7**

Chinatown Gate, **17**

Governor Tom McCall Waterfront Park and Salmon Street Plaza, **10**

Justice Center, **8**

Mill Ends Park, **11**

New Market Theater Village, **15**

Nike Town, **2**

Oregon Historical Center, **5**

Oregon Maritime Center and Museum, **12**

Pioneer Courthouse Square, **1**

Portland Art Museum, **4**

Portland Building, **6**

Portland Center for the Performing Arts, **3**

Portland/Oregon Visitors Association, **9**

Skidmore Fountain, **14**

kid-size versions of almost everything in the store. Don't expect any bargains—prices are full retail—and the word "sale" is almost as taboo around here as the word "Reebok." *930 S.W. 6th Ave., tel. 503/221-6453. Open Mon.–Thurs. 10–7, Fri. 10–8, Sat. 10–7, Sun. 11:30–6:30.*

❸ You are now in front of the **Portland Center for the Performing Arts** (corner of S.W. Broadway and S.W. Main St., tel. 503/ 248–4496). The "old building" and the hub of activity is the **Arlene Schnitzer Concert Hall,** host to the Oregon Symphony and musical events from classical recitals to rock concerts. Across Main Street, but still part of the center, is the 292-seat **Delores Winningstad Theater,** used for plays and lectures. Its stage design and dimensions are based on those of an Elizabethan-era stage. The 916-seat **Intermediate Theater,** the residence of Oregon Shakespeare Festival in Portland, is also part of the complex. The section of the street connecting the old and new buildings is often blocked off for food fairs, art shows, and other events.

One block west, at the tree-lined **South Park Blocks** you'll find a pleasant green-canopied place for a fine-weather stroll en route

❹ to the **Portland Art Museum.** The museum, which includes a film center, is the region's oldest visual- and media-arts facility. Its treasures span 35 centuries of Asian, European, and American art, with collections of Native American, regional, and contemporary art. The film center features the annual Portland International Film Festival in February and March, and the Northwest Film Festival in early November. *1219 S.W. Park Ave., tel. 503/226-2811; 503/221-1156 for film schedule. Admission: $4.50 nonmembers; senior citizens free Thurs.; $1.50 children 6–12; $2.50 students; free first Thurs. of the month 4–9 PM. Open Tues.–Sat. 11–5, Sun. 1–5.*

Across the South Park Blocks is an impressive six-story-high mural of Lewis and Clark and the Oregon Trail (the route the pioneers took from St. Joseph and Independence, Missouri, to the Oregon Territory). The paintings signal the entrance to the

❺ **Oregon Historical Center,** which documents the state's history from prehistoric times to the present. Permanent and special exhibits include archaeological and anthropological artifacts, ship models, and memorabilia from the Oregon Trail. A research library is open to the public. A bookstore (corner of Broadway and Madison St.) is the best source for maps and publications on Northwest history. *1200 S.W. Park Ave., tel. 503/222-1741. Admission: $3 adults, $1 students and senior citizens; senior citizens free Thurs. Open Mon.–Sat. 10–4:45, Sun. noon–5.*

❻ Follow Madison Avenue south to 5th Avenue, to the **Portland Building,** where *Portlandia,* the world's second-largest hammered-copper statue (after the Statue of Liberty) kneels on the second-story balcony. She stands 36 feet high and was installed in 1985. The building itself, one of the United States' first postmodern designs, generates strong feelings; chances are you'll either love it or hate it. The controversial structure, designed by architect Michael Graves, is buff-colored with brown trim and has what seems to be a wrinkled blue ribbon wrapped around its top. The **Metropolitan Center for Public Art,** on the second floor is well worth a visit. From a huge fiberglass mold of *Portlandia's* face to original works by local artists, the gallery specializes in images of Portland in sculpture, painting, and photography. *1120 S.W. 5th Ave., tel. 503/823–5111. Admission to museum free. Museum open weekdays 8–6.*

Time Out One block south and two blocks west from *Portlandia* is the **Broadway Revue** (1239 S.W. Broadway, tel. 503/227–3883) lounge, where you can relax with a cold soda or beer and admire the vintage B-movie posters adorning the walls.

7 South across 4th Avenue are **Chapman and Lownsdale squares,** between Madison and Salmon streets. During the 1920s these squares were segregated: Chapman was reserved for women, and Lownsdale for men. Beware the public rest rooms, which are grungy and considered unsafe by the locals. The elk statue on Main Street, which separates the parks, was given to the city by former mayor David Thompson; supposedly, it honors an elk that grazed here in the 1850s. Terry Shrunk Park, south across Madison Street, is a terraced amphitheater of green lawn and brick, shaded by flowering cherry trees, and a popular lunch spot for the office crowd.

8 Walking east on Main Street to 3rd Avenue will take you to the **Justice Center,** a beautiful building with glass bricks built into portions of the east and west sides. Because of a city ordinance requiring that 1% of the development costs of new buildings be allotted to the arts, the center's hallways are lined with travertine sculptures, ceiling mosaics, stained-glass windows, and photographic murals. Within the center is housed the county court, support offices, and the **Police Museum,** on the 16th floor, which has uniforms, guns, and badges worn by the Portland Police Department. Visitors are invited to view the artwork. *1111 S.W. 2nd Ave., tel. 503/796–3019. Admission free. Open Mon.–Thurs. 10–3.*

9 The **World Trade Center,** northeast of the Justice Center, is a trio of buildings connected by sky bridges and designed by prominent Portland architect Robert Frasca. On the ground floors of the buildings are retail stores, a restaurant, coffee shops, banks, and travel agencies. In World Trade Center Three is the **Portland/Oregon Visitors Association,** where you can pick up maps and literature about the state. *26 S.W. Salmon St., tel. 503/222–2223. Open weekdays 8:30–5, Sat. 9–3.*

10 Cross Front Avenue and enter **Governor Tom McCall Waterfront Park** and **Salmon Street Plaza.** The park stretches north for approximately a mile to Burnside Street and offers what may be the finest ground-level view of downtown Portland's river, bridges, and skyline. The broad, grassy park, which occupies the site of a former expressway, is the site of some of Portland's top special events—the Rose Festival, a series of classical and blues concerts, and the Oregon Brewers' Festival in July. At other times of the year, Waterfront Park is a favorite venue for bikers, joggers, and rollerskaters. The arching jets of water at the **Salmon Street Fountain** change configuration every few hours, and are a favorite cooling-off spot during the dog days of summer.

11 Follow the park one block north to where **Mill Ends Park** sits in the middle of a traffic island on Front Avenue. At 24 inches in diameter, it has been recognized by the *Guinness Book of World Records* as the world's smallest official city park.

You are now in the heart of the **Yamhill National Historic District,** a 6-square-block district in which many examples of 19th-century cast-iron architecture have been preserved. Since the cast-iron facade helped support the main structure, these buildings traditionally did not need big, heavy walls to bear the weight; the interior spaces could therefore be larger and more open.

North and west of this district, along 2nd Avenue, you'll find several galleries featuring fine art, ceramics, photography, and posters. On the first Thursday of each month, new shows and exhibits are unveiled and most galleries stay open until 9 PM. For details call the Portland Art Museum (tel. 503/226–2811).

Oak Street marks the southern boundary and Everett Street the northern boundary of the **Skidmore Old Town National Historic District.** Portland, the region settled in 1845 (chartered as a city in 1851) by New Englanders and named for Portland, Maine, began here, and the 20-square-block district includes a variety of buildings of varying ages and architectural designs. Before it was renovated, this was the city's skid row, and vestiges of that condition remain. Even in daylight, you may feel more comfortable sightseeing with a companion. Don't walk here at night.

The main mast of the battleship *Oregon*, which served in three wars, stands at the foot of Oak Street. Across Front Street is ⑫ the **Oregon Maritime Center and Museum,** whose exterior features prime street-level examples of cast-iron architecture. Inside, you'll find models of ships that plied the Columbia River, most of which were made from scratch by local model makers, some of whom work at the museum. Photographic displays cover World War II, when Portland was a major military shipbuilding center. *113 S.W. Front St., tel. 503/224–7724. Admission: $2 adults, $1.25 students and senior citizens, $4.50 families. Open Memorial Day–Labor Day, Fri.–Sun. 11–4; Labor Day–Memorial Day, Thurs.–Sun. 11–4.*

Take a moment to study the evocative figures cast into the bronze columns at the entrance to the block-square **Japanese-American Historical Plaza,** just north of the Burnside Bridge. They show Japanese-Americans before, during, and after World War II—living daily life, fighting in battle for the United States, marching off to internment camps. More than 110,000 Japanese-Americans were interned by the American government during the war, and this park was created to commemorate their experience and contributions. The park is an oasis of meticulous landscaping and flowering cherry trees; simple blocks of granite, carved with *haiku* poems describing the war experience offer powerful testimony to this dark episode in American history.

⑬ Next door, at the **Central Fire Station** (111 S.W. Front St.) is the Jeff Morris Memorial Fire Museum, where you can see antique pumps and other equipment through large plate-glass windows. Cast-iron medallions, capitals, and grillwork taken from other buildings are displayed on the north wall, which ⑭ faces **Skidmore Fountain,** built in 1888. Aside from being the centerpiece of the square around which many community activities take place, the fountain is renowned for its granite troughs and spouting lions' heads from which water was collected for quenching the thirsts of both men and horses.

From March through Christmas, the fountain's square is home to the **Portland Saturday Market** (also open on Sunday), North America's largest open-air handicraft market. Some 300 merchants sell an assortment of foods, produce, arts, and crafts, all one-of-a-kind creations by the artisans. If you're looking for crystals, yard goods, beaded hats, stained glass, jewelry, flags, wood and rubber stamps, or custom footwear and decorative boots, you stand a good chance of finding it here. An assortment of street entertainers and food booths adds to the festive atmosphere. *100 S.W. Ankeny St., tel. 503/222–6072. Open Sat. 10–5, Sun. 11–4:30. Closed Jan.–Feb.*

⑮ The **New Market Theater Building,** across 1st Avenue was considered the grandest theater in the West when it opened in 1875. During its heyday it staged everything from Shakespeare to a prize fight with John L. Sullivan. Today its splendidly restored interior houses fast-food restaurants, shops, and offices. The **Skidmore Fountain Building** (28 S.W. 1st Ave., tel. 503/–227–5305), also part of the square, has three floors of baskets, jewelry, pottery, women's wear, leather crafts, imports, and other specialty shops. *50 S.W. 2nd Ave., tel. 503/228–2392. Open daily 10–6.*

⑯ Northwest of the village is the **American Advertising Museum,** which bills itself as the only museum devoted exclusively to advertising. You may feel as though the museum has oversold itself a bit, because it isn't all that comprehensive, is in a very small space, and the exhibits are limited. There are, however, examples of memorable campaigns, print advertisements, radio and TV commercials, and a variety of novelty and specialty promotion products, along with changing exhibits. A gift counter stocks books and reproductions of such specialty items as pens, cups, and pins. *9 N.W. 2nd Ave., tel. 503/226–0000. Admission: $3 adults, $1.50 children 6–12 and senior citizens. Members and children under 6 free. Open Wed.–Fri. 11–5, weekends noon–5.*

Time Out If you need a break from sightseeing and shopping, the cool, dark oasis of **Kell's Irish Restaurant & Pub** (112 S.W. 2nd Ave., tel. 503/227–4057) is close at hand. Settle into this quiet pub for a pint of Guiness and authentic Irish pub fare, and be sure to ask the bartender how all those folded-up dollar bills got stuck to the ceiling.

During the 1890s, Portland had the second-largest Chinese community in the United States. Today the community is compressed into several blocks of northwest Portland and is known ⑰ for its restaurants, shops, and grocery stores. **Chinatown Gate** (N.W. 4th Ave. and Burnside St.) can be recognized by its five roofs, 64 dragons, and two huge lions, and is the official entrance to Chinatown.

If you are interested in art and architecture, you may wish to zigzag back and forth between S.W. 5th and S.W. 6th avenues and the intersecting streets of Oak and Yamhill. This is the heart of the **Glazed Terra Cotta National Historic District.** Buildings from the late 1890s to the mid-1910s still stand here, as commercial and public properties. At the turn of the century terra-cotta was an often-used material because of its availability and inexpensive cost; it could also be easily molded into decorative details that were popular at the time. Take time to look up at the elaborate lions' heads, griffins, floral displays, and other classical motifs that adorn the rooflines of many of these buildings.

Public art lines 5th and 6th avenues. On **5th Avenue** you'll find a sculpture that reflects light and changing colors, a nude woman made of bronze, a copper and redwood sculpture inspired by the Norse god Thor, and a large limestone cat in repose. Sixth Avenue has a steel-and-concrete matrix, a granite-and-brick fountain, and an abstract modern depiction of an ancient Greek defending Crete.

A short walk west will take you back to the beginning of the tour.

Tour 2: Outside City Center

Numbers in the margin correspond to points of interest on the Portland Outside City Center map.

Several of Portland's prime attractions are outside its city center and are not within walking distance. For 95¢ you can reach them via **Tri-Met Line 63** (tel. 503/238–7433 for schedule and route information). During summer a 4-mile round-trip narrow-gauge **train ride** operates from the zoo to the International Rose Test Garden and the Japanese Gardens. The fare is $2.50 adults, $1.75 children 3–11 and senior citizens. (*See* Getting Around, *above*.)

⓲ **Washington Park** covers 322 acres of Portland's western hills.
⓳ The **Washington Park Zoo,** established in 1887, has been a prolific breeding ground for Asian elephants. Major exhibits include an African section with rhinos, hippos, zebras, and pythons, plus an aviary with 15 species of birds. Other popular attractions include an Alaska Tundra exhibit, a penguinarium, bears, and animals such as beavers, otters, and reptiles that are native to the west side of the Cascade Mountains. *4001 S.W. Canyon Rd., tel. 503/226–ROAR. Admission: $5 adults; $3.50 senior citizens; $3 children 3–11; free second Tues. after 3 PM. Open daily at 9:30; closing hours vary from 4 to 6 PM with the season.*

⓴ Despite its name, the **International Rose Test Garden** isn't an experimental greenhouse laboratory but three breathtaking terraced gardens set on four acres on which 10,000 bushes and 400 varieties of roses are grown. The flowers, many of them new varieties, are at their peak in June and July, and September and October. This is one of the nation's oldest continually operating sites of its kind. *400 S.W. Kingston Ave., tel. 503/ 823–3636. Admission free. Open dawn–dusk.*

㉑ The **Japanese Gardens,** situated above the test garden, meander through 5½ acres of Washington Park. A ceremonial teahouse, an Oriental pavilion, a strolling pond, a sand-and-stone garden, and three other gardens are among the highlights. *611 S.W. Kingston Ave., tel. 503/223–4070. Admission: $5 adults, $2.50 senior citizens and students. Open Apr.–May and Sept., daily 10–6; June–Aug, daily 9–8; Oct.–Mar., daily 10–4.*

㉒ Across from the Washington Park Zoo is the **World Forestry Center,** whose spokesman is a 70-foot-tall talking tree. Outside, a 1909 locomotive and antique logging equipment are displayed, and inside are two floors of exhibits, a multi-image

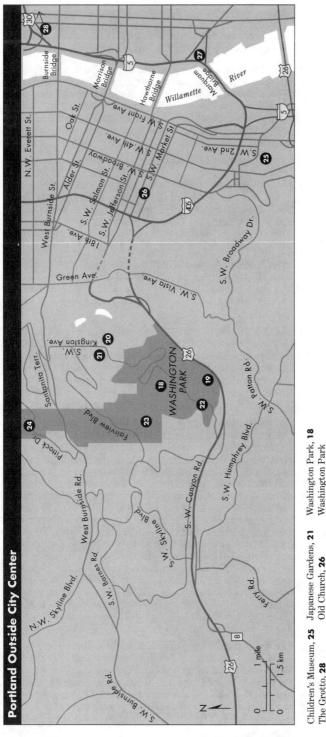

Portland Outside City Center

Children's Museum, **25**
The Grotto, **28**
Hoyt Arboretum, **23**
International Rose
Test Gardens, **20**

Japanese Gardens, **21**
Old Church, **26**
Oregon Museum of
Science and Industry
(OMSI), **27**
Pittock Mansion, **24**

Washington Park, **18**
Washington Park
Zoo, **19**
World Forestry
Center, **22**

"Forests of the World," a collection of 100-year-old wood, and a gift shop. *4033 S.W. Canyon Rd., tel. 503/228–1367. Admission: $3 adults, $2 children 2–18 and senior citizens. Open summer, daily 9–5; after Labor Day, daily 10–5.*

㉓ **Hoyt Arboretum,** adjacent to Washington Park, has more than 700 species of plants, plus one of the nation's largest collection of coniferous trees. Ten miles of trails wind through the park to the Winter Garden and a Vietnam memorial. The Visitor's Center is open most days 9–4 for information and trail maps. *4000 S.W. Fairview Blvd., tel. 503/228–8733. Admission free. Open daily dawn–dusk.*

㉔ **Pittock Mansion,** 1,000 feet above the city, offers superb views of the skyline, rivers, and Cascade Mountains. The 1909 mansion, which combines French Renaissance–and Victorian-style decor, was built by Henry Pittock, former editor of the *Oregonian.* Set in its own park, the opulent manor has been restored and is filled with art and antiques of the 1880s. *3229 N.W. Pittock Dr., tel. 503/823–3624. Admission: $3.50 adults, $3 senior citizens, $1.50 children 6–18. Open daily noon–4.*

㉕ The **Children's Museum** offers hands-on play for children (infant–10) through changing arts-and-crafts exhibits, a clay shop, and a child-size grocery store. *3037 S.W. 2nd Ave., tel. 503/823–2227. Admission: $3.50 adults, $3 children. Open daily 9–5.*

㉖ The **Old Church,** built in 1882, is a prime example of Carpenter Gothic architecture, demonstrated by the exterior's rough-cut lumber, tall spires, and original stained-glass windows. The acoustically resonant church hosts free classical concerts at noon each Wednesday. If you're lucky, you'll get to hear one of the few operating Hook and Hastings tracker pipe organs. *1422 S.W. 11th Ave., tel. 503/222–2031. Open weekdays 11–3.*

On the east side of the Willamette River, across the Morrison
㉗ Bridge, is the new home of the **Oregon Museum of Science and Industry** (OMSI). A great place for children, it houses the Northwest's largest astronomy educational facility, including an OMNIMAX theater and a 200-seat planetarium, a hands-on computer center, a space wing with a mission control center, and a variety of other permanent and touring exhibits, which explain things scientific to 1 million visitors a year. Beginning in the summer of 1994, a 240 foot submarine, the USS *Blueback*, will be moored in the Willamette as part of the museum. There's also a fine technology-oriented gift shop. *1934 S.E. Water Ave., tel. 503/797–4000. Admission museum only: $6.50 adults, $5.50 senior citizens, $4 children 3–17; museum and Omnimax: $9.75 adults, $8.25 senior citizens, $6 children; planetarium admission: $4 adults, $3.50 senior citizens, $3 children. Call for show times. Open June 20–Sept. 4, Mon.– Thurs. and weekends 9–7, Fri. 9–7; Sept. 3–May 24, Mon.– Thurs. and weekends 9–5, Fri. 9–7.*

㉘ The Sanctuary of Our Sorrowful Mother, also known as **The Grotto,** is a 64-acre tract staffed by the Order of the Servants of Mary. More than 100,000 visitors per year come here to walk the Stations of the Cross trail, which leads through a thick forest, and to visit a cave set in a 110-foot cliff that enshrines a marble replica of Michelangelo's *Pietà. Corner of N.E. 85th Ave. and Sandy Blvd., tel. 503/254–7371. Admission free; ele-*

vator fee: $1. Open May–Sept., daily 9–8; Oct.–Apr., daily 9–5:30.

Portland for Free

The **State of Oregon Sports Hall of Fame** houses 3,300 square feet of sports memorabilia associated with prominent Oregonian athletes and teams, including Heisman Trophy winner Terry Baker, and Mickey Lolich, who played for Detroit in three World Series. *900 S.W. 4th Ave. (concourse level of the Standard Insurance Ct.), tel. 503/227–7466. Admission free. Open Mon.–Sat. 10–3.*

The **Cowboys Then & Now Museum.** This brand-new specialty museum gives visitors an intimate glimpse of what life was *really* like for cowboys in the Old West (as well as today). A chronologically organized collection of authentic tack and other personal possessions, a 100-year-old chuck wagon (complete with cow pies) and exhibits on the 20 most popular cattle breeds enliven this small museum, which traces the evolution of the cowboy and the cattle industry from its Spanish roots. *729 N.E. Oregon, tel. 503/731–3333. Open Wed.–Fri. 11–5, weekends noon–5.*

What to See and Do with Children

Children's Museum (*see* Tour 2).

Japanese Gardens (*see* Tour 2).

Ladybug Theater (on Willamette River at the foot of S.E. Spokane St., tel. 503/232–2346 for showtimes) is exclusively for children and is located in Oaks Amusement Park.

Oaks Amusement Park may not be Disneyland, but it has a small-town charm that delights children and adults alike. There are thrill rides and miniature golf in summer, and rollerskating year-round. *At the foot of S.E. Spokane St., tel. 503/233–5777. Admission: $7.50. Open Memorial Day–Labor Day, daily noon–5; rest of year, weekends noon–5.*

Oregon Maritime Center and Museum (*see* Tour 1).

Oregon Museum of Science and Industry (*see* Tour 2).

Washington Park Zoo (*see* Tour 2).

World Forestry Center (*see* Tour 2).

Off the Beaten Track

Portland may be known as the City of Roses, but beer-lovers have come to regard it as the City of Microbreweries. At last count, there were more than a dozen small breweries operating in the metropolitan area, producing an astonishing variety of pale ales, bitters, bocks, barleywines, and stouts. Some have attached pub operations, where you can sample a foaming pint of house ale. **Bridgeport Brewing** (1313 N.W. Marshall, tel. 503/241–7179), **Portland Brewing** (1339 N.W. Flanders, tel. 503/222–7150) or **McMenamins on Broadway** (1504 N.E. Broadway, tel. 503/288–9498) are just a few among the many.

Ft. Vancouver National Historic Site. Ft. Vancouver is a reconstruction of the 1825 site that was the fur-trading headquarters of the Hudson's Bay Company. Tours, conducted by National Park Service staff and volunteers, take you into the smithy, the bakery, and other shops. Some furnishings are from the original fort. A visitor center has a museum, an audiovisual program, and a gift shop. *612 E. Reserve St., Vancouver, tel. 206/ 696–7655. Admission: $2 adults, $4 families Memorial Day– Labor Day; free the rest of the year. Open Memorial Day–Labor Day, daily 9–5; rest of year, daily 9–4.*

Officers' Row Historic District. Outside the front entrance of Ft. Vancouver is a string of 21 Victorian-style homes built between 1850 and 1906. Although they are not part of the fort, the houses were often occupied by officers stationed there. Some of the more notable residents include Ulysses S. Grant and George Marshall. Some of the houses are still private residences; others have been converted into restaurants and commercial businesses.

To reach the fort and Officers' Row, leave Portland northbound on I–5 (across the Columbia River toward Vancouver, WA); take Exit 1-C and follow the signs to Officers' Row.

Forest Park is one of the nation's largest (4,700 acres) urban wildernesses. It is home to more than 100 species of birds and 50 species of mammals, and it includes more than 50 miles of trails. *Take Lovejoy St. west to where it becomes Cornell Rd. and follow to the park, tel. 503/823–4492. Admission free. Open dawn–dusk.*

The **Portland Audubon Society** (5151 N.W. Cornell Rd., tel. 503/292–6855), within 4,500-acre Forest Park, offers a bevy of bird activities in the heart of the only old-growth forest left in any major U.S. city. Nature trails, guided bird-watching events, a hospital for injured and orphaned birds, and a gift shop stocked with books, feeders, and other bird lover's paraphernalia fill out the bill.

Oregon City (population 19,000) was the western terminus of the Oregon Trail. The city was founded in 1829, when Dr. John McLoughlin claimed the land for his employer, the Hudson Bay Co. In 1843, Oregon country's first provisional legislature was held here, and the town served as territorial capital from 1849 to 1852. McLoughlin's 1846 home, now the **John McLoughlin House National Historic Site,** contains many of his possessions and artifacts from the era. *713 Center St., Oregon City, tel. 503/ 656–5146. Admission: $3 adults, $2.50 senior citizens 62 and older, $1 students 6–17. Open Tues.–Sat. 10–4, Sun. 1–4.*

The **McLoughlin Historic District** that surrounds the home, originally part of McLoughlin's property, is now a neighborhood of picturesque houses and churches in architectural styles dating from the 1840s to the 1930s.

The **End of the Trail Interpretive Center** highlights Oregon Trail travel with displays that include covered wagons, river rafts, firearms, and other artifacts. *500 Washington St., Oregon City, tel. 503/657–9336. Admission: $2 adults, $1 students 6–17, $1.50 senior citizens. Open Mon.–Sat. 10–4, Sun. noon–4.*

From Portland take McLoughlin Boulevard (U.S. 99E) south 13 miles to Oregon City.

Shopping

Shopping Districts, Streets, and Malls

The main shopping area in the city center is concentrated between S.W. 3rd and 10th avenues and between S.W. Stark and Morrison streets.

Downtown/ City Center **The Galleria** (921 S.W. Morrison St., in Fareless Sq., tel. 503/228–2748) covers a full block, with three floors of 50 specialty stores, gift shops, and restaurants.

Pioneer Place (700 S.W. 5th Ave., in Fareless Sq., tel. 503/228–5800) has 70 specialty shops anchored by Saks Fifth Avenue, which offers two floors of high-quality men's and women's clothing and jewelry, among other merchandise. The Cascades Food Court, in the basement, offers good, inexpensive ethnic food from 18 different vendors.

Portland Saturday Market (100 S.W. Ankeny St., tel. 503/222–6072) is a good place to find unique handcrafted items. *(See* Tour 1, *above,* for details about the products sold here.)

Northwest Portland's funky and fashionable **Pearl District,** north of downtown along N.W. 21st and N.W. 23rd streets, is home to an eclectic array of clothing, gift, and food shops, as well as art galleries, ethnic restaurants, and bookstores. The quiet tree-shaded residential neighborhoods to the east and west make for pleasant walking tours.

Northeast Portland **Jantzen Beach Center** (1405 Jantzen Beach Ct., off I–5, tel. 503/289–5555) has 100 shops, three major department stores, a bowling alley, a triplex cinema, and an old, operating carousel.

In 1960, when it opened, **Lloyd Center** (adjacent to MAX light rail; bounded by E. Multnomah, Broadway, and 16th and 19th Aves., tel. 503/282–2511) was the largest shopping mall in the United States. Extensively remodeled in 1990, the center contains more than 170 stores, including four department stores, a large food court, multi-screen cinema, and an ice-skating pavilion.

Southwest Portland **Washington Square** (S.W. Hall Blvd. and Hwy. 217, tel. 503/639–8860) has five major department stores, 120 specialty shops, parking accommodations for more than 6,000 cars, vaulted skylights, and indoor landscaping. Washington Square Too has 15 additional stores.

John's Landing (5331 S.W. Macadam, tel. 503/228–9431) is a pleasant smaller mall with 35 specialty shops and six restaurants.

Southeast Portland **Sellwood** (S.E. 13th St., tel. 503/233–7334), 5 miles from the city center, offers a combination historical walking tour and venture into unusual antiques and collectibles. More than 50 antiques shops line S.E. 13th Street, along with shops specializing in specific products as well as outlet stores for sporting goods. Building dates and original occupants are identified by plaques at each store.

Clackamas Town Center (Exit 14 off I–205 at Sunnyside Rd., tel. 503/653–6913), with more than 180 shops and five major department stores, has one of the largest selections of merchandise in the Northwest.

Department **Meier and Frank** (621 S.W. 5th Ave., in Fareless Sq., tel. 503/
Stores 223–0512) dates from 1857 and offers 10 floors of general mer-
Downtown chandise at the main store downtown.

Nordstrom (701 S.W. Broadway, tel. 503/224–6666) features
fine-quality apparel, accessories, and a large footwear department.

Specialty Stores

Antiques **Portland Antique Company** (1211 N.W. Glisan St., tel. 503/223–
0999) spreads over 35,000 square feet and houses the
Northwest's largest selection of European and English antiques.

Sellwood Antique Row (*see* Shopping Districts, Streets, and
Malls, *above*).

Art Dealers/ Second Avenue, north and west of Yamhill Marketplace, has
Galleries many fine art galleries. Recommended downtown shops are
Jamison/Thomas Gallery (1313 N.W. Glisan St., tel. 503/222–
0063), representing contemporary West Coast artists and spe-
cializing in art for the knowledgeable collector, and **Quintana
Galleries of Native American Art** (139 N.W. 2nd Ave., tel. 503/
223–1729), which focuses on Native American, Southwest,
Navajo, and Hopi jewelry.

The **Photographic Image Gallery** (208 S.W. 1st Ave., tel. 503/
224–3543) features prints by nationally known nature photographers Ansel Adams and Ray Atkinson, among others.

Books **Powell's City of Books** (1005 W. Burnside St., tel. 503/228–
4651) is the largest bookstore in the United States, and features new and used books, and rare and hard-to-find editions.
Open 365 days a year.

Gifts Shoppers who wish to take home local products will want to
seek out the several **Made in Oregon** shops, at Portland International Airport, Lloyd Center, The Galleria, Old Town, Washington Square, or Clackamas Town Center. Merchandise
ranges from books to distinctive carvings made of myrtlewood,
local wines, and woolen products.

Jewelry **Zell Brothers Jewelers** (800 S.W. Morrison, tel. 503/227–8471)
has sold fine jewelry and other precious trinkets to Portlanders
since 1912.

Men's/Women's **Norm Thompson Outfitters** (1805 N.W. Thurman St., tel. 503/
Apparel 221–0764) offers classic fashions for men and women, innovative footwear, and one-of-a-kind gifts. A downtown store (at
420 S.W. Morrison, tel. 503/243–2680) opened in 1993.

Perfume **Perfume House** (3328 S.E. Hawthorne Blvd., tel. 503/234–
5375) has more than 600 brand-name fragrances for women and
200 for men.

Records **Django Records** (1111 S.W. Stark St., tel. 503/227–4381) is a
must for collectors of tapes, compact discs, 45s, and albums.

Toys **Finnegan's Toys and Gifts** (922 S.W. Yamhill St., tel. 503/221–
0306), downtown Portland's largest toy store, stocks artistic,
creative, educational, and other types of toys.

Sports and the Outdoors

Participant Sports

Bicycling Cyclists are common on Portland's streets, and numerous bike paths meander through parks and along the shoreline of the Willamette River. Designated routes include a 30-mile path along U.S. 30, through Forest Park into northwest and southwest Portland and on to the suburb of Lake Oswego. Other options are the 2 miles of promenade along the Willamette River between the Broadway and Marquam bridges and an eastside route between the Hawthorne and Burnside bridges. Bikes can be rented at **Cascaddens Outdoor Shop** (1533 N.W. 24th Ave., tel. 503/224–4746).

Fishing The Columbia and Willamette rivers are both major sport-fishing streams with opportunities for angling virtually year-round (*see* Excursions from Portland, *below*).

The Willamette River offers prime fishing for rainbow and cutthroat trout, as well as bass, channel cat-fish, and sturgeon. It is also a good winter steelhead stream, and salmon action lasts into June. June is also the top shad month, with some of the best fishing occurring below Willamette Falls at Oregon City. The Columbia River is known for its abundance of trout, salmon, and sturgeon.

Regulations Local sport shops are the best source of information on current fishing hot spots, which change from year to year. Detailed fishing regulations are available at local tackle shops or from the **Oregon Department of Fish and Wildlife** (2501 S.W. 1st Ave., Portland 97201, tel. 503/229–5403).

Outfitters There are numerous outfitters throughout Portland who offer guide services, including **Larry's Sport Center** (2205 E. Burnside St., tel. 503/665–6102), and **Stewart Fly Shop** (23830 N.E. Halsey St., tel. 503/666–2471). Few outfitters rent out equipment anymore, so either bring your own or be prepared to buy it.

Golf Golfers have a choice of 18 public courses in the greater Portland area. Among the best are **Broadmoor** (3509 N.E. Columbia Blvd., tel. 503/281–1337), 18 holes; **Colwood National** (7313 N.E. Columbia Blvd., tel. 503/254–5515), 18 holes; **Glendoveer** (14015 N.E. Glisan St., tel. 503/253–7507), two 18-hole courses; and **Heron Lakes** (3500 N. Victory Blvd., tel. 503/289–1818), 36 holes.

Skiing For detailed information on cross-country and downhill ski trails, *see* Excursions from Portland, *below*. Two places for ski rentals are **Cascadden's Outdoor Shop** (1533 N.W. 24th Ave., tel. 503/224–4746) and **The Mountain Shop** (628 N.E. Broadway, tel. 503/288–6768).

Tennis Public indoor tennis is available at **Glendoveer Golf Course**
Indoor (14015 N.E. Glisan St., tel. 503/253–7507) and at the **Lake Oswego Indoor Tennis Center** (2900 S.W. Diane Dr., tel. 503/635–5550). **Portland Parks and Recreation** (tel. 503/796–5193) operates 117 outdoor tennis courts (many with night lighting) on a first-come, first-served basis. **The Portland Tennis Center** (324 N.E. 12th Ave., tel. 503/823–3189) operates four indoor courts;

the **St. John's Racquet Center** (7519 N. Burlington Ave., tel. 503/823–3629) has three indoor courts.

Outdoor From May 1 to September 30, outdoor courts may be reserved at **Grant Park, Portland Tennis Center,** and **Washington Park.**

Spectator Sports

Auto Racing **Portland International Raceway** (N. Victory Blvd. at West Delta Park, tel. 503/285–6635) features bicycles, drag racing, and motocross on weeknights, and sports cars, motorcycles, and go-carts on weekends from April through September. **Portland Speedway's** (9727 N. Martin Luther King Blvd., tel. 503/285–2883) season runs April–September, with demolition derbies, NASCAR, and stock-car races. In June, it hosts the Budweiser Indy Car World Series, a 200-mile race featuring the top names on the Indy Car circuit.

Basketball Memorial Coliseum (1401 N. Wheeler Ave., tel. 503/248–4496) is home court for the NBA's **Portland Trail Blazers.**

Greyhound Racing The season at **Multnomah Kennel Club** (223rd and N.E. Glisan Sts., tel. 503/667–7700) starts in May and continues through September.

Hockey The **Portland Winter Hawks** of the Western Hockey League play home games at Memorial Coliseum (1401 N. Wheeler Ave., tel. 503/238–4636).

Horse Racing Thoroughbred and quarter horses race, rain or shine, at **Portland Meadows** (1001 N. Schmeer Rd., tel. 503/285–9144) from October through April.

Dining

First-time visitors to Portland are likely to be surprised by both the diversity of restaurants and the low prices. Although this city has never been known as a melting pot, lovers of ethnic foods can choose from regional Chinese, French, German, Indian, Mexican, Middle Eastern, Japanese, Thai, and Vietnamese. Of course, there's also Northwest cuisine, an emerging style that features local fish and domestic game, such as venison, duck, and pheasant, plus locally grown wild mushrooms and other produce. Northwest chefs try to avoid fats by searing and broiling meats.

Highly recommended restaurants are indicated by a star ★.

Category	Cost*
Very Expensive	over $25
Expensive	$20–$25
Moderate	$12–$20
Inexpensive	under $12

per person, excluding drinks and service charge

Very Expensive **Atwater's.** Perched on the 30th floor of the U.S. Bancorp Tower,
★ Atwater's has an outstanding view of the Willamette River, the Cascade Mountains, and the city's skyline. The decor is a mix of classical pillars, Oriental art, and tile. Northwest cuisine fea-

tures a variety of mushrooms, huckleberries, venison, Pacific salmon, lamb, and pheasant. A 300-label wine list of Northwest, California, and Italian vintages ranges in price from $15 to $800 per bottle. Sunday brunch is served. *111 S.W. 5th Ave., tel. 503/275–3600. Reservations advised. Dress: casual but neat. AE, D, DC, MC, V. Closed lunch.*

L'Auberge. In this French restaurant, you can dine à la carte beside the lounge fireplace or order a six-course meal in the formal dining room. The menu changes weekly and emphasizes seasonal specialties, but you can always count on main entrées of steak, rack of lamb or veal, and a poultry or fish offering that might include duckling, pheasant, squab, quail, sturgeon, or swordfish. *2601 N.W. Vaughn St., tel. 503/223–3302. Reservations recommended for dining room. Dress: casual. AE, D, DC, MC, V. Closed lunch.*

Genoa Restaurant. This crowded, intimate Italian restaurant seats only about 35 people and serves a four-course meal at 5:30, 6, and 10:30, and there's a seven-course dinner every half hour from 5:30 to 9:30. Since there are no windows in this somewhat dark dining room, the consistently delicious meals have become the attraction. Emphasizing fresh meat and seafood, the menu changes frequently but promises creative picks. Fillet of swordfish and veal loin chops are featured specials, along with fish soups and seafood ravioli. *2832 S.E. Belmont St., tel. 503/238–1464. Reservations required. Dress: casual. AE, D, DC, MC, V. Closed lunch and Sun.*

Expensive **Couch Street Fish House.** Long recognized as one of Portland's finest restaurants, the Fish House offers an elegant atmosphere in a building that dates from 1883. Watercolor seascapes hang on the dining-room walls, and antiques and greenery are interspersed with the tables and high-back chairs. Continental cooking includes mesquite broiled salmon, rack of lamb with port sauce and mint, prawns on chanterelles and apricots, and Maine lobster poached in court bouillon. *105 N.W. 3rd Ave., tel. 503/223–6173. Reservations advised. Dress: casual but neat. AE, MC, V. Closed lunch.*

Esplanade at Riverplace. Tall windows frame a view of the sailboat-filled marina and the Willamette River, providing a dramatic backdrop to this elegant restaurant in the Riverplace Alexis Hotel. The cuisine is gourmet Northwest—Dungeness crab cakes; plump scallops seared with fennel, red onion, and oyster mushrooms; duck with blackberry sauce—and the award-winning wine list features many hard-to-find Northwest vintages in a gratifyingly wide range of prices. *Riverplace Alexis Hotel, 1510 S.W. Harbor Way, tel. 503/228–3233. Reservations advised. Dress: casual but neat. AE, D, DC, MC, V. Closed Sat. lunch.*

★ **L'Etoile.** Intimate and romantic, filled with fresh flowers and flickering candlelight, this tiny (12-table) restaurant in Northeast Portland specializes in the delicately sauced pillars of classical French cuisine: *escargot*, rack of lamb, duck with cassis. Chef and owner John Zweben has a deft and artful touch with fresh local ingredients. Try the house specialty, veal sweetbreads in a truffle-infused sauce *Financier*. From Memorial Day to Labor Day (if the weather's good), be sure to get a table outside in the brick-terraced herb garden. *4627 N.E. Fremont St., tel. 503/281–4869. Reservations recommended. Dress: casual but neat. MC, V. Closed lunch; closed Sun.–Tues.*

Abou Karim, **11**
Alexis, **9**
Atwater's, **12**
Bangkok Kitchen, **19**
Bridgeport
Brew Pub, **2**
Couch Street Fish
House, **8**
Dan & Louis's
Oyster Bar, **10**
Esplanade at
Riverplace, **15**
Genoa Restaurant, **18**
Indigene, **17**
Jake's Famous
Crawfish, **7**
Kornblatt's, **4**
L'Auberge, **1**
L'Etoile, **23**
Newport Bay at
Riverplace, **16**
Panini, **14**
Papa Haydn, **3**
Pazzo, **13**
The Rheinlander
Restaurant, **22**
Ringside, **6**
Sylvia's Italian
Restaurant, **21**
Yen Ha, **20**
Zefiro, **5**

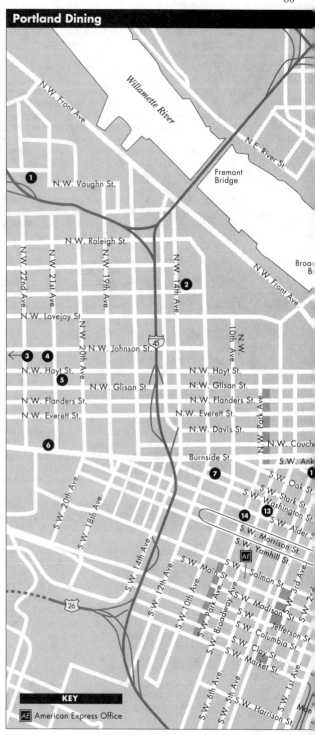

Portland Dining

KEY

AE American Express Office

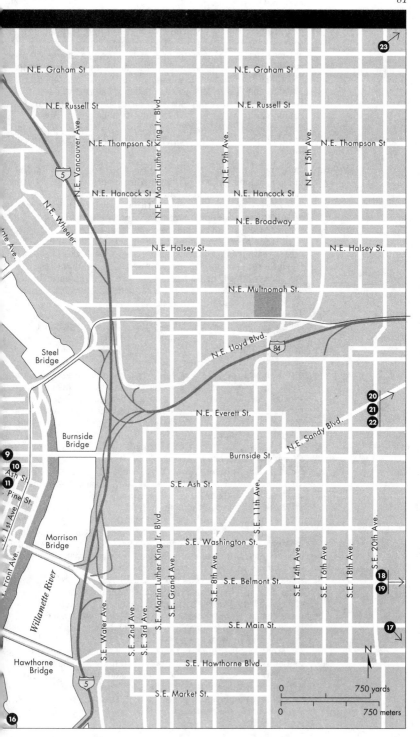

★ **Zefiro.** From its Scandanavian-blonde hardwood floors to its gracefully curved walls of honey-colored stucco, scrupulous attention to detail is what sets Zefiro apart. The meticulousness extends to the food, for example grilled prawns on a leafy, arrow-like skewer of rosemary. The menu here is primarily Northern Italian, with the emphasis on simple but impeccable preparation. The offerings change daily; one recent menu featured a T-bone of veal, grilled with sage and lemon butter, accompanied by a creamy potato and artichoke gratin. *500 N.W. 21st Ave., tel. 503/226–3394. Reservations necessary. Dress: casual but stylish. AE, DC, MC, V. Closed Sun., closed lunch Sat.*

Moderate **Indigene.** Chef/owner Millie Howe wows regulars with her unique cuisine, which draws on the flavors of India, Latin America, Indonesia, and Europe. Depending on the season, diners may encounter rabbit with mustard, fresh rosemary, cream and green peppercorns; fresh razor clams seared for 20 seconds a side in butter and garlic; or a four-course Indian feast with Howe's own fresh homemade chutneys. This intimate (11-table) restaurant has a pleasingly spare look, accented with fresh flowers and lots of natural wood. The small garden deck out back is one of the best places in town for a romantic dinner on a summer evening. *3725 S.E. Division, tel. 503/238–1470. Reservations recommended. MC, V. Closed Sun.–Mon. and Tues.–Sat. lunch.*

Jake's Famous Crawfish. When Jake's added crawfish to its menu in 1920, it gained a national reputation. When crawfish is in season (May–Sept.), you can have it Creole, as a pie, or étouffé (with a beef broth used for dipping). Jake's celebrated its 100th birthday in 1992. Here white-coated waiters serve up fresh Northwest seafood, selected from a lengthy sheet of daily specials, in a warren of small, individual, old-fashioned wood-paneled dining rooms. The back bar came around Cape Horn during the 1880s, and the chandeliers hanging from the high ceilings date from 1881. *401 S.W. 12th Ave., tel. 503/226–1419. Reservations advised. Dress: casual. AE, D, DC, MC, V. Closed weekends lunch.*

Newport Bay at Riverplace. When it comes to views, there's not a bad seat in this house; the restaurant literally floats on the water of the Willamette River. The circular glass dining room affords a 360° view of the marina, bridges, river, and city skyline. Newport Bay seeks out whatever is in season worldwide, which might include Oregon spring salmon, sturgeon, Maine lobster, Australian lobster tail, Alaskan halibut, or New Zealand roughy, as well as swordfish, marlin, and shark. *0425 S.W. Montgomery St., at Riverplace, tel. 503/227–FISH. Reservations advised. Dress: casual but neat. AE, D, DC, MC, V.*

Papa Haydn. This corner restaurant, situated near the center of N.W. 23rd Avenue's boutiques, makes a convenient lunch or dinner stop. Sandwiches are made with Gruyère cheese and Black Forest ham grilled on French bread, and with mesquite-grilled chicken breast on a roll with bacon, avocado, basil, and tomato. Favorite dinner entrées are the combination mesquite-grilled top sirloin, Italian sausage, and breast of chicken, and the sautéed veal chop in thyme and raspberry vinegar. Many patrons come here just for the luscious, fresh-baked desserts, temptingly displayed in glass cases. *701 N.W. 23rd Ave., tel. 503/228–7317. Reservations for Sun. brunch only. Dress: casual. AE, MC, V.*

Pazzo. The aromas of roasted garlic and wood smoke greet diners at the door of this bustling Italian restaurant, at street level of the swanky Hotel Vintage Plaza downtown. Relying on perfectly grilled meats, fish and poultry, deceptively simple nuovo cuisine, and pastas and risottos, Pazzo has quickly elbowed its way to the forefront of Portland's fine dining scene. The decor is a soothing mix of dark wood, terra-cotta, red-checkered tablecloths, and dangling Parma hams; booths and glass partitions keep the dining area surprisingly quiet. The menu is small and changes frequently, but get the grilled lamb chops with fennel and artichoke risotto when they're offered. *422 S.W. Broadway, tel. 503/228–1515. Reservations recommended. Dress: casual but neat. AE, D, DC, MC, V.*

★ **Rheinlander.** The Bavarian chalet-style building has dining areas crammed with steins, wood carvings, china, clocks, and figurines inside. Singing waiters and strolling musicians serenade at tables. All dinners start with Swiss-cheese fondue and Russian rye bread. If you're a first-timer, you may wish to sample the German cooking with a combination platter of roast pork, sauerbraten, bratwurst, and chicken Cordon Bleu. For lighter and less expensive meals, Gustav's, the operation's next-door beer garden, is a lively alternative. *5035 N.E. Sandy Blvd., tel. 503/288–5503. Reservations advised. Dress: casual but neat. AE, MC, V.*

Ringside. Waiters in tuxedos, a fireplace, and low lighting make this the perfect setting for romantic dining. The Ringside is known for its fine wine list, onion rings, rib-eye steaks, seafood, and chicken. *2165 W. Burnside St., tel. 503/223–1513. Reservations advised. Dress: casual but neat. AE, MC, V. Closed lunch.*

Sylvia's Italian Restaurant. This is really two restaurants. In the dining room you'll find Chianti bottles hanging from the ceiling and traditional red-and-white-check tablecloths. A separate dinner theater stages five musicals, comedies, and dramas a year—each with a run of eight weeks or longer; the $24.95 tab includes the meal and the show. Traditional entrées range from spaghetti and Italian sausage to shrimp Milano with fresh mushrooms and green peppers simmered in a red sauce and white wine. *5115 N.E. Sandy Blvd., tel. 503/288–6828. Reservations advised. Dress: casual. AE, D, MC, V. Closed lunch.*

Inexpensive **Abou Karim.** Although more than half of the Lebanese menu is vegetarian, the leg of lamb served on a bed of rice with lentil soup, including a full salad and pita bread, is a favorite. A special menu of meals low in saturated fats is also featured, and there is an outside area for dining in summer. The only nod to atmosphere or decor consists of a few plants, and a Lebanese sword or two hanging on a wall. *221 S.W. Pine St., tel. 503/223–5058. Reservations advised on weekends. Dress: casual. AE, D, MC, V.*

Alexis. The interior is as simple as the white walls and basic furnishings, but the authentic Greek flavor keeps the crowds coming. You'll find such traditional Greek food as *kalamarakia* (deep-fried squid served with *tzatziki*, a yogurt dip) and *horiatiki* (a green salad combination with feta cheese and Kalamata olives, tossed in olive oil, vinegar, and oregano). Greek beers and wines are served at the bar. *215 W. Burnside St., tel. 503/224–8577. Dress: casual. AE, D, DC, MC, V. Closed weekend lunch.*

Bangkok Kitchen. Chef/owner Srichan Miller juggles the lime, cilantro, coconut milk, lemongrass, curry, and (above all) hot peppers of classical Thai cuisine with great virtuosity. Pay no attention to the '60s diner decor, and be sure to try one of the noodle dishes—the tender rice stick noodles with shrimp, egg, fresh mint, chilies, and coconut are memorable. Order your dishes mild or medium-hot unless you have an asbestos tongue, and don't forget the cold Singh Ha beer. *2534 S.E. Belmont St., tel. 503/236-7349. Reservations advised. No credit cards. Closed Sat. and Sun. lunch.*

Bridgeport Brew Pub. The only food on the menu is thick, hand-thrown pizza on sourdough beer-wort crust, served up inside a cool, ivy-covered century-old industrial building near the Willamette River. The boisterous crowds wash down the pizza with frothing pints of Bridgeport's English-style ale, brewed on the premises (there's also wine and nonalcoholic seltzers, for the fainter of heart). During the summer, the flower-festooned loading dock is transformed into an outdoor beer garden. *1313 N.W. Marshall, tel. 503/241-7179. No reservations. Dress: ultracasual. MC, V. Closed lunch Mon.-Thurs.*

★ **Dan & Louis's Oyster Bar.** You can have your oysters fried, stewed, or on the half-shell. Crab stew—virtually impossible to find elsewhere—is also a specialty. You'll also find local wines and microbrews. Founder Louis Wachsmuth, who started his restaurant in 1907, was an avid collector of steins, plates, and marine art. The collection has grown over the years to fill nearly every inch of wall, beams, nooks, and crannies. Allow time to examine the ship models, paintings on glass, and the many photographs. *208 S.W. Ankeny St., tel. 503/227-5906. Reservations required for parties of 5 or more. Dress: casual. AE, D, DC, MC, V.*

Kornblatt's. You won't find a better bagel anywhere in Portland than the ones they serve at Kornblatt's—moist, chewy, still warm from the oven. This authentic kosher deli has been transplanted from New York to Northwest Portland's trendy 23rd Avenue. The decor is clean and modern; the fresh-cooked pastrami, corned beef, and tongue lean and tender; the home-smoked salmon and sablefish are simply the best. For breakfast, try the poached eggs with spicy homemade corned beef hash. *628 N.W. 23rd Ave., tel. 503/242-0055. No reservations. Dress: casual. MC, V.*

Panini. This minuscule restaurant, tucked away on a narrow downtown side-street, is a much-loved spot for breakfast, lunch, light suppers, and good wine by the glass. Panini—hearty sandwiches of fontina cheese, eggplant, fresh basil, and Parma ham pressed between hot grills until crisp and bubbly—are the house specialty. The fresh-baked desserts and unusual salads, on display in the dining room, change daily, as do the imaginative pasta specials. *620 S.W. 9th St., tel. 503/224-6001. No reservations. Dress: casual. No credit cards. Closed Sun.*

Yen Ha. The vibrant flavors of Vietnam find full expression at Yen Ha, which is thronged nightly with Asians and Americans alike. Superb rice-paper rolls—translucent cylinders filled with pungent bean threads, fresh mint and shrimp, and dipped in peanut sauce—and wonderful noodle dishes are among the star attractions. *8640 S.W. Canyon Rd., tel. 503/292-0616; 6820 N.E. Sandy Blvd., tel. 503/287-3698. Reservations recommended. Dress: casual. MC, V.*

Lodging

Travelers to Portland will find a variety of accommodations. Lodgings range from high-rise all-suite complexes near the airport, especially convenient for business travelers, to elegant hotels near the city center and waterfront, appealing because of their proximity to the city's attractions. For families, all-suite hotels in the southwest suburbs provide a lot of space without requiring you to give up the extras. Budget travelers will need to sacrifice convenience to the airport and downtown. Many places allow small pets, and some offer senior-citizen discounts and family plans.

Highly recommended lodgings are indicated by a star ★.

Category	Cost*
Very Expensive	over $110
Expensive	$80–$110
Moderate	$60–$80
Inexpensive	under $60

All prices are for a standard double room for two, excluding tax of 6%–9%, depending on the location of the property; unless noted, all places include room/valet service and color TVs.

Airport Area **Shilo Inn Suites Hotel.** This all-suites hotel provides amenities that border on the excessive. Each room has three TV sets, a VCR, a microwave, four telephones, refrigerator and wet bar, and two oversize beds. The contemporary decor runs to soothing pale blues, light pinks, and light grays in both public and private areas. *11707 N.E. Airport Way, 97220, tel. 503/252-7500 or 800/222-2244. 200 rooms; no-smoking rooms available. Facilities: restaurant, lounge, airport shuttle, complimentary Continental breakfast, indoor pool, spa, exercise room, steam room, business service center, free local telephone calls. AE, D, DC, MC, V. Expensive–Very Expensive.*

Days Hotel. This facility built in 1989 is conveniently located ¾ mile from I–205. Rooms are of average size and are brightly decorated in teals, maroons, and yellows. The lounge features a large TV screen and grill. *11550 N.E. Airport Way, 97220, tel. 503/252-3200 or 800/325-2525. 150 rooms; no-smoking rooms available. Facilities: restaurant, lounge, complimentary airport shuttle, free parking, Jacuzzi, outdoor pool. AE, D, DC, MC, V. Moderate.*

★ **Ramada Inn Airport.** This facility caters to business travelers; it has board and conference rooms and a business center with computers, fax machines, and individual work stations. The 108 execu-suites have microwaves, wet bars, refrigerators, and sitting areas. Spacious one- and two-bedroom suites come equipped with a Jacuzzi, and standard rooms, with king-size beds, are tastefully decorated in quiet grays, browns, and pinks. *6221 N.E. 82nd Ave., 97220, tel. 503/255-6511 or 800/228-2828, fax 503/255-8417. 202 rooms. Facilities: restaurant, lounge, complimentary limo service to airport and car-rental companies, free parking, Jacuzzi, pool, sauna, weight room. AE, D, DC, MC, V. Expensive.*

★ **Best Western/Fortniter Motel.** Each room has a living area with queen-size bed or queen-size hide-a-bed, coffee table, full

The Benson Hotel, **7**
Best Western/
Fortniter Motel, **24**
Best Western Inn at
the Convention
Center, **18**
Days Hotel, **22**
Embassy Suites, **4**
The Governor Hotel, **6**
Greenwood Inn, **3**
Heathman Hotel, **10**
Heron Haus, **1**
Hotel Vintage Plaza, **8**
Lamplighter Inn, **2**
Mallory Hotel, **5**
Marriott Hotel, **11**
Portland Guest
House, **19**
Ramada Inn
Airport, **23**
Red Lion/Coliseum, **15**
Red Lion/Columbia
River, **14**
Red Lion/Jantzen
Beach, **13**
Red Lion/Lloyd
Center, **20**
Riverplace Alexis
Hotel, **12**
Riverside Inn, **9**
Shilo Inn/Lloyd
Center, **17**
Shilo Inn Suites
Hotel, **21**
Travelodge Hotel, **16**

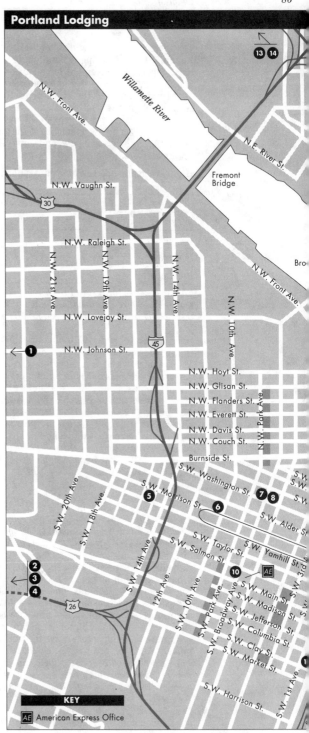

Portland Lodging

KEY

AE American Express Office

kitchenette, full-size refrigerator, and a separate bedroom. Rooms have a lived-in, put-your-feet-up feel. Although there is no room service, there is a nearby restaurant that can be reached by free shuttle provided by the motel. *4911 N.E. 82nd Ave., 97220, tel. 503/255–9771 or 800/528–1234. fax 503/255–9774. 52 rooms. Facilities: complimentary 24-hr shuttle to airport, shuttle transfers to restaurant, 1-wk free parking, outdoor pool, complimentary Continental breakfast, laundry room. AE, D, DC, MC, V. Inexpensive.*

Downtown **The Benson Hotel.** Portland's premier hotel, built in 1912, completed a $20 million restoration in 1990. Elegance has been maintained with the hand-carved Russian Circassian walnut paneling and Italian white-marble staircase. In the guest rooms expect to find small crystal chandeliers, inlaid mahogany doors, and original ceilings. All rooms have state-of-the-art movie systems. The London Grill and Trader Vic's are among the city's finest restaurants. *309 S.W. Broadway, 97205, tel. 503/228–2000 or 800/426–0670. 290 rooms. Facilities: coffee shop, lounge, gift shop, airport-shuttle service, valet/laundry, concierge service, exercise room. AE, D, DC, MC, V. Very Expensive.*

The Governor Hotel. The public rooms of this most atmospherically "Northwestern" of Portland's many renovated luxury hotels are an oasis of soft amber light, dark wood, crackling fireplaces, well-stocked bookshelves, and comfortable, old-fashioned furniture amid the modern highrises. The Governor is small and quiet, more like a rustic hunting lodge than a bustling downtown hotel. The 100 guest rooms and suites, in contrast, are furnished in '30s-flavored Wodehousian opulence, designed to soothe weary business travellers and vacationers alike. *S.W. 10th and Alder, 97205, tel. 503/224–3400 or 800/554–3456, fax 503/224–9426. 100 rooms, some with fireplaces. Facilities: athletic club, business center, restaurant, lounge. AE, D, DC, MC, V. Very Expensive.*

★ **Heathman Hotel.** Superior service, a renowned restaurant, a central downtown location (adjoining the Performing Arts Center) and elegantly beautiful public areas have earned the Heathman its reputation for quality. From the teak-paneled lobby hung with Warhol prints to the rosewood elevators and marble fireplaces, this hotel exudes elegance. The earth-toned guest rooms are luxuriously comfortable, if not overly spacious, and the bathrooms have lots of marble and mirrors. The Heathman's clientele, from wealthy Far Eastern businessmen to famous Italian tenors, is as select as its prices. *1009 S.W. Broadway, tel. 503/241–4100 or 800/551–0011. 152 rooms; no-smoking rooms available. Facilities: health club, restaurant, lounge. AE, D, DC, MC, V. Very Expensive.*

Heron Haus. This lovely B&B occupies a stately 90-year-old Tudor mansion, near Forest Park in Portland's West Hills. Each of the five large guest rooms has its own private bath, phone, and work desk, as well as such graceful touches as a tulip-shape bath tub, a tiled, seven-headed antique shower, and a graceful eyebrow window overlooking the downtown skyline and distant mountains. Breakfast (included in the price), is a gourmet Continental affair. *2545 N.W. Westover, Portland, OR 97210, tel. 503/274–1846, fax 503/274–1846. 5 double rooms, all with private baths. Facilities: heated pool, cable TV, phones in room, air-conditioning. No smoking. AE, MC, V. Very Expensive.*

Hotel Vintage Plaza. Completely renovated in 1991, this historic landmark took its theme from the area's vineyards and features rooms with four distinct styles. Two-story town-house suites are named after local wineries. Guests can fall asleep counting stars in top-floor rooms, where skylights and wall-to-wall conservatory-style windows rate highly among the special details. Hospitality suites feature extra-large rooms with a full living area, and the deluxe rooms have a bar. All rooms are appointed in hunter green, deep plum, cerise, taupe, and gold; and more than 20 rooms have hot tubs. In keeping with the theme, there's plenty of shrubbery in public areas, including the 10-story atrium. An extensive collection of Oregon wines is displayed in the tasting room. *422 S.W. Broadway, 97205, tel. 503/228–1212 or 800/243–0555. 88 rooms, 19 suites. Facilities: restaurant, piano lounge, complimentary coffee and newspaper in mornings and wine in evenings, minibars, valet parking, gym, business center, secretarial services. AE, D, DC, MC, V. Very Expensive.*

Marriott Hotel. Emphasis on service starts with uniformed doormen and continues to the 12th floor, the concierge level. The large rooms are decorated in off-whites; the best rooms look east to the Willamette and the Cascades. Champions Lounge, filled with sports memorabilia, is a singles hot spot on weekends. *1401 S.W. Front Ave., 97201, tel. 503/226–7600 or 800/228–9290. 500 rooms; handicapped and no-smoking rooms available. Facilities: 3 restaurants, coffee shop, lounge entertainment, 24-hr fitness center, gift shop, indoor pool, hair salon. AE, D, DC, MC, V. Very Expensive.*

Riverplace Alexis Hotel. The Alexis has the feeling of a private home, with its large, airy rooms, wing-back chairs, teak tables, and feather pillows. It has one of the best views in Portland, overlooking the river and the marina, the city skyline, and a courtyard. *1510 S.W. Harbor Way, 97201, tel. 503/228–3233 or 800/227–1333. 84 rooms; no-smoking rooms available. Facilities: 2 restaurants, lounge entertainment, athletic-club arrangement, complimentary Continental breakfast, parking in locked garage. AE, D, DC, MC, V. Very Expensive.*

Riverside Inn. This five-story hotel overlooking Waterfront Park and the Willamette is the top choice for visitors who want both location and value. The downtown core and the MAX light-rail line are right outside the back door; the hotel itself is scrupulously maintained—newly furnished, painted, and carpeted. East-facing rooms offer a good view of the river and park across busy Front Avenue; rooms on the west side are a trifle quieter and have views of the downtown skyline. The rooms themselves are clean and furnished in white, green, and rattan with comfortable beds and prints of modern artwork. The airy café and bar features a seafood-and-steak menu. *50 S.W. Morrison St., 97204, tel. 503/221–0711 or 800/648–6440. 138 rooms; no-smoking rooms available. Facilities: restaurant, lounge, free parking, athletic-club arrangement. AE, D, DC, MC, V. Expensive.*

Mallory Hotel. This older (20s vintage) hotel, eight blocks from the downtown core, has aged gracefully. Its gilt-ceilinged lobby received fresh white paint and floral carpet in 1993; crystal chandeliers and a leaded-glass skylight hark back to a more elegant era. The rooms, also undergoing a floor-by-floor upgrade, are old-fashioned but clean and cheerful; corner suites and rooms on the east side of the building have impressive skyline views. The hotel is a favorite with visiting singers, writers, and artists of every stripe. The staff is friendly and knowledgeable, and most of them have been here for years. *729 S.W. 15th Ave., 97205, tel. 503/223–6311 or 800/228–8657. 144 rooms. Facilities: restaurant, lounge, free parking. AE, DC, MC, V. Inexpensive.*

West Side   **Embassy Suites.** Every room here is a suite, and each has a separate sitting room, bedroom, wet bar with refrigerator, two color TVs, and two telephones. This nine-story structure, within a block of Washington Square shopping center, surrounds an atrium filled with tropical plants and waterfalls. Cooked-to-order breakfast, and a two-hour manager's reception with live entertainment, are included. *9000 Washington Sq. Rd., Tigard 97223, tel. 503/644–4000 or 800/EMBASSY, fax 503/641–4654. 353 rooms; no-smoking rooms available. Facilities: restaurant, lounge entertainment, courtesy limo to surrounding shops and restaurants, indoor pool, Jacuzzi, sauna, health-club arrangement, gift shop. AE, D, DC, MC, V. Very Expensive.*

Greenwood Inn. This large suburban Portland hotel (a 10-minute drive west of downtown) was completely remodeled in 1993. Some of its 253 guest rooms, now very comfortably furnished in southwestern shades of sand, ocher, pale green and red, have courtyard views; avoid the noisier rooms on the hotel's west side. The location is popular with both business and pleasure travelers. There is dancing to live bands six nights a week. *10700 S.W. Allen Blvd., Beaverton 97005, tel. 503/643–7444 or 800/289–1300. 253 rooms; handicapped and no-smoking rooms available. Facilities: dining room, lounge, free parking, athletic-club arrangement, weight room, 2 outdoor pools, Jacuzzi, gift shop, kitchens. AE, D, DC, MC, V. Expensive.*

Lamplighter Inn. Although it's close to the freeway, noise coming into the hotel is muffled by highway embankments. The inn's color scheme runs through blues and mauves. The small shopping mall across the street has a supermarket, lounge, and sporting-goods and equipment stores, and a Mongolian restaurant is nearby. *10207 S.W. Pkwy., Beaverton 97225, tel. 503/297–2211. 56 rooms. Facilities: 6 kitchen units. AE, D, DC, MC, V. Inexpensive.*

East Side   **Red Lion/Lloyd Center.** One of the largest hotels in the state,
   ★   this property is the flagship of the popular Northwest-based Red Lion chain. It's a busy and well-appointed business-oriented hotel, with a huge traffic in meetings and special events. The recently remodeled public areas are a tasteful mix of marble, rose-and-green carpet, and antique-style furnishings. The chain prides itself on its attentive service and its food. The MAX light-rail line runs along the south side of the hotel, Lloyd Center is next door, and the Oregon Convention Center is a five-minute walk away. The atmosphere is one of understated luxury. *1000 N.E. Multnomah St., 97232, tel. 503/281–6111 or 800/547–8010. 476 rooms; no-smoking rooms available. Facilities: 3 restaurants, 3 lounges, evening entertainment, airport shuttle, free parking, outdoor pool, weight room. AE, D, DC, MC, V. Expensive–Very Expensive.*

Portland Guest House. This Northeast Portland "working-class Victorian" house, with its coffee-and-cream-colored paint job, five guest rooms, and scarred oak floors, was transformed into a cozy B&B in 1987. There are no TVs, but each room has its own phone—a rarity among Portland's B&Bs, and a concession to business travelers. *1720 N.E. 15th St. (near Lloyd Center), Portland 97212, tel. 503/282–1402. 5 double rooms, 3 with private baths. Facilities: in-room phones. AE, DC, MC, V. Moderate.*

Travelodge Hotel. The light and airy rooms here come with king- or queen-size beds, sofas, and coffee table, plus full-length mirrors and cable TVs. The Coliseum and Convention Center are within walking distance. *1441 N.E. 2nd Ave., 97232, tel. 503/233–2401 or 800/255–3050. 237 rooms; no-smoking rooms available. Facilities: restaurant, lounge, airport shuttle. AE, D, DC, MC, V. Moderate–Expensive.*

Best Western Inn at the Convention Center. Rooms were redecorated in 1989 in pleasing creams and rusts. Rooms with king-size beds come with wet bars. Conveniently located, the inn is four blocks west of Lloyd Center, directly across the street from the Portland Convention Center, and on the MAX line. *420 N.E. Holladay St., 97232, tel. 503/233–6331 or 800/528–1234. 97 rooms. Facilities: restaurant (serving breakfast and lunch), free parking, free local telephone calls. AE, D, DC, MC, V. Moderate–Expensive.*

Red Lion/Coliseum. The restaurant and many of the rooms here overlook the Willamette River. Unfortunately, a railroad line is between the river and the hotel, making courtside rooms the better choice if you want peace and quiet. The rooms are standard but pleasing enough; decorated in pinks, whites, mauve, and sea-foam green, and modern oak furnishings. *1225 N. Thunderbird Way, 97227, tel. 503/235–8311 or 800/547–8010. 212 rooms. Facilities: 2 restaurants, lounge entertainment, airport shuttle, free parking, outdoor pool. AE, D, DC, MC, V. Moderate.*

Shilo Inn/Lloyd Center. The Coliseum and Convention Center are only three blocks away, and several dining establishments, including a Chinese restaurant/lounge, are within easy walking distance. Rooms have a comfortable, lived-in feeling and are equipped with only the basics. *1506 N.E. 2nd Ave., 97232, tel. 503/231–7665 or 800/222–2244. 44 rooms; no-smoking rooms available. Facilities: airport shuttle, free parking, complimentary Continental breakfast. AE, D, DC, MC, V. Moderate.*

North **Red Lion/Columbia River.** The rooms were completely refurbished in 1988, and public areas—with lots of brass, dark wood, green, and mauve colors—were redecorated in 1991. The rooms are quite large, overlooking the mighty Columbia River. The hotel is on Hayden Island, a 100-yard stroll away from Jantzen Beach Shopping Center and the tennis courts at neighboring Red Lion/Jantzen Beach (*see below*). *1401 N. Hayden Island Dr., 97217, tel. 503/283–2111 or 800/547–8010. 351 rooms; no-smoking rooms available. Facilities: 2 restaurants, lounge entertainment, airport shuttle, free parking, outdoor pool, putting green, gift shop, health-club arrangement. AE, D, DC, MC, V. Very Expensive.*

Red Lion/Jantzen Beach. Because it was designed and built by and for this West Coast chain, rather than purchased and refurbished, this property has been given special attention. The results are larger-than-average guest rooms with good views (particularly those facing the Columbia River and Vancouver, Washington), and public areas that glitter with brass and bright lights that accentuate the greenery and burgundy, green, and rose color scheme. Maxi's fine dining room features a seasonal menu made with ingredients fresh from Northwest fields, farms, and waters. *909 N. Hayden Island Dr., 97217, tel. 503/283–4466 or 800/547–8010. 320 rooms; no-smoking rooms available. Facilities: 2 restaurants, lounge entertainment, airport shuttle, free parking, outdoor pool, tennis courts, workout facilities, gift shop. AE, D, DC, MC, V. Very Expensive.*

The Arts

"The Arts and Entertainment Guide," published each Friday in The *Oregonian*, contains current listings of performers, productions, events, and club entertainment. *Willamette Week*, published free each Wednesday and widely available throughout the metro area, contains similar, but hipper, listings. For current information on theater productions, call **Portland Area Theatre Alliance Hot Line** (tel. 503/241–4903).

Theater **Artists Repertory Theatre** (1111 S.W. 10th Ave. in the YWCA's Wilson Center, tel. 503/242–9043) stages five productions a year, featuring regional premiers, occasional commissioned works, and selected classics appropriate to contemporary issues.

Oregon Puppet Theater (tel. 503/236–4034) stages five children's productions per year at different locations in town.

Oregon Shakespeare Festival Portland (1111 S.W. Broadway, tel. 503/248–6309) produces five contemporary and classical productions between November and April in the 916-seat Intermediate Theater.

Portland Center for the Performing Arts (1111 S.W. Broadway, tel. 503/248–4496) includes four theaters and schedules rock stars, symphonies, lectures, and Broadway musicals.

Portland Repertory Theater (World Trade Ctr., 25 S.W. Salmon St., tel. 503/224–4491) presents a varied season with six productions a year by the region's oldest professional theatrical company.

Tygres Heart Shakespeare Co. (1111 S.W. Broadway, tel. 503/222–9220) mounts Shakespearean production each in fall, winter, and spring.

Concerts **Arlene Schnitzer Concert Hall** (in Portland Center for the Performing Arts, S.W. Broadway and Main St., tel. 503/248–4496) hosts rock stars, Broadway shows, symphonies, and classical concerts.

La Luna (215 S.E. 9th Ave., tel. 503/241–5862) hosts rock, world beat, blues, and ethnic concerts in a nightclub setting.

Memorial Coliseum (1401 N. Wheeler Ave., tel. 503/248–4496) has 12,000 seats and books popular rock groups and touring shows.

Portland Civic Auditorium (222 S.W. Clay St., tel. 503/248–4496), with 3,000 seats and outstanding acoustics, attracts name country and rock performers and touring shows.

Roseland Theater (8 N.W. 6th St., tel. 503/224–2038) specializes in rock and blues in a club that accommodates up to 1,400 people.

Ballet **Oregon Ballet Theatre** (1120 S.W. 10th Ave., tel. 503/ 227–6867) produces four classical and contemporary works a year, including a much-beloved holiday *Nutcracker*. The affiliated ballet school offers drop-in classes for adults.

Opera **Portland Opera** (1516 S.W. Alder St., tel. 503/241–1401) and its orchestra and chorus stage five productions annually at the Portland Civic Auditorium.

Orchestral Music **Oregon Symphony** (711 S.W. Alder St., tel. 503/228–1353) presents more than 40 classical, pop, children's, and family concerts per season at the Arlene Schnitzer Concert Hall.

Nightlife

Except where noted, each of the following bars and cafés offer live music nightly.

Bars and **Dakota Café** (239 S.W. Broadway, tel. 503/241–4151). Ameri-
Nightclubs can cuisine and rock music have made this one of Portland's hot spots.
Key Largo Restaurant and Night Club (31 N.W. 1st Ave., tel. 503/223–9919) is a romantic night spot in an historic building with brick walls, outdoor courtyard, dance floor, and Cajun food. The club features a top-name lineup of local and national rock, blues, and folk acts.

Acoustic/Ethnic **Dublin Pub** (6821 Beaverton/Hillsdale Hwy., tel. 503/297–2889) has more than 100 beers on tap, plus wine, Irish bands, and rock groups.
East Avenue Tavern (727 E. Burnside St., tel. 503/236–6900) features a potpourri of styles from Cajun to Irish and from bluegrass to French acoustic-guitar music.

Blues **Candlelight Cafe and Bar** (S.W. 5th and Lincoln, tel. 503/222–3378) features blues seven nights a week.
Dandelion Pub (31 N.W. 23rd Pl., tel. 503/223–0099) offers blues nightly in a dark, *L*-shaped room with dance floor.

Country and **Jubitz Truck Stop** (33 N.E. Middlefield Rd., tel. 503/283–1111)
Western presents live country music nightly.
The Drum (146 S.E. Division St., tel. 503/760–1400) is Portland's top country club, with traditional country and contemporary country-rock played nightly.

Jazz **Brasserie Montmarte** (626 S.W. Park Ave., tel. 503/224–5552) presents duos on weeknights and quartets and larger groups on weekends.
Jazz de Opus (33 N.W. 2nd Ave., tel. 503/222-6077) features local musicians with national reputations Tuesday–Saturday.
Parchman Farm (1204 S.E. Clay St., tel. 503/235-7831) offers prominent local jazz performers Monday–Saturday.

Rock **Eli's** (424 S.W. 4th Ave., tel. 503/223–4241) is where to go for hard rock.

Comedy **The Last Laugh Comedy Club** (1130 S.W. Main St., tel. 503/295–2844) presents headliners with national reputations Tuesday–Sunday.

Excursions from Portland

The Columbia River Gorge and the Oregon Cascades

There's only one reason to drive to the Columbia River Gorge and Oregon Cascades: pleasure. Sightseers, sailboarders, hikers, skiers, waterfall lovers, and fans of the Old West will all find contentment in this rugged region. The following tour will take you through the highlights of the Columbia River Gorge, where America's second-largest river (after the Mississippi) slashes through the Cascade Range. Along the way you'll pass Multnomah Falls and Bonneville Dam, the world-class windsurfing hub and rich orchardland of Hood River, and skiing and other alpine attractions of the 11,245-foot-high Mt. Hood. Finally, you'll arrive in Bend, a stronghold of outdoor pleasures steeped in the traditions of the Old West.

An important note: The Columbia Gorge, the Mt. Hood area, and Bend all receive much heavier winter weather than does Portland. At times, even I–84—Oregon's main east–west highway—is closed because of snow and ice. If you're planning a winter visit, be sure your car has traction devices, and carry plenty of warm clothes with you.

Getting Around **Bend-Redmond Municipal Airport** (tel. 503/548–6059) is serv-
By Plane iced by Horizon Airlines (tel. 800/547–9308) and United Express (tel. 800/241–6522).

By Car Mt. Hood is about 50 miles from Portland; Bend is 160 miles away. Virtually all travel in eastern and central Oregon is by car. I–84 follows the Columbia River all the way to Idaho, terminating at Salt Lake City. U.S. 197 (later U.S. 97) leaves I–84 at The Dalles and heads south to California, passing Bend along the way.

By Train **Amtrak** (tel. 800/USA–RAIL) follows I–84 through the Columbia Gorge, to Boise and beyond. From Portland, stops include Hood River and The Dalles. Once you've reached Hood River, consider taking the **Mt. Hood Railroad** (tel. 503/386–3556 or 800/TRAIN61), built in 1906, on a 44-mile round-trip scenic tour to Parkdale. Call for schedule information.

By Bus **Greyhound** (tel. 503/243–2310) provides service the length of the gorge and to Bend.

Scenic Drives The **Scenic Gorge Highway** (Rte. 30) leaves I–84 at Troutdale and climbs past the lush, fern-covered greenery, awesome cliff-top vistas, and thundering waterfalls. The old highway, built in the 1910s by lumber magnate Simon Benson, is a narrow and serpentine 22-mile road made expressly for sightseeing. The route is especially lovely in the fall but often impassable in winter.

The **Highway 97–Highway 218 Loop** is a 25-mile tour through some of the state's most forbiddingly beautiful high desert country. From Shaniko, take Highway 218 south to Antelope, near the now-abandoned commune of Rajneeshpuram. Follow the signs back to Highway 97 and Bend.

Important **Bend Chamber of Commerce** (63085 N. Hwy. 97, Bend 97701,
Addresses and tel. 503/382–3221).
Numbers **Hood River County Chamber of Commerce** (Port Marina Park,
Tourist Information Hood River 97031, tel. 503/386–2000 or 800/366–3530).
Mt. Hood National Forest Ranger Stations are located in Gresham (tel. 503/666–0771), Troutdale (tel. 503/695–2276), Zigzag (tel. 503/666–0704), Mt. Hood Information Center (tel. 503/622–3191), and Hood River (tel. 503/352–6002).
Mt. Hood Recreation Association (65000 E. Hwy. 26, Welches 97067, tel. 503/622–3162 or 503/622–4822 for recreation information on recreational facilities).

Emergencies In most parts of the state, dialing 911 will connect you with **police, fire,** and **medical assistance.** In some rural areas, it may be necessary to call 800/452-7888, the **Oregon State Police** central dispatch line. Dial "0" to get an **operator.**

Exploring *Numbers in the margin correspond to points of interest on the Eastern Oregon map.*

❶ The tour begins at **Troutdale,** the gateway to the gorge, where the 22-mile-long Columbia River Scenic Highway leaves the interstate. Traveling on the well-signed route for a few miles will take you to Crown Point, a 730-foot-high bluff with an unparalleled 30-mile view down the gorge. Then the highway heads downhill, over graceful stone bridges built by Italian immigrant masons, past quiet forest glades and belichened cliffs, over which a dozen waterfalls pour in a single 10-mile stretch. Among the most spectacular are **Latourell, Bridal Veil, Wah-**
❷ **keena, Horsetail,** and—finest of all—**Multnomah Falls,** at 620 feet. All the falls have parking areas and hiking trails, so visitors can take a close look. Multnomah Falls is by far the most popular and accessible; there's a paved (but steep) hiking trail to the bridge over the lower falls.

A few miles farther along the old highway from Crown Point is
❸ **Oneonta Gorge.** During the hot summer months, you can walk up the bed of a shallow stream and through a cool green canyon that's hundreds of feet high (at other times of year, take the trail that follows along the west side of the canyon). The clearly marked trailhead is 100 yards west of the gorge, on the south side of the road. The walls of the narrow rift drip moisture year-round; hundreds of plant species—some found nowhere else—flourish under these conditions. About a half mile up the stream, the trail ends at lovely Oneonta Falls. You'll need boots or submersible sneakers—plus a strong pair of ankles—because the rocks are slippery.

Just past Oneonta Gorge, the old Scenic Highway rejoins I–84.
❹ Head east to **Bonneville Dam,** Oregon's most impressive manmade attraction. The first dam ever to span the Columbia, Bonneville was dedicated by President Franklin D. Roosevelt in 1937. Its great turbines (visible from special walkways during self-guided powerhouse tours) can produce nearly a million kilowatts, which is enough to supply 40,000 single-family homes. There is a modern visitor center on Bradford Island, complete with underwater windows for viewing migrating salmon and steelhead as they struggle up the fish ladders (April–October are the best viewing times). Nearby, **Bonneville Fish Hatchery** has ponds teeming with fingerling salmon, as well as fat rainbow trout and 6-foot-long sturgeon. A gift shop is on the premises. *Visitor center on Bradford Island, Bonneville Lock and Dam, Cascade Locks, OR 97014 (drive over powerhouse), tel. 503/374–8820. Admission free. Open summer, daily 9–8; rest of year, daily 9–5. Fish hatchery, Star Rte. B, Box 12, Cascade Locks, OR 97014 (on Oregon shore), tel. 503/374–8393. Admission free. Open daily dawn–dusk.*

The rapids that once bedeviled river travelers near the town of
❺ **Cascade Locks** have been inundated by the 48-mile-long **Lake Bonneville.** In pioneer days, boats needing to pass the rapids had to portage around them. In 1896, the locks that gave the town its name were completed, allowing waterborne passage for the first time. Today the locks are used by Native Ameri-

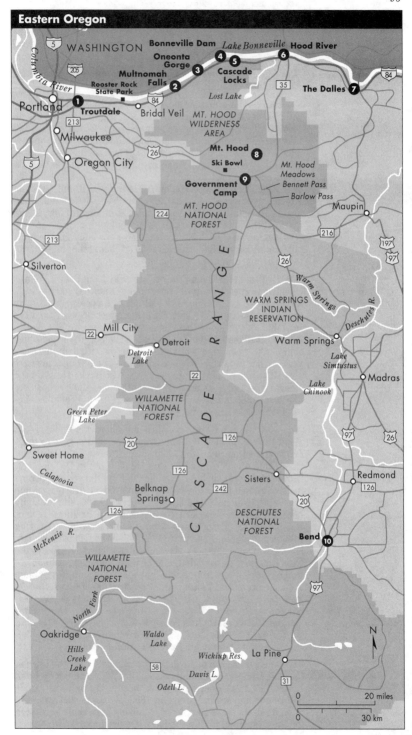

Eastern Oregon

cans for their traditional dip-net fishing, and Cascade Locks is notable mainly as the home port of the 600-passenger stern-wheeler *Columbia Gorge*. From June through September, the comfortable, pleasantly appointed ship churns its way upriver, then back again, on daily two-hour excursions through some of the gorge's most awesome scenery. The company also offers lunches and brunches, and dinner-and-dancing cruises in the evenings. *Cruises leave from Marine Park in Cascade Locks, tel. 503/223–3928 or 503/374–8427. Three departures daily for excursions June–Sept. at 10, 12:30, and 3. Admission: $10.95 adults, $5.45 children 4–12. Dinner cruises embark Wed.–Sat. 7 PM; weekends 6 PM. Cruises vary in length from 2 to 4 hrs. Meal and cruise prices range from $17.95 to $32.95 for adults. Reservations required for any cruise with meal. AE, MC, V.*

6 For years the incessant easterly winds at **Hood River,** where the gorge widens and the scenery changes to tawny, wheat-covered hills, were nothing but a nuisance. Then somebody bolted a sail to a surfboard, and a new recreational craze was born. A fortuitous combination of factors—mainly the reliable gale-force winds blowing against the current—have made Hood River the self-proclaimed boardsailing capital of the world. Now, especially in the summer, this once-somnolent fruit-growing town swarms with colorful "boardheads," many of whom have journeyed from as far away as Europe and Australia. A collection of restaurants, equipment shops, and inns have sprung up to service this trade, and Hood River is rapidly becoming one of the state's busiest tourist destinations.

Columbia Gorge Sailpark (Port Marina, tel. 503/386–2000), located on the river downtown, was one of the amenities added to encourage the boardsailing craze. It offers a boat basin, swimming beach, jogging trails, picnic tables, and rest rooms.

Situated 28 miles southwest of Hood River, via signed Forest Service roads, is **Lost Lake** (tel. 503/386–6366 for cabin reservations), one of the most photographed sites in the Pacific Northwest. Lake waters reflect the mountain and thick forests that line the shore.

7 **The Dalles,** 20 miles east, presents a placid alternative to frenetic, Californian Hood River. With its plethora of 19th-century brick storefronts and historic homes, The Dalles has a small-town, Old West feel to it, possibly because it's the traditional end of the Oregon Trail, where the wagons were loaded onto barges for the final leg of their 2,000-mile journey. The 130-year-old **Wasco County Courthouse** and the 1857-vintage **Ft. Dalles Surgeon's Quarters** have been converted into museums; both contain outstanding displays and collections illustrating the incredible pioneer ordeal. *The Courthouse Museum, 406 W. 2nd St., tel. 503/296–4798. Admission free; donations accepted. Open Apr.–May, Tues.–Sat. 11–3; June–Sept., Tues.–Sat. 10–4. Closed Oct.–Mar. Ft. Dalles Museum, 15th and Garrison Sts., tel. 503/296–4547. Admission: $2 adults, children free. Open Nov.–Feb., Wed.–Fri. noon–4, weekends 10–4; Mar.–Oct., weekdays 10:30–5, weekends 10–5.*

8 From Hood River, Highway 35 climbs south toward the regal snow-covered bulk of **Mt. Hood,** believed to be an active volcano, quiet now but capable of the same violence that decapitated nearby Mt. St. Helens in 1980. The mountain is just one feature of the 1,079,169-acre **Mt. Hood National Forest,** an all-season playground that attracts more than 4 million visitors annually. You'll find 95 campgrounds and 150 lakes stocked with brown, rainbow, cutthroat, brook, and steelhead trout. The Sandy, Salmon, and other rivers are known for their fishing, rafting, canoeing, and swimming. Both forest and mountain are crossed by an extensive trail system for hikers, cyclists, and horseback riders. Some are half-milers, while others are day-or-longer treks. The **Pacific Crest Trail,** which begins in British Columbia and ends in Mexico, crosses here at the 4,157-foot-high Barlow Pass, the highest point on the highway.

Two miles off Highway 26, near the pass, sits **Trillium Lake** (tel. 503/666–0771), a beautiful spot for picnicking, overnight camping, and fishing for brown and rainbow trout.

Farther on, Highway 35 joins Highway 26 at 4,670-foot-high **Bennett Pass.** Turning west, you'll encounter signs to historic **Timberline Lodge,** an exquisite 1930s stone and timber structure, graced with hand-forged wrought iron, intricately carved woodwork, and great stone fireplaces. The lodge has been used as a setting in many films, including *The Shining* with Jack Nicholson. At the front desk of the lodge you can pick up maps that will direct you along the network of trails, leading through alpine meadow and old growth forest. Today Timberline offers comfortable lodging and gourmet dining high (6,000 feet) on the mountain's flank and is a favorite destination of skiers, romantics, and sightseers alike (*see* Dining and Lodging, *below*).

⑨ Government Camp, just off Highway 26 west of the Timberline exit, is an alpine-flavored resort village with an abundance of lodging, restaurants, and nightlife. It's a convenient drive to each of Mt. Hood's five ski resorts: **Timberline, Mt. Hood Meadows, Summit Ski Area, Ski Bowl** and **Cooper Spur Ski Area** (*see* Sports and the Outdoors, *below*).

During the summer months, the **Alpine Slide** at Ski Bowl, just across Highway 26 from Government Camp, gives the intrepid a chance to whiz down the slopes on a European-style toboggan run. This is heady stuff, with a marvelous view. *Hwy. 26 at milepost 53, tel. 503/272–3206. Admission: $18/day. Open June–Sept., weekdays 11–6, weekends 10–7.*

⑩ Bend, a city of 20,000, very nearly sits in the center of Oregon, about two hours southeast of Mt. Hood. It occupies a countryside many visitors wouldn't even recognize as Oregon: a tawny high desert plateau, perfumed with juniper and surrounded by 10,000-foot Cascade peaks. Called Bend because it was built on Farewell Bend in the Deschutes River—here an easy-flowing river that becomes a roaring cataract a few miles downstream—the city is a good fueling-up spot. It's filled with decent restaurants, dance bars, pro shops and rental places, and a surprising number of good, reasonably priced hostelries.

While in Bend, visit the **High Desert Museum,** where you can walk through a stone-age Indian campsite, a pioneer wagon camp, a groaning, echoing old mine, an Old West boardwalk, and other lovingly detailed dioramas, complete with authentic relics, sounds, and even odors. There are outstanding exhibits on local Native American cultures as well. The high point of the complex is the 150-acre outdoor section, which features fat porcupines, baleful birds of prey, and crowd-pleasing river otters at play aboveground and underwater. *59800 S. Hwy. 97, 6 mi* *south of Bend, tel. 503/382–4754. Admission: $5.50 adults, $5 senior citizens, $2.75 children 5–12. Members and children under 4 free. Open daily 9–5; closed Thanksgiving, Christmas, and New Years.*

Sports and the Outdoors

Beaches The Columbia River is lined with sandy beaches, the most famous of which is at **Rooster Rock State Park** (tel. 503/695–2261), where both nudists and conventional bathers soak up the sun. There is a $3 daily-per-vehicle fee.

Bicycling With a wide bicycle path paralleling I–84, the entire length of the gorge is suitable for bicycling. The terrain is generally flat, but there are stiff and constant winds from the east. The Bend area offers many memorable venues for cyclists, including the entire **Sunriver complex** (tel. 503/593–1221 or 800/547–3922), with 26 miles of paved bike paths and rentals available. Also, Highway 97 north to the **Crooked River Gorge** and the spectacular **Smith Rocks** promise breathtaking scenery and a good workout.

Canoeing and Rafting The **Deschutes River** flows north from the Cascades west of Bend, gaining volume and momentum as it nears its rendezvous with the Columbia River at The Dalles. Its upper stretches, particularly those near Sunriver and Bend, are placid and suitable for leisurely canoeing. The stretch between Madras and Maupin offers some of Oregon's most famous white-water rafting. Due to heavy use, this portion of the Deschutes is accessible by permit only; for details, call the **Central Oregon Recreation Association** (tel. 503/389–8799 or 800/800–8334).

Skiing
Cross-country There are nearly 120 miles of cross-country ski trails in the **Mt. Hood National Forest;** try the trailheads at Government Camp, Trillium Lake, or the Cooper Spur Ski Area, on the mountain's northeast flank. The **Deschutes National Forest,** surrounding Bend, is even richer in Nordic trails, with more than 165 miles of them at last count. The **Mt. Bachelor Nordic Center** (tel. 503/382–2442), a lodge surrounded by 36 miles of trails, is an excellent place to begin. **Summit Ski Area** (tel. 503/272–0256) and Ski Bowl/Multipor (tel. 503/272–3206), among other resorts, can supply cross-country rentals, accessories, maps, and guidebooks. For ski conditions, call 503/222–2211, 503/222–BOWL, 503/227–SNOW.

Downhill **Cooper Spur Ski Area,** on the eastern slope of Mt. Hood, caters to families and has two rope tows and a T-bar. The longest run is ⅔ mile, with a 500-foot vertical drop. *Follow signs from Hwy. 35 for 3½ mi to ski area, tel. 503/352–7803. Facilities: rentals, instruction, repairs, ski shop, day lodge, snack bar, restaurant.*

Mt. Bachelor, which is generally regarded as one of the 10 best ski areas in the United States, is the Northwest's largest and most complete facility. The U.S. Ski Team trains here in the spring. There are 11 lifts, including one that takes skiers all the way to the mountain's 9,065-foot summit. The vertical drop is 3,100 feet; the longest of the 54 runs is 2½ miles. *22 mi southwest of Bend off Hwy. 97 (follow signs), tel. 503/382–7888 or 800/829–2442. Open weekdays 9–4, weekends 8–4. Facilities: 6 lodges (including the new mid-mountain Pine Marten Lodge* *at 7,700 feet), restaurants, bars, ski shop, equipment rental and repair, ski school, day care, Nordic skiing, weekly races.*

Mt. Hood Meadows is Mt. Hood's largest ski resort, with more than 2,000 skiable acres, dozens of runs, seven double chairs, one triple chair, one quad chair, a top elevation of 7,300 feet, a vertical drop of 2,777 feet, and a longest run of 3 miles. *10 mi east of Government Camp on Hwy. 35, tel. 503/337-2222. Open Mon. and Tues. 9-4, Wed.-Sat. 9 AM-10 PM, Sun. 9-7. Facilities: day lodge, 3 restaurants, 2 lounges, ski school, ski shop, equipment rental and repair.*

Ski Bowl, the ski area closet to Portland (only 50 miles away), boasts "the most extensive night skiing in America." The complex has 63 trails serviced by four double chairs and five rope tows, a top elevation of 5,050 feet, a vertical drop of 1,500 feet, and a longest run of 3 miles. *53 mi east of Portland, across Hwy. 26 from Government Camp, tel. 503/272-3206. Open Mon.-Thurs. 9 AM-10 PM, Fri. 9 AM-11 PM, Sat. 8:30 AM-11 PM, Sun. 8:30 AM-10 PM. Facilities: 2 day lodges, mid-mountain Warming Hut, 2 restaurants, 2 lounges, sleigh rides; summer: horseback rides, go-carts, mountain and alpine bike rentals. Alpine slide in summer (see Exploring, above).*

Summit Ski Area has one chairlift, 1 rope-tow. Its longest run is a half-mile, with a 400-foot vertical drop. *Box 250, Government Camp, tel. 503/272-0256. Facilities: rentals, instruction, ski shop, day lodge, cafeteria, Nordic rentals and trails. Bike rentals in summer.*

Timberline, a full-service family-oriented ski area, is also a favorite of snowboard skiers. The U.S. ski team conducts summer training at Timberline, a resort famous for its Palmer Chairlift, which takes skiers to a high glacier for summer skiing. There are five double chairs, including one quad chair; the top elevation is 8,500 feet, with 3,600 feet of vertical drop. *60 mi east of Portland on Hwy. 26, tel. 503/231-5400. Open Sun.-Tues. 9-5, Wed.-Sat. 9 AM-10 PM. Summer lift hours: 7 AM-1:30 PM Facilities: Timberline Lodge (see Dining and Lodging, below), day lodge with fast food, cross-country skiing, lessons, ski shop, equipment rental and repair.*

Dining and Lodging

Dining and Lodging ratings correspond to price charts for Portland restaurants and hotels.

Bend
Dining

Le Bistro. The best restaurant in Bend has prices to match the quality. The menu features traditional French cuisine with an emphasis on fresh Oregon meat and seafood. Try the critics' choices, the highly regarded seafood Wellington and roast rack of lamb. *1203 N.E. 3rd St. (Hwy. 97), tel. 503/389-7274. Reservations suggested. Dress: casual. AE, DC, MC, V. Closed for lunch. Expensive.*

Stuft Pizza. This new restaurant, located in a pleasant Old West Victorian storefront, specializes in hand-tossed pizza with fresh ingredients. There's also a good salad bar and regional microbrews and wines. There is entertainment, including comedy, on weekends. *125 Oregon Ave., tel. 503/382-4022. No reservations. Dress: casual. AE, MC, V. Closed major holidays. Inexpensive-Moderate.*

Deschutes Brewery & Public House. This cheery, popular brew pub features upscale Northwest cuisine and local ales and wines. Give close attention to the extensive list of lunch and dinner specials on the blackboard above the open kitchen, and try the admirable Black Butte Porter. Portions are large. *1044 N.W. Bond St., tel. 503/382–9242. No reservations. Dress: casual. MC, V. Inexpensive.*

Lodging **Sunriver.** Many residents consider this to be Oregon's premier outdoor resort destination, and with good reason. There's golf (two 18-hole championship courses designed by Robert Trent Jones); skiing at 9,000-foot Mt. Bachelor 20 minutes to the west; Class-4 white-water rafting on the Deschutes River, which flows right through the complex; high-desert hiking and mountain-biking; hunting; fishing; riding; tennis; and swimming. The Sunriver complex itself, once the site of an Army base, is now a self-contained community, with stores, restaurants, contemporary homes, condominiums, lodge and recreational facilities, all set in a warm, pine-scented desert landscape. Visitors can rent condos, hotel rooms, or houses, and a host of outdoorsy paraphernalia. *Sunriver, OR (just west of Hwy. 97, 15 mi south of Bend) 07707, tel. 503/593–1221 or 800/547–3922. 710 condos, 211 hotel rooms. Facilities: 2 18-hole golf courses, 28 tennis courts, 2 pools, 26 mi of paved bike paths, hot tubs, saunas, stables, racquet club, bike and canoe rentals, air strip, 8 restaurants, conference and meeting facilities. AE, D, DC, MC, V. Expensive.*

Lara House Bed & Breakfast Inn. This nicely restored former boardinghouse is in a residential district overlooking Drake Park and Mirror Pond, a five-minute walk from downtown. One of the six spacious rooms has a water bed. Public areas are sunny and inviting. *640 N.W. Congress St. (west on Franklin from Hwy. 97), 97701, tel. 503/388–4064. 5 rooms with private bath. Facilities: spa, fireplace. AE, D, MC, V. Moderate.*

The Riverhouse. This 1970s hotel is a cut or two above what you'd expect to find for the very reasonable price. The surprisingly large, well-appointed guest rooms are furnished in contemporary oak pieces, and many have river views (well worth the extra $5 charge). Perhaps the best feature is the sound of the rushing Deschutes River, which you can hear from your room. *3075 N. Hwy. 97, 97701, tel. 503/389–3111 or 800/547–3928. Facilities: 3 restaurants, lounge, entertainment, indoor and outdoor pools, weight room, sauna, Jacuzzi, tennis courts, 18-hole golf course, riverside jogging trail. AE, D, DC, MC, V. Moderate.*

Cascade Locks **Cascade Inn.** At this family-style restaurant you can eat break-
Dining fast, lunch, and dinner at the counter or in booths. Highlighting the home-cooked specials is the Captain's Platter, which includes prawns, fresh fish, oysters, and clams. *Columbia Gorge Ct., tel. 503/374–8340. No reservations. Dress: casual. AE, D, MC, V. Inexpensive.*

Char Burger Restaurant. In the 225-seat dining room overlooking the Columbia River you can enjoy a variety of hamburgers plus salmon, seafood, steak dinners, and a full breakfast menu. Indian arrowhead collections, rifles, and wagon-wheel chandeliers carry out the western motif. *745 S.W. Wanapa St., tel. 503/374–8477. Reservations required for Sun. brunch. Dress: casual. MC, V. Closed Thanksgiving and Christmas. Inexpensive.*

Lodging **Scandian Motor Lodge.** Oregon pine furniture and wood paneling, colorful bedspreads, and Scandinavian wall hangings brighten otherwise standard but inexpensive rooms. *Box 217, Columbia Gorge Ct. 97014, tel. 503/374–8417. 30 rooms with showers, no tubs. Facilities: adjacent to restaurant, lounge, and general store. AE, D, DC, MC, V. Inexpensive.*

The Dalles **Ole's Supper Club.** Local folk like this establishment for its ex
Dining cellent food, friendly and competent service, and its straightforward, no-nonsense approach. The menu of Western-style food with a Continental twist features specialties from thick slabs of prime rib to veal Oscar. It's hard to go wrong when choosing an entrée, especially when it's accompanied by a selection from the excellent wine list. *2620 W. 2nd St., tel. 503/296–6708. Reservations advised. Dress: casual. AE, MC, V. Closed Sun., Mon., and lunch. Moderate.*

Lodging **Williams House Inn.** This Victorian home furnished with antiques is on the Register of National Historic Places. Sitting on a city block of landscaped grounds, it has a three-room suite with private bath and two rooms, each with a private balcony and shared bath. *608 W. 6th St., 97058, tel. 503/296–2889. 3 rooms. AE, D, MC, V. Moderate.*

Hood River **6th Street Bistro and Loft.** The menu at this friendly local favor
Dining ite changes weekly but concentrates on Pacific Northwest flavors, right down to the coffee and salads. Depending on the season, choices may include local fresh steamer clams and wild coral mushrooms, along with grilled swordfish and chicken. *Corner of 6th and Cascade Sts., tel. 503/386–5737. Reservations recommended on weekends. Dress: casual. AE, MC, V. Moderate.*

The Mesquitery. You'll get fish of the season plus lean beef, chicken, and pork grilled over aromatic mesquite—without the usual rich, cloying sauces. Instead, the owners use fresh herbs and tangy marinades with satisfying results. There's also a modest wine and beer list at this sunny, western-flavored restaurant. *1219 12th St. (atop the hill south of the downtown core), tel. 503/386–2002. No reservations. Dress: casual. MC, V. Inexpensive–Moderate.*

White Cap Brew Pub. The largest microbrewery in Oregon, this glass-walled brew pub and windswept deck overlooking the Columbia won major awards in Denver (in 1989) at the Great American Beer Festival. The pub offers a variety of savory snack foods to complement the brewery-fresh ales. *506 Columbia St. (in the old Diamond cannery overlooking downtown Hood River), tel. 503/386–2247. No reservations. Dress: casual. No credit cards. Inexpensive.*

Lodging **Best Western-Hood River Inn.** This modern hotel, built on the river within paddling distance of Hood River's Columbia Gorge Sailpark, is the address of choice for visiting windsurfers. Be sure to ask for a room with a river view. *1108 E. Marina Way, 97031, tel. 503/386–2200 or 800/828–7873. 150 rooms. Facilities: restaurant, bar, live entertainment, outdoor pool, river access. AE, D, DC, MC, V. Moderate.*

Hood River Hotel. This local landmark, built in 1913 and abandoned for more than 20 years, reopened in December 1989 after undergoing a floor-to-ceiling restoration. The results are spectacular. Public areas are rich in beveled glass, warm wood, and tasteful jade-and-cream-colored fabrics. Each room is unique, but all have bare fir floors softened by Oriental carpets, four-poster beds, and skylights. There's a lively lobby bar and a Mediterranean-flavored kitchen, plus—a thoughtful touch—plenty of locked storage for boardsailors. *102 Oak St., 97031, tel. 503/386–1900. 33 rooms with private bath, plus 9 suites with kitchen and room for 5. Facilities: restaurant, outdoor café, entertainment, bar. AE, D, DC, MC, V. Moderate.*

★ **Lakecliff Estate.** This four-room bed-and-breakfast inn, just up the road from the Columbia Gorge Hotel, was a summer home designed by architect A. E. Doyle, who designed Portland's Classic Revival public library, U.S. Bank Building, and the Multnomah Falls Lodge. The 1908 house, built on a cliff overlooking the river, is beautifully maintained and exceptionally comfortable. A pleasant deck at the back of the house and wood-burning fireplaces in three of the rooms ensure a relaxing stay. *3820 Westcliff Dr. (Exit 62), 97031, tel. 503/386–7000. 4 rooms. No smoking. No credit cards. Moderate.*

Dining and Lodging **Columbia Gorge Hotel.** The grande dame of gorge hotels, built by lumber baron Simon Benson as the final destination of his Scenic Highway, was restored to its original magnificence in 1979. The ambience is a bit florid, but the major attraction—the 208-foot-high waterfall—is magnificent. Public areas are decorated in coral, green, and rose, and guest rooms reveal lots of brass, wood, and antiques. Rooms with two beds overlook the formal gardens. A huge seven-course breakfast—the World Famous Farm Breakfast—is included in the price of a room (nonguests pay $22.95 for the meal). While watching the sun set on the Columbia River, you can dine on breast of pheasant with pear wine, hazelnuts, and cream; grilled venison; breast of duck; Columbia River salmon; and sturgeon. *4000 Westcliff Dr. (take Exit 62), 97031, tel. 503/386–5566 or 800/345–1921. 46 rooms. Facilities: restaurant, lounge, gardens, waterfall. AE, D, DC, MC, V. Very Expensive.*

Mt. Hood **Valu-Inn/Mt. Hood.** The inn opened in 1990, and although
Lodging everything looks and smells new, it also has a comfortable, relaxed feel. The Mt. Hood National Forest is outside the east windows; rooms facing the southwest are great for watching the spectacle of night skiing at Ski Bowl, which is literally across the street. Accommodations come in a variety of sizes, from roomy standards to king-size suites with refrigerators and Jacuzzis to double queens with kitchenettes. *87450 Government Camp Loop, 97028, tel. 503/272–3205. 56 rooms; handicapped and no-smoking rooms available. Facilities: covered parking, laundry facilities, spa, free ski lockers, ski tuning room, Continental breakfast. AE, D, DC, MC, V. Expensive.*

Dining and Lodging **Timberline Lodge.** This National Historic Landmark, which
★ has withstood howling winter storms on an exposed flank of the mountain for more than 50 years, still manages to warm guests with its hospitality, hearty food, and guest rooms with fireplaces. Built as a WPA project during the Depression, everything about the lodge has a handcrafted, rustic feel, from the wrought-iron chairs with rawhide seats to the massive handhewn beams. The elegant Cascade Dining Room features expertly prepared cuisine made from the freshest Oregon products. *Follow the signs from Hwy. 26 a few mi east of Zig Zag; Timberline 97028, tel. 503/272–3311 or 800/547–1406. 71 rooms, some with fireplaces. Facilities: restaurant, bar, downhill and cross-country skiing, heated outdoor pool in summer, sauna, spa. AE, D, MC, V. Expensive.*

Troutdale **Multnomah Falls Lodge.** The lodge, with high, vaulted ceilings
Dining and classic stone fireplaces, was built in 1925. Freshwater
trout, salmon, and a platter of prawns, halibut, and scallops are
specialties. The lodge is justly famous for its wild-huckleberry
daquiris and desserts. A gift shop and nature center are part of
the complex. *Hwy. I–84 and Columbia River Scenic Hwy., tel.
503/695–2376. Reservations accepted. Dress: casual but neat.
AE, MC, V. Inexpensive–Moderate.*

Warm Springs **Kah-Nee-Tah Resort.** The culture of the native Wasco, Warm
Dining and Lodging Springs, and Paiute tribes permeates this luxurious resort 11
miles north of Warm Springs off Hwy. 26. Traditional Indian
salmon bakes, festivals, arts, and dances enliven an austerely
beautiful setting in the middle of the 640,000-acre high-desert
Warm Springs Reservation. Mineral hot springs bubbling up
from the desert floor fill baths and pools. If you don't mind
spending a little extra, reserve the splendid Warm Springs,
Wasco, or Paiute suites, with their tiled fireplaces and hot
tubs, big-screen TVs, king-size beds and spectacular desert
views. If you'd rather rough it (sort of), and don't mind bringing your own bedroll, check into one of the tepees here. Replicas of traditional native-American dwellings, these wood-
frame, canvas-covered conical structures are set on a concrete
slab with a fire pit in the center. Restrooms and shower facilities are campground-style. *Warm Springs, 97761, tel. 503/553–
1112 or 800/831–0100. 139 rooms, 21 tepees. Facilities: 2 outdoor pools, hot mineral baths, saunas and soak tubs, golf
course, weight room, hiking trails, fishing, kayak rentals, stables, water slide, tennis court, RV hookups, mountain-bike
rentals, cable TV, conference facilities, lounge, 2 restaurants,
poolside food and cocktail service. AE, DC, MC, V. Moderate–
Expensive.*

Welches **The Chalet Swiss.** The atmosphere is authentically alpine in this
Dining country-Swiss restaurant, but it's the food that will make you
want to yodel. From the creamy fondue to the nutty
buendnerfleisch—tissue-thin slices of dry-cured beef—to the
rich sautées and fresh seafood, the kitchen displays a sure and
artful hand. *Hwy. 26 at Welches Rd., tel. 503/622–3600. Reservations suggested. Dress: casual. AE, MC, V. Closed Mon.,
Tues., and lunch. Expensive.*

Dining and Lodging **The Resort at the Mountain.** This sprawling resort complex,
nestled among the burly Cascade foothills, has changed hands
more often than a track baton. Still, it offers the mountain's
most complete resort facilities, with attractive modern public
areas and reasonably well-appointed rooms. With the last renovation—in 1990—came the Scottish motif, including tartans on
lounge tables and light pink-and-teal floral patterns in guest
rooms. Accommodations include standard rooms, huge deluxe
rooms, and limited numbers of two-bedroom condos. The Highland Dining Room features Northwest cuisine, including fillet
of salmon with fresh herbs and Pinot Noir wine, venison with
black-currant sauce, and quail sautéed with mustard. *68010 E.
Fairway Ave. (follow the signs from Hwy. 26), 97067, tel. 503/
622–3101 or 800/669–7666. 158 rooms. Facilities: 2 restaurants, 2 lounges, live entertainment, 27 holes of golf, 6 tennis
courts (2 with lights), outdoor pool, outdoor spas, health club,
meeting facilities, bike paths and rentals. AE, D, DC, MC, V.
Very Expensive.*

4 Western Oregon

By Jeff Kuechle

At its eastern end, Oregon begins in a high, sage-scented desert plateau that covers nearly two-thirds of the state's 96,000 square miles (roughly the same size as the United Kingdom). Moving west, the landscape rises to 10,000-foot-high alpine peaks, meadows, and lakes; plunges to fertile farmland and forest; and ends, at last, at the cold, green Pacific.

Thus, within 90 minutes' drive from Portland or Eugene you can lose yourself in the recreational landscape of your choice: a thriving wine country; scenic and uncrowded ocean beaches; lofty, snow-silvered mountain wilderness; or a monolith-studded desert used as a backdrop for many a Hollywood western. Oregonians, who have been called both the hardest-working and the hardest-playing Americans, take full advantage of this bounty. They are uncomplicated people, with down-to-earth ideals. There is a story, never confirmed, that early pioneers arriving at a crossroads of the Oregon Trail found a pile of gold quartz or pyrite pointing the way south to California. The way north, on the other hand, was marked by a hand-lettered sign: TO OREGON. Thus, Oregonians like to think that the more literate of the pioneers found their way here, while the fortune hunters continued south.

It was, however, the promise—and achievement—of wealth that quite naturally fueled Oregon's early exploration. In 1792, Robert Gray, an American trading captain, followed a trail of debris and muddy water inland and discovered the Columbia River. Shortly thereafter, British Army Lieutenant William Broughton was dispatched to investigate Gray's find, and he sailed as far upriver as the rapids-choked mouth of the Columbia River Gorge.

Within a few years, a thriving seaborne fur trade sprang up, with both American and British entrepreneurs exchanging baubles, cloth, tools, weapons, and liquor with the natives for high-quality beaver and sea-otter pelts. By 1804, American explorers Meriwether Lewis and William Clark had arrived at the site of present-day Astoria after their epic overland journey, spurring an influx of white pioneers—clerks, trappers, and traders—sent by John Jacob Astor's Pacific Fur Company in 1810. They came to claim the land from the unfortunate natives for the United States and to trade for furs. The trading part was accomplished readily enough, but the massive fir trees—some so huge that the clasped arms of 10 men couldn't encircle their bases—proved formidable, and after two months Astor's men had managed to clear just an acre.

But the "soft gold" of the fur trade proved an irresistible attraction. The English disputed American claims to the territory, on the basis of Broughton's exploration, and soon after the War of 1812 began, they negotiated the purchase of Astoria from Astor's company. It wasn't until 1846 that they formally renounced their claims in the region with the signing of the Oregon Treaty.

"Oregon Country" grew tremendously between 1841 and 1860, as more than 50,000 settlers from the eastern United States made the journey over the plains in their 10- by 4-foot covered wagons. Most settled in the Willamette Valley, where the vast majority of Oregon's 2.7 million residents still live.

As settlers capitalized on gold-rush San Francisco's need for provisions and other supplies, Oregon reaped its own riches and the lawless frontier gradually acquired a semblance of civilization. The territory's 50,000 residents voted down the idea of statehood three separate times, but in 1859, Oregon became the 33rd U.S. state.

Today the state's economy is still heavily dominated by timber (Oregon is America's largest producer of softwood), agriculture (hazelnuts, fruit, berries, wine, seed crops, livestock, and dairy products), and fishing. A major high-tech center known as the Silicon Forest, producing high-speed computer hardware and sophisticated instruments, has taken root west of Portland in the Tualatin Valley, side by side with the wine industry. Its proximity to Pacific Rim nations such as Japan and Korea has made Portland one of the busiest port cities on the West Coast. Tourism grows in importance here every year— Oregonians have discovered that the scenic and recreational treasures that thrill them also thrill visitors from all over the world. To cater to visitors' needs, a sophisticated hospitality network has appeared, making Oregon more accessible than ever before.

Essential Information

Important Addresses and Numbers

Tourist Information All Oregon tourist information centers are marked with blue *I* signs from main roads. Opening and closing times vary, depending on season and individual office; call ahead for hours.

Willamette Valley/ Wine Country **Ashland Chamber of Commerce and Visitors Information Center** (110 E. Main St., 97520, tel. 503/482–3486).
Corvallis Convention and Visitors Bureau (420 N.W. 2nd St., 97330, tel. 503/757–1544 or 800/334–8118).
Eugene-Springfield Convention & Visitors Bureau (305 W. 7th Ave., Eugene 97401, tel. 800/452–3670, 503/484–5307).
Grant's Pass Visitor & Convention Bureau (1501 N.E. 6th St., 97526, tel. 503/476–7717 or 800/547–5927).
McMinnville Chamber of Commerce (417 N. Adams St., 97128, tel. 503/472–6196).
Roseburg Area Chamber of Commerce (410 S.E. Spruce St., 97470, tel. 503/672–2648).
Salem Convention & Visitors Center (Mission Mill Village, 1313 Mill St. SE, 97301, tel. 503/581–4325 or 800/874–7012).

The Oregon Coast **Astoria Area Chamber of Commerce** (111 W. Marine Dr., 97103, tel. 503/325–6311).
Brookings Harbor Chamber of Commerce (16330 Lower Harbor Rd., 97415, tel. 503/469–3181 or 800/535–9469).
Cannon Beach Chamber of Commerce (2nd and Spruce Sts., 97110, tel. 503/436–2623).
Florence Area Chamber of Commerce (270 Hwy. 101, 97439, tel. 503/997–3128).
Greater Newport Chamber of Commerce (555 S.W. Coast Hwy., 97365, tel. 503/265–8801 or 800/262–7844).
Lincoln City Visitors Center (801 SW Hwy. 101, 97367, tel. 503/994–8378 or 800/452–2151).
North Bend Tourist Information Center (1380 Sherman St., 97459, tel. 503/756–4613).
Seaside Visitors Bureau (7 N. Roosevelt Ave., 97138, tel. 503/738–6391 or 800/1444–6740).

Oregon

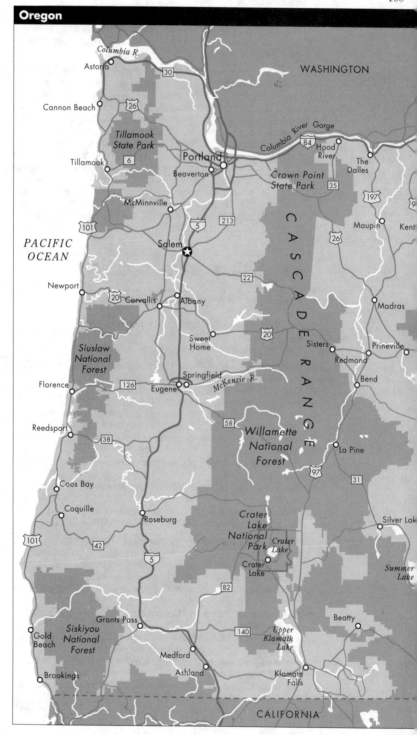

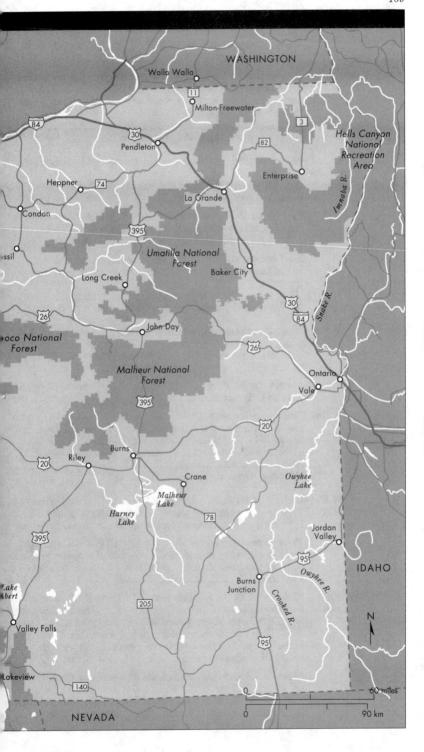

Tillamook Chamber of Commerce (3705 Hwy. 101 N, 97141, tel. 503/842–7525).

Yachats Chamber of Commerce (Hwy. 101, near 2nd St., 97498, tel. 503/547–3530).

Emergencies In most parts of the state, calling 911 will summon **police, fire,** or **ambulance** services; dialing "0" will give you the operator. In some rural areas, it may be necessary to dial the **Oregon State Police** (tel. 800/452–7888).

Arriving and Departing by Plane

Airports and Airlines **Eugene Airport** (tel. 503/687–5430), the best mid-valley air destination, is serviced by American (tel. 800/433–7300), Horizon (tel. 800/547–9308), United (tel. 800/241–6522), and United Express (tel. 800/241–6522).

Farther south, **Jackson County Airport** (tel. 503/772–8068), in Medford, is served by Horizon (tel. 800/547–9308), United (tel. 800/241–6522) and United Express (tel. 800/241–6522).

Most communities along the Oregon coast have municipal airports, but there is no major commercial service anywhere on the coast.

Arriving and Departing by Car, Train, and Bus

By Car If you are entering Oregon from the north or south, take I–5, which runs 300 miles through the Willamette Valley and the heart of Oregon. Entering from the east, take I–84, which runs from the Idaho border to Portland.

By Train **Amtrak** (tel. 800/USA–RAIL) services larger towns along the I–5 and I–85 corridors.

By Bus **Greyhound/Trailways** (call local listing) services the larger towns throughout the state, including Eugene (987 Pearl St., tel. 503/344–6265), La Grande (2108 Cove Ave., tel. 503/963–5165), and Medford (212 N. Bartlet St., tel. 503/779–2103).

Getting Around

By Car
Oregon Coast **Highway 101** runs the length of the coast, through vistas of shore pine and churning waves, sometimes turning inland for a few miles, then rewarding you with an awesome coastal vista.

Three Capes Loop leaves Highway 101 at Tillamook and winds past the dense forests and windswept cliffs of three protruding peninsulas: Capes Meares, Lookout, and Kiwanda (*see* Tour 1: The Oregon Coast in Exploring, *below*).

Willamette Valley/ Wine Country **Highway 34** leaves I–5 just south of Albany and heads west, past Corvallis and into the Coast Range, where it follows the fish-filled Alsea River. Watch for a sign marked Alsea Falls/ South Fork Road/Monroe a mile south of Alsea. It will take you to the lovely Alsea Falls, where salmon in the spring and steelhead in the fall make prodigious leaps to clear the falls.

Highway 138 leads you through the spectacular waterfall country of the Umpqua River, east of Roseburg (watch for signs along the road), to the back door of Crater Lake National Park (*see* National and State Parks, *below*); in the winter, however, the road to Crater Lake is closed.

By Bus **Greyhound** (800/231–2222) bus routes criss-cross the state from the I–5 and I–84 corridors to the Highway 101 coastal route and Highways 20 and 97 in central and eastern Oregon. Be warned, however, that buses—particularly those running on the less-populated routes—leave sporadically and at inconvenient hours.

By Train **Amtrak**'s (tel. 800/USA–RAIL) *Coast Starlight* follows I–5 south to Eugene, then enters the rugged Cascades at Oakridge; from there it follows Highways 58 and 97 south past Diamond Peak and Crater Lake, on its way to California. The *Pioneer* runs daily from Portland to the Columbia Gorge, and parallels I–84 to the Idaho border and beyond.

Guided Tours

Orientation **Gray Line Sightseeing Tours** (Box 17306, Portland 97217, 503/ 285–9845) offers guided tours of scenic Oregon for both individuals and groups. Regular destinations include the Mt. Hood Loop and Oregon Coast.

Special-Interest A copy of "Discover Oregon Wineries," the free map and guide
Tours published by the **Oregon Wine Center** (1200 N.W. Front Ave., Suite 400, Portland 97209, tel. 503/228–8336), is an indispensable tool for touring wineries. It provides profiles and service information about each winery and is available at no charge where Oregon wine is sold.

Exploring

Tour 1: The Oregon Coast

Numbers in the margin correspond to points of interest on the Oregon Coast and Willamette Valley/Wine Country map.

Oregon has 300 miles of white-sand beaches, not a grain of which is privately owned. Highway 101 parallels the coast from Astoria south to California, past stunning monoliths of sea-tortured rock, brooding headlands, hidden beaches, haunted lighthouses, tiny ports, and, of course, the Pacific, a gleaming gunmetal gray stretching to the horizon. With its charming hamlets (Coos Bay–North Bend–Charleston, the largest metropolis on the coast, has only 25,000 inhabitants) and endless small hotels and resorts, the Oregon Coast seems to have been created with pleasure in mind. That's even more true today, as the awesome forests and salmon runs that once produced immense fortunes dwindle and disappear. Now the locals pursue tourists who come for the endless miles of empty beaches, deep-sea charter fishing, golf, cycling, hiking, shopping, and eating.

Astoria to Newport Our journey begins in **Astoria,** where the mighty Columbia Riv-
❶ er meets the Pacific. Astoria, founded in 1811, was named for John Jacob Astor, then America's wealthiest man, who financed the original fur-trading colony here.

More than 2,000 ships have been lost at the mouth of the Columbia, where the river's powerful current meets the ocean surge over shallow sandbanks. Settlers built sprawling Victorian houses on the flanks of **Coxcomb Hill,** many of which have since been restored and are no less splendid as bed-and-breakfast

Oregon Coast and Willamette Valley/Wine Country

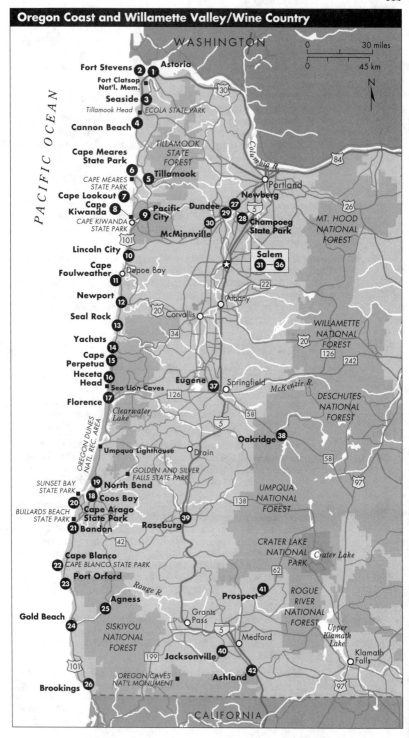

WASHINGTON

Fort Stevens ②①**Astoria**
Fort Clatsop
Nat'l. Mem.
Seaside ③
Tillamook Head ■ ECOLA STATE PARK
Cannon Beach ④

TILLAMOOK
STATE
FOREST

**Cape Meares
State Park**
⑥
CAPE MEARES ⑤ **Tillamook**
STATE PARK
Cape Lookout ⑦
**Cape
Kiwanda** ⑧ ⑨**Pacific
City** **Dundee** **Newberg**
CAPE KIWANDA ⑳ ㉗
STATE PARK ㉙
McMinnville ㉘ **Champoeg
State Park**
③⓪

PACIFIC OCEAN

Lincoln City ⑩
**Cape
Foulweather** Depoe Bay
⑪
Newport ⑫
Seal Rock
⑬
Yachats
⑭
**Cape
Perpetua** ⑮
**Heceta
Head** ⑯ ■ Sea Lion Caves
Florence ⑰
Clearwater
Lake

Portland
Columbia R.

MT. HOOD
NATIONAL
FOREST

Salem ㉛—㊱

Albany

Corvallis

WILLAMETTE
NATIONAL
FOREST

Eugene ㊲ Springfield
McKenzie R.

DESCHUTES
NATIONAL
FOREST

OREGON DUNES
NAT'L. REC. AREA
■ Umpqua Lighthouse ○ Drain

Oakridge ㊳

GOLDEN AND SILVER
FALLS STATE PARK
SUNSET BAY
STATE PARK
⑱ ⑲ **North Bend**
Coos Bay
⑳
BULLARDS BEACH
STATE PARK ■ **Cape Arago
State Park**
㉑**Bandon**

UMPQUA
NATIONAL
FOREST

Roseburg ㊴

Cape Blanco
㉒ CAPE BLANCO STATE PARK
Port Orford
㉓
Agness
㉕
Gold Beach
㉔

Rouge R.

SISKIYOU
NATIONAL
FOREST

OREGON CAVES
NAT'L MONUMENT ■

Brookings
㉖

CRATER LAKE
NATIONAL
PARK Crater Lake

Prospect ㊶
ROGUE
RIVER
NATIONAL
FOREST

Upper
Klamath
Lake

Grants
Pass

Medford
Klamath
Falls

Jacksonville ㊵

Ashland ㊷

CALIFORNIA

0   30 miles
0   45 km
N

inns. Modern Astoria is a placid amalgamation of turn-of-the-century small town and hardworking port city. With its museums, inns, and fine recreational offerings, it should be one of the Northwest's prime tourist destinations. Yet Astoria remains relatively undiscovered, even by Portlanders.

The **Columbia River Maritime Museum,** located on the downtown waterfront, is one of the two most interesting man-made tourist attractions on the Oregon Coast (Newport's Oregon Coast Aquarium is the other). It beguiles visitors—particularly young ones—with exhibits ranging from the observation tower of the World War II submarine USS *Rasher* (complete with working periscopes) and the fully operational U.S. Coast Guard lightship *Columbia* to the personal belongings of some of the ill-fated passengers of some of the ships that have been wrecked here since 1811. *1792 Marine Dr. at 17th St., tel. 503/325–2323. Admission: $5 adults, $4 senior citizens, $2 children 6–18. Open daily 9:30–5; closed Christmas and Thanksgiving.*

A mile up 16th Street from downtown, the **Astoria Column**—a 125-foot-high monolith atop Coxcomb Hill that was patterned after Trajan's Column in Rome—rewards the 164-step spiral stair climb with breathtaking views over Astoria, the Columbia River, the Coast Range, and the Pacific. *Follow signs from downtown. Admission free. Open daily 9–dusk.*

Follow 16th Street downhill to Duane Street, then walk west about seven blocks to the **Flavel House,** a prim and proper Victorian built between 1883 and 1885. The house's period furnishings, many selected by Captain George Flavel, give insight into the lifestyle of a wealthy 19th-century shipping tycoon. The admission price also includes a visit to the Heritage Museum, housed in the former City Hall. It's an interesting look at the history of Clatsop County, the oldest American settlement west of the Mississippi. *441 8th St., tel. 503/325–2203. Admission: $4 adults and senior citizens, $2 children 6–12. Open May–Sept., daily 10–5; Oct.–Apr., daily 11–4.*

"Ocean in view! O! The joy!" recorded William Clark, standing near this spot in the fall of 1805. After building a fort and wintering over here, however, the explorers wrote "O! How horrible is the day waves brakeing with great violence against the shore . . . all wet and confined to our shelters." **Ft. Clatsop National Memorial** is a faithful replica of the log stockade depicted in Clark's journal. Park rangers, who dress in period garb during the summer and perform such early 19th-century tasks as making fire with flint and steel, lend an air of authenticity, as does the damp and lonely ambience of the fort itself; a well-appointed visitors center tells the story of the great adventure. *Follow the signs 6 mi south of Astoria on Hwy. 101, tel. 503/861–2471. Admission $2 adults Apr. 1–Sept. 30, families $4; free the rest of the year. Open mid-June–Labor Day, daily 8–6; rest of year, daily 8–5.*

To round out your historical view of the West Coast's largest river, journey west on Highway 101, then follow signs to **❷** Warrenton Drive toward Oregon's northwestern tip and **Ft. Stevens,** in **Hammond.** The earthworks of this 37-acre fortress were mounded up during the Civil War, to guard the Columbia against a rather improbable Confederate attack. During World War II, Ft. Stevens became the only mainland U.S. military installation to come under enemy (Japanese submarine) fire since the War of 1812. Today the fort's abandoned gun mounts and eerie subterranean bunkers are a memorable destination, especially for children. The corroded skeleton of the *Peter Iredale*, a turn-of-the-century English four-master ship, protrudes from the sand just west of the campground, stark evidence of the malevolence of the Pacific. The nearby state park offers 605 campsites. *Ft. Stevens State Park, Hwy. 101 (follow signs toward Hammond), tel. 503/861–2000. Admission $3 per vehicle for historic area; summer guided truck tours of fort, $2, and underground Battery Mishler, $2.50. Open mid-May–Sept., daily 10–6; Oct.–mid-May, Wed.–Sun. 10–4.*

❸ For years, **Seaside,** 10 miles farther south on Highway 101, had a reputation as the sort of garish, arcade-filled town you would expect to find near Atlantic City, New Jersey. In the past decade it has cleaned up its act, and it now supports a bustling tourist trade with a cluster of hotels, condominiums, and restaurants surrounding the long beach. A 2-mile boardwalk parallels the shore and the stately old beachfront homes. Because it's only 90 miles from Portland, Seaside is often crowded, so it may not be the place for you if you crave solitude. Be especially wary in July, when the annual Miss Oregon Pageant is in full swing, and in February, during the Trail's End Marathon.

For more contemplative surroundings, go 10 miles south to ❹ Seaside's refined, artistic alter ego—**Cannon Beach**—a more mellow but trendier place for Portlanders to take in the sea air. With its tasteful, weathered, cedar downtown shopping district and beautiful beachfront homes, this tiny hamlet (population 1,200) is undoubtedly one of the most charming on the coast. However, the Carmel of the Oregon Coast is expensive, crowded, and afflicted with a subtle, moneyed hauteur (such as the town's recently enacted ban on vacation-home rentals) that may grate on less-aristocratic nerves.

The town got its name when a cannon from the wrecked schooner USS *Shark* washed ashore in 1846 (the piece is now on display a mile east of town on Highway 101). Towering over the broad sandy beach is **Haystack Rock,** a vast 235-foot-high monolith that is supposedly the most-photographed feature of the Oregon Coast. The rock is temptingly accessible during some low tides, but don't be beguiled: The Coast Guard regularly airlifts stranded climbers from its precipitous sides, and falls have claimed numerous lives over the years. Every May the town hosts the **Cannon Beach Sandcastle Contest,** when thousands throng the beach to view imaginative and often startling works in this most transient of art forms. While in the town, take a walk down the main thoroughfare, **Hemlock Street** (*see* Shopping, *below*), a fine shopping district of art galleries, clothiers, and gift shops.

About a mile north of Cannon Beach is **Tillamook Head** and **Ecola State Park,** a popular playground of sea-sculpted rock, sandy beach, tide pools, green headlands, and panoramic views. Less crowded **Indian Beach,** in the same park complex, is one of Oregon's rare rocky beaches. With its small, often deserted cove, mussel-encrusted rocks, and tide pools, this beach is a welcome departure from crowded Ecola.

A brisk 2-mile hike leads to the 1,100-foot-high viewpoint atop Tillamook Head. From there you'll see the old **Tillamook Rock Light Station,** which stands a mile or so out to sea. The lonely beacon, built in 1881 on a straight-sided rock, towers 41 feet above the surrounding ocean. In 1957, the lighthouse was abandoned; it is now a columbarium, or repository for the cremated remains of those who yearn for the sea.

Heading south again on Highway 101, follow signs for 10 miles to the trailhead at **Neahkahnie Mountain.** Cryptic carvings on beach rocks near here, and centuries-old Native American legends of shipwrecked Europeans, gave rise to a tale that the survivors of a wrecked Spanish mystery galleon buried a fortune in doubloons somewhere on the side of this 1,661-foot-high mountain. The treasure has never been found, but the trail to the summit provides the intrepid with a different kind of reward: unobstructed views over surf, sand, forest, and mountain. Those who visit in December and April often see pods of gray whales on their annual 14,000-mile migration.

Adventurous travelers will enjoy a sojourn at **Oswald West State Park** at the mountain's base, one of the best-kept secrets on the Pacific Coast. Park your car in the lot on Highway 101 and use a park-provided wheelbarrow to trundle your camping gear down a half-mile trail. There you'll find 36 campsites, surrounded by Cape Falcon's lush old-growth forest. The beach, with its caves and little-visited tide pools, is spectacular. There are no reservations for the campsites, but a call to the park office (tel. 503/731–3411) will yield information on vacancies.

More than 600,000 visitors annually press their noses against the spotlessly clean windows at the **Tillamook County Creamery,** the largest cheese-making plant on the West Coast. Here the rich milk from the area's thousands of holstein and brown Swiss cows becomes fine Cheddar and Monterey Jack cheeses, butter, and ice cream. There are wide display windows and exhibits on the cheese-making process at the visitor center, free samples, and, of course, a gift shop. *Hwy. 101, about 2 mi north of Tillamook, tel. 503/842–4481. Admission free. Visitors center open mid-Sept.–May, daily 8–6; June–early Sept., daily 8–8. Closed Thanksgiving and Christmas.*

Not to be outdone, **Blue Heron French Cheese Company,** a mile closer to Tillamook, specializes in such French-style cheeses as Camembert and Brie. There's a new petting zoo for kids, as well as a sit-down deli. The factory gift shop also sells a selection of Oregon wine and other Oregon products, such as jams and mustards. *2001 Blue Heron Dr., watch for signs from Hwy. 101, tel. 503/842–8281. Tasting room open Memorial Day–Labor Day, daily 8–8; rest of year, daily 9–5.*

⑤ Tillamook, south of Cannon Beach, is a kind of wet Wisconsin-on-the-Pacific. The town, situated about 2 miles inland, surrounded by rich dairyland, and blessed with abundant fresh and saltwater fishing, has some of the finest scenery on the Oregon Coast, which contributes to the placid atmosphere. It lacks the aristocratic charm of Cannon Beach but has much to offer the traveler in search of a quiet, natural retreat. In Tillamook's 1905 county courthouse, the **Pioneer Museum** has marvelous exhibits on local natural history, Native Americans, pioneers, and logging, as well as a collection of military artifacts dating back two centuries. *2106 2nd St., tel. 503/842–4553. Admission: $1 adults, 50¢ children 12–17, $5 family. Open Mar. 16–Sept. 30, Mon.–Sat. 8–5, Sun. noon–5; Oct. 1–Mar. 15, Tues.–Sat. 8–5, Sun. noon–5.*

Tillamook Bay, where the Miami, Kilchis, Wilson, Trask, and Tillamook rivers enter the Pacific, is a sportfishing mecca. The quarry includes silver and chinook salmon, steelhead, sea-run cutthroat trout, bottom fish, the delectable Dungeness crab, mussels, oysters, and a variety of clams. There are abundant charter-fishing services available at **Garibaldi,** a mast-filled fishing harbor just north of Tillamook. For some of the best rock fishing in the state, try Tillamook Bay's **North Jetty.**

Leaving downtown Tillamook, going west via 3rd Street, you'll find the start of scenic **Three Capes Loop,** one of the coast's most rewarding driving experiences. Turning west on Bay Ocean Drive will take you past what was once the thriving resort town of **Bay Ocean.** More than 30 years ago, Bay Ocean washed into the sea, taking with it lots, houses, a bowling alley—almost everything. Still on the loop, at **Cape Meares State Park,** you'll have a chance to climb 100-year-old **Cape Meares Lighthouse,** open to the public from May through September. From the tower, there's a spectacular view over the cliff of the caves and the sea-lion rookery on the rocks below. A titanic, many-trunked Sitka spruce known as the Octopus Tree grows near the lighthouse parking lot.

Cape Lookout, next on the loop, has equally fine views, as well as a year-round campground. **Cape Kiwanda,** 15 miles farther south, is a favorite spot for hang gliders and surf watchers. Some of the world's best nature photographers have fallen in love with **Cape Kiwanda State Park,** where huge waves pound jagged sandstone cliffs and caves. The beach at **Pacific City,** a mile or two farther south, is one of the only places in the state where fishing dories (flat-bottom boats with high flaring sides) are launched directly into the surf instead of from harbors or docks. During the commercial salmon season in late summer, it's possible to buy salmon directly from fishermen.

If you continue south on Highway 101, you'll encounter **Lincoln City,** the most popular destination city on the Oregon Coast. Here, clustered like barnacles on the offshore reefs, you'll find fast-food restaurants, gift shops, and supermarkets and hotels; Lincoln City even has its own brew pub, the westernmost outlet of Portland's McMenamin chain, as well as a bustling factory outlet mall. Lincoln City's only other real claim to fame is the 445-foot-long D River, stretching from its source in Devil's Lake to its mouth in the Pacific; *The Guinness Book of World's Records* lists this as the world's shortest river.

High above placid Siletz Bay, just south of Lincoln City, is **Salishan.** The most famous resort on the Oregon Coast. This elegant and expensive collection of guest rooms, vacation homes, condominiums, restaurants, golf fairways, tennis courts, and covered walkways blends into a 750-acre forest preserve; if it weren't for the signs, you would hardly be able to find it.

The tiny (six-acre) harbor at **Depoe Bay** may look vaguely familiar; it was used as a setting for the Academy Award–winning film *One Flew Over the Cuckoo's Nest.* With its narrow channel and deep water, the bay is one of the most protected on the coast, and it supports a thriving fleet of commercial- and charter-fishing boats. The **Spouting Horn,** a natural cleft in the basalt cliffs on the waterfront, blasts seawater skyward during heavy weather.

If you take the **Otter Crest Loop** a mile or two south of Depoe
Bay, you'll shortly arrive at **Cape Foulweather,** with its lighthouse gift shop and backward-leaning shore pines lending mute
witness to the 100-mile-an-hour winds that strafe this exposed
spot in winter. British explorer Captain James Cook named
this 500-foot-high headland on a blustery March day in 1778.

Rejoining the highway near **Yaquina Head,** you'll find the
northern city limits of **Newport,** a busy harbor and fishing town
with about 8,000 residents. Newport exists on two levels: the
highway above, threading its way through the community's
main business district; and the charming old bayfront below,
which you'll find by heading east on Herbert Street. With its
high-masted fishing fleet, well-worn buildings, art galleries
and shops, fragrantly steaming crab kettles, and the finest collection of fresh seafood markets on the coast, Newport's bayfront is an ideal place for an afternoon stroll.

Just across the Yaquina Bay is the most recent jewel in the
trove of Oregon Coast tourist attractions: the brand-new **Oregon Coast Aquarium.** This 2½-acre complex contains painstaking re-creations of a variety of offshore and near-shore Pacific
marine habitats, all teeming with life: playful sea otters, comi-
cal puffins, fragile jellyfish, even a 60-pound octopus, among
other creatures. Visitors follow a drop of rain from the forested
uplands of the Coast Range, through the tidal estuary and out
to sea. There's a salty, hands-on interactive area for children,
as well as North America's largest seabird aviary. *2820 SE
Ferry Slip Rd., Newport, tel. 503/867–3474. Admission: $7.35
adults, $5.25 senior citizens 60 and older, and children 13–18;
$3.15 children 4–12. Open mid-May–mid-Oct., daily 9–6; mid-
Oct.–mid-May, daily 10–4:30. Closed Christmas Day.*

Right next door to the Oregon Coast Aquarium, Oregon State
University's **Hatfield Marine Science Center** offers a different
kind of underwater experience. Interpretive exhibits in the
center's public aquarium explain the cycle of life in the North
Pacific, as well as the natural history of the Yaquina estuary.
The star of the show is the large octopus in a round low tank
near the entrance—he seems as interested in human visitors as
they are in him, and he has been known to reach up and gently
stroke children's hands with his suction-tipped tentacles. *2030
Marine Science Dr. (head south across Yaquina Bay Bridge—
Hwy. 101—and follow signs), tel. 503/867–0100. Admission
free. Open Memorial Day–Labor Day, daily 10–6; Labor Day–
Memorial Day, daily 10–4.*

**Newport to Coos
Bay**   South of Newport, following the highway, you'll enter a slower-
paced, less-crowded section of the Oregon Coast. The scenery,
fishing, and other outdoor activities are just as rich as those in
the other towns along the way, but the commercialism and the
crowds seem curiously absent.

At **Seal Rock,** chain-saw sculpture—a peculiar Oregon art
form—reaches its pinnacle in one of the state's most unusual
tourist attractions: **Sea Gulch,** a full-size ghost town inhabited
by more than 300 fancifully carved wood figures. Carver Ray
Kowalski wields his Stihl chain saw with virtuosity to create
unique cowboys, Indians, hillbillies, trolls, gnomes, and other
humorous figures. Visitors can watch him work in his adjoining
studio. *East side of Hwy. 101 in Seal Rock, tel. 503/563–2727.*

Admission: $4.50 adults, $3.50 senior citizens, $3 children. Open daily 8–5.

⑭ A few miles south of Seal Rock is **Yachats** (pronounced "Ya-hots"), an Indian word meaning "foot of the mountain." Among Oregon beach lovers, this tiny burg of 600 inhabitants has acquired a reputation that is disproportionate to its size. Yachats offers a microcosm of all the coastal pleasures: bed-and-breakfasts, excellent restaurants, deserted beaches, surf-pounded crags, fishing and crabbing. It is also one of the few places in the world where the silver smelt come inland. Every year, from May to September, hundreds of thousands of these delectable sardinelike fish swarm up the Yachats River, where dip-net fishermen eagerly await them. A community smelt-fry celebrates this bounty each July.

⑮ Three miles south of Yachats is **Cape Perpetua,** another lovely headland that towers hundreds of feet over the waves. Watch for the U.S. Forest Service Visitors Center on the east side of the highway, where you can obtain handy free maps of Cape Perpetua's miles of hiking trails, as well as of such geological features as the Devil's Churn, where the furious sea rushes into a volcanic fissure in the cliff.

⑯ Ten miles farther south, in **Heceta Head,** the lighthouse—visible for more than 21 miles—is the most powerful beacon on the Oregon Coast. The structure is said to be haunted by the wife of a lighthouse keeper, who fell to her death from the cliffs shortly after the beacon was built in 1874. Excellent views and photographic perspectives can be found at **Devil's Elbow State Park,** a few hundred yards to the south.

In 1880, a sea captain named Cox rowed a small skiff into a fissure in a 300-foot-high sea cliff. Inside, he was startled to discover a vaulted chamber in the rock, 125 feet high and 2 acres in area. Hundreds of massive sea lions—the largest bulls weighing 2,000 pounds or more—covered every available horizontal surface. Cox had no way of knowing it, but his discovery would eventually become one of the Oregon Coast's most venerable and popular tourist attractions, known today as **Sea Lion Caves,** located about a mile south of Heceta Head. Visitors ride an elevator from the cliff-top ticket office down to the floor of the cavern, near sea level, to watch the antics of the fuzzy pups and their parents from above. An ancient sea-lion skeleton is on display, proof that these animals have lived here for many centuries. *91560 Hwy. 101N, tel. 503/547–3111. Admission: $5.50 adults, $3.50 children ages 6–15. Open Oct.–June, daily 9–dusk; July–Sept., daily 8–dusk.*

Six miles south of the caves is **Darlingtona Botanical Wayside,** another surefire child pleaser. Here, a half-mile nature walk leads through clumps of carnivorous, insect-catching cobra lilies, so named because they look like spotted cobras ready to strike. This park is most interesting in May, when the lilies are in bloom. *Mercer Lake Rd., on the east side of Hwy. 101, no phone. Admission free.*

Just past Heceta Head, Highway 101 jogs inland, and the frowning headlands and cliffs of the north coast give way to the endless beaches and rolling dunes of the south. Here you'll en-**⑰** ter **Florence,** a popular destination for both tourists and retirees. The picturesque waterfront Old Town has restaurants, antiques stores, fish markets, and other wet-weather diversions.

Time Out While in Old Town, stop off at **Mo's** (1436 Bay St., tel. 503/997–2185) for a rich, creamy bowl of clam chowder and clear bayfront views. This coastal institution has been around for more than 40 years, consistently providing the freshest seafood and friendly, down-home service.

Florence is the gateway to the **Oregon Dunes National Recreation Area,** a 41-mile swath of undulating camel-colored sand. **Honeyman State Park,** 522 acres within the recreation area, is a popular base camp for the thousands of dune-buggy enthusiasts, mountain bikers, boaters, horseback riders, and dogsledders (the dunes are an excellent training ground) who converge here. The dunes, some more than 500 feet high, are a vast and exuberant playground for children, particularly the sandy slopes surrounding cool **Cleawox Lake.** Facilities in the park include 381 campsites, 66 with full hookups, showers, and a boat ramp; there are also numerous hiking trails. *Oregon Dunes National Recreation Area office, 84505, Hwy. 101, Florence 97439, tel. 503/997–3641. 381 campsites. Facilities: showers, boat ramp, 66 RV hookups, hiking. Reservations are a must for weekends and holidays. Admission: $3 per vehicle day use, $14–$16 overnight stays. Send request and a $20 deposit (check or money order only) to park address above. Open Apr.–Sept., Wed.–Sat. 10–5. Closed Oct.–Mar.*

For coastal sportsmen, **Winchester Bay's Salmon Harbor** is always spoken of with reverence. A public pier, built especially for crabbers and fishermen, juts out over the bay and yields excellent results. The rockfishing from the **Winchester Bay** jetty is also popular. Salmon Harbor's excellent full-service marina was designed to provide everything an avid fisherman could possibly need, including a fish market in case the day's quest was unsuccessful. For further information, the Lower Umpqua Chamber of Commerce (tel. 503/271–3495) can assist you.

The first **Umpqua River Lighthouse,** built on the dunes at the mouth of the Umpqua River in 1857, lasted only four years before it toppled over in a storm. It took chagrined local residents 33 years to build another one. The "new" lighthouse, built on a bluff overlooking the south side of Winchester Bay, is still going strong, flashing a warning beacon out to sea every five seconds. The adjacent **Douglas County Coastal Visitors Center** has a museum featuring local history exhibits. The 50-acre **Umpqua Lighthouse Park** contains 500-foot sand dunes, the highest in the United States. *On Umpqua Hwy., west side of Hwy. 101, tel. 503/271–4631. Admission free. Open Apr. 1–Oct 1., Wed.–Sat. 10–5, Sun. 1–5. Closed Sept. 30–Mar. 31.*

18 **Coos Bay,** synonymous with the tall timbers that thrive here, is located 20 miles farther on Highway 101. The largest metropolitan area on the Oregon Coast, it stands next to the largest natural harbor between the San Francisco Bay Area and Seattle's Puget Sound. Log trucks freighted with some of the biggest old-growth logs being cut anywhere in the world support Coos Bay's claim that it's still the world's largest lumber-shipping port. But the glory days of the timber industry are over, and Coos Bay has begun to look in other directions, such as tourism, for economic prosperity.

⑲ Fortunately, the Coos Bay and **North Bend** metro area is also the gateway to some of the coast's most rewarding recreational experiences. For one, the Golden and Silver Falls State Park is where Glenn Creek pours over a high rock ledge deep in the old-growth forest. The 210-foot-high **Golden Falls** is the more forceful, but 200-foot-high **Silver Falls,** plunging over the same abyss a quarter-mile to the northwest, is perhaps more beautiful. *Take the Eastside-Allegany exit from Hwy. 101 at the south end of Coos Bay; follow signs to Golden and Silver Falls State Park, about 24 mi northeast.*

Coos Bay to Brookings Backtrack to Coos Bay and head west, following signs from Highway 101 to **Charleston,** a fishing village at the mouth of Coos Bay that has an almost Mediterranean quaintness about it. Four miles farther south, on Seven Devils Road, is the **South Slough National Estuarine Reserve,** where the rich and productive mud flats and tidal estuaries of Coos Bay support life ranging from algae to bald eagles to black bear. More than 300 species of birds have been sighted here; an interpretive center, guided walks (summer only), and nature trails give visitors a chance to see things up close. *Seven Devils Rd., tel. 503/888–5558. Admission free. Trails open daily dawn–dusk; interpretive center open Memorial Day–Labor Day, daily 8:30–4:30; Labor Day–Memorial Day, weekdays 8:30–4:30.*

Returning to Charleston, follow the Cape Arago Highway south toward **Sunset Bay State Park.** This placid semicircular lagoon, protected from the sea by overlapping fingers of rock, is the safest swimming beach on the Oregon Coast. Leaving the park, you'll continue southbound to **Shore Acres State Park,** situated on the estate of lumber baron Louis J. Simpson. Today all that remains are the gardens, a beautifully landscaped swath of formal English and Japanese horticulture. *10965 Cape Arago Hwy., tel. 503/888–4902. Admission: $3 per vehicle May–Sept., otherwise free. Open daily 8–dusk.*

⑳ Just down the road from Shore Acres is **Cape Arago State Park** (end of Cape Arago Hwy., tel. 503/888–4902), surrounded by a trio of tide pool–pocked coves connected by short but steep trails. Here you'll find some of the richest and least-visited tidal rockery in the state.

㉑ Still traveling south on Highway 101, you'll reach **Bandon,** a small coastal village that bills itself as the Cranberry Capital of Oregon. Bandon, built above a walking beach with weathered monoliths, might be the most beautiful section along the coast. Follow the signs from Bandon south along Beach Loop Road to **Face Rock Wayside** and descend a stairway to the sand, where you can watch the sunset through a veritable gallery of natural sculptures, including Elephant Rock, Table Rock, and Face Rock. If the weather turns inclement, you might consider a stop at **Bullards Beach State Park,** which houses the photogenic **Bandon Lighthouse** as well as the **Bandon Historical Museum.** At the latter, a historic white clapboard Coast Guard station, you'll see exhibits on the three fires that have leveled Bandon. *1st St., tel. 503/347–2164. Admission: $1, children under 12 free. Open Tues.–Sat. noon–4.*

㉒ About 20 miles south of Bandon you'll come to **Cape Blanco,** the westernmost point in the continental United States. **Cape Blanco Lighthouse,** accessible after a pleasant 6-mile drive from Highway 101 (follow signs), has been in continual use since 1870. The 1,880-acre **Cape Blanco State Park** (tel. 503/ 332–6774) has campsites, hiking, and spectacular views of offshore rocks and reefs.

㉓ Many knowledgeable coastal travelers consider the stretch of Highway 101 between **Port Orford** and Brookings (*see below*) to be the most beautiful in all of Oregon, perhaps on the entire Pacific Coast. The ocean here is bluer and clearer—though not appreciably warmer—than it is farther north. The highway soars up green headlands, some hundreds of feet high, and past awesome sea-sculpted scenery: caves, towering arches, and bridges, including the man-made **Thomas Creek Bridge,** the highest span in Oregon. A word of caution: Take plenty of time to admire the scenery, but make use of the many turnouts and viewpoints along the way. This close to California, some stretches of Highway 101 are heavily trafficked, and rubbernecking can be dangerous. Ten-mile-long **Boardman State Park** offers particularly outstanding hiking trails and cliff-top views.

㉔ **Gold Beach,** about 20 miles north of the California border, is famous mainly as the place where the much-renowned Rogue River meets the ocean. Daily jet-boat excursions roar upstream from **Wedderburn,** Gold Beach's sister city across the bay, from
㉕ late spring to late fall. Some go to **Agness,** 32 miles upstream, where the riverside road ends and the wild and scenic portion of the Rogue begins. Other boats penetrate farther, to the wet-knuckle rapids at **Blossom Bar,** 52 miles upstream.

Gold Beach also marks the entrance to Oregon's banana belt, where mild, California-like temperatures take the sting out of winter and encourage a blossoming trade in lilies and daffodils. It's said that 90% of the pot lilies grown in the United States
㉖ come from a 500-acre area just inland from **Brookings.** You'll even see a few palm trees here, a rare sight in Oregon.

Brookings is equally famous as a commercial and sportfishing port at the mouth of the incredibly clear, startlingly turquoise-blue Chetco River. If anything, the Chetco is more highly esteemed among fishermen and wilderness lovers alike than is the Rogue. A short jetty, popular with local crabbers and fishermen, offers easy and productive access to the river's mouth; salmon and steelhead running 20 pounds or larger are caught here. At **Loeb State Park**—located on the north bank of the Chetco, 10 miles east of Brookings (follow signs from Highway 101)—with its impressive grove of myrtlewood trees (they grow nowhere else in the world), you'll find 53 riverside campsites and some fine hiking trails, including one that leads to a hidden, little-known redwood grove.

Tour 2: Willamette Valley/Oregon Wine Country

During the 1940s and 1950s, researchers at Oregon State University concluded that the Willamette Valley had the wrong climate for the propagation of fine varietal wine grapes. Fortunately for wine lovers everywhere, the researchers' techniques were faulty, which has been proven by the success of Oregon's burgeoning wine industry. More than 40 wineries dot the hills between Portland and Salem, and a dozen more are scattered from Roseburg along the I–5 corridor as far south as Ashland, on the California border. Their products—mainly cool-climate varietals such as Pinot Noir, chardonnay, and Riesling—have won numerous gold medals in blind tastings against the best wines that California or Europe have to offer. Oregon's wine country occupies the wet, temperate trough between the Coast Range to the west and the Cascades to the east. The main concentration lies in the north, among the Willamette and Yamhill Valleys, near Portland. The warmer, drier Umpqua and Rogue valleys, near Roseburg and Ashland—respectively—also produce their share of fine bottlings.

The best way to see the wine country here is to rent a car and map out your own itinerary. Strangely enough, there are no regularly scheduled bus tours at this time, though the Oregon Wine Center (*see* Special-Interest Tours in Guided Tours, *above*) may be able to arrange one for larger groups. Some of the state's most accomplished and hospitable wineries include (from the northern valley to the south) **Tualatin Vineyards** (Forest Grove, tel. 503/357–5005), **Shafer Vineyard Cellars** (Forest Grove, tel. 503/357–6604), Ponzi Vineyards (Beaverton, tel. 503/628–1227), **Laurel Ridge Winery** (Forest Grove, tel. 503/359–5436), **Rex Hill Vineyards** (Newberg, tel. 503/538–0666), **Veritas Vineyard** (Newberg, tel. 503/538–1470), **Autumn Wind Vineyard** (Gaston, tel. 503/538–6931), **Knudsen Erath** (Dundee, tel. 503/538–3318), **Yamhill Valley Vineyards** (McMinnville, tel. 503/843–3100), **Amity Vineyards** (Amity, tel. 503/835–2362), **Bethel Heights Vineyard** (Salem, tel. 503/581–2262), **Eola Hills Wine Cellars** (Rickreall, tel. 503/623–2405), **Tyee Wine Cellars** (Corvalis, tel. 503/753–8754), **Alpine Vineyards** (Alpine, tel. 503/424–5851), **Henry Estate Winery** (Umpqua, tel. 503/459–5120), **Girardet Wine Cellars** (Roseburg, tel. 503/679–7252), and **Callahan Ridge Winery** (Roseburg, tel. 503/673–7901). For opening times and tour schedules, call in advance.

The following tour suggests sightseeing stops, but does not incorporate wineries. Those who are interested can fit one or two wineries from the above list into this itinerary. The tour begins
㉗ in **Newberg,** a graceful old pioneer town, located at a broad bend in the Willamette River about a half hour southwest of Portland. The oldest and most significant of its original structures is the **Hoover-Minthorne House,** boyhood home of President Herbert Hoover. Built in 1881, the beautifully preserved and well-landscaped frame house includes many of the original furnishings, as well as the woodshed that no doubt played an important role in shaping young "Bertie" Hoover's character. *115 S. River St., tel. 503/538–6629. Admission: $1.50 adults, $1 senior citizens and students 12 and older. Open Mar.–Nov., Wed.–Sun. 1–4; Dec. and Feb., weekends 1–4. Closed Jan.*

From Newberg, Highway 219S (toward Donald) will take you
㉘ to lovely **Champoeg** (pronounced "shampooey") **State Park,** former seat of the first provisional government in the Northwest. The site of a Hudson's Bay Company trading post, grainery, and warehouse built in 1813, the settlement was abandoned after a catastrophic flood in 1861, then rebuilt and abandoned again after the flood of 1890. Now the park's wide-open spaces, groves of oak and fir, modern visitor's center, museum, and historic buildings (such as the Pioneer Mother's Memorial Cabin) give visitors a vivid glimpse of pioneer life. *8239 Champoeg Rd., NE, St. Paul, OR 97137, tel. 503/678–1251. Admission: $3 per vehicle May–Sept., free Oct.–Apr. Open Labor Day–Memorial Day, weekdays 8–4, weekends noon–4; Memorial Day–Labor Day, daily 10–6.*

29 If you retrace your route to Highway 99W and continue south, you'll pass through the idyllic orchardland around **Dundee:** A haven of produce stands and tasting rooms—home to 90% of America's hazelnut crop.

30 Twelve miles farther southwest is **McMinnville**—the largest (population 16,000) and most sophisticated of wine-country towns—which hosts a fine collection of bed-and-breakfasts, small hotels, and restaurants. **Linfield College,** a perennial football powerhouse, is an oasis of brick and ivy in the midst of McMinnville's farmers-market bustle and annually hosts Oregon's **International Pinot Noir Celebration.** The college, founded in 1849, is the second oldest in Oregon, next to Willamette University. *Admissions office, 900 S. Baker St., Melrose Hall, tel. 503/472-4121, ext. 213. Open weekdays 8–5. Free guided walking tours of the campus arranged by appointment.*

31 Continuing south on Highway 99W, take Highway 22 west toward **Salem**—the state capital—located precisely halfway between the North Pole and the equator on the 45th parallel, about 45 miles south of Portland, along I–5. The brightly gilded 23-foot-high bronze statue of the Oregon Pioneer atop the 140-foot capitol dome is the centerpiece of Salem's **Capitol Mall,** where Oregon's legislators convene every two years.

Numbers in the margin correspond to points of interest on the Salem map.

32 **Oregon's State Capitol complex**—graceless blocks of gray Vermont marble—looks as if it was designed by a committee of career bureaucrats to frighten away the commoners. But don't be deterred—the interior is softened by some fine relief sculptures and the surprisingly deft historical murals. Tours of the rotunda, the house and senate chambers, and the governor's office leave from the information counter under the dome. *900 Court St., tel. 503/378-4423. Admission free. Open weekdays 8–5, Sat. 9–4, Sun. noon–4. Guided capitol tours available Memorial Day–Labor Day, daily on the hour; Labor Day–Memorial Day by appointment.*

33 Just across State Street but half a world away are the tradition-steeped brick buildings and immaculate greens of **Willamette University,** the oldest college in the West. Founded in 1842, Willamette has long been a mecca for aspiring politicians (Oregon senators Mark Hatfield and Bob Packwood are alumni). Stunning **Hatfield Library,** built in 1986 of gracefully curved brick and glass, is an oasis of silent scholarship on the banks of the merry Mill Stream; tall, prim **Waller Hall,** built in 1841, is one of the five oldest buildings in the Pacific Northwest. The university hosts theatrical and musical performances, athletic events, guest lecturers, and art exhibits year-round. For information and tours, contact the university's public relations office (tel. 503/370-6340).

34 From 12th Street cross over to the **Mission Mill Village** and **Thomas Kay Woolen Mill Museum,** where teasel gigging, napper flock bins, and the patented Furber double-acting napper are but a few of the venerable machines and processes on display. The museum complex (circa 1889), complete with working waterwheels and mill stream, looks as if the workers have just stepped away for a lunch break, giving visitors a vivid glimpse of 19th-century manufacturing. In the same complex, the **Marion County Museum of History** (tel. 503/364-2128) dis-

Bush's Pasture
Park, **35**
Deepwood Estate, **36**
Mission Mill
Village, **34**
State Capitol, **32**
Willamette
University, **33**

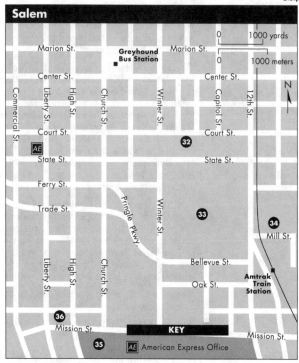

plays a fine collection of pioneer and Calipooya Indian artifacts.
The spare simplicity of the Jason Lee House, John D. Boon
Home, and Methodist Parsonage, also part of the village, invites the visitor to steal a glimpse of domestic life in the wilds of
Oregon in the 1840s. In the warehouse a few steps away, specialty shops offer antiques, clothing, quilts, toys, and other
handmade goods from local craftspeople. *Museum complex,
1313 Mill St. SE, tel. 503/585–7012. Admission: $5 adults,
$4.50 senior citizens 65 and older, $4 children 6–18 (includes
the tour). Open daily 10–4:30. Guided tours of historic houses
and woolen mill museum leave from the mill's admission tent
every hour on the hour.*

35 36 **Bush's Pasture Park** and **Deepwood Estate,** situated just south
of Salem's downtown district, include 105 acres of rolling lawn
and formal English gardens. Also on the grounds, the 1878
Bush House is a creaky, gaslit Italianate oddity with 10 marble
fireplaces. The fanciful 1894 **Deepwood Estate,** built in the
Queen Anne style, is worth a visit just for its splendid interior
woodwork and original stained glass. The houses and gardens
are all on the National Historic Register. *Bush House and
Bush's Pasture Park, 600 Mission St. SE, tel. 503/363–4714.
Admission: $1.50 adults, $1 senior citizens, 75¢ students, 50¢
children. Open Oct.–May, Tues.–Sun. 2–5; June–Sept.,
Tues.–Sun. noon–5. The Deepwood Estate, 1116 Mission St.
SE, tel. 503/363–1825. Admission: $2 adults, $1.50 senior citizens and students. Open Oct.–Apr., Sun., Mon., Wed., Fri.
1–4; May–Sept., Sun.–Fri. noon–4:30.*

Numbers in the margin correspond to points of interest on the Oregon Coast and Willamette Valley/Wine Country map.

37 Continuing south on I-5, you'll come to **Eugene,** 63 miles farther. The second-largest city in the state and the mid-valley's cultural hub, Eugene has more than 300 restaurants, a world-class performing-arts center, and outdoor recreation "from sea level to ski level." The centerpiece of the city is the **University of Oregon,** where Nike shoes founder Phil Knight attended school. The self-proclaimed sobriquet for Eugene—Tracktown USA—and the many joggers thronging the streets and parks of the city are part of his legacy. Also, visitors may recognize the campus as the location for the filming of National Lampoon's *Animal House.* However, Oregon's liberal arts university thrives on more than the reputation of one alumnus and recognition from Hollywood. The grounds are lush and green, with more than 400 varieties of trees shading the 250-acre brick-and-ivy campus. In addition to the athletic events at **Autzen Stadium, MacArthur Court,** and **Hayward Field,** where the U of O's perennially powerful track and field team holds its meets, there are visiting arts exhibits and lecturers at the **Maude I. Kerns Art Center,** as well as a highly regarded permanent collection of Oriental art at the **University of Oregon Museum of Art.** The university's **Museum of Natural History** is a small museum of Pacific Northwest anthropology and natural sciences. Its ever-changing exhibits are drawn from the university's own vast collections. *Admissions office: 1585 E. 13th Ave., tel. 503/346-3201. Open weekdays 8–noon and 1–5. Art Museum: 1430 Johnson La., tel. 503/346-3027. Natural History Museum: 1680 E. 15th Ave., tel. 503/346-3024. Admission: $1. Open Wed.–Sun. noon–5. Maps and guided tours of the campus available.*

If you're in the mood for a stroll or jog along the river, the **Willamette Science and Technology Center,** next to Autzen Stadium, is a good place to end your journeys. The city's well-equipped and imaginative hands-on scientific museum and planetarium (known to the locals as "Wiz-Tek") features rotating exhibits designed with children in mind; one recent offering, "Pets and People," brought forth lectures, demonstrations, and a petting zoo equipped with everything from puppies and kittens to pythons and cockroaches. The adjacent planetarium offers a rotating slate of stars and shows. *2300 Leo Harris Pkwy. Museum tel. 503/687-3619. Admission: $8 families, $3 adults 17 and older, $2 children 4–16. Open Wed.–Sun. noon–6. Planetarium tel. 503/689-6500; admission and hours vary.*

Time Out If you have hungry children, or have a tough time deciding what sounds good for lunch, the food options at the **5th Street Public Market Food Pavilion** (5th and High Sts., tel. 503/484-0383), a downtown landmark, will give you plenty of options. They range from sit-down restaurants (Mekala's Thai Cuisine, Casablanca Mediterranean Cuisine) to decadent bakeries (the Metropol Bakery on the building's lower level is especially fine) to the bewildering international diversity of the clean, airy second-floor food esplanade, offering Greek, Mexican, English, Chinese, Italian, and nouvelle American foods.

The wineries and memorable scenic drives continue both east and west of Eugene. Highway 58 climbs into the Cascades and the Deschutes Forest toward Willamette Pass east of the city. There, in addition to a popular ski area, you'll find the 286-foot-high Salt Creek Falls, not far from the town of **Oakridge.**

Westward, toward the coast, Highway 126 gives access to several wineries and trout-filled rivers before coming to Florence (*see* Tour 1: The Oregon Coast, *above*), on the central Oregon shore.

Following I–5, take note of **Roseburg,** where the highway crosses the Umpqua River, a name sacred to steelhead fishermen the world over. Six wineries (Callahan Ridge, Girardet, Henry Estate, Hillcrest, LaGarza, and Looking Glass) are within an easy drive west of this sleepy farming community.

In town, the **Douglas County Museum,** one of the best county museums in the state, gives visitors a window on 8,000 years of human activity in the region. Its fossil collection, which includes a million-year-old saber-toothed tiger, is worth a stop. *At the Douglas County Fairgrounds (take Exit 123 from I–5 and follow the signs), tel. 503/440–4507. Admission free; donations accepted. Open Tues.–Sat. 10–4, Sun. noon–4.*

If for no other reason, downtown **Jacksonville,** about 70 miles farther south and 5 miles west of I–5 on Route 238, deserves a visit for the simple reason that the entire hamlet is on the National Register of Historic Places. Clumping along the boardwalks, it's easy to imagine yourself in Jacksonville during its gold rush heyday in 1853, because several of the 80 privately owned historic structures date from this era. The **Jacksonville Museum,** located in the old Jackson County Courthouse, houses an intriguing collection of gold rush–era artifacts and a permanent exhibit called "Jacksonville! Boomtown to Home Town," outlining the rich local history. An exhibit installed in 1993 features the images of Peter Britt, the pioneer photographer who homesteaded here. The adjoining Children's Museum, occupying the 80-year-old Jackson County Jail, contains hands-on exhibits on pioneer life, as well as a splendid collection of antique toys. *206 N. 5th St., tel. 503/773–6536. Admission: $2 for both museums. Open Memorial Day–Labor Day, daily 10–5; Labor Day–Memorial Day, Tues.–Sun. 10–5.*

For free maps and guides to Jacksonville's many historic structures, stop by the **Jacksonville Chamber of Commerce** (185 N. Oregon St., tel. 503/899–8118).

In many ways the town has become more important to the cultural life of Oregon than has Portland or Eugene. Jacksonville hosts the **Peter Britt Festival** (*see* The Arts, *below*), which attracts some of the world's best-known classical, jazz, and popular musicians each summer.

Nature lovers who want a glimpse of Rogue River's loveliest angle should plan a side trip to the **Avenue of the Boulders, Mill Creek Falls,** and **Barr Creek Falls,** just off Highway 62, near **Prospect** (45 miles northeast of Jacksonville). Here the wild waters of the upper Rogue foam through volcanic boulders and the dense greenery of the **Rogue River National Forest.**

In spite of its small size and relative isolation from other towns in the state, **Ashland** is also a major cultural center for Oregon. Home to the Tony Award–winning **Oregon Shakespeare Festival,** Ashland draws more than 100,000 theater lovers to the Rogue Valley every year. The influx is especially dramatic during the peak festival months of June–September, when reservations get very tight. A critical mass of excellent restaurants, bed-and-breakfasts (more than 50 at last count), shops, and galleries combines with a salubrious climate to make Ashland one of Oregon's most popular tourist destinations.

At Ashland's **Shakespeare Festival Exhibit Center** in the festival complex, theater fans can try on costumes and view exhibits about the history of the festival. A visit to the center is included with a guided backstage tour, which takes you on a fascinating trip from the indoor Angus Bowmer Theatre, through backstage production shops, and all the way to the very heavens above the Elizabethan stage. *Festival box office, 15 S. Pioneer St., tel. 503/482–4331. Admission: $7.50 adults, $5 children 5–17 (under 5 not admitted). Exhibit center admission only: $2 adults, $1.50 children 5–17. Open Oct. 5–June 6, Tues.–Sun. 10:30–1:30; June 7–Oct. 4, Tues.–Sun. 10–4. Tours run Feb.–Oct., Tues.–Sun. at 10 AM; reservations necessary during summer months.*

The Elizabethan Theatre overlooks lovely **Lithia Park,** a 99-acre swath of green in the center of the town. An old-fashioned bandshell, a duck pond, a children's playground, nature trails, and **Ashland Creek** make this a perfect spot for a pretheater picnic. Each June, to mark the opening of the outdoor season, the festival hosts a Renaissance dinner (the Feast of Will) in the park, complete with period music, dancing, and food. Tickets ($12.50 per person) are available through the festival box office (*see above*).

What to See and Do with Children

Columbia River Maritime Museum (*see* Tour 1, *above*).

Ft. Stevens (*see* Tour 1, *above*).

The Hatfield Marine Science Center (*see* Tour 1, *above*).

Highway 101 between **Seal Rock** and **Honeyman State Park** (*see* Tour 1, *above*).

Oregon Vortex/The House of Mystery. This may be just a tourist trap, but then again, who knows? Peculiar kinks in the laws of physics seem to occur in this weathered old house, blithely explained by the management as the result of "a spherical field of force, half above ground and half below." The 45-minute guided tours depart frequently. *Sardine Creek Rd., near Gold Hill (take Exit 234 from I-5), tel. 503/855–1543. Admission: $6 adults, $4 children 5–11. Open Mar.–May and Sept.–Oct., daily 9–4:30; June–Aug, daily 8:30–5:30. Closed Nov.–Feb.*

Mission Mill Village (*see* Tour 2, *above*).

Oregon Caves National Monument (*see* National and State Parks, *below*).

Prehistoric Gardens. On a path that winds deep into the primeval old-growth forest along Oregon's coast, children come face-to-face with detailed, life-size models of such dinosaurs as Tyrannosaurus rex, brontosaurus, ankylosaur, and Plesiosaurus. It may not be *Jurassic Park*, but these painted concrete creatures are faithfully rendered, and give visitors an impressive sense of prehistoric scale. *13 mi south of Port Orford* *on Hwy. 101, tel. 503/332–4463. Admission: $5 adults, $4 senior citizens and children 12–18, $3 ages 5–11.*

Silver Falls State Park (*see* National and State Parks, *below*).

Wildlife Safari. In this 600-acre drive-through wildlife park, you'll motor past lions, tigers, rhinos, the largest collection of cheetahs in North America, elephants, and hundreds of other exotic creatures roaming the plains of Oregon's central valley. Children are especially enthralled with the park's petting zoo. *Follow the signs from I–5, Exit 119, about 6 mi south of Roseburg, tel. 503/679–6761. Admission: $8.95 adults, $7.50 senior citizens, $5.75 children 4–12, plus $1 per vehicle. Open daily 8:30 AM; closing times vary from 4–8 with the season.*

Off the Beaten Track

The Willamette Valley near Salem is known as the **"Bulb Basket of the Nation"** to local farmers. Irises and tulips create fields of brilliant color in near-perfect growing conditions. Two-hundred-acre **Schreiner's Iris Gardens** is especially esteemed. Established in 1925, this rhizome grower now ships bulbs all over the world; during the short spring growing season (mid-May to early June), the 10-acre display gardens are ablaze with such fancifully named varieties as Hello Darkness, Well Endowed, and Ringo. *3625 Quinaby Rd. NE (Brooks Exit off I–5, then West on Brooklake Rd., left on River Rd., then left on Quinaby), Salem, 97303, tel. 503/393-3232. Admission free. Display gardens open 8–dusk during the blooming season.*

National and State Parks

Crater Lake National Park. A cascade peak called Mt. Mazama decapitated itself 6,800 years ago in a volcanic explosion that spewed hot ash and pumice for hundreds of miles. Rain and snowmelt eventually filled the resulting caldera, creating a sapphire-blue lake so clear that sunlight penetrates to a depth of 400 feet. This geological curiosity, the crown jewel of the Cascades and Oregon's most famous tourist attraction, is now Crater Lake National Park. Oregon's only national park is accessible both from Roseburg (via Highway 138, about 85 miles) and from Medford (via Highway 62, about 71 miles). Visitors can drive, bicycle, or hike **Crater Lake's** 25-mile rim; feed the chipmunks along either Godfrey Glen Nature Trail or the 4-mile Castle Crest Wildflower Trail; or take a boat ride out to famous Wizard Island, a perfect miniature cinder cone protruding 760 feet above the surface of the lake. Private boats are not allowed on Crater Lake, so these tours, which leave every two hours (in the summer) from Cleetwood Cove on the lake's north side, offer a unique surface-level view of the caldera. Historic **Crater Lake Lodge,** perched on the rim of the Caldera, is undergoing a complete restoration, which may be finished as early as the summer of 1994. Until it reopens, overnight accommodations are available at the 40-room Forest Service rental-cabin complex at **Annie Creek Canyon,** south of the lake. These accommodations are far from luxurious, however; you might prefer one of the 198 campsites at nearby **Mazama Campground.** The surrounding National Forest campgrounds offer 900 additional sites. Due to conditions caused by the 6,000-foot elevation, access to the park in winter is restricted to the south and west entry roads. *Crater Lake Lodge,*

Box 128, Crater Lake 97604, tel. 503/594–2511. Boat tour cost: $10 adults, $5.50 children. Tours run late June–early Sept. Campsites are not reserved; first-come, first-served camping information available through lodge. MC, V. Moderate.

Oregon Caves National Monument. The "Marble Halls of Oregon," high in the verdant Siskiyou Mountains, have been entrancing visitors since local hunter Elijah Davidson chased a bear into them in 1874. Huge stalagmites and stalactites, the Ghost Room, Paradise Lost, and the River Styx are all part of a half-mile subterranean tour that lasts about 75 minutes. The tour includes more than 200 stairs and is not recommended for anyone who experiences difficulty in walking or has respiratory or coronary problems. The historic **Oregon Caves Chateau** offers food and lodging at the monument May 28–September 30. *20 mi southeast of Cave Jct. (between Ashland and Brookings) on Hwy. 46, tel. 503/592–3400. Admission: $6.75 adults, $3.75 children 6–11. Children 6 and under not allowed in cave; child care is available. Open June 13–Sept. 30, daily 8–7; Oct. 1–Apr. 30, daily 8:30–4; May 1–June 12, daily 9–5.*

Silver Falls State Park. In the lush Cascades, 26 miles east of Salem, shallow Silver Creek roars over the lip of a mossy basalt bowl and into a deep pool far below. The 177-foot South Silver Falls is the main attraction in the 8,700-acre park, the largest state park in Oregon. Thirteen other waterfalls—half of which are more than 100 feet high—are accessible to hikers within the park. There are picnic facilities and a WPA-era day lodge; during the winter, the cross-country skiing is excellent. Follow Highway 22 east to its junction with Highway 214 and follow the signs to Silver Falls. *Headquarters, 20024 Silver Falls Hwy. SE, Sublimity, tel. 503/873–8681. Admission $3 per vehicle May–Sept.*

Waldo Lake. This incredibly pure shield-shape lake situated deep in the old-growth forest, 50 miles east of Eugene, is thought by some to be the cleanest landlocked body of water in the world. The lake is accessible after a short hike, so bring comfortable walking attire. *Take Hwy. 58 to Oakridge, then follow signs northwest to Waldo Lake, no phone.*

Shopping

Shopping Districts/Streets

The Oregon Coast Hemlock Street, the main thoroughfare in **Cannon Beach,** is lined with shops and galleries selling everything from kites to upscale clothing, local artwork, gourmet food, wine, and coffee.

On **Newport's** Bay Boulevard, you'll find the finest group of fresh seafood markets on the coast, as well as wood crafts from **The Wood Gallery** (818 S.W. Bay Blvd., tel. 503/265–6843) and nautical supplies, including fishing equipment, hardware, and gear from **Englund Marine Supply** (424 S.W. Bay Blvd., tel. 503/265–9275).

Willamette Valley/ You'll find a cornucopia of handmade local toys, books, doll-
Wine Country houses, quilts, sweaters, and other items at Salem's **Mission Mill Village Warehouse** (1313 Mill St. SE, tel. 503/585–7012).

Eugene's **5th Street Public Market** (5th and High Sts., tel. 503/
484–0383) crams nearly 100 shops—specializing in everything
from clothing to local art—into a 60-year-old warehouse
surrounding a brick-paved courtyard. Every Saturday between April and Christmas (10–5), local craftsmen, farmers,
and chefs come together to create the weekly **Eugene Saturday
Market** (8th and Oak Sts., tel. 503/686–8885), where you can
buy local artwork, dine cheaply and well, or simply watch the
people go by.

Specialty Stores

Anglers   When you need to replenish your supply of mottled turkey-
wing quills, primed popper bodies, or bleached beaver, the
place to go to is the **Caddis Fly Angling Shop** (168 W. 6th Ave.,
Eugene, tel. 503/342–7005 or 800/825–7005).

Antiques   Oregon's largest permanent antiques show is housed in a
lovingly restored 1910 schoolhouse at the **Lafayette Schoolhouse Antique Mall** (Hwy. 99W, 5 mi north of McMinnville, tel.
503/864–2720). A vast assortment of antiquities, from china
and toys to Native American artifacts, are on sale in a three-
story showroom.

Food   **Josephson's** (106 Marine Dr., Astoria, tel. 503/325–2190 or 800/
772–3474 outside OR) is one of the Oregon Coast's oldest
commercial smokehouses (tours offered), preparing Columbia
River Chinook salmon in the traditional alder-smoked and lox
styles. Smoked shark, tuna, oysters, mussels, sturgeon, scallops, and prawns are also available by the pound or in sealed
gift packs.

Mail-order   **Harry and David's** and **Jackson & Perkins** (2518 S. Pacific Hwy.,
Medford, tel. 503/776–2121 or 800/345–5655) are two of the
largest mail-order companies in the world: Harry and David for
fruit and gift packs; Jackson & Perkins for roses. **Harry and
David's Country Store,** located in the same complex, is a retail
outlet for their products, most of which are grown in the famous Bear Creek Orchards. Free tours leave the store hourly
on the half hour on weekdays.

Sports and the Outdoors

Bicycling

For the past 20 years, Oregon has set aside 1% of its highway
funds for the development and maintenance of bikeways
throughout the state, resulting in one of the most extensive
networks of bicycle trails in the country. Write or call for the
free "Oregon Bicycling Guide" (Bicycle Program Manager,
Oregon Dept. of Transportation, Room 200, Transportation
Bldg., Salem 97310, tel. 503/378–3432). A second excellent
publication, "Mountain Bike Guide to Oregon" (Oregon Parks
and Recreation Dept., 525 Trade St. SE, Salem 97310, tel. 503/
378–6305), costs $5.50, plus postage.

The Oregon Coast   The **Oregon Coast Bike Route** parallels Highway 101 and the
coastline from Astoria to Brookings. There are numerous de-
tours for scenic loops, hikes, and waysides; though the terrain
is far from mountainous, it does have its share of hills and head-

lands. For mountain bikers, the **Oregon Dunes National Recreation Area** near Florence offers a unique challenge.

Willamette Valley/ Eugene is particularly esteemed as a cyclists' town. **Pedal Pow-**
Wine Country **er** (535 High St., downtown Eugene, tel. 503/687–1775) rents
Eugene bikes by the hour, day, or week. The **River Bank Bike Path,** originating in Alton Baker Park on the Willamette's north bank, is a level and leisurely introduction to this exercise-oriented city's two-wheel topography. Also in the park, try the **Prefontaine Trail,** which travels through level fields and forests for 1½ miles.

Yamhill Valley The 25 miles of Highway 18 between Dundee and Grand Ronde, in the Coast Range, roll through the heart of the Yamhill Valley wine country; wide shoulders and relatively light traffic earned the route a "most suitable" rating from the "Oregon Bicycling Guide."

Canoeing and Rafting

There is excellent canoeing on most coastal bays and tidal estuaries and lakes. Virtually all rivers flowing from the Willamette Valley and the I–5 corridor offer memorable rafting and canoeing experiences ranging from a placid float through lush forests to an adrenaline-pumping plunge through roaring maelstroms of rock and frigid water.

For wet-knuckle enthusiasts (rafters), two rivers stand out: the exuberant **McKenzie,** west of Eugene, and the especially challenging **Rogue,** near the California border. Many parts of the Rogue are still true wilderness, with no road access. Deer, bears, eagles, and other wild creatures are abundant here. Many guide services offer overnighters and longer trips, aboard either rafts or powerful jet boats, which roar upstream from Gold Beach on the coast. **Oregon Guides and Packers** (Box 10841, Eugene 97440, tel. 503/683–9552) publishes a free 80-page guide to Oregon guides and will help you find a professional guide service—an absolute necessity on both the McKenzie and the Rogue rivers.

Fishing

The mountains and bountiful rainfall in western Oregon have given birth to some of the finest fishing lakes and rivers in North America. Though overfishing and logging-caused siltation have vastly depleted the runs, many types of fish can still be caught: Native rainbow and sea-run cutthroat trout; wily steelhead reaching 20 pounds and larger; sturgeon; and, greatest prize of all, the fat chinook salmon (weighing up to 50 pounds) that return every spring. Silver and chinook salmon and the delectable Dungeness crab are the prime quarry the entire length of Oregon's shoreline. Steelhead, flounder, sea-run cutthroat trout, red snapper, lingcod, perch, greenling (whose flesh is a startling electric blue), and dozens of other species are accessible from jetties, docks, and riverbanks from Astoria to Brookings.

There are a bewildering number of options available to visiting fishermen, from self-guided boat and shore trips to guided adventures and seagoing charters. Major charter fleets are available from most towns along the coast; the amenities and fruitful waters of Astoria, Reedsport, and Brookings are particularly esteemed. Ocean salmon season begins in earnest in late June and usually runs through mid-September. For information about fishing options in the specific area you'll be visiting, it's best to contact the local chamber of commerce or visitor center (*see* Important Addresses and Numbers in Essential Information, *above*). Although it's hard to go wrong on any of the Coast Range streams or high-mountain lakes, fly-and-bait fishing is internationally famous on the **McKenzie, Umpqua, Rogue,** and **Chetco** rivers. In **Crater Lake,** massive rainbow trout, some 3 feet in length, cruise the depths in profusion. The fish thrive because there is no boat fishing allowed. You'll need to bring your own tackle, and no license is necessary, but you're not allowed to use organic baits that might cloud the lake—it's lure fishing only.

To fish in most areas of Oregon, out-of-state visitors need a yearly ($35.75), 10-day ($21.25), 3-day ($14.75), 2-day ($10), or daily ($5.25) nonresident angler's license; those fishing for salmon and steelhead need an additional salmon/steelhead tag ($5.50), available from any local sporting goods-store.

Golf

Oregon's 136 golf courses run the gamut from layouts designed by such top pros as Robert Trent Jones to easy pitch-and-putt par 3s, in settings ranging from the blue Pacific to high mountain meadows to the sagebrush and lodgepole pine of central Oregon.

The Oregon Coast
Florence
Ocean Dunes Golf Links (3345 Munsel Lake Rd., tel. 503/997–3232), 18 holes.

Gold Beach
Cedar Bend Golf Course (34391 Squaw Valley Rd., tel. 503/247–6911), 9 holes.

Lincoln City
Lakeside Golf & Racquet Club (3245 Clubhouse Dr., tel. 503/994–8442), 18 holes.

Neskowin
Neskowin Beach Golf Course (48405 Hawk St., tel. 503/392–3377), 9 holes.

Newport
Agate Beach Golf Club (4100 N. Coast Hwy., tel. 503/265–7331), 9 holes.

North Bend/
Coos Bay
Kentuck Golf Course (675 Golf Course La., North Bend, tel. 503/756–4464), 18 holes; **Sunset Bay Golf Course** (11001 Cape Arago Hwy., Coos Bay, tel. 503/888–9301), 9 holes.

Reedsport
Forest Hills Golf Club (1 Country Club Dr., tel. 503/271–2626), 9 holes.

Seaside
Seaside Golf Club (451 Ave. U, tel. 503/738–5261), 9 holes.

Tillamook
Alderbrook Golf Club (7300 Alderbrook Rd., tel. 503/842–6413), 18 holes.

Willamette Valley/
Wine Country
Corvallis
Trysting Trees Golf Club (34028 Electric Rd., Corvallis, tel. 503/752–3332), 18 holes; **Golf Club of Oregon** (905 Spring Hill Dr. N, Albany, tel. 503/928–8338), 18 holes; **Pineway Golf Club** (30949 Pineway Rd., Lebanon, tel. 503/258–8919), 9 holes.

Eugene/
Springfield
Fiddler's Green Golf Course (91292 Hwy. 99 N, tel. 503/689–8464), 18 holes; **Laurelwood Golf Course** (2700 Columbia St., tel. 503/687–5321), 9 holes; **Oakway Golf Course** (2000 Cal Young Rd., tel. 503/484–1927), 18 holes; **Riveridge Golf Course** (3800 N. Delta Hwy., tel. 503/345–9160), 18 holes; **McKenzie**

River Golf Course (41723 Madrone St., Springfield, tel. 503/896–3454), 9 holes; **Emerald Valley Golf Course** (83293 Dale Kuni Rd., Creswell, tel. 503/895-2174), 18 holes.

Medford/ Ashland **Bear Creek Golf Course** (2355 S. Pacific Hwy., Medford, tel. 503/773–1822), 9 holes; **Cedar Links Golf Course** (3155 Cedar Links Dr., tel. 503/773–4373), 18 holes; **Oak Knoll Golf Course** (3070 Hwy. 66, Ashland, tel. 503/482–4311), 9 holes.

Newberg/ McMinnville **Bayou Golf & Country Club** (9301 S.W. Bayou Dr., McMinnville, tel. 503/472–4651), 9 holes; **Riverwood Golf Club** (21050 S.E. Riverwood Rd., Dundee, tel. 503/864–2667), 9 holes.

Roseburg **Knolls Golf Club** (1919 Recreation La., Sutherlin, tel. 503/459–4422), 18 holes.

Salem **Salem Golf Club** (2025 Golf Course Rd., tel. 503/363–6652), 18 holes; **McNary Golf Club** (6255 River Rd. N, Keizer, tel. 503/393–4653), 18 holes; **Battle Creek Golf Club** (6161 Commercial St. SE, tel. 503/585–1402), 18 holes.

Skiing

Cross-country The Willamette Valley itself is temperate and generally receives only a few inches of snow a year, but the **Coast Range,** the **Cascades,** and, farther south, the **Siskiyous** are all Nordic skiers' paradises, crisscrossed by hundreds of miles of trails. Every major ski resort in the state offers Nordic skiing; you can also set off down your choice of Forest Service trails and logging roads. If you're unsure where to begin, the **City of Eugene Parks and Recreation Department** (tel. 503/687–5329) takes cross-country snow campers on overnight loops around both **Crater Lake** and **Waldo Lake.**

See also **Willamette Pass** and **Mt. Bailey,** *below.*

Downhill **Willamette Pass.** Though most Oregon downhillers congregate around Mt. Hood and Mt. Bachelor (*see* Chapter 3, Portland), there is excellent skiing to the south as well. Willamette Pass, 6,666 feet high in the Cascades Mountains, packs an annual average snowfall of 300 inches atop 18 runs. With a vertical drop of 1,563 feet, there are four triple chairs and one double chair; lift lines are refreshingly short. Other facilities include 13 miles of Nordic trails, Nordic and downhill rentals, repairs, instruction, ski shop, day care, bar, and restaurant. *Hwy. 58, 69 mi southeast of Eugene, tel. 503/484–5030. Open Nov.–Dec. 31, Wed.–Sun. 9–4; Jan. 1–Apr., Wed.–Sat. 9–9, Sun. 9–4; Apr.–June (depending on snow conditions), weekends only, 9–4.*

Mt. Ashland. This cone-shaped Siskiyou peak has some of the steepest runs in the state. There are two triple and two double chair lifts, accommodating a vertical drop of 1,150 feet; the longest of the 22 runs is 1 mile. Facilities include rentals, repair, instruction, ski shop, restaurant, and bar. *18 mi southwest of downtown Ashland; follow the signs from I–5, tel. 503/482–2897 or 800/547–8052. Open winter, daily 9–4; night skiing Thurs.–Sat. 4–10.*

Snowcat Skiing **Mt. Bailey.** If you *really* crave solitude (and detest lift lines), this is the guide service for you. First you ride in heated snowcats to the summit of Mt. Bailey, an 8,300-foot peak not far from Crater Lake. Then you attack the virgin powder on 4 miles of runs, with a vertical drop of 3,000 feet. The excursions are limited to 12 skiers a day, but be warned—this is downhill for advanced intermediates and experts only. Tours leave Diamond Lake Resort daily at 7 AM. Facilities at the resort include three restaurants, a bar, lodging, downhill and Nordic ski rentals, and Nordic trails. *Diamond Lake Resort, 76 mi east of Roseburg on Hwy. 138, tel. 503/793–3333. Reservations required. Season runs Nov.–May.*

Spectator Sports

Baseball The **Eugene Emeralds,** the Kansas City Royals' Northwest League (Class A) affiliate, play 38 home games at **Civic Stadium** (2077 Willamette St., Eugene, tel. 503/342–5367) from June to September.

Basketball The **Oregon State Beavers** play their home games at **Gill Coliseum** (26th and Washington Sts., on the OSU campus, Corvallis, tel. 503/737–4455). The **University of Oregon's Ducks** seldom fare as well as the Beavers, but seeing a home game at the eccentrically designed, and somewhat claustrophobic, **MacArthur Court** (1601 University St., on the U of O's campus, Eugene, tel. 800/932–3668) is a real experience.

Football The **University of Oregon Ducks** play their home games at **Autzen Stadium** (2700 Centennial Blvd., tel. 800/932–3668). The **Oregon State Beavers** play theirs at **Parker Stadium** (26th and Western Sts., on the OSU campus, tel. 503/737–4455).

Beaches

Virtually the entire 300-mile coastline of Oregon is a clean, quiet white-sand beach, publicly owned and accessible to all. A word of caution: The Pacific off the Oregon Coast is not the mild-mannered playmate it becomes in southern California. It is 45°–55°F year-round, a temperature that can be described as brisk at best and numbing at worst. Tides and undertows are strong, and swimming is not advised. When fishing from the rocks, always watch for sneaker or rogue waves, and never play on logs near the water—they roll in the surf without warning and have cost numerous lives over the years. Above all, watch children closely while they play in or near the ocean.

Everyone has a favorite beach, but Bandon's **Face Rock Beach** is justly renowned as perhaps the state's loveliest for walking, while the beach at **Sunset Bay State Park** on Cape Arago, with its protective reefs and encircling cliffs, is one of the few places along the Oregon Coast where you can swim without worrying about the currents and undertows, although the water temperature is still on the chilly side. Nearby, **Oregon Dunes National Recreation Area** adds extra cachet to Florence's beaches. Fossils, clams, mussels, and other aeons-old marine creatures, easily dug from soft sandstone cliffs, make **Beverly Beach State Park** (5 miles north of Newport) a favorite with young beachcombers.

Dining and Lodging

In wine districts everywhere, eating and living well is high on the list of priorities. The Oregon wine country, which includes the Willamette and Rogue valleys from Newberg to Ashland, is no exception. The regional gastronomy is enlivened by an extensive collection of excellent ethnic restaurants, from Italian to Vietnamese to Eastern European, as well as by some expert practitioners of nouvelle cuisine. Eugene, with its longtime emphasis on good living, and Ashland, with its world-famous Oregon Shakespeare Festival, are particularly noted for the excellence and diversity of their restaurants.

Lodging choices are equally varied. In addition to the ever-popular and flourishing number of bed-and-breakfasts, Wild West resorts (complete with buffalo and stagecoach), rustic fisherman's lodges, and plenty of chain facilities are available in all price ranges.

The Oregon Shakespeare Festival has stimulated one of the most extensive networks of B&Bs in the country—more than 50 in all. High season for Ashland-area B&Bs is June–October. Expect to pay $85–$110 per night, which includes breakfast for two; during the off-season, $50–$80. Deciding which one to patronize can be a bewildering task. The **Ashland B&B Clearinghouse** (tel. 503/488–0338) and **Ashland B&B Reservation Network** (tel. 503/482–2337) offer free, unbiased advice to connect travelers with more than 450 options available in the area.

Highly recommended restaurants and lodgings are indicated by a star ★.

Dining	Category	Cost*
	Expensive	over $20
	Moderate	$11–$19
	Inexpensive	$5–$10

per person, not including tip and beverages

Lodging	Category	Cost*
	Expensive	over $95
	Moderate	$50–$95
	Inexpensive	$30–$50

All prices are for a standard double room, excluding tax of 6%–9%, depending on the location of the property.

The Oregon Coast

Astoria
Dining

Pier 11 Feed Store Restaurant & Lounge. Housed in a renovated warehouse located on a pier, the windows of this spacious restaurant overlook the Columbia River. The tables are set with fine linen and crystal, and the friendly staff serves hearty and abundant fish, steaks, and prime rib. The cioppino is a massive helping packed with clams, crab, oysters, shrimp, and fish, and it is large enough to feed three people. *Foot of 11th St., tel. 503/*

325–0279. Reservations accepted. Dress: casual. D, MC, V. Moderate.

Columbian Café. The locals love this small, unpretentious diner with its tongue-in-cheek south-of-the-border decor that's heavy on the chili pepper–shaped Christmas lights and religious icons. Fresh, simple food—crepes with broccoli, cheese, and homemade salsa for lunch; grilled salmon and pasta with lemon-cream sauce for dinner—is served by a modest staff that usually includes the owner. Come early, though, since this place always draws a crowd. *1114 Marine Dr., tel. 503/325–2233. No reservations. Dress: casual. No credit cards. Closed Sun.; Mon.–Tues. dinner. Inexpensive.*

Lodging **Red Lion Inn.** The only north-coast outlet of this reliable regional chain sits right on the Columbia River, beneath the Astoria Bridge; there's a view of the river and the bridge from the guest-room balconies. The small rooms and public areas are decorated in soothing earth tones. *400 Industry St., 97103, tel. 503/325–7373 or 800/547–8010. 124 rooms. Facilities: restaurant, lounge, cable TV. AE, D, DC, MC, V. Moderate.*

★ **Franklin Street Station Bed & Breakfast.** The ticking of grandfather clocks and the mellow marine light filtered through leaded-glass windows set the tone at this quiet, velvet-upholstered Victorian, built in 1900 on the slopes above downtown Astoria. Each of the six immaculate guest rooms has a private bath. Breakfasts are huge, hot, and satisfying; there's always a plate of goodies and a pot of coffee in the kitchen. *1140 Franklin St., 97103, tel. 503/325–4314. 5 rooms. MC, V. Moderate.*

Grandview Bed & Breakfast. This huge, turreted mansion lives up to its name, and then some—decks and telescopes look out over Astoria, with the Columbia River and Washington beyond. The interior is bright and airy, with scrubbed hardwood floors and comfortable, lace-filled rooms. The breakfast specialty is bagels with cream cheese and smoked salmon from Josephson's (*see* Shopping, *above*). *1574 Grand Ave., 97103, tel. 503/325–5555 or 800/488–3250. 8 units (3 1-bedroom units, 3 2-bedroom units) with private bath. D, MC, V. Moderate.*

Bandon **Bandon Boatworks.** A local favorite, this romantic jetty-side
Dining eatery serves up its seafood, steaks, prime rib, and rack of lamb with a view of the Coquille River harbor and the historic Bandon Lighthouse. Try the panfried oysters flamed with brandy and anisette, or the quick-sautéed seafood combination that's heavy on scampi and scallops. *275 Lincoln SW, tel. 503/347–2111. Reservations suggested. Dress: casual. AE, D, MC, V. Closed Jan. on Mon. Moderate.*

Lord Bennett's. Some come to this modern cliff-top restaurant for the rich food; the prawns sautéed with butter, brandy, cream, and mustard are especially fine. Even better is the house lobster, sautéed with shallots, mushrooms, brandy, and cream, then broiled in hollandaise sauce. Most guests, however, come primarily for the sunsets seen through picture windows that overlook Face Rock Beach. The lounge features live music on weekends, and Sunday breakfasts are particularly good. *1695 Beach Loop Rd., tel. 503/347–3663. Reservations suggested. Dress: casual. AE, D, MC, V. Moderate.*

Lodging **Inn at Face Rock.** This modern, cheerful resort sits just across Beach Loop Drive from Bandon's fabulous walking beach. The rooms are spacious, soothing, and well furnished; nearly half have ocean views. The interior is clean and contemporary, decorated in a cream-and-sand color scheme, and some rooms have kitchenettes and fireplaces. *3225 Beach Loop Rd., 97411, tel. 503/347–9441. Facilities: restaurant, bar, spa, 9-hole golf course, some fireplace and kitchen units available, cable TV. AE, D, DC, MC, V. Moderate–Expensive.*

Brookings **Mama's Authentic Italian Food.** The decor is down-home
Dining trattoria, styled to accompany the homestyle Italian food served here. The tender pasta, crusty pizza, and slow-simmered sauces keep this small and simply furnished restaurant always busy. *703 Chetco Ave., tel. 503/469–7611. Reservations accepted. Dress: casual. AE, MC, V. Inexpensive.*

Lodging **The Chetco Inn.** Not to be confused with the Chetco River Inn (*see below*), this once-grand hotel was the destination of choice for a Who's Who of Hollywood stars in the 30s. It's a bit rough around the edges these days, but is nearing the end of a lengthy and detailed renovation. It's still not the Ritz, but it's a good choice for fishermen because of its central location and reasonable rates. *417 Fern St., 97415, tel. 503/469–5347. 41 rooms, some with kitchens. D, MC, V. Inexpensive.*

Dining and Lodging **Chetco River Inn.** Thirty-five acres of private forest surround
★ this splendidly remote inn, located 17 miles up the pale-blue Chetco River from Brookings. There are three guest rooms (all with private bath), plus a library, a comfortable common room, and a crackling fireplace. Guests come here to relax, hike, hunt wild mushrooms, and savor the gourmet dinners cooked by the host. The rooms feature thick comforters and panoramic views of river and forest; hearty dinners might star a nickel-bright salmon fresh from the stream. *21202 High Prairie Rd. (follow North Bank Rd; the road follows the north bank of the Chetco River), 97415, tel. 503/469–8128 (radio phone) or 800/327–2688. MC, V. Moderate.*

Cannon Beach **The Bistro.** Cannon Beach's most romantic restaurant is small
Dining and filled with flowers, candlelight, and classical music. The
★ menu features imaginative, Continental-influenced renditions of fresh local seafood dishes in a four-course fixed-price menu; expect monstrous scampi and Pacific seafood stew to appear as specials. This 12-table no-smoking establishment is not inexpensive, but it is arguably the best meal in town. *263 N. Hemlock St., tel. 503/436–2661. Reservations suggested. Dress: casual. MC, V. Expensive.*

Dooger's. The original Dooger's in Seaside, as well as the newer branch a few miles south in Cannon Beach, are both much beloved by local families. The seafood is fresh and expertly prepared, and the contemporary decor—warm floral tones and wood paneling—makes this a comfortable place in which to enjoy a meal. The creamy clam chowder may also be the best on the coast. *505 Broadway, tel. 503/738–3773; 1371 S. Hemlock St., tel. 503/436–2225. No reservations. Dress: casual. MC, V. No smoking. Inexpensive–Moderate.*

Lazy Susan Café. This no-smoking establishment is the place to come for breakfast in Cannon Beach, with its cheerful, wood-and-oilcloth decor. Excellent entrées include a substantial order of waffles topped with fruit and orange syrup, oatmeal, quiche, and omelets. Whatever your choice, don't leave without tasting the fresh-baked muffins and home fries. *126 N. Hemlock St., in Coaster Sq., tel. 503/436–2816. No reservations. Dress: casual. No credit cards. Closed Tues. and dinner.*

Lodging **Hallmark Resort at Cannon Beach.** Cozy rooms with fireplaces, spas, and the best views in Cannon Beach make this triple-decker oceanfront resort the destination of choice for the north coast. Rooms, adorned with oak-tiled baths and spacious balconies, favor a soothing color scheme. Their large size makes them ideal for families or couples looking for a romantic splurge. *1400 S. Hemlock St., 97110, tel. 503/436-1566 or 800/345-5676. 131 rooms, 5 oceanfront rental homes. Facilities: restaurant, lounge, indoor pool, sauna, spa, weight room, children's pool, cable TV, in-room refrigerators, covered parking, free newspaper delivered daily, laundry facilities. AE, D, DC, MC, V. Expensive-Very Expensive.*

Webb's Scenic Surf. This quiet, small family-operated hotel is a throwback to simpler times in Cannon Beach, before trendiness translated into big resorts and $500 weekends. Located on the beach, Webb's provides panoramic views of the ocean. The austerely furnished rooms, many with kitchens and fireplaces, are functional, clean, and have comfortable beds. For the budget traveler, this is the best deal in town, but call ahead—reservations are a must. *255 N. Larch St., 97110, tel. 503/436-2706. 14 rooms. Facilities: kitchens, cable TV. MC, V. Moderate.*

Charleston **The Portside Restaurant.** This unpretentious place overlooking
Dining the busy Charleston boat basin is a gem, with fresh fish brought to the kitchen straight from the dock outside. The nautical decor reinforces the view of the harbor through the restaurant's picture windows. Preparation is simple, usually with a touch of garlic butter, tomato, white wine, or cream. Try the steamed Dungeness crab with drawn butter or, better, come Friday night for the scrumptious all-you-can-eat seafood buffet. *8001 Kingfisher Rd. (follow Cape Arago Hwy. from Coos Bay), tel. 503/888-5544. Reservations accepted. Dress: casual. AE, DC, MC, V. Moderate.*

Coos Bay **The Blue Heron Bistro.** You'll get subtle preparations of local
Dining seafood, chicken, and homemade pasta with an international
★ flair at this busy bistro. There are no flat spots on the far-ranging menu; the innovative soups and desserts are also excellent. The skylit, tile-floor dining room seats about 70 amid natural wood and blue linen. The outside seating area's blue awnings and colorful Bavarian window boxes add a festive touch. For breakfast, the omelets are as filling as they are innovative. *100 Commercial St., tel. 503/267-3933. Reservations suggested for large groups. Dress: casual. MC, V. Moderate.*

Kum-Yon's. If you have a hankering for something Oriental but can't decide on a cuisine, this small multiethnic restaurant on Coos Bay's main drag will fit the bill. You'll find everything from sushi to *kung pao* shrimp to Korean short ribs on the voluminous menu. The preparations are average, and the ambience resembles nothing so much as a Seoul Burger King, but the portions are satisfying and the prices are ridiculously low. *835 S. Broadway, tel. 503/269-2662. Reservations accepted. Dress: casual. MC, V. Inexpensive.*

Lodging **This Olde House B&B.** The charm and care that have gone into
★ the creation of this sprawling Victorian, four blocks up the hill from downtown Coos Bay, are matched only by the charm and warmth of its owners. Each room is a treasure trove of antiques and oddities collected over the past 40 years. You'll never sleep better, or eat better when you awake; the breakfast, including

heavenly French toast with fresh berries, homemade caramel syrup, and great coffee, is included in the room rate. *202 Alder Ave., 97420, tel. 503/267–5224. 4 rooms, 1 with private bath. No credit cards; personal checks accepted. Moderate.*

Florence **Bridgewater Seafood Restaurant.** The venerably salty am-
Dining bience of Florence's photogenic bayfront Old Town permeates this spacious fish house. Fresh-caught seafood is the mainstay at this creaky-floored Victorian-era restaurant. On any given night, there are 25–30 fish dishes from which to choose. Try the shrimp and crab enchiladas, a house specialty. *1297 Bay St., tel. 503/997–9405. Reservations accepted. Dress: casual. MC, V. Moderate.*

The Windward Inn. One of the south coast's most elegant eateries, this tightly run ship prides itself on its vast menu, master wine list, home-baked breads and desserts, and array of fresh seafood. The rich, grand-piano atmosphere is, perhaps a bit florid, but the prices are quite reasonable. During the summer months, there's live jazz and classical music in the courtyard lounge on Friday and Saturday nights. *3757 Hwy. 101 N, tel. 503/997–8243. Reservations suggested. Dress: casual but neat. AE, D, MC, V. Moderate–Expensive.*

Lodging **Driftwood Shores Surfside Resort Inn.** The chief amenity at this resort is the location, just north of Florence and directly above one of the longest, emptiest walking beaches on the coast. The rooms and public areas fall a bit short of elegance but they're comfortable, and equipped with kitchens. Some rooms have fireplaces and balconies. *88416 1st Ave. (take Heceta Beach Rd. from Hwy. 101, about 3 mi north of Florence), 97439, tel. 503/997–8263 or 800/824–8774 outside OR. 136 rooms. Facilities: restaurant, bar, indoor pool, spa, sauna, in-room kitchens in most units, cable TV. AE, D, DC, MC, V. Moderate.*

Gleneden Beach **Chez Jeanette.** This whitewashed, French country cottage nes-
Dining tles in the shore pine between Highway 101 and the ocean, and seems a continent or so away from the frenetic tourism of downtown Lincoln City. The atmosphere is quiet, with fireplace, antiques, linen, and crystal. The food is wonderful: Try the carpetbagger steak, a thick fillet stuffed with tiny local oysters, wrapped in bacon and sauced with crème fraîche, scallions, spinach, and bacon. The rest of the menu puts a Parisian spin on the local bounty from the sea, sky, and pasture. *7150 Old Hwy. 101 (turn west from Hwy. 101 at the Salishan entrance; take the first left and go ¼ mi south), tel. 503/764–3434. Reservations necessary. Dress: casual but neat. AE, MC, V. Closed lunch; Sun.–Mon. Labor Day–June. Expensive.*

★ **Gourmet Dining Room at Salishan.** The Salishan resort's main dining room, a multilevel expanse of hushed waiters, hillside ocean views, and snow-white linen, has built an enviable reputation on its showy Continental cuisine. House specialties include fresh local fish, game, beef, and lamb; the fettuccine with fat scallops and salmon caviar is heavenly. By all means make a selection from the wine cellar, the largest in the state. *Hwy. 101 at Gleneden Beach, tel. 503/764–2371. Reservations advised. Jacket and tie suggested. AE, D, DC, MC, V. Closed lunch. Expensive.*

Lodging **Salishan Lodge.** For most visitors, this is *the* resort on the Oregon Coast. From the soothing, silvered-cedar ambience of its guest rooms, divided into eight complex units nestled into a 750-acre hillside forest preserve, Salishan embodies a uniquely

Oregonian elegance. Each of the quiet, spacious rooms has a wood-burning fireplace, a balcony , and artwork by Northwest artists. Add to this setting an impressive collections of wines (there are 20,000 bottles in the cellar here), original art, and you'll understand why the timeless atmosphere also carries what may well be the steepest price tag on the coast. *Hwy. 101 at Gleneden Beach, 97388, tel. 503/764–2371 or 800/547–6500 outside OR. 205 rooms. Facilities: 3 restaurants, bar, private beach access, indoor pool, spas and saunas, indoor and outdoor tennis courts, 18-hole golf course, men's and women's weight rooms, children's playground, conference facilities. AE, D, DC, MC, V. Expensive.*

Gold Beach
Dining

The Captain's Table. You can trust this popular local eatery for ultratender Midwest corn-fed beef, a solid touch with fresh seafood, and a nice view out over the ocean. The antique-filled dining room is on the smallish side, providing a cozy atmosphere; the service is excellent. *1295 S. Ellensburg Ave., tel. 503/247–6308. No reservations. Dress: casual. D, MC, V. Closed lunch. Moderate.*

Lodging

Ireland's Rustic Lodges. Seven original one- and two-bedroom cabins filled with rough-hewn charm, plus 28 newer motel rooms and two new cabins, are available in this spectacularly landscaped setting. Some units have fireplaces and a deck overlooking the sea, with venerable furnishings in a black, brown, rust, and beige color scheme. For the price, you can't beat this accommodation. *1120 S. Ellensburg Ave., 97444, tel. 503/247–7718. 40 units; no-smoking rooms available. Facilities: decks, some fireplaces, ocean views. No credit cards; personal checks accepted. Inexpensive–Moderate.*

Dining and Lodging
★

Tu Tu Tun Lodge. This famous, richly appointed fishing resort (pronounced "Too Tootin'") sits right on the clear-blue Rogue River, 7 miles upriver from Gold Beach. This is a small place, and all units were remodeled in 1992 and brought up to a new level of elegance. Some now have hot tubs, others have fireplaces, and a few have both. Private decks overlook the river and the surrounding old-growth forest. Two deluxe rooms have tall picture windows, tiled bath, and river-view outdoor soaking tub. The lodge dining room serves rib-sticking breakfast, lunch, and dinner; the latter are open to nonguests with reservations and consist of a five-course fixed-price meal that changes nightly. Portions are dauntingly huge. *96550 N. Bank Rogue, 97444, tel. 503/247–6664. 16 rooms, 2 suites, one 3-bedroom house. Facilities: restaurant, bar, heated outdoor pool, 4-hole golf course, horseshoes, hiking, boat dock and ramp, salmon and steelhead fishing, jet-boat excursions. MC, V. Expensive.*

Lincoln City
Dining
★

Lighthouse Brew Pub. This westernmost outpost of the Portland-based McMenamin brothers' microbrewery empire has the same virtues as their other establishments: fresh local ales, including several brewed on the premises; good unpretentious sandwiches, burgers, and salads; cheerfully eccentric decor— of particular note is the psychedelic artwork by Northwest painters. Be sure to try a house specialty, the stout ale milkshake. Families are welcome. *4157 N. Hwy. 101, tel. 503/994–7238. No reservations. Dress: casual. MC, V. Inexpensive.*

Lodging

Ester Lee Motel. Perched on a bluff overlooking the cold green Pacific through panoramic windows, this small whitewashed motel has attracted a devoted repeat business through a simple, elegant approach to the innkeeping business. For the price, there are some nice amenities, including wood-burning fireplaces and full kitchens. Be sure to request a unit in the older section of the hotel; the rooms are larger, furnished in rustic knotty pine, with brick fireplaces and picture windows. *3803 S.W. Hwy. 101, 97367, tel. 503/996–3606. 54 units. Facilities: kitchens, cable TV. D, MC, V. Moderate.*

Manzanita Dining **Blue Sky Café.** There is a quirky, cheerful atmosphere here, conveyed through the eclectic table furnishings, the jungle of plants, stained glass, and butcher paper–covered tables. Menu specialties such as pesto prawns; creamy homemade soups such as ham, apple, and blue-cheese bisque; and memorably rich desserts make this tiny hole-in-the-wall restaurant worth a trip from Cannon Beach or Tillamook. *154 Laneda St., tel. 503/ 368–5712. Reservations accepted. Dress: casual. MC, V. Closed breakfast and lunch. Moderate.*

Newport Dining **Tables of Content.** This restaurant at the outstanding Sylvia Beach Hotel offers a well-plotted eight-course, fixed-price ($16.50 per person) menu that changes nightly. Chances are the main character will be fresh local seafood, perhaps a moist grilled salmon fillet in sauce Dijonnaise, with a supporting cast of sautéed vegetables, fresh-baked breads, rice pilaf, and a decadent dessert. The interior is functional and unadorned, and features family-size tables, but, of course, decor isn't the reason to come here. *267 N.W. Cliff St. (from Hwy. 101, turn west on 3rd St., to Cliff St.), tel. 503/265–5428. Reservations necessary. Dress: casual. AE, MC, V. Closed lunch. Moderate–Expensive.*

Don Petrie's Italian Food Co. A little hole-in-the-sand place near the beach, with a strong local following, this tidy, Spartan restaurant serves some of the best seafood lasagna you'll ever eat. Get there early, especially on weekends, as the place fills up with locals. *613 N.W. 3rd St., tel. 503/265–3663. No reservations. Dress: casual. MC, V. Moderate.*

Mo's. There are several Mo's restaurants, scattered from Lincoln City to Coos Bay. All are always busy, attesting to the quality of the food and the friendly, hardworking staff. Mo's chowder, a creamy, velvet-textured potion flavored with bacon and onion and studded with tender potatoes and clams, is famous; her grilled oysters and cioppino are merely delicious. The decor is hoary and nautical, but never mind—just consider yourself lucky to get a table. Children love this place for its great chowder and picnic-table informality. *622 S.W. Bay Blvd., tel. 503/265–2979; 860 S.W. 51st St., Lincoln City, tel. 503/996–2535; 1436 Bay St., Florence, tel. 503/997–2185; 700 S. Broadway, Coos Bay, tel. 503/269–1323. No reservations. Dress: casual. D, MC, V. Inexpensive.*

Lodging **The Embarcadero.** This luxurious bayfront resort has everything you're looking for in coastal accommodations. The location—at the east end of Bay Boulevard—is outstanding, offering great views over Yaquina Bay and its graceful bridge. The rooms and public areas are modern and posh, heavily decorated with rough-hewn native woods and ceramic tiles. Spacious suites have one or two bedrooms, with bayside deck, fireplace, and kitchen. All the rooms have bay views; all have been freshly refurbished. *1000 S.E. Bay Blvd., 97365, tel. 503/ 265–8521 or 800/547–4779. 136 rooms. Facilities: restaurant,* *bar, indoor pool, sauna, spa, private marina, boats, fishing rentals, decks, harbor views, kitchen and fireplace units available, private crabbing and fishing dock. AE, D, DC, MC, V. Moderate–Expensive.*

★ **The Sylvia Beach Hotel.** Book a reservation far in advance for this unique beachfront hotel; some weekends are fully booked as much as a year in advance. The owners have restored this 1912-vintage hostelry along a literary theme; each of the 20 antique-filled guest rooms is named for a famous writer, and no two are decorated alike. The Poe Room, for instance, sports a pendulum swinging over the bed. The Christie, Twain, and Colette rooms are the most luxurious; all have fireplaces, decks, and great ocean views. Upstairs is a well-stocked, split-level library, with decks, a fireplace, slumbering cats, and too-comfortable chairs. Complimentary mulled wine is served there nightly at 10. And in the morning, a hearty breakfast buffet (included in the room rate) with homemade pastries, cereals, and hot entrée is offered. *267 N.W. Cliff St., 97365, tel. 503/ 265–5428. Facilities: restaurant, library. No smoking allowed inside; no TVs or phones. AE, MC, V. Moderate.*

Waldport **The Cliff House Bed-and-Breakfast.** The view from Yaquina
Lodging John Point (once an Indian chief's headquarters), on which this
★ extraordinary B&B sits, is exquisite. The huge romantic old house, once a bordello, is filled with an Aladdin's trove of antiques, a mishmash of Oriental and European items, including a 500-year-old sleigh bed that once adorned a French manor house. Lacquered screens, Chinese porcelains, deep, comfortable furnishings, and a garden filled with fairy lights complete the ambience. The breakfasts are as sumptuous as the surroundings. *1 block west on Adahi Rd. off Hwy. 101, 97394, tel. 503/563–2506. 4 rooms with private bath. Facilities: hot tub. MC, V. Moderate.*

Yachats **La Serre.** Don't be dismayed by the vaguely steak-and-salad-
Dining bar ambience at this skylit, plant-filled restaurant—the chef's
★ deft touch with impeccably fresh seafood attracts knowledgeable diners from as far away as Florence and Newport. Try the tender geoduck clam, breaded with Parmesan cheese and flash-fried in lemon-garlic butter. A reasonably priced wine list and mouth-watering desserts complete the package. La Serre also serves Sunday brunch. *2nd and Beach Sts., tel. 503/547–3420. Reservations recommended. Dress: casual. AE, MC, V. Closed lunch and Tues. Moderate.*

New Morning Coffeehouse. Exquisite fresh-baked breads and desserts, salads, sandwiches, and fine coffee make this airy sunlit café worth a stop. The spacious new deck makes for pleasant outdoor seating on fine days. *4th St. and Hwy. 101, tel. 503/547–3848. No reservations. Dress: casual. No credit cards. Closed dinner; Mon.–Tues. Oct.–June. Inexpensive.*

Lodging **Ziggurat.** You'll have to see this four-story cedar-and-glass pyramid, rising from the tidal grasslands, to believe it; and you'll need to spend a night or two here, serenaded by the wind and the sea, to fully appreciate it. Odd angles, Scandinavian furnishings, and artworks gathered from the owner's world travels lend an eccentric but welcoming air. Ask for the fourth-floor master bedroom if it's available, because the best views in the house make it the most romantic. One of the ground-floor rooms has its own sauna. *95330 Hwy. 101, 97498, tel. 503/547–*

3925. 3 rooms, all with private bath. No credit cards. No smoking inside. Moderate–Expensive.

Dining and Lodging **The Adobe.** Yachats is a beautiful and relaxed alternative to some of the more intensely touristy communities to the north, and this quiet, unassuming resort motel is right at home here. Many of the rooms have wood-burning fireplaces, and all have the low-key, knotty-pine, high-ceiling ambience you look for in a coastal getaway. Rooms are on the smallish side but warm and inviting, with high-beamed ceilings and picture windows framing noble views. Recent renovation has added 30 new guest rooms, as well as a handsome new lobby. The Adobe Restaurant offers sweeping views and quality Continental cuisine. The loft above the bar offers a panoramic vantage for storm- and whale-watching. *1555 Hwy. 101, 97498, tel. 503/547–3141 or 800/522–3623. 90 units. Facilities: restaurant, bar, spa, sauna, cable TV, refrigerators, coffee makers. Reservations accepted. Dress: casual. AE, D, DC, MC, V. Moderate.*

Willamette Valley/Wine Country

Ashland **Chateaulin.** One of southern Oregon's most romantic res-
Dining   taurants occupies a little ivy-covered storefront a block from
★   the Shakespeare Festival center, and dispenses elegant French food, local wine, and impeccable service with equal facility. Try the fresh loin of lamb with a sauce of balsamic vinegar, shallots, veal stock, and cream, accompanied by a bottle of Ponzi Pinot Noir. *50 E. Main St., tel. 503/482–2264. Reservations necessary, especially during Shakespeare season (June–Oct.). Dress: casual but neat; tie is acceptable. AE, DC, MC, V. Closed lunch. Expensive.*

Gepetto's. Kids love this unpretentious local favorite, open daily for breakfast, lunch and dinner. The vaguely Italian menu features hearty renditions of standard pasta dishes, as well as delicious and unusual sandwiches, salads, and soups. The staff is friendly and fast-moving. Try the fresh-grilled marinated turkey sandwich, served on the crispy house cheese bread. *345 E. Main, tel. 503/482–1138. Dress: casual. Reservations recommended. MC, V. Inexpensive–Moderate.*

Thai Pepper. Spicy Thai-style curries and stir-fries are the specialties at this elegantly appointed restaurant perched above musical Ashland Creek. With an interior filled with local art, rattan, linen, and crystal, the restaurant feels like a French café in downtown Bangkok. The house special is spicy curry, but try the coconut prawns as well as the Thai beef-salad appetizer for starters. *84 N. Main St., tel. 503/482–8058. Reservations suggested. Dress: casual. MC, V. Closed lunch Sun.–Mon. Moderate.*

Rogue Brewery & Public House. Ashland's first brew-pub (a no-smoking establishment indoors) serves pizza and other hearty pub food, as well as a rotating selection of 4–6 ales brewed on the premises, including Rogue Golden, Ashland Amber, and Shakespeare Stout. Two decks overhang the creek, a pleasant venue for ale and conversation during Ashland's warm summer evenings. *31 B Water St., tel. 503/488–5061. No reservations. Dress: casual. MC, V. Inexpensive.*

Lodging **Best Western Bard's Inn.** If you're looking for a nicely appointed commercial hotel, close to the theaters but not too expensive, this 79-unit property fits the bill. The pool's a little small if you've got kids along, but there are Rogue Valley views from every window. Inside, original artwork, created by contemporary local artists, hangs on the walls. The rooms, though on the small side, are freshly furnished in oak and knotty pine and neutral tones. *132 N. Main St., 97520, tel. 503/482–0049 or 800/ 528–1234. Facilities: restaurant, bar, outdoor pool, hot tub, in-room refrigerators. AE, D, DC, MC, V. Moderate–Expensive, depending on season (summer is most expensive).*

★ **The Mt. Ashland Inn.** Deserving special mention, this is one of the most unusual B&Bs in the area. The 5,000-square-foot lodge was hand-built from cedar logs cut from the owners' 160-acre property, located just a mile or two from the summit ski area on Mt. Ashland. The views of Mt. Shasta and the rest of the Siskiyou Mountains are as magnificent as the forested setting; the Pacific Crest Trail runs through the parking lot. On the inside, a huge stone fireplace, hand-stitched quilts, and natural wood provide welcoming warmth. *550 Mt. Ashland Rd. (take Exit 6 from I–5 and follow the signs toward the ski area), 97520, tel. 503/482–8707. 5 rooms with private bath, plus separate guest house with soaking tub, small meeting room. MC, V. Moderate–Expensive.*

Dining and Lodging **Winchester Country Inn.** Another favorite with locals and knowledgeable visitors, this 1886-vintage restaurant/inn, with guest rooms upstairs, serves superb food from a small but imaginative menu. The duck à la Bigarde (roast duck in a sauce of duck stock, caramel, brandy, and fresh fruit) is ambrosial; the homemade scones, crab Benedict, and duck hash with orange hollandaise, served for Sunday brunch, are equally memorable. Set among manicured gardens, the airy, high-windowed dining rooms lend a feeling of casual elegance. *35 S. 2nd St., 97520, tel. 503/488–1113 or 800/972–4991. 7 rooms, all with private bath, 2 suites in separate cottages. Reservations recommended. Dress: casual but neat. MC, V. Closed lunch; closed Mon. Nov.–May. Expensive.*

Bellevue **Augustine's.** First explore the Lawrence Gallery, with its fine *Dining* collection of local art. Then enter the adjoining Oregon Wine Tasting Room to sample the wares of more than 20 Yamhill Valley wineries. Finally, go upstairs to the tastefully decorated dining room, with its modern furnishings and rustic views, where you'll enjoy fresh local seafood, lamb, and beef, all simply prepared and lightly sauced. The wine list is as extensive as it is reasonably priced; many local vintages are available by the glass, a nice concession to those with moderation in mind. Give the Sunday brunch a try, too. *19706 Hwy. 18 (7 mi west of McMinnville), tel. 503/843–3225. Reservations suggested. Dress: casual. D, MC, V. Closed Tues.; Mon. Labor Day–Memorial Day. Moderate.*

Corvallis **The Gables.** This quiet, elegant eatery, with all dark wood, has *Dining* earned a reputation over the years as Corvallis's most romantic restaurant. The menu is about what you would expect: steaks, straightforward seafood, local lamb, and prime rib. The portions are huge and satisfying. The well-stocked wine cellar can be reserved as a dining room for small groups and special occasions. *1121 N.W. 9th St., tel. 503/752–3364. Reservations suggested. Dress: casual. AE, D, DC, MC, V. Closed lunch. Moderate–Expensive.*

Novak's Hungarian Paprikas. Locals can't say enough about this unpretentious family-run restaurant, located a few miles east of Corvallis in Albany. Its Hungarian owners turn out such native specialties as *kolbasz* (homemade sausages with sweet-and-sour cabbage) and beef *szelet* (crispy batter-fried cutlets) with virtuosity. The restaurant's only drawback is its lack of a liquor license, so no alcohol is permitted. *2835 Santiam Hwy., Albany, tel. 503/967–9488. Reservations suggested. Dress: casual. MC, V. Closed Sat. lunch. Inexpensive–Moderate.*

Lodging **Madison Inn.** One of the Willamette Valley's most venerable B&Bs—opened more than a decade ago by the current owner's mother—is this sprawling five-story Tudor that overlooks Central Park in downtown Corvallis. There's also a guest cottage. *660 S.W. Madison Ave., 97333, tel. 503/757–1274. 2 rooms with bath, 6 rooms share 3 baths. AE, D, DC, MC, V. Moderate.*

Eugene **Chanterelle.** In a city quietly renowned for its restaurants, this
Dining is where the smart money comes when it wants a superb meal in a memorably romantic setting. Seasonal, regional European-inspired cuisine is on the menu here; the chef's touch is equally deft with game and local beef or lamb as it is with seafood. The 14-table restaurant, in an old warehouse across from the 5th Street Public Market, is warm and intimate, and is filled with crystal and fresh flowers. *207 E. 5th Ave., tel. 503/484–4065. Reservations suggested. Dress: casual but neat. AE, DC, MC, V. Closed lunch; Sun.–Mon.; last 2 wks of Mar.; last week of Aug.; 1st week of Sept.; major holidays. Expensive.*

Café Zenon. You never know what you'll find on the menu here—Thai, Indian, Italian, South American, down-home barbecue—but it's sure to be both memorable and expertly prepared. The patio-slate floors, picture windows, Parisian street lamps, marble-topped cafe table and cafe chairs give this much-beloved local eatery a romantic, open-air bistro feel. There's an admirably stocked wine cellar, and the desserts are formidable—two full-time bakers produce an eye-popping array of some 20 to 30 desserts daily. Look for the zuccotto Fiorentino, a dove-shaped Italian wedding cake with rum, orange, and flavored whipped cream. *898 Pearl St., tel. 503/343–3005. No reservations. Dress: casual. MC, V. Moderate.*

The Excelsior Café. This elegant Victorian restaurant, with its hardwood floors, closet-size bar and accomplished chefs, is a university tradition. The sparely decorated dining room, shaded by blossoming cherry trees in the spring, has a quiet, scholarly ambience. Despite the simple setting, there is nothing spare about the food here: Glorious fresh-baked breads and desserts and imaginative, well-executed sandwiches, pastas, sautées, and grills form the backbone of the menu. Also try the excellent Sunday brunch. *754 E. 13th Ave., tel. 503/342–6963. Reservations accepted. Dress: casual but neat. AE, MC, V. Moderate.*

Poppi's Anatolia. For years a joyful, slightly seedy taverna called Poppi's near the University of Oregon's campus distributed home-style Greek food, retsina (very dry Greek white wine), Aegean beer, and music with equal liberality. Now Poppi's has moved downtown, altered its name slightly, and generally spruced up. The food—particularly a lovely moussaka and *kalamarakia* (fried squid)—is still great, even if the menu has something of a split personality—Poppi's also serves East Indian specialties from Monday to Saturday. *992 Willamette St., tel. 503/343–9661. Reservations accepted for parties of 6 or more. Dress: casual. MC, V. Closed Sun. lunch. Inexpensive.*

Lodging
★
Campus Cottage B & B. Eugene's first bed-and-breakfast, this 1922 French country–style cottage is within lecturing distance of the U of O campus and enjoys an enduring popularity with visiting academics and parents. The rustic European ambience extends to the four cozy guestrooms, furnished with antiques and fresh flowers; each has a private bath. *1136 E. 19th Ave., Eugene 97403, tel. 503/342–5346. 4 rooms, all with private bath. Facilities: phones in room, guest refrigerators, full breakfast included. No credit cards. Moderate.*

Eugene Hilton. Location, amenities, and a complete, room-by-room face-lift completed in 1993 make this property Eugene's finest hotel. All 270 rooms have been newly furnished and decorated in shades of rose and forest green; all have views. The hotel and its extensive convention facilities adjoin Eugene's Hult Center for the Performing Arts. *66 E. 6th Ave., Eugene 97401, tel. 503/342–2000 or 800/HILTONS, fax 503/342–6661. 270 rooms. Facilities: 2 restaurants, 2 lounges, indoor pool, outdoor spa, athletic facility, hair salon, free covered parking, free airport shuttle. AE, D, DC, MC, V. Expensive–Very Expensive.*

New Oregon Best Western. This handsomely appointed mid-sized motel is directly across Franklin Boulevard from the university. Furnishings—such as the leather couches in the lobby—are unexpectedly plush. Completely refurbished in 1992 with upgrades planned at two-year intervals, the property is clean, fresh, and modern. There are some surprising amenities for this price range. *1655 Franklin Blvd., Eugene 97401, tel. 503/683–3669 or 800/528–1234, fax 503/484–5556. 129 rooms. Facilities: 2 restaurants, bar, cable, TV, indoor pool, saunas, 2 racquetball courts. AE, D, DC, MC, V. Moderate.*

Jacksonville
Dining and Lodging
★
The Jacksonville Inn. The eight guest rooms and basement dining room of this 1863-vintage inn remind you of what the Wild West might have been, had Leona Helmsley been in charge. Four-poster beds, scrubbed floors, and spotless old antiques are maintained with scrupulous attention to detail. The Continental fare and 600-label wine cellar in the dining room are among the best in southern Oregon. Fresh razor clams and veal dishes are house specialties here. You'll need to book well in advance, particularly from late June to August, when the Peter Britt Festival draws thousands of visitors here. Those in a romantic frame of mind should try the new honeymoon cottage. *175 E. California St., 97530, tel. 503/899–1900 or 800/321–9344. Reservations suggested. Dress: casual but neat. AE, D, DC, MC, V. Closed Mon. lunch. Expensive–Very Expensive.*

McKenzie Bridge
Dining and Lodging
The Log Cabin Inn. This inn, on the banks of the wild, fish-filled McKenzie River, is an appropriate romantic weekend getaway. Inside the log cabin–style buildings, the inn is furnished with antique furniture, new beds and baths, and each room has a river view. The restaurant, featuring a decadent homemade beer-cheese soup, buffalo, wild boar, quail, salmon, and a famous marionberry cobbler, is delightful. *McKenzie Hwy., 97413, tel. 503/822–3432. 8 cabins. Facilities: excellent fishing, river views, restaurant, lounge. MC, V. Moderate.*

McMinnville
Dining
★
Nick's Italian Café. Ask any wine maker in the valley to name his favorite wine-country restaurant, and chances are that Nick's would head the list. It's not the decor—Nick's occupies a modestly furnished former dinette—but it might be Nick's

voluminous wine cellar, a veritable New York Public Library of local vintages. The food is spirited and simple, reflecting the owner's northern Italian heritage. The five-course fixed-price menu changes nightly. Diners have their choice of three entrées; there's always at least one fish choice. *521 E. 3rd St., tel. 503/434–4471. Reservations recommended. Dress: casual but neat. No credit cards; personal checks accepted. Closed lunch; Mon. Expensive.*

Roger's. With its emphasis on fresh fish, and its jaunty maritime decor and pleasant stream-side location (there's patio dining in the summer), this restaurant is a local family favorite. Great french fries and large, simply prepared seafood, coupled with reasonable prices, are the why. *2121 E. 27th St., tel. 503/472–0917. Reservations accepted. Dress: casual but neat. AE, D, DC, MC, V. Closed lunch. Moderate.*

Lodging **Mattey House Bed & Breakfast.** This 100-year-old Victorian-
★ style home was built by English immigrant Joseph Mattey, a prosperous local butcher. Its current owners, the Seeds, took over in 1993. The inn had been fully renovated in 1986, and the owners decorated the property with family antiques and hand-screened wallpapers. Now, with its cheerful faux-marble fireplace and gourmet breakfasts (poached pears with raspberry sauce and scrambled eggs with smoked salmon are typical fare), this B&B is an area favorite. *10221 N.E. Mattey La., off Hwy. 99 W, ¼ mi south of Lafayette, 97128, tel. 503/434–5058. 4 rooms, 1 with private bath. MC, V. No smoking allowed inside. Moderate.*

Safari Motor Inn. This motel on McMinnville's main drag is more functional than fancy. The clean, comfortable accommodation in a wonderfully central wine-country location has modest rates and modern, up-to-date furnishings. *345 N. Hwy. 99 W (corner of 19th St.), 97128, tel. 503/472–5187 or 800/472–5187. 90 rooms. Facilities: restaurant, bar, modest weight room, Jacuzzi. AE, D, DC, MC, V. Inexpensive.*

Medford **Under the Greenwood Tree.** Regular guests at this B&B are
Lodging hard-pressed to decide which they like most: the luxurious and
★ romantic rooms, the stunning 10-acre gardens, or the breakfasts cooked by the owner, a Cordon Bleu–trained chef. The interior is decorated with Renaissance splendor. Gigantic old oaks hung with hammocks shade the inn itself, a 130-year-old farmhouse exuding French Country charm. There's a manicured two-acre lawn and a creaky three-story barn for exploring; an outbuilding holds the buckboard wagon that brought the property's original homesteaders westward on the Oregon Trail. *3045 Bellinger La. (midway between Medford and Ashland; take Exit 27 from I–5 and follow Stewart to Bellinger, about 3 mi), 97501, tel. 503/776–0000. MC, V. Expensive.*

Motel 6. It's not the Savoy, but it's clean and cheap. Color schemes are primary; a typical room might contain a durable bed with a green bedspread and quarter-operated "magic fingers," a color TV, table and chairs, and a spartan bath. Perhaps one of the best attributes of this chain hotel is its close proximity to not only the Shakespeare Festival but also the Mt. Ashland ski area and Crater Lake. *950 Alba Dr. (off I–5 Exit 27), 97504, tel. 503/773–4290. 167 units. Facilities: outdoor pool, nearby skiing. AE, D, DC, MC, V. Inexpensive.*

Oakland **Tolly's.** Stroll past the Victorian ice-cream parlor downstairs to
Dining the opulent oak- and antique-filled dining room upstairs, where

steaks, chicken, veal, shellfish, and salmon receive tender and expert treatment. The menu features such favorites as lamb loin in a pan juice demiglaze and fillet royale, topped with scampi, artichoke hearts, and lobster sauce. *115 Locust St. (take Exit 138 from I–5 to Oakland), tel. 503/459–3796. Reservations recommended. Dress: casual. MC, V. Moderate.*

Salem
Dining
★

The Inn at Orchard Heights. This handsome hilltop restaurant is filled with the sound of trickling water and soft classical music, and panoramic views overlooking the lights of the capital city. The deftly handled Continental menu, relying heavily on fresh local seafood, beef, and pasta, is enlivened by the European chef/owner's rich sauces. Standbys include fresh prawns stuffed with crabmeat, and panfried New York steak with pepper-cream sauce. *695 Orchard Heights Rd. NW (across the Willamette River from downtown Salem off Hwy. 221), tel. 503/378–1780. Reservations advised. Dress: casual but neat. AE, DC, MC, V. Closed Sun. lunch. Moderate–Expensive.*

Gerry Frank's Konditorei. Furnished European sidewalk café-style in red, white, and black, with cheerful flower boxes out front, this is *the* place to go in Salem for rich desserts. Lunch and dinner (mostly simple sandwiches, salads, and soup), are also served but it's the tall glass cases piled high with homemade cakes, tortes, and cheesecakes, with names like "Orange Cloud" and "Blackout," that are the real draw. *310 Kearney St. SE, tel. 503/585–7070. D, MC, V. Inexpensive.*

Thompson Brewery & Public House. This atmospheric southern outpost of a Portland-based brew-pub empire is decked out with a funky mix of '60s-vintage rock-and-roll memorabilia and hand-painted woodwork through its series of small, intimate rooms. The food—mostly hearty sandwiches, salads, and pasta dishes—is good and remarkably cheap; families are welcome. There are 21 beer taps behind the bar, most pouring fresh local microbrews. Several, including Java Ale and Terminator Stout, are made on the premises in a tiny brewery enlivened by colorful original artwork. The surrealistic rendering of the state capitol as a spaceship, with Uncle Sam waving his hat astride the dome, is especially noteworthy. Tours are given gladly. *3575 Liberty Rd. S (a 10-min drive south of the Capitol Mall), tel. 503/363–7286. No reservations. Dress: casual. MC, V. Inexpensive.*

Lodging

Quality Inn. This is a clean, functional hotel about five minutes from the capitol, built in 1981; its chief virtue is its location, in addition to a few unexpected luxuries, such as the spacious Jacuzzis in the presidential suites. Views of the freeway are not particularly desirable, but a $1 million remodeling of the rooms and public areas, completed in late 1991, left them freshly modernized. *3301 Market St. NE, 97301, tel. 503/370–7888 or 800/248–6273. 146 rooms. Facilities: restaurant, lounge, no-smoking rooms, laundry facilities, free taxi service from airport, indoor pool, sauna. AE, D, DC, MC, V. Moderate.*

State House Bed & Breakfast. Though the capital's first B&B tends to get a bit of the State Street noise, it makes up for the inconvenience in location and luxury; it's a five-minute walk from the Capitol Mall and Willamette University, and it has a large hot tub overlooking Mill Creek. The decor, in lacy, floral fabrics of sky blue and salmon, is a little fussy but warm. Ask for the Grand Suite—Hank Aaron once slept there, and besides, it's the nicest room in Salem. Cabins, perfect for families, are available in addition to rooms in the main building. *2146*

State St., 97301, tel. 503/588–1340. 4 rooms, plus 2 cottages overlooking Mill Creek; 2 rooms with private bath. D, MC, V. Moderate.

Steamboat
Dining and Lodging
★

The Steamboat Inn. Oregon's most famous fishing lodge, first brought to the world's attention in travel articles by western writer Zane Grey in the 1930s, sits high above the emerald North Umpqua River. A veritable Who's Who of the world's top fly fishermen still converge on this very special nook in the Cascades every fall to try their luck against the 20-pound steelhead that haunt these waters. Others come simply to relax in the reading nooks or on the broad decks of the riverside guest cabins. Another renowned activity here is to partake in the nightly Fisherman's Dinner, a multicourse feast served around a massive 50-year-old sugar-pine dinner table. In all, there are eight riverside cabins, five forest bungalows, and two riverside suites (the bungalows and suites have their own kitchens). Especially during July–October, the prime fishing months, you'll need to make reservations well in advance. *Steamboat, 97447 (38 mi east of Roseburg on Hwy. 138), tel. 503/498–2411. Facilities: restaurant, library/conference room, world-class fishing, riverside location, nearby hiking, wildlife viewing, fishing equipment rentals and sales. Guide services available. MC, V. Moderate–Expensive.*

Talent
Dining

Chata. There are plenty of great restaurants in and around Ashland, but the locals rave about the food, the service, and the warm atmosphere at this Eastern European restaurant, run by a Polish immigrant couple and their children. Try the *piroshki* (meat or vegetable-filled dumplings in a delicate sour-cream sauce). *1212 S. Pacific Hwy. (Hwy. 99), about 2 mi north of Ashland, tel. 503/535–2575. Reservations suggested. Dress: casual. MC, V. Closed lunch. Moderate.*

Yamhill
Lodging
★

Flying M Ranch. The mysterious red *M* signs begin in downtown Yamhill and continue west for 10 miles into the Chehalem Valley, in the foothills of the Coast Range. Following them will bring you to the 625-acre Flying M Ranch, perched above the steelhead-filled Yamhill River. The centerpiece of this rustic complex is the great log lodge, decorated in a style best described as Daniel Boone eclectic and featuring a bar carved from a single six-ton tree trunk. Guests have their choice of the somewhat austere cabins (the cozy, hot tub–equipped Honeymoon Cabin is the nicest) or the 28 riverside hotel units. Parents should take note, however: There are no TVs or telephones. Be sure to book ahead for a Flying M specialty: the Steak Fry Ride, where guests, aboard their choice of horse or a tractor-drawn wagon, ride into the mountains to the ranch's elk camp for a feast of barbecued steak with all the trimmings. *From Newberg, take Hwy. 240 west to Yamhill, then follow the small red Flying M signs west to 23029 N.W. Flying M Rd., 97148, tel. 503/662–3222. 28 units, 7 cabins, more than 100 campsites. Facilities: restaurant, bar, live entertainment, swimming hole, tennis court, basketball court, horseshoe pits, horseback riding, fishing, hiking. AE, D, DC, MC, V. Moderate–Expensive. Closed Dec. 24–25.*

The Arts and Nightlife

The Arts

Ashland
Every year, more than 100,000 bard-quoting fanatics descend on Ashland for the **Oregon Shakespeare Festival** (Box 158, Ashland 97520, tel. 503/482–4331). In three different theaters from February through October, this accomplished repertory company stages some of the finest Shakespearean productions you're likely to see on this side of Stratford—plus works by Ibsen, Williams, and other more modern writers. There are backstage tours, noon lectures, and Renaissance music and dancing before each outdoor performance. The best time to go is from June through October, when the 1,200-seat Elizabethan Theatre, an atmospheric re-creation of Shakespeare's Globe, is operating. Be forewarned that tickets are difficult to come by—the festival generally operates at 98% of capacity, and you'll need to book ahead.

Eugene
The **Hult Center For the Performing Arts** (1 Eugene Ctr., Eugene 97401, tel. 503/342–5746) is an airy, spacious confection of glass and native wood, containing two of the most acoustically perfect theaters on the West Coast. In the course of a typical year, the complex hosts everything from Broadway shows to ballet, heavy-metal music to Haydn.

Jacksonville
Every summer some of the finest musicians in the world gather in this historic Wild West town for the **Peter Britt Festival** (Box 1124, Medford 97501, tel. 503/773–6077 or 800/882–7488), a weekly series of outdoor concerts and theater presentations lasting from mid-June to early September. Contemporary and classical performances are held in a natural amphitheater on the estate of early photographer Peter Britt.

Nightlife

Lounges, restaurants, and bars throughout western Oregon provide the outlet for the region's nightly entertainment. In Salem, visit the **Union Street Oyster Bar** (445 State St., tel. 503/362–7219). In Ashland, the after-theater crowd (including many of the actors) congregates in the bar at **Chateaulin** (50 E. Main St., tel. 503/482–2264) for a nightcap. The **Rogue Brewery and Public House** (31 B. Water St., tel. 503/488–5061) caters to a younger crowd.

5 Seattle

By Adam Woog
and Loralee
Wenger

*Adam Woog is a
Seattle-based
freelance writer
whose works have
appeared in the*
Village Voice,
Seattle Times, *and*
Japan Times.
*Loralee Wenger is
the former travel
editor for* Pacific
Northwest
*magazine and a
freelance writer
whose articles
have appeared in
the* San Francisco
Examiner,
Washington Post,
Parade *magazine,
and* Glamour
magazine.

Seattle is defined by water. There's no use denying the city's damp weather, or the fact that its skies are cloudy for much of the year. People in Seattle don't tan—goes the joke—they rust. Vendors at the city's waterfront Public Market sell T-shirts that read "Seattle Rain Festival: January through December."

But Seattle is also defined by a different kind of water. A variety of rivers, lakes, and canals bisect steep hills, creating a series of distinctive areas along the water's edge that provide for a wide range of activities. Funky fishing boats and floating homes, swank yacht clubs and waterfront restaurants, exist side by side.

But a city is defined by people as well as by its geography, and the people of Seattle—some half million within the city proper, another 2 million in the surrounding Puget Sound region—are a diversified bunch. Seattle has long had an active Asian and Asian-American population, as well as being home to well-established communities of Scandinavians, African Americans, Jews, Native Americans, Hispanics, and other ethnic groups.

Although it's impossible to accurately generalize about such a varied group, the prototypical Seattleite was once pithily summed up by a *New Yorker* cartoon in which one arch-eyebrowed East Coast matron says to another, "They're backpacky, but nice." And it's true, nearly everyone in Seattle shares a love for the outdoors.

Aided by the proximity of high mountains (the Cascades to the east, the Olympics to the west) and water (both salt water and fresh water are everywhere), Seattle's vigorous outdoor sports are perennial favorites. The city's extensive park system (designed by Frederick Law Olmsted, creator of New York City's Central Park) and miles of secluded walking and bicycling paths add to one's appreciation of its surroundings.

At the same time, the climate fosters an easygoing, indoor lifestyle as well. Overcast days and long winter nights help make Seattle a haven for movie-goers and book-readers—the city is often used by Hollywood as a testing ground for new films and, according to independent bookstore sales and per-capita book purchases, the city ranks in the highest category.

Shedding its sleepy-town image, Seattle is one of the fastest-growing cities in the United States. For years, giant aerospace manufacturer Boeing was the only major factor in the area's economy besides lumber and fishing—the staples of the Northwest. But as the 1962 World's Fair (and its enduring symbol, the Space Needle) signaled a change from small town to medium-size city, so the 1990 Goodwill Games announced the city's new role as a respected international hub. Seattle is now a major seaport and a vital link in Pacific Rim trade, and the evidence of internationalism is everywhere, from the discreet Japanese script identifying downtown department stores (i.e., "Nordstrom" written as "Katakana") to the multilingual recorded messages at Seattle-Tacoma International Airport.

The town that Sir Thomas Beacham once described as a "cultural wasteland" now has all the artistic trappings of a full-blown big city, with ad agencies and artists' co-ops, symphonies and ballet companies. Several magazines compete with the two daily newspapers. There's an innovative new convention center, a covered dome for professional sports, a world-renowned theater scene, an excellent opera company, and a strong music community.

As the city grows, though, it is also beginning to display full-blown big-city problems. Increases in crime, drug abuse, homelessness, and poverty are coupled with a decline in the quality of the public schools. Suburban growth is also rampant; nearby Bellevue, the largest suburb, has swollen in just a few years from a quiet farming community to the second-largest city in the state. Further, the area is plagued with one of the worst traffic problems in the country. But Seattleites are an active political bunch with a great love for their city and a firm commitment to maintaining its reputation as one of the most liveable in the country.

Essential Information

Arriving and Departing by Plane

Seattle-Tacoma International Airport is 20 miles from downtown Seattle and is served by Air BC (tel. 206/467–7928 or 800/663–8868), Air Canada (tel. 206/467–7928), Alaska (tel. 206/433–3100), American (tel. 800/433–7300), America West (tel. 800/247–5692), British Airways (tel. 206/433–6714), Continental (tel. 206/624–1740 or 800/525–0280), Delta (tel. 206/433–4711), EVA Airways (tel. 206/687–2833 or 800/695–2833), Hawaiian (tel. 800/367–5320), Horizon (tel. 800/547–9308), Japan (tel. 206/624–4737 or 800/225–2525), Northwest (tel. 206/433–3500 or 800/221–2000), TWA (tel. 206/447–9400), Thai Airways (tel. 800/426–5204), United (tel. 206/441–3700 or 800/241–6522), United Express (tel. 206/441–3700), and USAir (tel. 206/587–6229 or 800/428–4322).

Between the Airport and Center City
By Bus
Gray Line Airport Express (tel. 206/626–6088) operates buses from major downtown hotels from 6:10 AM to 11:45, with departures every 20–30 minutes, depending on the hotel. The fare is $7 one-way, $12 round-trip.

Shuttle Express (tel. 206/622–1424) offers service to and from the airport. Fares are $16 for singles one-way or $22 for two one-way tickets.

By Taxi Taxis to the airport take 30–45 minutes; the fare is about $25.

Arriving and Departing by Car, Bus, and Train

By Car I–5 enters Seattle from the north and south, I–90 from the east.

Washington law requires all passengers to be buckled into seat belts. Children under age five should use car seats. Cars are allowed to turn right at a red light after stopping to check for oncoming traffic.

By Bus Seattle is served by **Greyhound** (8th Ave. and Stewart St., tel. 800/231–2222), a nationwide bus line.

By Train **Amtrak** (303 S. Jackson St., tel. 800/USA–RAIL) provides rail transportation from Seattle.

Getting Around Seattle

By Car Many downtown streets are one-way, so a map with arrows is especially helpful. Main thoroughfares into downtown are Aurora Avenue (the part through downtown is called the Alaskan Way Viaduct) and I–5.

By Bus **Metropolitan Transit** (821 2nd Ave., tel. 206/553–3000) provides a free-ride service in the downtown waterfront area. Fares to other destinations range from 85¢ to $1.60, depending on the zone and time of day.

By Ferry The **Washington State Ferry System** (tel. 206/464–6400 or 206/464–2000, ext. 5500) is the largest in the U.S., (*see* Getting There, by Ferry, Bainbridge Island, in Excursions from Seattle, *below*). Ferries leave from downtown Seattle for Bainbridge Island and Bremerton (Kitsap Peninsula) several times daily. Ferries for pedestrians travel to Vashon Island and Southworth (Kitsap Peninsula). Car and passenger ferries leave from Fauntleroy, in West Seattle, to Vashon Island and Southworth; from Edmonds, north of Seattle, to Kingston; and from Mukilteo, farther north, to Clinton (Whidbey Island). In Anacortes, about 90 minutes north of Seattle, ferries depart for the San Juan Islands and Vancouver Island, British Columbia. Fares range from as low as $1.10 for children 5–11 and senior citizens traveling the Mukilteo to Clinton route, to $31.25 for a car and driver going one-way from Anacortes to Sydney.

Clipper Navigation, Inc.'s (tel. 206/448–5000) passenger catamarans leave from Pier 69. They make the trip to Victoria in under three hours and depart four times daily in the summer, two times daily in the spring and fall, and once daily in winter. The fares are $74–$85 round-trip. The ships offer summer sunset cruises. Clipper Navigation also makes runs to Port Townsend and Friday Harbor on San Juan Island in the summer. Reservations are necessary.

By Monorail The **Monorail** (tel. 206/684–7200), built for the 1962 World's Fair, runs direct from Westlake Center to the Seattle Center every 15 minutes. Hours are Sunday to Thursday 9–9 and Friday and Saturday 9 AM–midnight. The fare is 85¢ each way; free for children under 6.

By Trolley **Waterfront trolleys** (tel. 206/553–3000) run from Pier 70 into Pioneer Square. The fares (85¢ nonpeak and $1.60 for travel during peak hours) are the same as bus fares.

By Taxi Taxis can be hailed on the street, and the fare is $1.20 at the flag drop and $1.40 per mile. Major companies are **Farwest** (tel. 206/622–1717) and **Yellow Cab** (tel. 206/622–6500).

Important Addresses and Numbers

Tourist Information The **Seattle/King County Convention and Visitors Bureau** (800 Convention Pl., tel. 206/461–5840), at the I–5 end of Pike Street, can provide you with maps and information about lodging, restaurants, and attractions throughout the city.

Emergencies For **police, ambulance,** or **other emergencies,** dial 911.

Hospitals Area hospitals with emergency rooms include **Harborview Medical Center** (325 9th Ave., tel. 206/223–3074) and **Virginia Mason Hospital** (925 Seneca St., tel. 206/583–6433).

Pharmacies **Fred Meyer** (417 Broadway Ave. E, tel. 206/323–6586) is open until 10 PM.

Guided Tours

Orientation Several guided tours of Seattle's waterfront and nearby areas are available, primarily during summer months. From Pier 55, **Seattle Harbor Tours** offers one-hour tours exploring Elliott Bay and the Port of Seattle. Some seven vessels take visitors on trips through the Hiram Chittendan Locks and Lake Washington. Sailings vary according to season. *Pier 55, Suite 201, 98101, tel. 206/623–1445. Cost: $9.50 adults, $8.50 senior citizens, $7 youths 12–17, $5 children 5–12.*

Gray Line offers some 20 guided bus tours of the city and environs ranging in scope from a daily 2½-hour spin to a six-hour "Grand City Tour." The company also offers various specialized tours, including the Boeing 747-767 plants, Mt. Rainier, and Seattle's waterways by boat. From May to October, Gray Line also offers tours via Seattle Trolleys through downtown. *All departures from the downtown Sheraton, 1400 6th Ave., tel. 206/626–5208 (except Seattle Trolley tours and the* Victoria Star *service between Bellingham and Victoria that operates June 1–Oct. 15). Free transfer service from major downtown hotels. Reservations required.*

For an off-beat introduction to the Emerald City, try the *Name Dropper's Tour,* a Trivial Pursuits–style guided bus tour. Book dealers Jim and Carol Norman offer insider's insight, bits of juicy gossip, and orientation information and historical data about Seattle. The three-hour tour covers 36 miles of town. *Box 12918, Seattle 98111, tel. 206/625–1317. Cost: $25 per person.*

Special-Interest **Emerald City Charters** offers a unique look at Seattle's waterfront from beneath the sails of a refurbished 64-foot 1939 yawl. There are 90-minute harbor sails and a 2½-hour sunset sail. *Pier 56, tel. 206/624–3931. May–Oct. Cost: harbor sail $20, sunset sail $37.*

The *Spirit of Washington* is a diesel-powered dinner train that takes passengers on a 3½-hour, 44-mile round-trip excursion along the eastern shore of Lake Washington from the depot in Renton to the Chateau Ste. Michelle winery in Woodenville. Passengers ride in regular or domed dining cars and are served dinner on the first leg of the trip, then disembark for a self-guided tour and tasting, or a stroll through the gardens at the winery. Dessert and coffee are served on the return trip. The route offers views of Lake Washington, the Bellevue skyline, and Mt. Rainier. The menu includes prime rib, baked cherry-smoked salmon with pineapple chutney and a seafood fettuccine. Desserts are flavorful and usually decadent, and bar offerings include Washington wines, beers and ales. There are also Saturday lunch and Sunday brunch trips. *Renton Depot, tel. 800/876–7245. Reservations required. No runs Mon. mid-Sept.–mid-May. Cost: $55; $65 for dome-car seating.*

The *Spirit of Puget Sound* runs dinner cruises in Elliott Bay evenings 7–10 on a sleek, 175-foot yacht. The cruise includes beef, salmon, and chicken buffet dinner; a 30-minute Broadway revue; and one hour of dancing to a five-piece band. Summer moonlight cocktail cruises set sail at about 11:30 and return at 2 AM, and feature a nightclub atmosphere. *2819 Elliot Ave., Suite*

204, Seattle 98121, tel. 206/443–1439. Cost for dinner cruise is about $50, depending on weekends or weeknight travel; for moonlight cruises, $15.95 per person. Call for schedules.

From Pier 56, **Tillicum Village Tours** sails across Puget Sound to Blake Island, south of Bainbridge Island, for a four-hour examination of traditional Native American life. A dinner including steamed clams and salmon is served, and Native American dancers perform a new production, *Dance on the Wind. Pier 56, tel. 206/443–1244. Tour schedule varies during the year, with up to 3 tours leaving daily during peak months. Cost: $43.23 adults, $39.98 senior citizens, $28.08 youths 13–19, $17.26 children 6–12, $8.60 children 4–5; children 3 and under free.*

The ***Victoria Clipper*** offers two-hour sunset cruises with two itineraries. One sails down the east coast of Vashon Island and returns along areas of Greater Seattle, including Alki Point, in West Seattle. The other goes northwest to Agate Passage, then south along the western shore of Bainbridge Island through Rich Passage. *Pier 69, tel. 206/448–5000. Cost: $16 adults, $8.50 children.*

Gray Line (*see above*).

Seattle's Chinatown, known as the International District, reflecting its multicultural flavor, is one of the largest Asian-American enclaves in North America. **Chinatown Discovery Tours** offers groups (and individuals on a space-available basis) a three-hour tour of the area that includes such sights as a fortune cookie factory, a Chinese market, and an herb dispensary. Tours end with a traditional dim sum or dinner banquet. *Box 3406, 98114, tel. 206/236–0657. $27.50 for the tour, including dim sum lunch. Tours offered several times during the day and evening.*

One of the most beloved of Seattle's tours is the **Underground Tour,** begun in 1965 by feisty entrepreneur/historian Bill Speidel as an effort to help preserve the then-derelict Pioneer Square area. This 90-minute walking tour explores (with tongue-in-cheek narration) the rough-and-tumble history of early Seattle; the Great Fire of 1889, which destroyed most of downtown; and the fascinating below-ground sections of Pioneer Square that have been abandoned (and built on top of) since 1907. This tour, however, is not wheelchair- or stroller-accessible, as six flights of stairs are involved. *Departure from Doc Maynard's Public House, 610 1st Ave., tel. for reservations, 206/682–4646; tel. for schedules, 206/682–1511. Cost: $5.50 adults, $4.50 senior citizens, $4 youths 13–17 or with valid student ID, $2.25 children 6–12, children under 6 free. Reservations recommended. Tours run daily except Easter, Thanksgiving, Christmas Eve, Christmas Day, and New Year's Day. Tour schedule varies with season, with up to 7 tours daily in summer.*

Self-Guided Also worth exploring are the unusual self-guided tours found in "Steps to Enjoying Seattle's Public Art," an illustrated brochure published by the Seattle Arts Commission. It describes walks and drives to see more than 1,000 innovative works of **art in public places.** Among these treasures are brass dance-steps inlaid on the sidewalks of Broadway, whirligigs festooning a neighborhood electric power substation, an "ark" of animals at Woodland Park Zoo, murals on downtown high rises, and a "sound garden" of acoustical sculptures in a lakeside park.

"Steps to Enjoying Seattle's Public Art" is free from the Seattle Arts Commission (305 Harrison St., 98109, tel. 206/684–7171).

Ballooning **Balloon Depot** (16138 N.E. 87th St., Redmond 98052, tel. 206/881–9699) offers 60- to 90-minute balloon flights for $99–$145 per person depending on the length of flight and whether it's a weekday or weekend. **Lighter Than Air Adventures** (21808 N.E. 175th St., Woodinville 98072, tel. 206/788–2454) has evening flights that last 30 minutes–one hour for $125 per person, as well as morning flights that last one–two hours and feature a champagne brunch for $145 per person. The **Great Northwest Aerial Navigation Company** (7616 79th Ave. SE, Mercer Island 98040, tel. 206/232–2023) specializes in longer flights and gourmet picnics, lasting about four hours, surveying the Snohomish Valley north and east of Seattle. Morning and evening picnic flights, $145 on weekends, $120 weekdays; flights only, $105.

Highlights for First-time Visitors

Kingdome (*see* Exploring Seattle, *below*).
Seattle Center (*see* Exploring Seattle, *below*).
Space Needle (*see* Exploring Seattle, *below*).
Seattle's waterfront (*see* Exploring Seattle, *below*).

Exploring Seattle

Numbers in the margin correspond to points of interest on the Downtown Seattle map.

Downtown Downtown Seattle is bounded by the Kingdome to the south, the Seattle Center to the north, I–5 to the east, and the waterfront to the west. You can reach most points of interest by foot, bus, or the monorail. Bear in mind that Seattle is a city of hills, so comfortable walking shoes are a must.

❶ Start at the **Seattle Visitor Information Center** to pick up maps, brochures, and listings of events. *666 Stewart St., tel. 206/461–5840. Open weekdays 8:30–5. Other location at the Seattle Center, adjacent to the Space Needle. Open Memorial Day–Labor Day.*

From the Information Center, you can proceed either north or south. If you choose the latter, take Westlake Avenue to **❷** **Westlake Center** (*see* Shopping, *below*), a complex completed in 1989 in spite of the controversy surrounding its construction. The conflict was between city residents—some of whom objected to the 27-story office tower and three-story shopping structure with enclosed walkways—and favored, instead, the large grassy park without commercial buildings. In any case, the center is a major terminus for buses and the monorail, which goes north to Seattle Center. *1601 5th Ave., tel. 206/467–1600. Open weekdays 9:30–9.*

Make your way from 5th Avenue west to 2nd Avenue. The **❸** doors to the new **Seattle Art Museum** opened in 1991, and the five-story building, designed by postmodern theorist Robert Venturi, is a work of art in itself. The building features a limestone exterior with large-scale vertical fluting, accented by terra-cotta, cut granite, and marble. The museum has a café and gift shop, and displays an extensive collection of Asian, Native American, African, Oceanic, and pre-Columbian art. *1320*

Historical Marker, **7**
Omnidome Film
Experience, **6**
Pike Place Market, **4**
Pioneer Square, **8**
Seattle Aquarium, **5**
Seattle Art Museum, **3**
Seattle Visitor
Information Center, **1**
Westlake Center, **2**

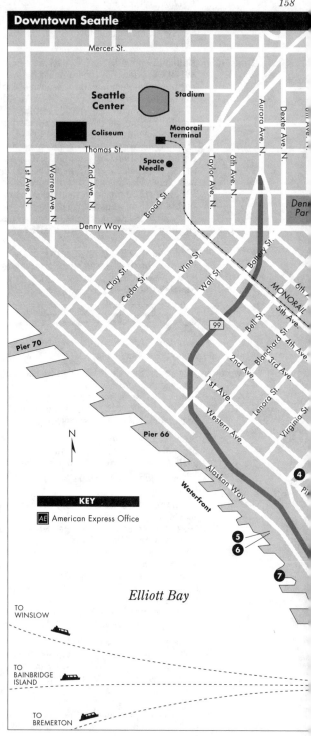

Downtown Seattle

*2nd Ave., tel. 206/625–8900. Admission: $5 adults, $3 senior
citizens and students, children under 12 free; admission free
first Tues. of the month; free tours daily at 2. Open Tues.–Sat.
10–5, Thurs. 10–9, Sun. noon–5. Closed Mon., Thanksgiving,
Christmas, and New Year's Day.*

❹ Go west one block to 1st Avenue and one block north to the **Pike
Place Market,** a Seattle institution. It began in 1907 when the
city issued permits to farmers allowing them to sell produce
from their wagons parked at Pike Place. Later the city built
stalls that were allotted to the farmers on a daily basis. At one
time the market was a madhouse of vendors hawking their produce, haggling over prices; some of the fishmongers still carry
on this kind of frenzied banter, but chances are you won't get
them to waver on their prices. Urban renewal almost killed the
market, but just as planners were about to do away with it, city
voters, led by the late architect Victor Steinbreuck (for whom
the park near the market was named), rallied and voted it a historical asset. Many of the buildings have been restored, and the
project is now connected to the waterfront by stairs and elevators. You can still find fresh seafood (which can be packed in dry
ice for your flight home), produce, cheese, Northwest wines,
bulk spices, tea, coffee, and arts and crafts here. *1st Ave. at
Pike St., tel. 206/682–7453. Open Mon.–Sat. 9–6, Sun. 11–5.*

From the market, take the stairs or elevator down to the waterfront. In the early days, the waterfront was the center of activity in Seattle; today it stretches some 19 blocks, from Pier 70
and Myrtle Edwards Park in the north, where there is a bicycle
and jogging trail, down to Pier 51 in Pioneer Square.

Pier 70, to the south of the park, is a large warehouse that has
been converted into shops, galleries, restaurants, and bars.

❺ At the base of the Pike Street Hillclimb at Pier 59 is the **Seattle
Aquarium,** showcasing Northwest marine life. The Discovery
Lab offers visitors a chance to see baby barnacles, minute jelly
fish, and other "invisible" creatures through high-resolution
video microscopes. The Tide Pool Exhibit re-creates
Washington's rocky coast and sandy beaches at low tide with a
6,000-gallon wave that sweeps over the underwater life—spectators standing close by may get damp from the simulated sea
spray. Sea otters and seals swim and dive in their pools, and the
"State of the Sound" exhibit shows the aquatic life and ecology
of Puget Sound. *Pier 59, tel. 206/386–4320. Admission: $6.50
adults, $5 senior citizens, $4 youngsters 6–18, $1.50 children
3–5, children under 2 free. Call for group rates. Open daily
10–5, 10–7 in summer.*

❻ Next to the aquarium is the **Omnidome Film Experience,** which
includes short films on such subjects as the eruption of Mt. St.
Helens, mountain gorillas, and the Great Barrier Reef. *Pier
59, tel. 206/622–1868. Admission: $5.95 adults, $4.95 youths
13–18 and senior citizens, $3.95 children 3–12, children under
3 free; phone for special combination ticket prices for the
Omnidome and aquarium. Open daily 10–5.*

North of the aquarium, at Pier 66 along Alaskan Way, is the
site of the **Odyssey Contemporary Maritime Museum,** scheduled
to open in 1995. This new center will feature cultural and educational maritime exhibits on Puget Sound and ocean trade,
and offer visitors tours of ships and boats docked nearby. The
development will also include a conference center, short-stay

boat basin, fish-processing and fisheries support terminals, and a restaurant.

7 The **historical marker** indicating the landing of the ship *Portland*, on July 17, 1897, is at Pier 58. The ship brought gold and news of the Klondike gold rush; shops at this pier continue to commemorate the event with gold-rush theme merchandise.

From Pier 51 at the foot of Yesler Way, walk a couple of blocks east to **Pioneer Park,** where an ornate iron-and-glass pergola stands. This was the site of Henry Yesler's (one of Seattle's first businesspeople) pier and sawmill, and Seattle's original business district. In 1889, a fire destroyed many of the wood-frame **8** buildings in the area now known as **Pioneer Square,** but the industrious residents and businesspeople rebuilt them with brick and mortar.

The term Skid Row originated here, when timber was logged off the hill and sent to the sawmill. The skid road was made of small logs laid crossways and greased so the freshly cut timber could slide down to the mill. With the Klondike gold rush, this area became populated with saloons and brothels; businesses gradually moved north, and the old pioneering area deteriorated. Eventually, only drunks and bums hung out on Skid Road, and the term changed to Skid Row and became synonymous with "down and out." Today's Pioneer Square encompasses about 18 blocks and includes restaurants, bars, shops, and the city's largest concentration of art galleries, but it is once again known as a hangout for those down on their luck. Incidents of crime in the neighborhood have increased lately, especially after dark. In Pioneer Square is the **Klondike Gold Rush National Historical Park** and interpretive center. The center provides insight into the story of Seattle's role in the 1897–98 gold rush through film presentations, permanent exhibits, and gold-panning demonstrations. *117 S. Main St., tel. 206/442–7220. Admission free. Open daily 9–5, except major holidays.*

Numbers in the margin correspond to points of interest on the Metropolitan Seattle map.

Walk a half block east on Main Street, and two blocks south on **9** Occidental Avenue to the **Kingdome,** Seattle's covered stadium where the Seattle Seahawks NFL team and the Seattle Mariners baseball team play. The 650-feet-diameter stadium was built in 1976 and has the world's largest self-supporting roof, which sits 250 feet high. If you're interested in the inner workings, take the one-hour guided tour. *201 S. King St., tel. 206/296–3111 for information. Tour admission: $3 adults, $1.50 children and senior citizens.*

10 To the east is a 40-square-block area known as the **International District** (the ID). Inhabited by about one-third Chinese and one-third Filipinos, other residents here come from all over Asia. The ID began as a haven for Chinese workers after they finished the Transcontinental Railroad. The community has remained largely intact, despite the anti-Chinese riots in Seattle during the 1880s and the World War II Japanese-American internment. The district, which includes many Chinese, Japanese, and Korean restaurants, also houses herbalists, massage parlors, acupuncturists, and about 30 private clubs for gambling and socializing. The most notorious club is the **Wah Mee Club,** on Canton Avenue, where a multiple murder linked to

Boeing Field, **21**
Henry Art Gallery, **18**
International
District, **10**
Kingdome, **9**
Museum of History
and Industry, **19**
Nippon Kan
Theater, **11**
Seattle Center, **13**
Space Needle, **14**
Thomas Burke
Memorial Washington
State Museum, **17**
University of
Washington, **16**
Washington Park
Arboretum, **20**
Wing Luke
Museum, **12**
Woodland Park
Zoo, **15**

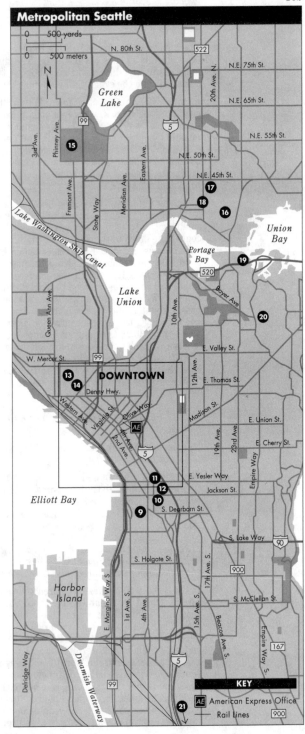

gangs and gambling occurred in 1983. **Uwajimaya** (519 6th Ave. S, tel. 206/624–6248), one of the—if not *the*—largest Japanese stores on the West Coast, is in this district as well. Here you will find china, gifts, fabrics, housewares, and a complete supermarket with an array of Asian foods.

Time Out If you need to rest your feet a bit by now, stop in at **Okazuya,** the Asian snack bar (tel. 206/624–6248) in Uwajimaya. You can get noodle dishes, sushi, tempura, *humbow,* and other Asian dishes for carryout or to eat in.

From Uwajimaya, continue north on 6th Street to Washington Street. In summer, as you walk up the hill, you can see the many gardens tended by residents of the ID.

⓫ Historically, the **Nippon Kan Theater** (628 S. Washington St., tel. 206/467–6807) was the focal point for Japanese-American activities, including Kabuki theater. Renovated and reopened in 1981 as a national historic site, it presents many Asian-interest productions, including the Japanese Performing Arts series, which runs from October through May.

The final stop on the southbound Downtown Seattle tour will
⓬ be at the **Wing Luke Museum,** named for the first Asian person to be elected to a Seattle city office, where exhibits emphasize Oriental history and culture. An acupuncture exhibit demonstrates how needles are inserted into parts of the body to release blocked energy and promote healing. Other elements of the permanent collection include costumes, fabrics, crafts, basketry, and Chinese traditional medicines. *407 7th Ave. S, tel. 206/623–5124. Admission: $2.50 adults, $1.50 senior citizens and students, 75¢ children. Open Tues.–Fri. 11–4:30, weekends noon–4; closed Mon.*

North of To explore outside the downtown area, take the 4th Avenue bus
Downtown to Westlake Center, where you can pick up the Monorail to
⓭ **Seattle Center,** a 74-acre complex built for the 1962 Seattle World's Fair. It includes an amusement park, theaters, the Coliseum, exhibition halls, museums, shops, and the popular Space Needle with its restaurant and observation deck. The
⓮ landmark **Space Needle** can easily be seen from almost any spot in the downtown area, and looks like something from the old "Jetsons" cartoon show. The glass elevator to the observation deck offers an expansive view of the city.

Time Out The **Space Needle Lounge** (tel. 206/443–2100), on the observation deck (one floor above the Space Needle Restaurant), offers fabulous views of Elliott Bay and Queen Anne Hill. The black-and-gray exterior decor emphasizes the '60s style of the Needle. Ask the bartender for the special "Spirit of the Needle" cocktail or choose from the full bar.

From downtown or from the Seattle Center, take Highway 99 (Aurora Ave. N) north across the Aurora Bridge to the 50th
⓯ Street exit; follow signs to the **Woodland Park Zoo,** where many of the animals are free to roam their section of the total of 92 acres. The African savanna, the new elephant house, and the new tropical rain forest are popular features. Wheelchairs and strollers can be rented. *N. 59th St. and Fremont Ave., tel. 206/684–4800. Admission: $4.50 adults, $2.25 children 6–17 and*

senior citizens, children under 5 free. Open summer, daily 9:30–6; winter, daily 10–4.

From the Woodland Park Zoo, take the 50th Street exit to 15th Avenue NE, then drive south to 45th Street. Turn east for a
16 few blocks to the entrance of the 33,500-student **University of Washington.** The U-Dub, as locals call it, was founded in 1861. On the northwestern corner of the beautifully landscaped cam-
17 pus is the **Thomas Burke Memorial Washington State Museum,** Washington's natural-history and anthropological museum. The museum has been renovated recently and features exhibits on cultures of the Pacific region and the state's 35 Native American tribes. *17th Ave. NE and N.E. 45th St., tel. 206/543–5590. Admission: $2.50 adults, $1.50 youth and senior citizens; children 5 and under free. Open daily 10–5, Thurs. 10–8.*

18 Going south, on the west side of the campus is the **Henry Art Gallery,** which displays paintings from the 19th and 20th centuries, textiles, and traveling exhibits. *15th Ave. NE and N.E. 41st St., tel. 206/543–2280. Admission: $3 adults, $1.50 senior citizens; students and children 12 and under free; free Thurs. Open daily 10–5, Thurs. 10–9; closed Mon.*

Close to the university's Husky Stadium, off Montlake and
19 Lake Washington boulevards, is the **Museum of History and Industry.** An 1880s-era room and a Seattle time-line depict the city's earlier days. Other displays from the permanent collection are shown on a rotating basis, along with traveling exhibits. *2700 24th Ave. E, tel. 206/324–1125. Admission: $3 adults, $1.50 children 6–12 and senior citizens, children under 6 free. Open daily 10–4:30.*

At the museum pick up a brochure of self-guided walking tours
20 of the nearby **Washington Park Arboretum.** The arboretum's Rhododendron Glen and Azalea Way are in full bloom from March through June. During the rest of the year, other plants and wildlife flourish. A new visitor center at the north end of the park is open to instruct you on the species of flora and fauna you'll see here. *2300 Arboretum Dr. E, tel. 206/325–4510. Admission free. Park open daily 7 AM–sunset; visitor center open weekdays 10–3:45, weekends noon–3:45.*

21 If you have your own plane, you can land at **Boeing Field** to see the **Museum of Flight.** The earthbound can get there by metro bus No. 174 that follows 2nd Avenue from downtown Seattle. The **Red Barn,** Boeing's original airplane factory, houses an exhibit on the history of aviation. The **Great Gallery,** a dramatic structure designed by Seattle architect Ibsen Nelson, contains more than 20 vintage airplanes—suspended from the ceiling and on the ground—dating from the Wright brothers. For a complete lesson, take the free hour-long Boeing tour. *9404 E. Marginal Way S, tel. 206/764–5720. Admission: $5 adults and senior citizens, $3 children 6–16, children under 6 free. Open Fri.–Wed. 10–5, Thurs. 10–9; closed Christmas.*

Seattle for Free

Rainier Brewery, located 2 miles south of the Kingdome on I–5, offers 30-minute tours of the premises that conclude with free samples of the locally made beer for adults. If you don't want to drive, take Bus 130 bus from downtown. *3100 Airport Way S, tel. 206/622–2600. Tours weekdays 1–6. No children under 3.*

Gallery Walk (begin at any gallery in Pioneer Square, tel. 206/ 587–0260), an open house hosted by Seattle's art galleries, explores new local exhibits the first Thursday of every month, starting at 5.

The **Charles and Emma Frye Art Museum** features a large collection of Munich School and American School paintings. *704 Terry Ave., tel. 206/622–9250. Open Mon.–Sat. 10–5, Sun. noon–5.*

The **Elliott Bay Book Company** (101 S. Main St., tel. 206/ 624– 6600) hosts lectures and readings by authors of local and international acclaim. Most are free, but phone ahead to be sure.

Recreational Equipment, Inc. (REI, tel. 206/323–8333), the largest consumer co-op in the United States, hosts free programs on travel, adventure, and outdoor activities in Seattle (1525 11th Ave.), Bellevue (15400 N.E. 20th St.), and Federal Way (2565 Gateway Center Blvd. S) locations, starting at 7 PM every Thursday, and at Lynnwood (4200 194th St. SW) at 7 PM on Tuesday.

Seattle's summer concerts, the **Out to Lunch Series** (tel. 206/ 623–0340), runs from mid-June to early September every weekday at noon in various parks, plazas, and atriums in downtown. Concerts feature local and national musicians and dancers. Call ahead for schedules and locations.

What to See and Do with Children

Burke-Gilman Trail (*see* Sports and the Outdoors, *below*) offers good bike trails for children.

Elliott Bay Book Company (*see* Seattle for Free, *above*) hosts a children's story hour at 11 AM on the first Saturday of the month.

Green Lake (*see* Sports and the Outdoors, *below*).

Museum of Flight (*see* Exploring Seattle, *above*).

Myrtle Edwards Park (*see* Sports and the Outdoors, *below*).

Seattle Aquarium (*see* Exploring Seattle, *above*).

Seattle Children's Museum is a colorful, spacious facility at the Seattle Center's Center House. An infant-toddler area features a giant, soft ferryboat for climbing and sliding. A bubble area helps children learn about shapes and gravity. The pretend neighborhood allows children to play in a post office, café, fire station, grocery store, and more. Intergenerational programs, special exhibits, and workshops are offered. *Fountain level of Seattle Center House, 305 Harrison St., tel. 206/441– 1768. Admission: $3.50 adults and children, children under 1 free. Open Tues.–Sun. 10–5.*

The $10 million **Charlotte Martin Theatre,** which opened in the fall of 1993, is the new home of Seattle Children's Theatre. The space includes carpeted seating tiers and a curved, 485-seat auditorium, classrooms, and offices. SCT, the second-largest professional resident children's theater company in the United States, has developed a national reputation for its high-quality and innovative productions and has commissioned more than 55 new plays, adaptations and musicals, many of which have gone on to be produced by theater companies across the nation. Their season runs September–June. *Charlotte Martin Theatre* *at Seattle Center, Box 9640, 2nd Ave. N and Thomas St., tel 206/441–3322.*

Thomas Burke Memorial Washington State Museum (*see* Exploring Seattle, *above*).

Off the Beaten Track

Touring **brew pubs**—drinking establishments attached to actual breweries—is a congenial and educational alternative to usual city attractions. Seattle, as well as a good portion of the Pacific Northwest, has become a hotbed for **microbrews** (high-quality beers made for local distribution). All of the pubs listed below also serve food and nonalcoholic beverages. If live music is performed, a cover charge may be required; otherwise admission is free.

The **Pacific Northwest Brewing Co.,** located in the heart of Pioneer Square, offers six mild beers that reflect the taste of its British owner. The elegantly decorated interior—smooth high-tech design, blended with antiques and brewing equipment in full view—fits not only the personality of proprietor Richard Wrigley, but the downtown location as well. *322 Occidental Ave. S, tel. 206/621–7002. Open Tues.–Sat. 11:30 AM–midnight.*

Near the north end of the Fremont Bridge, just 8 miles from downtown, is the **Trolleyman,** birthplace of the local-favorites Ballard Bitter and Red Hook Ale. The premises mix Northwest style—whitewashed walls and a no-smoking policy—with a cozy British pub atmosphere that includes a fireplace and ample armchairs. *3400 Phinney Ave. N, tel. 206/548–8000. Open weekdays 8:30 AM–11 PM, Sat. 11–11, Sun. noon–6. Tours given weekdays at 3, weekends at 1:30, 2:30, 3:30, and 4:30.*

Catering to the nearby university crowd, the **Big Time Brewery** resembles an archetypal college-town pub, with a moose head on the wall and co-ed decor. Pale ale, amber, and porter are always on tap; specialty brews change monthly. *4133 University Way NE, tel. 206/545–4509. Open daily 11:30 AM–1 AM.*

Technically not a brew pub, **Cooper's Northwest Alehouse,** located north of the University District, nonetheless deserves mention for featuring the products of so many regional microbreweries. Its more than 20 brews are specialties from all over the West Coast, and the staff is awesomely knowledgeable about the subtle distinctions between each brew. If you don't come for the drink, come for the dart tournaments that are played on a regular basis. *8065 Lake City Way NE, tel. 206/522–2923. Open weekdays 3 PM–2 AM, Sat. 1 PM–2 AM, Sun. 1 PM–midnight.*

If your preference is viticulture, visit **Ste. Michelle Winery,** one of the oldest wineries in the state. It's located 15 miles northeast of Seattle, nestled on 87 wooded acres that were once part of the estate of lumber baron Fred Stimson. Some of the original 1912 buildings are still on the property, including the family home—the manor house—which is on the National Register of Historic Places. Trout ponds, a carriage house, a caretaker's cottage, and formal gardens are part of the original estate. The landscaping, created by New York's Olmsted family (designers of New York City's Central Park), has been restored, and the gardens feature hundreds of trees, shrubs, and plants. Visitors are invited to picnic and explore the grounds. Delicatessen items, wines, and wine-related gifts are available at the winery shop. In the summer, the company hosts a series of nationally known performers and arts events in the amphitheater. *14111 N.E. 145th St., Woodinville, tel. 206/488–1133. From downtown Seattle take I–90 east, then go north on I–405. Take Exit 23 east (S.R. 522) to the Woodinville exit. Complimentary wine tastings and cellar tours are available daily 10–4:30, except holidays.*

Another option if you're looking to go off the beaten track is to visit the Hiram M. Chittenden Locks, more commonly called the **Ballard Locks,** part of the 8-mile Lake Washington Ship Canal linking lakes Washington and Union with the salt water of Shilshole Bay and Puget Sound. Completed in 1917, the locks currently service some 100,000 boats yearly by raising and lowering water levels anywhere from 6 to 26 feet.

The locks themselves are fascinating to watch as a variety of commercial fishing boats and pleasure craft go through them, but there are several other sights nearby that are well worth seeing. The **Fish Ladder** has 21 levels that allow fish to swim upstream on a gradual incline. A series of seaquariumlike viewing rooms that runs alongside the ladder below the waterline allows visitors to watch several varieties of salmon and trout—an estimated half-million fish yearly—struggle against the current as they migrate upstream. (This, by the way, is where various attempts are being carried out to prevent sea lions, including the locally notorious Herschel, from depleting the salmon population.)

On the north side of the locks is a fine 7-acre **ornamental garden** of native and exotic plants, shrubs, and trees. Also on the north side is a staffed visitor center with displays on the history and operation of the locks, and several fanciful sculptures by local artists. Along the south side is a lovely 1,200-foot promenade with a footbridge, fishing pier, and an observation deck. *North entrance, 3015 N.W. 54th St., west of the Ballard Bridge. Locks tel. 206/783–7001; visitor center tel. 206/783–7059. Visitor center open daily 10–7; closed in winter, Tues., Wed.; locks open year-round, except for maintenance.*

Two legendary performers—rock guitarist Jimi Hendrix and kung-fu movie star Bruce Lee—are buried in the Seattle area; their graves are popular sites for fans who wish to pay their respects. In addition, there is a memorial to Hendrix, a Seattle native, overlooking the African Savannah exhibit at Woodland Park Zoo; appropriately enough, it's a big rock.

Jimi Hendrix's grave site is at the Greenwood Cemetery, in Renton. *From Seattle, take I–5 south to the Renton exit, then I–405 past Southcenter to Exit 4B. Bear right under the freeway, take a right along Sunset Blvd. 1 block and right again up 3rd St. Continue 1 mi and go right at the 3rd light; the cemetery is on the corner of 3rd and Monroe Sts., tel. 206/255–1511. Open daily until dusk. Inquire at the office; a counselor will direct you to the site.*

Bruce Lee's grave site is at the Lakeview Cemetery on the north slope of Capitol Hill. *1554 15th Ave. E, directly north of Volunteer Park, tel. 206/322–1582. Open weekdays 9–4:30. Inquire at the office for a map.*

Shopping

Shopping Districts

Westlake Center (1601 5th Ave., tel. 206/467–1600) lies in the middle of downtown Seattle. The three-story steel-and-glass building contains 80 upscale shops, as well as covered walkways to Seattle's two major department stores, **Nordstrom's** and **The Bon.**

Pike Place Market (*see* Exploring Seattle, *above*).

The **University District** (University Ave., north and south of 45th St., tel. 206/527–2567) has an eclectic mixture of such student-oriented imports as ethnic jewelry and South American sweaters; a few upscale shops; and many bookstores.

Seattle's **Fremont area** (N. 35th St. and Fremont Ave. N, north of the ship canal and the Fremont Bridge), a remnant from hippie days, offers products of a different variety—namely funky and used. There's the **Daily Planet** (3416 Fremont Ave. N, tel. 206/633–0895), and **Guess Where** (615 N. 35th St., tel. 206/547–3793) for vintage clothing. At **Armadillo & Co.** (3510 Fremont Pl. N, tel. 206/633–4241), you'll find jewelry, T-shirts, and other armadillo-theme accessories and gifts. The **Frank & Dunya Gallery** (3418 Fremont Ave. N, tel. 206/547–6760) features unique art pieces, from furniture to jewelry. You'll also find **Dusty Strings** (3406 Fremont Ave. N, tel. 206/634–1656), a hammered dulcimer shop.

Capitol Hill's **Broadway Avenue** features clothing stores, high-design housewares shops, espresso bars, and restaurants. An unusual boutique is the **Bead Works** (233 Broadway Ave. E, tel. 206/323–4998).

Northgate Mall, located 10 miles north of downtown, encompasses 118 shops, including **Nordstrom's, The Bon, Lamonts,** and **J.C. Penney.** *I–5 and Northgate Way, tel. 206/362–4777. Open Mon.–Sat. 9:30–9:30, Sun. 11–6.*

Southcenter Mall contains 140 shops and is anchored by major department stores. *I–5 and I–405 in Tukwila, tel. 206/246–7400. Open Mon.–Sat. 9:30–9:30, Sun. 11–6.*

Bellevue Square, an upscale shopping center about 8 miles east of Seattle, houses more than 200 shops and includes a children's play area, the Bellevue Art Museum, and covered parking. *N.E. 8th St. and Bellevue Way, tel. 206/454–8096. Open Mon.–Sat. 9:30–9:30, Sun. 11–6.*

Specialty Stores

Antiques **Antique Importers** (640 Alaskan Way, tel. 206/628–8905) carries mostly English oak antiques.

Art Dealers **Michael Pierce Gallery** (600 Pine St., tel. 206/447–9166) specializes in limited-edition prints and paintings on paper.

Art Glass The **Glass House** (311 Occidental Ave. S, tel. 206/682–9939), Seattle's only working glass studio open for public viewing, features one of the largest displays of glass artwork in the city.

Chocolates **Cafe Dilettante** (416 Broadway Ave. E, tel. 206/329–6463) is well-known for its mouth-watering dark chocolates. Recipes come via Julius Rudolf Franzen, who obtained them from the kitchen of the imperial court of Russia when he was commissioned by Czar Nicholas II as master pastry chef. Franzen emigrated to the United States where he passed his recipes on to the grandfather of Cafe Dilettante's owner.

Crafts **Pike Place Market** (*see* Exploring Seattle, *above*).
Flying Shuttle Ltd. (607 1st Ave., tel. 206/343–9762) displays handcrafted jewelry, whimsical folk art, handknits, and handwoven garments.

Jewelry **Fireworks Gallery** (210 1st Ave. S, tel. 206/682–8707; 400 Pine St., tel. 206/682–6462) features whimsical earrings and pins.
Turgeon-Raine Jewelers (1407 5th Ave., tel. 206/447–9488) is an exceptional store with a sophisticated but friendly staff.

Leather and **Bergman Luggage Co.** (1930 3rd Ave., tel. 206/448–3000) fea-
Luggage tures luggage in a variety of prices and materials.

Men's Apparel **Joseph Abboud** (1335 5th Ave., tel. 206/682–4485) features his own sophisticated designer wear, as well as casual clothing predominantly for men.
Jeffrey-Michael (1318 4th Ave., tel. 206/625–9891) provides a fine line of traditional, business, and casual men's clothing.
Mario's (1513 6th Ave., tel. 206/223–1461) offers a wide selection of contemporary menswear.

Outdoor Wear and **REI** (1525 11th Ave., tel. 206/323–8333) sells clothing as well as
Equipment outdoor equipment, including water bottles, tents, bikes, and freeze-dried food in a creaky, funky building on Capitol Hill.
Eddie Bauer (5th Ave. and Union St., tel. 206/622–2766) features sports and outdoor apparel.

Toys **Magic Mouse Toys** (603 1st Ave., tel. 206/682–8097) carries two floors of toys, from small windups to giant stuffed animals.
Great Windup (Pike Place Market, tel. 206/621–9370) carries all sorts of windup action toys.

Wine **Delaurenti Wine Shop** (1435 1st Ave., tel. 206/340–1498) has a knowledgeable staff and a large selection of Northwest Italian wines.
Pike & Western Wine Merchants (Pike Pl. and Virginia St., tel. 206/441–1307 or 206/441–1308) carries a wide selection of Northwest wines from small wineries.

Women's Apparel **Boutique Europa** (1015 1st Ave., tel. 206/624–5582) features sophisticated clothing from Europe.
Littler's (Rainier Sq., tel. 206/223–1331) offers classic fashions for women.
Local Brilliance (1535 1st Ave., tel. 206/343–5864) showcases fashions from local designers.

Sports and the Outdoors

Participant Sports

"The best things in life are free" is a homily that holds true, at least in part, when it comes to keeping fit in this most health-oriented of cities. Walking, bicycling, hiking, and jogging require little money; pay-as-you-go alternatives such as golf, kayak, sailboat, or sailboard rentals require only marginally more.

Bicycling Although much of Seattle is so hilly that recreational bicycling is strenuous, many residents nonetheless commute by bike. The trail circling **Green Lake** and the **Burke-Gilman Trail** are popular among recreational bicyclists, although at Green Lake the crowds of joggers and walkers tend to impede fast travel. The Burke-Gilman Trail is a city-maintained trail extending 12.1 miles along Seattle's waterfront from Lake Washington nearly to Salmon Bay along an abandoned railroad line; it is a much less congested path. **Myrtle Edwards Park,** north of Pier 70, has a two-lane path for jogging and bicycling. For general information about Seattle's parks and trails, call the Seattle Parks Department (tel. 206/684–4075).

A number of shops around Seattle rent mountain bikes as well as standard touring or racing bikes and equipment. Among them are **Greg's Greenlake Cycle** (7007 Woodlawn Ave. NE, tel. 206/523–1822) and **Mountain Bike Specialists** (5625 University Way NE, tel. 206/527–4310).

Fishing There are plenty of good spots for fishing on **Lake Washington, Green Lake,** and **Lake Union,** and there are several fishing piers along the **Elliott Bay** waterfront. A number of companies operating from **Shilshole Bay** also offer charter trips for catching salmon, rock cod, flounder, and sea bass. A couple of the many Seattle-based charter companies are **Ballard Salmon Charter** (tel. 206/789–6202) and **Sport Fishing of Seattle** (tel. 206/623–4253). A two-day fishing license costs $3.50, and some charter companies include it in their charges.

Golf There are almost 50 public golf courses in the Seattle area. Among the most popular municipally run courses are **Jackson Park** (1000 N.E. 135th St., tel. 206/363–4747) and **Jefferson Park** (4101 Beacon Ave. S, tel. 206/762–4513). For more information, contact the Seattle Parks and Recreation Department (tel. 206/684–4075).

Jogging, Skating, **Green Lake** is far and away Seattle's most popular spot for jog-
Walking ging, and the 3-mile circumference of this picturesque lake is custom-made for it. Walking, bicycling, roller skating, fishing, and lounging on the grass and feeding the plentiful waterfowl are also popular pastimes here. In summer, a large children's wading pool on the northeast side of the lake is a popular gathering spot. Several outlets clustered along the east side of the lake offer skate and cycle rentals.

Other good jogging locales are along the **Burke-Gilman Trail,** around the reservoir at **Volunteer Park,** and at **Myrtle Edwards Park,** north of the waterfront.

Skiing Snoqualmie Pass in the Cascade Mountains, about an hour's drive east of Seattle on I-90, has a number of fine resorts offering both day and night downhill skiing. Among them: **Alpental, Ski Acres, Snoqualmie Summit** (for all areas: 3010 77th St. SE, Mercer Island 98040, tel. 206/232–8182). All of these areas rent equipment and have full restaurant/lodge facilities.

For ski reports for these areas and the more distant White Pass, Crystal Mountain, and Stevens Pass, call 206/634–0200 or 206/634–2754. For recorded messages about road conditions in the passes, call 206/455–7900.

Tennis There are public tennis courts in many parks around the Seattle area. For information, contact the King County Parks and Recreation Department (tel. 206/296–4258).

Water Sports

Boating It stands to reason that sailboating and powerboating are popular in Seattle. **Sailboat Rentals & Yachts** (301 N. Northlake Way, tel. 206/632–3302), on the north side of Lake Union near the Fremont area, rents sailboats, with or without skippers, 14–38 feet in length, by the hour or the day. **Wind Works Rentals** (7001 Seaview Ave. NW, tel. 206/784–9386), on Shilshole Bay, rents sailboats ranging from 25 to 40 feet on the more challenging waters of Puget Sound, with or without skippers and by the half-day, day, or week. **Seacrest Boat House** (1660 Harbor Ave. SW, tel. 206/932–1050), in West Seattle, rents 18-foot aluminum fishing boats, with or without motors, by the hour or the day.

Kayaking Kayaking—around both the inner waterways (Lake Union, Lake Washington, the Ship Canal) and open water (Elliott Bay)—is a terrific and easy way to get an unusual view of Seattle's busy waterfront. **The Northwest Outdoor Center** (2100 Westlake Ave. N, tel. 206/281–9694), on the west side of Lake Union, rents one- or two-person kayaks and equipment by the hour or week and provides both basic and advanced instruction. Canoes and rowing shells are also available.

Sailboarding Lake Union and Green Lake are Seattle's prime sailboarding spots. Sailboards can be rented year-round at the **Bavarian Surf Shop** (711 N. Northlake Way, tel. 206/545–9463) on Lake Union. Lessons are available.

Spectator Sports

Baseball The **Seattle Mariners,** an American-league team, play April through early October at the Kingdome (201 S. King St., tel. 206/628–3555).

Basketball The **Seattle SuperSonics,** an NBA team, play October through April at the Seattle Center Coliseum (1st Ave. N, tel. 206/281–5850).

Boat Racing The **unlimited hydroplane** (tel. 206/628–0888) races cap Seattle's Seafair festivities from mid-July through the first Sunday in August. The races are held on Lake Washington near Seward Park, and tickets cost $10–$20. Weekly **sailing regattas** are held in the summer on Lakes Union and Washington. Call the Seattle Yacht Club (tel. 206/325–1000) for schedules.

Football Seattle's NFL team, the **Seahawks,** play August through December in the Kingdome (201 S. King St., tel. 206/827–9777).

Dining

By John Doerper

John Doerper is a local food critic and travel writer whose pieces have appeared in Travel & Leisure *and* Pacific Northwest Magazine.

Highly recommended restaurants are indicated by a star ★.

Category	Cost*
Very Expensive	over $35
Expensive	$25–$35
Moderate	$15–$25
Inexpensive	under $15

*per person, excluding drinks, service, and sales tax (about 7.9%, varies slightly by community)

American/ Continental ★ **Canlis.** This sumptuous restaurant is almost more of a Seattle institution than a place of fine dining, dating from a time when steak served by kimono-clad waitresses was the pinnacle of high living in the city by the sound. Little has changed here since the '50s. The restaurant is still very expensive, very good at what it does, and very popular; and the view across Lake Union is as good as ever (though curtained off by a forest of recently built high rises on the far shore). Besides the famous steaks, there are equally famous oysters from Quilcene Bay and fresh fish in season, cooked to a turn. *2576 Aurora Ave. N, tel. 206/ 283–3313. Reservations advised. Jacket required. AE, DC, MC, V. Closed lunch and Sun. Very Expensive.*

Metropolitan Grill. This favorite lunch spot of the executive crowd serves custom-aged, mesquite-broiled steaks in a classic steakhouse atmosphere. The steaks—the best in Seattle— are huge and come with baked potatoes or pasta. This is not food for timid eaters: Even the veal chop is extra thick, and the hamburger ("Western Ground Sirloin Steak") is so big that one person may have problems finishing it. Among the accompaniments, the onion rings and sautéed mushrooms are tops. Don't be surprised if you hear more Japanese than English as you eat here: The place is so popular with visiting businessmen that there's a menu in Japanese, too. *818 2nd Ave., tel. 206/624– 3287. Reservations advised. Dress: casual but neat. AE, DC, MC, V. Closed Sun. lunch. Moderate.*

Place Pigalle. Despite its French name, this is a very American restaurant and a popular place with locals. Large windows look out over Elliott Bay and, in nice weather, are open to admit the salt breeze. Bright flower bouquets lighten up the café tables, and the friendly staff makes you feel right at home in this small, intimate restaurant located behind a meat market in the Pike Place Market's main arcade. Seasonal meals feature seafood and local ingredients. Go for the rich oyster stew, the fresh Dungeness crab (available only when it is truly fresh), or the fresh fish of the day baked in hazelnuts. *Pike Place Market, tel. 206/624–1756. Reservations advised. Dress: casual but neat. MC, V. Closed Sun. Moderate.*

Asian ★ **Wild Ginger.** This restaurant near the Pike Place Market specializes in seafood and Southeast Asian fare, ranging from mild Cantonese to spicier Vietnamese, Thai, and Korean dishes. The *satay* (chunks of beef, chicken, or vegetables skewered and grilled, and usually served with a spicy peanut sauce) bar, where you can sit to sip local brews and eat tangy, elegantly seasoned skewered seafood or meat until 2 AM, has quickly become a favorite local hangout. The dining room has an old-fashioned club-like decor of high ceilings, lots of mahogany, and Asian art. House specialties include satay, live crab, sweetly flavored duck, and a variety of wonderful soups. A number of vegetarian dishes also are offered. *1400 Western Ave., tel. 206/623–4450. Reservations advised. Dress: casual but neat. AE, CB, DC, MC, V. Closed Sun. lunch. Moderate.*

Chinese **Linyen.** This comfortable restaurant comes into its own late at night, when Seattle celebrities mingle here with chefs from Chinatown restaurants. The standard fare is light-style Cantonese, but you're best off sticking with the blackboard specials: clams in black-bean sauce, geoduck, spicy chicken, and fish dishes. The dart games in the bar are a popular—and heated—diversion. *424 7th Ave. S, tel. 206/622–8181. Reserva-*

tions advised. Dress: casual but neat. AE, DC, MC, V. Closed lunch. Moderate.

Chau's Chinese Restaurant. This small, very plain place on the outer limits of Seattle's Chinatown serves great seafood, such as steamed oysters in garlic sauce, Dungeness crab with ginger and onion, and geoduck. Avoid the standard dishes of the Cantonese repertoire that dominate much of the menu, and stick to the seafood and specials. *310 4th Ave. S, tel. 206/621–0006. Reservations advised. Dress: casual. MC, V. Closed weekend lunch. Inexpensive.*

Deli **A. Jay's.** This little deli has done so well that it's now open for dinner Tuesday–Saturday, serving eclectic bistro-style fare, but breakfast is still the big draw. Especially on weekends, people flock here for the eggs Benedict, blintzes, whitefish, and bagels piled high with cream cheese and lox. Service is friendly. You can sit and talk without being rushed. At lunch there are large sandwiches (good pastrami), pasta, burgers, and soup. *2619 1st Ave., tel. 206/441–1511. Reservations advised. Dress: casual. AE, MC, V. Closed Sun. night. Inexpensive.*

Three Girls Bakery. It's a 13-seat glassed-in lunch counter behind a bakery outlet, serving sandwiches and soups to hungry folks in a hurry. Go for the chili and a hunk of Sicilian sourdough. Another idea is to buy a loaf at the takeout counter, get smoked salmon at the fish place next door, and head for a picnic table in Waterfront Park. *Pike Place Market, 1514 Pike Pl., tel. 206/622–1045. No reservations. Dress: casual. No credit cards. No alcohol. Closed dinner and Sun. Inexpensive.*

French **Campagne.** Overlooking Pike Place Market and Elliott Bay, Campagne is intimate and urbane. The white walls, picture windows, white linens, candles, and fresh flowers evoke southern France. Start out with fresh oysters on the half-shell, calamari fillets with ground almonds, or Campagne's own seafood sausage. The restaurant's unique French country fare replaces the traditional cream and butter sauces with oils, light stocks, and vegetable essences to create such flavorful treats as apricot-cider and green peppercorn sauce that accompanies the Oregon rabbit, or the carrot and orange essence served with the cinnamon-roasted quail. Seafood entrées include panfried scallops with a green peppercorn tarragon sauce. *Inn at the Market, 86 Pine St., tel. 206/728–2800. Reservations advised. Jacket required. AE, MC, V. Expensive.*

Le Tastevin. This restaurant set a new tone for Seattle's French restaurants when it opened. Instead of dark wood and subdued lighting, you'll find a sunny, trellised dining room, bright with light wood and green plants, and racks of wine bottles along the far walls. The windows face west, toward the Olympic Mountains and colorful sunsets. Le Tastevin serves a combination of classic French and Northwest nouvelle cuisine. The house specialty is fresh salmon with herbs baked in a puff pastry and served with a chardonney-pomegranate sauce. The wide variety of dishes featuring this ubiquitous fish also includes salmon with plum tomatoes, garlic, and basil. Cream, the staple of traditional French cookery, is almost absent except for the Coquilles St. Jacques, with a champagne-cream sauce. For dessert, you should not miss the fresh fruit ices—made daily from scratch—or the wine sorbets. As an alternative to the expensive regular lunch menu, try the bar lunch, which is just as good. In the late afternoon, during happy hour, inexpensive

Campagne, **6**
Casa-U-Betcha, **3**
Chau's Chinese, **16**
El Puerco Lloron, **7**
Emmet Watson's
  Oyster Bar, **5**
Fuller's, **1**
Hunt Club, **19**
Il Terazzo
  Carmine, **15**
Kells, **4**
Linyen, **18**
Metropolitan Grill, **13**
Nikko, **2**
The Painted Table, **12**
Place Pigalle, **10**
Siam Gourmet, **17**
Takara, **8**
Three Girls Bakery, **9**
Trattoria Mitchelli, **14**
Wild Ginger, **11**

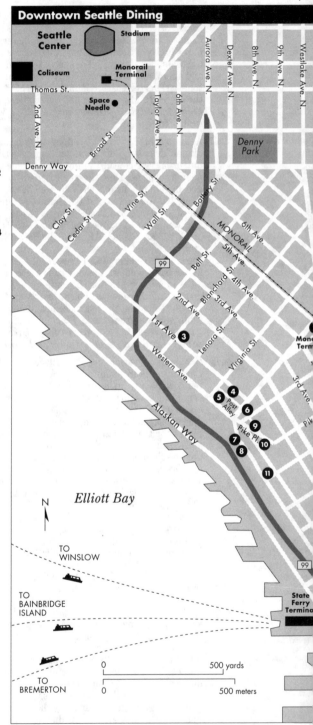

Downtown Seattle Dining

Seattle Center

Stadium

Coliseum

Monorail Terminal

Thomas St.

Space Needle

Denny Park

Aurora Ave. N.
Dexter Ave. N.
8th Ave. N.
9th Ave. N.
Westlake Ave. N.
Taylor Ave. N.
6th Ave. N.
2nd Ave. N.
Broad St.

Denny Way

Clay St.
Cedar St.
Vine St.
Wall St.
Bakery St.
Bell St.
Blanchard St.
2nd Ave.
3rd Ave.
4th Ave.
5th Ave.
6th Ave.

MONORAIL

99

1st Ave.
Western Ave.
Lenora St.
Virginia St.
Post Alley
Pike Pl.

Alaskan Way

Monorail Terminal

3rd Ave.

Pike

Elliott Bay

N

TO WINSLOW

TO BAINBRIDGE ISLAND

TO BREMERTON

99

State Ferry Terminal

0   500 yards
0   500 meters

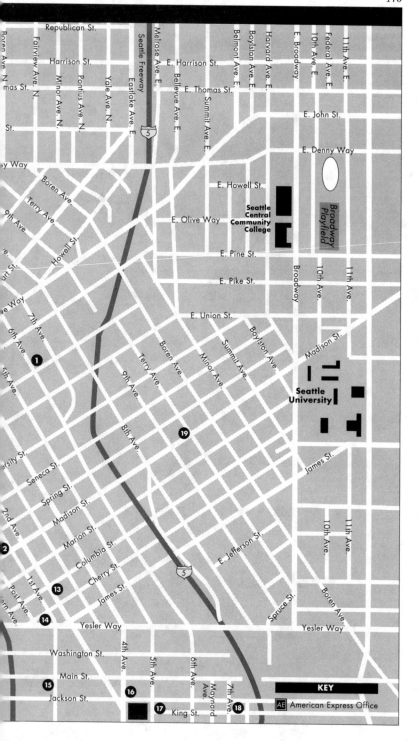

A. Jay's, **30**
Adriatica, **26**
Bahn Thai, **28**
Cafe Juanita, **27**
Canlis, **25**
Le Tastevin, **29**
Ray's Boathouse, **22**
Rover's, **31**
Saleh Al Lago, **20**
Santa Fe Cafe, **21, 24**

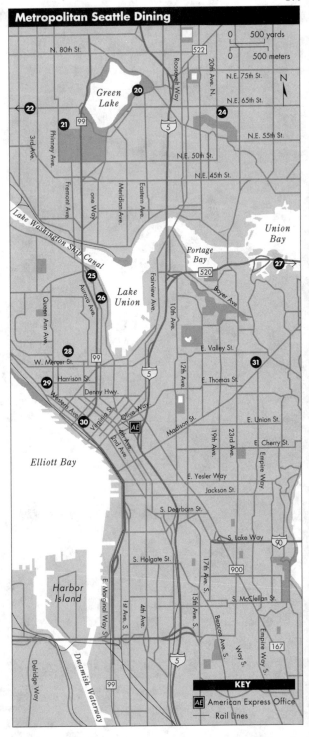

Metropolitan Seattle Dining

dishes and great snack food are served. The wine list is vast, spanning many countries and vintages, and quite reasonably priced. *19 W. Harrison St., tel. 206/283–0991. Reservations advised. Jacket required. AE, DC, MC, V. Closed Sat. lunch and Sun. Expensive.*

Rover's. This is French cooking at its best, with a daily menu based on what is locally available. Specialties include salmon, pheasant, quail, venison, and rabbit in elegant yet surprisingly light sauces. The enormous pasta dishes are among Seattle's best. Each of the dishes carries chef/owner Thierry Rautureau's Northwest-French stylings. The setting is highly romantic, in a small house with a garden. Herbs and flowers grow in flower beds just outside the windows. Service is excellent— friendly but unobtrusive. *2808 E. Madison St., tel. 206/325– 7442. Reservations advised. Dress: casual but neat. AE, MC, V. Closed lunch and Mon. Moderate.*

Irish **Kells.** Tucked into an old brick building along the Pike Place Market's most romantic thoroughfare, you'll forget you're in America when you step through the door of this pub. The accoutrements look like they've been brought over from the old country: bar, taps, wood paneling, sporting prints are all very Irish, down to the accents and politics. The food is simple but tasty: Irish stew, leg of lamb, meat pies, but there's also seafood and beef dishes. Fresh Guinness and Harp are on tap, as are hearty Northwest brews. The place rings with live Irish music Wednesday through Saturday nights. Kells is very friendly and feels an instant home away from home. In summer there's limited outdoor seating in the alley. *Pike Place Market, 1916 Post Alley, tel. 206/728–1916. Reservations advised. Dress: casual but neat. MC, V. Closed Sun. Moderate.*

Italian **Il Terrazo Carmine.** On the ground floor of a Pioneer Square office building, this restaurant surrounds diners with a comfortable, but refined atmosphere from the ceiling-to-floor draperies to the genteel service and quiet music. Chef-owner Carmine Smeraldo prepares flavorful chicken dishes with procuitto and fontina, and his veal baked with spinach and scallops is simply excellent. The pasta dishes, too, are superb. In the summer, you can choose to eat outdoors on the patio that faces a large fountain. *411 1st Ave. S, tel. 206/467–7797. Reservations advised. Dress: casual but neat. AE, D, DC, MC, V. Expensive.*

Saleh Al Lago. This restaurant north of downtown with a view of Green Lake and the park serves up some of the best Italian fare in the city. The well-lit dining room of soft colors invites simple, well-paced evening dining and choices such as the antipasti, fresh pasta, and veal dishes are always excellent. Be sure to try the *ravioli al mondo mio*, the chef's special ravioli (filling and sauce vary), or the *tagliatelle* (flat, ribboned egg pasta) with champagne and caviar. Even deceptively plain fare, like grilled breast of chicken with olive oil and fresh herbs, is superb here, with just the right—and a very light—touch. *6804 E. Greenlake Way N, tel. 206/522–7943. Reservations advised. Jacket required. AE, MC, V. Closed Sat. lunch and Sun. Expensive.*

Cafe Juanita. This comfortable, casual place—with wonderful views from the windows—is more than just a restaurant. There's a winery in the basement, and the vintages made there—bottled under owner/chef/winemaker Peter Dow's Cavatappi label—are available upstairs. The veal scaloppine and chicken dishes can be a bit on the rich and buttery side, but there's plenty of inexpensive Italian wine on the lengthy wine list to dilute the cream. Other entrées include lamb, salmon, fresh pastas, and veal. *9702 N.E. 120th Pl., Kirkland, tel. 206/ 823-1505. Reservations advised. Dress: casual but neat. MC, V. Closed lunch. Moderate.*

Trattoria Mitchelli. This archetypal Seattle storefront café is usually noisy and crowded, especially in the wee hours of the morning (the place stays open till 4 AM); and has an urban Bohemian atmosphere that's fast-paced and friendly, though you're never rushed. The food isn't haute cuisine, but it's tasty, moderately priced, and comes in generous portions: heaping servings of Italian pasta, sandwiches, and antipasti. *84 Yesler Way, tel. 206/ 623-3885. No reservations. Dress: casual. AE, DC, MC, V. Moderate.*

Japanese **Nikko.** Although Nikko has moved uptown from the International District into stylish quarters in the Westin Hotel, it continues to serve some of the best sushi and sashimi in town under the able direction of owner Shiro Kashiba. The sushi bar is the architectural centerpiece of the restaurant's sophisticated Japanese decor of low lighting and black lacquer-painted wood. The Kasuzuke cod and teriyaki salmon are both highly recommended. *Westin Hotel, 1900 5th Ave., tel. 206/322-4641. Reservations advised. Dress: casual but neat. AE, D, DC, MC, V. Closed lunch Sat., Sun. Moderate–Expensive.*

Takara. Sushi chef Kuma-san in full action can look like a character from a Japanese wood-block print: a master samurai swordsman preparing to fight heaven and earth. But there's nothing combative about the ever-smiling Kuma-san—except for his determination to serve only the freshest seafood for sushi and sashimi. It's the freshness of the raw materials and the quality of the knife handling (swordsmanship is more like it, actually) that's making him the hottest sushi chef in town. He's been known to create a perfect rose from translucent slices of raw tuna, and he can form a phoenix in full flight from a lump of rice (for the body), golden salmon caviar (to simulate the iridescent back feathers), and sparkling *nori* seaweed (for the head, beak, and wings). No wonder Japanese businessmen flock here for lunch. The dining room serves classic Japanese dishes using Northwest ingredients. The salmon teriyaki is superb, and so is the steamed black cod. *Pike Place Market Hillclimb, 1501 Western Ave., tel. 206/682-8609. Reservations advised for dining room, no reservations for sushi bar. Dress: casual but neat. AE, MC, V. Beer and sake. Closed Sun., except May–Labor Day. Moderate.*

Mediterranean **Adriatica.** This place gathered a loyal local following, becoming a virtual Seattle institution along the way, and was then discovered by visitors who spread the word. Located in a hillside Craftsman-style house, the dining room and upstairs bar offer views of Lake Union. Over several years, the fare here has evolved into a unique Pacific Northwest–influenced Greek and Italian cuisine. Regular offerings include daily fresh fish, a pasta, a risotto, and seafood souvlaki. Phyllo pastries with honey and nuts are among the tasty and interesting dessert choices. *1107 Dexter Ave. N., tel. 206/285-5000. Reservations advised. Dress: casual but neat. AE, DC, MC, V. Moderate–Expensive.*

Mexican **Casa-U-Betcha.** Colorful neon signs and faux granite sculptures standing in for room dividers create a fittingly lively atmosphere for the upscale crowd and cuisine at this trendy south of the border-themed spot. Familiar Mexican dishes are served using less grease, less cheese, and black beans rather than refried. But the menu isn't too strict, and it injects the influence of Caribbean, Central and South American cooking (south of the border here seems to mean anywhere between Texas and the equator) into such inventive offerings as Coyote Moon Carnitas—lean pork seasoned with herbs and marinated in lime juice, then grilled. *2212 1st Ave., tel. 206/441-1989. Reservations advised. Dress: casual but neat. AE, DC, MC, V. Moderate.*

El Puerco Lloron. Don't be put off by the cafeteria line and the studied "sleazy-south-of-the-border" bar look. The fresh, handmade tortillas have great texture, and the fillings are endowed with all the right flavors. The chili relleno is tops. But it almost doesn't matter what you order—tacos, *taquitos*, tamales—they're all good. The salsas are zesty and the beer is cold. *Pike Place Market Hillclimb, 1501 Western Ave., tel. 206/624-0541. No reservations. Dress: casual. AE, MC, V. Inexpensive.*

Northwest **Fuller's.** The works of northwest artists hang over the booths in
★ this dining room favored by locals for special occasions. Starter dishes include a sesame-crusted tuna pizza or a vegetable strudel with sun-dried tomatoes and goat cheese, and spinach salad with smoked duck and honey-mustard dressing. Entrées include pork loin with an apple-brandy bleu cheese sauce and monk fish with a wild mushroom-tomato ragu. All the dishes are enhanced by the elegant china and crystal settings atop linen tablecloths. Chef Monique Andree Barbeau specializes in low-fat sauces made from vegetable purées and natural reductions, but you'll forget all about that when you see the wonderfully decadent desserts. *1400 6th Ave. (in the Seattle Sheraton, at Pike St.), tel. 206/447-5544 or 800/325-3535. Reservations advised. Jacket required. AE, D, DC, MC, V. Closed Sat. lunch and Sun. Expensive.*

Hunt Club. This restaurant has gained tremendous popularity over the past few years. Located in the elegant Sorrento Hotel, the Hunt Club's traditional decor of dark wood and plush seats provides a comfortable if unlikely looking setting for the innovative and exciting cuisine. Chef Christine Cass uses fresh northwest produce in such Asian-inspired dishes as Thai-style crab cakes or Dungeness crab bisque. Entrées include tuna with a Szechuan-peppercorn sauce served with rice paper sushi. For the less adventurous, there is also rack of lamb, beef tenderloin, and salmon. The enticing desserts include gingersnap cannoli and lemon-pistachio cake. *Sorrento Hotel, 900 Madison St., tel. 206/622-6400. Reservations advised. Jacket required. AE, DC, MC, V. Expensive.*

★ **The Painted Table.** This sophisticated dining room in the Alexis Hotel opened in 1992 and is currently the only four-star restaurant in Seattle. Sand-colored walls and warm mahogany paneling and columns provide an elegant backdrop for the room's displays of works by local artists. Under the direction of French-trained executive chef Emily Moore, otherwise ordinary meats and vegetables are transformed into works of art, framed by the hand-painted plates. The northwest cuisine offers seasonal selections made from the freshest regional produce available from nearby small vendors, farms, and the Pike Place Market. Although you'll be tempted to order another bowl of the tasty crab and corn chowder and skip the entrées, make yourself try the crab cakes with aioli or the lightly smoked duck breast in ginger sauce. The wonderful and chewy walnut-onion bread is baked on the premises, and Moore, a former pastry chef, personally designed the desserts here, as well. *Alexis Hotel, 1007 1st Ave., tel. 206/624–3646. Reservations advised. Dress: casual but neat. AE, D, DC, MC, V. Closed weekend lunch. Moderate–Expensive.*

Seafood
★
Ray's Boathouse. The view of Puget Sound may be the drawing card here, but the seafood is impeccably fresh and well prepared. Perennial favorites include broiled salmon, sake kasu cod, teriyaki salmon fillets, blackened cod, and oysters prepared almost any way you could want them. Ray's has a split personality: a fancy dining room downstairs; a casual café and bar upstairs. Go for the café; the prices are lower and the food is just as good as it is downstairs. In warm weather, sit on the deck outside the café and watch a continuous parade of pilot boats, tugs, fishing boats, and pleasure yachts floating past almost below your table. You won't get bored. *6049 Seaview Ave. NE, tel. 206/789–3770. Reservations advised for window seats in dining room; no reservations for café. Dress: casual but neat. AE, DC, MC, V. Moderate.*

Emmet Watson's Oyster Bar. This small oyster bar may be a bit hard to find: It's in the back of the Pike Place Market's Soames-Dunn Building and fronts a small flower-bedecked (from spring through fall) courtyard. The decor is unpretentious, the inside booths are cramped, and a seat at the bar (in rainy weather) or in the courtyard (when the sun shines) is hard to find. But Seattleites know their oysters, and they know that this is where they'll find them. The place is worth the special effort, for the oysters are very fresh (and come in a great number of varieties) and the beer list is ample (50 or more selections, from local microbrews to fancy imports). Both oysters and beer are inexpensive. If you don't like oysters, try the salmon soup or the fish-and-chips (large flaky pieces of fish with very little grease). *Pike Place Market, 1916 Pike Pl., tel. 206/448–7721. No reservations. Dress: casual. No credit cards. Closed dinner and Sun. Inexpensive.*

Southwest
★
Santa Fe Cafe. The delicious, authentic southwestern fare here includes such spicy New Mexican dishes as green-chili burritos made with blue-corn tortillas. Interesting brews on tap help mitigate the heat of such fiery fare as the red-chili burrito (it's so hot, the waiter warns you as you order). Other choices are less *picante*, but still flavorful: the green-chili stew, the blue-corn crepes, the red or green enchiladas. Specialties are artichoke ramekin, chile relleno torte, and roasted garlic appetizer. Sauces are made from red and green chilis brought in from New Mexico. The 65th Street location offers a cozier, homey appeal, with its woven rugs and dried flowers, and is popular with graduate students and professors. The Phinney Avenue restaurant is slicker and more chic; skylights fill the place with light that brightens the soft pink-and-mauve color scheme. Visitors from Santa Fe admit that this is about as authentic as it gets. *Two locations: 2255 N.E. 65th St., tel. 206/524–7736; 5910 Phinney Ave. N, tel. 206/783–9755. Reservations advised. Dress: casual but neat. MC, V. Closed weekend lunch and Mon. Moderate.*

Thai **Bahn Thai.** Thai cooking is ubiquitous in Seattle—it can almost be considered a mainstream cuisine. Because of the variety of dishes and the quality of the preparations, the Bahn Thai, one of the pioneers of local Thai food, is still one of the best and most popular. Start your meal with a skewer of tangy chicken or pork satay, or with the *tod mun goong* (spicy fish cake), and continue with hot-and-sour soup and one of the many prawn or fish dishes. The deep-fried fish with garlic sauce is particularly good—and you can order it very hot. This restaurant promises a relaxed—particularly romantic—atmosphere in the evenings. *409 Roy St., tel. 206/283-0444. Reservations advised. Dress: casual but neat. AE, DC, MC, V. Closed weekend lunch. Inexpensive.*

Vietnamese **Saigon Gourmet.** Talk about unpretentious: This small café, set
★ in the International District, is about as plain as it gets in Seattle, but the food is superb. Aficionados make special trips for the Cambodian soup and the shrimp rolls. The peanut dipping sauce is more flavorful than usual. Do try the papaya with beef jerky—it's unusual but enjoyable. The prices are incredibly low, just one reason why this is one of the best lunch places in town. Parking, however, can be a problem. *502 S. King St., tel. 206/624-2611. No reservations. Dress: casual. No credit cards. No alcohol. Closed Tues. Inexpensive.*

Lodging

There is no shortage of lodging in Seattle. The variety ranges from the elegant deluxe hotels of downtown to the smaller, less expensive hotels in the University District; from a number of budget motels along Aurora Avenue North (Hwy. 99), many of which are legacies of the 1962 World's Fair, to the large, standard hotels strung along Pacific Highway South (Hwy. 99) that accommodate travelers near Seattle-Tacoma International Airport. Always inquire about special rates based on occupancy, weekend stays, or special packages. Also available are a number of bed-and-breakfast accommodations: For more information, contact the **Washington State Bed-and-Breakfast Guild** (2442 N.W. Market St., Seattle, WA 98107, tel. 509/548–7171) or the **Pacific Bed & Breakfast Agency** (701 N.W. 60th St., Seattle, WA 98107, tel. 206/784–0539).

Highly recommended hotels are indicated by a star ★.

Category	Cost*
Very Expensive	$180 and over
Expensive	$120–$179
Moderate	$70–$119
Inexpensive	under $70

per room, double occupancy, not including 14.1% combined hotel and state sales tax

Downtown Seattle **Alexis.** The Alexis is an intimate four-story, European–style
Very Expensive hotel in an artfully restored historic 1901 building on 1st Ave-
★ nue near the waterfront, the Public Market, and the Seattle Art Museum. Guests are greeted with complimentary sherry at this understated and elegant hotel. The rooms are decorated

Alexis, **13**
Doubletree, **22**
Edgewater, **2**
Four Seasons
Olympic Hotel, **11**
Holiday Inn
Sea-Tac, **25**
Hotel Vintage
Park, **16**
Hyatt Regency
Bellevue, **28**
Inn at the Market, **5**
Mayflower Park, **6**
Meany Tower, **19**
Pacific Plaza, **14**
Park Inn Club &
Breakfast, **1**
Red Lion Bellevue, **26**
Red Lion/Sea-Tac, **21**
Seattle Airport
Hilton, **23**
Seattle Hilton, **12**
Seattle International
Youth Hotel, **10**
Seattle Marriott, **24**
Seattle Sheraton Hotel
and Towers, **9**
Seattle YMCA, **15**
Sixth Avenue Inn, **4**
Sorrento, **18**
Stouffer Madison, **17**
University Plaza, **20**
Warwick, **3**
West Coast Bellevue
Hotel, **29**
WestCoast Camlin, **8**
Westin, **7**
Woodmark, **27**

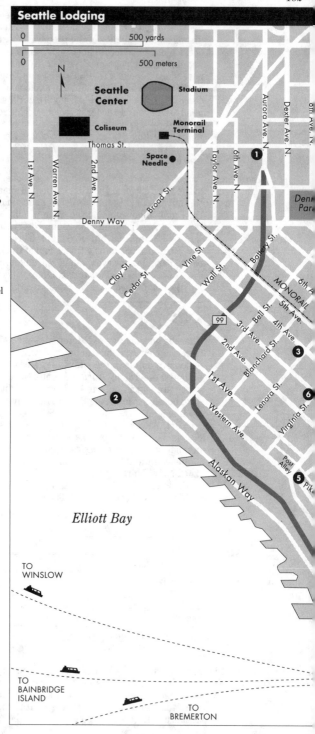

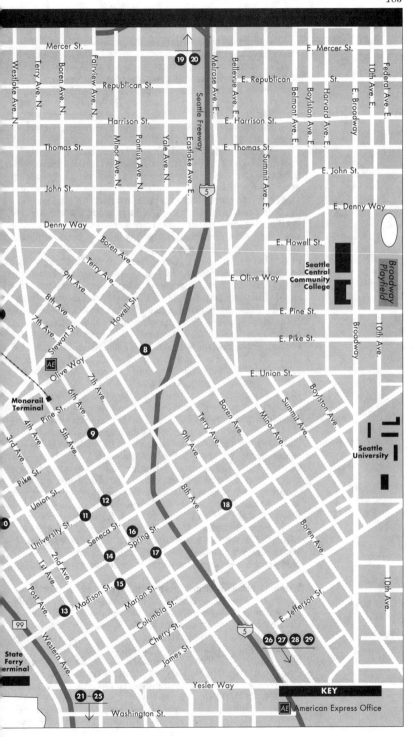

in subdued colors, with at least one piece of antique furniture in each. Some suites feature Jacuzzis, wood-burning fireplaces, and some have marble fixtures. Unfortunately, none of the rooms have any kind of view, and those facing the avenue can be noisy. Amenities include complimentary Continental breakfast, shoe shines, morning newspaper, and access to workout facilities and private steam room. The Painted Table restaurant is on the hotel's ground floor (*see* Dining, *above*). *1007 1st Ave., 98104, tel. 206/624–4844 or 800/426–7033; fax 206/621–9009. 54 rooms. Facilities: restaurant, café/bar, access to health club, steam room. AE, MC, V.*

★ **Four Seasons Olympic Hotel.** The Olympic is Seattle's most elegant hotel. In 1982, Four Seasons restored it to its 1920s Renaissance Revival–style grandeur, with the public rooms appointed with marble, wood paneling, potted plants, and thick rugs, and furnished with plush armchairs. Palms and skylights in the Garden Court provide a relaxing background for lunch, afternoon tea, or dancing to a live swing band on the weekends. The Georgian Room, the hotel's premier dining room, exudes Italian Renaissance elegance, while Shuckers oyster bar is more casual. Guest rooms are less luxurious than the public rooms and have a homey feel. They are furnished with sofas, comfortable reading chairs, and desks and decorated with period reproductions and floral print fabrics. Amenities include valet parking, 24-hour room service, stocked bar, chocolates on your pillow, complimentary shoe shines, and a bathrobe in the room for each guest. Locals drop in occasionally to pamper themselves with a massage and swim at the health club. *411 University St., 98101, tel. 206/621–1700 or 800/223–8772; fax 206/682–9633. 450 rooms. Facilities: 3 restaurants, health club, indoor pool. AE, DC, MC, V.*

Hotel Vintage Park. As tribute to the state's growing wine industry, each guest room in this small hotel is named for a Washington winery or vineyard. The theme is extended to complimentary servings of local wines each evening in the elegant lobby, where guests can relax on richly upholstered sofas and chairs arranged around the ornate marble fireplace. The rooms, which are decorated in rich color schemes of dark green, plum, deep reds, taupe and gold, are furnished with custom-made cherrywood pieces. Each room also contains original works by San Francisco artist Chris Kidd. For literary-minded guests, hotel staff will check out and deliver your choice of books from the nearby Seattle Public Library. *1100 5th Ave., 98101, tel. 206/624–8000 or 800/624–4433; fax, 206/623–0568. 129 rooms. No-smoking floors. Facilities: restaurant, health club access, secretarial services, room service. AE, DC, MC, V.*

Westin Hotel. This large high-rise hotel, located just north and east of the Pike Place Market and renovated in 1992, is easily recognizable by its twin-tower cylindrical shape. With this design, all rooms, equipped with balconies, make the most of the terrific views of the waterfront and Lake Union. The rooms themselves are airy and bright, though furnished in a plain but high-quality style. The informal Market Cafe, the more formal Palm Court, and Nikko, a stylish Japanese restaurant, as well as three lounges, are located in-house. *1900 5th Ave., 98101, tel. 206/728–1000 or 800/228–3000; fax 206/728–2259. 865 rooms, including 47 suites; no-smoking and handicapped rooms available. Facilities: 3 restaurants, 3 lounges, indoor* *pool, Jacuzzi, sauna, exercise and weight rooms, voice mail for guests, concierge service. AE, D, DC, MC, V.*

Expensive **Edgewater.** The only hotel on Elliott Bay, the Edgewater is an institution, known for the now-defunct tradition of guests' fishing from their waterside windows. In 1988 the new owners banned hotel fishing and remodeled the 238 rooms, and the results are magnificent. The lobby features oak furnishings and comfortable chairs and sofas, with a fireplace and a panoramic bay window from which you can sometimes see sea lions frolicking. Spacious rooms on the water provide views of ferries, barges, and the Olympic Mountains, and are decorated in rustic Northwest plaids and unfinished wood furnishings. *Pier 67, 2411 Alaskan Way, 98121, tel. 206/728–7000 or 800/624–0670; fax 206/441–4119. 238 rooms. Facilities: restaurant, bar. AE, DC, MC, V.*

Seattle Hilton. This Hilton is a favorite for conventions and meetings, especially because of its central location. Rooms are furnished in the same nondescript but tasteful style characteristic of Hiltons worldwide, and have soothing color schemes. One of its two restaurants, the Top of the Hilton, serves well-prepared variations of salmon steak and other local specialties, and has excellent views of the city. An underground passage connects the Hilton with a shopping concourse, Rainier Square, as well as with the 5th Avenue Theater and the Washington State Convention Center. *1301 University St., 98101, tel. 206/624–0500, 800/542–7700, or 800/426–0535; fax 206/682–9029. 237 rooms, including 6 suites; no-smoking floors available. Facilities: 2 restaurants, lobby, top-floor piano bar, gift shop. AE, D, DC, MC, V.*

Seattle Sheraton Hotel and Towers. The Sheraton is a modern, 840-room hotel (renovated in 1991) catering largely to conventioneers, as it is conveniently located near the Washington State Convention & Trade Center. The lobby features an art-glass collection by Dale Chihuly, a Northwest artist of international repute. The Towers (top five floors) feature larger, more elegant rooms with concierge service, and complimentary Continental breakfast. Within the complex is a diverse selection of restaurant entertainment options, including Banners, which offers an authentic Japanese breakfast, buffet luncheon, and Continental menu; Gooey's (named after the geoduck, a large, sausagelike northwestern clam that is the subject of many jokes), the bar/disco nighttime hot spot; and Fullers, one of the best restaurants in Seattle, serving nouvelle cuisine using local ingredients. *1400 6th Ave., 98101, tel. 206/621–9000 or 800/325–3535; fax 206/621–8441. 840 rooms. Facilities: 2 restaurants, 2 bars, health club, indoor pool. AE, D, DC, MC, V.*

★ **Sorrento.** This deluxe European-style hotel, built in 1909 for the Alaska-Yukon Exposition, was designed to look like an Italian villa. It has since been restored to its original elegance. The dramatic entrance is along a circular driveway around an Italian fountain, and ringed by palm trees. Sitting high on First Hill, it has wonderful views overlooking downtown and the waterfront. The rooms are smaller than a more modern hotel's, but are quiet and very comfortable; they're decorated in understated, elegant earth tones. The largest rooms are the corner suites with some antiques and spacious baths. The stylish Hunt Club (*see* Dining, *above*) restaurant features exquisite Northwest-Asian dishes by chef Christine Cass, while the dark-paneled Fireside Lounge in the lobby is a warm and inviting spot for sipping coffee, tea, or a cocktail. Other amenities include a complimentary limousine service within the downtown area, concierge, and guest privileges at a nearby athletic club. *900 Madison St., 98104, tel. 206/622–6400; fax 206/625–1059. 76 rooms, 42 suites. Facilities: restaurant, lounge, access to health club. AE, DC, MC.*

Stouffer Madison Hotel. This high-rise hotel, located between downtown and I–5, was built in 1983. Rooms are decorated in peach and green tones, and come equipped with wood cabinets and marble countertops, and those on the 10th floor and up have good views of downtown, Elliott Bay, and the Cascade Mountains. Views above the 20th floor are excellent. Club-level floors (25 and 26) feature their own concierge, complimentary Continental breakfast, and a library. Amenities on other floors include complimentary coffee, morning newspaper and shoe shines. The health club includes a 40-foot rooftop pool and a Jacuzzi. *515 Madison St., 98104, tel. 206/583–0300 or 800/468–3571; fax 206/622–8635. 554 rooms. Facilities: 2 restaurants, lounge, indoor pool, Jacuzzi, health club, indoor parking. AE, D, DC, MC, V.*

Warwick Hotel. The Warwick manages to combine its somewhat large size with intimate European-style charm. Service is friendly and leisurely (but not slow), and the rooms, renovated in 1991, are understated without being bland. All rooms have small balconies and good views of downtown. The lobby was renovated in 1993. There is live entertainment in the Liaison restaurant and lounge. *401 Lenora St., 98121, tel. 206/443–4300; fax 206/448–1662. 230 units, including 4 suites; no-smoking and handicapped rooms available. Facilities: 24-hr courtesy transportation within downtown, pool, Jacuzzi, exercise room, sauna. AE, D, DC, MC, V.*

Moderate–Expensive
★

Inn at the Market. This is a sophisticated but unpretentious hotel which opened in 1985 adjacent to the Pike Place Market. It combines the best aspects of a small, French country inn with the informality of the Pacific Northwest, offering a lively setting that's perfect for travelers who prefer originality, personality, and coziness to big-hotel amenities. The rooms are spacious and tastefully decorated with comfortable modern furniture and small touches such as fresh flowers and ceramic sculptures. Ask for a room with views of the Market and Elliott Bay. An added plus is a 2,000-square-foot deck, furnished with Adirondack chairs and overlooking the water and the market. There are three restaurants that are not part of the hotel but share the building: Campagne (*see* Dining, *above*); the Gravity Bar, an ultratrendy hangout with a variety of juices and coffees; and Cafe Dilettante for light meals, fine chocolates, and coffees. *86 Pine St., 98109, tel. 206/443–3600; fax 206/448–0631. 65 rooms; no-smoking rooms available. Facilities: 3 restaurants, access to health club and spa, room service, TV. AE, D, DC, MC, V.*

Mayflower Park Hotel. This pleasant older hotel, built in 1927, is conveniently connected with Westlake Center and the Monorail terminal to Seattle Center. Brass fixtures and antiques give both the public and private spaces a muted Oriental feel, and the service is similarly unobtrusive and smooth. The rooms are somewhat smallish, but the Mayflower Park is so sturdily constructed that it is much quieter than many modern downtown hotels. *405 Olive Way, 98101, tel. 206/623–8700; fax 206/382–6997. 182 units, including 14 suites; no-smoking rooms* available. *Facilities: restaurant, lounge, access to health club. AE, DC, MC, V.*

Moderate **Pacific Plaza.** Built in 1929 and refurbished in 1992, this hotel reflects its original character. The rooms and furnishings, reminiscent of the '20s and '30s, are appropriate for singles or couples but are too small to comfortably accommodate a family. Because of its downtown location and modest rates, the Plaza is a good choice for anyone who is not seeking contemporary luxury. *400 Spring St., 98104, tel. 206/623–3900 or 800/426–1165; fax 206/623–2059. 160 rooms. Facilities: 2 restaurants, complimentary Continental breakfast. AE, DC, MC, V.*

WestCoast Camlin Hotel. This 1926 Seattle apartment/hotel was remodeled in 1987 and resulted in a gracious lobby featuring Oriental carpets, large mirrors, and lots of marble. Located on the edge of the downtown office area, but close to the convention center, this reasonably priced hotel is popular with business travelers. Rooms ending with 10 are best because they feature windows on three sides, and all have working spaces with a chair and a table, along with cushioned chairs for relaxing. One drawback here, though, is the noisy heating, air-conditioning, and ventilation system. *1619 9th Ave., 98101, tel. 206/682–0100 or 800/426–0670; fax 206/682–7415. Facilities: restaurant, lounge, outdoor pool. AE, D, DC, MC, V.*

Inexpensive **Seattle YMCA.** This accommodation has 198 units and is a member of the American Youth Hostels Association. Rooms are clean and plainly furnished with a bed, phone, desk, and lamp. Rooms cost about $40; bunk units, designed to accommodate four people each, cost about $20. *909 4th Ave., 98104, tel. 206/382–5000. 198 units. Facilities: pool, health club. No credit cards.*

Youth Hostel: Seattle International. Situated near the Pike Place Market is a bright, clean youth hostel with 128 dormitory-style beds, kitchen, dining room, lounge, and small library for about $20 a night. It's closed between 11 and 4 daily for cleaning and has a 2 AM curfew. *84 Union St., 98101, tel. 206/622–5443. 128 units. No credit cards.*

Seattle Center **Meany Tower Hotel.** This pleasant hotel is just a few blocks from
Moderate the University of Washington's campus. Built in 1931 and re-
★ modeled many times since, it has managed to retain much of its old-fashioned charm, with a muted-peach color scheme throughout, brass fixtures, and careful, attentive service. The rooms, especially those on the higher floors, have good views of the college grounds with glimpses of Green Lake and Lake Union. Other amenities include room service and a complimentary morning paper. The Meany Grill on the ground floor serves breakfast, lunch, and dinner; there is a large street-level lounge as well. *4507 Brooklyn Ave. NE, 98105, tel. 206/634–2000; fax 206/634–2000. 55 rooms; no-smoking rooms available. Facilities: restaurant, lounge. AE, DC, MC, V.*

Sixth Avenue Inn. This small but comfortable motor hotel a few blocks north of downtown is a suitable location for families and business travelers. Rooms are pleasant, with wicker furnishings and standard-issue but well-maintained decor and color schemes; the service is cheerful. This is the hotel of choice for musicians playing at Dimitriou's Jazz Alley, the highly regarded club across the street. *2000 6th Ave., 98121, tel. 206/441–8300; fax 206/441–9903. 166 rooms; no-smoking rooms available. Facilities: restaurant, lounge. AE, DC, MC, V.*

University Plaza Hotel. This is a full-service motor hotel, just across I–5 from the University of Washington's campus, making it popular with families and others who have business in the area. The mock-Tudor decor gives its lobby and other public areas a slightly outdated feel, but the service is cheerful and the rooms are spacious and pleasantly decorated in teak furniture, with pale pinks and grays being the predominant colors. The rooms on the freeway side, however, can be noisy. *400 N.E. 45th St., 98105, tel. 206/634–0100; fax 206/633–2743. 135 rooms; no-smoking rooms available. Facilities: restaurant, lounge, outside heated pool, beauty parlor, fitness room. AE, D, DC, MC, V.*

Inexpensive **Park Inn Club & Breakfast.** This '60s-vintage motel, set off Aurora Avenue (Hwy. 99), is relatively close to Seattle Center. The decor is comfortable but not fancy, featuring nondescript contemporary furnishings and color schemes of beige and brown or pastels. Service is friendly and brisk. Continental breakfast, a cafeteria, weight room, and play area for children make this lodging a good value. *225 Aurora Ave. N, 98107, tel. 206/728–7666. 160 rooms, no-smoking rooms available. Facilities: complimentary Continental breakfast, indoor pool, Jacuzzi, parking. AE, MC, V.*

Seattle-Tacoma **Red Lion/Sea-Tac.** The Red Lion is a popular, hospitable 850-
Airport room, full-service convention hotel. Built in about 1970, it has
Expensive since been remodeled in mauve, teal, and gray. Rooms are spacious and bright, with large panoramic balconies; the corner "King Rooms" feature wraparound balconies and have the best views. Furnishings include chests of drawers, comfortable chairs, a dining table, and a desk; this is the perfect accommodation for the business traveler who plans on doing some work between meetings. *18740 Pacific Hwy. S, 98168, tel. 206/246–8600; fax 206/242–9727. 850 rooms. Facilities: 2 restaurants, coffee shop, 2 lounges, 24-hr workout facility with outdoor pool. AE, D, DC, MC, V.*

Seattle Airport Hilton. This relatively small hotel (for a Hilton) has an intimate, original feel accentuated by the lobby's oak furnishings, cozy fireplace, and paintings of Northwest scenery. The large rooms, renovated in 1993, are bright and decorated in pastel colors. This is also conveniently located: only a half-hour drive from downtown and a 10-minute drive from Southcenter shopping mall. *17620 Pacific Hwy. S, 98188, tel. 206/244–4800; fax 206/439–7439. 173 rooms. Facilities: restaurant, sports bar, health facilities, outdoor pool, complimentary shuttle to airport. AE, D, DC, MC, V.*

Moderate– **Doubletree Inn** and **Doubletree Suites.** These two hotels, situ-
Expensive ated across the street from each other, are adjacent to Southcenter shopping mall and convenient to the myriad of business-park offices there. The inn is a classic Pacific Northwest–style lodge. Rooms are smaller and less lavish than those at the Suites, but otherwise perfectly nice and cost at least $25 less. Suites, decorated in neutrals, mauves, and pinks, feature a sofa, table and chairs, and a wet bar in the living room. The vanity area includes a full-size closet with mirrored doors. *Doubletree Inn, 205 Strander Blvd., Tukwila 98188, tel. 206/246–8220. 198 rooms. Facilities: dining room, coffee shop, lounge, outdoor pool. Doubletree Suites, 16500 Southcenter Pkwy., Tukwila 98188, tel. 206/575–8220; fax 206/575–4743. 221 suites. Facilities: restaurant, lounge, health club, indoor*

pool, Jacuzzi, sauna, 2 racquetball courts. Doubletree Inn: Moderate; Doubletree Suites: Moderate–Expensive. AE, D, DC, MC, V (for both).

★ **Seattle Marriott.** A surprisingly luxurious and substantial hotel considering its non-downtown location, this Marriott, built in 1981, features a five-story-high, 20,000-square-foot tropical atrium that's complete with waterfall, dining area, indoor pool, and lounge. The rooms are decorated in greens and mauve with dark wood and brass furnishings. *3201 S. 176th St., 98188, tel. 206/241–2000, international reservations tel. 800/228–9290; fax 206/248–0789. 459 rooms; no-smoking rooms available. Facilities: restaurant, 2 whirlpools, health club, games room, airport shuttle, concierge service. AE, D, DC, MC, V. Special rates available to AAA and AARP members; package rates available for weekends.*

Moderate **Holiday Inn Sea-Tac.** This 260-room hotel, built in 1970, was remodeled in 1991, and a more private garden room, convenient for meeting people, was added to the atrium lobby. The Top of the Inn revolving-view restaurant features singing waiters. *17338 Pacific Hwy. S, 98188, tel. 206/248–1000 or 800/HOLIDAY; fax 206/242–7089. 260 rooms. Facilities: restaurant, coffee shop, gift shop, lounge, health club, indoor pool, Jacuzzi. AE, DC, MC, V.*

Bellevue/ **Hyatt Regency Bellevue.** This deluxe high-rise complex in the
Kirkland heart of downtown Bellevue, within a few blocks of Bellevue
Expensive Square and other fine shopping locales, opened in 1989. The exterior looks pretty much like any other sleek high rise, but the interior has such Oriental touches as antique Japanese *tansu* (wood chests of drawers) and huge displays of fresh flowers. The rooms are decorated in similarly understated ways, with floor-to-ceiling windows and dark wood and earth tones predominating the color scheme. The service is impeccable. Some rooms have been specially designed for Japanese travelers. Deluxe suites include two bedrooms, bar facilities, and meeting rooms with desks and full-length tables. The Eques restaurant serves excellent and reasonably priced breakfast, lunch, and dinner; an English-style pub serves a variety of drinks as well as lunch and dinner. *900 Bellevue Way NE, 98004, tel. 206/462–2626; fax 206/646–7567. 382 units, including 30 suites and deluxe suites; no-smoking rooms available. Facilities: restaurant, pub, 24-hr room service, access to health club and pool. AE, D, DC, MC, V.*

Red Lion Bellevue. This 10-story hotel was built in 1982 and has a large, airy atrium filled with trees, shrubs, and flowering plants. The property also has a formal dining room, a lounge with two dance floors, and 353 oversize rooms, many decorated in mauve and sea-foam green. Rooms have either king- or queen-size beds, and two-room suites feature wet bars and spas or Jacuzzis. A new Italian restaurant, Velato's, opened here in 1993. *300 112th Ave. SE, Bellevue 98004, tel. 206/455–1300 or 800/274–1415; fax 206/454–0466. 353 rooms. Facilities: 2 restaurants, lounge, health club, outdoor pool. AE, D, DC, MC, V.*

★ **Woodmark Hotel.** This hotel, built in 1989, is the only one on the shores of Lake Washington; downtown Kirkland is only a few steps away from the hotel. Its 100 contemporary-style rooms face the water, courtyard, or street and are tastefully furnished in European-style luxury, with earth tones, heavy comforters, and numerous amenities such as terry-cloth bathrobes and fragrant soaps. Comfortable chairs surround the fireplace in the large, open lobby; and a circular staircase descends to the lounge, passing a huge bay window and vast view of Lake Washington. The Carillon Room restaurant offers pasta and fresh fish dishes and excellent waterviews. *1200 Carillon Point, Kirkland 98033, tel. 206/822–3700 or 800/822–3700; fax 206/822–3699. 100 rooms. Facilities: restaurant, access to health club. AE, MC, V.*

Inexpensive **West Coast Bellevue Hotel.** This hotel/motor inn features 176 rooms, 16 of which are town-house suites, suitable for two to four people, with sleeping lofts and wood-burning fireplaces. Rooms are clean; those in the corporate wing face the courtyard and are larger and quieter than the others. The hotel is about eight blocks or a 20-minute walk from Bellevue Square. A complimentary appetizer buffet, offered in the lounge weekdays between 5 and 7 PM, is substantial and includes seafood and roast beef, and is sometimes built around a theme, such as Mexican or Scandinavian cuisine. *625 116th Ave. NE, Bellevue 98004, tel. 206/455–9444, fax 206/455–2154. 176 rooms. Facilities: restaurant, coffee shop, lounge, outdoor pool. AE, D, DC, MC, V.*

The Arts and Nightlife

The Arts

Seattle has gained a world-class reputation as a theater town, and it also has a strong music and dance scene for local, national, and international artists. A good handle on what's happening in town can be found in any of several periodicals. Both the *Seattle Times* and *Post-Intelligencer* have pull-out sections on Friday detailing most of the coming week's events. The *Seattle Weekly*, which hits most newsstands on Wednesday, has even more detailed coverage and arts reviews. *The Rocket*, a lively free monthly, covers music news, reviews, and concert information, with an emphasis on rock and roll.

Ticketmaster (tel. 206/628–0888) provides (for an added fee) tickets to most productions in the Seattle area through charge-by-phone. **Ticket/Ticket** (401 Broadway E, tel. 206/324–2744) or **Pike Place Market Information Booth** (1st Ave. and Pike St., tel. 206/682–7453 ext. 26) sell half-price tickets for most events on the day of the performance or the day before for matinees. Cash only, and in-person only.

Part of the legacy left by the 1962 World's Fair is a series of performance halls at **Seattle Center** (305 Harrison St., tel. 206/684–8582). Seattle also boasts two fine classic (and beautifully renovated) early 20th-century music halls—the **Fifth Avenue** (1308 5th Ave., tel. 206/625–1900) and the **Paramount** (907 Pine St., tel. 206/682–1414). Other prominent venues are the **Moore Theater** (1932 2nd Ave., tel. 206/443–1744), the small but acoustically outstanding **Broadway Performance Hall** (1625 Broadway, tel. 206/323–2623) at Seattle Central Community College, and **Kane** and **Meany halls** on the University of Washington campus (tel. 206/543–4880).

The **Cornish College of the Arts** (710 E. Roy St., tel. 206/323–1400) is an internationally recognized school that also serves as home to a number of distinguished professional performing groups. These groups stage productions September–May, ranging from dance and jazz to art lectures and multimedia performances. Of particular note are the Professional Acting Conservatory and the renowned Cornish New Performance Group, which often premieres important new pieces of music.

Theater **The Annex Theatre** (1916 4th Ave., Way, tel. 206/728–0933) is a cabaret-style, avant-garde, nonEquity theater specializing in new works and is run by a collective of 35 artists.

A Contemporary Theater (100 W. Roy St., tel. 206/285–5110) specializes in developing works by emerging playwrights, including at least one world premiere every year. The season runs May–November, and every December ACT mounts a popular production of Dickens's *A Christmas Carol*. There are tentative plans for a move in 1995 to the Eagles Auditorium site near the Convention Center.

The **Bathhouse Theater** (7312 W. Greenlake Dr. N, tel. 206/524–9108) produces six productions on a year-round schedule, specializing in innovative updates on classics. In addition, it mounts numerous free public shows in various Seattle parks.

Crêpe de Paris (1333 5th Ave., tel. 206/623–4111), a restaurant in the Rainier Tower building downtown, offers some side-splitting cabaret theater and musical revues, such as The Bouffants, an all-girl group complete with tall beehive hairdos and cat's-eye glasses.

The **Empty Space Theater** (3509 Fremont Ave., tel. 206/547–7500) has a reputation for introducing Seattle to new playwrights. The season generally runs Nov.–June, with five or six main-stage productions and several smaller shows throughout the season.

The **Fifth Avenue Musical Theater Company** (Fifth Avenue Theater, 1308 5th Ave., tel. 206/625–1468) is a resident professional troupe that mounts four lavish musicals between October and May each year, with each run lasting about two weeks. (During the rest of the year, this chinoiserie-style historical landmark, carefully restored to its original 1926 condition, hosts a variety of other traveling musical as well as theatrical performances.)

The **Group Theater** (305 Harrison St., on the fountain level of the Center House in Seattle Center, tel. 206/441–1299) is a multicultural troupe that prides itself on presenting socially provocative works—old and new—by artists of varied cultures and colors. The season runs September–June, and the Group also mounts a special summertime playwrights' festival. Of the regular season's six productions, one is always the popular *Voices of Christmas*, a study of the holidays with consideration to cultural differences and ethnic and emotional barriers.

The **Intiman Theater** (Playhouse at Seattle Center, 2nd and Mercer Sts., tel. 206/624–4541) presents the great plays with enduring themes of world drama in an intimate, high-quality setting. The season generally runs May–November.

The **New City Theater and Arts Center** (1634 11th Ave., tel. 206/323–6800) is home to a wide range of experimental performances, produced by a resident company as well as in conjunction with major national and international artists. Its yearly output includes six plays, a director's festival and a playwright's festival, three dance concerts, a monthly film showing, and a lively, late-night monthly cabaret.

The **Seattle Repertory Theater** (Bagley Wright Theater at Seattle Center, 155 Mercer St., tel. 206/443–2222) presents a variety of high-quality programming, from classics to new plays. During its October–May season, six main stage productions and three smaller shows (in the adjoining PONCHO Forum) are presented.

The **Village Theater** (120 Front St. N, Issaquah, tel. 206/392–2202) produces high-quality family musicals, comedies, and dramas September–May in Issaquah, a town east of Seattle.

Dance   **Allegro Dance Company** (Broadway Performance Hall, 1625 Broadway, tel. 206/32–DANCE) presents the best in local and regional choreography, with some productions that include other elements of the performing arts. It schedules about 10 concerts a year between September and June.

Meany Hall for the Performing Arts (University of Washington campus, tel. 206/543–4880) presents important national and international companies, September–May, with an emphasis on modern and jazz dance.

On the Boards (Washington Performance Hall, 153 14th Ave., tel. 206/325–7901) presents and produces a wide variety of contemporary performances, including not only dance but also theater, music, and multimedia events by local, national, and international artists. Although the main subscription series runs October–May, OTB events happen nearly every weekend year-round.

Pacific Northwest Ballet (Opera House at Seattle Center, tel. 206/547–5920) is a resident company and school that presents 60–70 performances annually. Its Christmastime production of *The Nutcracker*, with choreography by Kent Stowell and sets by Maurice Sendak, has become a beloved Seattle tradition.

Music   **Civic Light Opera** (11051 34th Ave. NE, tel. 206/363–2809) is a non-Equity, semipro company that offers three or four high-quality productions of large-scale American musical theater per season. The season runs roughly October–May.

Northwest Chamber Orchestra (tel. 206/343–0445) is the Northwest's only professional chamber-music orchestra. At the Moore Theater, the Nippon Kan, and other venues, it presents a full spectrum of music, from Baroque to modern. The season, generally September–May, includes a Bach festival every fall, a spring subscription series, and special holiday performances in December.

Seattle Symphony (Opera House at Seattle Center and other locations, tel. 206/443–4747) presents some 120 concerts September–June in Seattle and around the world and—under the musical direction of Gerard Schwartz—continues its long tradition of excellence.

A number of other organizations sponsor classical series throughout the year. An integral part of Seattle's strong early music scene is the **Early Music Guild** (tel. 206/325–7066), which presents regional, national, and international artists in various intimate settings during a season running roughly September–May. The 100-year-old **Ladies Musical Club** (tel. 206/328–7153), composed of professional or retired musicians, sponsors four or five recitals each year by internationally known artists.

For live rock concerts, the **Moore Theater** (1932 2nd Ave., tel. 206/443–1744) and the **Paramount** (907 Pine St.; for tickets and information, Ticketmaster, tel. 206/628–0888) are elegant former movie/music halls that now host visiting and national rock acts.

Opera **Seattle Opera** (Opera House at Seattle Center, Mercer St. at 3rd Ave., tel. 206/389–7676) is a world-class opera company, generally considered to be one of the top organizations in the United States. During the August–May season, it presents six performances of six productions.

Nightlife

For a city its size, Seattle has a remarkably strong and diverse music scene. On any given night, you can hear high-quality live sounds—ranging from traditional jazz and ethnic folk music to garage-punk rock—at a variety of venues. Jazz, blues, and R&B have long been Seattle favorites, and each year are showcased on major stages at the Labor Day Bumbershoot Festival at the Seattle Center. The Cornish School fosters a healthy jazz scene through its students and internationally known instructors. There is also a particularly strong blues circuit in and around town. Seattle is a center for grunge rock, as seen in the movie *Singles*, which was filmed on location here. Some of the better-known Seattle bands to spring from this scene include Nirvana, Screaming Trees, Pearl Jam, and Alice in Chains. Areas with high concentrations of clubs and taverns include Belltown, also known as the Denny Regrade, just north of the Pike Place Market, Ballard, Pioneer Square, and Capitol Hill. Many of these clubs feature a wide variety of live rock, including hard-rock, funk-rock, roots-rock, folk-rock, garage-punk, grunge, and probably whatever comes along next. (*see* Rock Clubs, *below*).

Bars and Bars with waterfront views are plentiful in Seattle. Among the
Lounges best: on Elliott Bay, **Ernie's Bar & Grill** (2411 Alaskan Way, Pier 67, tel. 206/728–7000) in the Edgewater Hotel (the hotel's lobby offers great views of the bay and the Olympic Mountains); on the Ship Canal, **Hiram's at the Locks** (5300 34th Ave. NW, tel. 206/784–1733); on Lake Union, **Triple's Seafood Bistro** (1200 Westlake Ave. N, tel. 206/284–2535) and **Arnie's** (1900 N. Northlake Way, tel. 206/547–3242); and on Shilshole Bay, **Ray's Boathouse** (6049 Seaview Ave. NW, tel. 206/789–3770) and **Anthony's Home Port** (6135 Seaview Ave. NW, tel. 206/783–0780).

Panoramic views of the city can be found at **Salty's** (1396 Harbor Ave. SW, tel. 206/937–1600), a noisy sprawling restaurant and lounge in West Seattle with unparalleled views of downtown, and at the **Space Needle** (Seattle Center, tel. 206/443–2100), where the revolving restaurant provides a 360-degree view during the course of an hour.

Other fine places for a drink downtown are the **Garden Court** (411 University St., tel. 206/621–1700) at the Four Seasons Olympic, a rather formal and elegant locale; the **J&M Cafe** (201 1st Ave. S, tel. 206/624–1670), a lively and casual Pioneer Square joint; and, near the Kingdome, **F. X. McRory's** (419 Occidental Ave. S, tel. 206/623–4800), famous for its huge selection of single-malt whiskies and the equally huge singing bartender.

Folk Clubs **Backstage** (2208 N.W. Market St., tel. 206/781–2805) is an often-packed basement venue in Ballard that has a lively mix of national and local acts with the emphasis on world music, offbeat rock, and new folk.

Kells (1916 Post Alley, tel. 206/728–1916), a snug Irish-style pub, is located near the Pike Place Market and plays live Celtic music Wednesday–Saturday starting at 9 PM.

Murphy's Pub (2110 45th St. NE, tel. 206/634–2110) features open-mike Wednesdays, with Irish and other folk music on Friday and Saturday in this cozy neighborhood bar.

Blues/R&B Clubs The **Ballard Firehouse** (5429 Russell St. NW, tel. 206/784–3516) is the music mecca in the heart of Ballard, with an emphasis on local and national blues acts.

Chicago's (315 1st Ave. N, tel. 206/282–7791) features Chicago-style pizza and other kinds of good, reasonably priced Italian food in this restaurant just west of the Seattle Center. Live blues is played on weekends.

Larry's (209 1st Ave. S, tel. 206/624–7665) features live R&B and blues nightly in an unpretentious, friendly, and usually jam-packed tavern/restaurant in Pioneer Square.

Old Timer's Cafe (620 1st Ave., tel. 206/623–9800) is a popular Pioneer Square restaurant and bar with live music—mostly R&B—nightly.

The **Scarlet Tree** (6521 Roosevelt Way NE, tel. 206/523–7153), a neighborhood institution, is a restaurant and bar just north of the University District. Great burgers and live R&B are offered nightly.

Jazz Clubs **Dimitriou's Jazz Alley** (2037 6th Ave., tel. 206/441–9729) is a downtown club with nationally known, consistently high-quality performers every night but Sunday. Excellent dinners are served before the first shows.

Latona Tavern (6423 Latona Ave. NE, tel. 206/525–2238) is a funky, friendly, often jazz-oriented, neighborhood bar at the south end of Green Lake that features a variety of local musicians playing folk, blues, and jazz nightly.

Lofurno's (2060 15th Ave., tel. 206/283–7980), located south of the Ballard Bridge, offers reasonably priced Italian food and jazz on Sunday nights.

New Orleans Creole Restaurant (114 1st Ave. S, tel. 206/622–2563) is a popular Pioneer Square restaurant with good food and live jazz nightly—mostly top local performers but occasionally national acts as well.

Rock Clubs **Central Tavern** (207 1st Ave. S, tel. 206/622–0209) is a crowded Pioneer Square tavern with an ever-changing roster of local and national rock acts.

The **Crocodile Cafe** (2200 2nd Ave., tel. 206/441–5611) is described by a local music critic as Seattle's "hippest hangout," with its variety of folk-rock, acoustic-rock, hard-rock, and new-wave groups every night but Monday.

Doc Maynard's (610 1st Ave., tel. 206/682–4649) is a classic rock-and-roll-oriented tavern with a small and always jam-packed dance floor.

The **Off-Ramp Music Cafe** (109 Eastlake E, tel. 206/628–0232) features a rock nightly, often the heavy-metal kind.

OK Cafe/Gallery & Club (212 Alaskan Way S, tel. 206/621–7903) offers rock, folk, and jazz nightly in a small venue near Pioneer Square.

Parker's (17001 Aurora Ave. N, tel. 206/542–9491) was a venerable North Seattle teen palace of the '50s and '60s but has since become a more sophisticated dinner-and-show venue for a variety of more traditional popular rock artists, often nationally known acts.

The **Re-Bar** (1114 Howell St., tel. 206/233–9873) presents an eclectic mix of music nightly including acid-jazz and soul-rhythm.

Vogue (2018 1st Ave., tel. 206/443–0673), a club in Belltown, the artists' community just north of the Public Market, presents a variety of au courant local and national rock.

Comedy Clubs **Comedy Underground** (222 S. Main St., tel. 206/628–0303), a Pioneer Square club (literally underground, beneath Swannie's), presents stand-up comedy nightly, with Monday and Tuesday reserved as open-mike nights; the other nights are mixtures of nationally known and local comics.

Giggles (5220 Roosevelt Way NE, tel. 206/526–JOKE), in the University District, presents the best of local and nationally known comedians five nights a week, with late shows on weekend nights. Closed Sunday and Monday.

Dance Clubs Several of the rock clubs listed above offer dancing (*see* Rock Clubs, *above*). In Pioneer Square there are several popular, chic clubs featuring recorded dance music, including the **Celebrity** (313 2nd Ave. S, tel. 206/467–1111).

In the downtown area, **Fitzgerald's on Fifth** (1900 5th Ave., tel. 206/728–1000) in the Westin Hotel and **Pier 70 Bay Cafe** (2815 Alaskan Way at Broad St., tel. 206/728–7071) are dance clubs that feature Top-40 music.

Ballroom Dancing The U.S. Amateur Ballroom Dancing Association's local chapter (tel. 206/822–6686) sponsors regular classes and dances throughout the year. These are either at the **Avalon Ballroom** (1017 Stewart St.) or at **Carpenter's Hall** (2512 2nd Ave.). The **Washington Dance Club** (1017 Stewart St., tel. 206/628–8939) sponsors nightly workshops and dances on various styles, and the **All-City Dance Club** (2245 N.W. 57th St., tel. 206/747–2707) hosts regular Saturday-night get-togethers.

Excursions from Seattle

The heavily developed I–5 corridor runs through Seattle, north to Vancouver, British Columbia, or south to Portland, Oregon. But venturing off this ribbon of highway—either toward the mountains in the east or the water to the west—will quickly bring the traveler to some relatively isolated areas. Four of the many excellent trips that can be taken from Seattle are to Bainbridge Island, a short but delightful ferry ride from downtown across Puget Sound; the scenic Snoqualmie Falls, where snowcapped mountains meet lush farmland; Whidbey Island and the San Juan Islands, with scenic beaches, rolling countryside, and good fishing; or Leavenworth, a mock Bavarian village high in the Cascade Mountains.

Bainbridge Island

On a nice day, there's no better way to escape Seattle than on board a Washington State Ferry for a trip across Puget Sound.

It's a great way to watch sea gulls, sailboats, and massive container vessels in the sound—not to mention the surrounding scenery, which takes in the Kitsap Peninsula and Olympic Mountains, Mt. Rainier, the Cascade Mountains, and the Seattle skyline. Even when the weather isn't all that terrific, travelers can stay snug inside the ferry, have a snack, and listen to the folk musicians who entertain the cross-sound commuters. Bainbridge Island combines a small-town atmosphere with scenic country surroundings.

Tourist Information **Bainbridge Island Chamber of Commerce** (590 Winslow Way, tel. 206/842–3700), just two blocks from the ferry dock, has free maps that detail shops, restaurants, and sights.

Getting There **By Ferry** Although there are several ferries that leave from the Seattle area (*see* Getting Around Seattle, *above*), probably the best one for a single-day excursion is the ferry to **Bainbridge Island.** The advantages of walking on board are obvious; it's cheap (only $3.30 for a round-trip ticket) and hassle-free (no long waits in lines of frustrated drivers during peak commute hours or on weekends).

The ferry leaves from Seattle's busy downtown terminal at Colman Dock (Pier 52, south of the Pike Place Market and just north of Pioneer Square), and the trip takes about a half-hour each way.

A word on ferries in general: The Washington State Ferry System, the biggest in the United States, includes vessels ranging from the 40-car *Hiyu* to jumbo ferries capable of carrying more than 200 cars and 2,000 passengers each. They connect points all around Puget Sound and the San Juan Islands. No smoking is allowed in public areas.

If you do take your car, there are several points to note: Passengers and bicycles always load first unless otherwise instructed. Prior to boarding, lower antennas. Only parking lights should be used at night, and it is considered bad form to start your engine before the ferry docks.

Sunny weekends are heavy traffic times all around the San Juan Islands, and weekday commuting hours for ferries headed into or out of Seattle are also crowded. Peak times on the Seattle runs are sunny weekends, eastbound in the morning and Sunday nights, as well as westbound Saturday morning and weekday afternoons. Since no reservations are accepted on Washington State Ferries (except for the Sidney–Anacortes run during summer), arriving at least a half hour before a scheduled departure is always advised. *Colman Dock, Pier 52, tel. 206/464–6400, 206/464–2000 (ext. 5500 for schedules), or 800/843–3779 and 800/542–7052 in WA. Cost: Bainbridge Island ferry auto and driver: $6.65; passenger (in car or as walk-on) $3.30; senior citizens and disabled persons half-fare; children under 5 free. Special rates for mobile homes and other oversize vehicles. Schedules vary according to season and time of day, but generally ferries leave daily every 30–40 min, early morning–2 AM.*

Once you reach the Bainbridge Island terminal, walk north up a short hill on Olympic Drive to Winslow Way; about ¼ mile farther north on Olympic is the Bainbridge Island Vineyard and Winery (682 S.R. 305, tel. 206/842–9463), which is open for tastings and tours Wednesday–Sunday noon–5.

Bloedel Reserve, the 150-acre estate of Vancouver, B.C. lumber baron Prentice Bloedel, was opened to the public in 1988. The grounds were designed to recapture the natural, untamed look of the island. Within the park are ponds with ducks and trumpeter swans, Bloedel's grand mansion, and 2 miles of trails. In spring the displays of blooming rhododendrons and azaleas are dazzling, and in fall the leaves of the Japanese maples and other trees colorfully signal the change of seasons. *7571 N.E. Dolphin Dr., Bainbridge Island 98110, tel. 206/842–7631. Admission: $4 adults, $2 senior citizens, children under 5 free. Reservations necessary. Open Sun.–Wed. 10–4.*

If you turn west on Winslow Way, you'll find yourself in town, with several square blocks of interesting antiques shops, clothing stores, gift shops, galleries, restaurants, and other services. Shopping in the town of Bainbridge Island is refreshingly slower than in downtown Seattle, but you will still find boutiques, designer housewares, and bookstores.

Whidbey Island

Whidbey Island, 30 miles northwest of Seattle, is one of the nearest "escapes" from the city. In fact, some folks escape to it from Seattle every night—they live on Whidbey and commute to work. The island is easily accessible via ferry from Mukilteo (pronounced muck-ill-TEE-oh) to Clinton on the southern part of the island or a drive across Deception Pass on the northern end of the island on Highway 20.

The first white settlers included Colonel Walter Crockett and Colonel Isaac Ebey, who came in the early 1850s. Their names are found on Crockett Lake and Ebey's Landing National Historic Reserve. On the west side of the island, visitors can watch container ships ply the waters of Puget Sound between Asia and ports in Seattle and Tacoma. Wildlife is plentiful. There are eagles and great blue herons; in the water, there are orcas, gray whales, dolphins, and otters.

At 60 miles long and 8 miles wide, Whidbey Island is the longest in the contiguous United States—the U.S. Supreme Court having decided that Long Island in New York was actually a peninsula. The island is a blend of bucolic rolling hills, forests, meadows, sandy beaches, and dramatic, high cliffs. It's a great place for country drives, bicycle touring, exploring the shoreline by boat or kayak, and viewing sunsets.

Tourist Information For information, contact the **Langley Chamber of Commerce** (Box 403, Langley 98260, tel. 206/221–6765) or **Central Whidbey Chamber of Commerce** (Box 152, Coupeville 98239, tel. 206/678–5434).

Getting There **Harbor Airlines** (tel. 800/359–3220) flies to Whidbey Island
By Plane from Friday Harbor and Sea-Tac Airport.

Kenmore Air (tel. 206/486–8400 or 800/543–9595) can arrange charter float plane flights to Whidbey Island.

By Car **Whidbey Island** can be reached via the Mukilteo-to-Clinton ferry, or you can drive from Seattle north along I–5, then heading west on Hwy. 20; cross the dramatic Deception Pass via the bridge at the north end of the island.

Maps of the island, helpful to motorists and cyclists, are available at realty offices in Clinton.

By Ferry The **Washington State Ferry System** (tel. 206/464–6400 or 800/
84-FERRY in WA) provides car and passenger service from
Mukilteo to Clinton (Whidbey Island).

Exploring *Numbers in the margin correspond to points of interest on the
Puget Sound map.*

This tour begins at the southern tip of Whidbey, a 50-mile,
mostly rural island of undulating hills, gentle beaches, and little coves. Naturally, on an island such as Whidbey, wildlife is
plentiful, and it's not unusual to see eagles, great blue herons,
and oyster catchers, as well as orcas, gray whales, dolphins,
and otters. Perhaps the best view of the sea creatures can be
❶ had from **Langley,** the quaint town that sits atop a 50-foot-high
bluff overlooking the southeastern shore. In the heart of town,
along **First Street** and **Second Street,** there are boutiques that
sell art, glass, antiques, jewelry, and clothing.

About halfway up this long, skinny island is Whidbey's town of
❷ **Greenbank,** home to the historically recognized **Loganberry
Farm.** The 125-acre site is now the place of production for the
state's unique spirit, Whidbey's Liqueur. *657 Wonn Rd., tel.
206/678–7700. Admission free. Tours offered daily 10–4.*

While in Greenbank, you may want to see the 53-acre **Meerkerk
Rhododendron Gardens,** with 1,500 native and hybrid species of
rhododendrons, numerous walking trails, and ponds. The best
time to view the flowers in full bloom is April and May. *Resort
Rd., Greenbank, tel. 206/321–6682. Admission: $2.*

❸ Farther north you'll come to **Keystone,** an important town because it is the port of call for the ferry bound for Port Townsend
on the Olympic Peninsula.

❹ **Ft. Casey State Park** (tel. 206/678–4519), just north of Keystone, is one of three forts built in 1890 to protect Puget Sound.
Today it offers a small interpretive center, camping, picnic
sites, fishing, and a boat launch.

❺ About two-thirds of the way up this long island is **Coupeville,**
home of many restored Victorian houses and one of the largest
National Historic Districts in the state. The town was founded
in 1852 by Captain Thomas Coupe; his house, built in 1853, is
one of the state's oldest. The town is also the site of the new **Island County Historical Museum** (908 N.W. Alexander St., tel.
206/678–3310).

❻ **Ebey's Landing National Historic Reserve** (tel. 206/678–4636),
west of Coupeville, is a 22-acre area that include Keystone,
Coupeville, and Penn Cove. Established by Congress in 1980,
the reserve is the first and largest of its kind. It is dotted with
some 91 nationally registered historical structures, farmland,
parks, and trails.

❼ About 11 miles farther north is **Oak Harbor,** which derived its
name from the Garry oaks in the area. It was settled by Dutch
and Irish immigrants in the mid-1800s, and several Dutch
windmills are still in existence. Unfortunately, the island's
largest city has not maintained the sleepy fishing-village pace
that much of the rest of the island follows. Instead, Oak Harbor
has the look of suburban sprawl, with strips of fast-food restaurants and service stations. Just north of Oak Harbor is **Whidbey
Island Naval Air Station** (tel. 206/257–2286), at which group
tours can be arranged. At **Deception Pass State Park,** 3 miles

Book Mark

American Express® Cardmembers Know 53 Ideal Places To Relax.

(With Or Without A Good Book.)

1. Red Lion Scottsdale *(Arizona)*
2. Red Lion Bakersfield *(California)*
3. Red Lion Eureka *(California)*
4. Red Lion Glendale *(California)*
5. Red Lion Los Angeles Airport *(California)*
6. Red Lion Modesto *(California)*
7. Red Lion Ontario *(California)*
8. Red Lion Orange County Airport *(California)*
9. Red Lion Redding *(California)*
10. Red Lion Sacramento *(California)*
11. Red Lion Sacramento Inn *(California)*
12. Red Lion San Diego *(California)*
13. Red Lion San Jose *(California)*
14. Red Lion Santa Barbara *(California)*
15. Red Lion Sonoma County *(California)*
16. Red Lion Colorado Springs *(Colorado)*
17. Red Lion Denver *(Colorado)*
18. Red Lion Durango *(Colorado)*
19. Red Lion Boise Downtowner *(Idaho)*
20. Red Lion Boise Riverside *(Idaho)*
21. Red Lion Omaha *(Nebraska)*
22. Red Lion Kalispell *(Montana)*
23. Red Lion Missoula Inn *(Montana)*
24. Red Lion Missoula Village Inn *(Montana)*
25. Red Lion Astoria *(Oregon)*
26. Red Lion Bend North *(Oregon)*
27. Red Lion Bend South *(Oregon)*
28. Red Lion Coos Bay *(Oregon)*
29. Red Lion Eugene *(Oregon)*
30. Red Lion Klamath Falls *(Oregon)*
31. Red Lion Medford *(Oregon)*
32. Red Lion Portland Coliseum *(Oregon)*
33. Red Lion Portland Columbia River *(Oregon)*
34. Red Lion Portland Downtown *(Oregon)*
35. Red Lion Portland Jantzen Beach *(Oregon)*
36. Red Lion Lloyd Center *(Oregon)*
37. Red Lion Pendleton *(Oregon)*
38. Red Lion Springfield *(Oregon)*
39. Red Lion Austin *(Texas)*
40. Red Lion Salt Lake City *(Utah)*
41. Red Lion Aberdeen *(Washington)*
42. Red Lion Bellevue *(Washington)*
43. Red Lion Bellevue Center *(Washington)*
44. Red Lion Kelso/Longview *(Washington)*
45. Red Lion Pasco *(Washington)*
46. Red Lion Port Angeles *(Washington)*
47. Red Lion Richland *(Washington)*
48. Red Lion Seattle Airport *(Washington)*
49. Red Lion Spokane *(Washington)*
50. Red Lion Vancouver Quay *(Washington)*
51. Red Lion Wenatchee *(Washington)*
52. Red Lion Yakima Inn *(Washington)*
53. Red Lion Yakima Valley Inn *(Washington)*

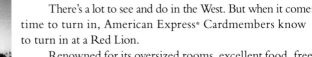

There's a lot to see and do in the West. But when it come time to turn in, American Express® Cardmembers know to turn in at a Red Lion.

Renowned for its oversized rooms, excellent food, free parking and incomparable service, Red Lion is a perfect place to kick back and get spoiled. Without spoiling your travel budget.

And when you make your reservation at a Red Lion Hotel, don't forget to use the American Express Card. With its wide acceptance and 24-hour customer service, the American Express Card is the perfect companion for your travel, dining and shopping needs.

Call your travel agent or 1-800-547-8010 for reservations. As you can see, chances are Red Lion is where you're headed.

 RED LION HOTELS & INNS

Don't Leave Home Without

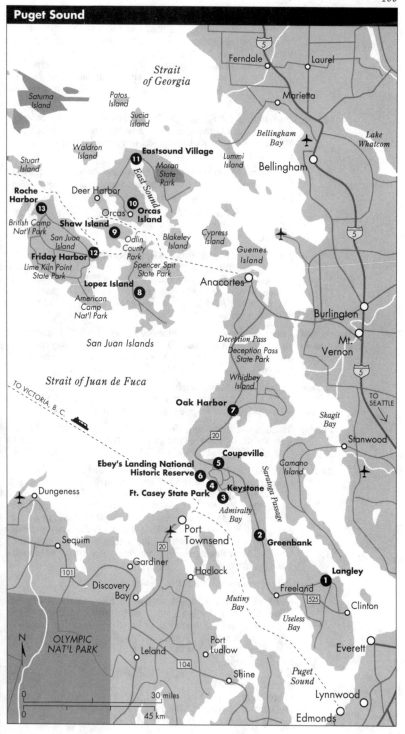

Puget Sound

from the naval base, take some time to notice the spectacular view and stroll among the madrona trees with their reddish-brown peeling bark. While walking across the bridge, you won't be able to miss seeing the dramatic gorge below, well-known for its tidal currents. The Deception Pass bridge links Whidbey to Fidalgo Island and the mainland. From here it's just a short distance to Anacortes and ferries to the San Juan Islands.

Shopping On Whidbey Island, **Langley's First Street** and **Second Street** offer a number of unique items. **Annie Steffen's** (101 1st St., tel. 206/321–6535) specializes in hand-painted, handwoven, and hand-knit apparel and jewelry.

You can meet the artist and shop owner, Gwenn Knight, at **The Glass Knight** (214 1st St., Langley, tel. 206/321–6283), where her glass art and jewelry are for sale.

The **Childers/Proctor Gallery** (302 1st St., Langley, tel. 206/321–2978) exhibits and sells paintings, jewelry, pottery, and sculpture.

Just outside of Langley is the **Blackfish Studio** (5075 S. Langley Rd., tel. 206/321–1274), where you can see works in progress as well as finished pieces by artist Kathleen Miller, who produces enamel jewelry and hand-painted clothing and accessories, and photographer Donald Miller's depictions of the land and people of the Northwest.

Sports and the Outdoors

Bicycling In the Bayview area of Whidbey Island, just off Highway 20, southeast of Anacortes, **The Pedaler** (5603½ S. Bayview Rd., tel. 206/321–5040) bicycle sales and service shop also has 25-or-so mountain bikes and hybrids for rent year-round.

Boating **Langley's small boat harbor** (tel. 206/221–6765) offers moorage for 35 boats, utilities, and a 160-foot fishing pier, all protected by a 400-foot timber-pile breakwater. No reservations.

Fishing You can catch salmon, perch, cod, and bottomfish from the Langley dock. Supplies are available from the **Langley Marina** (202 Wharf St., tel. 206/321–1771).

Beaches Beaches are best on Whidbey Island's west side, where the sand stretches out to the sea and you have a view of the shipping lanes and the Olympic Mountains. **Maxwelton Beach** (Maxwelton Beach Rd.), popular with the locals, is on the west side of the island. **Possession Point** (west on Coltas Bay Rd.) includes a park, a beach, and a boat launch. **Forts Casey** and **Ebey** offer more hiking trails and bluff outlooks than wide, sandy beaches. **West Beach,** north of the forts, is a stormy beach with lots of driftwood.

Dining *Rates correspond to Seattle Dining chart.*

Garibyan Brothers Café Langley. Terra-cotta tile floors, antique oak tables, Italian music, and the aromas of garlic, basil, and oregano set the tone for your lunch or dinner. Greek salads, vegetarian eggplant, fresh mussels, lamb loin chops, moussaka, and lamb shish kebabs are just a few of the offerings. *113 1st St., Langley, tel. 206/221–3090. Reservations suggested. Dress: neat but casual. MC, V. Moderate.*

Star Bistro. This black, white, and red bistro, atop the Star Store, serves up Caesar salads, shrimp-and-scallop linguine, and gourmet burgers. *201½ 1st St., Langley, tel. 206/221–2627. No reservations. Dress: casual. AE, MC, V. Moderate.*

Dog House Backdoor Restaurant. This extremely casual water-front tavern and restaurant serves large, juicy burgers, has a great view of Saratoga Passage, and a pool table. *230 1st St., Langley, tel. 206/321–9996. No reservations. Dress: casual. No credit cards. Inexpensive.*

Lodging *Rates correspond to Seattle Lodging chart.*

Cliff House. This luxury house, situated near Freeland, sleeps one to two couples in a secluded setting overlooking Admiralty inlet. The three-story house, one side nearly all glass, affords romantic views to the couple enjoying the elegant bedroom loft. Rain and occasionally snow whisk through the open-air atrium in the middle of the house. Guests are pampered with fresh flowers, a huge stone fireplace, and miles of driftwood beach. *5440 Windmill Rd., Freeland 98249, tel. 206/321–1566. 1 room. Facilities: fireplace, spa, art collection. No credit cards. Very Expensive.*

Guest House Cottages. This B&B, just outside Greenbank, in-cludes a luxurious log lodge for one couple, four private cot-tages, and a three-room suite in a farmhouse located on 25 acres of forest and pastureland. The accommodations are cozy, with fireplaces, stained-glass pieces, and country antique furnish-ings. *835 E. Christianson Rd., Greenbank 98253, tel. 206/678–3115. 6 units. Facilities: fireplaces, microwaves, some kitch-ens, swimming pool, exercise room, spa. Expensive.*

Fort Casey Inn. These restored, two-story, Georgian Revival officers' quarters were built in 1909. Each has two bedrooms, a living room and full country kitchen, and are perfect for fami-lies. Owners Gordon and Victoria Hoenig have restored the tin ceilings and decorated the units with rag rugs, old quilts, hand-painted furniture, and sundry Colonial touches. *1124 S. Engle Rd., Coupeville, 98239, tel. 206/678-8792. 9 units. Facilities: fireplaces in each, use of bicycles. Fixings for breakfast are provided. AE, MC, V. Moderate.*

Twickenham House. The weekend-in-the-country ambience of this new cedar-sided inn takes hold as soon as you catch sight of the sheep grazing and ducks wandering in the surrounding pasture. This inn makes for a quiet country retreat, and the rooms are decorated simply with trunks, pine armoires, and matching duvets and pillow shams. One of the highlights of a stay here is the gourmet breakfasts, made from fresh, local in-gredients and reflecting the English and French Canadian her-itage of the inn's owners. *5023 Langley Rd., Langley, WA 98260, tel. 800/874–5009. 2 suites, 4 double rooms. MC, V. Moderate.*

Dining and Lodging
★

Inn at Langley. This concrete-and-wood Frank Lloyd Wright–inspired structure perches on the side of a bluff that descends to the beach. Guest rooms feature Asian-style decor using neu-tral colors, wood and glass, and spectacular views of Saratoga Passage and the Cascade Mountains. Entering the inn's Coun-try Kitchen restaurant you first see a fireplace, and what looks like a living room, until you notice the tables for two unobtru-sively lining the walls. On the other side of the fireplace is the "great table," which seats 10. Dinner may include locally gath-ered mussels in a black-bean sauce, breast of duck in a logan-berry sauce, or rich Columbia River salmon. Appetizers, side dishes, salad greens so fresh they've never seen the inside of a refrigerator, and desserts such as a bowl of island-grown strawberries with cream complement the entrées. Continental breakfast (for guests) is served Monday–Wednesday, 8–10. Dinner starts promptly at 7, with a glass of sherry and a tour of the wine cellar. *400 1st St., Langley, tel. 206/221–3033. 24 rooms. Facilities: restaurant. Reservations for restaurant necessary. Jacket and tie suggested. MC, V. Expensive.*

Captain Whidbey Inn. This inn offers a wide variety of accommodations, including the original madrona log inn (listed on the National Register of Historic Places), cottages, a duplex, and houses with views of Penn Cove. Inn rooms are rustic, though they feature a few antiques, but do have feather beds and shared baths. Lagoon rooms are large and have private baths. Cottages and the duplex have one or two bedrooms, sitting rooms, and some have kitchens, fireplaces, and private baths. The dining room, serving breakfast, lunch, and dinner, is cozy, with dark paneling, soft lighting, and several tables overlooking Penn Cove. *2072 W. Captain Whidbey Inn Rd., Coupeville 98239, tel. 206/678–4097. 33 units. Facilities: bicycles and rowboats available. Reservations for restaurant suggested. Dress: neat but casual. MC, V. Moderate.*

The San Juan Islands

The San Juan Islands are the jewels of the Northwest. Because the islands are reachable only by ferry or airplane, they beckon to souls longing for a quiet change of pace, whether it be kayaking in a cove, walking a deserted beach, or nestling by the fire in an old farmhouse.

Unfortunately, solitude becomes a precious commodity in summer when the San Juan's are overrun with tourists. On weekends and even some weekdays, expect to wait at least three hours in line once you arrive at the ferry terminal. You will face the same challenge or worse if you return on Sunday afternoon or evening.

Island residents enjoy their peace and quiet; while some of them rely on tourism, many do not, and they would just as soon not have their country roads and villages jammed with "summer people." So it should come as no surprise that tourism and development are hotly contested issues on the islands.

One way to avoid crowds and the possibility of a cantankerous island resident is to plan a trip in the spring, fall, or winter. Reservations are a must anytime in the summer and are advised for weekends in the off-season, too.

Tourist Information For information on the San Juan Islands, contact the **San Juan Islands Visitor Information Service** (Box 65, Lopez 98261, tel. 206/468–3663).

Getting There
By Plane **West Isle Air** (tel. 800/874–4434) flies to Friday Harbor on San Juan Island from Sea-Tac and Bellingham airports; **Harbor Airlines** (tel. 800/359–3220) also flies from Friday Harbor to Whidbey Island.

Kenmore Air (tel. 206/486–8400 or 800/543–9595) flies float planes from Lake Union in Seattle to the San Juan Islands.

By Car To reach the **San Juan Islands** from Seattle, drive north on I–5 to Mt. Vernon, Exit 230, go west and follow signs to Anacortes; pick up the Washington State Ferry (*see below*).

By Ferry The **Washington State Ferry System** (tel. 206/464–6400 or 800/84-FERRY in WA only) provides car and passenger service from Anacortes, about 90 miles north of Seattle, to the San Juan Islands.

Island Shuttle Express (tel. 206/671–1137) takes passengers from Bellingham to Orcas Island and Friday Harbor. The San Juan *Express* (tel. 800/888–2535) leaves from Seattle and travels routes to Friday Harbor and Port Townsend.

Getting Around It is convenient to have a car in the San Juan Islands, but taking your car with you may mean waiting in long lines at the ferry terminals. In addition to the car-passenger ferries, the **Washington State Ferry System** (tel. 206/464–6400 or 800/84–FERRY) provides passenger-only service among the various islands. With prior arrangement, most bed-and-breakfast owners can pick up walk-on guests at the ferry terminals.

Car rentals are available from the **Inn at Friday Harbor** (tel. 206/378–4351) on San Juan Island. **West Isle Air** (tel. 206/378–2440 or 800/874–4434) serves both Friday Harbor and the Orcas Island Airport. Rentals are about $30 per day.

Guided Tours **Gray Line Cruises** (355 Harris Ave., Bellingham, 98225, tel. 800/443–4552) operates 3½-hour nature cruises through the San Juan Islands.

The **Rosario Princess** (5 Harbor Esplanade, Bellingham 98225, tel. 206/734–8866) conducts whale-watching, nature, and island cruises on an 83-foot tour boat.

Western Prince Cruises (tel. 206/378–5315) charters boats for half-day whale-watching cruises during the summer; in the spring and fall, bird-watching and scuba-diving tours are offered. Cruises depart from Friday Harbor.

Exploring *Numbers in the margin correspond to points of interest on the Puget Sound map.*

There are 172 named islands in the San Juan archipelago, although at low tide the islands total 743 and at high tide, 428. Sixty are populated, and 10 are state marine parks. Ferries stop at Lopez, Shaw, Orcas, and San Juan; other islands, many privately owned, must be reached by private plane or boat. In any case, the San Juan Islands are a gold mine for naturalists, because they are home to more than 94 orcas, a few minke whales, seals, dolphins, otters, and more than 100 active pairs of breeding bald eagles.

❽ The first ferry stop is **Lopez Island,** with old orchards, weathered barns, and pastures of sheep and cows. Because of the relatively flat terrain, this island is a favorite for bicyclists. Two popular parks to note are **Odlin County Park** and **Spencer Spit State Park.**

❾ At the next stop, **Shaw Island,** Franciscan nuns wear their traditional habits while running the ferry dock. You may notice that few people get off here; the island is mostly residential, and tourists rarely stop.

❿ **Orcas,** the next in line, is a large, mountainous, horseshoe-shape island. Roads sweep down through wide valleys and rise to marvelous hilltop views. A number of little shops featuring the island's cottage industries—jewelry, weaving, pottery—

⓫ are in **Eastsound Village,** the island's business and social center situated in the middle of the horseshoe. Walk along Prune Alley, where you'll find a handful of small shops and restaurants.

Skippered sailing charters are available through **Amante Sail Tours** (tel. 206/376–4231), **Custom Designed Charters** (tel. 206/376–5105), **Harmony Sailing Charters** (tel. 206/468–3310), **Kismet Sailing Charters** (tel. 206/468–2435), **Nor'wester Sailing Charters** (tel. 206/378–5478), and **Wind N' Sails** (tel. 206/378–5343).

Bare-boat sailing charters are available through **Wind N' Sails** (tel. 206/378–5343).

If you are kayaking on your own, beware of ever-changing conditions, ferry and shipping landings, and strong tides and currents. Go ashore only on known public property. Day trips and longer expeditions are available from **Shearwater Sea Kayak Tours** (tel. 206/376–4699), **Doe Bay Resort** (tel. 206/376–2291), **Black Fish Paddlers** (tel. 206/376–4041), **San Juan Kayak Expeditions** (tel. 206/378–4436), and **Seaquest** (tel. 206/378–5767).

Fishing You can fish year-round for bass and trout at **Hummel Lake** on Lopez Island, and at **Egg** and **Sportsman lakes** on San Juan Island. On Orcas, there are three lakes at **Moran State Park** that are open to fishing from late April through October.

You can go saltwater fishing through **Buffalo Works** (tel. 206/378–4612), **Captain Clyde's Charters** (tel. 206/378–5661), and **King Salmon Charters** (tel. 206/468–2314).

Beaches Lopez Island: The best beaches on this island include the low-bank beach at **Odlin County Park** (Rte. 2, Box 3216, tel. 206/468–2496) and a mile of waterfront at **Spencer Spit State Park** (Rte. 2, Box 3600, tel. 206/468–2251).

San Juan Island: You'll find 10 acres of beachfront at the **San Juan County Park** (380 Westside Rd. N, Friday Harbor, tel. 206/378–2992).

Dining *Rates correspond to Seattle Dining chart.*

Lopez Island **Bay Cafe.** A varied, seasonal menu of soups, salads, and entrées of seafood, pasta, chicken, and beef is served with an international flair. This restaurant is a special treat for the locals, who must otherwise choose between rather uninspired burgers and pizza. *Lopez Village, tel. 206/468–3700. Reservations accepted. Dress: casual. MC, V. Dinner only. Inexpensive–Moderate.*

Orcas Island **Christina's.** The atmosphere here is elegant whether you dine inside, on the enclosed porch, or on the rooftop terrace with views of East Sound. The emphasis is on fresh, local seafood, with some of the best salmon entrées in the Northwest. Other specialties include grilled breast of chicken with an eggplant-and-pepper stuffing and mouth-watering desserts. *North Beach Rd. and Horseshoe Hwy., tel. 206/376–4904. Reservations suggested. Dress: neat but casual. AE, DC, MC, V. Moderate–Expensive.*

Bilbo's Festivo. This house with a courtyard features stucco walls, Mexican tiles, wood benches, and weavings from New Mexico. The menu features burritos, enchiladas, and other Mexican favorites such as orange-sauce-marinated chicken grilled over mesquite and served with fresh asparagus, potatoes, and salad. *Northbeach Rd. and A St., Eastsound, tel. 206/376–4728. No reservations. Dress: casual. AE, MC, V. Closed Mon.; lunch Tues.–Wed. Inexpensive–Moderate.*

San Juan Island **Duck Soup Inn.** This Mediterranean-inspired kitchen makes the most of fresh local fish in dishes such as squid sautéed in butter and olive oil and served in a fresh tomato sauce, Wescott Bay oysters from across the island, and mussels in a tomato-wine sauce. There is also a good list of Northwest, California, and European wines. *3090 Roche Harbor Rd., tel. 206/378–4878. Reservations suggested. Dress: casual. MC, V. Closed winter; rest of year, closed dinner Mon.–Tues. Expensive.*

Springtree Eating Establishment and Farm. Meals are prepared from organically grown produce on the farm, and entrées include such items as cod with a fresh citrus and garden mint sauce, seafood chowder, and meal-size salads. Lots of plants and chintz fabrics decorate the interior, patio dining is available, and the service has improved under new management. *Spring St., tel. 206/378–4848. Reservations suggested. Dress: casual. MC, V. Moderate.*

Front Street Ale House. This English-style pub features sandwiches, salads, as well as such traditional pub fare as lamb stew, meat pasties, steak-and-kidney pie, and trifle. For vegetarians, there's the Hooley Burger, a quarter-pound of vegetable patty lightly sautéed, then stacked with cheese, mushrooms, lettuce, tomato, and onions. The pub wouldn't be complete without local brews from the San Juan Brewing Company, and with names such as Pig War Stout, they don't get much more local. *1 Front St., Friday Harbor, WA 98250, tel. 206/378–2337. No reservations. Dress: casual. MC, V. Inexpensive.*

Lodging *Rates correspond to Seattle Lodging chart.*

Lopez Island **Edenwild.** The imposing gray Victorian-style farmhouse, surrounded by rose gardens, looks as if it's a restored island building, but dates only from 1990, not 1890. Rooms feature whitewashed oak floors, a muted gray interior, and white painted woodwork, along with botanical prints, lace curtains from Scotland, leaded-glass windows, and some antiques. A three-course breakfast is served in the dining room. *Box 271, Lopez Island, WA 98261, tel. 206/468–3238. 7 double rooms with baths. MC, V. Expensive.*

Inn at Swifts Bay. Robert Herrman and Chris Brandmeir take guests into their sumptuously comfortable Tudor-style home as if they were welcoming old friends. Here you will find an English country ambience with electic furnishings, including antiques and well-stocked book and video libraries. Bay windows in the living and dining areas overlook well-kept gardens, and a crackling fire warms the living room on winter evenings. Thick terry robes, flip-flops, and flashlights are available for your walk down the garden path to the hot tub under the stars. The rooms and suites are all decorated tastefully and without fussiness. In the morning, Chris treats you to a gourmet breakfast, such as eggs Dungeness (poached eggs with hollandaise and fresh crab). *Rte. 2, Box 3402, Lopez Island, WA 98261, tel. 206/468–3636. 2 double rooms, 3 suites with bath. Facilities: hot tub. AE, D, MC, V. Moderate–Expensive.*

Mackaye Harbor Inn. At the south end of Lopez Island, across the road from MacKaye Harbor, is this inn, a two-story frame 1920s sea captain's house with ½ mile of beach. Rooms features golden oak and brass details and wicker furniture; three have views of the harbor. Owners Robin, who is Swedish, and Mike Bergstrom take turns cooking breakfast, which often includes Scandinavian specialties such as *aebleskiver* (apple pancake)

6 Washington State

By Loralee
Wenger and
Adam Woog

Thirty years ago, Washington State and Seattle were virtual backwaters in the country's landscape. The nation had first awakened to this corner of the world via the press given the 1962 Seattle World's Fair, but even so, Seattle was still nowheresville, stuck on the corner of the continental map.

For the most part, Washingtonians didn't care what the rest of the country thought of them; they were too busy hiking, backpacking, mountain climbing, and sailing. Before outdoor adventures became popular in the rest of the country, they were commonplace for Washington residents. For northwesterners, adventuring isn't so much the in thing to do as it is the expression of a yearning to join with the mighty and majestic forces of nature. Now the Northwest is one of the country's foremost locations for outdoor activities.

Washington boasts a host of scenic attractions that beckon the sightseer as well as the adventurer. To the west, the Olympic Peninsula's rain forest drips with moss, waterfalls, and sprawling greenery. The 5,200-foot-high Hurricane Ridge offers spectacular views of the Olympic Mountains and the Straits of Juan de Fuca. The state's coastline along the western shores of the Olympic Peninsula and the Long Beach Peninsula is punctured with inlets, coves, and secluded harbors.

Across Puget Sound, Mt. Rainier reigns over the Cascade Mountains. The mild climate and regular rainfall of western Washington make for lush stands of Douglas fir, western red cedar, and the Renoiresque washes of color with the springtime blossoming of rhododendrons and azaleas. Crossing the Cascades into central and eastern Washington, patchwork quilts of irrigated fruit orchards; miles of rolling, treeless prairie; and stands of golden grain prevail—and so does eastern Washington's extreme weather.

The state's contrasts in landscape have spilled over to its residents. Battles have been hard-fought between Native American and non–Native American fishermen, between land developers and environmentalists, and now, between residents and an influx of prospective residents, purportedly Californians hellbent on Los Angelesizing Puget Sound. These conflicts underscore the vigor with which Washingtonians defend their turf. Visitors can expect to feel welcome here as long as they continue to respect the state's bounty and leave it intact for others to enjoy.

Essential Information

Important Addresses and Numbers

Tourist
Information
State Offices

Washington State Department of Tourism (Dept. of Trade and Economic Development, General Administration Bldg., Olympia 98504, tel. 206/753–5600).

Bellingham/
Whatcom/Skagit
Counties

Bellingham/Whatcom County Convention and Visitors Bureau (904 Potter St., Bellingham 98226, tel. 206/671–3990). **North Cascades National Park** (2105 Hwy. 20, Sedro Woolley 98264, tel. 206/856–5700).

Long Beach
Peninsula

Long Beach Peninsula Visitors Bureau (Intersection of Hwys. 101 and 103, Box 562, Long Beach 98631, tel. 206/642–2400 or 800/451–2542).

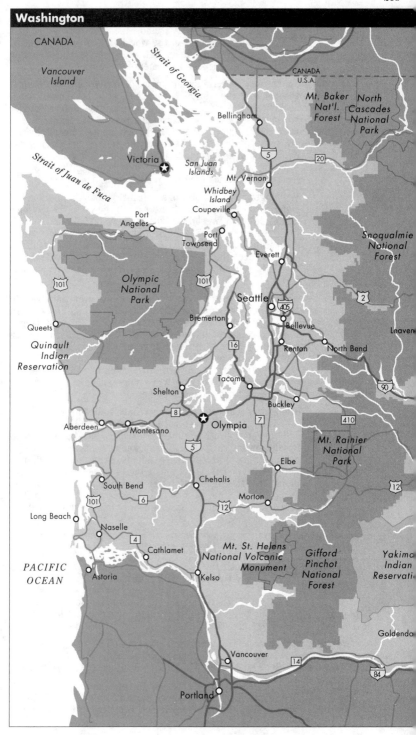

Washington

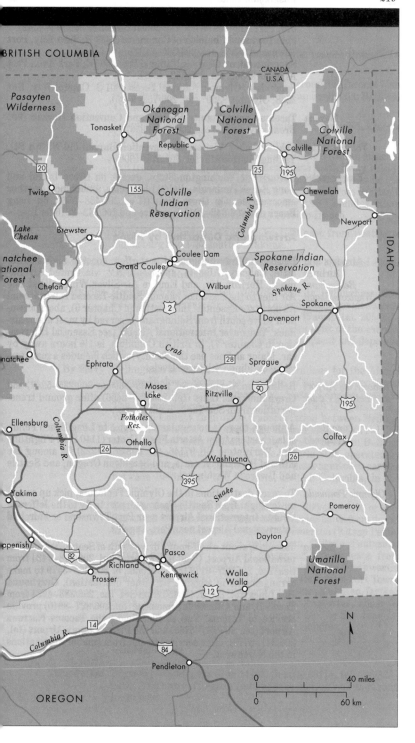

Christy's Escorted Tours (4655 Guide Meridian, Bellingham 98226, tel. 206/734–9361) organizes 2- to 5-day trips and extended United States/Canada tours of 10–38 days.

Gray Line Water Sightseeing (500 Wall St., Suite 310, Seattle 98121, tel. 206/441–1887) offers two-hour cruises of the Seattle waterfront and five-hour combination land/water tours.

Guided Historical Tours (820 Tyler St., Port Townsend 98368, tel. 206/385–1967) offers a number of tours, the most popular of which is a one-hour walking tour of Port Townsend's waterfront and downtown, focusing on its architecture, history, and humor (although not always in that order).

Hellelgrave International (1268 M. Baker Highway, Bellingham 98226, tel. 206/734–3570) provides a variety of trips in the Northwest, varying from one to five days.

Northwest Adventures, Inc. (7616 79th Ave. S.E., Mercer Island 98040, tel. 206/232–1490) represents tour operators throughout the state.

Peninsula Tours (Box 1923, Port Townsend 98368, tel. 206/385–6346) offers a two-hour tour of the town, three Victorian homes, and historic F. Worden.

Sunshine Ventures (Box 1372, Milton 98354, tel. 206/927–4605 or 206/572–9330) runs a multitude of tours, including tours of Tacoma, Mt. Rainier, and Mt. St. Helens.

Special-Interest **Evergreen Travel Service** (19505 44th Ave. W, Lynnwood 98036, tel. 206/766–1184) specializes in tours for the disabled.

Island Mariner Cruises (5 Harbor Esplanade, Bellingham 98225, tel. 206/734–8866) conducts whale-watching, nature, and island cruises on an 83-foot tour boat.

Wineries **Accent! Tours & Charters** (3701 River Rd., Suite B, Yakima 98907, tel. 509/452–9402) provides informative tours of Yakima-area wineries.

Blue Mountain Express (1037 Winslow Ave., Richland 99352, tel. 509/946–7375) visits wineries throughout eastern Washington.

Transcascade (609 E. Yakima Ave., Yakima 98907, tel. 509/452–9402) tours Yakima Valley wineries.

Exploring Washington State

Bellingham/Whatcom and Skagit Counties

Numbers in the margin correspond to points of interest on the Bellingham/Whatcom and Skagit Counties map.

North of Seattle on the way to Vancouver, British Columbia, I–5 passes through the beautiful Skagit River valley and Skagit and Whatcom counties. The gentle farmlands and low foothills along this route are often wrapped in mist, resembling a delicate Japanese pen-and-ink landscape drawing. To the east, however, rising sharply from the foothills, are the anything-but-delicate Cascade Mountains.

Aside from the natural beauty, there are many interesting sights in the area, and a good place to start—and a perfect launching point for exploration—is the town of **Bellingham**, where you'll witness the best of several worlds, including an intellectual college atmosphere and a bustling fishing and lumber industry in a lush and beautiful setting.

There are a variety of places to visit in and around Bellingham, but a convenient starting point is downtown, at the **Whatcom Museum of History and Art.** The expanded, four-building campus includes a beautiful, huge redbrick Victorian building housing permanent exhibits of the early coal and lumbering industries, Native American artifacts, and local waterfowl; other traveling exhibits, on a variety of subjects, are shown on a regular basis. The complex includes a children's museum, too. *121 Prospect St., tel. 206/676-6981. Admission free; children's museum admission: $2; ARCO Exhibits Building: $2 adults, $1 children, free Tues. Open Tues.–Sun. noon–5.*

Traveling by car or on foot, go northwest from downtown to Holly Street, across the mouth of Whatcom Creek. Turning right on C Street will bring you to the **Maritime Heritage Center,** an urban park that pays tribute to Bellingham and its fishing industry. Self-guided tours allow visitors to learn about hatcheries and salmon life cycles, see salmon-rearing tanks and fish ladders, go angling for salmon and trout, and watch salmon spawning. *1600 C St., tel. 206/676-6806. Admission free. Open weekdays 9–5.*

Go about ¼ mile down Holly Street or Roeder Avenue to F Street and Bellingham's northern waterfront. The harbor here, including the Squalicum Harbor Marina (Roeder Ave. and Coho Way, I–5 Exits 253 and 256), the second-largest marina on Puget Sound and home to more than 1,700 commercial and pleasure boats, makes for good dock-walking, fishing, lounging, and picnicking. There are several other points on Bellingham's shoreline from which to engage in any of these activities, including Boulevard Park (S. State St. and Bayview Dr., tel. 206/676-6985), an excellent waterfront park with 14 acres and a ½ mile of shoreline located midway between downtown and Old Fairhaven; and Marine Park (foot of Harris St., in Old Fairhaven), a small but popular spot for sunset-watching and crabbing that is close to the Alaska Marine Highway terminal.

On a hill, overlooking downtown and Bellingham Bay, is the picturesque campus of **Western Washington University** (516 High St., tel. 206/650-3000). To get there, take Garden Street from the north or College Drive from the south. The collection of outdoor sculptures scattered around the campus includes works by Mark DiSuvero, Isamu Noguchi, Richard Serra, and George Rickey.

Before leaving downtown Bellingham, pick up Alabama Street going east. Just before reaching Lake Whatcom, turn left onto Sylvan Street, which will take you to the **Big Rock Garden.** This extensive and unusual nursery, and its **Garden of Art,** feature an outdoor retail sculpture gallery with hundreds of azaleas, rhododendrons, Japanese maples, and other plants and trees, as well as trails interspersed with multimedia fountains, bells, and sculpture. The best time to visit is May–June, peak season for the shrubs. *2900 Sylvan St., Bellingham, tel. 206/*

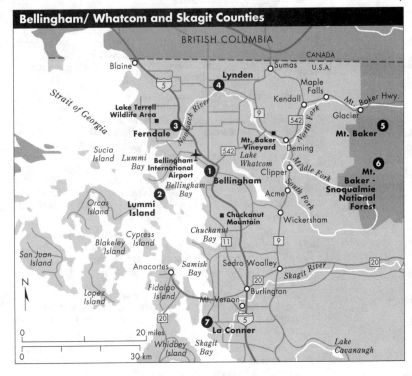

Bellingham/ Whatcom and Skagit Counties

734–4167. Admission free. Open Mar.–Nov., Mon.–Sat. 9–5:30, Sun. 11–5.

At the beginning of Chuckanut Drive is **Fairhaven**, home base for the Bellingham Cruise Terminal, the Alaska Marine Highway System, the 120-foot schooner the *Zodiac*, and seasonal cruise vessels that go to the San Juan Islands. The historic district of Fairhaven includes many Victorian homes and several commercial buildings, including restaurants, shops, galleries and bookstores.

An option out of the city is to take Highway 11 (Chuckanut Dr.) south for a 23-mile drive into Skagit County, alongside beautiful **Chuckanut Bay.** On one side is the steep and heavily wooded Chuckanut Mountain; on the other are stunning views westward over Puget Sound and the San Juan Islands. Many university professors and others have attractive houses built along this stretch of road. Beginning by **Fairhaven Park** in the Old Fairhaven neighborhood and joining up with I–5 in the flat farmlands near Bow, in Skagit County, the full loop can be made in a few hours. Several good restaurants are located toward the southern end of the drive, so planning your excursion to include a lunch stop is a good idea.

While in the area, stop at the **Rose Garden** at Fairhaven Park. It was developed in the early 1900s and is used as a testing site by the American Rose Society. Fairhaven Park also has numerous hiking trails and picnic grounds, a playground, tennis courts, playing fields, a wading pool, and a youth hostel. *107*

Chuckanut Dr., tel. 206/676–6985. Admission free. Open year-round; roses are best seen in summer months.

At the southern end of Chuckanut Drive is the **Rock Point Oyster Company,** a wonderfully funky and friendly operation where visitors can watch oysters being harvested, sorted, shucked, and sent on their way. Fresh Pacific oysters and a variety of other shellfish are sold by a very helpful staff. Ask to see the incredible pink scallops; they swim in their tanks by "biting" the water. *188 Chuckanut Dr., Bow, tel. 206/766–6002. Admission free. Open weekdays 8–5, weekends 1–5.*

Another alternative route from Bellingham is to take Exit 260 west off I–5 to the ferry terminal at Fisherman's Cove dock on the Lummi Indian Reservation. The dock is the site of the **Lummi Casino** (2559 Lummi View Dr., Bellingham 98226, tel. 206/758–7559), where there is gambling (poker and blackjack) 24 hours a day, as well as restaurant service, but no alcohol is allowed. The passenger/car ferry will take you on a 10-minute ride across to **Lummi Island.** The 10-mile-long mountainous and largely uninhabited spot in Bellingham Bay makes a great day trip, especially if you're going to bike or hike.

Farther north off I–5 is **Ferndale** (Exit 262), a charming town and longtime dairy-farming community in the Nooksack Valley, 18 miles north of Bellingham. Among its chief attractions is **Pioneer Park,** which features a number of 1870s log buildings, including a granary, Whatcom County's first church, a hotel, and several historic houses. The buildings have been restored and converted into period museums through which the public can wander and learn about the town's history. *1st and Cherry Sts. (2 blocks south of Main St.), tel. 206/384–3042. Admission free. Open May–Oct., Tues.–Sun. noon–5; tours run daily on the hour.*

Also in Ferndale is the **Hovander Homestead Park,** a National Historic Site with a model farm complete with Victorian-era farmhouse, barnyard animals, water tower, vegetable gardens, and antique farm equipment. Surrounding it are 60 acres of walking trails, picnic grounds, and access to fishing in the Nooksack. *5299 Nielsen Rd., Ferndale, tel. 206/384–3444. Admission free. Park open Thurs.–Sun. noon–6. Tours of farmhouse May, weekends; June–Sept. Thurs.–Sun.*

About a mile away is **Tennant Lake Natural History Interpretive Center,** situated in the Nielsen House, an early homestead. There are exhibits and nature walks around the lake within these 200 acres of marshy habitat, where eagles and other wildlife can be seen. The unusual **Fragrance Garden**—with herbs and flowers—is designed for the sight-impaired and can be explored by following Braille signs. *5236 Nielsen Rd., Ferndale, tel. 206/384–3444. Admission free. Open Thurs.–Sun. noon–4.*

At **Lake Terrell Wildlife Preserve,** visitors can observe a wide variety of waterfowl that live throughout this 11,000-acre spread. In the fall you can hunt pheasants and western Washington waterfowl; catfish, perch, bass, and cutthroat can be fished year-round. *5975 Lake Terrell Rd., Ferndale, tel. 206/384–4723. Admission free. Open weekdays 8–5.*

From Ferndale, take Highway 539 north and east to **Lynden**—a small dairying town that has preserved its conservative Dutch heritage. Sunday retail-store closure has only recently become voluntary instead of mandatory, and drinking alcoholic beverages is still prohibited in establishments where dancing occurs. **Lynden Farm Tours** (7026 Noon Rd., tel. 206/354–3549) offers tours of working farms in the area. Efforts to keep the Dutch heritage alive have resulted in much kitschy-cuteness, but several good examples of traditional Dutch architecture are also evident. **Downtown Lynden** features a four-story windmill (which doubles as an inn), a minimall called Delft Square, the Dutch Village Shopping Mall, and a miniature indoor canal. On special occasions, shopkeepers wear traditional Dutch clothing, right down to the wood clogs.

Probably the single biggest tourist attraction near Bellingham ❺ is **Mt. Baker,** part of the Cascade range. At 10,778 feet high, this sharp peak is visible from virtually everywhere in the area, as is the adjacent and photogenic **Mt. Shuksan,** which stands at ❻ an elevation of 9,038 feet. **Mt. Baker–Snoqualmie National Forest,** as well as the foothills, forests, streams, and country villages you will pass through on the road from Bellingham, provides endless opportunity for exploration. Along the 60-mile route east from Bellingham (on the Mt. Baker Highway, also called Highway 542) are several excellent stopping points. Among the pleasant mountain towns are **Deming, Kendall, Maple Falls,** and **Glacier,** all of which have a variety of good, old-fashioned cafés and shops. Near Deming, the small **Mt. Baker Vineyards** (4298 Mt. Baker Hwy., Everson, tel. 206/592–2300) is open to the public, with tours and a tasting room open Wednesday–Sunday. Be sure to try the plum wine.

Just past the town of Glacier is the turnoff to **Coleman Glacier;** the thundering, 170-foot-high **Nooksack Falls,** only a short walk from the road; and **Mt. Baker's Heather Meadows ski area** (*see* Sports and the Outdoors, *below*).

Time Out | If you're about ready for a mountain picnic, at Deming go south on Highway 9 to the town of **Van Zandt. Everybody's Store** (the only public building in town) is a long-standing local favorite place to stock up on exotic foods and goodies. Everything from dill pickles to homemade sausage, cheeses, bialys—not to mention toys, imported clothes, and regular foodstuffs—can be found here.

Continue south along the **Nooksack River valley,** through the small towns of **Clipper** and **Acme,** then cut over at **Wickersham** and back to Bellingham along **Lake Whatcom** for a splendid afternoon's drive. Special tours by the **Lake Whatcom Steam Train** (Box 91, Acme, WA 98220, tel. 206/595–2218) offer picturesque rides behind a restored, vintage steam engine through the woods at the south end of Lake Whatcom during the summer and holidays.

Driving south for about 30 miles on I–5 and Route 1 from Bel- ❼ lingham will bring you to **La Conner,** a small fishing village and arts community west of Mount Vernon, at the mouth of the Skagit River. Such painters as Morris Graves, Kenneth Callahan, Guy Anderson, and Mark Tobey set up shop here in the '40s, and it has been an artist's haven ever since. A concerted effort has been made in recent years to make La Conner a tourist destination; the number of good shops and restaurants has increased, but so has the traffic, and in summer this usually sleepy town becomes clogged and congested.

Many of the shopkeepers and gallery owners in La Conner carry free copies of a helpful visitor's guide, published by the **Chamber of Commerce** (Lime Dock, 109 N. 1st St., tel. 206/466–4778). Interesting attractions that you won't want to miss are the **Volunteer Fireman's Museum** (1st St., no phone), with turn-of-the-century equipment on display; the **Gaches Mansion** (2nd and Calhoun Sts., tel. 206/466–4288), a Victorian house that is now an exhibition space and museum for area artists, called the Northwest School of La Conner; and the **Skagit County Historical Museum** (501 4th St., tel. 206/466–3365).

Outside the village of La Conner is the fertile flatland of the Skagit River valley. Many farms grow huge batches of commercial flowers—especially daffodils and tulips—and depending on the season, it is possible to view these huge fields of bright colors as you drive the back roads. One of the commercial gardens open to the public is **La Conner Flats** (1588 Best Rd., tel. 206/424–8531). At various times throughout the year, tulips (the main crop), rhododendrons, roses, and flowering cherry trees may be seen. Another garden is **Roozengaarde** (1587 Beaver Marsh Rd., tel. 206/424–8531), one of the largest growers of tulips, daffodils, and irises in the United States.

Tacoma

Numbers in the margin correspond to points of interest on the Tacoma map.

Like many towns in the Northwest, Tacoma's history is tied inextricably with lumber and fishing, and with the two-fisted men and women who did the labor. Today Tacoma is still a hardworking, largely blue-collar town, and it is fighting to upgrade its downtown and its image. Although the reputation—based on the city's smell and pollution resulting from the many nearby pulp mills and smelters—is partly deserved, Tacoma is doing much to clean up its act; it appears that the self-proclaimed "City of Destiny" is finally getting a little respect.

Tacoma deserves this respect, too. Looking beyond the surface of this city of 179,000, the visitor will find lovely residential neighborhoods, handsome brick buildings, fine views of Commencement Bay, a world-class zoo, a tremendously active port (so busy, in fact, that it's stealing the thunder of its larger neighbor to the north), and the dominating presence of nearby Mt. Rainier. The city is also a convenient jumping-off point for exploring some wonderful locations in south-central Washington: the Cascade Mountains, the state capital of Olympia, and—across the Tacoma Narrows Bridge—the small fishing villages of the Kitsap Peninsula.

8 While downtown visit the **Tacoma Art Museum,** where you'll find a rich collection of American and French paintings, as well as Chinese jades and imperial robes. There is a permanent children's gallery with work stations for creating impromptu art and an ongoing series of high-quality changing exhibitions. The museum features a comprehensive collection of work by native Tacoman Dale Chihuly, generally recognized as the greatest living glass sculptor. *12th St. and Pacific Ave., tel. 206/272–4258. Admission $3 adults, $2 senior citizens, students, and children 6–12. Open Tues.–Sat. 10–5, Sun. noon–5.*

Camp Six Logging Museum, **16**

Ft. Nisqually, **15**

Gig Harbor, **17**

Northwest Trek Wildlife Park, **18**

Pantages Theater, **9**

Point Defiance Park, **13**

Point Defiance Zoo and Aquarium, **14**

Stadium High School, **10**

Tacoma Art Museum, **8**

Washington State Historical Society, **11**

Wright Park, **12**

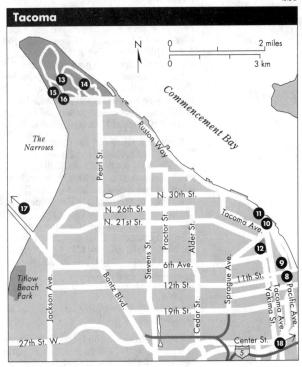

9 The **Pantages Theater,** designed by the famous theater architect B. Marcus Pritica, is a beautifully restored example of early 20th-century Greco-Roman music-hall style, which features classical figures, ornate columns, arches, and reliefs. Once the locale of performances by such varied entertainers as W.C. Fields, Mae West, Charlie Chaplin, Bob Hope, and Stan Laurel, it is now the home of the Tacoma Symphony and BalleTacoma, as well as visiting musical and theatrical productions. The Pantages is part of the Broadway Center for the Performing Arts, which also includes the 748-seat Rialto Theater, once home to vaudeville performances and showings of silent films, and reopened in 1991 to house the Tacoma Youth Symphony. **Theatre on the Square** opened in 1993 with the Tacoma Actors Guild as its resident company. *901 Broadway, tel. 206/ 591–5890. Tours Thurs. 1–4, free with reservations.*

West of the Pantages building, the **Children's Museum of Tacoma** offers hands-on exhibits in science, the arts, and creative play, especially for children ages 4–12. *925 Court St., tel. 206/ 627–2436. Admission: $3, children 2 and under free.*

10 At the north end of downtown is **Stadium High School,** an elaborate building designed in 1891 as a luxury hotel for the Northern Pacific Railroad (Tacoma was once the railroad's terminus); it was converted into a high school in 1906 after a fire left only the outer shell. The château-style building, with classic European details, is still used as such by the Tacoma School District. *111 N. E St., tel. 206/596–1325.*

⑪ The nearby **Washington State Historical Society,** housed in a newly remodeled building, features exhibitions on the natural, Native American, pioneer, maritime, and industrial history of the state. Its pioneer, Alaskan, and Native American displays are the largest on the Pacific Coast. The permanent exhibit, "Home, Frontier, Crossroads," depicts the many roles the state of Washington has played for its residents. *315 N. Stadium Way, tel. 206/593–2830. Admission: $2. Open Tues.–Sat. 10–5, Sun. 1–5.*

Time Out If the weather's cooperative, pick up a sandwich to go at the **Judicial Annex** (311 S. 11th St., tel. 206/272–3501) or at the **Ark Delicatessan** (1140 Court C, tel. 206/383–3354) and take it to Wright Park (*see below*) for a picnic.

⑫ **Wright Park** is a pleasant 28-acre park in the middle of town, just north of the downtown area. Lawn-bowling, a children's playground, and picnicking are big attractions here. The park's chief feature is the **W. W. Seymour Botanical Conservatory,** a lovely Victorian-style greenhouse with an extensive collection of exotic flora. *Park, between 6th and Division Sts., Yakima and Tacoma Aves. Conservatory, nearest corner on 4th and G Sts., tel. 206/591–5331. Admission free; donations accepted. Open daily 8:30–4:20.*

For a look at a variety of working boats, including container ships, bulk carriers, barges, tug boats, and fire boats, visit the **Port of Tacoma's** Interpretive Center. An observation tower allows for views of the harbor, one of the five best and naturally deep harbors in the world. Videos and displays explain the workings, activities, and history of the port. *Exit 136 off I–5 to Port of Tacoma Rd., turn left (S.W.) onto E. 11th St. and continue to the observation tower, tel. 206/383–5841. Admission free.*

The Port of Tacoma created Gog-Le-Hi-Te to replace a small intertidal wetland that had been filled to construct a major container terminal. The name, Gog-Le-Hi-Te, means "where the land and waters meet." The wetland comprises 9 ½ acres of land, marsh, mudflat, fresh water from the Puyallup River, and brackish water from Commencement Bay. There are viewing platforms and interpretive displays. The Tahoma Audubon Society has recorded more than 100 different types of migratory and resident birds, and there are salmon and steelhead there, as well. *Exit 135 off I–5 and follow Portland Ave. to Lincoln Ave.*

Leave the heart of the city by driving northeast along Commencement Bay or Ruston Way and turning right on Pearl Street, which will take you to the entrance of one of Tacoma's ⑬ most interesting attractions: 700-acre **Point Defiance Park,** one of the largest urban parks in the country. In addition to its various museums, this huge tract of land that juts out into the western part of Commencement Bay offers extensive footpaths and hiking trails, a variety of flower gardens, the densely wooded Five Mile Drive, and spectacular views of the waterfront. *5400 N. Pearl St., tel. 206/591–5335. Admission free. Open June–Aug., daily 10–7; Sept.–May, weekdays 10–4, weekends 10–7.*

⑭ On the grounds of the park is the **Point Defiance Zoo and Aquarium,** founded in 1888 and generally considered one of the top zoos in the country. Using the Pacific Rim as its theme, it has blossomed (since an extensive renovation in 1986) into an impressive example of humane and innovative trends in zoo administration. Natural habitats and superclose vantage points allow visitors to observe a wide variety of whales, walruses, sharks, polar bears, octopuses, apes, reptiles, and birds. Both the zoo and the aquarium have gained an international reputation for the expert caretakers who treat injured wildlife. *Tel. 206/591–5335. Admission: $6.25 adults, $5.75 senior citizens and disabled persons, $4.50 children 5–17, $2.25 children 3–4. Open Sept.–May, daily 10–4; June–Aug., daily 10–7; closed Thanksgiving and Christmas.*

⓯ Part of Point Defiance is **Ft. Nisqually.** This painstakingly restored Hudson Bay Trading Post was originally built as a British outpost on the Nisqually Delta in the 1830s and relocated as a WPA project to Point Defiance in 1935. Tours of the fort are offered, in which guides point out kitchens, stables, bunkhouses, and other parts of the fur-trading post. *Ft. Nisqually, tel. 206/591–5339. Admission: $1 adults, 50¢ children; free Mon.–Tues. in summer and Labor Day–Memorial Day noon–4 (when buildings are closed but grounds remain open). Open Memorial Day–Labor Day, Wed.–Sun. 11–6.*

⓰ Near the fort is the **Camp Six Logging Museum,** a 15-acre museum featuring restored original bunkhouses, hand tools, and historic logging equipment. A 1½-mile-long steam donkey train ride takes you around old bunk cars and a 240-ton skidder. *Logging museum, tel. 206/752–0047. Admission free; train ride $2 adults, $1 children 3–12 and senior citizens. Open Memorial Day–Sept., Wed.–Sun. 10–5. Special Santa trains run in Dec.*

⓱ From Point Defiance, take Highway 16 8 miles to **Gig Harbor,** once the home and fishing grounds for a small band of Nisqually Indians. Now it is a tiny village retreat inhabited by musicians, artists, sailing enthusiasts, and general layabouts. The beautiful and well-protected harbor is home to a number of unusual bed-and-breakfasts, a string of boutiques and antiques shops, and a lively marina full of both working fishing boats and pleasure crafts. Continuing north along the highway you'll pass many small farms, rolling hills, and fine beaches that are good for beachcombing and clamming.

⓲ Although the 35-mile drive southeast along Route 161 will take you away from the city, a trip to the **Northwest Trek Wildlife Park** is time well spent. The land, administered by the Metropolitan Park District of Tacoma, is 600 acres of forest and meadow in which bison, beavers, bobcats, bighorn goats, moose, elk, bald eagles, and more can be observed from a guided tram tour. The **Cheney Discovery Center,** in the park, features a live butterfly atrium and a 150-gallon fish tank with many varieties of native fish, such as salmon and trout. *11610 Trek Dr. E, Eatonville, tel. 206/832–6116 or 800/433–8735. Admission: $7.50 adults, $6.50 senior citizens, $5 children 5–17, $3 children 3–4. Open year-round at 9:30 AM; closing times vary, so call ahead. Tram tours run hourly from 10 AM.*

The Olympic Peninsula

Numbers in the margin correspond to points of interest on the Olympic Peninsula map.

American Express offers Travelers Cheques built for two.

American Express® Cheques *for Two*. The first Travelers Cheques that allow either of you to use them because both of you have signed them. And only one of you needs to be present to purchase them.

Cheques *for Two* are accepted anywhere regular American Express Travelers Cheques are, which is just about everywhere. So stop by your bank, AAA* or any American Express Travel Service Office and ask for Cheques *for Two*.

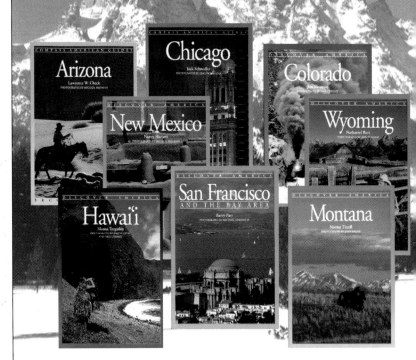

The rugged Olympic Peninsula is the most northwestern corner of the continental United States. Much of it is wilderness, with the magnificent Olympic National Park and National Forest at its heart. The peninsula has tremendous variety: the wild Pacific shore, the sheltered waters along the Hood Canal and the Strait of Juan de Fuca, the rivers of the Olympic Rain Forest, and the towering Olympic Mountains.

Although the region's economy—primarily lumber and fishing—assures some ties to the outside world, the peninsula is in many ways isolated and largely self-sufficient. Its inaccessible terrain and the unique climates caused by the Olympic Mountains add to this feeling of separateness: The mountains trap incoming clouds, creating both a rain forest to the west and a dry "rain shadow" area on the east. As a result, the peninsula has both the wettest and the driest climates in the entire coastal Pacific Northwest.

A benefit of this somewhat ambiguous environment is that wildlife takes to it—and flourishes. Visitors in search of the great outdoors, however, should be aware that much of the Olympic Peninsula is stringently protected. Within the National Park, all hunting, firearms, and off-road vehicles are prohibited, as is any disturbance to plants or wildlife. Although hunting and fishing are permitted in portions of the National Forest, many areas are maintained as complete wilderness. Furthermore, Native American tribal regulations restrict access to, and activity within, certain parts of reservations; check with local authorities for details.

Because of the rugged terrain and some difficult roads, much of the peninsula is accessible only to backpackers, but the 300-mile loop made by Highway 101 provides glimpses of some of its most interesting features. The various side roads off 101, meanwhile, offer excellent (if sometimes unpaved) opportunities for further exploration of more remote towns, beaches, and mountains. This section describes a journey clockwise, primarily around Highway 101 (although jaunts from the main drag are suggested), beginning and ending in Olympia.

⑲ Olympia, Washington State's capital, is often overrun with government activity; the legislative season determines whether this town at the southern end of Puget Sound is bustling or somnolent. But even in full swing, the city still retains a relaxed air. While you are in the capitol area, consider taking a tour of the stately **Legislative Building.** This handsome Romanesque structure boasts a 287-foot dome that closely resembles the Capitol Building in "the other Washington." State Senate and Representative sessions can be viewed from visitors' galleries. The surrounding grounds feature carefully maintained rose gardens (best in summer) and Japanese cherry trees that are in glorious bloom around the end of April. Also worth a look is the modern **State Library,** located directly behind the Legislative Building. It is open to the public during regular business hours and boasts a variety of artwork, including murals by two renowned Washington artists, Mark Tobey and Kenneth Callahan, and exhibits devoted to early state history. *Legislative Bldg., Capitol Way between 10th and 14th Aves., tel. 206/ 586–TOUR. Admission free. Tours offered daily, on the hour 10–3.*

Olympic Peninsula

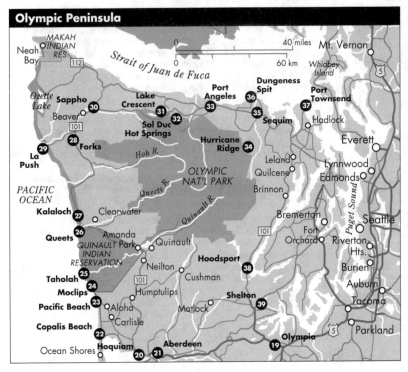

Traveling south along Capitol Way to 21st Street—a pleasant walk or a short drive—will bring you to the **State Capitol Museum,** housed in a handsome building that dates from the 1920s and was once the mansion of a local banker. Exhibits of local art, history, and natural history are on display, including a permanent collection of rare local Native American baskets. *211 W. 21st St., tel. 206/753–2580. Admission free; donations accepted. Open Tues.–Thurs. 10–4, weekends noon–4; closed Mon.*

A few blocks east of the Capitol campus on Union Avenue, at its intersection with Plum Street and adjacent to City Hall, the sister cities of Olympia and Yashiro, Japan, have recently collaborated on a beautiful **Japanese garden** complete with a waterfall, bamboo grove, carp pond, and stone lanterns. *Corner of Union and Plum Sts., tel. 206/357–3370. Admission free. Open daily 10–10.*

Wolfhaven, just 15 miles south of the city on Old Highway 99, is a unique facility offering walk-through guided tours on the hour of a 60-acre refuge and sanctuary primarily for wolves. On Friday and Saturday evenings in the summer, the facility reopens at 7 PM for the public Howl-in featuring tours, musicians performing around a campfire, and howling with the wolves. *3111 Offut Lake Rd., tel. 206/264–HOWL. Admission for daily tours: $5 adults, $2.50 children 5–12, children under 5 free; for Howl-in: $6 adults, $3 children 5–12. Open May–Sept., daily 10–5; Oct.–Apr., Wed.–Sun. 10–4.*

Leaving Olympia, travel west along Highway 101 and State Routes 8 and 12 to Gray's Harbor and the twin seaports of **Hoquiam** and **Aberdeen.** In spring, thousands of migratory shorebirds and peregrine falcons come to Bowerman Basin, west of Hoquiam on State Route 109.

An option from Hoquiam would be to drive north on Route 109, passing through resorts and ample beach areas such as **Copalis Beach, Pacific Beach,** and **Moclips** on your way to the Quinault Indian Reservation and the tribal center of **Taholah.** You should know, however, that access to the coastline at some points here is restricted to tribal members. Taholah is a rustic town, and the main attraction for tourists here, as elsewhere on the peninsula, is the vast amount of pristine scenery, rather than a commercialized town center.

Another route to follow from Hoquiam is Highway 101 north, along the west fork of the Hoquiam River (through the wonderfully named town of Humptulips) to picturesque Quinault Lake and west to the ocean at **Queets** and **Kalaloch.** The stretch of coastal highway north of Kalaloch has many well-marked trails—each ¼ mile or less in length—that lead to spectacular Pacific beaches.

Continue north on 101 for about 20 miles before taking the Hoh Road east to the spectacular Hoh Rain Forest, a complex and rich ecosystem of conifers, hardwoods, grasses, mosses, and other flora that shelter such wildlife as elk, otters, beavers, salmon, and even flying squirrels. The average rainfall here is 145 inches a year. The **Hoh Visitor Center,** located at the campground and ranger center at road's end, has information, nature trails, and a museum. There are several interpretive facilities to help visitors prepare for the nature trails, and naturalist-led campfire programs and walks are conducted daily in July and August. *Hoh Rd., 1½ mi north of the Hoh River Bridge; the Visitor Center is 20 mi farther. Tel. 206/374-6925. Park admission: $3. Visitor Center open June–Aug., daily 9–7; Sept.–May, daily 9–5 (staff often not available in winter, but center remains open).*

North on Highway 101 is the little town of **Forks,** famous throughout the Northwest for its lavish and enjoyable Fourth of July celebrations (which actually last three days). This is classic Americana with a Northwest twist: parades featuring giant logging trucks along with the Shriners and royalty, demolition derbies, marathon runs and dances, arts and crafts, fireworks, and lots of food. Every year one lucky tourist family is showered with free food, lodging, and gifts for being selected "Tourist of the Day." For details about festivities, write to Forks Old Fashioned Fourth of July (Box 881, 98331) or Forks Chamber of Commerce (Box 1249, 98331, tel. 206/374-2531).

From Forks, take La Push Road west for about 15 miles to the town of the same name. **La Push** is a coastal village and the tribal center of the Quileute Indians. (One theory about the town's name is that it is a variation on the French *la bouche,* "the mouth"; this makes sense, since it's located at the mouth of the Quilayute River.) Several points along this road have short trails with access to the ocean, fabulous views of offshore islands, and stark rock formations. The north branch of the La Push detour is the road to **Rialto Beach,** a picnic area and campsite.

30 North and east, Highway 101 enters the **Soleduck River valley,** which has been known for its salmon fishing. At **Sappho,** Burnt Mountain Road branches northward off to Route 112 (paved but slow) and eventually leads to **Neah Bay, Capes Flattery** and **Alava, Shi-Shi Beach,** and **Ozette Lake** (the largest body of fresh water in the state). Eight miles east of Sappho is the **Soleduck Hatchery** (tel. 206/327–3246), operated by the Washington State Department of Fisheries and offering a variety of interpretive displays about the many aspects of fish breeding.

31 The deep azure of **Lake Crescent,** about 12 miles farther along, is outstandingly beautiful, and the area has abundant campsites, resorts, trails, canoeing, and fishing. Among Lake Crescent's famous guests was Franklin D. Roosevelt, whose negotiations with U.S. senators and Park Department officials at the Lake Crescent Lodge in 1937 led directly to the creation of the Olympic National Forest. The original lodge buildings of 1915 are still in use, well-worn but comfortable.

32 Twelve miles south on Soleduck Road (which meets Highway 101 a mile west of the western tip of Lake Crescent) is **Sol Duc Hot Springs.** Native Americans have known about the soothing waters of these springs for generations, and since the first resort opened there tourists have learned about it as well. There are three hot sulfur pools, ranging in temperature from 98° to 104°. The Sol Duc Hot Springs Resort, a venerable institution dating from 1910, has a series of cabins, a restaurant, and a hamburger stand. It is not necessary to stay at the resort to use the hot springs. *Soleduck Rd. and Hwy. 101, tel. 206/327–3583. Admission: $4.75. Open mid-May–late Sept., daily 9–9.*

33 Back on Highway 101 east, you will soon come to **Port Angeles,** a bustling commercial fishing port and an access route to Canada. Directly across the Strait of Juan de Fuca is Victoria, British Columbia, which can be reached via the private Black Ball Ferry Line (tel. 206/457–4491). Among the points of interest in P.A., as its residents fondly refer to it, is the **Clallam County Historical Museum.** This handsome Georgian building, constructed in 1914 as a courthouse, has exhibitions of artifacts and photo displays detailing the lifestyles of the people, both Native American and white, who lived in this timber-rich and seagoing community. *4th and Lincoln Sts., tel. 206/452–7831, ext. 364. Admission free; donations accepted. Open June–Aug., Mon.–Sat. 10–4; Sept.–May, weekdays 10–4.*

Also interesting is the casual but well-appointed **aquarium** of the Arthur D. Feiro Marine Laboratory, operated as a joint venture by the City of Port Angeles and Peninsula College. Many kinds of local sea life, including octopuses, scallops, rockfish, and anemones, are on display, with new varieties and specimens arriving often. The tour is self-guided, but friendly volunteers are always on hand to answer questions. *Port Angeles City Pier, tel. 206/452–9277. Admission: $1 adults, 50¢ children 6–12, children 5 and under free. Open June–Aug., daily 10–8; Sept.–May, weekends noon–4.*

34 **Hurricane Ridge,** 17 miles south of Port Angeles, rises nearly a mile above sea level and offers spectacular views of the Olympics, the Strait of Juan de Fuca, and Vancouver Island. Despite the point's height, the road grade leading to it is easily negotiated by car. In the summer, rangers lead hikes and give interpretive talks on local geology and flora and fauna. The numerous nature trails range in difficulty from disabled-accessible paths to advanced climbs, and provide an opportunity to see wildflowers such as glacier lilies and lupine, as well as animals such as deer and marmots. In winter, when accessible, the area has miles of cross-country ski routes and a modest downhill ski operation. *3002 Mt. Angeles Rd., tel. 206/452-4501, ext. 230. Visitor center open daily 9-4.*

A wide variety of animal life, present and past, can be found in **35** the charming town of **Sequim,** 17 miles east of Port Angeles on Highway 101, and in the fertile plain at the mouth of the **36** Dungeness River to the north of the town. **Dungeness Spit,** part of the Dungeness National Wildlife Refuge and one of the longest natural spits in the world, is home to thousands of migratory waterfowl as well as clams, oysters, and seals. This picturesque locale features a lighthouse at the end of the spit in addition to its abundant natural beauty; there is no formal interpretive center, but large displays provide information about what can be seen. A 65-site campground nearby is operated by Clallam County. *About 3 mi north on Kitchen Rd. (4 mi west of Sequim). Campground tel. 206/683-5847. Wildlife Refuge tel. 206/683-5037. Admission: $2 per family per day.*

In 1977, 12,000-year-old mastodon remains were discovered near Sequim and today are displayed at the **Sequim-Dungeness Museum,** where you can look at these Ice Age creatures as well as at exhibits on Captain Vancouver, the early Klallam Indians, and the area's pioneer towns. *175 W. Cedar St., tel. 206/683-8110. Admission free; donations accepted. Open May-Sept., Wed.-Sun., noon-4; Oct.-Nov. and mid-Feb.-Apr., weekends noon-4; closed Dec.-mid-Feb.*

About 10 miles east of Sequim, State Route 20 turns northward **37** another 12 miles to **Port Townsend,** a charming town with a fine waterfront along which runs a series of handsome brick buildings that date from the 1870s. These have been carefully restored and now house a variety of attractive shops, restaurants, and services. High up on the bluff are several large gingerbread-trimmed Victorian homes, many of which have been turned into elegant B&Bs. Although Port Townsend is a flourishing arts community, with a high proportion of writers, musicians, and artists in residence, the restored buildings of **Fort Worden,** a former coast artillery army base, are the center for a variety of popular annual arts festivals.

Backtracking from Sequim, Highway 101 travels south along the west side of Hood Canal, past abundant oyster-picking and clam-digging areas. The **Hamma Hamma Oyster Company** is a retail store south of the town of Eldon, where you can buy fresh salmon, mussels, crab, shrimp, and other seafood, as well as a variety of pickled and smoked items. Picnic tables outside provide a fine place in which to have an al fresco meal. Especially worth a look and maybe a sample are the store's live examples of geoducks (pronounced gooey-ducks), giant cousins to the clam. *N. 35959 Hwy. 101, tel. 206/877-5811. Admission free. Open daily 8:30-5:30.*

About 10 miles farther, near the southern bend of the canal and **38** the town of **Hoodsport,** is the **Hoodsport Winery,** which produces a number of fine wines—from chardonnays and Reislings to gooseberry and rhubarb. The winery is open to the public; the friendly staff gives tours and tastings on an informal basis as requested. *N. 23501 Hwy. 101, tel. 206/877–9894. Admission free. Open daily 9–7.*

Branching off to the west from the middle of town is the Staircase Road, which leads to **Lake Cushman.** This is not only an important source of water for Tacoma's powerhouse on Hood Canal, but it is also the trailhead to numerous hiking trails, including one to the spectacular **Staircase Rapids** on the Skokomish River. Here the steep country gives rise to rushing cataracts and boulder-strewn rapids, broken up by deep pools where Dolly Varden trout rest.

Driving south on Highway 101 through the sawmill town of **39** **Shelton** will take you back to Olympia.

Long Beach Peninsula

Numbers in the margin correspond to points of interest on the Long Beach Peninsula map.

If the waters of the Pacific and the mighty Columbia River had met in a less turbulent manner, a huge seaport might sit at the river's mouth. Instead, the entrance to the Columbia is only sparsely populated. Dotted with fishing villages and cranberry bogs, it is worlds apart from Seattle—3½ hours southwest—and Portland—two hours away. Long Beach Peninsula, just north of the river's mouth, is rich for the naturalist who enjoys bird-watching, hiking, or beachcombing; the history buff; or the gourmet. It is the perfect place for holing up in front of a crackling fire and indulging in a good book or venturing out to witness a winter storm (of which there are plenty). Locals warn that it is not a place for swimming. Shifting sands underfoot and tremendous undertows account for several drownings each year.

Long Beach Peninsula's natural bounty comes from its water and coastline. The peninsula boasts the longest uninterrupted stretch (28 miles) of sandy beach in North America. Unfortunately, the locals act as if it were private property, greedily claiming their right to drive cars, trucks, recreational vehicles, and motorcycles up and down this pristine belt of sand. Despite what the practice may do to clamming beds or the psyche of solitary beachcombers, it continues. At least in 1990 the state legislature decided to close about 40% of the beach to motor vehicles from April through Labor Day.

In 1990, a ½-mile-long wood boardwalk (stretching from Bolstad Street south to South 10th Street) was installed, along with stairs to the beach access, disabled-accessible ramps, plenty of benches, and telescopes. Since no vendors are permitted, the addition allows for unobstructed views of the beach and bird life.

Inland a mile or two, the peninsula-area marshes are a haven to migrating birds, particularly the graceful, white trumpeter swans. The old-growth red-cedar grove on Long Island is believed to have sprouted some 4,000 years ago and is home to the endangered spotted owl, the marbled murelet, and other birds and small mammals. Following this tour will allow you to take in some of the unique features of Long Beach Peninsula.

40 **Fort Columbia State Park and Interpretive Center,** one of 27 coastal defense units of the U.S. Army, was built in 1903 to

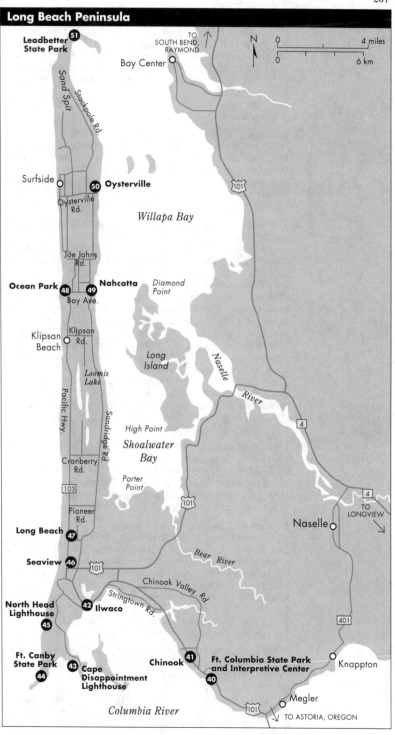

Long Beach Peninsula

Leadbetter State Park **51**

TO SOUTH BEND, RAYMOND

Bay Center

N

0 — 4 miles
0 — 6 km

Sand Spit

Stackpole Rd.

Surfside

50 Oysterville

Oysterville Rd.

Willapa Bay

Joe Johns Rd.

Diamond Point

Ocean Park **48** **49** Nahcotta

Bay Ave.

Klipsan Beach

Klipsan Rd.

Long Island

Naselle

River

4

Loomis Lake

Pacific Hwy.

Sandridge Rd.

High Point

Shoalwater Bay

Cranberry Rd.

Porter Point

101

4

TO LONGVIEW

Naselle

103

Pioneer Rd.

Long Beach **47**

Seaview **46**

101

Bear River

Chinook Valley Rd.

North Head Lighthouse **45**

42 Ilwaco

Stringtown Rd.

401

Ft. Canby State Park **43**

44 Cape Disappointment Lighthouse

Chinook **41**

40 Ft. Columbia State Park and Interpretive Center

Knappton

Megler

101

TO ASTORIA, OREGON

Columbia River

house as many as 200 men at one time. Many of the fort's 30 structures have been restored to their original state. Illustrating barracks life at the fort is an interpretive center in one of the old accommodations, and a museum in the fort commander's quarters depicts military family life. A hike up Scarborough Hill behind the fort gives a breathtaking view of the peninsula and the Columbia River. *Hwy. 101, 2 mi east of Chinook, tel. 206/777–8221. Admission free. Call the Long Beach Visitors Bureau for hours.*

④① Two miles farther is **Chinook,** named for a Native American tribe that helped William Clark and Meriwether Lewis during their stay on the Pacific Coast. The **Sea Resources Hatchery Complex** offers tours of the hatchery and fish-rearing ponds that are used to teach high-school students the basics of salmon culturing and marine industrial arts. *Houchen St., tel. 206/ 777–8229. Admission free. Phone ahead to arrange a tour.*

④② The next town along the coast is **Ilwaco,** a small fishing community of about 600. From 1884 to 1910, gill-net and trap fishermen around here fought one another with knives, rifles, and threats of lynchings over access to and ownership of the fishing grounds. Today, the port is home to salmon, crab, tuna, charter fishing, and other commercial boats. The **Ilwaco Heritage Museum** uses excellent dioramas to present the history of southwestern Washington, beginning with the Native Americans; moving on to the influx of traders, missionaries, and pioneers; and concluding with the contemporary industries of fisheries, agriculture, and forests. The museum also houses a model of the peninsula's "clamshell railroad," a narrow-gauge train that transported passengers and mail along the beach. The railbed on which the tracks were laid was made of ground-up clam and oyster shells. *115 S.E. Lake St., tel. 206/642–3446. Admission: $1.25 adults, $1 senior citizens, 50¢ children under 12. Open May–Aug., Mon.–Sat. 9–5, Sun. noon–4; Sept.– Apr., Mon.–Sat. 9–5, Sun. noon–5.*

④③ **Cape Disappointment Lighthouse,** first used in 1856, is one of the oldest lighthouses on the West Coast. The cape was named by English fur trader Captain John Meares in 1788 because of his unsuccessful attempt to find the Northwest Passage. Construction of the lighthouse suffered when the boat *Oriole,* carrying materials for the project, sank 2 miles offshore.

④④ **Ft. Canby State Park** was an active military installation until 1957, when it was turned over to the Washington State Parks and Recreation Commission, and many of the bunkers that guarded the mouth of the Columbia remain today. The park attracts beachcombers, ornithologists, and fishermen, and offers viewing spots for watching huge waves crash against the Columbia River bar during winter storms. *Robert Gray Dr. (Box 488), 2½ mi southwest of Ilwaco, off Hwy. 101; tel. 206/642– 3078 or 800/562–0990. Admission free. Call the Long Beach Visitors Bureau for hours.*

In the park is the **Lewis & Clark Interpretive Center,** which was built in 1976 and covers the 8,000-mile round-trip journey of the Corps of Volunteers for Northwest Discovery from Wood River, Illinois, to the mouth of the Columbia River. Artwork, photographs, and original journal entries are arranged along a series of ramps and take visitors from the planning of the expedition to a view of the Pacific from Cape Disappointment. *Tel.*

206/642–3029 or 604/642–3078. Check with the Long Beach Visitors Bureau for hours.

The U.S. Coast Guard Station Cape Disappointment is the largest search-and-rescue station on the Northwest coast, and its operations saved or assisted some 3,000 people in 1989. The **National Motor Life Boat School** is a graduate course in conquering fear. The only school of its kind, it teaches elite rescue crews from around the world advanced skills in navigation, mechanics, firefighting, lifesaving, the capabilities and limitations of motor lifeboats, and safe rescues. The rough conditions of the Columbia River bar provide a practical training for the regular surf drills. The observation platform on the North Jetty at Ft. Canby State Park is a good viewing spot for watching the motor lifeboats. *Tel. 206/642–2384. Informal tours may be available, but phone ahead of time.*

45 **North Head Lighthouse,** also one of the oldest lighthouses in the area, was built in 1899 to help skippers sailing from the north who could not see the Cape Disappointment Lighthouse. Before the lighthouses were built, a variety of less sophisticated signals, such as notched trees, white rags, or bonfires, were used. Volunteers residing in Astoria had to paddle across the river and hike 12 miles up the cape to place the signals.

46 **Seaview** is an unincorporated community that includes several homes dating from the 1800s. The **Shelburne Inn** (*see* Dining and Lodging, *below*), built in 1896, is the last turn-of-the-century hotel that still accommodates visitors. Another historic building is the **Sou'wester Lodge,** built by U.S. Senator Henry Winslow Corbett in 1892.

47 **Long Beach,** a community of 1,400, caters to tourists with its go-carts, bumper cars, amusement park, and beach activities.

48 **Ocean Park** is the commercial center of the peninsula's north end. It was founded as a camp for the Methodist Episcopal Church of Portland in 1883, but the law that once prohibited the establishment of saloons and gambling houses no longer exists. The **Taylor Hotel,** built in 1892 on Bay Avenue and N Place, houses retail businesses and is the only structure from the early days that is open to the public.

49 Across the way, on the bay side, is **Nahcotta,** the site of an active oyster industry. Oysters are shucked and canned on the docks on Willapa Bay, and you can sample them at the **Ark** (273 Sandridge Rd., tel. 206/665–4133), a restaurant on the old Nahcotta Dock. Named for a Native American chief, Nahcotta was once the northernmost point on the peninsula's narrow-gauge railway, and the schedule is still posted in the Nahcotta Post Office. The town's port is a good place from which to view Long Island, home of an old-growth cedar forest that can be reached only by private boat.

50 The town of **Oysterville,** established in 1854, did not survive the oyster industry's decline in the late 1800s. The native shellfish were fished to extinction and, although replaced with a Japanese oyster, Oysterville never made a comeback. Tides have washed away homes, businesses, and a Methodist church, but the village still exists, and free maps inside the vestibule of the restored **Oysterville Church** direct you through this town, which is now on the National Register of Historic Places. For more information on the town, write to the **Oysterville Restoration Foundation** (Box 1, Oysterville, WA 98641).

51 **Leadbetter State Park,** at the northernmost tip of the peninsula, is a wildlife refuge and good spot for bird-watching, and the dune area at the very tip of the point is closed from April to August to protect the nesting snowy plover. Black brants, sandpipers, turnstones, yellowlegs, sanderlings, knots, and plovers are among the 100 species biologists have recorded at the point. *Off Stackpole Rd. at the northern tip of the peninsula, tel. 206/ 642–3078. Call this number or the Long Beach Visitors Bureau for hours.*

Yakima Valley Wine Country

Numbers in the margin correspond to points of interest on the Yakima Valley map.

America's second-largest producer of wines, Washington state has been blessed with just the right soil, latitude, growing season, and climate that work together for premium grape and wine production. Its vineyards share the same latitude (46 degrees) and growth cycle of the great French wine-producing regions of Bordeaux and Burgundy. The Columbia and Yakima valleys have a low average rainfall, and irrigation allows for careful moisture control during critical growth phases. Warm, sunny days build heavy sugars and cool nights help to retain high acids in the grapes. The results are balanced wines of superior flavor and quality.

Eastern Washington has some 11,000 acres planted in vineyards of cabernet sauvignon, Johannesburg Riesling, chardonnay, sauvignon blanc, chenin blanc, grenache, merlot, semillon, muscat, and Gewürztraminer grapes. Yakima Valley, the viticultural center of the state, is home to the largest group of wineries. Wine operations vary from small wineries on the back of residential property to large, commercial operations. Barrels are tapped and wine tasting begins about the last week of April. The **Yakima Valley Wine Grower Association** (Box 39, Grandview, WA 98930) publishes a brochure that lists local wineries with tasting-room tours and maps of the region.

52 The first stop is 10 minutes south of Yakima at **Staton Hills Winery** (2290 Gangl Rd., Wapato, tel. 509/877–2112), just east of I–82. The building, with a huge stone fireplace and commanding view of the valley, is surrounded by three vineyard trellis systems, showing an efficient method of grape growing.

Zillah, a town named after the daughter of a railroad manager,
53 features six wineries. Small **Bonair Winery** (500 S. Bonair Rd., Zillah, tel. 509/829–6027), which specializes in chardonnay, is run by the Puryear family who, after 10 years of amateur wine making in California, took up commercial production in the
54 Yakima Valley. **Hyatt Vineyards Winery** (2020 Gilbert Rd., Zillah, tel. 509/829–6333) specializes in estate-bottled table wines, and premium dessert wines are produced under the
55 Thurston Wolfe label. **Zillah Oakes Winery** (Box 1729, Zillah, tel. 509/829–6990) produces wine from vineyards on the south-
56 ern slopes of the Rattlesnake Mountains. **Quail Run Vintners** (1500 Vintage Rd., Zillah, tel. 509/829–6235), producers of Covey Run wines, is one of the valley's largest wineries, with expansive decks and grounds offering commanding views of the

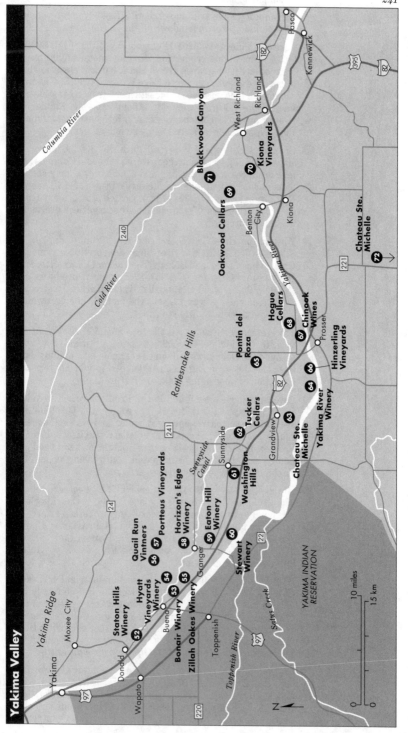

Yakima Valley

Columbia River

Yakima Ridge

Moxee City

Yakima

Donald

Wapato

Staton Hills Winery **52**

Hyatt Vineyards Winery **53**

Bonair Winery **53**

Zillah Oakes Winery **55**

Buena

Granger

Quail Run Vintners **56**

Porteus Vineyards **57**

Horizon's Edge Winery **58**

Eaton Hill Winery **59**

Stewart Winery

Toppenish

Toppenish River

Satus Creek

YAKIMA INDIAN RESERVATION

60

61

Washington Hills

Sunnyside

Sunnyside Canal

62

Tucker Cellars

Grandview

Chateau Ste. Michelle

63

64

Yakima River Winery

Hinzerling Vineyards

65

Pontin del Roza

66

Prosser

67

Chinook Wines

Hogue Cellars **68**

69

Oakwood Cellars

Benton City

Kiona

Yakima River

70

71

Blackwood Canyon

Kiona Vineyards

West Richland

Richland

Kennewick

Pasco

Cold River

Rattlesnake Hills

Chateau Ste. Michelle **72**

N

0   10 miles

0   15 km

surrounding vineyards and orchards. Inside you can watch the winemaking through windows off the tasting room.

57 **Portteus Vineyards** (5201 Highland Dr., Zillah, tel. 509/829–6970) limits its production to cabernet sauvignon and chardonnay from grapes grown at a 1,440-foot elevation in the **58** hills above Zillah. **Horizon's Edge Winery** (4530 E. Zillah Dr., Zillah, tel. 509/829–6401) takes its name from its tasting-room view of the Yakima Valley, Mt. Adams, and Mt. Rainier. The winery produces champagne, barrel-fermented chardonnays, Pinot Noir, cabernet sauvignon, and muscat canelli.

59 Granger's **Eaton Hill Winery** (530 Gurley Rd., Granger, tel. 509/854–2508), located in the restored Rinehold Cannery building, produces white Riesling and semillon. You may see fruit **60** pickers working outside the **Stewart Winery** (1711 Cherry Hill Rd., Granger, tel. 509/854–1882), located atop Cherry Hill. In sunny weather, tastings are held on the large deck overlooking the cherry orchard.

61 **Washington Hills** (111 E. Lincoln Ave., Sunnyside, tel. 509/839–9463), in the little town of Sunnyside, produces a variety of **62** white wines, a red, and a blush. The **Tucker Cellars** (Rte. 1, Box 1696, Sunnyside, tel. 509/837–8707) family produces some 20,000 gallons of wine annually. Their market, just east of Sunnyside on Highway 12, sells the family's homegrown fruit and vegetables in addition to wine.

63 The state's oldest winery is **Chateau Ste. Michelle** (W. 5th and Ave. B, Grandview, tel. 509/882–3928), in Grandview, where many of the company's red wines are made in a building dating from the '30s. The European-style open-top fermenters and a collection of wood aging tanks are featured.

64 Several wineries are found in the Prosser area. The **Yakima River Winery** (Rte. 1, Box 1657, Prosser, tel. 509/786–2805), specializing in barrel-aged red wines and dessert wines, is **65** southwest of town. The name **Pontin del Roza** (Rte. 4, Box 4735, Prosser, tel. 509/786–4449) comes from the owners, the Pontin family, and the Roza, the irrigated, south-facing slopes of the Yakima Valley where the grapes are grown.

66 **Hinzerling Vineyards** (1520 Sheridan Rd., Prosser, tel. 509/786–2163), operated by the Wallace family, is the valley's oldest family-owned winery, specializing in estate-grown cab-**67** ernets and late-harvest wines. East of Prosser is **Chinook Wines** (Wine Country Rd., Box 387, Prosser, tel. 509/786–2725), operated by Kay Siman and Clay Mackey, vintners known for their dry wines.

68 **Hogue Cellars** is housed at the Prosser Industrial Park, east of Chinook Wines. Three generations of the Hogue family have farmed in the Yakima Valley, and in 1982 they produced their first wine in the family's mint shed. Hogue Cellars includes a tasting room, reception room, and gift shop featuring Hogue Farm's foods and wines and other locally made products. *Box 31, Prosser, tel. 509/786–4557. Gift shop open daily 10–5.*

69 Farther east are three small wineries, including **Oakwood Cellars** (Rte. 2, Box 2321, Benton City, tel. 509/588–5332), where **70** almost all the work is done by hand; **Kiona Vineyards** (Rte. 2, Box 2169E, Benton City, tel. 509/588–6716), producers of the first commercial Lemberger released in this country; and

71 **Blackwood Canyon** (Rte. 2, Box 2169H, Benton City, tel. 509/588–6249), known for its Old World wine-making techniques.

72 The largest winery in the area is **Chateau Ste. Michelle** (Box 231, Hwy. 221, Columbia Crest Dr., tel. 509/875–2061) at Patterson. The imposing 16-acre estate is situated in the hills above the Columbia River near the Washington–Oregon border, and the winery itself is in a building that covers more than 9 acres.

What to See and Do with Children

Children's Museum Northwest is a hands-on exploratory museum for children. Exhibits include a fire station, TV station, puppet-making workshop, and science center. *106 Prospect St., Bellingham, tel. 206/733–8769. Admission: $2 adults, $1 children. Open Tues.–Fri. noon–5, Sat. 10–5, Sun. noon–5.*
Ilwaco Heritage Museum (*see* Long Beach Peninsula, *above*).
Lewis & Clark Interpretive Center (*see* Long Beach Peninsula, *above*).
Northwest Trek Wildlife Park (*see* Tacoma, *above*).
Point Defiance Zoo and Aquarium (*see* Tacoma, *above*).
Sequim-Dungeness Museum (*see* The Olympic Peninsula, *above*).

Shopping

Bellingham

Shopping Districts and Malls
The **Old Fairhaven District** (12th and Harris Sts.) is a number of square blocks of beautifully restored 1890s brick buildings housing a variety of restaurants, taverns, galleries, and specialty boutiques. To get there, take Exit 250 from I–5, then take Old Fairhaven Parkway west.

In **Old Town** (Lower Holly St.), in downtown Bellingham, there are a number of good antiques shops, second-hand stores, fish markets, hobby shops, and outdoor recreation equipment suppliers. The surrounding area also has small shops and a pleasant small-town atmosphere. Public parking is available on the street or at the Parkade (corner of Commercial and Holly Sts.).

Bellis Fair (I–5 Exits 256 and 256B, jct. I–5 and Guide Meridian, tel. 206/734–5022) is a glossy new regional shopping mall a few miles north of downtown. It has five department stores, several restaurants, and more than 120 other shops, including a multiplex movie theater.

Long Beach Peninsula

Specialty Shops
The Bookvendor (101 Pacific Ave., Long Beach, tel. 206/642–2702) stocks an extensive supply of children's books, classics, and travel books as well as art supplies.
Gray Whale Gallery & Gifts (105 Pacific Ave., Long Beach, tel. 206/642–2889) features Northwest art, cards, jewelry, and cranberry products from the peninsula.
Long Beach Kites (104 Pacific Ave. N, Long Beach, tel. 206/642–2202) offers myriad kites, from box kites, dragons, and fighters to 19 varieties of stunt kites, *and* free repairs are made.

North Head Gallery (600 S. Pacific Ave., Long Beach, tel. 206/642–8884) has the largest selection of Elton Bennett originals, plus Bennett's reproductions and works from other Northwest artists.

The Olympic Peninsula

Shopping Districts The single best locale for the confirmed shopaholic is the waterfront array of boutiques and stores in **Port Townsend,** all of which feature a good selection of Northwest arts and crafts. Additional shops are uptown on **Lawrence Street,** near the Victorian houses.

Tacoma

Shopping Districts **Freighthouse Square Public Market,** on the corner of 25th and D
and Malls streets, is a former railroad warehouse that's been converted into several small, unpretentious shops. The emphasis is on local arts and crafts, and there's also a weekend farmers market, several informal snack bars, and restaurants. For a small town ambience within the city, shop the **Proctor District,** with more than 60 businesses, in Tacoma's north end. The **Specialty Shop** (2702 N. Proctor St., tel. 206/752–2242) features apparel, books, pottery, food, and wine from more than 800 Northwest artisans and producers. The biggest shopping mall in the Pacific Northwest is the **Tacoma Mall** (tel. 206/475–4565), 1½ miles south of Tacoma Dome. The mall has more than 150 department stores, specialty shops, services, and restaurants for the devoted shopper.

Specialty Shops **Antique Row** (Broadway and St. Helens St., between 7th and
Antiques 9th Sts.) is made up of some 30 high-quality antiques stores: perfect for browsing on a rainy afternoon. A surprisingly wide variety of items is available—from high-quality to decidedly funky, Native American crafts to antique fishing gear, circus memorabilia to fine furniture. Proprietors are generally friendly and knowledgeable.

Sports and the Outdoors

Bicycling

Bellingham/ **Chuckanut Drive** and **Lummi Island** are favorite bicycling
Whatcom/ routes. Also good is the flat land around **La Conner,** to the
Skagit Counties south of Bellingham. To the north, **Lynden** is beautiful country, where tulip farms enliven the scenery in the spring. For rentals, try **Fairhaven Bicycle and Ski** (1103 11th St., tel. 206/733–4433) and **Yeager's Sporting Goods** (3101 Northwest Ave., Bellingham, tel. 206/733–1080).

Long Beach Good areas for bicycling include Ft. Canby and North Head roads, Sandridge Road to Ocean Park and Oysterville, and Highway 101 from Naselle to Seaview along Willapa Bay.

Tacoma Bicycling is especially popular in the **Puyallup Valley** to the east and the **Kitsap Peninsula.** A number of shops in Tacoma, Puyallup, Gig Harbor, and Port Orchard rent bicycles and equipment.

Climbing

Bellingham/ The **American Alpine Institute** (1212 24th St., Bellingham
Whatcom 98225, tel. 206/671–1505) is one of the most prestigious moun-
Skagit Counties tain- and rock-climbing schools around.

Tacoma **Rainier Mountaineering** (tel. 206/627–6242) offers one-day
snow and ice courses during the summer. This group also sponsors guided summit climbs and five-day climbing seminars. The
summit climb is not necessarily restricted to experienced
climbers, but it is not for people who are out of shape.

Fishing

Long Beach Salmon, rock cod, lingcod, flounder, perch, sea bass, and stur-
Peninsula geon are popular and plentiful for fishing. A free fishing guide
is available from the **Port of Ilwaco** (Box 307, 98624, tel. 206/
642–3143).

The clamming season varies depending on the supply but is a
popular pastime here. For details, call the **Washington Department of Fisheries** (tel. 206/753–6552) or the **fisheries shellfish
lab** (tel. 206/665–4166) in Nahcotta.

The Olympic Trout and salmon fishing is particularly abundant in rivers
Peninsula throughout the peninsula. In **Neah Bay,** halibut and salmon are
the target of charter fishing operations such as **Olson's Resort**
(Box 216, Sekiu 98381, tel. 206/963–2311). In **Aberdeen** and
Hoquiam, bottomfish and salmon are the primary catches. For
information concerning fishing in the Olympic Peninsula, contact **North Olympic Peninsula Visitors and Convention Bureau**
(Box 670, Port Angeles 98362, tel. 206/452–8552 or 800/942–
4042).

Tacoma The snow-fed lakes and streams of **Mt. Rainier** are a
fisherman's dream. Among the varieties available are cutthroat, rainbow, steelhead, and eastern brook trout; bass,
bluegill, crappie, and perch; and chinook salmon. Licenses are
available at most sporting-goods stores, or through the **Washington Department of Fisheries** (115 General Adm. Bldg.,
Olympia 98504, tel. 206/753–6552).

Golf

Bellingham A public course designed by Arnold Palmer is at the **Inn at
Semiahmoo Golf Club** (tel. 206/371–7005), a luxury resort near
Blaine and the Canadian border on Semiahmoo Spit. There are
also public 18-hole courses at **Birch Bay** (tel. 206/371–2026),
Sudden Valley (tel. 206/734– 6435), and **Lake Padden Park** (tel.
206/676–6989).

Long Beach The peninsula has two nine-hole golf courses, the **Peninsula
Golf Course** (tel. 206/642–2828), on the northern edge of Long
Beach, and the **Surfside Golf and Country Club** (tel. 206/665–
4148), located 2 miles north of Ocean Park.

Tacoma Tacoma has several fine golf courses, including **North Shore**
(tel. 206/927–1375), with 18 holes and several small unpretentious shops; **Allenmore** (tel. 206/627–7211), with 18 holes; **High-
lands** (tel. 206/759–3622), a 9-hole course; and **Meadowpark**
(tel. 206/473–3033), with 18 holes plus a 9-hole course.

Hiking

Long Beach Hiking trails are available at **Ft. Canby** (tel. 206/642–3078 or 800/562–0990) and **Leadbetter** (tel. 206/642–3078) state parks.

The Olympic Both the ocean and mountain areas offer numerous hiking trails
Peninsula for all levels of ability. For details, contact the **National Park Service** (600 E. Park Ave., Port Angeles 98362, tel. 206/452–0330).

Tacoma **Mt. Rainier National Park** (tel. 206/569–2211) has more than 300 miles of hiking trails, from easy to advanced.

Horseback Riding

Long Beach Horseback riding is popular on the beach, and rentals are available at **Skippers** (S. 9th St. and Beach Access Rd., tel. 206/642–3676). For beach access, riders are asked to use South 10th Street rather than Bolstad Street. Also, **Double "D" Horse Rides** (on 10th St., tel. 206/642-2576) takes phone reservations.

Skiing, Cross-Country

Bellingham/ Mt. Baker's **Heather Meadows** (1017 Iowa St., tel. 206/734–
Whatcom/ 6771) offers cross-country terrain. For rentals, try **The Great**
Skagit Counties **Adventure** (201 E. Chestnut, Bellingham, tel. 206/671–4615).

The Olympic **Hurricane Ridge,** south of Port Angeles, offers miles of cross-
Peninsula country ski trails. Contact **Port Angeles Visitor Center** (121 E. Railroad St., 98362, tel. 206/452–2363) for information.

Tacoma **Mt. Tahoma Trails System** (Box 942, Eatonville 98328) is a non-profit group of volunteers that has organized a series of trails near Mt. Rainier for more than 100 miles of cross-country skiing, most of which is beginner to intermediate terrain, and huts for basic overnight accommodations, available by reservation.

The **Ski Touring Center** (Box 108, Ashford 98304, tel. 206/569–2283) at Longmire, operated by Mt. Rainier Guest Services, rents cross-country ski equipment and provides lessons for those who want to explore the isolated meadows and forests of Mt. Rainier in winter.

Skiing, Downhill

Bellingham Mt. Baker's **Heather Meadows** (1017 Iowa St., tel. 206/734–6771) facility has the longest ski season in the state, lasting from roughly November–March. It has new chair lifts, day lodge facilities, and parking areas.

The Olympic **Hurricane Ridge** (tel. 206/452–4501) has a modest ski opera-
Peninsula tion, with two rope tows and a poma lift and cross-country trails.

Tacoma Sixty-four miles east of Tacoma is **Crystal Mountain** (Rtes. 410 and 123 at Crystal Mountain Rd., tel. 206/663–2265), a world-class ski resort with activities year-round. The elevation is 7,000 feet, with 34 runs and 2,300 acres of skiable terrain for all levels. Services include full resort amenities and equipment rentals. **Crystal Mountain Express** (tel. 206/455–5505 or 206/626–5208 in Tacoma) coaches leave from six locations, including Sea-Tac Airport, every morning.

Water Sports

Bellingham/ Whatcom/ Skagit Counties Several lakes near Bellingham offer ample opportunity for water sports, including **Lake Padden Park** (4882 Samish Way, tel. 206/676–6989) and **Bloedel Donovan Park** (2214 Electric Ave., tel. 206/676–6888), on the northwest shore of Lake Whatcom. **Island Mariner Cruises** offers scheduled summer whale-watching trips to the San Juan Islands. (No. 5 Esplanade, Bellingham 98225, tel. 206/734–8866). For a list of fishing and sailing charter companies, contact the Bellingham/Whatcom County CVB (tel. 206/671–3990).

Long Beach Peninsula **Whale-watching** is a popular activity on Long Beach Peninsula. Gray whales pass by here twice a year: December through February, on their migration from the Arctic to their winter breeding grounds in Californian and Mexican waters; and March through May, on the return trip north. At press time no charters were being offered in the Long Beach area, but the Northhead Lighthouse offers the best viewpoint. The best conditions exist in the mornings, when seas are calm and overcast conditions reduce the glare. Look on the horizon for a whale blow—the vapor, water, or condensation that spouts into the air when the whale exhales. Once a blow is spotted, there are likely to be others. Whales often make up to six shorter, shallow dives before a longer dive that can last as long as 10 minutes.

Spectator Sports

Bellingham/ Whatcom/ Skagit Counties The **Bellingham Mariners** are a class-A affiliate of the Seattle Mariners. Games are played June–September (Joe Martin Stadium, 1500 Orleans St., Bellingham, tel. 206/671–6347). The **Bellingham Ice Hawks** play in the British Columbia Junior Hockey League September–March (Whatcom Sports Arena, 1801 W. Bakerview Road, Bellingham, tel. 206/676–8080).

The Tacoma Dome is home to the **Tacoma Rockets**, an expansion team of the Western Hockey League. The Rockets play about 37 home games, October through March (tel. 206/627–3653). The **Tacoma Tigers,** a Pacific Coast League Triple-A baseball team, plays 72 home games a year at the 10,000-seat Cheney Stadium (Rte. 16, just west of Tyler St., tel. 206/752–7700 or 800/281–3834). The **Spanaway Speedway,** 7 miles south of Tacoma, has featured the region's most exciting auto racing for more than 30 years. Midweek competition features amateurs racing their "street legal" automobiles. The racetrack offers family packages and a supervised play area for children (16413 22nd Ave. E., Spanaway, tel. 206/537–7551).

National and State Parks and Forests

Birch Bay State Park (5105 Helwig Rd., Blaine 98230, tel. 206/371–2800), an official Audubon Society bird sanctuary 10 miles from the Canadian border, encompasses almost 200 acres, including a large campground and plenty of room for clamming, fishing, golf, swimming, and hiking.

Dash Point State Park (5700 S.W. Dash Pt. Rd., tel. 800/562–0990), 5 miles northeast of Tacoma, is a fine beach for picnicking, camping, or beachcombing, and it has excellent views of nearby Vashon Island.

Larrabee State Park (245 Chuckanut Dr., tel. 206/676–2093), 6 miles from Bellingham, has nearly 1,900 acres of forest and park and 3,600 feet of shoreline. The **Interurban Trail** is 6 miles of former train track along the water, paralleling part of Chuckanut Drive. It's now devoted to nonmotorized biking, walking, jogging, and horseback riding. The trailhead begins in the north near 24th Street and Old Fairhaven Parkway, and in the south near Larrabee State Park.

Mt. Baker–Snoqualmie National Forest (*see* Bellingham/Whatcom/Skagit Counties, *above*).

Mt. Rainier National Park, located 74 miles southeast of Tacoma, features the magnificent 14,411-foot Mt. Rainier—the fifth-highest mountain in the lower 48 states. It's so big that it creates its own weather system. But the park isn't just this incredible volcanic peak; it also encompasses nearly 400 square miles of surrounding wilderness. Within its boundaries are more than 300 miles of hiking trails, from easy to advanced, as well as good lakes and rivers for fishing, glaciers, isolated cross-country skiing spots, and ample camping facilities. Among the wildlife in the park are bears, mountain goats, deer, elk, eagles, beavers, and mountain lions; the abundant flora includes Douglas fir, hemlock, cedar, ferns, and wildflowers. The aptly named **Paradise,** at an altitude of 5,400 feet, is the usual starting point for climbs to Rainier's summit during the summer months. The **Henry M. Jackson Visitor's Center** has exhibits, films, and a 360-degree view of the summit and surrounding peaks. A number of hiking trails lead off from here. (*See* Dining and Lodging, *below*, for accommodations.) *To Mt. Rainier, follow Hwy. 5 south and east, or Hwy. 410 east and south. Both roads meet up at Cayuse and Chinook passes (often closed in winter) to form a full circle around the park. Henry M. Jackson Visitor's Center, tel. 206/ 569–2211. Jackson open Memorial Day–Labor Day, weekdays 9–7, weekends and holidays 10–5.*

Olympic National Park and Olympic National Forest, two of the most outstanding pieces of natural beauty in America, were established in 1938, and feature such diversified areas as the wind-swept beaches at La Push and Cape Alava, the lush green of the Hoh Rain Forest, the 60-odd active glaciers of the Olympic Mountains, and the high alpine beauty of Hurricane Ridge. Wildlife such as elk and eagle, as well as plant life such as wildflowers and Douglas fir, flourish here, in large part due to the prohibition of all hunting, firearms, and offroad vehicles, as well as any disturbance of plants or wildlife. Fishing, however, is permitted within the park without a state license, though punchcards for salmon and steelhead are required and certain waters are subject to regulation. In the National Forest, hunting and fishing are permitted in areas, though some portions are maintained as complete wilderness. For more information, contact Superintendent, Olympic National Park (600 E. Park Ave., Port Angeles 98362, tel. 206/452–4501) or Forest Supervisor, Olympic National Forest (Box 2288, Olympia 98507, tel. 206/753–9535).

Dining and Lodging

Dining Highly recommended restaurants are indicated by a star ★.

Category	Cost*
Very Expensive	over $35
Expensive	$25–$35
Moderate	$15–$25
Inexpensive	under $15

cost per person, excluding drinks, service, and 8.1% sales tax

Lodging Highly recommended hotels are indicated by a star ★.

Category	Cost*
Very Expensive	over $140
Expensive	$90–$140
Moderate	$50–$90
Inexpensive	under $50

All prices are for a double room, excluding 8.1% tax and service charge.

Anacortes
Dining and Lodging

Majestic Hotel. An old mercantile has been turned into one of the finest small hotels in the Northwest. From the elegant, two-story lobby with Victorian furnishings, guests can enter the Rose & Crown pub, banquet rooms, or walk up the sweeping stairway to the 23 guest rooms and the dark, English-style library. The top-floor gazebo features views of the marina, Mt. Baker, and the Cascades. Rooms are individually decorated with European antiques, down comforters, and several contain spa tubs. Complimentary Continental breakfast is served in the dining room. The full-service restaurant, Janot's Bistro, turns out excellent meals, with a variety of seafood, as well as chicken, pasta, and beef entrées. *419 Commercial Ave., Anacortes, 98221, tel. 206/293-3355. 23 rooms. Restaurant: Reservations recommended. Dress: casual. Dinner daily, lunch Mon.–Sat., Sun. brunch. MC, V. Restaurant: Inexpensive–Moderate. Hotel: Expensive–Very Expensive.*

Ashford
Dining and Lodging
★

Alexander's Country Inn. Built in 1912 as a luxury hotel, this bed-and-breakfast near the southwest entrance to the park has attracted a fiercely loyal clientele since its recent restoration to grandeur. Carefully decorated rooms have choice antiques and added touches, such as hand-sewn quilts and delicate floral wallpaper. A wheelchair-accessible suite with a separate entrance has recently been added, but it blends in well with the original building. Breakfasts (price included) are simple but well done, and might feature omelets, French toast, fruit, croissants, juice, and coffee. The excellent restaurant, open to guests and non-guests, bakes its own bread and desserts; a variety of fresh fish and pasta dishes, such as chicken fettuccine, are also specialties. *37515 Star Rte. 706 E., tel. 206/569-2300. Reservations in restaurant recommended. Dress: casual. Restaurant closed weekdays in winter. MC, V. Moderate–Expensive.*

Bellingham
Dining
★

Il Fiasco. Although the food can be pricey, this restaurant (the name means "the flask") is considered one of the best in Bellingham, offering an ambitious northern Italian menu, a sophisticated decor, knowledgeable staff, and a good wine list that mixes Italian and local vintages. Many of the entrées, such as the fresh-crab ravioli or a luscious lasagne made with lamb, fontina cheese, spinach, and polenta, can be ordered as appetizers; an entire meal can thus be concocted entirely from the appetizer list, a practice that is not only accepted but encouraged by the friendly waiters and waitresses. *1309 Commercial St., tel. 206/676–9136. Reservations advised. Dress: casual. MC, V. Closed Sat., Sun. lunch. Expensive–Very Expensive.*

La Belle Rose. This is a very good French country restaurant, run by an expatriate Frenchwoman, Mariette Wood, who emphasizes fresh ingredients and home baking. The extremely small dining room with just six tables is cozily and romantically decorated. Seafood is the specialty, reflecting the restaurant's waterfront location in the Harbor Center Building, though there are choice meat dishes as well. Typical menu listings may include salmon *en sauce verte* (herb mayonnaise sauce) or sausage prepared Alsatian style and accompanied by crisp sauerkraut. *1801 Roeder Ave., suite 102, tel. 206/647–0833. Reservations necessary. Dress: casual. MC, V. Closed Sun.–Mon. dinner; Sun.–Wed. lunch. Expensive.*

Douglas House. This renovated 1904 house with lots of windows that offer great views of Mt. Baker and the Cascade Mountains also serves some great meals. The restaurant specializes in seafood and incorporates many fresh Northwest products into its salads, entrées, and desserts. *2254 Douglas Dr., Ferndale, tel. 206/384–5262. Reservations advised. Dress: casual. MC, V. Closed lunch. Moderate–Expensive.*

Oyster Creek Inn. This small eatery, best described as Northwest eclectic, is set in a sharp switchback near the southern end of Chuckanut Drive in nearby Skagit County. The window tables overlook the creek and bay, to compliment the already wonderful atmosphere. Oysters, cooked in a variety of imaginative ways, stand out, while an excellent wine list—drawn exclusively from Washington State vineyards—is also featured. Sunday brunch, with classic dishes such as salmon omelets and fries, is offered. *190 Chuckanut Dr., Bow, tel. 206/766–6179. Reservations suggested. Dress: casual. AE, MC, V. Moderate.*

Pacific Café. This restaurant, next door to the historic Mt. Baker Theater in downtown Bellingham, features a variety of seafood and pasta dishes with an Asian twist; typical menu listings include such dishes as Alaska spot prawns in a garlicky blackbean sauce and rib steak with a plum-oyster sauce. Portions are large (but the spicing can be mild), but you'll want to save room for one of the wickedly good desserts, such as the chocolate éclairs. The café's understated decor, like the food, is Asian-influenced: white walls, rice-paper screens, wood shutters. *100 N. Commercial St., tel. 206/647–0800. Reservations advised. Dress: casual. AE, MC, V. Closed Sat. lunch, Sun. dinner. Moderate.*

Rhododendron Café. Homemade soups, seafood, and fresh salads comprise the foundations upon which the ever-changing specials menu is built in this generally excellent restaurant. Specials vary according to the market and may include marinated snapper with a toasted nut sauce or mussel-vegetable soup. The locally famous pies and other luscious desserts should be sampled. The restaurant, located at the very southern (and out of the way) end of Chuckanut Drive—near the tiny town of Bow in Skagit County—is pleasant and unpretentious in its decor; the service is usually cheerful and fast, though when things get crowded it can slow up. *553 Chuckanut Dr.,*

Bow, tel. 206/766–6667. Reservations accepted. Dress: casual.
MC, V. Closed Mon., Tues. Moderate–Inexpensive.

Colophon Cafe. Incorporated into the Village Bookstore, this restaurant offers such hearty soups as Brazilian peanut butter, as well as good sandwiches and ice cream. *1208 11th St., Old Fairhaven, tel. 206/647–0092. No reservations. Dress: casual. MC, V. Inexpensive.*

Archer Ale House. This smoke-free English-style pub features Northwest microbrews and pub food. Try the pasties and vegetarian pizza. *1212 10th St., Bellingham, tel. 206/647–7002. No reservations. Dress: casual. Inexpensive.*

Lodging **Loganita.** On Lummi Island just northwest of Bellingham, this sparkling white, rambling farmhouse offers accommodations with spectacular, 180-degree west-facing marine views, and opportunities for biking, eagle-watching, and beach-combing. The interior is decorated in an elegant but comfortable style, with large windows, Oriental rugs, lots of wood, antiques, and fireplaces. *2825 W. Shore Dr., Lummi Island, 98262, tel. 206/758-2651. 2 B&B rooms, 2 suites. Facilities: hot tub, pool table, ping-pong, volleyball, soccer, bike rentals; meals available by prior request. No smoking or pets. MC, V. Expensive.*

Schnauzer Crossing. A meticulously kept garden surrounds three sides of this elegant B&B, with Lake Whatcom on the fourth. Besides a large and gracious common sitting room, each of its two guest rooms offers something different: The larger has a huge bed, garden views, a fireplace, and a small sitting room, while the smaller has a view of the lake and a choice little library. Friendly owners Donna and Vermont McAllister serve ample gourmet breakfasts. *1807 Lakeway Dr., 98226, tel. 206/733–0055 or 206/734–2808. 2 rooms. Facilities: Jacuzzi, tennis court, outdoor hot tub, boating facilities. No smoking or pets. MC, V. Expensive.*

Best Western Lakeway Inn. A large, bustling hotel in downtown Bellingham, this accommodation is popular with tourists, especially those from Vancouver. Located near the big Fred Meyers shopping complex, there are plenty of things to keep the whole family occupied. Children under 12 stay for free when sharing a room with their parents. *714 Lakeway Dr., 98225, tel. 206/671–1011 or 800/547–0106; fax 206/676–8519. 132 rooms. Facilities: café, piano lounge, indoor pool, sauna, weight room, free shuttle service to airport or ferry. AE, D, DC, MC, V. Moderate.*

Park Motel. Because of its "children under 12 free" policy, this is a popular family motel, and since it's close to the university, it's also often occupied by the visiting parents of students. The strictly standard-issue decor and furnishings are functional but comfortable, and some are equipped with kitchens. *101 N. Samish Way, 98225, tel. 206/733–8280; fax 206/738–9186. 56 rooms; no-smoking rooms available. Facilities: Jacuzzi, sauna. AE, DC, MC, V. Moderate.*

Blaine **The Inn at Semi-ah-moo.** At the tip of a sandspit on the U.S.–
Lodging Canadian border, the Inn at Semi-ah-moo (a coastal Native American word for "clam eaters") is housed in the old Semiahmoo Salmon Cannery building. Extensively renovated and refitted to be a hostelry, the inn's guest rooms range from standard motellike accommodations to rooms and suites with fireplaces, balconies, and expansive views. The draw here, however, is the dramatic waterside location and the plethora of outdoor activities available at this 800-acre resort. Guests can bike, jog, or hike around the nearby nature trails; join a fishing

charter or sightseeing cruise; golf a course designed by Arnold Palmer; recreate indoors at the health club; and swim in heated pools indoors or out. *9565 Semiahmoo Pkwy., Blaine, WA 98230, tel. 206/371–2000, 800/854–2608, or 800/854–6742 in Canada; fax 206/371–5490. 188 rooms, 12 suites. Facilities: 2 restaurants, bar, health club, 2 heated pools, indoor running track, indoor tennis, racquetball, squash, golf course, marina, bike rentals. AE, MC, V. Expensive.*

Cle Elum
Dining and Lodging

Mama Vallone's Steakhouse and Inn. The Vallones use traditional recipes from their Italian homeland to design the menu for this cozy and informal restaurant. Although it's renowned for its great pasta, the pasta and *fagioli* soup (a tomato-based soup with vegetables and beans) and the *bagna calda* (a bath of olive oil, garlic, anchovies, and butter for dredging vegetables and meat) are also worthy favorites. Also try the Sunday brunch, which may feature ravioli or tortellini along with a standard eggs-and-ham buffet. The inn upstairs was built in 1906 as a boardinghouse for unmarried miners; today three moderately priced rooms with private baths and antique reproduction furnishings are available. *302 W. 1st St., tel. 509/674–5174. 3 rooms. No facilities. Reservations for restaurant suggested. Dress: casual. AE, DC, MC, V. Closed Mon. and lunch. Moderate.*

Copalis Beach
Lodging

Iron Springs Resort. Located 3 miles north of Copalis Beach on Route 109, this string of 25 individual cottages can accommodate anywhere from 2 to 10 people—perfect for families. Each has its own fireplace and kitchen; older cabins are decorated in a dimly lit but pleasantly funky style, while newer ones (Nos. 22–25) are spiffier; only No. 6 has no view, but others have superb beach, river, and forest views and access. *Box 207, Copalis Beach 98535, tel. 206/276–4230. 25 units. Facilities: heated and covered pool. AE, MC, V. Moderate.*

Forks
Dining and Lodging

Kalaloch Lodge. This facility, set in the lush Olympic National Forest, is a hodgepodge of old cabins, new log cabins, an old lodge, and a new hotel. Lodge rooms are clean, airy, and comfortable, and most have terrific ocean views. Some of the rooms in the modern part—Sea Crest House—have fireplaces and decks. The old cabins can be pretty basic (drafty in winter, with minimal kitchens and other amenities), but they are fine for informal stays and for a sense of what the wild Washington coast was like in "the good old days." The new log cabins convey a similar feeling but are a little spiffier, and the lodge offers few resort-type amenities but abundant opportunities for beachcombing, hiking, and other robust activities. Good, fresh salmon and oysters highlight the menu in the restaurant, though the rest of the fare can be disappointingly ordinary. *Hwy. 101 (HC 80, Box 1100), Forks-Kalaloch 98331, tel. 206/962–2271. 58 rooms and cabins. Facilities: restaurant. Reservations accepted. Dress: casual. AE, MC, V. Moderate–Expensive.*

Gig Harbor
Dining
★

Neville's Shoreline. This pleasant, accommodating restaurant in the heart of Gig Harbor's marina is rather dark inside, but window tables offer excellent views of the water. Northwest seafood is the specialty here—try especially the simply but well-prepared salmon and clams. There is a fine Sunday brunch. *8827 N. Harborview Dr., tel. 206/851–9822. Reservations advised. Dress: casual. AE, D, MC, V. Moderate.*

Tides Tavern. This noisy, cheerful waterfront bar-cum-restaurant has been going strong since 1904. The menu features standard tavern grub—sandwiches, burgers, pizza—but is much better than average; shrimp salad is a house specialty. When the sun's out, the deck is the most popular seating area. If you happen to arrive by boat or seaplane, no problem—you can tie up right at the tavern. *2925 Harborview Dr., tel. 206/858-3982. No reservations. Dress: casual. MC, V. Inexpensive.*

La Conner
Lodging

Hotel Planter. This renovated hotel is the oldest in La Conner and is on the National Register of Historic Places. Bright and airy rooms are filled with attractive handmade furniture, and offer fine views of either La Conner's main street or the waterfront. *715 1st St., 98257, tel. 206/466-4422. 12 rooms, some with private bath. Facilities: hot tub. AE, MC, V. Moderate.*

Rainbow Inn. This B&B is in a stately looking, restored three-story turn-of-the-century country house a half-mile east of La Conner. Hosts Sharon Briggs and Ron Johnson left corporate careers in the Bay Area to pursue their love of cooking, gardening, and entertaining. The main floor's parlor has a tile fireplace, antiques, and views out onto open fields. From the enclosed porch where breakfast is served, guests can see the gardens and neighboring farms. Rooms are large and are furnished with antiques and new furniture. One room has its own whirlpool tub, but all guests can soak while gazing at Mt. Baker from the hot-tub in the gazebo behind the house. Gourmet dinners can be arranged for groups by reservation. *1075 Chilberg Rd., LaConner 98257, tel. 206/466-4578. 5 rooms with bath, 3 rooms share 1 bath. Facilities: hot tub. MC, V. Moderate.*

Long Beach Peninsula Area
Dining

The Ark. The Ark, sitting adjacent to the Nahcotta oyster dock, has excellent cuisine. The house specialty is seafood—especially oysters, but leave room for the splendid desserts—cranberry Grand Marnier mousse and blackberry bread pudding, for example. The bar presents less expensive, lighter fare, including soup and sandwiches. *273 Sandridge Rd., Nahcotta, tel. 206/665-4133. Closed Jan.-Feb. Call ahead for hours. Reservations recommended. Dress: casual. AE, MC, V. Expensive.*

Columbia Lightship. This restaurant, on the beach side of Nendel's Inn, affords some of the best views of the beach and surf in the area. Huge windows and high ceilings lend an open, airy feeling to the place, and the atmosphere is casual and low-key. Don't be surprised to see kites or a large wind sock floating in the air as you gaze out at the beach from the open-air bar, which serves an assortment of Washington wines and local microbrews. The lunch menu offers fish-and-chips, fresh salads, quiche, pasta, and sandwiches. Dinner entrées include grilled fresh salmon, fresh Willapa Bay oysters, Cajun chicken, Manilla clams, pasta primavera, and prime rib. Try the Chicken Radiator Pasta, accordian-shaped noodles in a white Parmesan cheese sauce, with chicken and artichokes. Breakfast (served in summer only) options include a buffet with meat, eggs, fruit, waffles, pancakes, biscuits, muffins, and porridge. *409 10th St. SW, Long Beach, tel. 306/542-2311. Reservations suggested. Dress; casual but neat. MC, V. Moderate-Expensive.*

The Sanctuary. This restaurant, in a turn-of-the-century church building, offers fine cuisine and a quiet atmosphere with soft lighting and stained-glass windows. Swedish meatballs are a specialty, but the menu also features local seafood, prime rib, veal, an extensive wine list, and delicious homemade desserts. *Hwy. 101 and Hazel St., Chinook, tel. 206/777-8380.*

Reservations recommended. Dress: neat but casual. AE, MC, V. Dinner only starting at 5 PM. Moderate–Expensive.

★ **The Shoalwater Restaurant.** The Shoalwater Restaurant at the Shelburne Inn has been acclaimed by *Gourmet, Bon Appétit,* and *Travel & Leisure,* so you dine in good company here. Seafood, bought from the fishing boats to the restaurant's back door, is as fresh as it can be; local mushrooms and salad greens are gathered from the peninsula's woods and gardens. Exquisite desserts are the creation of Ann Kischner, a master pastry chef, and an extensive wine list and Northwest microbrews on tap in the Heron & Beaver Pub are featured. Also try the Sunday brunch offered on Easter, Mother's Day, and throughout the summer. *Pacific Hwy. and N. 45th St., Seaview, tel. 206/642–4142. Reservations recommended. Dress: casual but neat. AE, MC, V. Restaurant open daily for dinner starting at 5:30 PM. Pub offers lunch. Moderate–Expensive.*

Dog Salmon Cafe & Lounge. Even if you don't eat here, have a look inside this family restaurant, decorated with replicas of Northwest Coast Native American carvings and paintings of bears, beavers, and salmon on wood-paneled walls. The fare ranges from hamburgers to spicy Cajun shrimp linguini. *113 Hwy. 103, in downtown Long Beach, tel. 206/642–2416. No reservations. Dress: casual. MC, V. Inexpensive–Moderate.*

42nd Street Cafe. This much-needed, middle-of-the-road restaurant is nestled comfortably between deep-fried seafood and fries at one end of the peninsula's restaurant spectrum and expensive gourmet fare on the other. The café, which opened last year, emphasizes home-cooked food and features a new menu daily. Owner Robert Guy's father bakes the restaurant's breads and makes the tasty corn relish and conserves. Grilled Willapa Bay oysters are tender and succulent, and halibut and salmon are grilled or poached. The raisin cream pie for dessert is heavenly. Prices include soup, salad, vegetable, potato, entrée, and dessert. *Hwy. 103 and 42nd St., Seaview, tel. 206/642–2323. Reservations accepted for 5 or more persons. Dress: casual. V. Open from 4:30 PM for dinner. Closed Tues. Inexpensive–Moderate.*

My Mom's Pies. Although this lunch spot is in a mobile home, and keeps *very* irregular hours, it's worth dropping by for the specialty pies, such as the banana whipped cream, chocolate almond, pecan, sour-cream raisin, and fresh raspberry. They also serve clam chowder and quiche. *Hwy. 103 and 12th St. S, tel. 206/642–2342. No reservations. Dress: casual. MC, V. Closed dinner and Mon. Inexpensive.*

Lodging **Shelburne Inn.** This bright and cheerful antiques-filled inn was built in 1896 by Charles Beaver and is now listed on the National Register of Historic Places. It is also right on the highway, which can make it noisy, so the best picks are rooms on the west side. The indefatigable team of David Campiche and Laurie Anderson have the inn to its current high level of comfort and quality. Most of the rooms have balconies, private baths, queen-size beds with handmade quilts or hand-crocheted bedspreads, and some have lovely stained glass. The gourmet breakfast is unforgettable. *Hwy. 103 and N. 45th St., Seaview, 98644, tel. 206/542–2442. 16 rooms. Facilities: pub, restaurant. AE, MC, V. Expensive.*

The Breakers Motel and Condominiums. These contemporary condominiums have one- and two-bedroom units and are located on the beach. Since they are individually owned, the decor varies, but all are modern, comfortable, and clean. *Box 428, 98631, tel. 206/642-4414 or 800/288-8890. 114 rooms, some with kitchenettes. Facilities: indoor heated pool and spa, playground. MC, V. Moderate-Expensive.*

Inn at Ilwaco. This New England–style church, built in 1928, has been renovated as a B&B. All but two of the nine guest rooms are upstairs in the old Sunday-school rooms and all are cozily furnished with some antiques, armoires, and eyelet or printed chintz curtains and coverlets. The lobby, with upholstered sofas, chairs, and tables with loads of books, and the breakfast area are in the former church parlor. For performances, meetings, classes, and weddings, the inn makes use of its converted sanctuary, which is now a 120-seat theater. Breakfast may include such delicacies as apple-walnut pancakes, homemade muffins, fresh fruit, and cereal. *120 Williams St. NE, Ilwaco, 98624, tel. 206/642-8686. 9 rooms, 7 with private bath. No facilities. MC, V. Moderate-Expensive.*

Nendels. This modern motel (formerly the Edgewater Inn), set just behind the sand dunes and very close to the beach, presents a variety of rooms with different views, but those in the newer building offer the best scenery. *Box 793, 98631, tel. 206/642-2311 or 800/547-0106. 72 rooms. Facilities: restaurant, lounge, outdoor heated spa. Moderate-Expensive.*

Sandpiper Beach Resort. This resort is a modern, four-story complex of clean, attractive, and fully equipped suites; most have a sitting room, dining area, fireplace, small kitchen, porch, bedroom, and bath. Penthouse suites have an extra bedroom and cathedral ceilings. There are also five cottages and a few one-room studios. Despite a downright ugly playground that mars the beach view, the building is attractive, with the wood exterior blending well with the surrounding woods and water. This is definitely the place for a getaway: no in-room phones, no pool, no TV, no restaurant. *Rte. 109 (1½ mi south of Pacific Beach), Box A, 98571, tel. 206/276-4580. 30 rooms. No facilities. MC, V. Moderate.*

Sou'wester. A stay at the Sou'wester promises a bohemian experience that begins with your choice of accommodation: rooms and apartments in a historic lodge, cabins, or classic mobile-home units on the surrounding property just behind the beach. The lodge was built in 1892 as the summer retreat for Henry Winslow Corbett, a Portland banker, timber baron, shipping and railroad magnate, and U.S. senator. Units in the lodge are not "decorated"—instead they are the repository of things carefully collected over the years, including handmade quilts and original paintings and drawings. Stays of at least a month are welcomed in the lodge. Proprietors Len and Miriam Atkins came to Seaview from South Africa, by way of Israel and Chicago, where they worked with the late psychologist Bruno Bettelheim, and they are always up for a stimulating conversation. Soirees and chamber-music concerts sometimes occur in the parlor. Cabins and trailers have cooking facilities and instead of a B&B downstairs, there is a B&MYODB—"make your own damned breakfast" (in the Atkins' homey kitchen). *Beach Access Rd. (Box 102), Seaview, 98644, tel. 206/642-2542. 3 rooms with shared bath and kitchen; 4 cabins; 6 trailers. Facilities: adjacent to beach. MC, V. Inexpensive-Moderate.*

Moclips
Dining and Lodging

Ocean Crest Resort. Set high on a bluff above a spectacular stretch of the Pacific, this resort hotel has one- and two-bedroom units with airy decor, fireplaces, cedar paneling, and superb views. Some have kitchens and/or fireplaces; access to the beach is down a steep wooded walkway. The Ocean Crest restaurant also features panoramic ocean views, along with standard but well-prepared food in ample portions: eggs, hash browns, good coffee and muffins at breakfast, fresh seafood for lunch and dinner. There's also a gift shop and a snug bar decorated with Native American artifacts. *Hwy. 109 (18 mi north of Ocean Shores), 98562, tel. 206/276–4465. 45 rooms. Facilities: recreation area with pool, Jacuzzi, weight room. AE, MC, V. Moderate.*

Mt. Baker **Mt. Baker Lodging & Travel.** These self-contained cabins and
Lodging chalets nestled in a lovely wooded setting 17 miles west of the Mt. Baker National Forest offer units of varying sizes, from snug hideaways suitable for couples to larger chalets suitable for families or groups. Each unit is rustic, but clean and charming and has a wood-burning stove or fireplace, and comes stocked with linen, firewood, and towels. For families with children, cribs and toys are available. *Box 472, Glacier 98244, tel. 206/599–2453. Facilities: some units equipped with VCRs, hot tub, sauna. MC, V. Moderate.*

Olympia **La Petite Maison.** Imaginative French food is the specialty in
Dining this converted 1890s farmhouse, generally considered to be Olympia's premier fine-dining establishment. The ambience—one of quiet elegance—is created by the classical music, unobtrusive service, and crisp linens. Entrées range from delicately prepared local seafood (look especially for the Shelton clams) to marinated lamb or duck with blackberry sauce. A good wine list and excellent desserts, such as a Grand Marnier torte, round out the menu. *2005 Ascension Way, tel. 206/943–8812. Reservations recommended. MC, V. Closed Sun.; Sat. lunch, Mon. dinner. Moderate–Expensive.*

Lodging **Westwater Inn.** This is a large but friendly hotel, close to downtown Olympia and the capitol grounds, with striking views of Capitol Lake, the Capitol Dome, and the surrounding hills. The rooms are spacious and comfortable; those facing the water are especially appealing. There are two good restaurants on the premises: a modest coffee shop called Tiffin's, and Ceazan's, a restaurant with a fine view that serves decent sandwiches and full meals, mostly imaginative American fare, for modest prices. *2300 Evergreen Park Dr., 98502, tel. 206/943–4000. 191 rooms; disabled and no-smoking rooms available. Facilities: 2 restaurants, coffee shop, lounge, outdoor pool, Jacuzzi. AE, D, MC, V. Moderate.*

Paradise **Paradise Inn.** At an elevation of 5,400 feet, this large, old-fash-
Dining and Lodging ioned lodge offers excellent views of Mt. Rainier and Nisqually Glacier from nearly every one of its rooms. The best part about it, aside from its splendid location, is the spacious common lobby, which has exposed wood-beam construction, two huge stone fireplaces, Indian rugs, and western decor. The full-service dining room, with a menu that leans toward heavy and rather bland meat or frozen-fish dishes, is a famous gathering place for leisurely Sunday brunches in summer; in addition, the lodge has a small snack bar and a snug, crowded lounge with plenty of rough natural wood for decor. *Hwy. 706 (c/o Mt. Rainier Guest Services, Box 108, Star Rte., Ashford 98304), tel. 206/569–2275. Reservations recommended. Dress: casual. MC, V. Closed Nov.–mid-May. Moderate–Expensive.*

Port Angeles **C'est Si Bon.** This is a locally famous French restaurant run by
Dining a French expatriate couple, Norbert and Michele Juhasz. Probably the most elegant restaurant on the decidedly informal
Olympic Peninsula, C'est Si Bon has bold art on the walls, fine
linen on the tables, and a good view of rose gardens and the
Olympic Mountains. Sophisticated and generally good service
complements the classic menu. *Escargots en Pernod, fruits de
mer au gratin,* or a hearty onion soup are typical appetizers;
entrées include salmon, duck, and prawns with tomato and garlic. There is an excellent wine list, and desserts are also good,
especially the chocolate mousse. *2300 Hwy. 101E (4 mi east of
Port Angeles), tel. 206/452–8888. Reservations advised. Dress:
casual. AE, DC, MC, V. Closed Mon. and lunch. Expensive.*
First Street Haven. Small and informal, this place is tucked quietly into the storefronts of downtown Port Angeles but is a
good place for high-quality breakfasts and lunch. The service
is always friendly and fast, the decor cheerful but unpretentious.
Fresh salads, thick sandwiches, well-prepared fajitas and chili,
and homemade quiche are featured; good espresso drinks and
desserts are offered, too. Sunday brunches include well-prepared, hearty standard fare. *107 E. 1st St. (at Laurel), tel. 206/
457–0352. No reservations. Dress: informal. No credit cards.
No alcohol. Closed dinner. Inexpensive.*

Lodging **Sol Duc Hot Springs Resort.** This is a comfortable, casual resort, dating from the turn of the century, but managing to be
spiffed-up just enough without becoming slick and soulless.
Consisting of 32 minimally outfitted cabins, the resort presents
a pleasant and cheery atmosphere. All units have separate
bathrooms, and some have kitchens. There is also an outdoor
hamburger stand and an attractive inside dining room that
serves unpretentious meals (breakfast, lunch, and dinner)
drawing on the best of the Northwest: salmon, crab, fresh vegetables, and fruit. *12 mi south of Hwy. 101 on Soleduck Rd.
(Box 2168), 98362, tel. 206/327–3583. 32 units and camping
and RV facilities. Facilities: restaurant, hot springs, outdoor
pool. Reservations for restaurant necessary. Dress: casual.
MC, V. Closed mid-Oct.–mid-May. Moderate.*
Tudor Inn. This 1910 Tudor-style house, fully refurbished and
turned into a pleasant B&B, is only about 12 blocks from the
Victoria-bound ferry dock. Adding to the quiet style of this inn
are the antique furnishings and library; from the biggest and
most pleasant of the five guest rooms you get spectacular water
views (and private bath). The cheerful and efficient owners—
the Glasses—serve breakfast in classic English style, which includes eggs, bacon, and muffins, as well as a generous afternoon tea with plenty of fresh scones and other goodies. *1108 S.
Oak St., 98362, tel. 206/452–3138. 5 units. No facilities. No
smoking. MC, V. Moderate.*

Dining and Lodging **Lake Crescent Lodge.** This old but comfortable accommodation
with a big main lodge and small cabins overlooks the beautiful
deep-blue Lake Crescent. Units in the lodge are minimal—
bathrooms down the hall, dimly lit rooms—but the setting
makes up for sparse amenities. Trout fishing, hiking, evening
nature programs, and boating are all on the bill. The food in the
restaurant is nothing special, but the service is cheerful and efficient, appealing to young college students enjoying a summer
away from the city. *6540 E. Beach Rd., 98362, tel. 206/928–
3325. Facilities: restaurant, fishing, boating. AE, DC, MC, V.
Closed mid-Nov.–Apr. Inexpensive.*

Port Townsend **Fountain Café.** This small café, set off the main tourist drag, is
Dining one of the best restaurants in Port Townsend. Fine linens and
★ fresh flowers dress up the unpretentious dining room, and a
cheerful staff furthers the welcoming tone of this café. You can
count on seafood and pasta specialties with imaginative and al-
ways-changing twists: smoked salmon in black porter sauce,
for instance. This is a local hotspot, as evidenced by the occasional wait for a table. *920 Washington St., tel. 206/385–1364.
Reservations advised. Dress: casual. MC, V. Moderate.*

Salal Café. Featuring home-style cooking and daily specials,
this cooperatively run restaurant shines among early morning
breakfast joints. Try one of many variations on the potato-egg
scramble. For lunch, seafood and regional American-style
meals are good, portions ample, and prices reasonable. Try to
get a table in the glassed-in back room, which faces a plant-
filled courtyard. *634 Water St., tel. 206/385–6532. No reservations. Dress: casual. No credit cards. Closed dinner and Tues.
Inexpensive.*

Lodging **James House.** A splendid antiques-filled Victorian-era B&B, located on the bluff overlooking downtown Port Townsend and
the waterfront, this inn presents an elegant atmosphere in a
terrific location. Each of the two parlors has a fireplace and a
library, and several of the guest rooms feature waterfront
views. Elegant Continental cuisine breakfasts, inspired by the
owners' garden and love for herbs, are served in the formal dining room. In addition to being on the National Register of Historic Places, the James lays claim to being the first B&B in the
Northwest. *1238 Washington St., 98368, tel. 206/385–1238. 12
rooms. No facilities. Call for restrictions. MC, V. Moderate–
Expensive.*

Palace Hotel. This friendly, small hotel in the historic downtown section of Port Townsend is tastefully decorated to reflect
its 1889 construction date and its former history as a bordello.
The narrow, steep brick facade is pleasant to look at, but there
is no elevator, a consideration if getting around is difficult for
you. On the up side, the Palace is conveniently located close to
the town's shopping and sightseeing district. *1004 Water St.,
98368, tel. 206/385–0773. 15 units, 1 with kitchenette. No facilities. AE, D, MC, V. Moderate.*

Tides Inn. You might recognize this place from the movie *An
Officer and a Gentleman,* which was filmed around Port Townsend and Fort Worden. (The hotel is the setting for those
steamy love scenes between Richard Gere and Debra Winger.)
There are even *Officer and a Gentleman*–theme rooms available, complete with stills from the movie and a VCR for private
viewing of the film. Along the waterfront, about six blocks
from downtown, the Tides is a comfortable, unfancy place, with
good views of the water. An informal but adequate Continental
breakfast is served every morning, and kitchens are available
in both single rooms and suites; all the rooms have TVs and
phones, and some have private decks. *1807 Water St., 98368,
tel. 206/385–0595. 21 units. Facilities: Jacuzzis in some rooms.
AE, DC, MC, V. Moderate.*

Quinault **Lake Quinault Lodge.** This lodge is set on a perfect glacial lake
Lodging in the midst of the Olympic National Forest. Spectacular old-
growth forests are an easy hike away, and there is abundant
salmon and trout fishing. The medium-size and quite deluxe
lodge, built in 1926 of cedar shingles, includes delightful public

rooms decorated with antiques and a fireplace. The restaurant food is expensive but generally bland and unadventurous; the old-fashioned bar is lively and pleasant. Hiking and jogging trails are within easy access. Lake Quinault Lodge is especially popular with conventions and other groups. *S. Shore Rd. (Box 7), 98575, tel. 206/288–2571. 89 rooms. Facilities: restaurant, bar, Jacuzzi, indoor pool, sauna, golf course, games room. MC, V. Expensive.*

Roslyn
Dining

Roslyn Café. This funky café has gained notice from its exterior's appearances on TV's "Northern Exposure," but it's the trappings from its real-life past that, along with its good food, make it popular. High ceilings, a jukebox with the original 78s, and neon in the window bring nostalgia to the place. The hamburgers with spinach and onions are mouthwatering, but entrées also include such offerings as fresh halibut in dill sauce. Desserts are decadent. *28 Pennsylvania Ave., tel. 509/649–2763. No reservations. Dress: casual. No credit cards. Closed Mon. Inexpensive–Moderate.*

Sequim
Lodging

Greywolf Inn. Peggy and Bill Melang, lately of North Carolina and still brimming with southern hospitality, have obviously had fun turning this B&B into the showplace it is. Each room is (very) individually decorated—one looks imported from China, with a black lacquer four-poster and wardrobe; another room is Bavarian themed, with a feather bed under a pine canopy. One room with a gas fireplace can be combined with the adjacent room to create a two-bedroom suite with its own entrance. A Japanese-style bathhouse outside holds a hot tub. The dining room and decks overlook meadows, and a woodland trail winds through the property's idyllic five acres. *395 Keeler Rd., tel. 206/683–5889 or 206/683–1487. 6 rooms with bath. Facilities: year-round outdoor hot tub. AE, MC, V. Moderate.*

Tacoma
Dining

Pacific Rim Restaurant. This much-praised sophisticated restaurant, undoubtedly the best in Tacoma, has an inventive menu, genuinely friendly staff, and the atmosphere of an elegant turn-of-the-century San Fancisco club. Fresh seafood and Italian fare are the specialties, and chef and co-owner Lenore Nolan-Ryan prepares some favorites with an Asian influence, culminating in such unusual dishes as grilled salmon in a cucumber-wasabi sauce. The desserts are also grand, especially the cremé brûlée. *100 S. 9th St., tel. 206/627–1009. Reservations advised. Dress: casual. AE, MC, V. Expensive.*

E.R. Rogers Restaurant. Housed in an 1891 mansion 10 miles southwest of Tacoma, the restaurant overlooks Puget Sound and historic Steilacoom, with views of the Tacoma Narrows Bridge. The restaurant, one of the best in the Tacoma area, is decorated in a Victorian theme, with lace valances, brass fixtures, some antiques, and the original tongue-in-groove ceiling in the bar. The menu features a wide array of seafood—try the salmon with strawberry butter glaze—as well as steaks, prime rib with Yorkshire pudding, poultry, and an extensive list of wines to accompany them. The restaurant is open seven nights a week and for Sunday buffet brunch. *1702 Commercial St., Steilacoom, tel. 206/582–0280. Reservations advised. Dress: casual to dressy. MC, V. Moderate–Expensive.*

Harbor Lights. This waterfront institution, appropriately adorned with nautical furnishings, including glass floats, stuffed fish, and life preservers, hasn't changed since the '50s. The specialties are also classics—seafood, steaks, chops, and shellfish—but the steamed clams (in season) and good, ungreasy fish-and-chips are particular favorites. Service is generally efficient despite the crowds usually found here. There's a good waterfront view of Commencement Bay if you're lucky enough to snag a window seat. *2761 Ruston Way, tel. 206/752–8600. Reservations advised. Dress: casual. AE, DC, MC, V. Moderate.*

The Lobster Shop. This classic seafood restaurant has two locations; the older, on Dash Point, is cozier than the newer in-town spot, although both have fine views of Commencement Bay. Dash Point's rustic feel makes for an especially good spot to while away a long winter evening. Both restaurants specialize in simply prepared seafood, with salmon the perennial favorite. There's a cocktail lounge in the newer location, and beer and wine are available in the older. *6912 Soundview Dr. NE (off Dash Point Rd.), tel. 206/927–1513; and 4013 Ruston Way, tel. 206/759–2165. Reservations advised. Dress: casual. AE, DC, MC, V. Moderate.*

Grazie Ristorante. In the heart of Old Town in a refurbished 1896 building with a waterfront view, this northern Italian restaurant features homemade pasta, chicken, and seafood dishes, predominantly with white sauces. You will also find a variety of salads and veal entrées. For those sunny, summer days, there is a comfortable deck outside. *2301 N. 30th St., tel. 206/627–0231. Reservations advised. Dress: casual. MC, V. Inexpensive–Moderate.*

The Antique Sandwich Company. Open daily for breakfast, lunch, and dinner, this pleasant deli-style café specializes in hearty soups and sandwiches, classic children's food such as waffles and PB&J sandwiches, and well-prepared espresso drinks. Old posters on the walls, plastic bears for serving honey on the tables, and a toy-covered play area for children (which doubles as a music stage) help set the restaurant's cheerful, casual mood. On weekends come hear live folk and classical music; Tuesday evening is open-mike night. *5102 N. Pearl St., 2 blocks from the entrance to Point Defiance Park, tel. 206/752–4069. No reservations. Dress: casual. AE, MC, V. No alcohol. Inexpensive.*

Dining and Lodging   **Sheraton Tacoma Hotel.** This attractive high rise is located in the heart of downtown and is a popular site for conventions. The executive suites on the top floors (24th and 25th) have concierge service and Continental breakfasts. Amenities for the other rooms include great views of Commencement Bay and/or Mt. Rainier from almost every angle, and modern decor in elegant muted tones. Also on hand in the hotel are a lively European-style café, the Wintergarden, as well as a less formal restaurant and a lobby-level cocktail lounge. Altezzo, a moderately priced rustic Italian restaurant at the top of the hotel, features large paintings of Italian city and country scenes and great views of Mt. Rainier and Commencement Bay. It is open for dinner only with an à la carte menu of salads, individual pizzas, pasta dishes, fresh seafood, chicken, and meat entrées. *1320 Broadway Plaza, 98402, tel. 206/572–3200. 319 rooms. Facilities: restaurants, lounge, health-club privileges. AE, DC, MC, V. Expensive.*

Quality Hotel–Tacoma Dome. Situated near the Tacoma Dome, this hotel caters to people coming to see the musical, sporting, and other events held there. Basic, standard-issue rooms are offered, with few amenities, but there is free airport service and pets are allowed. *2611 E. E St., 98421, tel. 206/572-7272. 163 rooms. Facilities: restaurant, lounge. AE, MC, V. Moderate-Expensive.*

Tenino **Alice's Restaurant.** This homey restaurant, set in a rural farm-
Dining house adjacent to the Johnson Creek Winery in the lovely
★ Skookumchuck Valley, offers a cheerful, simple ambience reminiscent of a Norman Rockwell rendering. The food is surprisingly sophisticated, and fixed-price dinner costs vary
depending on the entrée. These elegant six-course meals are
innovative takes on classic American cuisine and are accompanied, naturally, by Johnson Creek wines. Vegetable appetizers, soup, a fish course, and home-baked bread are among the
preludes to the robust entrées, which might be anything from
wild game to oysters or steak. *19248 Johnson Creek Rd. E, tel.
206/264-2887. Reservations required. Dress: casual. MC, V.
Closed Mon., Tues., and lunch. Moderate.*

The Arts and Nightlife

The Arts

In Bellingham, the **Whatcom Museum of History and Art** (121
Prospect St., tel. 206/676-6981) sponsors regular walks downtown, among the many art galleries. The **Mt. Baker Theater**
(104 N. Commercial St., tel. 206/734-6080) is a restored 62-
year-old theater from vaudeville days with a 110-foot Moorish
tower and a lobby fashioned after a Spanish galleon. The theater features movies and national and international touring performances. **Western Washington University** (College of Fine
Performing Arts, Western Washington College, 516 High St.,
tel. 206/676-3866) has a high-quality performing-arts scene
with classical music and theater presentations by local and national performers.

On Long Beach Peninsula, call **The Playhouse Community Theater** (120 William St., NE, Ilwaco 98624, tel. 206/642-8686) for
a calendar of events.

In Port Townsend, contact **Centrum** (Box 1158, Port Townsend
98368, tel. 800/733-3608), the town's well-known and respected
performing-arts organization, which features a variety of performances, workshops, and conferences each year.

Nightlife

In Bellingham, **Speedy O. Tubs Rhythmic Underground** (1305
11th St., Old Fairhaven, tel. 206/734-1539) features rock and
blues, rock and roll, and a drumming circle.

On the Olympic Peninsula, the **Fourth Avenue Tavern** (210 E.
4th Ave., Olympia, tel. 206/786-1444), a cheerful beer-and-
wine joint, offers live rock music on weekends. A favorite with
locals, featuring live rock and roll on weekends, is **Back Alley**
(923 Washington St., Port Townsend, tel. 206/385-2914).

7 Vancouver

*Updated by
Loralee Wenger*

Vancouver is a young city, even by North American standards. While three to four hundred years of settlement may make cities like Québec and Halifax historically interesting to travelers, Vancouver's youthful vigor attracts visitors to its powerful elements that have not yet been ground down by time. Vancouver is just over a hundred years old; it was not yet a town in 1870, when British Columbia became part of the Canadian confederation. The city's history, such as it is, remains visible to the naked eye: Eras are stacked east to west along the waterfront like some century-old archaeological dig—from cobbled, late-Victorian Gastown to shiny postmodern glass cathedrals of commerce grazing the sunset.

The Chinese were among the first to recognize the possibilities of Vancouver's setting. They came to British Columbia during the 1850s seeking the gold that inspired them to name the province *Gum-shan*, or Gold Mountain. They built the Canadian Pacific Railway that gave Vancouver's original townsite a purpose—one beyond the natural splendor that Royal Navy Capt. George Vancouver admired during his lunchtime cruise around its harbor on June 13, 1792. The transcontinental railway, along with its Great White Fleet of clipper ships, gave Vancouver a full week's edge over the California ports in shipping tea and silk to New York at the dawn of the 20th century.

Vancouver's natural charms are less scattered than in other cities. On clear days, the mountains appear close enough to touch. Two 1,000-acre wilderness parks lie within the city limits. The salt water of the Pacific and fresh water direct from the Rocky Mountain Trench form the city's northern and southern boundaries.

Bring a healthy sense of reverence when you visit: Vancouver is a spiritual place. For its original inhabitants, the Coast Salish peoples, it was the sacred spot where the mythical Thunderbird and Killer Whale flung wind and rain all about the heavens during their epic battles—how else to explain the coast's occasional climatic fits of temper? Devotees of a later religious tradition might worship in the sepulchre of Stanley Park or in the polished, incense-filled quiet of St. James Anglican Church, designed by English architect Sir Adrian Gilbert Scott and perhaps Vancouver's finest building.

Vancouver has a level of nightlife possible only in a place where the finer things in life have never been driven out to the suburbs and where sidewalks have never rolled up at 5 PM. There is no shortage of excellent hotels and restaurants here either. But you can find good theater, accommodations, and dining almost anywhere these days. Vancouver's *real* culture consists of its tall fir trees practically downtown and its towering rock spires close by, the ocean at your doorstep, and people from every corner of the earth all around you.

Essential Information

Arriving and Departing by Plane

*Airport and
Airlines
International
Airports*

Vancouver International Airport is on an island about 14 kilometers (9 miles) south of downtown. The main terminal building has three levels: departures, international arrivals, and domestic arrivals; a small south terminal building services flights

Vancouver Exploring *(Boxes Refer to Detail Maps)*

Tour 2

Lions Gate Br.

1A
99A

STANLEY PARK

Denn

Burrard Inlet

English Bay

Planetarium ■

Burra

Kitsilano Beach Park

Point Grey Rd.

Jericho Beach Park

Burrard St.

G

4th Ave.

4th Ave.

Alma St.

Balsam St.

8th Ave.

Broadway

Granville St.

10th Ave.

Connaught Park

12th Ave.

Macdonald St.

16th Ave.

She

Carnarvon Park

Trafalgar St.

Arbutus St.

Wallace St.

Dunbar St.

Blenheim St.

Valley Dr.

Cypress St.

Matthews

King Edward Ave.

Chaldercott Park

27th Ave.

McKenzie St.

Eddington Dr.

99

Balaclava Park

Quilchena Park

Memorial Park West

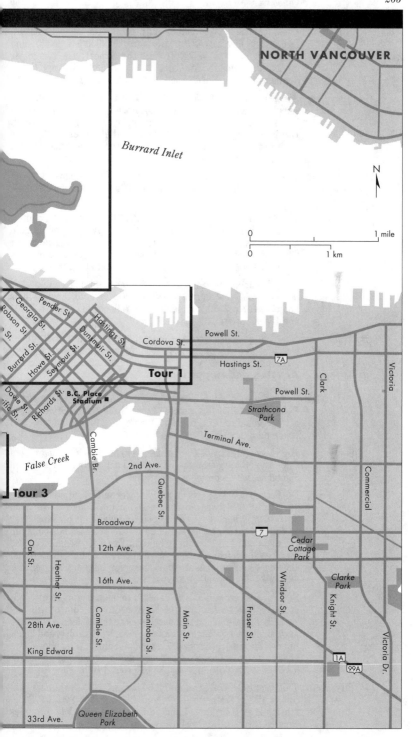

NORTH VANCOUVER

Burrard Inlet

N

0   1 mile
0   1 km

Pender St.
Georgia St.
Robson St.
_ St.
Burrard St.
Howe St.
Seymour St.
Dawie St.
ific St.
Richards St.
B.C. Place Stadium ■
Hastings St.
Dunsmuir St.
Cordova St.
Powell St.
Hastings St.   7A
Powell St.
Clark
Victoria
Tour 1
Strathcona Park
Terminal Ave.
False Creek
Cambie Br.
2nd Ave.
Quebec St.
■ **Tour 3**
Broadway
12th Ave.
Commercial
Oak St.
Heather St.
16th Ave.
7
Cedar Cottage Park
Clarke Park
28th Ave.
Cambie St.
Manitoba St.
Main St.
Fraser St.
Windsor St.
Knight St.
King Edward
1A
99A
Victoria Dr.
33rd Ave.
Queen Elizabeth Park

to secondary destinations within the province. **American Airlines** (tel. 800/433–7300), **Continental** (tel. 800/525–0280), **Delta** (tel. 604/221–1212), **Horizon Air** (800/547–9308), and **United** (tel. 800/241–6522) fly into the airport. The two major domestic airlines are **Air Canada** (tel. 604/688–5515) and **Canadian Airlines** (tel. 604/279–6611).

Other Facilities Air BC (tel. 604/688-5515) offers 30-minute harbor-to-harbor service (downtown Vancouver to downtown Victoria) several times a day. Planes leave from near the Bayshore Hotel. Helijet Airways (tel. 604/273–1414) has helicopter service from downtown Vancouver to downtown Victoria and Whistler. The heliport is near Vancouver's Pan Pacific Hotel.

Between the Airport and Downtown The drive from the airport to downtown is 20–45 minutes, depending on the time of day. Airport hotels offer free shuttle service to and from the airport.

By Bus The **Airport Express** (tel. 604/261–2299) bus leaves the domestic arrivals level of the terminal building every 15 minutes in summer and every 30 minutes in winter, stopping at major downtown hotels and the bus depot. It operates from 5:30 AM until 12:30 AM. The fare is $8.25 one-way and $14 round-trip.

By Taxi Taxi stands are in front of the terminal building on domestic and international arrivals levels. Taxi fare to downtown is about $24. Area cab companies are Yellow (tel. 604/681–3311) and Black Top (tel. 604/681–2181).

By Limousine Limousine service from **Airlimo** (tel. 604/273–1331) costs about the same as a taxi to downtown: The current rate is about $28.

Arriving and Departing

By Car From the south, I–5 from Seattle becomes **Highway 99** at the U.S.–Canada border. Vancouver is a three-hour drive from Seattle. Avoid border crossings during peak times: holidays and weekends.

Highway 1, the **Trans-Canada Highway,** enters Vancouver from the east. If you enter the city after rush hour (8:30 AM), you should not have a problem with traffic.

By Ferry **BC Ferries** operates two major ferry terminals outside Vancouver. From Tsawwassen to the south (an hour's drive from downtown), ferries sail to Victoria and Nanaimo on Vancouver Island and through the Gulf Islands (the small islands between the mainland and Vancouver Island). From Horseshoe Bay (30 minutes north from downtown), ferries sail a short distance up the coast and to Nanaimo on Vancouver Island. Call (tel.604/ 685–1021) for departure and arrival times.

Sealink Express (tel. 604/687–6925) takes passengers by high-speed catamaran from downtown Vancouver to downtown Victoria in 2½ hours. The two boats each seat 302 people and have such airplane-type amenities as movies, work tables, and headphones for music; there are also fax machines, telephones, two snack bars, a children's playroom, and a newsstand on board. Tickets cost $32.95 one-way, $59.95 round-trip.

By Train The Pacific Central Station (1150 Station St.) is the hub for rail, bus, and SkyTrain service. The **VIA Rail** (tel. 800/561–8630) station is at Main Street and Terminal Avenue. VIA provides service through the Rockies to Banff. Passenger trains leave the **BC Rail** (tel. 604/631–3500) station in North Vancouver for Whistler and the interior of British Columbia. There is no Amtrak service from Seattle.

By Bus   **Greyhound** (tel. 604/662–3222) is the biggest bus line servicing Vancouver. The Pacific Central Station (1150 Station St.) is the depot. **Quick Shuttle** (tel. 604/526–2836) bus service runs between Vancouver and Seattle six times a day.

Getting Around

By Car   Although no freeways cross Vancouver, rush-hour traffic is not yet horrendous. The worst rush-hour bottlenecks are the North Shore bridges, the George Massey Tunnel on Highway 99 south of Vancouver, and Highway 1 through Coquitlam and Surrey.

By Subway   Vancouver has a one-line, 25-kilometer (15-mile) rapid transit system called **SkyTrain,** which travels underground downtown and is elevated for the rest of its route to New Westminster and Surrey. Trains leave about every five minutes. Tickets must be carried with you as proof of payment, and are sold at each station from machines; correct change is not necessary. You may use transfers from SkyTrain to SeaBus and BC Transit buses (*see below*) and vice versa.

By Bus   Exact change is needed to ride the buses: $1.50 adults, 75¢ for senior citizens and children 5–13. Books of 25 tickets are sold at convenience stores and newsstands; look for a red, white, and blue "Fare Dealer" sign. Day passes, good for unlimited travel after 9:30 AM, cost $4.50 for adults. They are available from fare dealers and any SeaBus or SkyTrain station. Transfers are valid for 90 minutes and allow travel in both directions.

By Taxi   It is difficult to hail a cab in Vancouver; unless you're near a hotel, you'd have better luck calling a taxi service. Try **Yellow** (tel. 604/681–3311) or **Black Top** (tel. 604/681–2181).

By SeaBus   The **SeaBus** is a 400-passenger commuter ferry that crosses Burrard Inlet from the foot of Lonsdale (North Vancouver) to downtown. The ride takes 13 minutes and costs the same as the transit bus. With a transfer, connection can be made with any BC Transit bus or SkyTrain.

Important Addresses and Numbers

Tourist   **Vancouver Travel Infocentre** (200 Burrard St., tel. 604/683–
Information   2000) provides maps and information about the city and is open in summer, daily 8–6; in winter, Monday–Saturday 9–5. A kiosk in Pacific Centre Mall is open daily in summer, Monday–Saturday 9:30–5, Sunday noon–5; in winter, Monday–Saturday 9–5. Eaton's department store downtown also has a tourist information counter that is open all year.

Embassies   There are no embassies in Vancouver, only consulates and trade commissions: **United States** (1075 W. Pender St., tel. 604/685–4311) and **United Kingdom** (800–1111 Melville St., tel. 604/683–4421). For a complete listing, see the Yellow Pages.

Emergencies   Call 911 for **police, fire department,** and **ambulance.**

Hospitals and   **St. Paul's Hospital** (1081 Burrard St., tel. 604/682–2344), a
Clinics   downtown hospital, has an emergency ward. **Medicentre** (1055

Dunsmuir St., lower level, tel. 604/683–8138), a drop-in clinic on the lower level of the Bentall Centre, is open weekdays.

Dentist The counterpart to Medicentre is **Dentacentre** (1055 Dunsmuir St., lower level, tel. 604/669–6700), which is next door and is also open weekdays.

Late-night **Shopper's Drug Mart** (1125 Davie St., tel. 604/685–6445) is open
Pharmacy until midnight every night except Sunday, when it closes at 9.

Road Emergencies **BCAA** (tel. 604/293–2222) has 24-hour emergency road service for members of AAA or CAA.

Travel Agencies **American Express Travel Service** (1040 W. Georgia St., tel. 604/669–2813), **Hagen's Travel** (210–850 W. Hastings St., tel. 604/684–2448), and **P. Lawson Travel** (409 Granville St., tel. 604/682–4272).

Opening and Closing Times

Banks traditionally are open Monday–Thursday 10–3 and Friday 10–6, but many banks have extended hours and are open on Saturday, particularly outside of downtown.

Museums are generally open 10–5, including Saturday and Sunday. Most are open one evening a week as well.

Department store hours are Monday–Wednesday and Saturday 9:30–6, Thursday and Friday 9:30–9, and Sunday noon–5. Many smaller stores are also open Sunday. Robson Street and Chinatown are particularly good for Sunday shopping.

Guided Tours

Orientation **Gray Line** (tel. 604/879-3363), the largest tour operator, offers the 3½-hour Grand City bus tour year-round. Departing from the Hotel Vancouver, the tour includes Stanley Park, Chinatown, Gastown, English Bay, and Queen Elizabeth Park and costs about $31. **Westcoast City and Nature Sightseeing** (tel. 604/451-5581) accommodates up to 24 people in vans that run a 3½-hour City Highlights Tour for $27 (pickup available from any downtown location). A short city tour (2½ hours) is offered by **Vance Tours** (tel. 604/941-5660) in minibuses and costs $29.

The **Vancouver Trolley Company** (tel. 604/451-5581) runs turn-of-the-century–style trolleys through Vancouver from April to October on a 1½-hour narrated tour of Stanley Park, Gastown, English Bay, the Vancouver Museum, Granville Island, Queen Elizabeth Park, Science World, and Chinatown, among other sights. A day pass allows you to complete one full circuit, getting off and on as often as you like. Start the trip at any of the sights and buy a ticket on board. It's a perfect way to deal with a rainy day in Vancouver. Adult fare is $15, children's $7.

North Shore tours usually include any or several of the following: a gondola ride up Grouse Mountain, a walk across the Capilano Suspension Bridge, a stop at a salmon hatchery, the Lonsdale Quay Market, and a ride back to town on the SeaBus. Half-day tours cost about $35 and are offered by **Landsea Tours** (tel. 604/255–7272), **Harbour Ferries** (tel. 604/687–9558), **Gray Line** (tel. 604/879–3363), and **Pacific Coach Lines** (tel. 604/662–7575).

Air Tours   Tour the mountains and fjords of the North Shore by helicopter for $165 per person (minimum of three people) for 45 minutes: Vancouver Helicopters (tel. 604/270–1484) flies from the Harbour Heliport downtown. Or see Vancouver from the air for $60 for 20 minutes: Harbour Air's (tel. 604/688–1277) seaplanes leave from beside the Bayshore Hotel.

Boat Tours   The Royal Hudson, Canada's only functioning steam train, heads along the mountainous coast up Howe Sound to the logging town of Squamish. After a break to explore, you sail back to Vancouver via the MV *Britannia*. This highly recommended excursion costs about $45, takes 6½ hours, and is organized by **Harbour Ferries** (tel. 604/687–9558). Reservations are necessary.

The **SS *Beaver*** (tel. 604/682–7284), a replica of a Hudson Bay fur-trading vessel that ran aground here in 1888, offers two trips. One is the Harbour Sunset Dinner Cruise, a four-hour trip with a barbecue dinner; the other is a four-hour daytime trip up Indian Arm with salmon for lunch. Each is about $50 and reservations are necessary for both.

Harbour Ferries (tel. 604/687–9558) takes a 1½-hour tour of Burrard Inlet in a paddlewheeler, and costs about $20.

Fraser River Connection (tel. 604/525–4465) will take you on a four-hour tour of a fascinating working river—past log booms, tugs, and houseboats. Ride from New Westminster to Fort Langley, aboard a convincing replica of an 1800s-era paddlewheeler, for about $25.

Personal Guides   **Early Motion Tours** (tel. 604/687–5088) covers Vancouver in a Model-A Ford convertible that comfortably seats about four people. For about $60, up to four people can take an hour-long trip around downtown, Chinatown, and Stanley Park.

AAA Horse & Carriage (tel. 604/681–5115) has a 50-minute tour of Stanley Park, along the waterfront, and through a cedar forest and a rose garden for about $10.

Exploring Vancouver

The heart of Vancouver—which includes the downtown area, Stanley Park, and the West End high-rise residential neighborhood—sits on a peninsula bordered by English Bay and the Pacific Ocean to the west; by False Creek, an inlet on which you will find Granville Island, to the south; and to the north by Burrard Inlet, the working port of the city, past which loom the North Shore mountains. The oldest part of the city—Gastown and Chinatown—lies at the edge of Burrard Inlet, around Main Street, which runs north–south and is roughly the dividing line between the east side and the west side. All the avenues, which are numbered, have east and west designations.

Highlights for First-time Visitors

Chinatown, Tour 1: Downtown Vancouver
English Bay, Tour 2: Stanley Park
Granville Island, Tour 3: Granville Island
Stanley Park, Tour 2: Stanley Park

Tour 1: Downtown Vancouver

Numbers in the margin correspond to points of interest on the Tour 1: Downtown Vancouver map.

❶ You can logically begin your downtown tour in either of two ways. If you're in for a day of shopping, amble down **Robson Street** (*see* Shopping, *below*), where you'll find any item from souvenirs to high fashions, from espresso to sushi.

❷ If you opt otherwise, start at **Robson Square,** built in 1975 and designed by architect Arthur Erickson to be the gathering place of downtown Vancouver. The complex, which functions from the outside as a park, encompasses the Vancouver Art Gallery and government offices and law courts that have been built under landscaped walkways, a block-long glass canopy, and a waterfall that helps mask traffic noise. An ice-skating rink and restaurants occupy the below-street level.

❸ The **Vancouver Art Gallery** that heads the square was a neoclassical-style 1912 courthouse until Erickson converted it in 1980. Notice some details: lions that guard the majestic front steps and the use of columns and domes—features borrowed from ancient Roman architecture. In back of the old courthouse, a more modest staircase now serves as a speakers' corner. *750 Hornby St., tel. 604/682–5621. Admission: $4.50 adults, $2.50 students and senior citizens; free Thurs. eve. Open Mon.–Wed., and Sat. 10–5; Thurs. 10–9; Sun. noon–5.*

❹ Directly across Hornby Street is the **Hotel Vancouver** (1939), one of the last of the railway-built hotels. (The last one built was the Chateau Whistler, in 1989.) Reminiscent of a medieval French castle, this château style has been incorporated into hotels throughout almost every major Canadian city. With the onset of the depression, construction was halted here, and the hotel was finished only in time for the visit of King George VI in 1939. It has been renovated twice: During the 1960s it was unfortunately modernized, but the more recent refurbishment is more in keeping with the spirit of what is the most recognizable roof on Vancouver's skyline. The exterior of the building has carvings of malevolent gargoyles at the corners, an ornate chimney, Indian chiefs on the Hornby Street side, and an assortment of grotesque mythological figures.

❺ **Christ Church Cathedral** (1895), across the street from the Hotel Vancouver, is the oldest church in Vancouver. The tiny church was built in a Gothic style with buttresses and pointed arched windows and looks like the parish church of an English village. By contrast, the cathedral's rough-hewn interior is that of a frontier town, with Douglas-fir beams and carpenter woodwork that offers excellent acoustics for the frequent vespers, carol services, and Gregorian chants presented here. *690 Burrard St., tel. 604/682–3848.*

❻ **Cathedral Place,** on the corner of Hornby and Georgia streets, is a spectacular office tower adjacent to Christ Church Cathedral. Three large sculptures of nurses at the corners of the building are replicas of the statues that graced the art deco Georgia Medical-Dental Building, the site's previous structure.

A restored terra-cotta arch—formerly the front entrance to the medical building—and frieze panels showing scenes of indi-

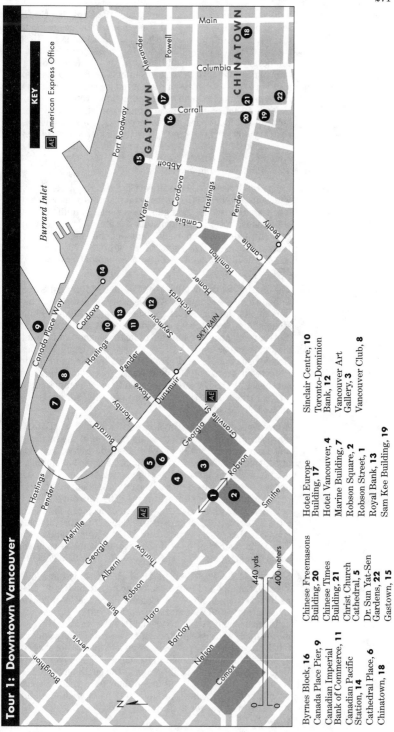

Tour 1: Downtown Vancouver

KEY

AE American Express Office

Byrnes Block, **16**
Canada Place Pier, **9**
Canadian Imperial
Bank of Commerce, **11**
Canadian Pacific
Station, **14**
Cathedral Place, **6**
Chinatown, **18**

Chinese Freemasons
Building, **20**
Chinese Times
Building, **21**
Christ Church
Cathedral, **5**
Dr. Sun Yat-Sen
Gardens, **22**
Gastown, **15**

Hotel Europe
Building, **17**
Hotel Vancouver, **4**
Marine Building, **7**
Robson Square, **2**
Robson Street, **1**
Royal Bank, **13**
Sam Kee Building, **19**

Sinclair Centre, **10**
Toronto-Dominion
Bank, **12**
Vancouver Art
Gallery, **3**
Vancouver Club, **8**

440 yds

400 meters

viduals administering care now grace the **Canadian Craft Museum,** across the courtyard. Originally founded in 1980, but opened on this site in 1992, the Craft Museum is the first national cultural facility dedicated to craft—historical and contemporary, functional and decorative. Craft embodies the human need for artistic expression in everyday life, and examples here range from elegantly carved utensils with decorative handles to colorful hand-spun and hand-woven garments. The three-level museum offers exhibits, workshops, and the Gallery Shop, which specializes in, of course, Canadian crafts. The restful courtyard is a quiet place to take a break. *639 Hornby St., tel 604/687–8266. Admission: $2.50 adults, $1.50 senior citizens and students, children under 12 free. Open Mon.–Sat. 9:30–5:30, Sun. and holidays noon–5.*

Cathedral Place also is the site of the **Sri Lankan Gem Museum,** which opened in 1993. The museum features a floor of 900 polished agates set in aggregate, and some $5 million worth of gemstones, including moonstones, rubies, lapis, diamonds, garnets, jade, and emeralds. Many of the gems are from Sri Lanka. *150 925 W. Georgia St., tel. 604/662–7708. Admission: $5 (proceeds go to the Vancouver Symphony Orchestra). Open Mon.–Sat. 10:30–5:30.*

❼ The **Marine Building** (1931), at the foot of Burrard Street, is Canada's best example of Art Deco style. Terra-cotta bas reliefs depict the history of transportation: Airships, biplanes, steamships, locomotives, and submarines are figured. These motifs were once considered radical and modernistic adornments, because most buildings were still using classical or Gothic ornamentation. From the east, the Marine Building is reflected in bronze by 999 West Hastings, and in silver from the southeast by the Canadian Imperial Bank of Commerce. Stand on the corner of Hastings and Hornby streets for the best view of the Marine Building.

A nice walk is along Hastings Street—the old financial district. Until the 1966–1972 period, when the first of the bank towers and underground malls on West Georgia Street were developed, this was Canada's westernmost business terminus. The temple-style banks, businessmen's clubs, and investment houses survive as evidence of the city's sophisticated architec-
❽ tural advances prior to World War I. The **Vancouver Club,** built between 1912 and 1914, was a gathering place for the city's elite. Its architectural design is reminiscent of private clubs in England that were inspired by Italian Renaissance palaces. The Vancouver Club is still the private haunt of some of the city's businessmen. *915 W. Hastings St., tel. 604/685–9321.*

❾ The foot of Howe Street, north of Hastings, is **Canada Place Pier.** Originally built on an old cargo pier to be the off-site Canadian pavilion in Expo '86, Canada Place was later converted into Vancouver's Trade and Convention Center. It is dominated at the shore end by the luxurious Pan Pacific Hotel (*see* Lodging, *below*), with its spectacular three-story lobby and waterfall. The convention space is covered by a fabric roof shaped like 10 sails, which has become a landmark of Vancouver's skyline. Below is a cruise ship facility, and at the north end are an Imax theater, a restaurant, and an outdoor performance space. A promenade runs along the pier's west side with views of the Burrard Inlet harbor and Stanley Park. *999 Canada Pl., tel. 604/688–8687.*

Time Out Across the street and accessible via an enclosed walkway is the luxurious **Waterfront Centre Hotel,** a 23-story glass structure that opened in 1992. The lobby, lounge, and restaurant offer stunning views of Burrard Inlet; at night, the casual Herons Lounge with a fireplace features relaxing piano music. Weather permitting, you can enjoy the view even more from the patio outside Herons Restaurant, where the menu offers local and regional Pacific Rim specialties. *900 Canada Place Way, tel. 604/691-1991.*

Just next door to the Waterfront Centre Hotel is the **Tourism Vancouver Infocentre** (200 Burrard St., tel. 604/682–2222), with brochures and personnel to answer questions, as well as an attractive Northwest Coast native art collection.

⑩ Walk back up to Hastings and Howe streets to the **Sinclair Centre.** Vancouver's outstanding architect, Richard Henriquez, has knitted four government office buildings (built 1905–1939) into an office-retail complex. The two Hastings Street buildings—the 1905 post office with the elegant clock tower and the 1913 Winch Building—are linked with the Post Office Extension and Customs Examining Warehouse to the north. Painstaking and very costly restoration involved finding master masons—the original terrazzo suppliers in Europe—and uncovering and refurbishing the pressed-metal ceilings.

Walking a bit farther up Hastings, at Granville Street, will reveal one of Vancouver's oldest and most impressive charter
⑪ banks, the former **Canadian Imperial Bank of Commerce** headquarters (1906–1908); the columns, arches, and details are of
⑫ typically Roman influence. The **Toronto–Dominion Bank,** one block east, is of the same style but was built in 1920.

⑬ Backtrack directly across from the CIBC on Hastings Street to the more Gothic **Royal Bank.** It was intended to be half of a symmetrical building that was never completed, due to the depression. Striking, though, is the magnificent hall, ecclesiastical in style, reminiscent of a European cathedral.

⑭ At the foot of Seymour Street is the **Canadian Pacific Station,** the third and most pretentious of three Canadian Pacific Railway passenger terminals. Constructed in 1912–1914, this terminal replaced the other two as the western terminus for Canada's transcontinental railway. After Canada's railways merged, the station became obsolete until a 1978 renovation turned it into an office-retail complex and SeaBus terminal. Murals in the waiting rooms show passengers what kind of scenery to expect on their journeys across Canada.

⑮ From Seymour Street, pick up Water Street, on your way to **Gastown.** Named after the original townsite saloon keeper, "Gassy" Jack Deighton, Gastown is where Vancouver originated. Deighton arrived at Burrard Inlet in 1867 with his Indian wife, a barrel of whiskey, and few amenities. A statue of Gassy Jack stands on the north side of Maple Tree Square, the intersection of five streets, where he built his first saloon.

When the transcontinental train arrived in 1887, Gastown became the transfer point for trade with the Orient and was soon crowded with hotels and warehouses. The Klondike gold rush encouraged further development until 1912, when the "Golden Years" ended. The 1930s–1950s saw hotels being converted into rooming houses and the warehouse district shifting elsewhere. The area gradually became unattended and run-down. However, both Gastown and Chinatown were declared historic areas and have been revitalized.

⑯ The **Byrnes Block** building was constructed on the corner of Water and Carrall streets (the site of Gassy Jack's second saloon) after the 1886 Great Fire. The date is just visible at the top of the building above the door where it says "Herman Block," which was its name for a short time. The extravagantly detailed Alhambra Hotel that was situated here was luxury class for the time, at a cost of a dollar a night.

Tucked behind 2 Water Street are **Blood Alley** and **Gaoler's Mews.** Once the site of the city's first civic buildings—the constable's cabin and courthouse, and a two-cell log jail—today the cobblestone street with antique streetlighting is the home of architectural offices.

⑰ The **Hotel Europe** (1908–1909), a flatiron building at Powell and Alexander streets, was billed as the best hotel in the city and was Vancouver's first reinforced concrete structure. Designed as a functional commercial building, the hotel lacks ornamentation and fine detail, a style unusually utilitarian for the time.

From Maple Tree Square, walk three blocks up Carrall Street
⑱ to Pender Street, where **Chinatown** begins. There was already a sizable Chinese community in British Columbia because of the 1858 Cariboo gold rush in central British Columbia, but the biggest influx from China occurred in the 1880s, during construction of the Canadian Pacific Railway, when 15,000 laborers were imported. The Chinese were among the first inhabitants of Vancouver, and some of the oldest buildings in the city are in Chinatown.

Even while doing the hazardous work of blasting the railbed through the Rocky Mountains, the Chinese were discriminated against. The Anti-Asiatic Riots of 1907 stopped growth in Chinatown for 50 years, and immigration from China was discouraged by more and more restrictive policies, climaxing in a $500 head tax during the 1920s.

In the 1960s the city council was planning bulldozer urban renewal for Strathcona, the residential part of Chinatown, and freeway connections through the most historic blocks of Chinatown were charted. Fortunately, the plans were halted, and today Chinatown is an expanding, vital district fueled by investment from Vancouver's most notable newcomers—immigrants from Hong Kong. It is best to view the buildings in Chinatown from the south side of Pender Street, where the Chinese Cultural Center stands. From here you'll get a view of important details that adorn the upper stories. The style of architecture in Vancouver's Chinatown is patterned on that of Canton and won't be seen in any other Canadian cities.

The corner of Carrall and East Pender streets, now the western boundary of Chinatown, is one of the neighborhood's most his-
⑲ toric spots. Standing at 8 West Pender Street is the **Sam Kee Building,** recognized by *Ripley's Believe It or Not!* as the narrowest building in the world, at just 6 feet wide. The 1913 structure still exists, with its bay windows overhanging the street and a basement that burrows under the sidewalk.

⑳ The **Chinese Freemasons Building** (1901) at 1 West Pender Street has two completely different styles of facades: The side facing Chinatown displays a fine example of Cantonese-imported recessed balconies; on the Carrall Street side, the standard Victorian style common throughout the British Empire is displayed. It was in this building that Dr. Sun Yat-sen hid for months from the agents of the Manchu dynasty while he raised funds for its overthrow, which he accomplished in 1911.

㉑ Directly across Carrall Street is the **Chinese Times Building,** constructed in 1902. Inside, there is a hidden mezzanine floor from which police officers could hear the clicking sounds of clandestine mah-jongg games played after sunset. Attempts by vice squads to enforce restrictive policies against the Chinese gamblers proved fruitless, because police were unable to find the players, who were hidden on the secret floor.

㉒ Planning for the **Chinese Cultural Center** and **Dr. Sun Yat-sen Gardens** (1980–1987) began during the late 1960s; the first phase was designed by James Cheng, a former associate of Arthur Erickson. The cultural center has exhibition space, classrooms, and meeting rooms. The Dr. Sun Yat-sen Gardens, located behind the cultural center, were built by 52 artisans from Suzhou, the Garden City of the People's Republic. The gardens incorporate design elements and traditional materials from several of that city's centuries-old private gardens and are the first living classical Chinese gardens built outside China. As you walk through the gardens, remember that no power tools, screws, or nails were used in the construction. Free guided tours are offered throughout the day; telephone for times. *Dr. Sun Yat-sen Gardens. 578 Carrall St., tel. 604/689–7133. Admission: $3.50 adults, $2.50 senior citizens and students, $7 families. Open May–Sept., daily 10–8; Oct.–Apr., daily 10–4:30.*

Tour 2: Stanley Park

Numbers in the margin correspond to points of interest on the Tour 2: Stanley Park map.

A 1,000-acre wilderness park just blocks from the downtown section of a major city is a rarity but is one of Vancouver's major attractions. In the 1860s, due to a threat of American invasion, the area that is now Stanley Park was designated a military reserve (though it was never needed). When the city of Vancouver was incorporated in 1886, the council's first act was to request that the land be set aside for a park. In 1888 permission was granted and the grounds were named Stanley Park after Lord Stanley, then governor general of Canada (the same person after whom hockey's Stanley Cup is named).

An afternoon in Stanley Park gives you a capsule tour of Vancouver that includes beaches, the ocean, the harbor, Douglas fir and cedar forests, and a good look at the North Shore mountains. The park sits on a peninsula, and along the shore is a pathway 9 kilometers (5½ miles) long called the seawall. You can walk or bicycle all the way around or follow the shorter route suggested below.

Bicycles are for rent at the foot of Georgia Street near the park entrance. Cyclists must ride in a counterclockwise direction and stay on their side of the path. A good place for pedestrians

Tour 2: Stanley Park

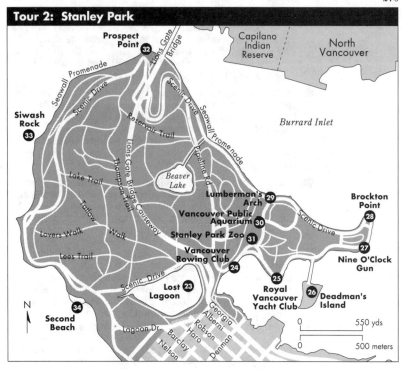

㉓ to start is at the foot of Alberni Street beside **Lost Lagoon.** Go through the underpass and veer right to the seawall.

㉔ The old wood structure that you pass is the **Vancouver Rowing Club,** a private athletic club (established 1903); a bit farther **㉕** along is the **Royal Vancouver Yacht Club.**

㉖ About ½ kilometer (⅛ mile) away is the causeway to **Deadman's Island,** a former burial ground for the local Salish Indians and the early settlers. It is now a small naval training base called the HMCS *Discovery* that is not open to the public. Just ahead **㉗** is the **Nine O'Clock Gun,** a cannonlike apparatus that sits by the water's edge. Originally used to alert fishermen to a curfew ending weekend fishing, now it automatically signals every night at 9.

㉘ Farther along is **Brockton Point** and its small but functional lighthouse and foghorn. The **totem poles,** which are situated more inland, make a popular photo spot for tourists. Totem poles were not carved in the Vancouver area; they were brought to the park from the north coast of British Columbia and were carved by the Kwakiutl and Haida peoples late in the last century. These cedar poles with carved animals, fish, birds, or mythological creatures were like family coats-of-arms or crests.

㉙ At kilometer 3 (mile 2) is **Lumberman's Arch,** a huge log archway dedicated to the workers in Vancouver's first industry. Beside the arch is an asphalt path that leads back to Lost Lagoon, for those who want a shorter walk. (It's about a third of the dis- **㉚** tance.) This path also leads to the **Vancouver Public Aquarium.**

Also part of this attraction is the humid Amazon rain-forest gallery, through which you can walk, with its piranhas, giant cockroaches, alligators, tropical birds, and jungle vegetation. Other displays show the underwater life of coastal British Columbia, the Canadian arctic, and other areas of the world. The Clamshell Gift Shop next to the aquarium is one of the best spots in town for high-quality souvenirs and gifts, most with an emphasis on natural history. *Aquarium, tel. 604/682–1118. Admission: $8.50 adults, $7.25 senior citizens and youths, $5.25 children 5–12. Open daily in summer 9:30–8; daily in winter 10–5:30. Clamshell open July–Labor Day, daily 9:30–8; rest of year, daily 10–5:30.*

③ Next to the aquarium is the **Stanley Park Zoo,** a friendly place, easily seen in an hour or two. Except for the polar bears, most of the animals are small—monkeys, seals, exotic birds, penguins, and playful otters.

About 1 kilometer (¾ mile) farther is the **Lions Gate Bridge**—the halfway point of the seawall. On the other side of the bridge **②** is **Prospect Point,** where you can see cormorants in their seaweed nests on the ledges along the cliffs. The large black diving birds are recognized by their long necks and beaks; when not nesting, they often perch atop floating logs or boulders. Another remarkable bird found along the shore in the park is the beautiful great blue heron, which reaches up to 4 feet tall and has a wing span of 6 feet. The heron preys on passing fish in the waters here; the oldest heron rookery in British Columbia is in the trees around the zoo.

Continuing around the seawall you will come to the **English Bay** side and the beginning of sandy beaches. The imposing **③** rock just offshore is **Siwash Rock.** Legend tells of a young Indian who, about to become a father, bathed persistently to wash his sins away so that his son could be born pure; for his devotion he was blessed by the gods and immortalized in the shape of Siwash Rock. Two small rocks, said to be his wife and child, are just up on the cliff above the site.

Time Out Along the seawall is one of Vancouver's best restaurants, the **Teahouse at Ferguson Point.** Set on the great lawn among Douglas fir and cedar trees, the restaurant is the perfect stopover for a summer weekend lunch or brunch. If you want just a snack, a park concession stand is also at Ferguson Point.

The next attraction along the seawall is the large saltwater pool **③** at **Second Beach.** In the summer it is a children's pool with lifeguards, but during winter the pool is drained and skateboarders perform stunts. At the pool you can take a shortcut back to Lost Lagoon. To take the shortcut, walk along the perpendicular road behind the pool, which cuts into the park. The wood footbridge that's ahead will lead you to a path along the south side of the lagoon and to your starting point at the foot of Alberni or Georgia street.

If you continue along the seawall, it will emerge out of the park into a high-rise residential neighborhood, the **West End.** You can walk back to Alberni Street along Denman Street, where there are plenty of places to stop for coffee, ice cream, or a drink.

Tour 3: Granville Island

Numbers in the margin correspond to points of interest on the Tour 3: Granville Island map.

Granville Island was just a sandbar until World War I, when the federal government dredged False Creek for access to the saw-mills that lined the shore. The sludge from the creek was heaped up onto a sandbar to create Granville Island so that it could house the much-needed industrial- and logging-equipment plants for British Columbia. By the late 1960s, however, many of the businesses that had once flourished on Granville Island had deteriorated. Buildings were rotted, rat-infested, and dangerous. In 1971, the federal government bought up leases from businesses that wanted to leave, and offered an imaginative plan to refurbish the island. A public market was introduced, and marine activities and artisans' studios were supported. The opposite shore of False Creek was the site of the 1986 World's Fair and is now part of the largest urban redevelopment plan in North America.

The small island has no residents except for a small houseboat community. Most of the previously used industrial buildings and tin sheds have been retained but are painted in upbeat reds, yellows, and blues. Through a committee of community representatives, the government regulates the types of businesses that settle on Granville Island; most of the businesses permitted here involve food, crafts, marine activities, and the arts.

Access on foot to Granville Island starts with a 15-minute walk from downtown Vancouver to the south end of Thurlow Street. From a dock behind the Vancouver Aquatic Center, the Granville Island ferry leaves every six minutes for the short trip across False Creek to the Granville Island Public Market. These pudgy boats are a great way to see the sights on False Creek, but for a longer ferry ride, go to the Maritime Museum (1905 Ogden St., tel. 604/737–2211), where visitors can board the wheelhouse of a tugboat and chart the coastal waters of British Columbia. For more information, call Granville Island Ferries (tel. 604/684–7781).

Another way to reach the island is to take a 20-minute ride on a BC Transit (tel. 604/261–5100) bus. Take a UBC, Granville, Arbutus, Cambie, or Oak bus from downtown to Granville and Broadway, and transfer to the Granville Island bus No. 51. Parking is limited, but if you must take a car, go early in the week and early in the day to avoid crowds. Parking is free for one to three hours; an alternative is to pay for parking in the garages on the island if you can find a space.

35 The ferry to Granville Island will drop you off at the **Granville Island Public Market,** where food stalls are enclosed in the 50,000-square-foot building. Since the government allows no chain stores, each outlet is unique, and most are of good quality. You probably won't be able to leave the market without a snack, espresso, or fixings for a lunch out on the wharf. Don't miss the charcoal-grilled oysters from **Sea-kist,** fish chowder or bouillabaisse from the **Stock Market,** fresh fudge at **Olde World Fudge,** or smoked salmon from the **Salmon Shop.** Year-round you'll see mounds of raspberries, strawberries, blueberries, and even more exotic fruits like persimmons and lychees. On

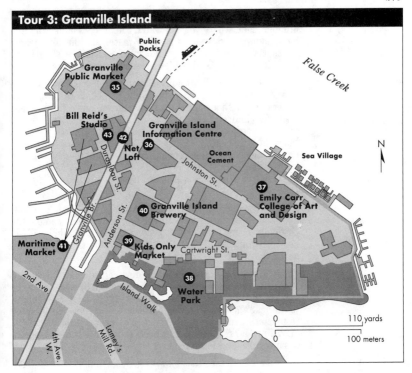

Tour 3: Granville Island

Public Docks

False Creek

Granville Public Market **35**

Bill Reid's Studio **43** **42**

Granville Island Information Centre **36**

Net Loft

Ocean Cement

Johnston St.

Sea Village

Duranleau St.

N

Granville Br.

Anderson St.

Granville Island Brewery **40**

Emily Carr College of Art and Design **37**

Maritime Market **41**

2nd Ave.

39 Kids Only Market

Cartwright St.

Island Walk

Water Park **38**

Lamey's Mill Rd.

4th Ave. W.

0   110 yards

0   100 meters

the water side of the market is lots of outdoor seating. *Public Market, tel. 604/666–6477. Open June–Aug., daily 9–6; closed Mon. Sept.–May except holidays.*

36 The **Granville Island Information Centre,** kitty-corner to the market, is a good place to get oriented to the island. Maps are available, and a slide show depicts the evolution of Granville Island. Ask here about special-events days; perhaps there's a boat show, outdoor concert, dance performance, or some other happening. *1592 Johnston St., tel. 604/666–5784. Open daily 9–6.*

Continue walking south on Johnston Street, along a clockwise loop of the island. Next is **Ocean Cement,** one of the last of the island's former industries; its lease does not expire until the year 2004.

37 Next door is the **Emily Carr College of Art and Design.** Just inside the front door, to your right, is the **Charles H. Scott Gallery,** which hosts contemporary multimedia exhibits. *1399 Johnston St., tel. 604/687–2345. Admission free. Open daily 11–5, Thurs. 11–8.*

Past the art school, on the left, is one of the only **houseboat communities** in Vancouver; others have been banned by the city because of problems with sewage and property taxes. The owners of this community appealed the ban and won special status. Take the boardwalk that starts at the houseboats and continues partway around the island.

As you circle around to Cartwright Street, stop in **Kakali** at number 1249, where you can watch the process of making fine handmade paper from all sorts of materials like blue jeans, herbs, and sequins. Another unusual artisan on the island is the **glassblower** at 1440 Old Bridge Street, around the corner.

The next two attractions will make any child's visit to Granville Island a thrill. First, on Cartwright Street, is the children's **38 water park,** with a wading pool, sprinklers, and a fire hydrant made for children to shower one another. A bit farther down, **39** beside Isadora's restaurant, is the **Kids Only Market,** with two floors of small shops selling toys, arts-and-crafts materials, dolls, records and tapes, chemistry sets, and other sorts of kid stuff. *Water park. 1318 Cartwright St., tel. 604/665–3425. Admission free. Open June–Aug., daily 10–6. Kids Only Market. 1496 Cartwright St., tel. 604/689–8447. Open daily 10–6.*

40 At the **Granville Island Brewery,** next door, you can take a half-hour tour every afternoon; at the end of the tour, sample the Granville Island lager that is produced here and sold locally in most restaurants. *Tel. 604/688–9927. Admission free. Tours daily at 1 and 3.*

Cross Anderson Street and walk down Duranleau Street. On your left, the scuba-diving pool in **Adrenalin Sports** marks the **41** start of the **Maritime Market,** a string of businesses all geared to the sea. The first walkway to the left, Maritime Mews, leads to marinas and dry docks. There are dozens of outfits in the Maritime Market that charter boats (with or without skippers) or run cruise-and-learn trips.

Another way to take to the water is by kayak. Take a lesson or rent a kayak from **Ecomarine Ocean Kayak Center** (1668 Duranleau St., tel. 604/689–7575). Owner John Dowd is considered *the* expert on Pacific Northwest ocean kayaking.

Time Out **Bridges** (1696 Duranleau St., tel. 604/687–4400), in the bright yellow building across from the market, is a good spot to have lunch, especially on a warm summer's day. Eat on the spacious deck that looks out on the sailboats, fishing boats, and other water activities.

The last place to explore on Granville Island is the blue building **42** next to Ecomarine on Duranleau Street, the **Net Loft.** The loft is a collection of small, high-quality stores—good places to find a gift to take home: a bookstore, crafts store/gallery, kitchenware shop, postcard shop, custom-made hat shop, handmade paper store, British Columbian native Indian gallery, do-it-yourself jewelry store, and more reside here.

43 Behind Blackberry Books, in the Net Loft complex, is the **Bill Reid's studio,** belonging to British Columbia's most respected Haida Indian carver. His *The Raven and the First Men*, which took five carvers more than three years to complete, is in the Museum of Anthropology (*see* Other Museums, *below*); Reid's Pacific Northwest Coast Indian artworks are world renowned. Although you can't visit the studio, there are large windows through which you can look.

Since you have come full circle, you can either take the ferry back to downtown Vancouver or stay for dinner and catch a play at the **Arts Club** (tel. 604/687–1644) or the **Waterfront Theater** (tel. 604/685–6217).

Other Museums

The **Maritime Museum** traces the history of marine activities on the west coast. Permanent exhibits depict the port of Vancouver, the fishing industry, and early explorers; the model ships on display are a delight. Traveling exhibits vary but always have a maritime theme. Guided tours are led through the double-masted schooner *St. Roch,* the first ship to sail in both directions through the treacherous Northwest Passage. A changing variety of restored heritage boats from different cultures are moored behind the museum, and a huge Kwakiutl totem pole stands out front. *North foot of Cypress St., tel. 604/737–2211. Admission: $5 adults, $2.50 children, students, and senior citizens, $8 families. Open daily 10–5, closed Mon. in winter. Access available by the Granville Island Ferries.*

The **Museum of Anthropology,** focusing on the arts of the Pacific Northwest Indians, is Vancouver's most spectacular museum. It's situated on the campus of the University of British Columbia and housed in an award-winning glass-and-concrete structure designed by Arthur Erickson. In the Great Hall are large and dramatic totem poles, ceremonial archways, and dugout canoes—all adorned with carvings of frogs, eagles, ravens, bears, and salmon. Also showcased are exquisite carvings of gold, silver, and argillite (a black stone found in the Queen Charlotte Islands), as well as masks, tools, and costumes from many other cultures. Also in the museum is a ceramics wing, which houses about 600 pieces from 15th- to 19th-century Europe. *6393 N.W. Marine Dr., tel. 604/822–3825. Admission: $5 adults, $2.50 students 6–18 and senior citizens; free Tues. evenings. Open Tues. 11–9, Wed.–Sun. 11–5.*

Science World is in a gigantic shiny dome that was built for Expo 86 for an Omnimax Theater—the world's largest dome screen. The hands-on museum encourages visitors to touch and participate in the theme exhibits. A special gallery, the Search Gallery, is aimed at younger children, as are the fun-filled demonstrations given in Center Stage. *1455 Quebec St., tel. 604/687–7832. Admission to Science World: $7 adults, $4.50 senior citizens and children. Admission to Omnimax is the same; for admission to both you get a discount. Open weekdays 10–5, Sat. 10–9.*

Vancouver Museum displays permanent exhibits that focus on the city's early history and native art and culture. Life-size replicas of an 1897 Canadian Pacific Railway passenger car, a trading post, and a Victorian parlor, as well as a real dugout canoe are highlights. Also on the site are the Planetarium and Observatory (*see* Off the Beaten Track, *below*). *1100 Chestnut St., tel. 604/736–7736. Admission: $5 adults, $2.50 senior citizens and children. Open Tues.–Sun. 10–5 in winter, daily 10–5 in summer.*

Other Parks and Gardens

Nitobe Garden is a small (2.4-acre) garden that is considered the most authentic Japanese garden outside Japan. The circular path around the park symbolizes the cycle of life and provides a tranquil view from every direction. In April and May cherry blossoms are the highlight, and in June the irises are magnificent. *1903 West Mall, Univ. of B.C., tel. 604/822–4208.*

Admission: $2 adults, $1.25 senior citizens and students, free Wed. and every day Oct. 11–Mar. 17. Open daily 10–dusk in summer; Mon.–Fri. in winter; phone for specific closing times.

Pacific Spirit Park (W. 16th Ave., tel. 604/224–5739) is a 1,000-acre park that is bigger and more rugged than Stanley Park. Pacific Spirit's only amenities are 61 kilometers (30 miles) of trails, a few washrooms, and a couple of signboard maps. Go for a wonderful walk in the west coast woods—it's hard to believe that you are only 15 minutes from downtown Vancouver.

Queen Elizabeth Park has lavish gardens and lots of grassy picnicking spots. Illuminated fountains; the botanical Bloedel Conservatory, with tropical and desert zones and 20 species of free-flying tropical birds; and other facilities including 20 tennis courts, lawn bowling, pitch and putt, and a restaurant are on the grounds. *Cambie St. and 25th Ave., tel. 604/872–5513. Admission to conservatory: $2.85 adults, $1.40 senior citizens and students, $5.70 families. Open May–Sept., weekdays 9–8, weekends 10–9; Oct.–Apr., daily 10–5.*

Van Dusen Botanical Garden was a 55-acre golf course but is now the grounds of one of the largest collections of ornamental plants in Canada. Native and exotic plant displays include the shrubbery maze and the rhododendrons in May and June. For a bite to eat, stop into Sprinklers Restaurant (tel. 604/261–0011), on the grounds. *5251 Oak St. at 37th Ave., tel. 604/266–7194. Admission: $4.50 adults, $2.25 senior citizens and children 13–18, $9 families; half-price off-season. Garden open 10–dusk.*

Vancouver for Free

Among the public galleries and museums that offer free admission on certain days are: The **Vancouver Art Gallery** (750 Hornby St., tel. 604/682–5621) is free on Thursday evenings; the **Museum of Anthropology** (6393 N.W. Marine Dr., tel. 604/822–3825) is free Tuesday evenings; the **Vancouver Museum** (1100 Chestnut St., tel. 604/736–7736) is free on the first Thursday evening of every month (it is also free every Tuesday for senior citizens).

The **University of British Columbia Botanical Garden** and **Nitobe Garden** (tel. 604/822–4208), a well-established Japanese garden also at UBC, are free on Wednesday and all winter.

What to See and Do with Children

Take your pint-size chef out to Sunday brunch at **Griffin's** (900 W. Georgia St., tel. 604/684–3131), the bistro-style restaurant in the Hotel Vancouver, where the little ones don small-person-size aprons and make their own pancakes and churn ice cream.

Stanley Park Zoo (*see* Tour 2: Stanley Park, *above*).

The **miniature steam train** in Stanley Park, just five minutes northwest of the aquarium, is a big hit with children as it chugs through the forest.

Splashdown Park (Hwy. 17, just before the Tsawwassen Ferry causeway, tel. 604/943–2251), 38 kilometers (24 miles) outside

Vancouver, is a giant waterslide park with 11 slides (for toddlers to adults), heated water, picnic tables, and minigolf.

Richmond Nature Park (No. 5 Rd. exit from Hwy. 99, tel. 604/273–7015), with its displays and games in the Nature House, is geared toward children. Guides answer questions and give tours. Since the park sits on a natural bog, rubber boots are recommended if it's been wet, but a boardwalk around the duck pond makes some of the park accessible to strollers and wheelchairs.

Maplewood Farms (405 Seymour River Pl., tel. 604/929–5610), a 20-minute drive from downtown Vancouver, is set up like a small farm, with all the barnyard animals for children to see and pet. Cows are milked every day at 1:15.

Kids Only Market (*see* Tour 3: Granville Island, *above*).

The Planetarium (1100 Chestnut St., tel. 604/736–3656), on the same site as the Vancouver Museum in Vanier Park, has astronomy shows each afternoon and evening, and laser rock music shows later in the night.

Science World (*see* Other Museums, *above*).

Vancouver Aquarium (*see* Tour 2: Stanley Park, *above*).

Off the Beaten Track

On the North Shore you can get a taste of the mountains and test your mettle at the **Lynn Canyon Suspension Bridge** (Lynn Headwaters Regional Park, North Vancouver, tel. 604/987–5922), which hangs 240 feet above Lynn Creek. Also on the North Shore is the **Capilano Fish Hatchery** in the Regional Park (4500 Capilano Park Rd., tel. 604/666–1790), with exhibits about salmon.

If the sky is clear, the telescope at the **Gordon Southam Observatory** (1100 Chestnut St., in Vanier Park, tel. 604/738–2855) will be focused on whatever stars or planets are worth watching that night. While you're there, visit the planetarium on the site. Open Friday, Saturday, Sunday, and holiday evenings.

The **Beatles Museum** (456 Seymour St., tel. 604/685–8841) exhibits memorabilia from the early years of the Fab Four. Admission is $3, and the museum is open daily 10–6, Sunday noon–6.

Shopping

Unlike many cities where suburban malls have taken over, Vancouver has a downtown area that is still lined with individual boutiques and specialty shops. Stores are usually open daily and on Thursday and Friday nights, and Sundays noon to 5.

Shopping Districts

The immense **Pacific Center Mall,** in the heart of downtown, connects Eaton's and The Bay department stores, which stand at opposite corners of Georgia and Granville streets. Pacific Center is on two levels and is mostly underground.

A new commercial center has developed around **Sinclair Center** (*see* Tour 1, *above*), which caters to sophisticated and upscale tastes.

On the opposite side of Pacific Center is **Robson Street,** stretching from Burrard to Bute streets, and chockablock with small stores and cafés. Vancouver's liveliest street is not only for the fashion conscious, it also provides many excellent corners for people watching.

Two other shopping districts, one on **West 41st Avenue** between West Boulevard and Larch Street in Kerrisdale and the other on **West 10th** from Discovery Street west, are both in upscale neighborhoods and have high-quality shops and restaurants.

Fourth Avenue, from Burrard to Balsam streets, offers an eclectic mix of stores (from sophisticated women's clothing to surfboards and Jams).

In addition to the Pacific Center Mall, **Oakridge Shopping Center** at Cambie Street and 41st Avenue has chic, expensive stores that are fun to browse.

Ethnic Districts   **Chinatown** (*see* Tour 1, *above*)—centered on Pender and Main streets—is an exciting and animated place for restaurants, exotic foodstuffs, and distinctive architecture.

Commercial Drive (around East 1st Avenue) is the heart of the Italian community, here called **Little Italy.** You can sip cappuccino in coffee bars where you may be the only one speaking English, or buy sun-dried tomatoes, real Parmesan, or an espresso machine.

The **East Indian shopping district** is on Main Street around 50th Avenue. Curry houses, sweet shops, grocery stores, and sari shops abound.

A small **Japantown** on Powell Street at Dunlevy Street is made up of grocery stores, fish stores, and a few restaurants.

Department Stores

The biggest department stores in Vancouver, **Eaton's, Holt Renfew,** and **The Bay,** are Canadian owned and located downtown and at most malls.

Flea Markets

A huge flea market (703 Terminal Ave., tel. 604/685–0666), with more than 300 stalls, is held Saturday, Sunday, and holidays from 8 to 4. It is easily accessible from downtown via SkyTrain, if you exit at the Main Street station.

Auctions

On Wednesday at noon and 7 PM, auctions are held at Love's (1635 W. Broadway, tel. 604/733–1157). Maynard's (415 W. 2nd Ave., tel. 604/876–6787) has home furnishings auctions on Wednesday at 7 PM. Phone for times of art and antiques auctions.

Specialty Stores

Antiques   A stretch of antiques stores runs along Main Street from 19th to 35th avenues. On 10th Avenue near Alma are a few antiques stores that specialize in Canadiana, including **Folkart Interiors** (3715 W. 10th Ave.) and **Old Country Antique Co.** (3720 W. 10th Ave.). Also try **Canada West** (3607 W. Broadway). For very refined antiques, see **Artemis** (321 Water St.) in Gastown. For Oriental rugs, go to Granville Street between 7th and 14th avenues.

Art Galleries There are many private galleries throughout Vancouver. The best of them are **Buschlen-Mowatt** (1445 W. Georgia St., tel. 604/682–1234), **Diane Farris** (1565 W. 7th Ave., tel. 604/737–2629), **Equinox** (2321 Granville St., tel. 604/736–2405), and the **Heffel Gallery** (2247 Granville St., tel. 604/732–6505). Call all galleries before visiting to make sure they are open.

Books The best general bookstores are **Duthie's**, located downtown (919 Robson St.) and near the university (4444 W. 10th Ave.), and **Blackberry Books** (1663 Duranleau St.) on Granville Island.

Specialty bookstores include **The Travel Bug** (2667 W. Broadway) and **World Wide Books and Maps** (736 Granville St., downstairs) for travel books, **Vancouver Kidsbooks** (3083 W. Broadway), **Sportsbooks Plus** (230 W. Broadway), and **Pink Peppercorn** (2686 W. Broadway) for cookbooks, and **William McCarley** (213 Carrall St.) for design and architecture.

Most of the secondhand and antiquarian dealers, such as **William Hoffer** (60 Powell St.) and **Colophon Books** (407 W. Cordova St., upstairs), are in the Gastown area. A block or two away are **McLeod's** (455 W. Pender St. and around the corner at 432 Richards St.), **Ainsworth's** (321 W. Pender St.), and **Bond's** (319 W. Hastings St.). **Lawrence Books** (3591 W. 41st Ave.) is out of the way but is probably the best used-books bookstore in town.

Children's Stores An unusual children's store worth checking out is **The Imagination Market** (528 Powell St.), an oddball warehouse-type store selling recycled industrial goods for arts-and-crafts materials: barrels of metallic plastic, feathers, fluorescent-colored paper, buttons, bits of Plexiglas, and other materials by the bagful.

Clothing Several high-quality men's clothing stores are in the business
Men district: **Edward Chapman** (833 W. Pender St.) has conservative looks; **E.A. Lee** (466 Howe St.) is stylish; **Leone** (757 W. Hastings St.) is ultrachic.

A few blocks away, at Pacific Center, are **Harry Rosen, Eddie Bauer,** and **Holt Renfrew.** If your tastes are traditional, don't miss **George Straith** (900 W. Georgia St.) in the Hotel Vancouver.

On Robson Street, a more trendy shopping area, are **Boy's Co.** (No. 1080) and **Club Monaco** (No. 1153), for casual wear.

Outside downtown Vancouver there are two men's boutiques selling Italian imports: **Mondo Uomo** (2709 Granville St.) and **Boboli** (2776 Granville St.).

In Kerrisdale, three excellent men's clothing stores are **Finn's** (2159 W. 41st Ave.), **Hill's** (2125 W. 41st Ave.), and, across the street, **S. Lampman** (2126 W. 41st Ave.).

Women For women's fashions, visit **E.A. Lee** (466 Howe St.), **Wear Else?** (789 W. Pender St.), **Leone** (757 W. Hastings St.), and the more conservative **Chapy's** (833 W. Pender St.), all in the business district.

On Robson Street, look for **Margareta** (No. 948), **Alfred Sung** (No. 1143), **Club Monaco** (No. 1153), and a lingerie shop, **La Vie en Rose** (No. 1001). The two blocks between Burrard and Bute have six shoe stores.

Two expensive and very stylish import stores in South Granville are **Boboli** (2776 Granville St.) and **Bacci** (2788 Granville St.). Nearby, one of the largest and best shoe stores in town is **Freedman Shoes** (2867 Granville St.).

On the west side **Enda B.** (4346 W. 10th Ave.) and **Wear Else?** (2360 W. 4th Ave.) are the largest and best stores for high-quality fashions, but there's also **Bali Bali** for the more exotic (4462 W. 10th Ave.) and **Zig Zag** (4424 W. 10th Ave.) for fashion accessories.

Gifts Want something special to take home from British Columbia? The best places for good-quality souvenirs are the Vancouver Art Gallery (750 Hornby St.) and the Clamshell Gift Shop at the aquarium in Stanley Park. The Salmon Shop in the Granville Island Public Market will wrap smoked salmon for travel. In Gastown, Haida and Salish Indian art is available at Images for a Canadian Heritage (164 Water St.). Near Granville Island is Leona Lattimer (1590 W. 2nd Ave.), where the inside of her shop is built like an Indian longhouse and is full of Indian arts and crafts ranging from cheap to priceless.

Sports and the Outdoors

Participant Sports

Biking **Stanley Park** (*see* Tour 2 in Exploring Vancouver, *above*) is the most popular spot for family cycling. Rentals are available here from **Bayshore Bicycles** (745 Denman St., tel. 604/688–2453) or around the corner at **Stanley Park Rentals** (676 Chilco St., tel. 604/681–5581).

Another biking route is along the north or south shores of **False Creek.** Rent bikes at **Robson Cycles** (1840 Fir St., tel. 604/731–5552), near Granville Island.

Fishing You can fish for salmon all year in coastal British Columbia. **Sewell's Marina Horseshoe Bay** (6695 Nelson St., Horseshoe Bay, tel. 604/921–3474) organizes a daily four-hour trip on Howe Sound or has hourly rates on U-drives. **Bayshore Yacht Charters** (1601 W. Georgia St., tel. 604/691–6936) has a daily five-hour fishing trip; boats are moored five minutes from downtown Vancouver. **Island Charters** (Duranleau St., Granville Island, tel. 604/688–6625) arranges charters or boat shares and supplies all gear.

Golf Lower Mainland golf courses are open all year. **Fraserview Golf Course** (tel. 604/327–3717), a spacious course with fairways well defined by hills and mature conifers and deciduous trees, is the busiest course in the country. Fraserview is also the most central, about 20 minutes from downtown. **Seymour Golf and Country Club** (tel. 604/929–5491), on the south side of Mt. Seymour, on the North Shore, is a semiprivate club that is open to the public on Monday and Friday. One of the finest public courses in the country is **Peace Portal** (tel. 604/538–4818), near White Rock, a 45-minute drive from downtown.

Health and Fitness Clubs Both the **YMCA** (955 Burrard St., tel. 604/681–0221) and the **YWCA** (580 Burrard St., tel. 604/683–2531) downtown have drop-in rates that let you participate in all activities for the day. Both have pools, weight rooms, and fitness classes; the YMCA has racquetball, squash, and handball courts. Two other recommended clubs are **Chancery Squash Club** (202–865 Hornby St., tel. 604/682–3752) and **Tower Courts Racquet and Fitness Club** (1055 Dunsmuir St., lower level, tel. 604/689–4424), both with racquetball courts, weight rooms, and aerobics.

Hiking **Pacific Spirit Park** is a 1,000-acre wilderness park with 48 kilometers (30 miles) of hiking trails (*see* Other Parks and Gardens in Exploring Vancouver, *above*).

The **Capilano Regional Park** (*see* Off the Beaten Track, in Exploring Vancouver, *above*), on the North Shore, provides a scenic hike.

Jogging The seawall around **Stanley Park** (*see* Tour 2 in Exploring Vancouver, *above*) is 9 kilometers (5½ miles) and gives an excellent minitour of the city. A shorter run of 4 kilometers (2½ miles) in the park is around **Lost Lagoon.**

Skiing The best cross-country skiing is at **Cypress Bowl Ski Area** (tel. *Cross-country* 604/926–6007).

Downhill Vancouver is two hours away from **Whistler/Blackcomb** (Whistler Resort Association, tel. 604/685–3650; snow report, tel. 604/687–7507), one of the top ski spots in North America.

There are three ski areas on the North Shore mountains, close to Vancouver, with night skiing. The snow is not as good as at Whistler, and the runs are generally used by novice, junior, and family skiers or those who want a quick ski after work. **Cypress Bowl** (tel. 604/926–5612; snow report, tel. 604/926–6007) has the most and the longest runs; **Grouse Mountain** (tel. 604/984–0661; snow report, tel. 604/986–6262) has extensive night skiing, restaurants, and bars; and **Mt. Seymour** (tel. 604/986–2261; snow report, tel. 604/986–3444) is the highest in the area, so the snow is a little better.

Water Sports Rent a kayak from **Ecomarine Ocean Kayak Center** (tel. 604/*Kayaking* 689–7575) on Granville Island (*see* Tour 3 in Exploring Vancouver, *above*).

Rafting The Thompson, the Chilliwack, and the Fraser are the principal rafting rivers in southwestern British Columbia. The Fraser River has whirlpools and big waves, but for frothing white water, try the Thompson and Chilliwack rivers. Trips range from three hours to several days. Some well-qualified outfitters that lead trips are **Kumsheen** (Lytton, tel. 604/455–2296; in British Columbia, 800/482–2269), **Hyak Wilderness Adventures** (Vancouver, tel. 604/734–8622), and **Canadian River Expeditions** (Vancouver, tel. 604/738–4449).

Sailing Several charter companies offer a cruise-and-learn vacation, usually to the Gulf Islands. The five-day trip is a crash course teaching the ins and outs of sailing. **Sea Wing Sailing Group, Ltd.** (Granville Island, tel. 604/669–0840) and **Pacific Quest** (Granville Island, tel. 604/682–2205) offer this package.

Windsurfing Boards can be rented at **Windsure Windsurfing School** (Jericho Beach, tel. 604/224–0615) and **Windmaster** (English Bay Beach, tel. 604/685–7245).

Spectator Sports

The **Vancouver Canucks** (tel. 604/254–5141) of the National Hockey League play in the Coliseum October–April. The **Canadians** (tel. 604/872–5232) play baseball in an old-time outdoor stadium in the Pacific Coast League. Their season runs April–September. The **B.C. Lions** (tel. 604/585–3323) football team scrimmages at the B.C. Place Stadium downtown June–November. Tickets are available from Ticketmaster (tel. 604/280–4444).

Beaches

An almost continuous string of beaches runs from Stanley Park to the University of British Columbia. Children and hardy swimmers can take the cool water, but most others prefer to sunbathe; these beaches are sandy, with grassy areas running alongside. Note that liquor is prohibited in parks and on beaches. For information on beaches, call the **Parks Department of the City of Vancouver** (tel. 604/681–1141).

Kitsilano Beach. Kits Beach, with a lifeguard, is the busiest of them all—transistor radios, volleyball games, and sleek young people are ever present. The part of the beach nearest the Maritime Museum is the quietest. Facilities include a playground, tennis courts, heated saltwater pool (good for serious swimmers to toddlers), concession stands, and many nearby restaurants and cafés.

Point Grey Beaches. Jericho, Locarno, and Spanish Banks begin at the end of Point Grey Road. This string of beaches has a huge expanse of sand, especially in the summer and at low tide. The shallow water here is warmed slightly by the sun and the sand and so is best for swimming. Farther out, toward Spanish Banks, you'll find the beach becomes less crowded, but the last concession stand and washrooms are at Locarno. If you keep walking along the beach just past Point Grey, you'll hit Wreck Beach, Vancouver's nude beach. It is also accessible from Marine Drive at the university, but there is a fairly steep climb from the beach to the road.

West End Beaches. Second Beach and Third Beach, along Beach Drive in Stanley Park, are large family beaches. Second Beach has a guarded saltwater pool. Both have concession stands and washrooms. Farther along Beach Drive, at the foot of Jervis Street, is Sunset Beach, a surprisingly quiet beach, considering the location. A lifeguard is on duty, but there are no facilities.

Dining

Among other allures, experiencing Vancouver's diverse gastronomical pleasures makes a visit to the city worthwhile. Restaurants appear throughout Vancouver—from the bustling downtown area to trendy beachside neighborhoods—making the diversity of the establishments' surroundings as enticing as the succulent cuisine they serve. A new wave of Chinese immigration and Japanese tourism has brought a proliferation of upscale Chinese and Japanese restaurants, offering dishes that would be at home in their own leading cities. Restaurants featuring Pacific Northwest fare—including homegrown regional favorites such as salmon and oysters, accompanied by British Columbia and Washington State wines—have become some of the city's leading attractions.

Highly recommended restaurants in each price category are indicated by a star ★.

Category	*Cost
Very Expensive	over $40
Expensive	$30—$40
Moderate	$20—$30

per person, including appetizer, entrée and dessert; excluding drinks, service, and sales tax

American **Isadora's.** Not only does Isadora's offer good coffee, a menu that ranges from samosas to lox and bagels, and children's specials, but there is also an inside play area packed with toys. Rest rooms with changing tables accommodate families. In the summer, the restaurant opens onto Granville Island's waterpark, so kids can entertain themselves. Service can be slow, but Isadora's staff is friendly. *1540 Old Bridge St., Granville Island, tel. 604/681–8816. Reservations required for 6 or more. Dress: casual. MC, V. Closed dinner Mon. Sept.–May. Inexpensive.*

Nazarre BBQ Chicken. The best barbecued chicken in several hundred miles comes from this funky storefront on Commercial Drive. Owner Gerry Moutal massages his chickens for tenderness before he puts them on the rotisserie and bastes them in a mixture of rum and spices. Chicken comes with roasted potatoes and a choice of mild, hot, extra hot, or hot garlic sauce. You can eat in, at one of four rickety tables, or take out. *1408 Commercial Dr., tel. 604/251–1844. No reservations. Dress: casual. No credit cards. Inexpensive.*

Cambodian/ **Phnom Penh Restaurant.** A block away from the bustle of
Vietnamese★ Keefer Street, the Phnom Penh is part of a small cluster of Southeast Asian shops on the fringes of Chinatown. Simple, pleasant decor abounds: arborite tables, potted plants, and framed views of Ankor Wat on the walls. The hospitable staff serves unusually robust Vietnamese fare, including crisp, peppery garlic prawns fried in the shell and slices of beef crusted with ground salt and pepper mixed in the warm beef salad. The decor in the new Broadway location is fancier and the food is every bit as good as at East Georgia Street. *244 E. Georgia St., tel. 604/682–5777; 955 W. Broadway, tel. 604/734–8898. No reservations for lunch; reservations for 5 or more only for dinner. Dress: casual. DC, MC. Closed Tues. Inexpensive.*

Chinese **Kirin Mandarin Restaurant.** Kirin, located two blocks from
★ most of the major downtown hotels, presents attentively served Chinese food in posh, elegant surroundings. Live fish in tanks set into the slate green walls remind one of an aquarium displayed in a lavishly decorated home. Drawn from a smattering of northern Chinese cuisines, dishes include Shanghai-style smoked eel, Peking duck, and Szechuan hot-and-spicy scallops. *1166 Alberni St., tel. 604/682–8833. Reservations advised. Dress: neat but casual. AE, DC, MC, V. Moderate.*

★ **The Pink Pearl.** In the world of Cantonese restaurants, biggest may very well be best: This 650-seat restaurant certainly wins

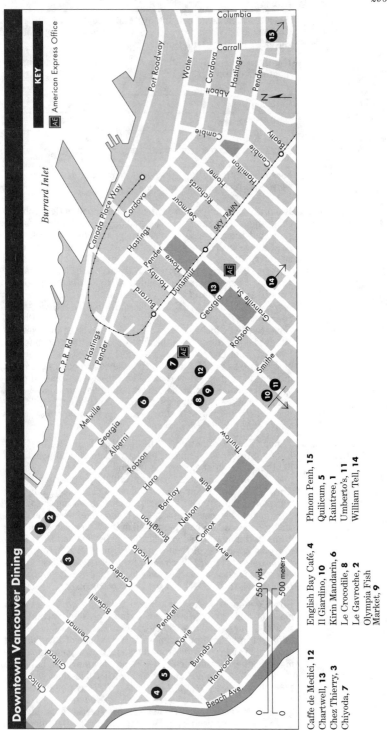

Downtown Vancouver Dining

KEY

AE American Express Office

Caffe de Medici, **12**
Chartwell, **13**
Chez Thierry, **3**
Chiyoda, **7**

English Bay Café, **4**
Il Giardino, **10**
Kirin Mandarin, **6**
Le Crocodile, **8**
Le Gavroche, **2**
Olympia Fish Market, **9**

Phnom Penh, **15**
Quilicum, **5**
Raintree, **1**
Umberto's, **11**
William Tell, **14**

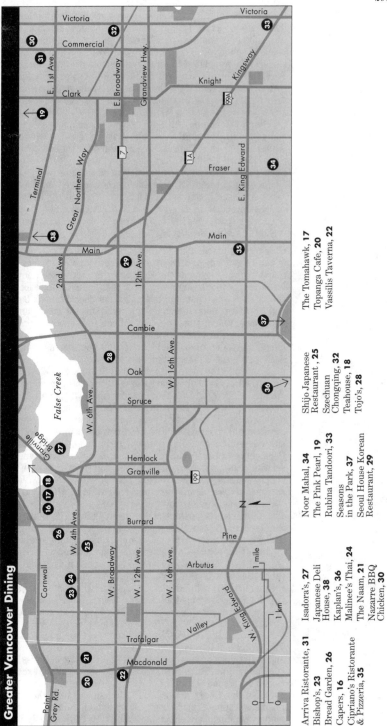

Greater Vancouver Dining

Arriva Ristorante, **31**
Bishop's, **23**
Bread Garden, **26**
Capers, **16**
Cipriano's Ristorante
& Pizzeria, **35**

Isadora's, **27**
Japanese Deli
House, **38**
Kaplan's, **36**
Malinee's Thai, **24**
The Naam, **21**
Nazarre BBQ
Chicken, **30**

Noor Mahal, **34**
The Pink Pearl, **19**
Rubina Tandoori, **33**
Seasons
in the Park, **37**
Seoul House Korean
Restaurant, **29**

Shijo Japanese
Restaurant , **25**
Szechuan
Chongqing, **32**
Teahouse, **18**
Tojo's, **28**

The Tomahawk, **17**
Topanga Cafe, **20**
Vassilis Taverna, **22**

the prize in this city. The huge, noisy room features tanks of live seafood—crab, shrimp, geoduck, oysters, abalone, rock cod, lobsters, and scallops. Menu highlights include clams in black bean sauce, crab sautéed with five spices (a spicy dish sometimes translated as crab with peppery salt), and Pink Pearl's version of crispy-skinned chicken. Arrive early for dim sum on the weekend if you don't want to be caught in the lineup. *1132 E. Hastings St., tel.604/253–4316. Reservations advised. Dress: casual. AE, DC, MC, V. Moderate.*

Szechuan Chongqing. Although fancier Szechuan restaurants can be found, the continued popularity of this unpretentious, white-tablecloth restaurant in a revamped fried-chicken franchise speaks for itself. Try the Szechuan-style fried green beans, steamed and tossed with spiced ground pork, or the Chongqing chicken—a boneless chicken served on a bed of spinach cooked in dry heat until crisp, giving it the texture of dried seaweed and a salty, rich, and nutty taste. *2495 Victoria Dr., tel. 604/254–7434. Reservations advised. Dress: casual. AE, MC, V. Inexpensive.*

Continental **Chartwell.** Named after Sir Winston Churchill's country home
★ (a painting of which hangs over the green marble fireplace), the flagship dining room at the Four Seasons Hotel (*see* Lodging, *below*) looks like an upper-class British men's club. Floor-to-ceiling dark wood paneling, deep leather chairs to sink back in and sip claret, plus a quiet setting make this the city's top spot for a power lunch. The chefs cook robust, inventive Continental food with lighter offerings and a variety of low-calorie, low-fat entrées. A salad of smoked loin of wild boar comes sprinkled with hazelnuts; Wiener schnitzel with roast potatoes is a favorite. Conclude the meal with port and Stilton. *791 W. Georgia St., tel. 604/844–6715. Reservations advised. Jacket suggested. AE, DC, MC, V. Closed weekends for lunch. Expensive.*

Seasons in the Park. Seasons has a commanding view over the park gardens to the city lights and the mountains beyond. A comfortable room with lots of light wood, white tablecloths, and deep-pile carpeting, this restaurant in Queen Elizabeth Park serves a conservative Continental menu with standards such as grilled salmon with fresh mint and roast duck with Bing cherry sauce. *Queen Elizabeth Park, tel. 604/874–8008. Reservations advised. Dress: neat but casual. AE, MC, V. Closed Christmas Day. Expensive.*

★ **The Teahouse Restaurant at Ferguson Point.** The best of the Stanley Park restaurants is perfectly poised for watching sunsets over the water, especially from its newer wing, a glassed-in room that conveys a conservatorylike ambience. Although the teahouse has a less innovative menu than its sister restaurant—Seasons in the Park—certain specialties such as the cream of carrot soup, duck in cassis, and the perfectly grilled fish don't need any meddling. For dessert, there's baked Alaska—a natural for this restaurant. *Ferguson Point in Stanley Park, tel. 604/669–3281. Reservations required. Dress: neat but casual. AE, MC, V. Closed Christmas Day. Expensive.*

The William Tell. Silver underliners, embossed linen napkins, and a silver flower vase on each table set the tone of Swiss luxury. The William Tell's well-established reputation for excellent Continental food continues at its quarters on the main floor of the Georgian Court Hotel, located 10 minutes from the central business district. Chef Pierre Dubrelle, a member of the gold medal–winning Canadian team at the 1988 Culinary Olympics, offers locally raised pheasant with glazed grapes and red wine sauce, sautéed veal sweetbreads with red onion marmalade and marsala sauce, and the Swiss specialty *Buendnerfleisch* (paper-thin slices of air-dried beef). Professional and discreet service contributes to the restaurant's excellence. *765 Beatty St., tel. 604/688–3504. Reservations advised. Jacket required at dinner. AE, DC, MC, V. Expensive.*

★ **English Bay Café.** Downstairs, the English Bay Café is a noisy bistro serving eggs Benedict, pasta, and fish specialties such as snapper or clam-and-sausage pasta. Upstairs, in the more serious dining room, you'll find the chef's fondness for venison and racks of lamb. Regardless of the level, however, when you look out the windows, it's all the same: With English Bay just two lanes of traffic away, you're guaranteed a glorious view of the sunset. Both bars are substantial; the bistro offers a large choice of imported beers. Valet parking is available and well worth the money. *1795 Beach Ave., tel. 604/669–2225. Reservations required. Dress: casual downstairs; neat but casual upstairs. AE, DC, MC, V. Moderate.*

Deli/Bakery **The Bread Garden Bakery, Café & Espresso Bar.** What began as a croissant bakery has taken over two neighboring stores and is now the ultimate Kitsilano 24-hour hangout. Salads, smoked salmon pizzas, quiches, elaborate cakes and pies, giant muffins, and cappuccino bring a steady stream of the young and fashionable. The Bread Garden To Go, next door, serves over-the-counter, but you may still be subjected to an irritatingly long wait in line; things just don't happen fast here. *1880 W. 1st Ave., tel. 604/ 738–6684; 812 Bute St., tel. 604/688–3213. No reservations. Dress: casual. MC, V. Inexpensive.*

★ **Kaplan's Deli, Restaurant and Bakery.** Tucked into a minimall on Oak Street (the road that leads to the Tsawwassen ferries and Seattle), Kaplan's is the traveler's last chance for authentic Jewish deli food before leaving town. Eat in at booths, or take your chopped liver, chopped herring, lox, and homemade corned beef with you. The bakery makes justly famous cinnamon buns. *5775 Oak St., tel. 604/263–2625. No reservations. Dress: casual. MC, V. Closed Jewish holidays. Inexpensive.*

East Indian **Rubina Tandoori.** If one must single out the best East Indian
★ food in the city, then Rubina Tandoori, 20 minutes from downtown, ranks as a top contender. The large menu spans most of the subcontinent's cuisines, and the especially popular *chevda* (East Indian salty snack) gets shipped to fans all over North America. Maître d' Shaffeen Jamal has a phenomenal memory for faces. Nonsmokers get the smaller, funkier back room with the paintings of coupling gods and goddesses; smokers get the big, upholstered banquettes in the new room. *1962 Kingsway, tel. 604/874–3621. Reservations advised on weekends. Dress: casual. MC, V. Closed lunch and Sun. Moderate.*

Noor Mahal. The only Lower Mainland restaurant that specializes in South Indian food, the Noor Mahal provides good-size portions at a reasonable price in authentic surroundings. The pink walls help to create the light and airy decor. Try a *dosa*—a lacy pancake made from bean, rice, and semolina flour, stuffed with curried potatoes, shrimp, or chicken—for lunch. Owners Susan and Paul Singh double as staff, so service can be slow and harried during busy periods. *4354 Fraser St., tel. 604/873–9263. Reservations advised on weekends. Dress: casual. AE, MC, V. Closed lunch. Inexpensive.*

French
★
Le Gavroche. Time has stood still in this charming turn-of-the-century house, where a woman dining with a man will be offered a menu without prices. Featuring classic French cooking, lightened—but by no means reduced—to nouvelle cuisine, Le Gavroche's menu also includes simple listings such as smoked salmon with blinis and sour cream. Other options may be as complex as smoked pheasant breast on a puree of celeriac, shallots, and wine with a light truffle sauce. The excellent wine list stresses Bordeaux. No reservations are necessary after 9:30, when the late-dessert menu is offered. Tables by the front window promise mountains-and-water views. *1616 Alberni St., tel. 604/685–3924. Reservations advised on weekends. Jacket and tie advised. AE, MC, V. Closed lunch, Sun., and holidays. Expensive.*

Chez Thierry. This cozy bistro on the Stanley Park end of Robson Street adds pizzazz to a celebration: Owner Thierry Damilano stylishly slashes open champagne bottles with a sword on request. The country-style French cooking emphasizes seafood. Try watercress and smoked salmon salad; fresh tuna grilled with artichokes, garlic, and tomatoes; and apple tarte Tatin for dessert. During the week the intimate dining room promises a relaxing meal; on the weekend, however, with every one of the 16 tables jammed, the restaurant gets noisy. *1674 Robson St., tel. 604/688–0919. Reservations required on weekends. Dress: casual. AE, DC, MC, V. Closed lunch and Dec. 24–26. Moderate.*

★ **Le Crocodile.** Why do people want to sit packed tighter than sardines in this tiny bistro? Because chef Michael Jacob serves extremely well cooked, simple food at very moderate prices. His Alsatian background shines with the caramelly, sweet onion tart. Anything that involves innards is superb, and even old standards such as duck à l'orange are worth ordering here. The one flaw? A small, overpriced wine list. *909 Burrard St., tel. 604/669–4298. Reservations required. Dress casual. AE, DC, MC, V. Closed Sat. lunch and Sun. Moderate.*

Greek
Vassilis Taverna. The menu in this family-run restaurant, located in the heart of the city's small Greek community, is almost as conventional as the decor: checked tablecloths and mandatory paintings of white fishing villages and the blue Aegean Sea. At Vassilis, though, even standards become memorable due to the flawless preparation. The house specialty is a deceptively simple *kotopoulo* (a half-chicken, pounded flat, herbed, and charbroiled); the lamb fricassee with artichoke hearts and broad beans in an egg-lemon sauce is more complicated, though not necessarily better. Save room for a *navarino*, a creamy custard square topped with whipped cream and ground nuts. *2884 W. Broadway, tel. 604/733–3231. Reservations advised on weekends. Dress: casual. AE, DC, MC, V. Closed Mon. and lunch Sat. and Sun. Moderate.*

Health Food
★
Capers. Hidden in the back of the most lavishly handsome health food store in the Lower Mainland, Capers (open for breakfast, lunch, and dinner) drips with earth-mother chic: wood tables, potted plants, and heady smells from the store's bakery. Breakfast starts weekdays at 7:30, weekends at 8. Eggs and bacon? Sure, but Capers serves free-range eggs, as well as bacon without additives. Feather-light blueberry pancakes crammed with berries star here. The view of the water compensates for service that can be slow and forgetful. *2496*

Marine Dr., W. Vancouver, tel. 604/925–3316. No reservations. Dress: casual. MC, V. Closed dinner Sun. Inexpensive.

The Naam Restaurant. Vancouver's oldest alternative restaurant is now open 24 hours, so those needing to satisfy a late-night tofu-burger craving, rest easy. The Naam has left its caffeine- and alcohol-free days behind and now serves wine, beer, cappuccino, and wicked chocolate desserts, along with the vegetarian stir-fries. Wood tables and kitchen chairs make for a homey atmosphere. On warm summer evenings, the outdoor courtyard at the back of the restaurant welcomes diners. *2724 W. 4th Ave., tel. 604/738–7151. Reservations required for 6 or more. Dress: casual. MC, V. Inexpensive.*

Italian
★
Caffe de Medici. It takes shifting gears as you leave the stark concrete walls of the Robson Galleria behind and step into this elegant restaurant with its ornate molded ceilings, rich green velvet curtains and chair coverings, and portraits of the de Medici family. But after a little wine, an evening's exposure to courtly waiters, and a superb meal, you may begin to wish the outside world conformed more closely to this peaceful environment. Although an enticing antipasto table sits in the center of the room, consider the *Bresaola* (air-dried beef marinated in olive oil, lemon, and pepper) as a worthwhile appetizer. Try the rack of lamb in a mint, mustard, and Martini & Rossi sauce. Any of the pastas is a safe bet. *1025 Robson St., tel. 604/669–9322. Reservations advised. Jacket advised. AE, DC, MC, V. Closed lunch Sat. and Sun. Expensive.*

Il Giardino di Umberto, Umberto's. First came Umberto's, a Florentine restaurant serving classic northern Italian food, installed in a century-old Vancouver home at the foot of Hornby Street. Then, next door, Umberto Menghi built Il Giardino, a sunny, light-splashed restaurant styled after a Tuscan house. This restaurant features braided breast of pheasant with polenta and reindeer fillet with crushed peppercorn sauce. Il Giardino attracts a regular young, moneyed crowd, while Umberto's is more quiet and sedate. Fish is treated either Italian style—rainbow trout grilled and served with sun-dried tomatoes, black olives, and pine-nuts—or with a taste of the Far East, as in yellow-fin tuna grilled with wasabi butter. *Il Giardino, 1382 Hornby St., tel. 604/669–2422. Umberto's, 1380 Hornby St., tel. 604/687–6316. Reservations advised. Dress: neat but casual. AE, DC, MC, V. Umberto's closed lunch and Sun., Mon. Il Giardino closed lunch Sat. and Sun. Expensive.*

Arriva Ristorante. Commercial Drive Italian restaurants, like Chinese restaurants in Chinatown, are best looked at with a skeptical eye. The best of the breed are elsewhere, and what's left is often found cranking out North Americanized travesties of the home country's food. Arriva is one Little Italy restaurant that's worth the drive, and it's a welcome find if you've spent the day shopping in Italian groceries. There's a version of spaghetti and meatballs on the menu, ziti with spicy squid sauce, and a fusili with wild game—"Bambi and Bugs Bunny," as the waiters have affectionately coined it. The antipasto plate includes a heaping order of octopus, shrimp, roasted red peppers, cheese, sausage, and fat lima beans in an herby marinade. Don't miss the orange sherbet served in a hollowed-out orange for dessert. *1537 Commercial Dr., tel. 604/251–1177. Reservations advised. Dress: casual. AE, DC, MC, V. Closed lunch Sat. and Sun. Moderate.*

Griffin's. Sunday brunch here was rated as top entertainment in 1992 by the daily newspaper, *The Province*. The ambience is fun, energetic, and kid-oriented: Kids in aprons (provided by the restaurant) whip up their own pancakes and take turns churning ice cream for dessert. The rest of the week the emphasis is on the adult crowd. This brasserie uniquely blends the charm of old Italy with the flair of sophisticated design and fresh, regional ingredients. Squash-yellow walls, bold black-and-white tiles, and splashy food art by Mary Frances Tuck enhance Griffin's liveliness. The hotel's gargoyles are repeated in stenciling on the walls and in the red, yellow, and green carpet. The brasserie features an open kichen that prepares inspirational cuisine, including buffet selections such as convict bread, a round loaf stuffed with soft, fresh goat cheese, olives, tomatoes, and peppers in olive oil; smoked salmon; chicken pasta al pesto; and baked Pacific black cod with herbed crumbs. There's a pizza buffet on Saturday. *900 W. Georgia St., tel. 604/684-3131. Reservations advised. Dress: casual but neat. AE, DC, MC, V. Moderate*

Cipriano's Ristorante & Pizzeria. Formerly a Greek pizza parlor, Cipriano's has been transformed into an Italian restaurant, with green-white-and-red walls representing the Italian flag, Mama-mia!—inexpensive and hearty Italian food is the mainstay here, including good pizza, even better pasta, and the "Pappa" lasagna. *3995 Main St., tel. 604/879-0020. Reservations accepted. Dress: casual. V. Closed lunch and Mon. Inexpensive.*

Japanese **Tojo's.** Hidekazu Tojo is a sushi-making legend here. His handsome blond-wood tatami rooms, on the second floor of a new
★ green-glass tower in the hospital district on West Broadway, provide proper ambience for intimate dining, but Tojo's 10-seat sushi bar stands as the centerpiece. With Tojo presiding, it is a convivial place for dinner and offers a ringside seat for watching the creation of edible art. Although tempura and teriyaki dinners will satisfy, the seasonal menu is more exciting. In October, ask for *dobbin mushi,* a soup made from pine mushrooms that's served in a teapot. In spring, try sushi made from scallops and pink cherry blossoms. *777 W. Broadway, No. 202, tel. 604/872-8050. Reservations advised on weekends. Dress: neat but casual. AE, DC, MC, V. Closed lunch and Sun.; Dec. 24-26. Expensive.*

Chiyoda. The robata bar curves like an oversize sushi bar through Chiyoda's main room: On one side are the customers and an array of flat baskets full of the day's offerings; on the other side are the robata chefs and grills. There are 35 choices of things to grill, from squid, snapper, and oysters to eggplant, mushrooms, onions, and potatoes. The finished dishes, dressed with sake, soy, or *ponzu* sauce, are dramatically passed over on the end of a long wooden paddle. If Japanese food means only sushi and tempura to you, check this out. *1050 Alberni St., tel. 604/688-5050. Reservations accepted. Dress: casual. AE, MC, V. Closed lunch Sat. and Sun.; closed Sun. off-season. Moderate.*

Shijo Japanese Restaurant. Shijo has an excellent and very large sushi bar, a smaller robata bar, tatami rooms, and a row of tables overlooking bustling Fourth Avenue. The epitome of modern urban Japanese chic is conveyed through the jazz music, handsome lamps with a patinated bronze finish, and lots of black wood. Count on creatively prepared sushi, eggplant *dengaku* topped with light and dark miso paste and broiled, and shiitake *foil yaki* (fresh shiitake mushrooms cooked in foil with *ponzu* sauce). *1926 W. 4th Ave., tel. 604/732–4676. Reservations advised. Dress: casual. AE, MC, V. Closed lunch, Sat. and Sun. Moderate.*

Japanese Deli House. The least expensive sushi in town is served in this high-ceilinged room on the main floor of a turn-of-the-century building on Powell Street, once the heart of Vancouver's Japantown. Along with the standard sushi-bar menu, Japanese Deli House makes a pungent but tender, hot ginger squid appetizer from baby squid caught off the Thai coast, and a geoduck appetizer in mayonnaise worth wandering off the beaten path for. The food is especially fresh and good if you can make it an early lunch: Nigiri sushi and sushi rolls are made at 11 AM for the 11:30 opening. *381 Powell St., tel. 604/681–6484. No reservations. Dress: casual. No credit cards. Closed lunch Mon. Inexpensive.*

Korean **Seoul House Korean Restaurant.** The shining star in a desperately ugly section of East Broadway, Seoul House is a bright restaurant, decorated in Japanese style, that serves a full menu of Japanese and Korean food. The best bet is the Korean barbecue, which you cook at your table. A barbecue dinner of marinated beef, pork, chicken, or fish comes complete with a half dozen side dishes—*kim chee* (Korea's national pickle), salads, stir-fried rice, and pickled vegetables—as well as soup and rice. Service can be chaotic in this very popular restaurant. *36 E. Broadway, tel. 604/874–4131. Reservations advised. Dress: casual. MC, V. Closed lunch Sun. Inexpensive.*

Mexican **Topanga Cafe.** Arrive before 6:30 or after 8 PM to avoid waiting in line for this 40-seat Kitsilano classic. The California-Mexican food hasn't changed much in the 15 years the Topanga has been dishing up fresh salsa and homemade tortilla chips. Quantities are still huge and prices are low. Kids can color blank menu covers while waiting for food; a hundred or more of the clientele's best efforts are framed and on the walls. *2904 4th Ave., tel. 604/733–3713. No reservations. Dress: casual. MC, V. Closed Sun. Inexpensive.*

Nouvelle **Bishop's.** John Bishop established Vancouver's most influential
★ restaurant in 1987 by serving West Coast Continental cuisine with an emphasis on British Columbia seafood. Penne with grilled eggplant, roasted peppers, and basil pasta cohabit the menu with medallions of venison, rack of lamb, and beef tenderloin. The small white rooms—their only ornament some splashy, expressionist paintings—are favored by Pierre Trudeau and by Robert De Niro when he's on location in Vancouver. *2183 W. 4th Ave., tel. 604/738–2025. Reservations required. Dress: casual. AE, DC, MC, V. Closed 1st week in Jan., lunch Sat. and Sun. Expensive.*

Pacific Northwest **Quilicum.** Only a few blocks from English Bay, this downstairs "longhouse" serves the original Northwest Coast cuisine: bannock bread, baked sweet potato with hazelnuts, alder-grilled salmon, and soapberries for dessert. Try the authentic but odd dish—oolichan grease—that's prepared from candlefish. Native music is piped in, and Northwest Coast masks (for sale) peer out from the walls. *1724 Davie St., tel. 604/681–7044. Reservations advised. Dress: casual. AE, MC, V. Closed lunch Sat.–Tues. Moderate.*

★ **The Raintree.** This cool, spacious restaurant offers a local menu and wine list, which features vintages from British Columbia, Washington, and Oregon. Raintree bakes its own bread, makes luxurious soups, and offers old favorites such as a slab of apple pie for dessert. With main courses, which change daily depending on market availability, the kitchen, focusing on healthy choices, teeters between willfully eccentric and exceedingly simple. Specials could include Queen Charlotte abalone and side-stripe shrimps, stir-fried with scallions and spinach in chamomile essence; and grilled lamb chops with a mint and pear puree. Leon's Bar and Grill, on the ground floor, stocks local beers and a respectable number of single-malt scotches. The pub-food menu includes organic-beef burgers and vegetarian chili. The $14 fixed-price Sunday brunch features ricotta and apple-stuffed French toast, sockeye salmon hash, and apricot-hazelnut pancakes, plus several other courses. *1630 Alberni St., tel. 604/688–5570. Reservations advised on weekends. Dress: casual. AE, DC, MC, V. Closed lunch Sat. and Dec. 24–26. Moderate.*

The Tomahawk. North Vancouver was mostly trees 66 years ago, when the Tomahawk first opened. Over the years, the original hamburger stand grew and mutated into part Northwest Coast Indian kitsch museum, part gift shop, and part restaurant. Renowned for its Yukon breakfast—five slices of back bacon, two eggs, hash browns, and toast—the Tomahawk also serves gigantic muffins, excellent French toast, and pancakes. The menu switches to oysters, trout, and burgers named after Indian chiefs for lunch and dinner. *1550 Philip Ave., tel. 604/ 988–2612. No reservations. Dress: casual. AE, MC, V. Inexpensive.*

Seafood **Olympia Fish Market and Oyster Co. Ltd.** Some of the city's best fish-and-chips are fried in this tiny shop located behind a fish store in the middle of the Robson Street shopping district. The choice is halibut, cod, prawns, calamari, and whatever's on special in the store, served with genuine—never frozen—french fries. *1094 Robson St., tel. 604/685–0716. No reservations. Dress: casual. DC, V. Inexpensive.*

Thai **Malinee's Thai.** The city's most consistently interesting Thai
★ food can be found in this typically Southeast Asian–style room, tapestries adorning the walls. The owners, two Canadians who lived several years in Thailand, can give you detailed descriptions of every dish on the menu. Steamed fish with ginger, pickled plums, and red chili sauce is on the regular menu; a steamed whole red snapper marinated in oyster sauce, ginger, cilantro, red pepper, and lime juice is a special worth ordering when available. *2153 W. 4th Ave., tel. 604/737–0097. Reservations advised. Dress: casual. AE, DC, MC, V. Closed lunch. Moderate.*

Lodging

Lodging has become a major business for Vancouver, a fairly young city that hosts a lot of Asian businesspeople who are used to an above-average level of service. Although by some standards pricey, properties here are highly competitive, and you can expect the service to reflect this trend.

Highly recommended lodgings in each price category are indicated by a star ★.

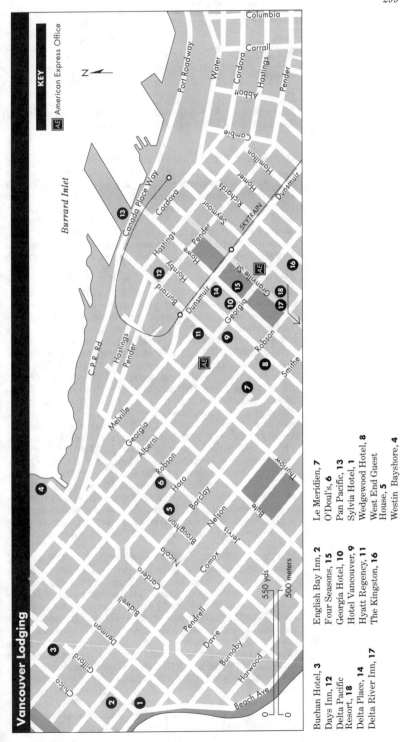

Vancouver Lodging

KEY

AE American Express Office

Burrard Inlet

Buchan Hotel, **3**
Days Inn, **12**
Delta Pacific
Resort, **18**
Delta Place, **14**
Delta River Inn, **17**

English Bay Inn, **2**
Four Seasons, **15**
Georgia Hotel, **10**
Hotel Vancouver, **9**
Hyatt Regency, **11**
The Kingston, **16**

Le Meridien, **7**
O'Doul's, **6**
Pan Pacific, **13**
Sylvia Hotel, **1**
Wedgewood Hotel, **8**
West End Guest
House, **5**
Westin Bayshore, **4**

Category	Cost*
Very Expensive	over $180
Expensive	$140–$180
Moderate	$90–$139
Inexpensive	under $90

All prices are for a standard double room for two, excluding 10% provincial accommodation tax, 15% service charge, and 7% GST.

Very Expensive **Four Seasons.** This 28-story hotel is adjacent to the Vancouver Stock Exchange and is attached to the Pacific Centre shopping mall. Standard rooms are not large; corner deluxe or deluxe Four Seasons rooms are recommended. Expect tasteful and stylish decor in the rooms and hallways, providing a calm mood despite the bustling hotel. A huge sun deck and indoor-outdoor pool are part of the complete health club facilities. Service is outstanding, and the Four Seasons has all the amenities. The formal dining room, Chartwell (see Dining, above), is one of the best in the city. *791 W. Georgia St., V6C 2T4, tel. 604/689–9333; in Canada, 800/268–6282; in the U.S., 800/332–3442; fax 604/844–6744. 317 rooms, 68 suites. Facilities: restaurant, café, bars, indoor-outdoor pool, sun deck, weight room, aerobics classes, sauna, Jacuzzi, ping-pong. AE, DC, MC, V.*

★ **Le Meridien.** This property feels more like an exclusive guest house than a large hotel: Its lobby has sumptuously thick carpets, enormous displays of flowers, and a newsstand situated discreetly down the hall. The rooms are even better, furnished with rich, dark woods reminiscent of 19th-century France. Bathrobes, slippers, and umbrellas in the room attest to the attention to detail here. Despite the size of this hotel, the Le Meridien in Vancouver has achieved and maintained a level of intimacy and exclusivity. The **Café Fleuri** serves one of the best Sunday brunches in town (plus a chocolate buffet on Thursday, Friday, and Saturday evenings), and **Le Club,** a fine French restaurant, is a special-occasion place. Lots of leather, dark wood, wingback chairs, and a fireplace give the **Gerard** bar the feel of a refined gentlemen's club. *845 Burrard St., V6Z 2K6, tel. 604/682–5511, fax 604/682–5513. 350 doubles, 47 suites. Facilities: restaurant, café, bar, business center, health club with pool, Jacuzzi, sauna, steam room, tanning bed, masseuse, salon, weights, exercise equipment, adjoining apartment hotel. AE, DC, V.*

★ **Pan Pacific.** Canada Place sits on a pier right by the financial district and houses the luxurious Pan Pacific Hotel (built in 1986 for the Expo), the Vancouver Trade and Convention Centre, and a cruise-ship terminal. The lobby has a dramatic three-story atrium with a waterfall, and the lounge, restaurant, and café all have huge expanses of glass, so that you are rarely without a harbor view or mountain backdrop. Earthtones and Japanese detail give the rooms an understated elegance. Make sure you get a room that looks out on the water. The health club has a $15 fee that's well worth the price. The Pan Pacific is a grand, luxurious, busy hotel, but it is not a pick for an intimate weekend getaway. *300–999 Canada Pl., V6C 3B5, tel. 604/662–8211; in Canada, 800/663–1515; in the U.S., 800/937–1515; fax 604/685–8690. 468 doubles, 40 suites. Facilities: 3 restaurants, bar, health club with indoor track, sauna, steam room, state-*

of-the-art aerobics equipment, weights, massage and Shiatsu, sports lounge with wide-screen TV, squash, racquetball, and paddle-tennis courts, heated outdoor pool. AE, DC, MC, V.

Expensive–
Very Expensive
Westin Bayshore. This hotel is the closest thing to a resort that you'll find in the downtown area. Because the Bayshore is perched right on the best part of the harbor, because it is a five-minute walk from Stanley Park, because of the truly fabulous view, and because of its huge outdoor pool, sun deck, and grassy areas, it is the perfect place to stay during the summer, especially for a family. The tower is the newer section, so rooms there are better furnished and larger and offer the best views of the water. The café is okay, and Trader Vic's, the hotel's dining room, is a pleasant, Polynesian-style experience. There are also several neighborhood restaurants. *1601 W. Georgia St., V6G 2V4, tel. 604/682–3377 or 800/228–3000; fax 604/691–6959. 481 doubles, 38 suites, 2 floors for the disabled. Facilities: restaurant, café, bars, free shuttle service downtown, bicycle rentals, marina with fishing and sailing charters, health club with indoor and outdoor pools, Jacuzzi, sun deck, masseur, sauna, pool table. AE, DC, MC, V.*

Expensive
Delta Pacific Resort & Conference Center. It's not a view or a shoreline that makes this place (five minutes from the airport) a resort, it's the facilities on the 12-acre site: three swimming pools (one indoor), four all-year tennis courts with a pro (matching list for partners), an outdoor fitness circuit, squash courts, aqua-exercise classes, outdoor volleyball nets, golf practice nets, a play center for children, summer camps for 5- to 12-year-olds, and a playground. In spite of the hotel's enormity, the atmosphere is casual and friendly. There are two guest-room towers and a few low-rise buildings for convention facilities. The resort was renovated in 1991–92, so guest rooms are modern with contemporary decor and pleasant color schemes. The Japanese restaurant is expensive and not the best value. *10251 St. Edwards Dr., V6X 2M9, tel. 604/278–9611; in Canada, 800/268–1133; in the U.S., 800/877–1133; fax 604/276–1122. 460 doubles, 4 suites. Facilities: restaurant, café, bar, shuttle to airport and shopping center, meeting rooms. AE, DC, MC, V.*

Delta Place. This 18-story hotel was built in 1985 by the luxurious Hong Kong Mandarin chain but was sold to Delta Hotels in 1987. Although the rates went down, the surroundings did not change: The lobby is still restrained and tasteful—one has to look for the registration desk. A slight Oriental theme is given to the deluxe furnishings, and dark, rich mahogany is everywhere. Most rooms have small balconies, and the studio suites are recommended since they are much roomier and only slightly more expensive than a standard room. Continental breakfast is included with your stay. The business center has secretarial services, work stations, cellular phones for rent, and small meeting rooms. The restaurant and bar are adequate and the location is perfect; the business and shopping district is a five-minute walk away. *645 Howe St., V6C 2Y9, tel. 604/687–1122; in Canada, 800/268–1133; in the U.S., 800/877–1133; fax 604/643–7267. 181 doubles, 16 suites. Facilities: restaurant, bar, squash and racquetball courts, lap pool, weight room. AE, DC, MC, V.*

Delta River Inn. This hotel, on the edge of the Fraser River, is two minutes from the airport. Rooms on the south side get the best view. Although renovations began in 1990, the River Inn still has a way to go to compete with others in the price range: The rooms here just don't have the style and pizzazz of the others. The hotel's draw lies in its proximity to the airport and its attachment to the marina, which organizes fishing charters so there are things for guests to do here. Food does not seem to be a priority with Delta. *3500 Cessena Dr., V7B 1C7, tel. 604/278–1241; in Canada, 800/268–1133; in the U.S., 800/877–1133; fax 604/276–1975. 410 doubles, 6 suites. Facilities: jogging route, outdoor pool, free shuttle to airport, shopping center, and extensive health club at the nearby Delta Pacific Resort. AE, DC, MC, V.*

★ **Hotel Vancouver.** The Hotel Vancouver, which opened in 1939 by the Canadian National Railway, is one of the grand old ladies of the chateau-style hotels that appear across Canada. Its copper roof dominates the city's skyline, and the hotel itself commands a regal position in the center of town across from the art gallery and Cathedral Place. Even the standard guest rooms lend an air of prestige with mahogany furniture, TVs in armoires, attractive linens, and the original, deep bathtubs. The whole design is by far more classic than what you'll find at the Hyatt Regency or the Four Seasons. The hotel's two floors of Entrée Gold feature extra services and amenities, including complimentary breakfast in a private, luxurious lounge. Entrée Gold suites are spacious with French doors, graceful wing-back chairs, and fine mahogany furniture. The style and elegance of the Hotel Vancouver especially leave their mark on these floors. The hotel features the Roof Restaurant, which offers spectacular views with fine dining and dancing to live entertainment nightly. Reservations for Griffin's, the hotel's bistro-style restaurant—one of the most popular eateries in the city—are a must; there's a pizza buffet Saturday and a Tex-Mex Sunday brunch where children get into the act, making pancakes and churning ice cream. *900 W. Georgia St., V6C 2W6, tel. 604/684–3131 or 800/441–1414; fax 604/662–1937. 466 doubles, 42 suites, rooms for guests with disabilities. Facilities: 2 restaurants, 2 bars, two-line telephones, health club with lap pool, exercise machines, tanning bed, sun deck. AE, CB, DC, MC, V.*

Hyatt Regency. The 34-story hotel, which opened in 1973, completed an $11 million renovation in 1992. The Hyatt's standard rooms are the largest in the city and have been decorated in deep, dramatic colors and dark wood. Ask for a corner room with a balcony on the north or west side. The lobby, with its four-story atrium, however, can't escape the feel of a large convention hotel. For a small fee, the Regency Club gives you the exclusivity of three floors accessed by keyed elevators, your own concierge, a private lounge with a stereo and large TV, complimentary breakfast, 5 PM hors d'oeuvres, and evening pastries. Robes and special toiletries are also in the Regency Club rooms. For a hotel restaurant, Fish & Co. is unusual in that the room is casual, the atmosphere fun, and the food good. The Gallery Lounge is one of the most pleasant in town. Health club facilities include outdoor heated pool, saunas, exercise machine, and access to a nearby fitness center with racquetball and squash courts. *655 Burrard St., V6C 2R7, tel. 604/687–6543 or 800/233–1234, fax 604/689–3707. 612 doubles, 34 suites. Facilities: restaurant, café, 2 bars, health club. AE, DC, MC, V.*

O'Doul's. This conveniently situated hotel on a lively street, with loads of shops and restaurants, is only a five-minute walk from either the heart of downtown or Stanley Park. It's a great location if you're traveling with teenagers who want time on their own. Among mid-range hotels, this is one of the more thoughtful: Public areas are very well maintained, and to insure extra security guests must use their room keys to operate the elevators. The rooms aren't what you'd expect, either: The decor is modern, with pastel color schemes. Deluxe rooms (with king-size beds) face Robson Street and are worth the price, especially off-season, when rates plummet. *1300 Robson St., V6E 1C5, tel. 604/684–8461 or 800/663–5491, fax 604/684– 8326. 119 doubles, 11 suites. Facilities: 3 telephones in every room, pool, Jacuzzi, steam rooms, exercise machines. AE, DC, MC, V.*

Waterfront Centre Hotel. This dramatically elegant, 23-story glass hotel opened in 1991 across from Canada Place, the Convention Centre, and the cruise-ship terminal—all of which can be reached from the hotel by an enclosed walkway. Views from the caramel-colored lobby and many of the guest rooms are of Burrard Inlet; other guest rooms look out onto the mountains. The Entrée Gold floor has a lounge, terrace, and includes a concierge, board room, shoe-shine service, deluxe breakfast, cocktail-hour canapes, and honor bar. All guest rooms are attractively furnished with contemporary artwork, minibars, and armoires concealing the TV. A pleasant place for guests to enjoy a drink is Herons Lounge, off of the lobby area. But as the evening progresses, the activity usually moves into Herons Restaurant, where a Mediterranean ambience prevails and guests can watch their meals being prepared in the open kitchen and rotisserie. Sundays here are high spirited, as live Gospel singers entertain and inspire during a lavish brunch that includes imaginative dishes and decadent desserts. The property's health club includes a whirlpool, enclosed walkway to an outdoor heated pool, a variety of exercise equipment, a steam room, and massage services. *900 Canada Place Way, V6C 3L5, tel. 604/691–1991 or 800/441–1414; fax 604/691–1999. 460 doubles, 29 suites. Facilities: restaurants, health club, whirlpool, heated outdoor pool, steam room. AE, CB, DC, MC, V.*

★ **Wedgewood Hotel.** This hotel upholds its reputation for being a small, elegant property run by an owner who fervently cares about her guests. The intimate lobby is decorated in fine detail with polished brass, beveled glass, a fireplace, and tasteful artwork. All the extra touches are here, too: nightly turndown service, afternoon ice delivery, dark-out drapes, flowers growing on the balcony, terry-cloth robes, and morning newspaper. No tour groups or conventions stop here; the Wedgewood's clients are almost exclusively corporate, except on weekends, when the place turns into a couple's retreat. Health facilities are next door at the excellent Chancery Squash Club. The lounge and restaurant couldn't be better. It's a treasure. *845 Hornby St., V6Z 1V1, tel. 604/689–7777 or 800/663–0666, fax 604/688–3074. 60 doubles, 33 suites. Facilities: 2 restaurants, bar, use of the adjacent Chancery Squash Club with 7 squash courts, weight room, aerobics, sauna, and whirlpool. AE, DC, MC, V.*

Moderate **Days Inn.** For the businessperson looking for a bargain, this location is tops. The six-story hotel, which opened as the Abbotsford in 1920, is the only moderately priced hotel in the business core. Recent renovations of the guest rooms and the lobby have made this accommodation even more agreeable. Although it's a basic hotel, rooms are bright, clean, and functional; standard units are very large, but there is no room service and few amenities. Suites 310, 410, 510, and 610 have a harbor view. The bar, the **Bombay Bicycle Club,** is a favorite with businesspeople. *921 W. Pender St., V6C 1M2, tel. 604/681–4335, fax 604/681–7808. 74 doubles, 11 suites. Facilities: restaurant, 2 bars, free overnight parking. AE, DC, MC, V.*

★ **English Bay Inn.** The newly renovated 1930s Tudor house in which this inn sits is one block from the ocean and Stanley Park in a quiet residential part of the West End. The five small guest rooms—each with private bath—have wonderful sleigh beds with matching armoires, Ralph Lauren linen, and alabaster lighting fixtures. The common areas are generous and elegantly furnished: The sophisticated but cozy parlor has wingback chairs, a fireplace, and French doors opening onto the front garden. A small, sunny English country garden graces the back of the inn. Breakfast is served in a rather formal dining room furnished with a Gothic dining room suite, a fireplace, and an 18th-century grandfather clock. *1968 Comox St., V6G 1R4, tel. 604/683–8002. 5 rooms. Facilities: off-street parking. AE, MC, V.*

★ **Hotel Georgia.** This handsome 12-story hotel, built in 1927, has such Old World features as a dark-wood-paneled lobby, ornate brass elevators, and a subdued, genteel atmosphere. Although it's lacking in extra amenities, the Georgia is a reliable and satisfactory deal. Rooms are small but well furnished, with nothing worn around the edges. Executive rooms have an almost separate seating area; rooms facing the art gallery have the best views. From this hotel (situated across from the Four Seasons) it's a five-minute walk to the business district. *801 W. Georgia St., V6C 1P7, tel. 604/682–5566 or 800/663–1111, fax 604/682–8192. 310 doubles, 4 suites. Facilities: restaurant, 3 bars. AE, DC, MC, V.*

★ **West End Guest House.** Judge this lovely Victorian house, built in 1906, by its gracious front parlor, cozy fireplace, and early 1900s furniture rather than by its bright pink exterior. Most of the small but extraordinarily handsome rooms have high brass beds, antiques, gorgeous linens, and dozens of old framed pictures of Vancouver. However, avoid the basement rooms. All units have phones, TVs, modern bathrooms, and newly papered walls. There's a veranda for people watching, and a back deck for sunbathing. A full breakfast is included and can be served in bed. The inn's genial host, Evan Penner, has learned that it is the little things that make the difference, including a predinner glass of sherry, duvets and feather mattress-pads, terry bathrobes, hand-knit slippers, turn-down service, and a goodnight tart. The inn is in a residential neighborhood that is a 15-minute walk from downtown and Stanley Park and two minutes from Robson Street. This is a nonsmoking establishment. *1362 Haro St., V6E 1G2, tel. 604/681–2889, fax 604/688–8812. 7 rooms. Facilities: off-street parking. AE, MC, V.*

Inexpensive **Buchan Hotel.** This three-story 1930s building is conveniently
★ set in a tree-lined residential street a block from Stanley Park, a block from shops and restaurants on Denman Street, and a 15-minute walk from the liveliest part of Robson Street. The hallways appear a bit institutional, but the rooms are bright and clean. Furnishings, in good condition, consist of a color TV and a wood-grained arborite desk and chest of drawers. The

rooms are small and the bathrooms tiny. None of the rooms have phones and you have to park on the street, but with this location you probably won't use your car much. Rooms on the east side are brightest and overlook a park; front corner rooms are the biggest. A popular restaurant with an eclectic menu is in the basement and is open for dinner. *1906 Haro St., V6G 1H7, tel. 604/685-5354 or 800/668-6654, fax 604/685-5367. 60 rooms, 30 with private bath. Facilities: TV lounge, laundry room. AE, DC, MC, V.*

The Kingston. The Kingston is a small budget hotel in a location convenient for shopping. It is an old-style, four-story hotel, with no elevator—the type of establishment you'd find in Europe. The Spartan rooms are small and immaculate and share a bathroom down the hall. All rooms have phones but no TVs. Rooms on the south side are brighter. Continental breakfast is included. *757 Richards St., V6B 3A6, tel. 604/684-9024, fax 604/684-9917. 60 rooms, 7 with bath. Facilities: sauna, coin-op laundry, TV lounge, free nighttime parking. AE, MC, V.*

★ **Sylvia Hotel.** Perhaps the Sylvia Hotel is the best bargain in Vancouver, but don't count on staying here June–August unless you've booked six months ahead. What makes this hotel so popular are its low rates and near-perfect location: about 25 feet from the beach, 200 feet from Stanley Park, and a 20-minute walk from downtown. Vancouverites are particularly fond of the eight-story ivy-covered brick building—it was once the tallest building in the West End and the first to open a cocktail bar in the city, in 1954. It's part of the local history and was declared a protected heritage building in the 1970s. Rooms are unadorned and have basic plain furnishings that have probably been around for more than 20 years—not much to look at, but the view and price make it worthwhile. Suites are huge, and all have kitchens, making this a perfect family accommodation. There is little difference between the old and new wings. *1154 Gilford St., V6G 2P6, tel. 604/681-9321. 97 doubles, 18 suites. Facilities: restaurant, lounge, parking. AE, DC, MC, V.*

The Arts and Nightlife

For information on events, look in the entertainment section of the *Vancouver Sun;* also, Thursday's paper has complete listings in the **"What's On"** column, and there's the **Arts Hotline** (tel. 604/684–ARTS). For tickets to major events, book through **Ticketmaster** (tel. 604/280–3311).

The Arts

Theater The **Vancouver Playhouse** (Hamilton St., tel. 604/872–6622) is the most established venue in Vancouver. The **Arts Club Theatre** (tel. 604/687–1644), with two stages on Granville Island (1585 Johnston St.) and performances all year, is the most active. Both feature mainstream theatrical shows. **Carousel Theater** (tel. 604/669–3410), which performs off-off Broadway shows at the Waterfront Theatre (1405 Anderson St.) on Granville Island, and **Touchstone** (tel. 604/687–8737), at the Firehall Theater (280 E. Cordova St.), are smaller but lively companies. The **Back Alley Theatre** (751 Thurlow St., tel. 604/688–7013) hosts **Theatresports,** a hilarious improv event. The **Vancouver East Cultural Centre** (1895 Venables St., tel. 604/254–9578) is a multipurpose performance space that always hosts high-caliber shows.

Music The **Vancouver Symphony Orchestra** (tel. 604/684–9100) and the **CBC Orchestra** (tel. 604/662–6000) play at the restored **Orpheum Theatre** (601 Smithe St.). Choral groups like the **Bach Choir** (tel. 604/921–8012), the **Cantata Singers** (no tel.), and the **Vancouver Chamber Choir** (tel. 604/738–6822) play a major role in Vancouver's classical music scene. The **Early Music Society** (tel. 604/732–1610) performs medieval, renaissance, and baroque music throughout the year and hosts the Vancouver Early Music Summer Festival, one of the most important early music festivals in North America. Concerts by the **Friends of Chamber Music** (no tel.) and the **Vancouver Recital Society** (tel. 604/736–6034) are always of excellent quality.

Vancouver Opera (tel. 604/682–2871) stages four productions a year, usually in October, January, March, and May, at the **Queen Elizabeth Theatre** (600 Hamilton St.). Productions are high caliber with both local and imported talent.

Dance Watch for **Ballet BC's Dance Alive!** series, presenting visiting or local ballet companies (from the Kirov to Ballet BC). Most performances by these companies can be seen at the Orpheum or the Queen Elizabeth Theatre (*see above*). Local modern dance companies worth seeing are **Karen Jamison, Judith Marcuse,** and **JumpStart.**

Film Two theaters have distinguished themselves by avoiding the regular movie fare: **Ridge Theatre** (3131 Arbutus St., tel. 604/738–6311), which generally plays foreign films and rerun double-bills, and **Pacific Cinématèque Pacifique** (1131 Howe St., tel. 604/688–3456), which goes for even more esoteric foreign and art films. The **Vancouver International Film Festival** (tel. 604/685–0260) is held in September and October in several theaters around town.

Nightlife

Bars and Lounges The **Gérard Lounge** (845 Burrard St., tel. 604/682–5511) at Le Meridien Hotel is probably the nicest in the city because of its fireplaces, wingback chairs, dark wood, and leather. For spectacular views, head up to the **Roof Lounge** (900 W. Georgia St., tel. 604/684–3131), in the Hotel Vancouver, where a pianist plays nightly. The **Bacchus Lounge** (845 Hornby St., tel. 604/689–7777) in the Wedgewood Hotel is stylish and sophisticated. The **Gallery Lounge** (655 Burrard St., tel. 604/687–6543) in the Hyatt is a genteel bar, with lots of windows letting in the sun and giving views of the action on the bustling street. The **Garden Lounge** (791 W. Georgia St., tel. 604/689–9333) in the Four Seasons is bright and airy with greenery and a waterfall, plus big soft chairs you won't want to get out of. For a more lively atmosphere, try **Joe Fortes** (777 Thurlow St., 604/669–1940), or **Night Court** (801 W. Georgia St., tel. 604/682–5566) in the Georgia Hotel.

The **English Bay Café** (1795 Beach Ave., tel. 604/669–2225) is the place to go to catch the sunset over English Bay. **La Bodega** (1277 Howe St., tel. 604/684–8815), beneath the Château Madrid, is a popular Spanish tapas bar.

Two bars on Granville Island catering to the after-work crowd are **Bridges** (tel. 604/687–4400), near the Public Market, and the upscale **Pelican Bay** (tel. 604/683–7373), in the Granville Island Hotel, at the other end of the island. The **Backstage Lounge** (1585 Johnston St., tel. 604/687–1354), behind the main stage at the Arts Club Theatre, features one of the largest selections of scotches in town, and is the hangout for local and touring musicians and actors.

Music While discos come and go, lines still form every weekend at
Discos **Richard's on Richards** (1036 Richards St., tel. 604/687–6794) for live and taped Top-40 music.

Jazz A jazz and blues hotline (tel. 604/682–0706) gives you current information on concerts and clubs. **Carnegie's** (1619 W. Broadway, tel. 604/733–4141), and the **Alma Street Café** (2505 Alma St., tel. 604/222–2244), both restaurants, are traditional venues with good mainstream jazz. The **Glass Slipper** (185 E. 11th Ave., tel. 604/877–0066) has mainstream to contemporary jazz with a more underground atmosphere.

Rock The **Town Pump** (66 Water St., tel. 604/683–6695) is the main venue for local and touring rock bands. The **Soft Rock Café** (1925 W. 4th Ave., tel. 604/736–8480) is decidedly more upscale. There's live music with dinner. The **86th Street Music Hall** (750 Pacific Blvd., tel. 604/683–8687) serves up big-name bands. The **Commodore Ballroom** (870 Granville St., tel. 604/681–7838), a Vancouver institution, has been restored to its original, art deco style and offers live music ranging from B.B. King to zydeco bands.

Casinos A few casinos have been licensed recently in Vancouver, and proceeds go to local charities and arts groups. No alcohol is served. Downtown there are the **Royal Diamond Casino** (535 Davie St., tel. 604/685–2340) and the **Great Canadian Casino** (2477 Heather St., tel. 604/872–5543) in the Holiday Inn.

Comedy Yuk Yuks (750 Pacific Blvd., tel. 604/687–5233) is good for a few laughs. Punchlines Comedy Theatre (15 Water St., tel. 604/684–3015), another fun place, is in Gastown.

Excursion to Victoria

Important Addresses and Numbers

Tourist **Tourism Victoria** (812 Wharf St., Victoria V8W 1T3, tel. 604/
Information 382–2127 or 800/663–3883).

Emergencies Dial **911** in Victoria.

Hospitals **Victoria General Hospital** (35 Helmcken St., tel. 604/727–4181).

Late-night All-night pharmacies are unknown in British Columbia, even in
Pharmacies the largest cities, although some pharmacies do offer after-hours emergency numbers. Generally, emergency prescriptions can be filled through major hospitals. McGill and Orme Pharmacies (649 Fort St., tel. 604/384–1195) could provide assistance.

Arriving and Departing by Plane

Airports and **Victoria International Airport** serves Victoria. **Air Canada** (tel.
Airlines 604/360–9074; in the U.S., 800/458–5811) and **Canadian Airlines International** (tel. 604/382–6111; in the U.S., 800/426–

7000) are the two dominant carriers. **Air B.C.** (tel. 604/360–9074; in the U.S., 800/663–0522) provides both airport-to-airport and harbor-to-harbor service from Vancouver to Victoria at least hourly. Both flights take about 35 minutes. **Air B.C.** is the major regional line and runs daily flights between Seattle and Victoria. **Helijet Airways** (tel. 604/382–6222) helicopter service is available from downtown Vancouver to downtown Victoria.

Arriving and Departing by Car, Bus, and Boat

By Car The TransCanada Highway, Route 1, runs south from Nanaimo to Victoria. Route 14 connects Sooke to Port Renfrew, on the West Coast of Vancouver Island, with Victoria.

By Bus **Greyhound** (tel. 604/388–5348; in Seattle, 206/624–3456) connects destinations throughout British Columbia with cities and towns throughout the Pacific North Coast.

By Boat **BC Ferries** (tel. 604/656–0757) travel year-round from Tsawwassen, just south of Vancouver, to Swartz Bay, a 30-minute trip by car or bus from Victoria.

Sealink Express (tel. 604/687–6925) offers high-speed (2 ½-hour) catamaran service between downtown Vancouver and downtown Victoria. One-way fares for adults are $32.95, and round-trip is $59.95.

There is year-round passenger service (closed Christmas) between Victoria and Seattle via the *Victoria Clipper* (tel. 800/888–2535).

Washington State Ferries (tel. in Victoria, 604/656–1551; in Seattle, 206/464–6400) cross daily, year-round, between Sidney, just north of Victoria, and Anacortes, WA. **Black Ball Transport** (tel. in Victoria, 604/386–2202; in Seattle, 206/622–2222) operates between Victoria and Port Angeles, WA.

Getting Around

For the most part, Victoria is a walker's city; most of its main attractions are downtown or are a few blocks from the core. Attractions on the outskirts of downtown can easily be reached by bus or a short cab ride (though taxis can be alarmingly expensive). In the summer you have the added option of horse-drawn carriage, bicycle, boat, or double-decker bus tours.

By Bus The **BC Transit System** (tel. 604/382–6161) runs a fairly extensive service throughout Victoria and the surrounding areas, with an all-day pass that costs $4 for adults, $3 for students and senior citizens. Passes are sold at many outlets in downtown Victoria, including Eaton Centre and Harbour Square Ticket Centre.

Guided Tours

Tally-ho Horsedrawn Tours (tel. 604/479–1113) offers visitors a get- acquainted session with downtown Victoria that includes Beacon Hill Park.

Exploring Victoria

Numbers in the margin correspond to points of interest on the Downtown Victoria map.

Victoria, originally Fort Victoria, was the first European settlement on Vancouver Island and is the oldest city on Canada's west coast. It was chosen in 1842 by James Douglas to be the Hudson's Bay Company's most western outpost, and it became the capital of British Columbia in 1868. Today it's a compact seaside town laced with tea shops and gardens. Though it's quite touristy during the high summer season, it's also at its prettiest, with flowers hanging from turn-of-the-century building posts and strollers feasting on the beauty of Victoria's natural harbor.

❶ A logical place to begin this tour is at the **Visitors Information Centre,** located on the waterfront. *812 Wharf St., tel. 604/382–2127. Open July, Aug., daily 9–9; May, June, Sept., Oct., daily 9–7; Nov.–Apr., daily 9–5.*

❷ Just across the way is the **Empress Hotel,** which originally opened in 1908, and is a symbol both of the city and of the Canadian Pacific Railway. Designed by Francis Rattenbury, whose works dot Victoria, the property is another of the great châteaux built by Canadian Pacific, the still-current owners who also built the Château Frontenac in Québec City, Château Laurier in Ottawa, and Château Lake Louise in Alberta. The $45 million face-lift was a hot topic of discussion in traditional Victoria, though not all of the comments have been positive: For contrast, take a pleasant stroll through the modern, elegantly designed Victoria Conference Centre at the south end of the Empress. Criticism aside, the ingredients that made the 488-room hotel a tourist attraction in the past are still alive. Stop in for high tea—served at hour-and-a-half intervals during the afternoon. *721 Government St., tel. 604/384–8111. Proper dress required; no jeans, shorts, or T-shirts.*

Around the corner from the Empress is **Miniature World,** on Humboldt Street, where small replicas of people, trains, and historic events are displayed. The exhibit seems at times like a mix of fact and fiction, with the models laid out so delicately. *649 Humboldt St., tel. 604/385–9731. Admission: $6.50 adults, $5.50 children 12–17, $4.50 children 4–11, disabled persons with escort free. Open mid-June–mid-Sept., daily 8:30–10 PM; mid-Sept.–mid-June, daily 9–5.*

❸ A short walk around the harbor leads you to the old CPR Steamship Terminal, also designed by Rattenbury and completed in 1924. Today it is the **Royal London Wax Museum,** housing more than 200 wax figures, including replicas of Queen Victoria, Elvis, and Marilyn Monroe. *470 Belleville St., tel. 604/388–4461. Admission: $6.50 adults, $5.50 students and senior citizens, $3.50 children 5–12. Open May–Aug., daily 9–9; Sept.–Apr., daily 9–5.*

❹ Next to the wax museum is the **Pacific Undersea Gardens,** where more than 5,000 marine specimens are on display in their natural habitat. You also get performing scuba divers and a giant Pacific octopus. Unfortunately, there are no washrooms, and the site is not wheelchair accessible. *490 Belleville St., tel. 604/382–5717. Admission: $6 adults, $5.50 senior citizens, $4.50 children 12–17, $2.75 children 5–11. Open Oct.–end of*

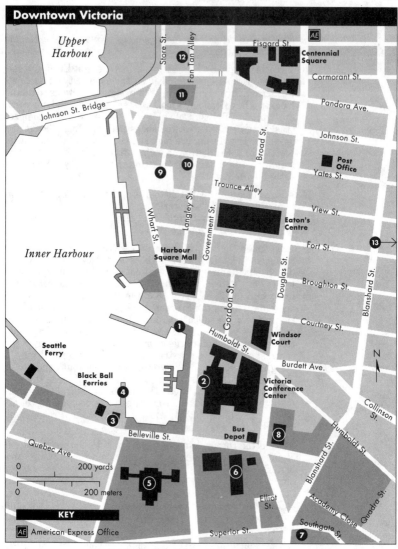

Downtown Victoria

Upper Harbour

Inner Harbour

Johnson St. Bridge

Store St.

Fan Tan Alley

Fisgard St.

Centennial Square

Cormorant St.

Pandora Ave.

Johnson St.

Post Office

Yates St.

Broad St.

Trounce Alley

View St.

Eaton's Centre

Langley St.

Government St.

Wharf St.

Fort St.

Harbour Square Mall

Broughton St.

Blanshard St.

Gordon St.

Douglas St.

Courtney St.

Humboldt St.

Windsor Court

Seattle Ferry

Black Ball Ferries

Belleville St.

Burdett Ave.

Victoria Conference Center

N

Collinson St.

Quebec Ave.

Bus Depot

0   200 yards

0   200 meters

Elliot St.

Humboldt St.

Blanshard St.

Academy Close

Quadra St.

Southgate St.

Superior St.

KEY

AE American Express Office

Bastion Square, **9**

Beacon Hill Park, **7**

Chinatown, **12**

Craigdarroch Castle, **13**

Crystal Gardens, **8**

Empress Hotel, **2**

Legislative/ Parliament Buildings, **5**

Maritime Museum, **10**

Market Square, **11**

Pacific Undersea Garden, **4**

Royal British Columbia Museum, **6**

Royal London Wax Museum, **3**

Visitors Information Centre, **1**

May, daily 10–5; summer, daily 9–9; closed Christmas. Shows run about every 45 minutes.

❺ Across Belleville Street is the **Legislative Parliament Buildings** complex. The stone-exterior building, completed in 1897, dominates the inner harbor and is flanked by two statues: Sir James Douglas, who chose the location of Victoria, and Sir Matthew Baille Begbie, the man in charge of law and order during the gold-rush era. Atop the central dome is a gilded statue of Captain George Vancouver, who first sailed around Vancouver Island; a statue of Queen Victoria stands in front of the complex; and outlining the building at night are more than 3,000 lights. Another of Rattenbury's creations, the complex gives a good example of the rigid symmetry and European elegance that characterize much of the city's architecture. The public can watch the assembly, when it's in session, from the galleries overlooking the Legislative Chamber. *501 Belleville St., tel. 604/387–3046. Admission free. Tours run several times daily and are conducted in at least 4 languages in summer and 3 in winter. Open Sept.–June, weekdays 8:30–5; summer, daily 8:30–5:30.*

❻ Follow Belleville Street one block east to reach the **Royal British Columbia Museum.** Adults and children can wander for hours through the centuries, back 12,000 years. In the prehistoric exhibit, you can actually smell the pines and hear the calls of mammoths and other ancient wildlife. Other exhibits allow you to explore a turn-of-the-century town, with trains rumbling past; in the Kwakiutl Indian Bighouse, the smell of cedar envelops you, while piped-in potlatch songs tell the origins of the genuine ceremonial house before you. *675 Belleville St., tel. 604/387–3014. Admission: Free Mon., Oct.–Apr.; otherwise $5 adults, $3 students and senior citizens, $2 children 6–18 and disabled persons. Open Oct.–Apr., daily 10–5:30; May–Sept., daily 9:30–7; closed Christmas.*

The **Newcombe Theatre** behind the museum presents slide talks and films. *Tel. 604/387–5822. Admission by donation.*

❼ A walk east on Belleville Street to Douglas Street will lead you to **Beacon Hill Park,** a favorite place for joggers, walkers, and cyclists. The park's southern lawns offer one of the best views of the Olympic Mountains and the Strait of Juan de Fuca. There are also lakes, walking paths, abundant flowers, a wading pool, petting zoo, and an outdoor amphitheater for Sunday-afternoon concerts.

❽ From the park, go north on Douglas Street and stop off at the **Crystal Gardens.** Opened in 1925 as the largest swimming pool in the British Empire, this glass-roof building—now owned by the provincial government—is home to flamingos, macaws, 75 varieties of other birds, hundreds of blooming flowers, penguins, and monkeys. At street level there are several boutiques and Rattenbury's Restaurant, one of Victoria's well-frequented establishments. *713 Douglas St., tel. 604/381–1213. Admission: $3 adults, $2 children 6–16 and senior citizens. Open Oct.–Apr., daily 10–5:30; summer, daily 9–9.*

❾ From Crystal Gardens continue on Douglas Street going north to View Street, west to **Bastion Square,** with its gas lamps, restaurants, cobblestone streets, and small shops. This is the spot James Douglas chose as the original Fort Victoria in 1843 and the original Hudson's Bay Company trading post. Today fashion boutiques and restaurants occupy the old buildings. At the Wharf Street end of the square are some benches where you can rest your feet and catch a great view of the harbor. While you're here, you may want to stop in at what was Victoria's original courthouse but is now the **Maritime Museum of British Columbia.** Dugout canoes, model ships, Royal Navy charts, photographs, uniforms, and ship's bells chronicle Victoria's seafaring history. A seldom-used 100-year-old cage lift, believed to be the oldest in North America, ascends to the third floor. In 1995, however, a new museum is scheduled to open and replace this facility. *28 Bastion Sq., tel. 604/385–4222. Admission: $5 adults, $3 children 12–17, $2 children 6–11. Open Oct. 1–May 31, daily 9:30–4:30; June 1–Sept. 30, daily 9–6. Closed Christmas and New Year's Day.*

West of Government Street, between Pandora Avenue and Johnson Street, is **Market Square,** offering a variety of specialty shops and boutiques and considered one of the most picturesque shopping districts in the city. At the turn of the century this area—once part of Chinatown—provided everything a visitor desired: food, lodging, entertainment. Today the square has been restored to its original, pre-1900s character.

Just around the corner from Market Square is Fisgard Street, the heart of one of the oldest **Chinatown**s in Canada. It was the Chinese who were responsible for building much of the Canadian Pacific Railway in the 19th century, and their influences still mark the region. If you enter Chinatown from Government Street, you'll walk under the elaborate **Gate of Harmonious Interest,** made from Taiwanese ceramic tiles and decorative panels. Along the street, merchants display fragile paper lanterns, embroidered silks, imported fruits, and vegetables. **Fan Tan Alley,** situated just off Fisgard Street, holds claim not only to being the narrowest street in Canada but also to having been the gambling and opium center of Chinatown, where mahjongg, fantan, and dominoes games were played.

A 15-minute walk or a short drive east on Fort Street will take you to Joan Crescent, where **Craigdarroch Castle** stands. This lavish mansion was built as the home of British Columbia's first millionaire, Robert Dunsmuir, who oversaw coal mining for the Hudson's Bay Company. (He died before the castle's completion in about 1890.) Recently converted into a museum depicting turn-of-the-century life-style, the castle is strikingly authentic, with elaborately framed landscape paintings, stained-glass windows, carved woodwork—precut in Chicago for Dunsmuir and sent by rail—and rooms for billiards and smoking. The location offers a wonderful view of downtown Victoria from the fifth-floor tower; guided tours are given. *1050 Joan Crescent, Victoria, tel. 604/592–5323. Admission: $5.50 adults, $4.50 students, children under 12 by donation. Open mid-June–Aug., daily 9–7:30; Sept.–mid-June, daily 10–5.*

What to See and Do with Children

Anne Hathaway's Cottage, tucked away in a unique English village complex, is a full-size replica of the original thatched home in Stratford-Upon-Avon, England. The building and the 16th-century antiques inside are typical of Shakespeare's era. The Olde England Inn, on the grounds, is a pleasant spot for tea or a traditional English-style meal. You can also stay ($68–$184;

AE, DC, MC, V) in one of the 50 antiques-furnished rooms, some complete with four-poster beds. *429 Lampson St., Victoria, V9A 5Y9, tel. 604/388–4353. Admission: $5.75 adults, $3.50 senior citizens and children 8–17, children under 8 free. Open June–Sept., daily 9–9; rest of year, daily 10–4. Guided tours leave from the inn during the winter and directly from the cottage in summer. From downtown Victoria, take the Munro bus to the door.*

Pacific Undersea Gardens (*see* Exploring Victoria, *above*).

Swan Lake Christmas Hill Nature Sanctuary. This 23-acre lake, set within 110 acres of open fields and wetlands out Blanshard Street, is 10 minutes from downtown. From the 1½-mile chip trail and floating boardwalk, birders can spot a variety of waterfowl in winter and nesting birds in the tall grasses. Children will enjoy the displays and games in the nature house. *3873 Swan Lake Rd. (take the No. 70/No. 75 bus), tel. 604/479–0211. Admission free. Open year-round; nature House open Mon.–Fri. 8:30–4; weekends and holidays 12–4.*

Off The Beaten Track

Butchart Gardens, situated on the 130-acre Butchart estate about 21 kilometers (13 miles) north of downtown Victoria, offers more than 700 varieties of flowers and includes Italian, Japanese, and English rose gardens. During the summer, many of the exhibits are illuminated at night. Once a limestone quarry, the grounds were transformed in 1904 when Canadian cement pioneer Robert Butchart began building bridges and walkways and planting shrubs and flowers on the 50-acre (20-hectare) site. The grounds are lighted with beautiful displays during the Christmas season. Also on the premises are a gift shop, teahouse, and restaurants. *800 Benvenuto Ave., Victoria, tel. 604/652–5256. Admission: $9.50 adults, $5 children 12–17, $1 children under 12 excluding GST.*

Shopping

Shopping in Victoria is easy: Virtually everything can be found in the downtown area, beginning at the Empress and walking north along Government Street. In succession you'll hit **Roger's Chocolates** (tel. 604/384–7021), for fine chocolates; **George Straith Ltd.** (tel. 604/384–6912), for woolens; **Edinburgh Tartan Shop** (tel. 604/388–9312), for traditional Scottish clothing and accessories; **Gallery of the Arctic** (tel. 604/382–9012), for good-quality Inuit art; **Munro's Books** (tel. 604/382–2464), for the best selection of Victoriana in the city; and **Old Morris Tobacconist, Ltd.** (tel. 604/382–4811), for unusual pipe tobacco blends.

On the block of Douglas Street behind the Empress are shops like the exclusive **G. Gagliano of Florence,** with beautiful Italian leather goods; **LeJame Fashions,** with clothing designed and manufactured in Victoria, and the **Stephen Lowe Art Gallery.** Handy, also, is the **Currency Exchange,** which is open daily. The **Eaton Centre** at Government and Fort streets is both a department store and a series of small boutiques, with a total of 140 shops and restaurants. Market Square, between Johnson and Pandora, has three stories of specialty shops.

At last count, Victoria had 60-plus **antiques shops** specializing in coins, stamps, estate jewelry, rare books, crystal, china, furniture, or paintings and other works of art. A short walk on Fort Street going away from the harbor will take you to **Antique Row** between Blanshard and Cook streets. **Waller Antiques** (tel. 604/388–6116) and **Newberry Antiques** (tel. 604/388–7732) offer a wide selection of furniture and collectibles. You will also find antiques on the west side of Government Street near the **Old Town.**

A 10-minute drive (or the No. 1/No. 2 bus) from downtown out Fort Street to Oak Bay Avenue will take you to one of the few residential shopping areas that is not a mall. The **Oak Bay Village** is great for browsing, buying, or an afternoon *cuppa'*. Start at the corner of Oak Bay and Foul Bay and work your way east toward the water.

Sports and Outdoor Activities

Golf   Though **Victoria Golf Club** (1110 Beach Dr., Victoria, tel. 604/598–4321) is private, it's open to other private-club members. This windy course is the oldest (built in 1893) in British Columbia and offers a spectacular view of the Strait of Juan de Fuca. **Uplands Golf Club** (3300 Cadboro Bay Rd., Victoria, tel. 604/592–1818) is a flat, semiprivate course (it becomes public after 2). **Cedar Hill Municipal** (1400 Derby Rd., Victoria, tel. 604/595–3103) is a public course with up-and-down terrain. **Royal Oak Golf Club** (4680 Elk Lake Dr., Victoria, tel. 604/658–1433) is the newest nine-hole course in the area. **Gorge Vale Golf Club** (1005 Craigflower Rd., Victoria, tel. 604/386–3401) is a semiprivate course but is open to the public. It has punitive traps and a deep gorge that eats up golf balls. **Glen Meadows Golf and Country Club** (1050 McTavish Rd., Sidney, tel. 604/656–3921), situated near the ferry terminal, is a semiprivate course that's open to the public at select times.

Dining and Lodging

Dining   For prices see Dining chart for Vancouver, *above.*

Chez Daniel. One of Victoria's old standbys, Chez Daniel offers dishes that are rich, though the nouvelle influence has found its way into a few of the offerings. The interior, following a burgundy color scheme, seems to match the traditional rich, caloric cuisine. The wine list is varied, and the menu has a wide selection of basic dishes: rabbit, salmon, duck, steak. This is a restaurant where you linger for the evening in the romantic atmosphere. *2524 Estevan Ave., tel. 604/592–7424. Reservations advised. Jacket advised. AE, MC, V. Closed lunch and Sun.–Mon. Expensive.*

Chez Pierre. Established in 1973, this is the oldest French restaurant in Victoria, and the downtown location, combined with an intimate, rustic decor, creates a pleasant ambience. House specialties include *canard à l'orange* (duckling in orange sauce), rack of lamb, and British Columbia salmon. Although a tourist destination, this restaurant has managed to maintain its high quality over the years. *512 Yates, tel. 604/388–7711. Reservations advised. Dress: casual but neat. AE, MC, V. Closed lunch and Sun.–Mon. Moderate–Expensive.*

Swan's Café. Here's a good choice for a casual meal with Mediterranean and pan-Pacific flair. Inside the historic building in which the café is housed are lavish bouquets of fresh flowers and original artwork collected by owner Michael Williams. Creatively prepared salads and succulent stir-fries are recommended. The brew pub on the premises sometimes features live music and is the busiest pub in the city. *506 Pandora Ave., tel. 604/361-3310. Reservations accepted. Dress: casual. MC, V. Moderate–Expensive.*

Camilles. This restaurant is romantic, intimate, and one of the few West Coast–cuisine restaurants in Victoria. House specialties such as chicken Napoli, papaya brochettes (prawns wrapped around chunks of papaya in a lime and jalapeño marinade), phyllo-wrapped salmon (fresh fillet of salmon in phyllo pastry) are all served in generous portions. Camilles also has an extensive wine cellar, uncommon in Victoria. *45 Bastion Sq., tel. 604/381-3433. Reservations advised. Dress: casual but neat. MC, V. Closed lunch and Sun.–Mon. Moderate.*

French Connection. Located in one of Victoria's Heritage homes, built in 1884, the restaurant has maintained the character of the time. From the outside, ornate details indicate the French tradition that you will find in the service and on the menu. The food is prepared with care, with an emphasis on the sauces. *512 Simcoe St., tel. 604/385-7014. Reservations required. Dress: casual. AE, MC, V. Closed Sat.–Mon. lunch and Sun. Moderate.*

★ **La Ville d'Is.** This historic brick building houses one of the best seafood restaurants in Victoria. Both the quality and price are right. Run by Michel Duteau, a Brittany native, the restaurant is cozy and friendly, with an outside café open May–October. An extensive, imaginative wine list features bottles from the Loire Valley that go well with the seafood, rabbit, lamb, and beef tenderloin specials. Try the *perche de la Nouvelle Zélande* (orange roughie in muscadet with herbs) or lobster soufflé for a unique taste. *26 Bastion Sq., tel. 604/388-9414. Reservations advised. Dress: casual but neat. AE, MC, V. Closed Sun. and Jan. Moderate.*

★ **Pagliacci's.** If you want Italian food, Pagliacci's is a must. Featured are dozens of pasta dishes, quiches, veal, and chicken in marsala sauce with fettuccine. The pastas are freshly made in-house. The orange-color walls are covered with photos of Hollywood stars, so there's always something to look at here. *1011 Broad St., tel. 604/386-1662. No reservations. Dress: casual. MC, V. Moderate.*

Blethering Place. Next to a teddy bear shop in Oak Bay is this clubby, neighborhood restaurant populated by dignified ladies sipping afternoon tea and blethering over crumpets, tarts, and scones. The menu points out that "blethering" is Scottish for "voluble, senseless talking." Later, neighborhood families stroll in for a dinner of steak-and-kidney pie, East Indian curries, and wonderfully rich desserts. Wines from British Columbia are featured. *2250 Oak Ave., tel. 604/598-1413. Reservations advised. Dress: casual but neat. AE, MC, V. Inexpensive–Moderate.*

Don Mee's. A large neon sign signals guests to Don Mee, a traditional Chinese restaurant. The long, red staircase leads to an expansive, comfortable restaurant for entrées such as sweet-and-sour chicken, almond duck, and bean curd with broccoli. *538 Fisgard St., tel. 604/383-1032. Reservations accepted. Dress: casual. MC, V. Inexpensive–Moderate.*

Le Petite Saigon. This is a small, intimate café-style restaurant, offering a quiet dining experience with beautifully presented meals and a fare that is primarily Vietnamese, with a touch of

French. The crab, asparagus, and egg swirl soup is a specialty of the house, and combination meals are cheap and tasty. *1010 Langley St., tel. 604/386–1412. Dress: casual. AE, MC, V. Closed Sat. lunch and Sun. Inexpensive–Moderate.*

Cafe Mexico. Hearty portions of Mexican food, such as *pollo chipolte* (grilled chicken with melted cheddar and spicy sauce, on a bed of rice) are served inside this spacious, redbrick dining establishment, situated just off the waterfront. Bullfight ads and cactus plants decorate the restaurant and reinforce its character and Mexican theme. *1425 Store St., tel. 604/386–5454. Reservations accepted. Dress: casual. AE, MC, V. Inexpensive.*

Periklis. Standard Greek cuisine is offered in this warm, taverna-style restaurant, but there are also steaks and ribs on the menu. On the weekends you can enjoy Greek and belly dancing, but be prepared for the hordes of people who come for the entertainment. *531 Yates St., tel. 604/386–3313. Reservations accepted. Dress: casual. Closed weekend lunch; during summer, open Sat. lunch. AE, MC, V. Inexpensive.*

★ **Six-Mile-House.** This 1855 carriage house is a Victoria landmark. The brass, carved oak moldings and stained glass set a festive mood for the evening. The menu is constantly changing but always features seafood selections and burgers. Try the cider or one of the many international beers offered. *494 Island Hwy., tel. 604/478–3121. Reservations accepted. Dress: casual. MC, V. Inexpensive.*

Lodging

Category	Cost*
Very Expensive	over $180
Expensive	$110–$179
Moderate	$70–$109
Inexpensive	under $70

*All prices are for a standard double room for two, excluding 10% provincial accommodation tax, service charge, and 7% GST.

★ **The Empress Hotel.** This is Victoria's dowager queen with a face-lift. First opened in 1908, the hotel underwent a $45 million dollar renovation in 1989 that enhanced its Edwardian charm, updated existing guest rooms, and added some 45 new ones. Stained glass, carved archways, and hardwood floors are used effectively. The Empress dominates the inner-harbor area and is the city's primary meeting place for politicians, locals, and tourists. From the Lobby Lounge, guests can have a splendid view of the harbor. Afternoon tea has been a tradition here since 1908, but it's so popular today, reservations are a must. The Bengal Lounge is full of colonial charm from British India, including a stuffed Bengal tiger, overhead fans, and mosquito netting. *721 Government St., V8W 1W5, in Canada, tel. 604/384–8111 or 800/268–9411; in the U.S., 800/828–7447; fax 604/381–4334. 481 rooms. Facilities: 2 restaurants, café, 2 lounges, conference center, indoor pool, sauna, health club, in-room movies, cable TV, Christmas discount, family discount. AE, DC, MC, V. Very Expensive.*

★ **Abigail's.** A Tudor country inn with gardens and crystal chandeliers, Abigail's is not only lovely but also conveniently located four blocks east of downtown. All guest rooms are prettily detailed with a contemporary color schemes. Down comforters, together with Jacuzzis and fireplaces in some, add to the pampering atmosphere. There's a sense of elegant informality about the hotel, noticed especially in the guest library and sitting room, where you'll want to spend an hour or so relaxing in the evening. Breakfast, included in the room rate, is served from 8 to 9:30 in the downstairs dining room. *906 McClure St., V8V 3E7, tel. 604/388–5363; fax 604/361–1905. 16 rooms. MC. Expensive.*

★ **The Beaconsfield Inn.** Built in 1875 and restored in 1984, the Beaconsfield has retained its Old World charm. Dark mahogany wood appears throughout the house; down comforters and some canopy beds and claw-foot tubs adorn the rooms, reinforcing the Edwardian style of this residentially situated inn. Some of the rooms have fireplaces and Jacuzzis. An added plus is the guest library and conservatory/sun room. Full breakfast, with homemade muffins, and a cocktail hour (6–7 PM), with sherry, cheese, and fruit, are included in the room rates. *998 Humboldt St., V8V 2Z8, tel. 604/384–4044; fax 604/361–1908. 12 rooms. Facilities: library, Jacuzzi. MC. Expensive.*

The Bedford Hotel. This European-style hotel, located in the heart of downtown, is reminiscent of San Francisco's small hotels, with personalized service and strict attention to details. In keeping with the theme, rooms follow an earthen color scheme, and many have goose-down comforters, fireplaces, and Jacuzzis. Meeting rooms and small conference facilities are available also, making this a good businessperson's lodging. An extensive breakfast is included in the room rate. *1140 Government St., V8W 1Y2, tel. 604/384–6835 or 800/665–6500; fax 604/386–8930. 40 rooms. Facilities: restaurant, pub. AE, MC, V. Expensive.*

Chateau Victoria. This 19-story hotel, situated across from Victoria's new Conference Centre, near the inner harbor and the Royal British Columbia Museum, promises wonderful views from its upper rooms and its rooftop restaurant. Following a Victorian motif, the rooms are warm and spacious, some with balconies or sitting areas and kitchenettes. *740 Burdett Ave., V8W 1B2, tel. 604/382–4221 or 800/663–5891; fax 604/380–1950. 178 rooms. Facilities: restaurants, lounge, indoor pool, whirlpool, meeting rooms, courtesy vans to ferry, access to health club. AE, MC. Expensive.*

Dashwood Manor. If you want a quiet place with a great view, this is it. Located on the waterfront next to Beacon Hill Park, this Heritage Tudor mansion, built in 1912 on property once owned by Governor Sir James Douglas, offers panoramic views of the Strait of Juan de Fuca and the Olympic Mountains. This B&B lacks some of the charm that many offer because the parlor and dining rooms have been made into guest quarters. The only place for guests to congregate is in the tiny office, where sherry or wine is offered in the afternoon. Three guest rooms have fireplaces, and all rooms come with a fully stocked frig; and breakfast is "make your own." *1 Cook St., V8V 3W6, tel. 604/385–5517. 14 rooms. AE, MC. Expensive.*

Mulberry Manor. This Tudor mansion is a special place for a number of reasons: It is the last building to have been designed by Victoria architect Simon McClure; the grounds were designed and, until recently, maintained by a gardener at the world-famous Butchart Gardens; the manor has been restored and decorated to magazine-cover perfection with antiques, sumptuous linens, and tiled baths. Hosts Susan and Tony Temple are charming and provide gourmet breakfasts with home-made jams and great coffee. *611 Foul Bay Rd., V8S 1H2, tel. 604/370–1918. 2 rooms, 2 suites. MC, V. Expensive.*

★ **Holland House Inn.** Two blocks from the inner harbor, legislative buildings, and ferry terminals, this nonsmoking hotel has a sense of casual elegance. Some of the individually designed rooms have original fine art created by the owner, and some have four-poster beds and fireplaces. All rooms have private baths, and all but two have their own balconies. A gourmet breakfast is served and included in room rates. You'll recognize the house by the picket fence around it. *595 Michigan St., V8V 1S7, tel. and fax 604/384–6644. 10 rooms. Facilities: lounge. AE, DC, MC, V. Expensive.*

★ **Hotel Grand Pacific.** This is one of Victoria's newest and finest hotels, with a lot of mahogany woodwork and an elegant ambience. Overlooking the harbor, and adjacent to the legislative buildings, the hotel accommodates business and vacationing people looking for comfort, convenience, and great scenery; all rooms have terraces, with views of either the harbor or the Olympic Mountains. The health club is elaborate, equipped with Nautilus, racquetball court, and sauna. *450 Québec St., V8V 1W5, tel. 604/386–0450 or 800/663–7550; fax 604/383–7603. 149 rooms. Facilities: restaurant, lounge, sauna, whirlpool, fitness center, convention facilities, underground parking, indoor pool. AE, D, DC, MC, V. Expensive.*

Ocean Pointe Resort. Set across the "blue bridge" from downtown Victoria, the resort, with a northern European ambience, opened in the summer of 1992 on the site of an old shingle mill and an area once claimed by the Songhees natives. Public rooms and half of the guest rooms offer romantic evening views of downtown Victoria and the parliament buildings, bedecked with some 3,000 twinkling lights. Guest rooms are spacious and some feature floor-to-ceiling windows and small balconies. The property offers a rich cache of amenities, including hydrotherapy, micronized marine algae body wrap, massages, aerobics, and beauty treatments in the spa. There are salads and sandwiches in the Boardwalk Café; steaks and seafood in the Boardwalk Brasserie; and Pacific Northwest and Continental entrées, along with low-calorie, low-fat spa cuisine in the Victorian Restaurant. *45 Songhees Rd., Victoria V9A 6T3, tel. 604/360–2999 or 800/667–4677; fax 604/360–1041. 213 rooms, 37 housekeeping suites w/kitchens. Facilities: 3 restaurants, lounge, 3 tennis courts, whirlpool, sauna, exercise room, indoor pool, squash and racquetball court, beauty parlor, supervised playroom. Reservations advised in restaurant. MC, V. Expensive.*

Victoria Regent Hotel. Originally built as an apartment, this is now a posh, condo-living hotel that offers views of the harbor or city. The outside is plain, with a glass facade, but the interior is sumptuously decorated with warm earth tones and modern furnishings; each apartment has a living room, dining room, deck, kitchen, and one or two bedrooms with bath. *1234 Wharf St., V8W 3H9, tel. 604/386–2211 or 800/663–7472; fax 604/386–2622. 47 rooms, including 32 suites. Facilities: restaurant, free parking, laundromat. AE, D, DC, MC, V. Expensive.*

Oak Bay Beach Hotel. This Tudor-style hotel in Oak Bay, on the southwest side of the Saanich Peninsula, is well removed from the bustle of downtown. There's a wonderful atmosphere here, though; the hotel, situated oceanside, overlooks the Haro Strait and catches the setting sun. The interior decor is as dreamy as the grounds, with antiques and flower prints decorating the rooms. The restaurant, Tudor Room by the Sea, is average, but the bar with its cozy fireplace is truly romantic. *1175 Beach Dr., V8S 2N2, tel. and fax 604/598–4556. 51 rooms. Facilities: restaurant, pub, yacht for cruises, access to health club. AE, DC, MC, V. Moderate–Very Expensive.*

Admiral Motel. Located on the Victoria harbor and along the tourist strip, this motel is right where the action is, although it is relatively quiet in the evening. If you're looking for a basic, clean lodging, the Admiral is just that. The amicable owners take good care of the newly refurbished rooms, and small pets are permitted. *257 Belleville St., V8V 1X1, tel. 604/388–6267. 29 rooms, 23 with kitchens. Facilities: cable TV, free parking, laundry. AE, D, MC, V. Inexpensive–Moderate.*

★ **Craigmyle Guest House.** At this typical English-style bed-and-breakfast you'll find a casual, homey feeling without expensive designer touches. In the shade of Craigdarroch Castle, about 2 kilometers (1 mile) from the downtown core, this lodge, built in 1913, has a special view of the castle. The rooms are small and simple, but most units have a private bath. The main lounge features high ceilings and a huge fireplace. A hearty English-style breakfast, with homemade preserves, porridge, and eggs is served. Hosts are very friendly and chatty. *1037 Craigdarroch Rd., V8S 2A5, tel. 604/595–5411, fax 604/370–5276. 19 rooms, 15 with private bath. MC, V. Inexpensive–Moderate.*

The Arts and Nightlife

The Arts

Galleries

The **Art Gallery of Greater Victoria** is considered one of Canada's finest art museums and is home both to large collections of Chinese and Japanese ceramics and other art and to the only authentic Shinto shrine in North America. The gallery hosts about 40 different temporary exhibitions yearly. *1040 Moss St., Victoria, tel. 604/384–4101. Admission: $3 adults, $1.50 students and senior citizens, children under 12 free; free Thurs. after 5, though donations are accepted. Open Mon.–Wed. and Fri.–Sat. 10–5, Thurs. 10–9, Sun. 1–5.*

The **Emily Carr Gallery** (under the auspices of the Greater Victoria Gallery) presents the art of and films about this renowned artist, who was a contemporary of the Group of Seven. *1107 Wharf St., Victoria, tel. 604/384–3130.*

Among the numerous commercial galleries, the **Fran Willis North Park Gallery** (200–1619 Store St., tel. 604/381–3422) is a good bet. In a gorgeously restored warehouse near the waterfront, it shows contemporary paintings and sculpture by local artists; music is performed from time to time. For a further look at what's going on in Victoria's art scene, try the **Winchester Galleries** (tel. 604/595–2777), the **Nunavut Gallery** (tel. 604/598–1344), and the **Barton Leir Gallery** (tel. 604/383–6477).

Music

The **Victoria Symphony** has a winter schedule and a summer season, playing in the recently refurbished **Royal Theatre** (805 Broughton St., Victoria, tel. 604/361–0820) and at the **University Centre Auditorium** (Finnerty Rd., Victoria, tel. 604/721–8480). The **Pacific Opera Victoria** performs three productions a year in the 800-seat **McPherson Playhouse** (3 Centennial Sq., tel. 604/386–6121), adjoining the Victoria City Hall. The **Victoria International Music Festival** (tel. 604/736–2119) features internationally acclaimed musicians, dancers, and singers each summer from the first week in July through late August.

The **Victoria Jazz Society** (tel. 604/388–4423) organizes an annual **JazzFest International** in late June, which in the past has featured jazz, blues, and world-beat artists such as Dizzy Gillespie, Frank Morgan, Ellis Marsalis, and Aster Aweke.

For listings of clubs and restaurants featuring jazz during the year, call **Jazz Hotline** (604/658–5255).

Theater Live theater can be seen at the **Belfry Theatre** (1291 Gladstone Ave., Victoria, tel. 604/385–6815), **Phoenix Theatre** (Finnerty Rd., tel. 604/721–8000) at the University of Victoria, **Victoria Theatre Guild** (805 Langham Ct., tel. 604/384–2142), and **McPherson Playhouse** (3 Centennial Sq., tel. 604/386–6121).

Nightlife After 8 PM, **Tudor House Hotel Pub** (533 Admirals Rd., tel. 604/389–9943) becomes a pub attracting the younger set. There's a dance floor and large screen for disco and video entertainment nightly.

Harpo's (15 Bastion Sq., tel. 604/385–5333) features live rock, blues, and jazz, with visits from internationally recognized bands.

Excursion to Whistler

Important Addresses and Numbers

Tourist Information Contact the **Whistler Resort Association** (4010 Whistler Way, Whistler V0N 1B4; in Whistler, tel. 604/932–3928; reservations, tel. 604/932–4222; in the U.S. and Canada, tel. 800/944–7853). In Whistler Village an information booth at the front door of the Conference Center is open 8:30–8.

A provincial government **Travel Infocentre** (tel. 604/932–5528) is on the main highway, about 1 ½ kilometers (a mile) south of Whistler.

Emergencies Dial 0 for **police, ambulance,** or **poison control.**

Arriving and Departing by Car

By Car Arriving time from Seattle to Vancouver is about three hours. Whistler is 1½ to two hours north of Vancouver via Route 99, the Sea-to-Sky Highway.

Getting Around

By Bus **Maverick Coach Lines** (tel. 604/932–5031) has buses leaving every couple of hours from the bus depot in downtown Vancouver. The bus stops at Whistler Village and the fare is under $14 one way. During ski season, the last bus leaves Whistler at 10PM.

Perimiter Bus Transportation (tel. 604/266–5386) has daily service, November–April and June–September from Vancouver Airport to Whistler. Reservations are necessary 24 hours in advance; the ticket booth is on the arrivals level of the airport.

By Train **BC Rail** (tel. 604/932–2134) travels north from Vancouver to Whistler along a beautiful route. The Vancouver Bus Terminal and the North Vancouver Station are connected by bus shuttle.

Exploring Whistler

If you think of skiing when you hear mention of **Whistler,** British Columbia, you're thinking on track. Whistler and Blackcomb mountains, part of the Whistler Resort Association, are the two biggest ski mountains in North America; there's summer glacier skiing, the longest vertical drop in North America, and the most advanced lifts in the world. At the base of the mountains is Whistler Village—a small community of lodgings, restaurants, pubs, gift shops, and boutiques. With more than 60 hotels, most of which are arranged within a five-minute walk between the mountains, the site is frenzied with activity. Culinary options within the village range from burgers to French, Japanese to deli cuisine; and nightly entertainment runs the gamut from sophisticated piano bars to casual pubs.

In the winter, the village buzzes with skiers taking to the slopes in vibrantly colored attire, but as the scenery changes from winter's snow-white to summer's lush-green landscapes, the mood of Whistler changes, too. Things seem to slow down a bit, and the resort sheds some of its competitive edge and welcomes a more relaxed, slower-paced environment. Even the local golf tournaments and the triathlon are interspersed with Mozart and bluegrass festivals.

Adjacent to the area is the 78,000-acre (31,579-hectare) **Garibaldi Provincial Park,** with dense mountainous forests splashed with hospitable lakes and streams. But even if you don't want to roam much farther than the village, there are five lakes for canoeing, fishing, swimming, and windsurfing, and many nearby hiking and mountain-bike trails.

No matter what the season, though, Whistler Village is very accessible to the pedestrian. Anywhere you want to go within the resort is at most five minutes away, and parking lots are just outside the village. The bases of Whistler and Blackcomb mountains are also just at the edge; in fact, you can ski right into the lower level of the Chateau Whistler Hotel, and all 2,700 of the village's hotel rooms are less than 1,000 feet from the lifts.

If you are interested in a tour of the area, **Alpine Adventure Tours** (tel. 604/932–2705) has a Whistler history tour of the valley and a Squamish day trip.

Scenic Drives

Completion of a new highway opened the **Coast Mountain Circle,** linking Vancouver to Cariboo Country. This 702-kilometer (435-mile) route takes in spectacular Howe Sound, the deep-water port of Squamish, Whistler Resort, and Pemberton Valley before heading back to Vancouver through scenic Fraser Canyon and Harrison Hot Springs. The loop makes a comfortable two- to three-day journey. For more information contact the **Tourism Association of Southwestern B.C.** (304–828 W. 8th Ave., Vancouver V52 1E2, tel. 604/876–3088 or 800/667–3306).

Sports and the Outdoors

Canoeing and Kayaking You'll see lots of canoes and kayaks at the many lakes and rivers near **Whistler.** If you want to get in on the fun, rentals are available at Alta Lake at both **Lakeside Park** and **Wayside Park.** Another spot that's perfect for canoeing is the **River of Golden Dreams,** either from Meadow Park to Green Lake or upstream to Twin Bridges. Kayakers looking for a thrill may want to try **Green River** from Green Lake to Pemberton. Call **Whistler Outdoor Experience** (tel. 604/932–3389) or **Sea to Sky Kayaking** (tel. 604/8989–5498) for equipment or guided trips.

Fishing **Whistler Backcountry Adventures** (tel. 604/938–1410) or **Whistler Fishing Guides** (tel. 604/932–4267) will take care of anything you need—equipment, guides, and transportation. All five of the lakes around Whistler are stocked with trout, but the area around **Dream River Park** is one of the most popular fishing spots. Slightly farther afield, try **Cheakamus Lake, Daisy Lake,** and **Callaghan Lake.**

Golf Arnold Palmer designed the par-72 championship **Whistler Golf Course** (tel. 604/932–4544), which is said to be a "good four-iron shot from the village." The course is very scenic, fairly flat, and challenging for the experienced, but pleasant for beginners. The relatively new **Predator Ridge Golf Resort** (360 Commonage Rd., Vernon, tel. 604/542–3436) is a very challenging public course. The area's newest offering, the **Robert Trent Jones Jr. Golf Course** (4599 Chateau Blvd., tel. 604/938–8000), is equally scenic, nestled at the foot of the mountain on the opposite side of Whistler Village.

Skiing Whistler Resort has more than 200 runs along with hotels and
Downhill restaurants, and, like Whistler, is in the process of rapidly expanding. The vertical drops and elevation at **Blackcomb** and **Whistler** mountains are, perhaps, the most impressive features to skiers. Blackcomb has a 5,280-foot vertical drop (North America's longest); Whistler has a 5,020-foot drop. The top elevation is 7,494 feet on Blackcomb and 7,160 on Whistler. These mountains also have the most advanced ski-lift technology, with lift capacity on Blackcomb being 26,350 skiers per hour; on Whistler, 22,295 per hour. Blackcomb and Whistler have more than 100 marked trails each and receive an average of 450 inches of snow per year; Blackcomb is open June–August for summer glacier skiing. **Whistler Ski School** (tel. 604/932–3434) and **Blackcomb Ski School** (tel. 604/932–3141) offer lessons to skiers of all levels.

Heli- and Snowcat In Whistler, **Mountain Heli-Sports** (tel. 604/932–2070 or 604/
Skiing 932–3512), **Tyax Heli-Skiing** (tel. 604/932–7007), and **Whistler Heli-Skiing** (tel. 604/932–4105) have day trips with up to four glacier runs, or 12,000 vertical feet of skiing for experienced skiers; the cost is about $300.

Dining and Lodging

For prices *see* Dining chart for Vancouver, *above.*

Dining **Il Caminetto Di Umberto; Trattoria di Umberto; Settebello's.** Umberto Menghi is Vancouver's best-known restaurateur because of his fabulously successful Italian restaurants. Now there are three in Whistler. Il Caminetto and the Trattoria are in the village, and Settebello's is in Whistler Creek, about 3 kilometers (about 2 miles) south. Umberto offers home-style Italian cooking and specializes in pasta dishes like crab-stuffed cannelloni or a four-cheese lasagna that mix well with the relaxed atmosphere. The Trattoria has a Tuscan-style rotisserie, featuring a pasta dish served with a tray of chopped tomatoes, hot pepper, basil, olive oil, anchovies, and Parmesan so that you can mix it as spicy and flavorful as you like. Settebello's specialty is lean grilled beef and chicken, and Il Caminetto, perhaps the best restaurant in the Whistler area, is known for its veal, osso buco, and zabaglione. *Il Caminetto: 4242 Village Stroll, tel. 604/932–4442; Trattoria: Mountainside Lodge, tel. 604/ 932–5858; Settebello's: Whistler Creek Lodge, tel. 604/932– 3000. Reservations advised for dinner. Dress: neat but casual. AE, DC, MC, V. Expensive.*

★ **Les Deux Gros.** The name means "the two fat guys," which may explain the restaurant's motto, "Never trust a skinny chef." Portions of the country French cuisine are generous indeed. The spinach-and-warm-duck salad, steak tartare, juicy rack of lamb, and salmon Wellington are all superbly crafted and presented, and the service is friendly but unobtrusive. Located just southwest of the village, this is the spot for that special romantic dinner; request one of the prime tables by the massive stone fireplace. *1200 Alta Lake Rd., tel. 604/932–4611. Dinner only. Reservations advised. Dress: neat but casual. AE, DC, MC, V. Expensive.*

The Wildflower Cafe. Although this is the main dining room of the Chateau Whistler, it's an informal, comfortable restaurant. Huge picture windows overlook the ski slopes and let in the bright sun reflected off the snow. The rustic effect of the Chateau Whistler lobby continues in the Wildflower—more than 100 antique wood birdhouses decorate the room, and chairs and tables have that farmhouse look. Although there is an à la carte menu that focuses on Pacific Northwest cuisine, the restaurant features terrific breakfast, lunch, and dinner buffets that may include fresh crepes and omelets, sweet potato–and–parsnip soup, barbecued salmon, smoked halibut, artichoke-and-mushroom salad, pepper salad, seafood pâté, pasta in a spicy tomato sauce, and cold meats. *Chateau Whistler Hotel, tel. 604/938– 8000. Reservations advised for dinner. Dress: neat but casual. AE, DC, MC, V. Expensive.*

Lodging All lodgings can be booked through the Whistler Resort Association (tel. 604/932–4222 or 800/944–7853).

For prices *see* Lodging chart for Victoria, *above.*

★ **Le Chamois.** Sharing the prime ski-in, ski-out location at the base of the Blackcomb runs is this elegant, new luxury hotel. Of the 50 spacious guest rooms with convenience kitchens, the most popular are the studios with Jacuzzi tubs set in the living room in front of bay windows overlooking the slopes and lifts. Guests can keep an eye on the action also from the glass elevators and the heated outdoor pool. *4557 Blackcomb Way, tel. 604/932–8700; in the U.S. and Canada, 800/777–0185; fax 604/ 938–1888. 50 suites and studios, rooms for the disabled. Facilities: 2 restaurants, outdoor heated pool, Jacuzzi, fitness room, laundry room, complimentary valet skilocker, parking, shuttle to village. AE, DC, MC, V. Very Expensive.*

Chateau Whistler. Whistler's most extravagant hotel is a large and friendly looking fortress, just outside the village. It was built and run by Canadian Pacific Railway. It is the same style as the Banff Springs Hotel and the Jasper Park Lodge; the marvelous lobby is filled with rustic Canadiana, handmade Mennonite rugs, enormous fireplaces, and enticing overstuffed sofas. Floor-to-ceiling windows in the lounge, the health club, and the Wildflower Cafe overlook the base of Blackcomb Mountain. It's possible to schuss from there right into the basement of the hotel. The standard rooms are called premier and are fairly small, but the suites are fit for royalty, with specially commissioned quilts and artwork, and are complemented by antique furnishings. Both the Wildflower Cafe (*see* Dining, *above*) and La Fiesta, a tapas bar, are very good choices for a meal. Look for summer rates that drop by 50%. *4599 Chateau Blvd., Box 100, V0N 1B0, tel. 604/938–8000; in the U.S., 800/828–7447; in Canada, 800/528–0444; fax 604/938–2020. 303 doubles, 40 suites, rooms for the disabled. Facilities: 2 restaurants, bar, indoor-outdoor pool, indoor and outdoor Jacuzzis, morning stretch classes for skiers, 3 covered tennis courts, golf course. AE, DC, MC, V. Expensive.*

Pension Edelweiss. The Edelweiss is one of seven charming and very European bed-and-breakfasts around Whistler, and it's within walking distance of Whistler Village. Rooms have balconies and fireplaces and that crisp, northern European spic-and-span feel, in keeping with the Bavarian chalet style of the house. Each morning a different breakfast (included in room rate) is served: Scandinavian, American, French, German. *7162 Nancy Greene Way, Box 850, tel. 604/932–3641, fax 604/932–3776. 8 rooms, all with private bath. Facilities: sauna, Jacuzzi, transportation to lifts. MC, V. Inexpensive–Moderate.*

8 British Columbia

By Ray Chatelin

Canada's third-largest province (only Québec and Ontario are bigger), British Columbia occupies almost 10% of Canada's total surface area, stretching from the Pacific Ocean to the provinces of Alberta, Saskatchewan, and Manitoba, and from the U.S. border to the Yukon and Northwest Territories. It spans more than 360,000 square miles, making it larger than every American state except Alaska.

But size alone doesn't account for British Columbia's popularity as a vacation destination. Even easterners, content in the fact that Ontario and Québec form the industrial heartland of Canada, admit that British Columbia is the most spectacular part of the nation, with salmon-rich waters, abundant coastal scenery, and stretches of snow-capped peaks.

The region's natural splendor has ironically become the source of one of its more serious conflicts. For more than a century, logging companies have depended on the abundant supply of British Columbia wood, and whole towns are still centered on the industry. But environmentalists and many residents see the industry as a threat to the natural surroundings. Compromises have been achieved in recent years, but the issue is far from resolved.

The province used to be very British and predictable, reflecting its colonial heritage, but no longer. Vancouver, for example, has become an international city whose relaxed lifestyle is spiced by a rich and varied cultural scene embracing large Japanese, Chinese, Italian, and Greek communities. Even Victoria, which clings with restrained passion to British traditions and life-styles, has undergone an international metamorphosis in recent years.

No matter how modern the province, evidence remains of the earliest settlers, Pacific Coast natives (Haida Gwaii, Kwakiutl, Nootka, Salish, and others), who occupied the land for more than 12,000 years before the first Europeans arrived en masse in the late 19th century.

But material proof of their heritage may not be enough for today's native residents, who often face social barriers that have kept them from the mainstream of the province's rich economy. Although some have gained university educations and have fashioned careers, many are just now beginning to make demands on the nonnative population. In dispute are thousands of square miles of land claimed as aboriginal territory, some of which is located within major cities such as Vancouver, Prince George, and Prince Rupert.

Although the issue of ownership remains inconclusive, testimony of British Columbia's roots is apparent throughout the province, from small-town boutiques to big-city dining establishments. Native arts, such as wood-carved objects and silver-etched pendants, fetch top dollar from visitors and residents alike, and native Canadian restaurants prepare authentic culinary delights from traditional recipes.

Essential Information

Important Addresses and Numbers

Tourist Information
For information concerning the province contact the **Ministry of Tourism and Provincial Secretary** (Parliament Buildings, Victoria V8V 1X4, tel. 604/387–1642 or 800/663–6000). More than 140 communities in the province have **Travel Infocentres.**

The principal regional tourist offices are: **Tourism Association of Southwestern B.C.** (304–828 W. 8th Ave., Vancouver V5Z 1E2, tel. 604/876–3088; in the U.S., 800/667–3306, fax 604/876–8916); **Tourism Association of Vancouver Island** (302–45 Bastion Sq., Victoria V8W 1J1, tel. 604/382–3551, fax 604/382–3532); **Okanagan–Similkameen Tourist Association** (104–515 Hwy. 97 S, Kelowna V1Z 3J2, tel. 604/769–5959, fax 604/861–7493); **High Country Tourist Association** (403–186 Victoria St., Box 962, Kamloops V2C 6H1, tel. 604/372–7770, fax 604/828–4656); **North By Northwest Tourism** (3840 Alfred Ave., Box 1030, Smithers V0J 2N0, tel. 604/847–5227, fax 604/847–7585); **Rocky Mountain Visitors Association** (495 Wallinger Ave., Box 10, Kimberley V1A 2Y5, tel. 604/427–4838, fax 604/427–3344); **Prince Rupert Convention and Visitors Bureau** (100 McBride St., Box 669 CMG, Prince Rupert V8J 3S1, tel. 604/624–5637); **Kootenay Country Tourist Association** (610 Railway St., Nelson V1L 1H4, tel. 604/352–6033, fax 604/352–1656); **Cariboo Chilcotin Coast Tourist Association** (190 Yorston St., Box 4900, Williams Lake V2G 2V8, tel. 604/392–2226 or 800/663–5885, fax 604/392–2838); **Peace River Alaska Highway Tourist Association** (106319–100th St., Box 6850, Fort St. John V1J 4J3, tel. 604/785–2544, fax 604/785–4424).

Emergencies
Dial **911** in Vancouver and Victoria; dial **0** elsewhere in the province for **police, ambulance,** or **poison control.**

Hospitals
British Columbia has hospitals in virtually every town, including: in Prince George, **Prince George Regional Hospital** (2000 15th Ave., tel. 604/565–2000 or for emergencies, 604/565–2444); in Chilliwack, **Chilliwack General Hospital** (45600 Menholm, tel. 604/795–4141); in Kamloops, **Royal Inland Hospital** (311 Columbia St., tel. 604/374–5111); in Kelowna, **Kelowna General Hospital** (2268 Pandosy St., tel. 604/862–4000).

Late-night Pharmacies
All-night pharmacies are unknown in British Columbia, even in the largest cities, although some pharmacies do offer after-hours emergency numbers. Generally, emergency prescriptions can be filled through major hospitals. The following is a list of some pharmacies that could provide assistance: in Prince George, **Hart Drugs** (3789 W. Austin Rd., tel. 604/962–9666); in Kamloops, **Kipp-Mallery I.D.A. Pharmacy** (273 Victoria St., tel. 604/372–2531); in Hope, **Pharmasave Drugs** (240 Wallace St., tel. 604/869–2486).

Arriving and Departing by Plane

Airports and Airlines
British Columbia is served by **Victoria International Airport** and **Vancouver International Airport.** Domestic airports are in most cities. **Air Canada** (tel. in Vancouver, 604/688–5515; in the U.S., 800/776–3000) and **Canadian Airlines International** (tel. in Vancouver, 604/279–6611; in the U.S., 800/426–7000) are the two dominant carriers. **Air B.C.** (tel. in Vancouver, 604/688–

5515; in Victoria, 604/360–9074; in the U.S., 800/776–3000) is the major regional line and runs daily flights between Seattle and Victoria.

Arriving and Departing by Car, Bus, and Boat

By Car Driving time from Seattle to Vancouver is about 2½ hours. From other Canadian regions, there are three main routes leading into British Columbia: through Sparwood, in the south, take Highway 3; from Jasper and Banff, in the central region, travel on Route 1 (Trans-Canada) or Highway 5; and through Dawson Creek, in the north, follow Highways 2 and 97.

By Bus **Greyhound** (tel. in Vancouver, 604/662–3222; in Seattle, 206/ 624–3456) connects destinations throughout British Columbia with cities and towns throughout the Pacific North Coast.

By Boat There is year-round passenger service (closed Christmas) between Victoria and Seattle via the *Victoria Clipper* (tel. 800/ 888–2535).

Washington State Ferries (tel. in Victoria, 604/656–1531; in Seattle, 206/464–6400) cross daily, year-round, between Sidney, just north of Victoria, and Anacortes, WA. **Black Ball Transport** (tel. in Victoria, 604/386–2202; in Seattle, 206/622–2222) operates between Victoria and Port Angeles, WA.

Getting Around

By Air **Trans Provincial Airlines** (tel. in Prince Rupert, 604/627–1341;
Queen Charlotte in Sandspit, 604/637–5355) runs scheduled floatplanes between
Islands Sandspit, Masset, Queen Charlotte City, and Prince Rupert daily except Christmas, December 26, and New Year's Day.

Air B.C. provides both airport-to-airport and harbor-to-harbor service from Vancouver to Victoria at least hourly. Both flights take about 35 minutes.

Vancouver Island **Helijet Airways** (tel. 604/273–1414 or 604/382–6222) helicopter service is available from downtown Vancouver to downtown Victoria.

By Car Major roads in British Columbia, and most secondary roads, are paved and well engineered. Mountain driving is slower but more scenic. There are no roads on the mainland coast once you leave the populated areas of the southwest corner near Vancouver.

Car Rentals Most major agencies, including **Avis, Budget,** and **Hertz,** service cities throughout the province (*see* Chapter 1).

By Bus **Greyhound Lines of Canada** (tel. 604/662–3222 or 604/388– 5248) serves the area with hundreds of stops in the province.

North of Vancouver **Farwest Bus Lines** (tel. 604/624–6400) serves Prince Rupert,
Island Terrace, Kitimat, Stewart, and Smithers.

Vancouver Island **Pacific Coach Lines** (tel. 800/661–1725) operates daily connecting service between Victoria and Vancouver via B.C. Ferries. **Island Coach Lines** (tel. 604/385–4411) serves the Vancouver Island area. **Maverick Coach Lines** (tel. 604/255–1171) services Nanaimo from Vancouver, via B.C. Ferries (*see below*).

By Ferry **B.C. Ferries** (tel. in Vancouver, 604/685–1021; in Victoria, 604/656–0757; in Nanaimo, 604/753–6626) has an efficient cross-strait ferry service from Tsawwassen and Horseshoe Bay (both just outside of Vancouver) to Vancouver Island (Victoria and Nanaimo), and the Gulf Islands. Ferries usually depart on the hour 7 AM–9 PM and can carry about 360 cars and 1,500 passengers. Ferries also run from Powell River, Campbell River, Comox, and Port McNeill to the Gulf Islands; from Port Hardy to Prince Rupert; and from Prince Rupert to the Queen Charlotte Islands, although schedules vary greatly. When traveling with a car during summer months, expect a long line and delays. For schedule information call the numbers above for a 24-hour recorded message.

Royal Sealink Express (tel. 604/687–6925) is a new passenger service (no cars) that takes people by high-speed catamaran between downtown Victoria and downtown Vancouver in 2½ hours.

By Train **BC Rail** (in Vancouver, tel. 604/984–5246 or 604/631–3500; in Prince George, tel. 604/564–9080) travels from Vancouver to Prince George, a 747-kilometer (463-mile route) including daily service to Whistler. **Via Rail** (tel. 800/561–8630 in B.C.) offers service between Prince Rupert and Prince George.

Vancouver Island **Esquimalt & Nanaimo Rail Liner** (450 Pandora Ave., Victoria V8W 3L5, tel. 604/383–4324; in B.C., 800/561–8630), operated by Via Rail, travels from Victoria to Courtenay and returns. It leaves Victoria's Pandora Avenue Station daily at 8:15 AM, arrives in Courtenay by 12:50 PM, and departs 25 minutes later for a 5:45 PM return.

Guided Tours

Orientation The following operators offer tours throughout the province: Classic Holidays Tour & Travel (102–75 W. Broadway, Vancouver V5Y 1P1, tel. 604/875–6377); Klineburger Worldwide Travel (3627 1st Ave. S, Seattle, WA 98134, tel. 206/343–9699); and Sea to Sky (1928 Nelson Ave., W. Vancouver V7V 2P4, tel. 604/984–2224).

Special-interest A few Vancouver Island–based companies that conduct whale-watching tours are: **Subtidal Adventures** (Box 253, Ucluelet V0R 3A0, tel. 604/726–7336), **Inter-Island Excursions** (Box 393, Tofino V0R 2Z0, tel. 604/725–3163), **Jamie's Whale Station** (Box 590, Tofino V0R 2Z0, tel. 604/725–3919), **Tofino Sea-Kayaking Company** (Box 620, Tofino, VOR 2Z0, tel. 604/725–4222), and, near Port Hardy, **Stubbs Island Charters** (Box 7, Telegraph Cove V0N 3J0, tel. 604/928–3185).

Ecosummer Expeditions (1516 Duranleau St., Vancouver V6H 3S4, tel. 604/669–7741) runs ecological tours of the Queen Charlotte Islands.

Exploring British Columbia

When traveling by car, keep in mind that more than three-quarters of British Columbia is mountainous terrain. Trips that appear relatively short may take longer, especially in the northern regions and along the coast, where roads are often narrow and winding. In certain areas—most of the uninhabited west coast of Vancouver Island, for example—roads do not exist.

Within British Columbia, there is a vast range of climates, largely a result of the province's size, its mountainous topography, and its border on the Pacific. Vancouver Island, surrounded by Pacific waters, experiences relatively mild winters and summers (usually above 32 degrees winter, below 80 degrees summer), although it rains a lot in the winter. Likewise, the northern coast around Prince Rupert and the Queen Charlotte Islands has wet winter months and few extremes in temperature. But as you move inland, and especially toward the Peace River region in the north, the climate becomes much colder. In the southern interior, the Okanagan Valley has an arid climate, with temperatures dropping below the freezing level in winter and sometimes reaching 90 degrees during the summer.

Highlights for First-time Visitors

Kilby General Store Museum, Tour 3: Okanagan Valley and Environs
Mintner Gardens, Tour 3: Okanagan Valley and Environs
Naikoon Provincial Park, Tour 2: North of Vancouver Island
O'Keefe Historic Ranch, Tour 3: Okanagan Valley and Environs
Pacific Rim National Park, Tour 1: Vancouver Island

Tour 1: Vancouver Island

Vancouver Island, the largest island on the west coast, stretches 450 kilometers (280 miles) from Victoria in the south to Cape Scott, although 97% of the population live between Victoria and Campbell River (halfway up the island); 50% of them live in Victoria itself. Geographically, the differences between the east and west are impressive. The western side is wild, often inhospitable, with just a handful of small settlements. Virtually all of the island's human habitation is on the eastern coast, where the weather is gentler and the topography is lowlying.

The cultural heritage of the island is from the Kwakiutl, Nootka, and Coastal Salish native groups. Native art and cultural centers flourish throughout the region, especially in the lower section of the island. These centers enable visitors to catch a glimpse of contemporary native culture.

Mining, logging, and tourism are the important island industries. But environmental issues, such as logging practices by British Columbia's lumber companies, are becoming important to islanders—both native and nonnative. Residents are working to reach a happy coexistence with the island's wilderness and its economy, which is dependent on industrial development and tourism.

Numbers in the margin correspond to points of interest on the Vancouver Island map.

Beginning your driving tour from Victoria (*see* Chapter 5), take Highway 14 west to **Sooke** (26 miles, or 42 kilometers, west of Victoria), a logging, fishing, and farming community. **East Sooke Park,** on the east side of the harbor, offers 3,500 acres of beaches, hiking trails, and meadows with wildflowers.

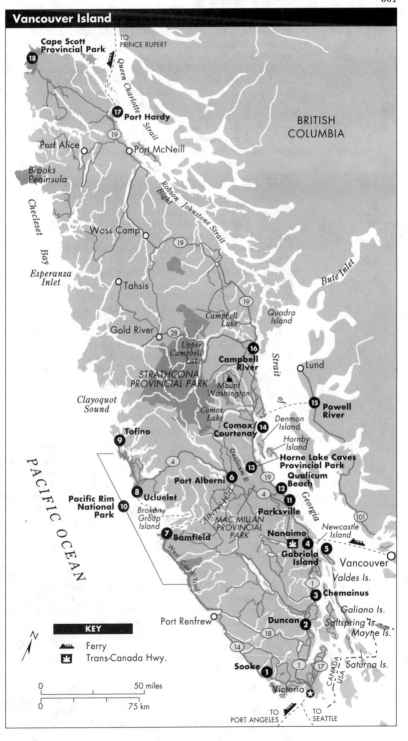

Vancouver Island

Cape Scott Provincial Park — 18

TO PRINCE RUPERT

Queen Charlotte Strait

Port Hardy — 17

(19)

Port Alice

Port McNeill

BRITISH COLUMBIA

Brooks Peninsula

Checleset Bay

Robson Bight

Esperanza Inlet

Johnstone Strait

Woss Camp

(19)

Tahsis

Bute Inlet

Gold River

(28)

Campbell Lake

Quadra Island

Upper Campbell Lake

Campbell River — 16

Lund

STRATHCONA PROVINCIAL PARK

Mount Washington

Strait of Georgia

Powell River — 15

Clayoquot Sound

Comox Lake

Comox/ Courtenay — 14

Denman Island

Hornby Island

Tofino — 9

Qualicum R.

Horne Lake Caves Provincial Park — 13

(4)

Port Alberni — 6

(19)

Qualicum Beach — 12

Ucluelet — 8

Pacific Rim National Park — 10

Broken Group Island

Alberni Inlet

MAC MILLAN PROVINCIAL PARK

Parksville — 11

(101)

(4)

PACIFIC OCEAN

Bamfield — 7

Newcastle Island

Nanaimo — 4

Gabriola Island

— 5

Vancouver

West Coast Trail

Valdes Is.

Chemainus — 3

Galiano Is.

Port Renfrew

Duncan — 2

(18)

Saltspring Is.

Mayne Is.

(14)

(1)

Saturna Is.

Sooke — 1

(1)

(17)

CANADA / USA

Victoria ★

KEY

⛴ Ferry
🍁 Trans-Canada Hwy.

N

| 0 | | 50 miles |
| 0 | | 75 km |

TO PORT ANGELES

TO SEATTLE

You can also visit the **Sooke Region Museum and Travel Infocentre,** with Salish and Nootka crafts, artifacts from 19th-century Sooke, barbecued salmon, and strawberry shortcake on the front lawn during the summer, and plenty of information about the region. *2070 Phillips Rd., Box 774, V0S 1N0, tel. 604/642–6351. Admission free; donations accepted. Open summer, daily 9–6; winter, Tues.–Sun. and holiday Mon., 9–5; closed Christmas and Boxing Day (Dec. 26).*

Time Out **Seventeen Mile House** (5121 Sooke Rd., Sooke, tel. 604/642–5942) is on the road to Sooke from Victoria. Stop here for English pub fare, a beer, or fresh local seafood. Built as a hotel, the house is an education in turn-of-the-century island architecture, as well.

The adventurous can continue on Highway 14 west and pick up the logging road from Port Renfrew back to the east coast, although conditions on the gravel road may be hazardous, especially on weekdays with the trucks rolling by. The more reliable route backtracks to Victoria, then follows the Trans-Canada Highway up the eastern coast toward Nanaimo, the mid-island B.C. Ferries terminal point. On your way you'll pass ❷ through the town of **Duncan** (about 60 kilometers, or 37 miles, north of Victoria), nicknamed City of Totems for the many totem poles that dot the small community. The two carvings behind the City Hall are worth a short trip off the main road. Duncan is also home to the **Native Heritage Centre.** Covering 13 acres of land on the banks of the Cowichan River, the center features a native big house, fantastic theater and interpretive dance presentations, an arts-and-crafts gallery that focuses on carvings and weaving traditions, and picnic meals of smoked salmon next to the river. *200 Cowichan Way, Duncan, tel. 604/746–8119. Admission: $6 adults, $5.50 senior citizens and students, $2 children 6–12, children under 5 free. Open May–Sept., daily 9:30–5:30; Oct.–Apr., 10–4:30.*

Also in Duncan is the **B.C. Forest Museum.** More a park than a museum, the attraction spans more than 40 hectares (100 acres), combining indoor and outdoor exhibits that focus on the history of forestry in British Columbia. You ride an original steam locomotive around the property and over an old wood trestle bridge. The exhibit feature logging and milling equipment. *RR 4 Trans-Canada Hwy., tel. 604/746–1251. Admission: $5 adults, $4 senior citizens and children 13–18, $2.50 children 6–12. Open May–late Sept., daily 9:30–6. For off-season visits, call for an appointment.*

❸ Just north of Duncan, the small town of **Chemainus** has become known recently for the bold epic murals that decorate its landscape. Once dependent on the lumber industry, the town began to revitalize in the early 1980s when its mill closed down. Since then, more than 25 murals depicting local historical events have been painted around town by international artists. Restaurants, shops, cafés, and coffee bars have added to the town's growth. Footsteps on the sidewalk lead you on a self-guided tour of the murals.

❹ **Nanaimo,** across the strait of Georgia from Vancouver, is about an hour's drive from Victoria. Throughout the Nanaimo region, petroglyphs (rock carvings) representing humans, birds, wolves, lizards, sea monsters, and supernatural creatures can be found. The **Nanaimo Centennial Museum** (100 Cameron St., tel. 604/753–1821) will give you information about local carvings. Eight kilometers (5 miles) south of town is the **Petroglyph Provincial Park,** where designs estimated to have been carved thousands of years ago can be seen along the marked trails that begin at the parking lot.

Nanaimo is a convenient departure point for other island activities. A 20-minute ferry ride leaves from town for **Gabriola Island,** a rustic, rural island with lodging; and a 10-minute ferry takes you to **Newcastle Island,** where you can picnic, ride your bicycle, walk on trails leading past old mines and quarries, and wait for glimpses of deer, rabbits, and eagles.

As you continue north on Highway 19, you have the option of taking Highway 4 west to Port Alberni and the lower west-coast towns. **Port Alberni** is about an 80-kilometer (49-mile) drive from Nanaimo and is mainly a pulp-and-saw-mill town and a stopover for those on the way to Ucluelet and Tofino, though fishermen will want to take advantage of the salmon-rich waters. While you're there, consider taking a breathtaking trip down the Alberni Inlet to Barkley Sound aboard the *Lady Rose*, a Scottish ship, built in 1937. The *Lady Rose* leaves the Argyle Street dock Tuesday, Thursday, and Saturday (and Friday and Sunday in July and August) for the four-hour cruise to **Bamfield,** a remote village of about 200. Bamfield's seaside boardwalk affords an uninterrupted view of ships heading up the inlet to Port Alberni. Oddly, for a place this small, it is well equipped to handle overnight visitors. The west coast is invaded every summer by fishermen, kayakers, scuba divers, and hikers. Bamfield is also a good base from which to take boating trips to the Broken Group Islands and hikes along the West Coast Trail (*see below*). From early June to mid-September the *Lady Rose* and *Francis Barkley* sail for Ucluelet on Monday, Wednesday, and Friday. It's a unique trip and deserves all the accolades it receives. Most of the trips, to both Bamfield and Ucluelet, stop at the Broken Group Islands, but call ahead to make sure. *Argyle St. dock, tel. 604/723–8313. Bamfield fare: $32; Broken Group Islands fare: $34; Ucluelet fare: $36. Sailings depart daily at 8 AM.*

North of Bamfield are Ucluelet and Tofino—the whale-watching capitals of Canada, if not of the whole west coast of North America. The two towns are quite different in character, though both are relaxed in the winter and swell to several times their sizes in summer. **Ucluelet,** which in the native language means "people with a safe landing place," is totally focused on the sea. Fishing, water tours, and whale watching are the primary activities. Whale watching is big business, with a variety of charter companies that take tourist boats to greet the 20,000 gray whales that pass within a very short distance of Ucluelet on their migration to the Bering Sea every March–May. Sometimes the migrating whales can even be seen from the Ucluelet shore.

Tofino, on the other hand, is more commercial, with beachfront resorts, motels, and several unique bed-and-breakfast establishments. But the surrounding area remains natural. You can walk along the beach discovering caves on the way, cruise around the ancient forests of Meares Island, or take an hour-long water taxi to the hot springs north of town.

Ucluelet and Tofino bookend the Long Beach section of the
⑩ Pacific Rim National Park (Box 280, Ucluelet, V0R 3A0, tel.
604/726–7721), the first national marine park in Canada. The
park itself comprises three separate areas—Long Beach, the
Broken Group Islands, and the West Coast Trail. Each accommodates a specific interest.

The unit of **Long Beach** gets its name from an 11-kilometer (7-
mile) strip of hard-packed white sand strewn with twisted
driftwood, shells, and the occasional Japanese glass fishing
float. The beach is a favorite spot during the summer, and you
often have to fight heavy traffic along the twisting 85 kilometers (53 miles) of Highway 4 from Port Alberni.

The 100 islands of the **Broken Group Islands** can be reached
only by boat. Many boating tours are available from Ucluelet,
which rests at the southern end of Long Beach, and from
Bamfield and Port Alberni. The 100 islands are alive with sea
lions, seals, and whales. The sheltered lagoons of Gibraltar,
Jacques, and Hand islands offer protection and good boating
conditions, but go with a guide.

The third element of the park is the **West Coast Trail** (*see* Hiking, *below*), which stretches along the coast from Bamfield to
Port Renfrew. After the SS *Valencia* ran aground in 1906, kill-
ing all the crew and passengers, the Canadian government constructed the lifesaving trail to help future victims of
shipwrecks reach safe ground. The trail remains, with demanding bogs, steep slopes and gullies, cliffs (with ladders),
slippery boardwalks, and insects. Although it presents many
obstacles for hikers, the rewards are the panoramic views of
the sea, dense rain forest, sandstone cliffs with waterfalls, and
wildlife that includes gray whales and seals.

Heading back to the east coast from Port Alberni, stop off at
Cathedral Grove, located in MacMillan Provincial Park on Highway 4. Walking trails lead you past Douglas fir trees and western red cedars, some about 800 years old. Their remarkable
height creates a spiritual effect, as though you were gazing at a
cathedral ceiling. Another stop along the way is **Butterfly
World** (Alberni Hwy., Box 36, Coombs, V0R 1M0, tel. 604/248–
7026), an enclosed tropical garden housing a massive collection
of exotic, free-flying tropical butterflies.

⑪ At the junction of Highways 4 and 19 is **Parksville**—one of the
east island's primary resort areas with lodges and waterfront
motels catering to families, campers, and boaters. In **Rathtrevor Provincial Park,** 1½ kilometers (about 1 mile) south of
Parksville, high tide brings ashore the warmest ocean water in
British Columbia. Swimmers should time their visits accord-
ingly.

⑫ Just 12 kilometers (7 miles) north of Parksville is **Qualicum
Beach,** known largely for its salmon fishing and opportunities
for beachcombing along the long, sandy beaches. The nonprofit
Old School House Gallery and Art Centre (122 Fern Rd. W, tel.
604/752–6133), with nine working studios, shows and sells the
work of local artists and artisans.

Continue north, then head west off the highway and follow
signs for about 15 kilometers (9 miles) to Horne Lake and the
⑬ Horne Lake Caves Provincial Park. Three of the six caves are
open at all times. If you decide to venture in, bring along a

flashlight, warm clothes, and a hard hat, and be prepared to bend and even crawl. Riverbend Cave, spanning 383 meters (1,259 feet), requires ladders and ropes in some parts, and can only be explored with a guided tour. Spelunking lessons and tours are offered for all levels, from beginner to advanced. *Tel. 604/248–3931. Fees for tours vary depending on ability level. Reservations suggested for tours.*

Between the Horne Lakes turnoff and the twin cities of Comox and Courtenay is tiny Buckley Bay, where ferries leave for **Denman Island,** with connecting service to **Hornby Island.** Denman offers old-growth forests and long sandy beaches, while Hornby's spectacular beaches have earned it the nickname the Undiscovered Hawaii of British Columbia. Many artists have settled on the islands, establishing studios for pottery, jewelry, wood carving, and sculpture.

⓮ **Comox** and **Courtenay** are near **Strathcona Provincial Park** and are commonly used as a base for anyone skiing Mt. Washington in the winter. Strathcona, the largest provincial park on Vancouver Island, encompasses **Mt. Golden Hinde,** at 2,200 meters (7,218 feet) the island's highest mountain; and **Della Falls,** Canada's highest waterfall, reaching 440 meters (1,443 feet). The park's multitude of lakes and 161 campsites attract summer canoers, fishermen, and wilderness campers, and the **Strathcona Park Lodge and Outdoor Information Center,** well known for its wilderness-skills programs, provides information on the park's facilities. *Information Center, Hwy. 28, on Upper Campbell Lake, about 45 km (28 mi) west of Hwy. 19, Box 2160, Campbell River, V9W 5C9, tel. 604/286–3122.*

⓯ From Comox, you can take a 75-minute ferry east across the Strait of Georgia to **Powell River,** a city established around the MacMillan pulp-and-paper mill, which opened in 1912. Renowned as a year-round salmon-fishing destination, the mainland's Sunshine Coast town has 30 regional lakes that offer exceptional trout fishing, as well. For information contact **Powell River Travel Info Center** (6807 Wharf St., tel. 604/485–4051).

⓰ **Campbell River** is ringed by shopping centers that make it look like a free-zoned mess. But people don't come here for the aesthetics, they come for the fish; some of the biggest salmon ever caught on a line have been landed just off the coast at Campbell River. At the mouth of the town's namesake, you can try for membership in Campbell River's Tyee Club, which would allow you to fish in a specific area, and possibly land a giant chinook. Requirements for membership in the club include registering and landing a tyee (a spring salmon weighing 30 pounds or more). Coho salmon and cutthroat trout are also plentiful in the river. *Travel Information Center, 1235 Island Hwy., Box 400, Campbell River, V9W 5B6, tel. 604/287–4636. Open late June–Labor Day, daily 8–6; rest of year, Mon.–Fri. 9–5.*

Pods of resident Orcas live nearby year-round in Johnstone Strait; and in Robson Bight they like using the beaches to rub against. Because of their presence, Robson Bight has been made into an ecological preserve: Whales must not be disturbed by human observers there. Some of the island's best whale-watching tours, however, are conducted nearby, out of Telegraph Cove, a village built on pilings over water.

⓱ Farther north is **Port Hardy,** the departure and arrival point for B.C. Ferries going through the Inside Passage to and from Prince Rupert, the coastal port serving the Queen Charlotte Islands. During the summer the town can be crowded, so book your accommodations well in advance.

If you choose to continue to the northernmost point on Vancouver Island, drive about 60 kilometers (about 37 miles) on logging roads to reach **Cape Scott Provincial Park,** a wilderness
⓲ camping region designed for well-equipped and experienced hikers. At Sand Neck, a strip of land that joins the cape to the mainland of the island, you can see both the eastern and western shores at once.

Tour 2: North of Vancouver Island

Numbers in the margin correspond to points of interest on the British Columbia map.

⓳ Cruising the 274-nautical-mile **Inside Passage,** between Port Hardy on northern Vancouver Island and Prince Rupert, is a sail through a sheltered marine highway that follows a series of natural channels behind protective islands along the green-and-blue shaded British Columbia coast. The undisturbed landscape of rising mountains and humpbacked islands has a prehistoric look that leaves an indelible impression.

After a short segment in the open ocean, the 410-foot MV *Queen of the North* ducks in behind Calvert Island into Fitz Hugh Sound. From there, its route is protected from ocean swells all the way through Finlayson and Grenville channels, which are flanked by high, densely wooded mountains that rise steeply, in places, from narrow gorges. The *Queen of the North* carries up to 800 passengers and 157 vehicles, and takes close to an entire day to make the Port Hardy to Prince Rupert trip. The ship has plenty of deck space plus lounge areas, a self-serve cafeteria, and a satisfactory restaurant that offers a plentiful buffet. Day-use cabins are available for an additional fee. Children can play in the Captain Kids Room. *British Columbia Ferry Corporation, 1112 Fort St., Victoria V8V 4V2, tel. 604/ 386–3431. Cost varies according to cabin, vehicle, and time of season. Reservations required for the cruise and advised for hotel accommodations at ports of call. Oct. 1–Apr. 30 sailings are once weekly; May 1–May 31 sailings twice-weekly; June 1– Sept. 30 sailings daily, departing on alternate days from Port Hardy and Prince Rupert; departure time 7:30 AM, arrival time 10:30 PM. Schedule and fares subject to change.*

An alternative to the ferry cruise along the Inside Passage is one of the more expensive luxury-liner cruises that sail along the B.C. coast (*see* Chapter 1) from Vancouver to Alaska.

⓴ **Prince Rupert,** the final stop on the B.C. Ferries route through the Inside Passage, is about 750 air kilometers (465 miles) northwest of Vancouver, though it takes more than 20 hours to drive the mountainous 1,500 kilometers (936 miles). Prince Rupert has a mild but wet climate, so take rain gear.

The town lives off fishing, fish processing, logging, saw-and-pulp-mill operations, and deep-sea shipping. A gondola ride to the top of Mt. Hays, located just outside the downtown area, offers magnificent views on a clear day of the industrial harbor, the Queen Charlotte Islands, and the mountains of Alaska. You can ski Mt. Hays during the winter and picnic in the summer. Prince Rupert is also a place where British Columbia's cultural heritage is quite evident. The **Museum of Northern British Columbia** has one of the finest collections throughout the province of coastal native art, some artifacts dating back 10,000 years. Native artisans carve totem poles in the carving shed and, during the summer, the museum runs a 2½-hour boat tour of the harbor and Metlakatla native village. *1st Ave. and McBride St., Prince Rupert, tel. 604/624–3207. Admission: free; donations accepted. Open Sept–May, Mon.–Sat. 10–5; June–Aug., Mon–Sat. 9–9, Sun. 9–5.*

From Prince Rupert you can continue on to explore either the Alaskan Panhandle, the Queen Charlotte Islands, or interior British Columbia. If you wish to proceed north through the Alaskan waterways to Skagway, board the **Alaska Marine Highway System ferry** (tel. in Prince Rupert, 604/627–1744 or 800/642–0066), which docks alongside the *Queen of the North* in Prince Rupert. Alaska ferries travel this route four times a week in the summer, twice a week otherwise.

㉑ The popular vacation destination, the **Queen Charlotte Islands,** or misty islands, though once the remote preserve of the Haida Gwaii natives, is now easily accessible by ferry. Today the Haida Gwaii make up only one sixth of the population, but they continue to infuse the island with a sense of the Haida Gwaii past and contribute to the logging and fishing industries, and to tourism, as well. Haida Gwaii elders lead tours—an essential service if you want to reach the isolated, abandoned villages. Though the region has become a popular tourist destination, limited accommodations make it necessary to reserve guest rooms well in advance.

The *Queen of Prince Rupert* (tel. in Prince Rupert, 604/624–9627) sails four to five times a week between June and September, and can easily accommodate recreational vehicles. Crossing the Hecate Strait from Prince Rupert to Skidegate, near Queen Charlotte on Graham Island, takes about six hours. Schedules vary, so call ahead—a good idea anyway because the boat fills up quickly. The **MV** *Kwuna,* a B.C. Ferries ship, connects Skidegate Landing to Alliford Bay on Moresby Island, with 12 20-minute sailings daily. Access to smaller islands off Graham Island (the northernmost and largest of the group of 150) and Moresby Island is by boat or air, but plans should be made in advance through a travel agent.

In the Queen Charlottes, there are 150 kilometers (93 miles) of paved road, most of it on Graham Island, connecting Queen Charlotte in the south to Masset in the north. Some of the other islands are laced with gravel roads, most of which can be accessed with any sturdy car or RV. The rugged, rocky west coast of the archipelago faces the ocean; the east coast has many broad sandy beaches. Throughout, the mountains and shores are often shrouded in fog and rain-laden clouds, adding to the mysteriousness of the islands.

Naikoon Provincial Park (tel. 604/557–4390), in the northeast corner of Graham, preserves a large section of the unique wilderness found here, where low-lying swamps, pine and cedar forests, lakes, beaches, trails, and wildlife combine to create an intriguing environment. Take the 5-kilometer (3-mile) walk from the Tlell Picnic Site to the beach, and on to the bow section

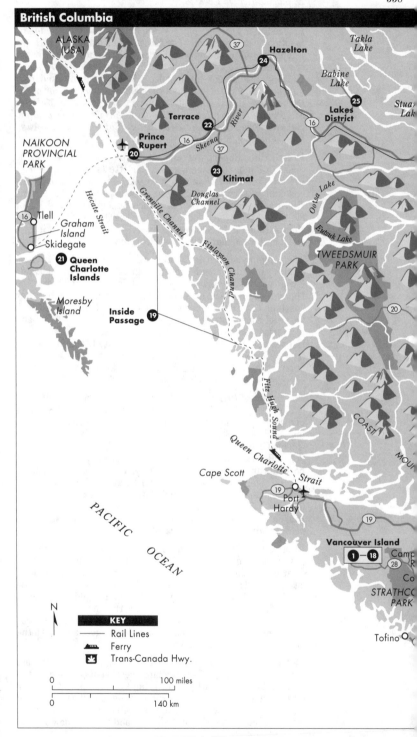

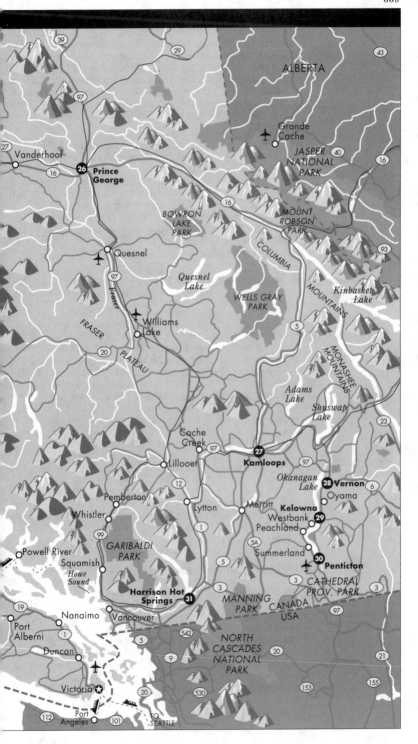

ALBERTA

(39)
(29)
(43)

(97)

Grande
Cache

(27) Vanderhoof

(16)

JASPER
NATIONAL
PARK
(40)

(16)

(26) **Prince George**

(16)

BOWRON
LAKE
PARK

MOUNT
ROBSON
PARK

(93)

Quesnel

(97)

Quesnel
Lake

COLUMBIA

WELLS GRAY
PARK

Kinbasket
Lake

Williams
Lake

FRASER

MOUNTAINS

(20)

FRASER
PLATEAU

(5)

MONASHEE
MOUNTAINS

Adams
Lake

Shuswap
Lake

(23)

Cache
Creek

(97)

(27) **Kamloops**

(97)

Okanagan
Lake

(28) **Vernon** (6)

Lillooet

Oyama

(12)

Pemberton

(1)

Merritt

Kelowna

Westbank (29)

Whistler

Lytton

Peachland

(99)

GARIBALDI
PARK

(5A)

Summerland

Powell River

(5)

(30) **Penticton**

Squamish
*Howe
Sound*

**Harrison Hot
Springs** (31)

(3)

CATHEDRAL
PROV. PARK

(3)

(19)

Nanaimo
Vancouver

MANNING
PARK

CANADA
USA

(97)

Port
Alberni

(1)

(5)

(542)

NORTH
CASCADES
NATIONAL
PARK

(20)

(21)

Duncan

(9)

(153)

(155)

Victoria

(20)

(530)

(112)

Port
Angeles

(101)

TO
SEATTLE

of the old wooden shipwreck of the *Pezuta*, a 1928 log-hauling vessel. On the southern end of Graham Island, the **Queen Charlotte Islands Museum** has a small but impressive display of Haida Gwaii totem poles, masks, and carvings of both silver and argillite (a hard black slate). There is also a natural-history exhibit, which gives interesting background on the wildlife of the islands. *Box 1373, Skidegate V0T 1S1, tel. 604/559-4643. Admission: $2.25 adults, children 13 and under free. Open Apr.–late Oct., weekdays 9–5, weekends 1–5; winter, Wed.–Sun. 1–5.*

If you have time on Graham Island, drive up to Old Masset on the northern coast, site of the **Ed Jones Haida Museum.** Exhibits here include totems and artifacts. Nearby, artists sell their work from their homes. South of Graham, in and around South Moresby National Park Reserve, lie most of the better-known abandoned Haida Gwaii villages, which are accessible by water. Visiting some of the villages requires at least several days, and lots of planning for the wilderness. You (or your tour) need to contact the Skidegate Band Council and the Canadian Parks Services before you go.

For more information on the Queen Charlotte Islands, contact the **Queen Charlotte Islands Travel Information Center** (Box 337, Queen Charlotte V0T 1S0, tel. 604/559–4742).

To see interior British Columbia, take Highway 16 east from Prince Rupert. En route you'll pass through or near such communities as **Terrace,** with a hot-springs complex at the Mt. Layton Resort, skiing at Shames Mountain, and excellent fishing in the Skeena River; and **Kitimat** (on Highway 37, south of Terrace), at the head of the Douglas Channel, where the fishing is superb. At **Hazelton,** a town rich in the culture of the Gitksan and Wet'suwet'en peoples you must visit **'Ksan,** just outside town, a re-created Gitksan village. The brightly painted community of six longhouses is a replica of the one that stood on the same site when the first explorers arrived in the last century. The **National Exhibition Centre and Museum** displays works and artifacts from the Upper Skeena River region. A workshop, often used by 'Ksan artists, is open to the public, and three other longhouses can be visited on a 45-minute tour: One features contemporary masks and robes, another has song-and-dance dramas in the summer. A gift shop and museum are on the grounds. *Box 333, Hazelton, V0J 1Y0, tel. 604/842–5723. Admission: $5 adults, $3.50 senior citizens, $3 students, $2 children 5–12. Open May–mid-Oct., daily 9–6; mid-Oct.–Apr., weekdays 9–5. Tours given May–mid-Oct., on the hour.*

North of Highway 16 you pass by the serene **Lakes District,** which is popular for camping, fishing, and water sports, before coming to **Prince George** (Tourism Prince George, 1198 Victoria St., V2L 2L2, tel. 604/562–3700), British Columbia's third-largest city. This provincial hub contains a regional historic museum (tel. 604/562–1612), a railroad museum (tel. 604/563–7351; open May–Labor Day), and the Prince George Native Art Gallery (tel. 604/562–7385). From Prince George you can turn south on Highway 97 for Kamloops and the Okanagan Valley (*see* Scenic Drives, *below*), or you can continue on Highway 16, then on 5 for a longer (some say even more spectacular) route to the same place.

Tour 3: Okanagan Valley and Environs, Including Rainbow and High Country

The Okanagan Valley is part of a highland plateau between the Cascade range of mountains on the west and the Monashee mountains on the east. Though small in size (only 3% of the province's total land mass), the area contains the interior's largest concentration of people. Dominating the valley is Okanagan Lake, a vacation hot-spot for tourists from the west coast and Alberta. In summer months it can be difficult to find rooms. The largest towns along the lake are Vernon at the north end, Kelowna in the middle, and Penticton at the south. Between, and along the lake, are the recreational and resort communities of **Summerland, Peachland, Westbank,** and **Oyama,** which are popular tourist destinations and have camping facilities, motels, and cabins. Favorite local lore tells of the legendary Ogopogo, a snakelike creature that inhabits the lake between Peachland and Summerland.

The valley is the fruit-growing capital of Canada, producing apricots, cherries, pears, plums, apples, and peaches. A visit to the region from mid-April through early June promises to jolt your senses with the brightness and fragrance of the spring blossoms.

27 We arrive in the valley by way of **Kamloops** (which is officially a part of High Country, not Okanagan), a convenient passageway from Fraser Canyon and Thompson Valley, and a stop on the Canadian Pacific Railroad. The town is 50 minutes northeast of Vancouver by air and 425 kilometers (260 miles) by road and is surrounded by 500 lakes, which provide an abundance of trout, Dolly Varden, and kokanee. During late September and October, however, attention turns to the sockeye salmon, when thousands of these fish—intent on breeding—return home to their birth waters in Adams River (only 65 kilometers, or 40 miles, east of Kamloops off the Trans-Canada Highway).

Once every four year—the last time was 1990—the sockeye run reaches a massive scale, as more than a million salmon pack the waters and up to 500,000 visitors come to observe. The **Roderick Haig-Brown Conservation Area,** which protects the 11-kilometer (7-mile) stretch of Adams River, is the best place to watch.

Wildlife enthusiasts will also enjoy the **Kamloops Wildlife Park** (Box 698, Kamloops, V2C 5L7, tel. 604/573–3242), a 55-acre compound housing 71 species in fairly natural habitats. Canyon hiking trails, a miniature railway, and adjacent waterslides provide something for everyone in the family.

Vernon, Kelowna, and Penticton, running south along Highway 97, like to believe each has a distinct personality, but local rivalries aside, the towns are actually one large unit. Okanagan Lake is their glue, offering recreation, lodging, and restaurants.

28 Of the three, **Vernon** is the least dependent on tourism, organized instead around forestry and agriculture. The city borders on two other lakes besides Okanagan, the most enticing of which is Kalamalka Lake. The **Kalamalka Lake Provincial Park** has warm waters, and some of the most scenic viewpoints and hiking trails in the region. Twelve kilometers (7.5 miles) north of Vernon, the **O'Keefe Historic Ranch** gives visitors a window on cattle-ranch life at the turn of the century. The O'Keefe house is a late 19th-century Victorian mansion opulently furnished with original antiques. On the grounds, which now are 50 acres (20 hectares), there are a Chinese cooks' house, St. Ann's Church, a blacksmith shop, a reconstructed general store, and a display of the old Shuswap and Okanagan Railroad. Also featured are a contemporary restaurant and gift shop. *9830 Hwy. 97, 12 km (8 mi) north of Vernon, tel. 604/542–7868. Admission: $4.50 adults, $3.50 senior citizens and children 13–18, $2.50 children 6–12; family and group rates available. Open mid-May–mid-Oct., daily 9–5.*

㉙ **Kelowna,** the largest city in the Okanagan, is home to **Father Pandosy's Mission,** the first nonnative settlement in the region, founded in 1859. *3685 Benvouline Rd., tel. 604/860–8369. Admission free. Open daily 9–5.*

The city also offers the area's only tour of a **fruit orchard;** a covered wagon, pulled by a tractor, takes you on the hour-long narrated excursion. *2750 KLO Rd., East Kelowna, tel. 604/ 769–4719. Admission: $6.50 adults, $5.50 senior citizens, accompanied children free. Open July 1–early Sept., weekdays 10–4, weekends 10–12.*

Kelowna is the geographic center of the valley's wine industry, with **Calona Wines Ltd.** (1125 Richter St., tel. 604/762–3332), British Columbia's oldest and biggest winemaker. Also around Kelowna are smaller but more intimate wineries, including **Gray Monk Cellars** (1051 Camp Rd., 8 km, or 5 mi, west of Winfield, off Hwy. 97, tel. 604/766–3168), and **Cedarcreek Estate Winery** (5445 Lakeshore Rd., 12 km, or 7.5 mi, south of Kelowna, off Hwy. 97 on the corner of Pandosy and Lakeshore Rds., tel. 604/764–8866).

㉚ **Penticton** is the most tourist-oriented of the three. While its winter population is about 25,000, its population in summer nears 130,000. An 11-kilometer (5-mile) drive south on Highway 97 takes you to the **Okanagan Game Farm** (tel. 604/497–5405), with more than 650 species of wild animals from around the world. Farther south, off Highway 3 and along the U.S. border, **Cathedral Provincial Park** (tel. 604/494–0321) features 82,000 acres (33,198 hectares) of lakes and rolling meadows, teeming with mule deer, mountain goats, and California bighorn sheep. To reach the main part of the park, either take the steep, eight-hour hike, or arrange (and pay in advance) for the Cathedral Lake Resort (in the park, tel. 604/499–5848) to transport you by four-wheel drive. There are 16 campsites in the park.

Winding farther south, Highway 3 connects with the Trans-Canada Highway (Highway 1), which parallels the Fraser River through the region known as **Rainbow Country.** A glimpse through the mists above roiling **Hell's Gate,** off Highway 1 in Fraser Canyon, hints at how the region got its name. An airtram carries visitors across the foaming canyon, above the fishway, where millions of sockeye salmon fight their way upriver to spawning grounds each September. In addition to interpretive displays on the life cycle of the salmon, you'll find a fudge factory, gift shop, and restaurant at the lower airtram terminal. *Box 129, Hope, tel. 604/867–9277. Admission: $8 adults, $7 senior citizens, $4 children. Open mid-Apr.–mid-*

June and mid-Sept.–mid-Oct,, Mon.–Thurs. 9–5 and Fri.–
Sun. 9–7; mid-June–early Sept., daily 9–7.

Continue southwest on Highway 1 to the well-signed **Mintner Gardens** at Exit 135 in Rosedale. This 27-acre compound contains 11 beautifully presented theme gardens—Chinese, rose, English, fern, fragrance, and more—along with aviaries and ponds. There are even farmyard animals, playgrounds, and a giant evergreen maze to entertain the kids. *52892 Bunker Rd., Rosedale, tel. 604/794–7191. Admission: $7.50 adults, $6.50 senior citizens, $3.50 children 6–12, children under 6 free. Open Apr.–Oct., daily 9–dusk.*

It's hard to miss the **Trans-Canada Waterslides,** just across the highway. This tremendously popular waterpark features slides with names such as Kamikaze, Cannonball, Super Heroes, and Flash Flood, along with wave and soaking pools, snack bars, and sunbathing areas to provide plenty of warm-weather fun. *Bridal Falls Rd., Rosedale, tel. 604/794–7455. Admission: $10.75 adults, $7.50 children, children under 3 free. Open mid-May–mid-June, weekends 10–8, mid-June–mid- Aug., daily 10–9.*

31 The same exit also leads to **Harrison Hot Springs,** a small resort community at the southern tip of picturesque Harrison Lake. Vacationers flock here to relax and rejuvenate in this almost pristine natural setting. Mountains surround the (64-kilometer, or 40-mile) lake that is ringed by pretty beaches and provides a broad range of outdoor activities to enjoy, in addition to the hot springs. Located across from the beach in the large building to the left of the Harrison Hot Springs Hotel is a spring-fed public pool. *100 Esplanade, Harrison Hot Springs, tel. 604/796–2244. Admission: $5 adults, $3.50 senior citizens and children, children under 5 free; unlimited-entry day passes $7 adults, $5 children. Open Sun.–Thurs. 8 AM–9 PM, Fri.–Sat.8–10.*

A tour of the **Kilby General Store Museum,** a heritage attraction in nearby Harrison Mills, takes you back in time to British Columbia as it was in the 1920s. Visitors tour the general store and hotel of T. Kilby, a pioneer of the area, and chat with the shopkeeper, sniff whatever is simmering on the wood-burning stove, and tramp through the orchards, stockroom, fueling station, barn, and dairy house on the grounds. This is a fine slice of living history. *215 Kilby Rd. (1.6 km [1 mi] off Hwy. 7 on north shore of Frazer River; follow signs), Harrison Mills, tel. 604/ 796–9576. Admission: $4.50 adults, $4 senior citizens, $2.50 children, children under 5 free. Open May–June and Labor Day–mid-Oct., Thurs.–Mon. 10–4; July–Aug., daily 10–5, and mid-Oct.–Nov. 1, daily 10–4.*

Scenic Drives

The **Gold Rush Trail** is a 640-kilometer (400-mile) route along which the frontiersmen traveled in search of gold in the 19th and early 20th centuries. The interior British Columbia trail begins just below Prince George in the north, and extends to Lillooet in the south, but juts off at points in between. Following the route you can travel through Quesnel, Williams Lake, Wells, Barkerville, along the Fraser Canyon, and Cache Creek. Most towns and communities through which the trail passes have re-created villages, history museums, or historic sites that help to tell the story of the gold-rush era. For more information contact the **Cariboo Chilcotin Coast Tourist Association** (Box 4900, Williams Lake V2G 2V8, tel. 604/392–2226; in U.S. 800/663–5885, fax 604/392–2838).

Completion of a new highway opened the **Coast Mountain Circle,** linking Vancouver to Cariboo Country. This 702-kilometer (435-mile) route takes in spectacular Howe Sound, the deep-water port of Squamish, Whistler Resort, and Pemberton Valley before heading back to Vancouver through scenic Fraser Canyon and Harrison Hot Springs. The loop makes a comfortable two- to three-day journey. For more information contact the **Tourism Association of Southwestern B.C.** (304–828 W. 8th Ave., Vancouver V5Z 1E2, tel. 604/876–3088 or 800/667–3306).

Shopping

Okanagan Valley The **Peter Flanagan Okanagan Pottery Studio** (tel. 604/767–2010), located on Highway 97 in Peachland, sells handcrafted ceramics.

Geert Maas Sculpture Gardens, Gallery, and Studio. World-class sculptor Geert Maas exhibits his art in an indoor gallery and a one-acre garden, in the hills above Kelowna. Maas, who works in bronze, stoneware, and mixed media, creates distinctive abstract figures with a round and fluid quality. He also sells medallions, original paintings, and etchings. *R.R. 1250 Reynolds Rd., Kelowna, V1Y 7P9, tel. 604/860–7012. Admission free. Open year-round; call for exact hours.*

Prince Rupert Native art and other local crafts are available at **Studio 9** (516 3rd Ave. W, tel. 604/624–2366).

Queen Charlotte Islands The Haida Gwaii carve valuable figurines from the hard, black slate called argillite. The specific variety used by the Haidas is found only on the islands. Their works can be found at the **Adams Family House of Silver** (tel. 604/626–3215), in Old Masset, behind the Ed Jones Haida Museum, and at **Joy's Island Jewellers** (tel. 604/559–4742) in Queen Charlotte. Other island specialties are silk-screen prints and silver jewelry.

Vancouver Island Duncan is the home of Cowichan wool sweaters, handknitted by the Cowichan people. A large selection is available from **Hills Indian Crafts** (tel. 604/746–6731) and **Big Foot Trading Post** (tel. 604/748–1153), both on the main highway, about 1½ kilometers (1 mile) south of Duncan. Also check out **Modeste Wool Carding** (2615 Modeste Rd., Duncan, tel. 604/748–8983), about a half mile off the highway in nearby Koksilah.

Sports and Outdoor Activities

Canoeing and Kayaking Canoeing and kayaking are favorite ways to explore the miles of extended, interconnected waterways and the breathtaking coastline of British Columbia. The **Inside Passage, Queen Charlotte Strait, Georgia Strait,** and the other island-dotted straits and sounds that border the mainland provide fairly protected sea-going from Washington State to the Alaskan border, with numerous marine parks to explore along the way. Another particular favorite among paddlers is the **Powell Forest Canoe**

Route, an 80-kilometer (50-mile) circuit of 12 lakes connected by streams, rivers, and well-maintained portage trails.

For rentals on Vancouver Island, contact **Tofino Sea-Kayaking Company** (Box 620, Tofino, tel. 604/725–4222) and **Stubbs Island Charters** (Box 7, Telegraph Cove, tel. 604/928–3185). On the mainland, try **Clipper Canoes** (1717 Salton Rd., Box 115, Abbotsford, tel. 604/853–9320) or **Lavington Rental** (5562 Hwy. 6, Vernon, tel. 604/542–4788).

Fishing Miles of coastline and thousands of lakes, rivers, and streams bring more than 750,000 fishermen to British Columbia each year. The waters of the province hold 74 species of fish (25 of them sport fish), including Chinook salmon and rainbow trout. An annual freshwater-fishing license is about $19 for Canadians, $17 for B.C. residents. For a nonresident or non-Canadian, it's $10–$15 for six days, and $27 annually. A saltwater-fishing license for one day costs $3.75 for Canadian residents and non-Canadians, and is available at virtually every fishing lodge and sporting-goods outlet along the coast. Annual licenses are about $11 for non-B.C. Canadians and $38 for non-Canadians.

For updated fishing information and regulations, contact the **B.C. Fish Branch** (Ministry of Environment, 810 Blanshard St., Victoria V8V 1X5, tel. 604/387–4573). For a guide to saltwater fishing, contact the **Department of Fisheries and Oceans** (Recreational Fisheries Div., Station 415, 555 W. Hastings St., Vancouver V6B 5G3, tel. 604/666–3271).

Golf There are more than 200 golf courses in British Columbia, and the figure is growing. The province is now an Official Golf Destination of the PGA Tour in Canada and of the American PGA tour. Greens fees are about $20–$40. The topography in British Columbia tends to be mountainous, and many courses have fine views as well as treacherous approaches to greens.

Okanagan Valley The Okanagan has a central tee-time booking service for out-
and Environs of-town golfers that lists all of the Okanagan/Interior British Columbia courses below. *Box 342, Westbank V0H 2A0, tel. 604/768–7500, call collect. Open May 15–Oct. 15, Mon.–Fri. 9–5; leave message if no one is there.*

Gallaghers Canyon Golf Resort (4320 McCulloch Rd., Kelowna, tel. 604/861–4240) is one of the most challenging courses in British Columbia, with long, rolling, and twisting fairways. **Kelowna Golf and Country Club** (1297 Glenmore Dr., Kelowna, tel. 604/763–2736) is a private club that favors straight drivers; visitors are welcome but advised to avoid weekends. **Osoyoos Golf and Country Club** (20th Ave., Osoyoos, tel. 604/495–7003) provides a green setting in the dry, parched hills; only two of the 12 par-fours on the course are under 350 yards. Visitors are welcome. **Penticton Golf and Country Club** (799 Eckhardt Ave. W, Penticton, tel. 604/492–8727) has 10 acres of water hazards, challenging traps, and bunkers; it is a semi-private club that welcomes visitors. **Rivershore Golf Club** (off Old Shuswap Rd., Kamloops, tel. 604/573–4622) is a Robert Trent Jones–designed course and is one of British Columbia's longest, at 7,007 yards. Visitors are welcome. **Salmon Arm Golf Course** (3400 Hwy. 97B, Salmon Arm, tel. 604/832–4727) welcomes visitors to its hilly terrain. **Shadow Ridge Golf Club** (3770 Bullman Rd., Kelowna, tel. 604/765–7777) is a relatively new course, set in a valley and surrounded by orchards. **Summerland Golf and Country Club** (2405 Mountain Rd., Summerland, tel. 604/494–

9554) is slightly off the beaten track but has two distinctly different nines with the front nine clear and the back nine cut through a pine forest. **Twin Lakes Golf and Country Resort** (Hwy. 3A, Kaleden, tel. 604/497–5359) has an on-site RV park.

Vancouver Island   Golf is also very popular on Vancouver Island, so there are many good courses to choose from, including: the **Glen Meadows Golf Club** (1050 McTavish Rd., Sidney, tel. 604/656–3136) on the Saanich Peninsula; the **Morningstar Golf Course** (525 Lowery St., Parksville, tel. 604/248–8161) not far from Nanaimo; and the **Long Beach Golf Course** (Pacific Rim Hwy., Tofino, tel. 604/725–3332) on the west side of the island.

Hiking   One of the most challenging hikes in British Columbia is along the **West Coast Trail** (*see* Exploring, Tour 1) in Pacific Rim National Park (tel. 604/726–4212), on Vancouver Island. The demanding 77-kilometer (47-mile) trail is for experienced hikers and follows part of the coast dubbed the "Graveyard of the Pacific," so-called because of the large number of shipwrecks that have occurred there. It can be traveled only on foot, takes an average of six days to complete, and is open from mid-May to late September. A permit is necessary to hike this trail; reservations are available from March through September.

In the Okanagan Valley, hikers will enjoy exploring the railbeds, trestles, tunnels, and abandoned stations of the **Kettle Valley Railway** network, stretching along Lake Okanagan between Penticton and Kelowna. The going is mild; just remember to make enough noise to let the rattlesnakes and bears know you're coming. The Chambers of Commerce for Kelowna (tel. 604/861–1515) and Penticton (tel. 604/492–4103) can provide maps and information.

Virtually all of British Columbia's provincial parks have fine hiking trail networks. The **Ministry of Parks** (1610 Mt. Seymour Rd., N. Vancouver V7G 1L3, tel. 604/929–1291) offers detailed information on those in the area you plan to visit.

Heli-hiking   Heli-hiking is very popular in this province; helicopters deliver hikers to untouched high alpine meadows and verdant mountain tops that have remained virtually untouched because of their inaccessibility. **Alpine Rafting Company** (Box 1409, Golden V0A 1H0, tel. 604/344–5016), **Fraser River Raft Expeditions Ltd.** (Box 10, Yale V0K 2S0, tel. 604/863–2336), **Highland Helicopter** (1685 Tranmer, Agassiz V0M 1K0, tel. 604/796–9610), and **Mount Robson Adventure Holidays** (Box 687, Valemount V0E 2Z0, tel. 604/566–4386) can provide further information.

Rafting   With beautiful rivers such as Adams, Clearwater, Fraser, Illecillewaet, and Thompson interlacing the High Country, Okanagan Valley, and Fraser Canyon, there is a diverse range of rafting trips from which to choose. Operators such as **Clearwater Expeditions** (613 Bissette Rd., Kamloops V2B 6L3, tel. 604/579–8360), **Fraser River Raft Expeditions Ltd.** (Box 10, Yale V0K 2S0, tel. 604/863–2336), **Hyak Rafting** (1975 Maple St., Vancouver V6J 3S9, tel. 604/734–8622), and **Alpine Rafting Company** (Box 1409, Golden V0A 1H0, tel. 604/344–5016) provide options from lazy, half-day floats to exhilarating whitewater journeys of up to a week.

Skiing   British Columbia has hundreds of kilometers of groomed cross-
Cross-country   country (Nordic) ski trails in the provincial parks and more than 40 cross-country resorts. Most downhill destinations have

carved out Nordic routes along the valleys, and there are literally thousands more trails in unmanaged areas of British Columbia.

For cross-country enthusiasts, two of the finest in the province are **Lac le Jeune** (Box 3215, Kamloops V2C 6B8, tel. 604/732–2722), 30 kilometers (18 miles) southwest of Kamloops, and **Manning Park Resort** (Manning Park V0X 1R0, tel. 604/840–8822) en route to the Okanagan, about 200 kilometers (124 miles) east of Vancouver. Manning Park also has downhill facilities, which are just as popular as the nordic program. On Vancouver Island, **Mt. Washington** and **Mt. Cain Alpine Park** (*see below*) have nordic facilities, as do **Apex Alpine** and **Silver Star Mountain Resort** (*see below*) in the Okanagan Valley.

Downhill   With more than half the province situated higher than 4,200 feet above sea level, new downhill courses are constantly opening. At the moment, more than 40 major resorts have downhill facilities.

On Vancouver Island, **Mt. Washington Ski Resort Ltd.** (Box 3069, Courtenay V9N 5N3, tel. 604/338–1386), with more than 40 runs and an elevation of 5,200 feet, is the largest ski area on Vancouver Island, and the third-largest in terms of visitors, in the province. Located in the Comox Valley, it's a modern, well-organized mountain with snowpack averaging 472 inches a year. It also has 30 kilometers (19 miles) of double trackset Nordic trails. Other island ski areas are **Forbidden Plateau** (2050 Cliffe Ave., Courtenay V9N 2L3, tel. 604/334–4744), located near Mt. Washington, with 15 runs and a fall of 1,150 feet; and **Mt. Cain** (Box 1225, Port McNeill V0N 2R0, tel. 604/956–3849), on the northern part of the island near the community of Sayward off Highway 19, with 16 runs and a fall of 1,500 feet.

The Okanagan Valley region, four hours east by car from Vancouver, or one hour by air, offers some of the best ski bargains in the province. **Big White Ski Resort** (Box 2039, Station R, Kelowna V1X 4K5, tel. 604/765–3101) is the highest ski area in British Columbia, though Whistler has a longer free fall. The resort has more than 45 runs along with hotels, restaurants, and, like Whistler, is in the process of rapidly expanding. **Silver Star Mountain Resort** (Box 2, Silver Star Mountain V0E 1G0, tel. 604/542–0224), with more than 61 runs, offers well-lighted night skiing. The complete village at the base of the mountain has enough hotels to accommodate 725 people. **Apex Alpine** (Box 1060, Penticton V2A 7N7, tel. 604/493–3200) has 45 runs and is the largest ski resort in South Okanagan. On-mountain condominiums—many for rent—can accommodate a total of 350.

Kootenay Country, a southeastern section of British Columbia that includes the Rockies, Purcells, Selkirks, and Monashees, features two major resorts: **Whitewater** (Box 60, Nelson V1L 5P7, tel. 604/354–4944), with more than 20 runs and a lot of powder skiing; and **Red Mountain Resorts** (Box 670, Rossland V0G 1Y0, tel. 604/362–7384), which spans two mountains and three mountain faces, and has 30 marked runs.

The resorts in the High Country reflect British Columbia's most diverse topographical area. At 3,100 feet of vertical drop, **Tod Mountain** (Box 869, Kamloops V2C 5M8, tel. 604/578–7222) has 47 runs. On-mountain accommodations are limited to private condominium rentals and a bed-and-breakfast that accommodates up to 32 people. **Mt. Mackenzie** (Box 1000, Revelstoke V0E 2S0, tel. 604/837–5268) has 20 runs and offers deep- powder skiing. Revelstoke, located 5 kilometers (3 miles) from the base, has a wide selection of lodging.

Heli- and Snowcat Skiing Heli-skiing operators are often located at well-established resorts, taking clients into otherwise inaccessible deep-powder regions of the mountains. Others operate as independents and offer accommodations, dining, and recreational facilities in their deluxe lodges. Some companies offer Snowcat skiing, in which an enclosed all-terrain vehicle takes you into the wilderness areas.

In Kootenay Country, try **Kootenay Helicopter Skiing** (Box 717, Nakusp V0G 1R0, tel. 604/265–3121; in B.C., Alberta, and the U.S., 800/663–0100). With accommodations at Kuskanax Lodge, they run seven-day packages to and from Kelowna, Spokane, WA, and Castlegar. **Selkirk Wilderness Skiing** (1 Meadow Creek Rd., Meadow Creek V0G 1N0, tel. 604/366–4424) offers six-day packages (including remote lodging) to and from Nelson.

In the High Country, **Cat Powder Skiing** (Box 1479, Revelstoke V0E 2S0, tel. 604/837–9489) organizes two-, three-, and five-day, all-inclusive packages that run into the Selkirks and on the upper slopes of Mt. MacKenzie in Revelstoke.

Dining and Lodging

Dining

Throughout British Columbia you'll find a variety of cuisines, from Vancouver Island's seafood places to interior British Columbia's wild game–oriented menus. Prices vary from location to location, but ratings reflect the categories listed on the dining chart.

Category	Cost*
Very Expensive	over $35
Expensive	$25–$35
Moderate	$15–$25
Inexpensive	under $15

per person, excluding drinks, service, and 7% GST, in Canadian dollars

Highly recommended restaurants in each price category are indicated by a star ★.

Lodging

The lodging possibilities across the region are as diverse as the restaurant menus. Accommodations range from bed- and-breakfast inns and rustic cabins to deluxe chain hotels. In the cities, especially, there is an abundance of accommodations, but once you get off the beaten track, guest rooms are often a rare commodity and may require advance booking.

Category	Cost*
Very Expensive	over $125
Expensive	$90–$125
Moderate	$50–$90
Inexpensive	under $50

All prices are for a standard double room, excluding 7% GST. Prices are in Canadian dollars.

Highly recommended lodgings in each price category are indicated by a star ★.

Vancouver Island

Campbell River
Dining
★

Royal Coachman Inn. This is another of those informal, blackboard-menu restaurants that dot the landscape of the island. The menu is surprisingly daring for what is essentially a high-end pub, and the inn draws crowds nightly, especially on Tuesday and Saturday (prime rib nights). The menu, however, changes daily, so if ribs aren't your favorite, try one of the other specials. Come early for both lunch and dinner to beat the crowds. *84 Dogwood St., tel. 604/286–0231. No reservations. Dress: casual. AE, MC, V. Inexpensive–Moderate.*

Dining and Lodging

Tsa-Kwa-Luten Lodge. This resort, operated by members of the Kwakiutl tribe, offers authentic Pacific Coast native food and cultural activities. It is located on a high bluff amid 1,100 acres of forest on Quadra Island, a 10-minute ferry ride from Campbell River. Each room in the main lodge has a sea view from a deck or patio; many have a fireplace and loft. There are also four beachfront cabins with fireplace, whirlpool tub, kitchen facilities, and private veranda. Guests are invited to take part in traditional dances in the resort's lounge, which resembles a longhouse, and to visit nearby petroglyphs to make rubbings. *Box 460, Quathiaski Cove, VOP 1NO, tel. 604/285–2042 or 800/665–7745, fax 604/285–2532. 26 rooms, 4 cabins. Facilities: restaurant, lounge, fitness room, sauna, Jacuzzi, mountain bikes, guided salmon fishing. AE, DC, MC, V. Very Expensive.*

★ **April Point Lodge and Fishing Resort.** Operated for almost 50 years by the friendly Peterson family, it comes as no surprise that April Point Lodge has developed a tremendous reputation and whopping amount of repeat business among vacationers. Spread across a point of Quadra Island, and stretching into Discovery Passage across from Campbell River, the 1944 cedar lodge is surrounded by refurbished fishermen's cabins and guest houses that have been added over the years. For the most part, the accommodations are tidy and comfortable rather than fancy; most have kitchen facilities, fireplaces, and sun decks, and a few are equipped with Jacuzzi baths and hot tubs. Kwakiutl and Haida Gwaii art adorn the comfortable lounge and dining room where fine regional cuisine is featured. Special native feasts on the beach on warm summer nights are especially memorable, with spitted salmon roasted over an open fire; fresh steamed scallops, prawns, and clams; and one of the wines from the extensive cellar. *1000 April Point Rd., Box 1, V9W 4Z9, tel. 604/285–2222; fax 604/285–2411. 33 units. Facilities: restaurant, lounge, gift shop, universal gym, pool, nature trails, bikes marina, sea plane dock, salmon charters and*

nature tours available. AE, D, DC, MC, V. Some units closed
Oct.–Apr. Expensive.

Comox/Courtenay **The Old House Restaurant.** This split-character restaurant of-
Dining fers both formal and casual dining, in a restored 1938 home
★ with large cedar beams and a stone fireplace. Upstairs, among
linen and fresh flowers, you select from an innovative Continental menu, with a delightful pepper steak leading as the house
specialty. Downstairs, where it is decidedly more informal, you
can get sandwiches, pastas, and salads. *1760 Riverside La.,
Courtenay, tel. 604/338–5406. Reservations advised upstairs;
no reservations downstairs. Dress: casual but neat upstairs;
casual downstairs. AE, DC, MC, V. Moderate.*

Lodging **The Greystone Manor.** This nonsmoking bed-and-breakfast, set
in a 70-year-old house with period furnishings, looks right out
on Comox Harbor, where a playful colony of seals is often visible from the house. The antiques, wood stove, and wood paneling add to the hospitable, cozy feel of this inn. Breakfast, which
includes fresh fruit, muffins, fruit pancakes, or quiche, is
enough to keep you filled most of the day. *4014 Haas Rd.,
Courtenay V9N 8H9, tel. 604/338–1422. 4 rooms share 2 baths.
Facilities: garden, walking trails. MC. Moderate.*

★ **The Kingfisher.** This hotel, situated among trees and overlooking the Strait of Georgia, is located five minutes south of
Courtenay, but still has some nice touches. The inn's solid
furnishings, clean white-stucco walls, bright lobby with lots of
greenery, and rooms with mountain and ocean views offer a
nice change from the majority of plain accommodations lining
the main drag. *Site 672, RR 6, Courtenay V9N 8H9, tel. 604/
338–1323. 30 units. Facilities: restaurant, lounge, 2 tennis
courts, outdoor pool, sauna, whirlpool. AE, D, DC, MC, V.
Moderate.*

Malahat **The Aerie.** The million-dollar view of Finlayson Arm and the
Dining and Lodging Gulf Islands persuaded Austrians Leo and Maria Schuster to
★ build their small, luxury resort. In this Mediterranean-style
villa, some rooms have a patio; others have whirlpool tubs
tucked into window nooks to take advantage of the scenery.
The dining room is open to the public for stunning dinner views
and outstanding cuisine. The maple-smoked salmon, pheasant
consommé, medallions of venison in morel sauce, and crème
brûlée with fruit sorbet are more than worth the short drive
from Victoria. *600 Ebedora Ln., V0R 2L0, tel. 604/743–7115 or
604/743–4055; fax 604/743–4766. 8 rooms, 5 suites. Facilities:
restaurant, indoor and outdoor Jacuzzis, sauna, exercise
room, library, heli-pad, nature trails. Reservations advised
for restaurant. AE, MC, V. Expensive–Very Expensive.*

Nanaimo **The Mahle House.** This casually elegant place serves innovative
Dining Northwest cuisine, such as braised rabbit with Dijon mustard
★ and red wine sauce. Twelve items adorn the regular menu, including a succulent carrot and ginger soup, and a catch of the
day. Care to detail, an intimate setting, and a new addition to
the three country-style rooms make this one of the finest dining
experiences in the region. *Cedar and Heemer Rds., tel. 604/
722–3621. Reservations advised. Dress: casual but neat. MC,
V. Closed lunch and Mon.–Tues. Moderate.*

★ **The Grotto.** A perennial favorite, The Grotto is a Nanaimo institution that specializes in a variety of seafood. The restaurant
is set against a waterfront background, and dining here is relaxed and casual. Try the spare ribs, gourmet pizzas, or the

seafood platter—zum-zum—that's big enough for two. *1511 Stewart Ave., tel. 604/753–3303. Reservations accepted. Dress: casual. AE, MC, V. Closed lunch and Sun. Inexpensive–Moderate.*

Dining and Lodging **Yellow Point Lodge.** Yellow Point is a spit of land south of Nanaimo, east of Ladysmith, that has a series of luxurious rustic lodges of which this is the finest example. Rebuilt in 1986 after a fire destroyed the original, the lodge lost almost nothing in ambience and gained a great deal: Nine larger rooms have better facilities (all have private baths and are available year-round). Situated on a rocky knoll overlooking the Stuart Channel are beach cabins, field cabins, a range of different-size cottages, and beach barracks (closed mid-October to mid-April) for the hardy (the summer-use cabins, cottages, and barracks have no running water and share a central bathhouse). Beach cabins can be private and include tree-trunk beds and wood-burning stoves; beach barracks are not as sound, and noises carry from unit to unit, but the location along the shore makes them popular. One hundred eighty acres of land allows for strolling and exploring. Three full meals and snacks are included in the tariff. *Yellow Point Rd., RR 3, Ladysmith V0R 2E0, tel. 604/245–7422. 50 rooms. Facilities: restaurant (for guests only), 2 tennis courts, seawater pool, hot tub, sauna, canoes, mountain bikes. MC, V. Inexpensive–Expensive.*

Dorchester Hotel. Upbeat Mediterranean tones of champagne, ochre, and teal replace the old drab blue exterior of the Dorchester. Once the Nanaimo Opera House, this elegant hotel overlooking the harbor has a distinctive character, with gold knockers on each of the doors, winding hallways, and a spacious library. The rooms are small but exceptionally comfortable, and most have views of the harbor. *70 Church St., V9R 5H4, tel. 604/754–6835; fax 604/754–2638. 70 rooms. Facilities: restaurant, meeting rooms, fitness room, lounge, library, rooftop patio. AE, DC, MC, V. Moderate.*

Dining and Lodging **La Coast Bastion Inn.** This hotel is conveniently located downtown near the ferry terminal, train, and bus stations. All rooms with balconies have views of the old Hudson's Bay fort and the ocean and are modernly furnished. The three eating/entertainment establishments located within the hotel make this a self-sufficient accommodation. *11 Bastion St., V9R 2Z9, tel. 604/753–6601, or 800/663–1144 in the U.S. 179 rooms. Facilities: restaurant, lounge, Irish deli/pub, gift shop, boutique, convention rooms, sauna, hot tub, gym. AE, DC, MC, V. Expensive–Very Expensive.*

Parksville **Beach Acres Resort Hotel.** For a family vacation, this collection *Dining and Lodging* of cottages set in the woods facing the Georgia Strait is both charming and practical. Each unit has one or two bedrooms, living room, kitchen, fireplace, and storage areas. *1015 E. Island Hwy., V9P 2E4, tel. 604/248–3424; fax 604/248–6145. 60 cottages. Facilities: restaurant, indoor pool, sauna, whirlpool, playground, 3 tennis courts, health club. AE, DC, MC, V. 1-week minimum July–Aug. Very Expensive.*

The Roadhouse Inn. This Swiss chalet, set on three acres, is central to four of the region's golf courses. There are only a limited number of rooms, but all are comfortable. *1223 Smithers Rd., V9P 2C1, tel. 604/248–2912. 6 rooms. Facilities: restaurant. MC, V. Inexpensive–Moderate.*

Port Hardy
Dining and Lodging

Glen Lyon Inn. All of the rooms have a full ocean view of Hardy Bay and, like most area motels, have clean, modern amenities. Eagles are often on the premises, eyeing the water for fish to prey on. It's a short ride from the inn to the ferry terminal. *6345 Hardy Bay Rd., Box 103, V0N 2P0, tel. 604/949–7115; fax 604/949–7415. 29 rooms. Facilities: restaurant, lounge, nearby marina, boat launch. AE, DC, MC, V. Moderate.*

Sidney
Lodging
★

Borthwick Country Manor. Flower boxes and awnings adorn the windows of this Tudor home, built in 1979 on Vancouver Island's Saanich Peninsula. It is ideally located in the quiet countryside within minutes of Victoria, Butchart Gardens, the airport, and Washington and British Columbia ferries. Owners Joyce and Watson Borthwick's interest in collecting and refinishing antiques is evident throughout the house, from the elaborately carved 17th-century mahogany table and Victorian balloon-back chairs and sideboard in the dining room, to a Canadian bedstead and early American dresser, both of mahogany, in the largest guest room. French doors lead to the backyard, with gardens to admire and a hot tub to enjoy. *9750 Ardmore Dr., RR 2,, V8L 3S1, tel. 604/656–9498; fax 604/474–7250. 5 rooms. Facilities: hot tub, fishing charters available. MC, V. Closed Dec. Moderate–Expensive.*

Sooke
Dining and Lodging
★

Ocean Wilderness. This large 1940s log cabin sits on five forested, beachfront acres, 13 kilometer (8 miles) west of Sooke. Owner Bill Paine, a retired sea captain, and his wife, Marion, added seven guest rooms in a rough cedar addition in 1990. The pair of auction buffs has furnished their home with a fine collection of Victorian antiques. Romantic canopies and ruffled linens on high beds dominate the spacious guest rooms, which have sitting areas with views of either the Strait of Juan de Fuca or the gardens in the back. Just outside, stepping stones lead to a hot tub housed in a Japanese-style gazebo near awinding path that descends to the beach cove. *109 W. Coast Rd., RR 2, V0S 1N0, tel. and fax 604/646–2116. 7 rooms. Facilities: private decks or patios, hot tub, hiking trails, meal service available. MC, V. Moderate–Expensive.*

★ **Sooke Harbour House.** This original 1931 clapboard farmhouse turned inn presents three suites, a 10-room addition, and a dining room—all of which exude elegance. One of the finest restaurants in British Columbia, it is well worth the trip to Sooke, from Victoria. The fish is just-caught fresh, and the herbs, picked from some 200 varieties, are grown on the property. Four chefs sharing the kitchen guarantees an abundance of creative dishes. On a nice summer evening you may want to sit on the terrace, where you can catch a glimpse of the sea mammals that play by the spit of land in front of the restaurant. Equally exquisite are the romantic guest rooms, with natural wood and white finishes adding to each unit's unique theme. Rooms range from the Herb Garden Room—decorated in shades of mint, with French doors opening onto a private patio—to the Longhouse Room, complete with Native American furnishings. All units, with fireplaces and either ocean or mountain views, come with fresh flowers, a decanter of port, and wet bars that include herbal teas and cookies. Breakfast and lunch are included in your room rate, but you must make a reservation for your meals. Likewise, reservations for nonguests for dinner are essential. Hosts Fredrica and Sinclair Philip have been paying attention to details here since 1979. *1528 Whiffen Spit Rd., RR 4, V0S 1N0, tel. 604/642–3421; fax 604/642–6988.*

13 rooms. Facilities: restaurant. Closed lunch except for hotel guests. Dress: casual but neat. AE, MC, V. Very Expensive.

Ucluelet/Tofino
Dining

Whale's Tale. This is a no-frills, dark but warmly decorated down-to-earth place where cooking and the rustic decor go hand-in-hand. The view isn't much, but the cedar-shingle building, set on pilings, shakes with a good gust of wind. The menu is highlighted by prime rib and a variety of local seafood. *1861 Peninsula Rd., Ucluelet, tel. 604/726–4621. Dress: casual. MC, V. Closed lunch and Nov.–Jan. Moderate.*

★ **The Wickaninnish Restaurant.** Before the Canadian government acquired this wonderful wood building for its interpretive center, it was a unique inn. It is still a restaurant, with an ambience—the beach setting, combined with the building's glass exterior and stone-and-beam interior, accented by a stone fireplace—that cannot be matched anywhere else in the area. Seafood is the primary choice here—especially the West Coast chowder—but if you take the chicken-and-prawn stir-fry, you won't be disappointed. *On Long Beach, 16 km (11 mi) north of Ucluelet, tel. 604/726–7706. Reservations advised for 7 or more. Dress: casual. AE, MC, V. Closed mid-Oct.–mid-Feb. Moderate.*

Lodging

★ **Chesterman's Beach Bed and Breakfast.** This is one of several small, romantic bed-and-breakfasts located on the beach, but the front yard—which is the rolling ocean surf—makes this one unique. You can walk away the hours just walking the beach, searching the tidal pools, or—from March to October—watching whales migrating by the front door. The self-contained suite in the main house and the separate Lookout Suite are romantic, cozy, and unique; both have comfortable beds and a view of the beach. The self-sufficient one-bedroom garden cottage offers no ocean view but accommodates up to four; it's a good option for a family vacation. Owner Joan Dublanko makes hot muffins every morning. *1345 Chesterman's Beach Rd., Tofino V0R 2Z0, tel. 604/725–3726. 3 suites. Facilities: bikes, surfboards, beach. MC, V. Expensive–Very Expensive.*

Canadian Princess Fishing Resort. If old ships are to your liking, book a berth on this converted survey ship which has 30 comfortable, but hardly opulent, staterooms. Each offers one to four berths, and all share washrooms; for something a bit more spacious, request the captain's cabin. Roomier than the ship cabins and complete with more contemporary furnishings are the resort's deluxe shoreside rooms. Promising an unusual experience, this Spartan resort provides the bare necessities—mostly to the many fishermen who flock here during the summer. *The Boat Basin, Box 939, Ucluelet V0R 3A0, tel. 604/726–7771 or 800/663–7090; fax 604/726–7121. 76 sleeping units. Facilities: 10 charter boats. AE, MC, V. Moderate–Expensive.*

Pacific Sands Beach Resort. Just a mile north of Pacific Rim National Park is this rustic resort with motel suites and individual two-bedroom cottages. The motel rooms are basic with modern furnishings, but fireplaces make them seem cozier. Some of the rooms in the new, three-story addition have Jacuzzi tubs. Pacific Sands is close to Long Beach golf course and is on the ocean. *1421 Pacific Rim Hwy., Box 237, Tofino V0R 2Z0, tel. 604/725–3322; fax 604/725–3155. 66 rooms. AE, MC, V. Moderate–Expensive.*

North of Vancouver Island

Prince Rupert
Dining

Smile's Seafood Café. If you don't mind walking among the fish-processing plants by the railway, you'll find this place a real change of pace. It has been a mainstay of Prince Rupert since 1935 and has succeeded because it provides small-town friendly service along with its seafood menu. Favorites include the halibut cheeks and the fisherman's platter. *113 George Hills Way, tel. 604/624–3072. No reservations. Dress: casual. MC, V. Moderate.*

Lodging

Highliner Inn. This modern high rise near the waterfront is conveniently situated and relatively well priced. It's in the heart of the downtown shopping district and is only one block from the airline terminal building. Ask for a room with a private balcony and view of the harbor. *815 1st Ave. W, V8J 1B3, tel. 604/624–9060; fax 604/627–7759. 96 rooms. Facilities: restaurant, lounge, convention rooms, beauty salon, laundromat. AE, DC, MC, V. Moderate.*

Dining and Lodging
★

Crest Motor Hotel. It may surprise you to find a four-diamond AAA hotel in this small community, but this warm, modern hotel is probably the finest in the north. It's one block away from the two shopping centers but is situated on a bluff overlooking the harbor. The pleasantly decorated restaurant has brass rails, beam ceilings, and a waterfront view, and specializes in seafood; particularly outstanding are the salmon dishes. *222 1st Ave. W, V8J 3P6, tel. 604/624–6771; in Canada, 800/663–8150; fax 604/627–7666. 103 rooms. Facilities: restaurant, lounge, coffee shop. Reservations required for restaurant. Dress: casual but neat. AE, D, DC, MC, V. Moderate–Expensive.*

Queen Charlotte Islands
Lodging

Alaska View Lodge. On a clear day, you can step onto your porch at this bed-and-breakfast and see the mountains of Alaska in the distance. The lodge is bordered by a long stretch of sandy beach on one side and by woods on the other. Eliane and Charly Feller, both European by origin, offer simple beachhouse rooms with few of the amenities you're likely to find in a Hilton; but the private balconies more than compensate. For an additional cost, Eliane makes a three-course dinner, using classical recipes based on Queen Charlotte fare, such as home-smoked salmon, scallops, and Dungeness crab. *Tow Hill Rd., Box 227, Masset V0T 1M0, tel. 604/626–3333. 4 rooms. No credit cards. Moderate.*

Spruce Point Lodge. This cedar-sided building, encircled by a balcony, attracts families and couples because of its inexpensive rates and down-home feel. Like most Queen Charlotte accommodations, this one is more rustic than luxurious and features locally made pine furnishings that go with the northern-woods motif. For the money you get a Continental breakfast and an occasional seafood barbecue, with a menu that depends on the daily catch. Kayakers and hikers on a budget should ask about the bunk rooms, usually available at a low nightly rate. *609 6th Ave., Queen Charlotte V0T 1S0, tel. 604/559–8234. 7 rooms. MC, V. Inexpensive.*

Dining and Lodging

Tlell River House. The smell of fresh-cut wood welcomes you into this new, secluded lodge overlooking the Tlell River. From the property in the middle of the woods, it's only a few hundred feet to the beach (and the shipwreck of the *Pezuta*). The rooms feature all-wood paneling, floral curtains, and thick down com-

forters; many have views of the river. The restaurant serves
excellent seafood and a variety of deliciously rich cheesecakes.
*Beitush Rd., just south of the Tlell River Bridge on Hwy. 16,
Box 56, Tlell V0T 1Y0, tel. 604/557-4211, fax 604/557-4622. 10
rooms. Facilities: restaurant, lounge, meeting room, laundromat, boat rentals, guided fishing trips. MC, V. Moderate.*

Okanagan Valley and Environs, Including Rainbow and High Country

Harrison Hot
Springs
Dining
★

The Black Forest. Ask the locals where to dine and they'll send
you here, a charming Bavarian dining room on Harrison Village Esplanade, overlooking the lake. It comes as no surprise
that the specialties here are German standards, from schnitzels
to Black Forest cake, with a few Continental dishes (mainly
steaks and seafood) thrown in for good measure. Hearty
German beer and an array of wines round out the selection. *180
Esplanade, tel. 604/796-9343. Reservations advised. Dress:
casual but neat. MC, V. Closed lunch. Moderate–Expensive.*

Dining and Lodging
★

Harrison Hot Springs Hotel. Ever since fur traders and gold
miners discovered the soothing hot springs in the late 1800s,
Harrison has been a favored stopover spot. The St. Alice Hotel,
built in 1896 to accommodate these weary travelers, was destroyed by fire, and from its ashes rose the Harrison Hot
Springs Hotel in the 1920s. The property has continued to
grow over the decades, and, for the most part, you can tell from
the decor when sections were built. The most reasonably
priced rooms located in the original building and west tower are
dated, with worn furnishings, fixtures, and carpets; those in
the new east tower (added in 1989) are much more modern and
plush, with a heftier price tag. The long list of amenities and
scenic lakeside location give the hotel a resort feel; plans to add
a PGA-rated 18-hole golf course are underway. Bring a robe to
make the trip from your room to the indoor hot spring-fed pools
or heated outdoor pool. *100 Esplanade, Harrison Hot Springs
V0M 1K0, tel. 604/796-2244; in the Pacific Northwest, 800/
663-2266; fax 604/796-9374. 290 rooms, 12 cottages. Facilities:
2 restaurants, lounge, 2 indoor pools, 1 outdoor pool, saunas, 3
tennis courts, 9-hole executive golf course, games room, gift
shops, beauty salon, health club, complimentary afternoon
tea, bike rentals, hiking trails. Reservations advised for restaurant. Dress: neat. AE, DC, MC, V. Moderate–Very Expensive.*

Kamloops
Dining and
Lodging
★

Lac le Jeune Resort. This is the property that locals use when
they want to combine the outdoors and sophisticated, modern
surroundings. With 160 kilometers (99 miles) of cross-country
skiing, a lake stocked with trout, and a restaurant that serves
robust helpings, this is a good choice for an accommodation.
The rustic, self-sufficient cabins are perfect for families because of their ample size and amenities, and pets are permitted. There are also comfortable, spacious rooms in the main
lodge, with no phones or televisions to distract from the beauty
of the setting. *Off Coquihala Hwy., 29 km (18 mi) southwest of
Kamloops, Box 3215, Kamloops V2C 6B8, tel. 604/372-2722 or
800/561- 5253, fax 604/372-8755. 28 rooms, 4-plex chalet, 6
cabins. Facilities: restaurant, lounge, meeting room, gift shop,
theater, games room, indoor whirlpool, sauna, boat and ski
rentals. AE, D, DC, MC, V. Moderate–Expensive.*

Kelowna **Papillon.** This contemporarily furnished restaurant features a
Dining Continental menu that offers pasta, seafood, and steak. While
seafood is not necessarily the specialty here, the prawns and
scallops Caribbean is superb and highly recommended. The
wine list includes a wide selection of imported and local wines
that work nicely with the meals. *375 Leon Ave., tel. 604/763–
3833. Reservations advised. Dress: neat but casual. AE, MC,
V. Closed weekend lunch. Moderate–Expensive.*

Dining and Lodging **Hotel Eldorado.** In 1989, the owners bought the old Eldorado
Arms, built in 1926, and floated it by barge to its present location. Shortly thereafter, the old property burned down, but a
new Eldorado has been built in its place, with much of the old-
style charm intact. Rooms tend to be small and cozy, with light
carpets, floral patterns, and antique furnishings; many have
balconies affording superb views of Okanagan Lake. The
Boardwalk Restaurant has earned a fine reputation, serving
fresh rack of lamb and seafood dishes. Ask for a seat on the waterfront patio. *500 Cook Rd., V1W 9L5, tel. 604/763–7500, fax
604/861–4779. 20 rooms. Facilities: restaurant, lounge, conference room, marina, Jacuzzi suite. Dress: casual but neat. AE,
MC, V. Expensive.*

Dining and Lodging **Lake Okanagan Resort.** This well-acclaimed Hotels and Re-
★ sorts property is a popular, self-contained destination on the
west side of Okanagan Lake. All rooms have either kitchens or
kitchenettes and range in size from one-room suites in the main
hotel to spacious three-room chalets situated around the 300
acres. The resort shows some signs of age, particularly in the
worn floors; but functional, earthtone furnishings, wood-burning fireplaces, perfect views of the lake, and all the resort activities make this a good choice of accommodations. Lakeside
Terrace rooms renovated in 1993 are the best choice. *2751
Westside Rd.,V1Y 8B2; tel. 604/769–3511 or 800/223–0888, fax
604/769–6655. 150 rooms. Facilities: restaurant, café, poolside
lounge, Jacuzzi and saunas, 3 pools, par-3 9-hole golf course, 7
tennis courts, stables, marina, scuba shop, pro shop, hiking/
biking trails, nature and dinner cruises. AE, D, DC, MC, V.
Very Expensive.*

Merritt **Corbett Lake Country Inn.** The locals want to keep this one a
Dining and Lodging secret, but not owner Peter McVey, a French-trained chef. His
★ restaurant offers a different fixed menu every night; favorites
include rack of lamb and chateaubriand. The six single cabins
(with extra beds) and two duplexes are comfortable, but not
plush, and there are also three rooms in the main lodge. Small
pets are allowed. *Off Hwy. 5A, 11 km (6.8 mi) south of Merritt,
Box 327, V0K 2B0, tel. 604/378–4334. 10 cabins, 3 rooms. Facilities: boat rentals, cross-country ski trails. Reservations required for restaurant. Dress: casual. No credit cards. Closed
Mar.–Apr., Oct. 15–Dec. 23. Moderate.*

Penticton **Granny Bogner's.** The decor in this mostly Continental restau-
Dining rant is a bit contrived, with flowing lace curtains, Oriental
★ rugs, wood chairs, cloth-covered tables, and waitresses
adorned in long paisley skirts, conveying that this is a "homey"
place. But the food is excellent and prepared meticulously to
order. The poached halibut and roasted duck have contributed
to the widely held belief that this is the best restaurant in the
Okanagan. *302 Eckhardt Ave. W, tel. 604/493–2711. Reservations advised. Dress: casual. AE, MC, V. Closed lunch; Sun.
and Mon.; Jan. Moderate–Expensive.*

Lodging **Coast Lakeside Resort.** On the shore of Okanagan Lake, the inn is both a peaceful retreat and right in the center of the action. The waterfront offers relaxation, and the nearby Penticton Golf and Country Club invites a competitive round of golf. Vancouver businesspeople love this place because it provides comfort and convention facilities. The newly renovated rooms are bright and airy, and half of them have lake views. *21 Lakeshore Dr. W, V2A 7M5, tel. 604/493–8221 or 800/663–1144; fax 604/ 493–0607. 204 rooms. Facilities: 2 restaurants, lounge, beauty salon, 2 tennis courts, volleyball, windsurfing, sailing, waterskiing, indoor pool, health club, sauna, Jacuzzi, games room, shuffleboard, masseuse. AE, DC, MC, V. Very Expensive.*

★ **Riordan House.** When John and Donna Ortiz bought and restored the former Tiffin Tea House/Riordan Restaurant for their residence, they didn't expect to give guided tours to the newly spiffed-up 1921 house. But people seemed to like the place, built by a Prohibition rum-runner and furnished now with family antiques, so the Ortizes bowed to the inevitable and opened it as a bed-and-breakfast. One bedroom has a fireplace and one a sitting area; all look out on the surrounding hills. The Continental breakfast stars house-baked croissants, scones, muffins, and a selection of seasonal fruit; box lunches are packed on request (and Granny Bogner's is 60 paces away). Lake Okanagan is only a short walk, and you can drift on a rubber raft down the canal that connects it with Skaha Lake. *689 Winnipeg St., V2A 5N1, tel. 604/493–5997. 3 rooms share 3 baths. Facilities: airport pickup, shuttle to lake beach, robes and slippers, fresh flowers. MC, V. Inexpensive–Moderate.*

For bed-and-breakfast information contact **Okanagan Bed and Breakfast** (Box 5135, Kelowna V1Y 8T9, tel. 604/868–2700).

Silver Star **Craigellachie Dining Room.** The home-cooked meals in the din-
Mountain ing room of the Putnam Station Hotel are filling rather than
Dining fancy. Soups and sandwiches are on the lunch menu, while old
★ favorites like barbecue ribs, lasagne, pork chops, steaks, and pastas are offered in the evenings. The daily three-course special is generally a good deal. *Silver Star Mountain Resort, Box 4, Silver Star Mountain, tel. 604/542–2459. Reservations accepted. Dress: casual. AE, MC, V. Moderate.*

Dining and Lodging **Vance Creek Hotel.** Looking more like the set of a spaghetti
★ Western than a modern hotel, the Vance Creek enjoys a prime location in the heart of the *Gaslight*-era-themed village resort, atop Silver Star Mountain. Rooms are simple, with coordinated decor, long vanities in the entryway, and boxy bathrooms. Those on the first floor are popular with families because they are equipped with kitchenettes, bunk beds for the kids, and private entrances that open outside the hotel. Willow furniture and fireplaces add a touch more comfort to rooms in the annex completed in 1993. *Silver Star Mountain Resort, Box 3, Silver Star Mountain V0E 1G0, tel. 604/549–5191; fax 604/549–5177. 84 rooms. Facilities: 2 restaurants, lounge, bar, hot tubs, ski locker, meeting room, resort amenities including hiking/biking trails, indoor pool, horseback riding, bike and in-line skate rentals. Reservations accepted in restaurants. Dress: casual. Closed mid-Apr.–mid-May. AE, D, MC, V. Expensive.*

★ **Silver Lode Inn.** To complete the alpine experience on Silver Star Mountain, head to the Silver Lode Restaurant for raclette or fondue. Owners Max Schlaepfer and Trudi Amstutz, originally from Berne, Switzerland, serve hearty helpings of the real thing in the cheerful restaurant of their inn. No-frills rooms offer the basic comforts and are the most reasonably priced in the village. *Silver Star Mountain Resort, Box 5, Silver Star Mountain V0E 1G0, tel. 604/549–5105; fax 604/549–2163. Facilities: restaurant, bar, lounge, ski locker, hot tub, meeting room, resort amenities including hiking/biking trails, indoor pool, horseback riding, bike and in-line skate rentals. Reservations accepted in restaurant. Dress: casual. AE, MC, V. Moderate–Expensive.*

Vernon
Dining **Intermezzo.** This intimate Italian restaurant combines dim lighting, high-backed chairs, olive-green wall paneling, and a lounge with a fireplace. The effect is formal and old European, although the service is anything but stiff. Owner Jean DeLisle offers standard veal, fish, and pasta dishes, and an excellent selection of wines, as displayed in the wood cabinet of the main dining room. *3206 34th Ave., Box 22, Vernon V1T 6M1, tel. 604/542–3853. Reservations accepted. Dress: casual but neat. AE, MC, V. Inexpensive.*

Lodging **Village Green Hotel.** This hotel offers access to four golf courses and to the Silver Star Ski Resort, just 22 kilometers (14 miles) away. The bright, pleasant decor and reasonable prices make this hotel a good alternative to the other accommodations that line Highway 97. The rooms are spacious and the service is personal and friendly. *4801 27th St., V1T 4Z1, tel. 604/542–3321; fax 604/549–4252. 138 rooms. Facilities: restaurant, coffee shop, gift shop, lounge, night club, 4 tennis courts, volleyball, indoor and outdoor pools, sauna, Jacuzzi, shuttle to ski resort and golf courses. AE, D, DC, MC, V. Moderate.*

9 Southeast Alaska

By Mike Miller

Updated by
Mary Engel

Southeast, as Alaskans call the region, stretches below the state like the tail of a kite. It is a world of massive glaciers, fjords, and snowcapped peaks. Thousands of islands are blanketed with lush stands of spruce, hemlock, and cedar. Bays, coves, lakes of all sizes, and swift, icy rivers provide some of the continent's best fishing grounds—and scenery as majestic and unspoiled as any in North America.

Like anywhere else, the region has its drawbacks. For one thing, it rains a lot. If you plan to spend a week or more here, you can count on showers during at least a few of those days. Loyal Southeasterners simply throw on a light slicker and shrug off the rain. Their attitude is philosophical: without the rain, there would be no forests, no lakes, and no streams running with world-class salmon and trout, no healthy populations of brown and black bear, moose, deer, mountain goat, and wolves.

Another disadvantage—or advantage, depending on your point of view—is an almost total lack of connecting roads between the area's communities. To fill this void, Alaskans created the Marine Highway System of fast, frequent passenger and vehicle ferries. The ships, complete with staterooms, observation decks, cocktail lounges, and heated, glass-enclosed solariums, connect Bellingham, WA, and Prince Rupert, BC, with Southeast's Ketchikan, Wrangell, Petersburg, Sitka, Juneau, Haines, and Skagway. Smaller vessels connect remote towns and villages.

Beyond the ferries, there are the big cruise ships that ply Southeast waters, about 20 or so of them during the height of the summer. Regular jet service also provides access from the lower 48 states and from mainland Alaska to the north. Closer to the lower 48 states than any other Alaskan region, Southeast is therefore the least costly to reach.

The native peoples you'll meet in the Southeast coastal region are Tlingit, Haida, and Tsimshian Indians. These peoples, like their coastal neighbors in British Columbia, continue a culture rich in totemic art forms, including deeply carved poles, masks, baskets, and ceremonial objects.

Southeast Alaska is a busy and bustling region; it's a place of commercial fishermen, loggers, pulp-mill workers, government civil servants, modern-day miners, merchants, and white-collar professionals. It's a region vastly different from South Central or Interior Alaska, just as those regions differ dramatically from Alaska's Arctic or Canada's Yukon.

Essential Information

Getting Around

By Plane **Alaska Airlines** (tel. 800/426–0333) operates several flights daily from Seattle and dozens of other Pacific Coast and Southwestern cities to Ketchikan, Wrangell, Petersburg, Sitka, Glacier Bay, and Juneau. The carrier connects Juneau to the North with Yakutat, Cordova, Anchorage, Fairbanks, Nome, Kotzebue, and Prudhoe Bay. **Delta Airlines** (tel. 800/221–1212) has at least one flight daily from Seattle to Juneau and from Juneau to Fairbanks.

By Car Only Skagway and Haines, in the northern Panhandle, and tiny little Hyder, just across the border from Stewart, BC, are accessible by conventional highway. To reach Skagway or Haines, take the Alaska Highway to the Canadian Yukon's Whitehorse or Haines Junction, respectively, then drive the Klondike Highway or Haines Highway southwest to the Alaska Panhandle. You can reach Hyder on British Columbia's Cassiar Highway, which can be reached, in turn, from Highway 16 just north of Prince Rupert.

By Ferry From the south, the **Alaska Marine Highway System** (tel. 800/642–0066) operates stateroom-equipped vehicle and passenger ferries from Bellingham, WA, and from Prince Rupert, BC. The vessels call at Ketchikan, Wrangell, Petersburg, Juneau, Haines, and Skagway, and they connect with smaller vessels serving Bush communities. One of the smaller ferries also operates between Hyder and Ketchikan. In the summer, staterooms on the ferries are always sold out before sailing time; reserve months in advance. For those planning to take cars on the ferry, early reservations are also highly recommended for vehicle space.

BC Ferries (1112 Fort St., Victoria, BC, Canada V8V 4V2, tel. 604/669–1211) operates similar passenger and vehicle ferries from Vancouver Island, BC, to Prince Rupert.

By Train At present, Southeast Alaska's only railroad, the **White Pass Yukon Route** (tel. 800/343–7373), operates round-trip summer sightseeing excursions between Skagway and the White Pass summit and Fraser, BC, a mountain-climbing, cliff-hanging route of 28 miles each way. Bus connections are available at Fraser to Whitehorse, Yukon.

By Bus Year-round service between Whitehorse and Anchorage (including Fairbanks) is available from **Alaska Direct Bus Lines** (Box 501, Anchorage 99510, tel. 907/277–6652 or 800/328–9730). Service to and from Minneapolis is also available most of the year. For Minneapolis information call 612/228–1009 or 800/328–9730. **Gray Line of Alaska** (tel. 800/544–2206) offers summertime connections from these same cities to Anchorage, Fairbanks, and other stops en route. **Alaska–Yukon Motorcoaches** (tel. 800/637–3334) offers similar seasonal service between Haines and Anchorage. Though it's a long ride, you can travel **Canadian Greyhound** (tel. 604/662–3222) from Vancouver or Edmonton to Whitehorse and make connections there with Gray Line buses to Southeast Alaska.

By Cruise Ship Southeast waters attract cruise ships varying in size from 65 feet, with capacity for a few dozen passengers, to nearly 800 feet, with beds for more than a thousand.

Scenic Drives The descent (or ascent, depending on which direction you're traveling) from the high, craggy Canadian mountain country to the Southeast Alaska coast makes both the **Klondike Highway** into Skagway or the **Haines Highway** to Haines especially memorable traveling. At the top of the respective passes, vegetation is sparse and pockets of snow are often present, even in summertime. The scenery is stark, with mountains and major features silhouetted sharply against frequently blue skies. As you near the saltwater coast of the Panhandle, the forest cover becomes tall, thick, and evergreen. Both drives are worth an excursion, even if you don't intend to drive any farther than the

Canadian border and return. (*See* Car Rentals in Chapter 1, Essential Information, if you need to rent a vehicle.)

Every city, town, and village in Southeast Alaska has one or more waterfront drives that take in hustling, bustling dock scenes and tranquil bays and beaches, and they also offer the possibility of seeing wildlife. Inquire at local information centers.

Guided Tours

The operators listed below offer mainly day trips. For a list of operators offering longer trips, *see* Tours and Packages in Chapter 1, Essential Information, and Chapter 4, Parks, Wildlife Refuges, and Wilderness Adventures. For more information on cruises in Southeast Alaska, *see* Chapter 3, Cruising in Alaska. For a more complete listing of yacht charters in Southeast communities, contact visitor information offices in these towns (*see* Important Addresses and Numbers, below).

Haines   **Alaska Nature Tours** (tel./fax 907/766–2876) conducts bird-watching and natural-history tours through the Chilkat Bald Eagle Preserve, home of the largest concentration of bald eagles in the world. Tours include viewing of brown bears, wolves, and other wildlife.

Alaska Cross-Country Guiding and Rafting (tel. 907/767–5522) offers fly-in, raft-out trips down the Tsirku River, plus photo trips in the eagle preserve for small groups only.

Alaska Sightseeing Tours (tel. 907/766–2435 or 800/637–3334). Visitors travel by motor coach to historic Ft. Seward, the Alaska Indian Arts Center, Sheldon Jackson Museum, and the bald eagle-viewing grounds.

Haines Street Car Company (tel. 907/766–2819) offers tours of Haines, Ft. Seward, Chilkoot, and Chilkat state parks, and the Chilkat Bald Eagle Preserve. It also provides bus service between the state ferry terminal and town.

Juneau   **Alaska Rainforest Treks** (tel. 907/463–3466) schedules daily escorted hikes on trails around Juneau. Terrain includes mountains, glaciers, forests, and ocean shores. Food and rain gear are provided.

Alaska Travel Adventures (tel. 907/789–0052) packages a half-day guided raft trip (bumpy enough to be exciting but well short of a white-knuckle ride) down the Mendenhall River; it includes a mid-trip snack of Alaska smoked salmon, reindeer sausage, cheeses, apple cider, and an alcoholic brew called Mendenhall Madness. The company also offers tours in Sitka and Ketchikan.

Alaska Sightseeing Tours (tel. 907/586–6300 or 800/637–3334) and Gray Line of Alaska (tel. 907/586–3773, summer; or 800/544–2206, winter) both offer motor-coach sightseeing tours of Juneau, Mendenhall Glacier, and other points of interest.

Alaska Up Close (tel. 907/789–9544) provides custom sightseeing tours in small vans, specializing in natural history and fine art.

Juneau Carriage Company (tel. 907/586–2121) offers Southeast Alaska's newest horse-drawn carriage tour, 45 minutes through and around downtown Juneau's historic district.

Phillips Cruises & Tours (tel. 907/276–8023 or 800/544–0529) schedules daily six-hour cruises from Juneau to the twin glaciers at Tracy Arm fjord. It also offers nightly dinner cruises in waters around Alaska's capital city.

Ptarmigan Ptransport and Ptours (tel. 907/789–5427) has sightseeing tours to Juneau, neighboring Douglas, and Mendenhall Glacier in a bright red double-decker bus.

Temsco Helicopters (tel. 907/789–9501) pioneered helicopter sightseeing over Mendenhall Glacier with an actual touchdown and a chance to romp on the glacier. Era Helicopters (tel. 907/586–2030) offers a similar trip.

Ketchikan **Alaska Sightseeing Tours** (tel. 907/225–2740 or 800/637–3334) offers sightseeing motor-coach tours of downtown Ketchikan, Totem Bight State Historical Park, and Totem Heritage Center. Boat tours of Misty Fjords and the Inside Passage are also available.

Gray Line of Alaska (tel. 907/225–5930 or 800/544–2206) offers a city tour comparable to the above, plus a day tour to nearby Annette Island and the Tsimshian Indian community of Metlakatla.

Outdoor Alaska (tel. 907/225–6044) provides cruise or cruisefly daylong excursions from downtown Ketchikan to Misty Fjords National Monument, a wilderness of steep-walled fjords, mountains, and islands. Harbor cruises of the Ketchikan waterfront are also available.

Petersburg **LeConte Cruises** (Box 913, Petersburg, 99833, tel. 907/772–4790) offers yacht tours for sightseeing, photography, and fishing.

Pacific Wing, Inc. (tel. 907/772–9258) gets high marks from locals for its flightseeing tours over LeConte Glacier.

Sitka **Alaska Travel Adventures** (tel. 907/789–0052) operates boat and motorized Zodiac raft excursions to a seal rookery and bird refuge; en route, see porpoises, sea lions, and (if you're lucky) whales.

Baidarka Boats (tel. 907/747–8996) rents sea kayaks and offers guided custom trips in the island-dotted waters around Sitka.

Prewitt Enterprises (tel. 907/747–8443) meets state ferries and provides short city tours while vessels are in port, with stops at Sitka National Historical Park, Sheldon Jackson Museum, and the downtown shopping area. It also offers three-hour tours that visit St. Michael's Cathedral, Old Sitka, Castle Hill, and the old Russian cemetery.

Skagway **Alaska Sightseeing Tours** (tel. 907/983–2828 or 800/637–3334) and **Gray Line of Alaska** (tel. 907/983–2557 or 800/544–2206) provide motor-coach tours through Skagway's historic district, Gold-Rush Cemetery (where frontier "bad guy" Soapy Smith lies buried), and the trailhead of the Chilkoot Trail to the Yukon gold fields.

Gold Rush Tours (tel. 907/983–2289) provides a spectacular drive across the Canadian border to a picnic in the world's smallest desert. This is no joke—there really is a tiny desert a few miles north of Carcross, Yukon.

Wrangell **TH Charters** (tel. 907/874–2085) provides a fast-pace jet-boat ride into the Stikine River wilderness country to Shakes Glacier, Shakes Hot Springs, and other historic and natural attractions.

Important Addresses and Numbers

Tourist Information Southeast Alaska Tourism Council (Box 710, Juneau 99802, tel. 907/586–4777).

Gustavus Visitors Association (Box 167, Gustavus 99826, tel. 907/697–2358).

Glacier Bay National Park and Preserve (Gustavus 99826, tel. 907/697–2230).

Haines/Fort Seward Visitor Information Center (2nd Ave. near Willard St., Box 518, Haines 99827, tel. 907/766–2234 or 800/458–3579). Open June–Aug., daily 8 AM–8 PM; winter hours posted.

Juneau Convention and Visitors Bureau (369 S. Franklin St., Suite 201, Juneau 99801, tel. 907/586–1737) and Davis Log Cabin Visitor Center (134 3rd St., tel. 907/586–2201). Information also available at the kiosk on the cruise-ship dock, downtown at Marine Park.

Ketchikan Visitors Bureau (131 Front St., Ketchikan 99901, tel. 907/225–6166). Open daily May 15–Sept. 30, 8–5; winter, weekdays 8–5.

Petersburg Chamber of Commerce Visitor Center (221 Harbor Way, Box 649, Petersburg 99833, tel. 907/772–3646) is located downtown in the Harbormaster Building overlooking the boat harbor.

Sitka Convention and Visitors Bureau (Box 1226, Sitka 99835, tel. 907/747–5940). Open weekdays 8–5 and when cruise ships are in port. The Greater Sitka Chamber of Commerce (Box 638, Sitka 99835, tel. 907/747–8604). Open weekdays 9–5. Both are located in the Centennial Building on Harbor Drive downtown.

Skagway Convention and Visitors Bureau (City Hall, 7th Ave. and Spring St., Box 415, Skagway 99840, tel. 907/983–2854). Open 8:30–noon and 1–5.

The Klondike Gold Rush National Historical Park visitor center (2nd Ave. and Broadway, Box 517, Skagway 99840, tel. 907/983–2921) which has lots of information on the city as well, is housed in the old White Pass Yukon Route railroad terminal downtown. Open 8–5.

Wrangell Chamber of Commerce Visitors Center (Box 49, Wrangell 99929, tel. 907/874–3901) is in the A-frame on the waterfront next to City Hall. Open when cruise ships or ferries are in port, and at other posted times in summer.

Emergencies
Police and Ambulance In Haines/Ft. Seward, Juneau, Ketchikan, Petersburg, Sitka, and Skagway, dial 911. Gustavus EMS (tel. 907/697–2222). Wrangell: Police (tel. 907/874–3304); Ambulance, Fire Department (tel. 907/874–2000).

Physician and Dentist Haines/Ft. Seward Health Clinic, next to the Visitors Information Center, tel. 907/766–2521. Pharmacy needs also are cared for. Skagway Health Clinic, on 11th Avenue between State Street and Broadway, tel. 907/983–2255. Wrangell Hospital, on the airport road, next to the elementary school, tel. 907/874–3356.

Pharmacy Juneau: Juneau Drug Co., 202 Front Street, downtown, across from McDonald's, tel. 907/586–1233. Ron's Apothecary, 9101 Mendenhall Mall Road, located about 10 miles north of downtown in Mendenhall Valley, next to the Super Bear market, tel. 907/789–0458; afterhours emergencies, 907/789–9522. Ketchikan: Downtown Pharmacy, 300 Front Street, tel. 907/225–3144. Race Pharmacy, 2300 Tongass Avenue, across from the

Plaza Portwest shopping mall, tel. 907/225–4151. After hours, call the hospital, tel. 907/225–5171. **Petersburg: Rexall Drugs** (tel. 907/772–3265). After hours, call the hospital. **Sitka: White's Pharmacy**, 705 Halibut Point Road, tel. 907/747–5755. **Harry Race Drug**, 106 Lincoln Street, tel. 907/747–8666. **Wrangell: Wrangell Drug**, Front Street, tel. 907/874–3422.

Exploring Southeast Alaska

The Southeast Panhandle stretches some 500 miles from Yakutat at its northernmost to Ketchikan and Metlakatla at the southern end. At its widest the region measures only some 140 miles, and in the upper Panhandle just south of Yakutat it's a skinny 30 miles across. Most of the Panhandle consists of a sliver of mainland buffered by offshore islands.

There are, in fact, more than a thousand islands up and down the Panhandle coast—most of them mountainous with lush covers of timber. Collectively they constitute the Alexander Archipelago. On the mainland to the east of the U.S.–Canadian border lies British Columbia.

You can get to and around the area by ship or by plane, but forget the highway. The roadways that exist in these parts run at most a few dozen miles out from towns and villages, then they dead-end.

Not surprisingly, most of the communities of the region are located on islands rather than on the mainland. The principal exceptions are Juneau, Haines, Skagway, and the Indian village of Klukwan. Island outposts include Ketchikan, Wrangell, Petersburg, Sitka, Metlakatla, and a number of other towns, Indian villages, and logging camps.

If shipboard sightseeing is your pleasure, more than two dozen cruise ships and state ferries await your booking. The usual (though not the only) pattern is for cruising visitors to board ship at Vancouver, BC, or San Francisco, then to set sail on an itinerary that typically includes Ketchikan, Juneau, Skagway, and Sitka. Other itineraries go to Glacier Bay as well. Cruise-ship travel includes a mix of sailing and port visits, which can vary from a few hours to a full day. The state ferries (southern ports of origin: Bellingham, WA, or Prince Rupert, BC) rarely spend much time in the cities where they call, but you can get off one ship, spend a day or more ashore, then catch another vessel heading north or south to your next destination.

Don't overlook the region's alternative means of travel. Small float planes, some carrying five or fewer passengers, and yachts sleeping a half dozen or so ply the routes from the larger population centers to tiny settlements and even more remote sites where there are no permanent residents at all (unless you count bears).

If you're interested in fishing, you have a number of options to choose from (or mix). There are saltwater salmon charter boats, salmon fishing lodges (some near the larger communities, others remote and accessible by float plane), fly-in mountain-lake lodges where the fishing is for trout and char, and—

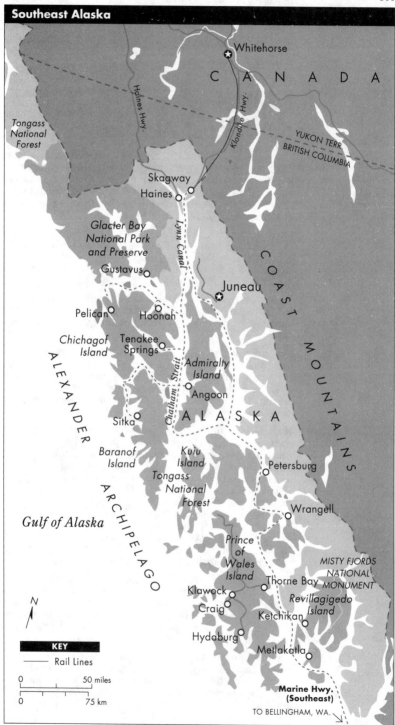

bargain hunters take special note—more than 150 remote but weather-tight cabins operated by the U.S. Forest Service. The USFS rents these units for the absurdly reasonable rate of $20 per night per group (*see* Off the Beaten Track, *below*).

Ketchikan

Numbers in the margin correspond to points of interest on the Ketchikan map.

Alaskans call Ketchikan "the First City," not because of size or population, but because in the days before air travel it was always the first Alaskan port of call for northbound steamship passengers. For many travelers today—arriving by air, cruise ship, or ferry—the tradition continues.

Ketchikan is perched on a large island at the foot of Deer Mountain (3,000 feet). The island's name is Revillagigedo (Alaskans just say "Revilla"), named by English mariner George Vancouver, who was exploring the Inside Passage in 1793. He often named things after his crew and friends; in this case it was named after the viceroy of Mexico.

The site at the mouth of Ketchikan Creek was a summer fish camp of the Tlingit Indians until white miners and fishermen came to settle in the town in 1885. Gold discoveries just before the turn of the century brought more immigrants, and valuable timber and commercial fishing resources spurred new industries. By the 1930s the town bragged it was the "Salmon Canning Capital of the World." Today Ketchikan ranks fourth among Alaskan cities in size (7,600 residents in the city proper, 5,000 in the borough, or county). Fishing and timber are still the mainstays of Ketchikan's economy, although tourism contributes.

There's a lot to be seen on foot in downtown Ketchikan. The
❶ best place to begin is at the **Ketchikan Visitors Bureau** on the dock, where you can pick up a free historic-walking-tour map. From there head up Mission Street, past the sub–post office located in the Trading Post (the main post office is inconveniently located several miles south, near the ferry terminal), to
❷ Bawden Street and **St. John's Church and Seaman's Center**. The 1903 church structure is the oldest remaining house of worship in Ketchikan, its interior formed from red cedar cut in the native-operated sawmill in nearby Saxman. The Seaman's Center, next door to the church, was built in 1904 as a hospital. It later housed the *Alaska Sportsman Magazine* (now *Alaska Magazine*), which began publication in Ketchikan in 1936.

❸ At Dock Street, your tour passes the ***Ketchikan Daily News***
❹ building, then, east, to the **Tongass Historical Museum and Totem Pole**. Here you can browse among Indian artifacts and pioneer relics of the early mining and fishing era. Among the exhibits: a big and brilliantly polished lens out of Tree Point Lighthouse, the bullet-riddled skull of a notorious and fearsome old brown bear called Old Groaner, Indian ceremonial objects, and a Chilkat blanket. There's even a 14-foot model of a typical Alaskan salmon-fishing seine vessel. *Museum admission: $1.50 Mon.–Sat., free on Sun. Open Mon.–Sat. 8–5, Sun. 9–4.*

Continuing north on Bawden, then east on Park Street, you can
❺ see **Grant Street Trestle**, constructed in 1908. At one time virtu-

City Park, **7**

Creek Street, **13**

Creek Street
Footbridge, **15**

Deer Mountain
Hatchery, **8**

Dolly's House, **14**

Federal Building/ U.S.
Forest Service, **16**

Grant Street Trestle, **5**

*Ketchikan Daily
News*, **3**

Ketchikan Indian
Corporation, **10**

Ketchikan Visitors
Bureau, **1**

Knox Bros. Clock, **17**

Kyan Totem Pole, **18**

Monrean House, **19**

*Return of the
Eagle*, **11**

St. John's Church and
Seaman's Center, **2**

Salmon Falls, **6**

Scenic lookout, **20**

Thomas Street, **12**

Tongass Historical
Museum and Totem
Pole, **4**

Totem Heritage
Center and Nature
Path, **9**

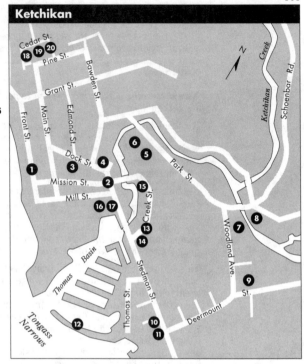

Ketchikan

ally all of Ketchikan's walkways and streets were wooden trestles. This is the last remaining example of the city's early road system. Get out your camera and set it for fast speed at the **6** **Salmon Falls, Fish Ladder, and Salmon Carving** just off Park Street. When the salmon start running in midsummer and later, thousands literally leap the falls (or take the easier ladder route) to spawn in Ketchikan Creek's waters farther upstream. **7** Many can be seen in the creek feeding the falls. At **City Park** you can see small ponds that were once holding areas for the first hatchery that operated in the area, from 1923 to 1928. The **8** modern **Deer Mountain Hatchery** now disperses tens of thousands of salmon annually into local waters, much to the satisfaction of local sport and commercial fishermen. Also at the park is **9** the **Totem Heritage Center and Nature Path**. Definitely plan to spend some time in the center viewing authentic ancient examples of the carver's art. *Admission: $1.50. Open Mon.–Sat. 8–5, Sun. 9–4.*

Continuing south to Deermount Street and then west on **10** Stedman Street, you pass the **Ketchikan Indian Corporation**, site of a former Bureau of Indian Affairs school, and a colorful **11** wall mural called *Return of the Eagle*. It was created by 21 native artists on the walls of the Robertson Building of the Ketchikan campus, University of Alaska–Southeast.

12 Next comes **Thomas Street** and **Thomas Basin**. The street was constructed in 1913 to be part of the New England Fish Company's cannery here; Thomas Basin is a major, and picture-worthy, harbor. One of four harbors in Ketchikan, it is home port to a wide variety of pleasure and work boats.

⑬ You will be passing **Creek Street,** former site of Ketchikan's in-famous red-light district; today its small, quaint houses, built on stilts over the creek waters, have been restored as trendy
⑭ shops. The street's most famous brothel, **Dolly's House,** has been preserved as a museum, complete with furnishings, beds, and a short history of the life and times of Ketchikan's best-known madam. *Admission: $2. Open when cruise ships are in port.*

Farther up Creek Street, there's more good salmon-viewing in
⑮ season at the **Creek Street Footbridge.** Head south to Mill Street
⑯ and see the **Federal Building/U.S. Forest Service** and historic
⑰ **Knox Bros. Clock,** a large outdoor timepiece. It's one of three that once served the city's downtown business district.

If you're into steep street climbing, head west on Mill Street, then north up Main Street past the Ketchikan Fire Depart-
⑱ ment to the **Kyan Totem Pole,** a replica of a 1913 carving that once stood near St. John's Church. Local legend says "Rub its tummy, you'll surely have money" within 24 hours. Nearby is
⑲ the **Monrean House,** a 1904 structure that is included in the Na-
⑳ tional Register of Historic Places, and a **scenic lookout** that looks down on City Float and the waters of Tongass Narrows.

Ketchikan's two most famous totem parks (there are more to-tems in Ketchikan than anywhere else in the world) are, re-spectively, **Totem Bight State Historical Park,** 10 miles north on North Tongass Highway, and the park at **Saxman Indian Vil-lage,** 2 miles south on South Tongass Highway. The poles at both parks are, for the most part, 50-year-old replicas of even older totems brought in from outlying villages as part of a fed-eral government works/cultural project during the 1930s.

Totem Bight, with its many totems and hand-hewn Indian tri-bal house, sits on a particularly scenic spit of land facing the waters of Tongass Narrows.

Saxman Village (named for a missionary who helped Indians settle there before 1900) has recently added new totems to its collection, as well as a new, large tribal house believed to be the largest in the world. There's also a carver's shed nearby where new totems and totemic art objects are created, and a stand-up theater where a multimedia presentation tells the story of Southeast Alaska's Indian peoples.

Out the highway in either direction, you won't go far before you run out of road. The North Tongass Highway ends about 18 miles from downtown, at Settler's Cove Campground. The South Tongass Highway terminates at a power plant. Side roads soon terminate at campgrounds and trailheads, view-points, lakes, boat-launching ramps, or private property.

If you're a tough hiker, the 3-mile trail from downtown to the top of **Deer Mountain** will repay your effort with a spectacular panorama of the city below (facing the water), and the wilder-ness behind. **Ward Cove Recreation Area,** about 6 miles north of town, offers easier hiking beside lakes and streams and be-neath towering spruce and hemlock trees.

Wrangell

Numbers in the margin correspond to points of interest on the Wrangell map.

Next up the line is Wrangell, located on an island near the mouth of the fast-flowing Stikine River. A small, unassuming timber and fishing community, the town has had three flags flown over it since the arrival of the Russian traders. Known as Redoubt St. Dionysius when it was part of Russian America, the town was renamed Fort Stikine after the British took it over. The name was changed to Wrangell when the Americans bought it.

❶ You can see a lot in Wrangell on foot, and a good place to start your tour is the A-frame **Chamber of Commerce Visitor Information Center** (tel. 907/874–3901) close to the docks at Front **❷** Street and Outer Drive. It's near **City Hall** and its very tall totem pole. The visitor center is open when cruise ships and the ferries are in port and at other times throughout the summer. If you need information and the A-frame is closed, drop by the City Museum (122 2nd St.). The Wrangell Convention and Visitors Bureau is located there. *Open summer, Mon.–Sat. 1–4, and whenever cruise ships or ferries are in port.*

❸ **KikSadi Indian Park,** a "pocket park" of Alaska greenery and impressive totem poles at St. Michael's and Front streets, is a pleasant place to stroll through.

On your way to Wrangell's number one attraction—Chief **❹** Shakes Island—stop at **Chief Shakes's gravesite,** uphill from Hansen's Boat Shop on Case Avenue. Buried here is Shakes V, one of a number of local chiefs to bear that name. He led the local Tlingits during the first half of the 19th century. Two killer-whale totems mark the chief's burial place.

❺ On **Chief Shakes Island,** reached by a footbridge off the harbor dock, you can see some of the finest totem poles in Alaska, as well as a tribal house constructed in the 1930s as a replica of one that was home to many of the various Shakes and their peoples. The interior contains six house totems, two of them more than 100 years old; unfortunately the house is open rarely, when ships are in port or by appointment. *Tel. 907/874–3503 or 907/874–3747. A donation of $1 is requested.*

After your visit to the island, wander out to the end of the dock **❻ ❼** for the view and picture taking at the **seaplane float** and **boat harbor.**

North and west from the A-frame infomation center are the **❽ ❾** **cruise-ship dock;** the **public library** (tel. 907/874–3535), with its small collection of ancient petroglyphs (more about these curi- **❿** ous rock carvings later), and the **Wrangell City Museum** (2nd St. and Bevier St., tel. 907/874–3770). Since its construction in 1906, the museum building has served as a library, a morgue, a doctor's office, and city hall. Now it contains a historical collection that ranges from totem fragments, petroglyphs, and other Indian artifacts to a bootlegger's still and even a vintage 1800s linotype and presses.

⓫ Beyond the **state ferry terminal** lies another museum, called **⓬** **"Our Collections"** by its owners, Bolly and Elva Bigelow. It's located in a barnlike building on the water side of Evergreen Avenue. To some, the artifacts that comprise the collection constitute less a museum than a garage sale waiting to happen. Still, large numbers of viewers seem quite taken by the literally thousands of unrelated collectibles (clocks, animal traps, waffle irons, tools, etc.) that the Bigelows have gathered in half a cen-

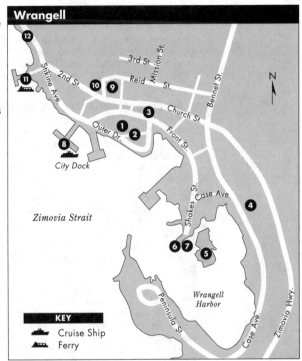

Boat harbor, **7**

Chamber of Commerce Visitor Information Center, **1**

Chief Shakes's gravesite, **4**

Chief Shakes Island, **5**

City Hall, **2**

Cruise-ship dock, **8**

KikSadi Indian Park, **3**

"Our Collections", **12**

Public library, **9**

Seaplane float, **6**

State ferry terminal, **11**

Wrangell City Museum, **10**

tury of Alaska living. *Tel. 907/874–3646. Call before setting out to visit.*

A five-minute walk beyond the Bigelows' brings you (at low tide only) to **Petroglyph Beach,** one of the more curious sights in Southeast Alaska. Here, scattered among other rocks, are three dozen or more large stones bearing designs and pictures chiseled by unknown, ancient artists. No one knows why the rocks were etched the way they are. Perhaps they were boundary markers or messages; possibly they were just primitive doodling. If you want a unique souvenir of your Wrangell visit, go to **Norris Gifts** on Front Street and buy rice paper and crayon-rubbing supplies. The staff at the city museum will demonstrate the proper rubbing technique for recording your own copy of the petroglyph designs. Do not, of course, attempt to move any of the petroglyph stones.

There are other stones in Wrangell that you can take with you. These are natural garnets, gathered at Garnet Ledge, facing the Stikine River. The semiprecious gems are sold on the streets for 50¢ or a dollar.

Petersburg

Numbers in the margin correspond to points of interest on the Petersburg map.

Getting to Petersburg is an experience, whether you take the "high road" by air or the "low road" by sea. Alaska Airlines claims the shortest jet flight in the world from takeoff at Wrangell to landing at Petersburg. The schedule calls for 20 minutes of flying, but it's usually more like 10. At sea level, ferries and smaller cruisers squeak through Wrangell Narrows with the aid of more than 50 buoys and range markers along the 22-mile crossing. At times the channel seems too incredibly narrow for ships to pass through, making for a breathtaking—though safe—trip.

At first sight of Petersburg you may think you're in the old country. Neat, white, Scandinavian-style homes and store-fronts with steep roofs and bright-colored swirls of leaf and flower designs (called "rosemaling") and row upon row of sturdy fishing vessels in the harbor invoke the spirit of Norway. No wonder. This prosperous fishing community was founded by Norwegian Peter Buschmann in 1897.

You may occasionally even hear some Norwegian spoken, especially during the Little Norway Festival held here each year on the weekend closest to May 17. If you're in town during the festival, be sure to partake in one of the fish feeds that highlight the Norwegian Independence Day celebration. You won't find better beer-batter halibut and folk dancing without going to Norway itself.

Petersburg, like Wrangell, is a destination for travelers who prefer not to be hand-held, or spoon-fed information by a tour guide. On your own, sample the brew at **Kito's Kave** bar on Sing Lee Alley (in the afternoon if you don't like your music in the high-decibel range) and examine the outrageous wall decor there, which varies from Mexican painting on black velvet to mounted Alaska king salmon and two stuffed sailfish from a tropical fishing expedition. Wander, at high tide, to **Hammer Slough** for a vision of houses and buildings on high stilts reflected perfectly in still slough waters. Or simply stroll down Nordic Drive, the city's main shopping street, to see shops displaying imported Norwegian wool sweaters or metal Viking helmets, complete with horns.

One of the pleasantest things to do in Petersburg is to roam among the fishing vessels tied up at dockside. This is one of Alaska's busiest, most prosperous fishing communities, and the variety of seacraft is enormous. You'll see small trollers, big halibut vessels, and sleek pleasure craft as well. Wander, too, around the fish-processing structures. Just watching shrimp, salmon, or halibut coming ashore, you'll get a real appreciation for this vibrant industry and the hardworking people who engage in it.

❶ From the **visitor center** overlooking the city harbor there are great viewing and picture-taking vantage points. Go north on **❷** Nordic Drive to get to **Sandy Beach**, where there's frequently good eagle-viewing and access to one of Petersburg's favorite picnic and recreation locales.

Heading northeast up the hill from the visitor center brings **❸** you to the **Clausen Museum** (tel. 907/772–3598) and the bronze *Fisk* (Norwegian for "fish") sculpture at Second and Fram streets. The monument, featuring literally scores of separately sculpted salmon, halibut, and herring, celebrates the bounty of the sea. It was created in 1967 as part of Petersburg's celebration of the 100th anniversary of the Alaska Purchase from Russia.

Catholic church, **4**

Clausen Museum, **3**

Hammer Slough
reflecting pool, **8**

Lutheran church, **5**

Presbyterian church, **6**

Sandy Beach, **2**

Sons of Norway Hall, **7**

Visitor center, **1**

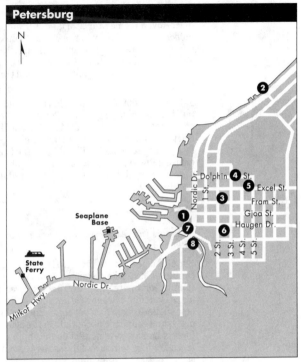

The museum—not surprising in this busiest of Southeast Alaska's commercial fishing ports—devotes a lot of its space to fishing and processing. There's an old "iron chink" used in the early days for gutting and cleaning fish, as well as displays that illustrate the workings of several types of fishing boats. A 126½-pound king salmon, the largest ever caught when it came out of a fish trap on Prince of Wales Island in 1939, is on exhibit, as is the world's largest chum salmon—a 36-pounder. Indian history and artifacts are included, as is an old Indian canoe.

4 5 6 Three pioneer churches—**Catholic, Lutheran,** and **Presbyterian**—are located nearby at Dolphin and 3rd streets, Excel and 5th streets, and on Haugen Street between 2nd and 3rd streets, respectively. Of the three, the 50-year-old Lutheran edifice is the oldest. It is said that boys wheelbarrowed fill from elsewhere in the city for landscaping around the foundation. Their compensation? Ice-cream cones. The enticement was so successful that after three years of ice cream rewards, it was necessary to bring in a bulldozer to scrape off the excess dirt.

7 The large, white, barnlike structure on stilts that stands in Hammer Slough off Indian Street is the **Sons of Norway Hall,** the headquarters an organization devoted to keeping alive the traditions and culture of the old country. North of the hall, **8** from the Nordic Drive bridge, is the high-tide **Hammer Slough reflecting pool.**

Petersburg's other attractions are located south of the city along the Mitkof Highway, where you will pass seafood processing plants and the state ferry terminal (at Mile .8) en route to the **Frank Heintzleman Nursery** at Mile 8.6 (named for a much-loved former territorial governor); the **Fall's Creek fish ladder** at Mile 10.8, where coho and pink salmon migrate upstream in late summer and fall; and the **Crystal Lake State Hatchery/Blind Slough Recreation Area** at Mile 17.5, where more than 60,000 pounds of salmon and trout are produced each year.

Petersburg's biggest attraction lies about 25 miles east of town but is accessible only by water or air. **LeConte Glacier** is the continent's southernmost tidewater glacier and one of its most active, often calving off so many icebergs that the lake at its face is carpeted bank-to-bank with floating bergs. Ferries and cruise ships pass it at a distance. Sightseeing yachts, charter vessels, and flightseeing tours are available; contact the Visitors Bureau.

Sitka

Numbers in the margin correspond to points of interest on the Sitka map.

For centuries before the Russians came at the end of the 18th century, Sitka was the ancestral home of the Tlingit Indian nation. Unfortunately for the Tlingits, Russian Territorial Governor Alexander Baranov (often spelled Baranof, as the island is now spelled) came to covet the Sitka site for its beauty, mild climate, and economic potential. In the island's massive timbered forests he saw raw materials for shipbuilding; its location offered trading routes as far east as Hawaii and the Orient, and as far south as California.

In 1799 Baranov negotiated with the local chief to build a wooden fort and trading post some 6 miles north of the present town. He called the outpost St. Michael Archangel and moved a large number of his Russian and Aleut fur hunters there from their former base on Kodiak Island.

The Indians soon took exception to the ambitions of their new neighbors, and in 1802 they attacked Baranov's people, burned his buildings, and assumed they were done with the troublesome outsiders.

Fortunately for Baranov, he was away at Kodiak at the time. He returned in 1804 with a formidable force including shipboard cannons, attacked the Indians at their fort near Indian River, and drove them to the other side of the island.

Under Baranov and succeeding managers, the Russian-American Company and the town prospered until, in the middle of the 19th century, it could be called "the Paris of the Pacific." Besides the fur trade, the community contained a major shipbuilding and repair facility, boasted sawmills and forges, had a salmon saltery, and even initiated an ice industry. The Russians shipped blocks of ice from nearby Swan Lake to the booming San Francisco market. Baranov shifted the capital of Russian America to Sitka from Kodiak.

Amenities of the town included schools, a library, a hospital, and the crown jewel of the Russian Orthodox Church in Russian America—St. Michael's Cathedral.

A good place to begin a tour of modern-day Sitka is at the Sitka **Visitors Bureau** headquarters, located in the **Centennial Build-**

Castle Hill, **2**

Centennial Building/
Visitors Bureau, **1**

Russian Bishop's
House, **7**

Russian blockhouse, **5**

Russian cemetery, **6**

St. Michael's
Cathedral, **4**

Sheldon Jackson
College, **9**

Sheldon Jackson
Museum, **10**

Sitka National
Cemetery, **8**

Sitka National
Historical Park, **11**

Sitka State Pioneers'
Home, **3**

Tlingit Fort, **12**

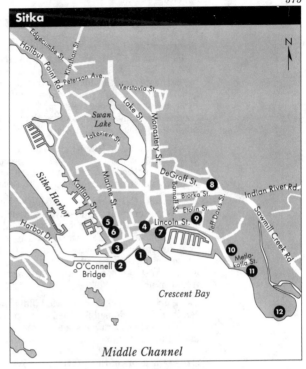

ing on Harbor Drive. A big Tlingit Indian war canoe rests nearby, while inside the building you'll find a museum, an auditorium, an art gallery, and lots of advice on what to see and how to see it. The staff will know if the colorfully costumed New Archangel Russian Dancers are performing, if concerts or recitals are on tap for the annual Sitka Summer Music Festival, or if logging competitions or the community's annual salmon derby is scheduled soon.

In the Centennial Building there's also an accurate model of New Archangel, as the Russians called their colony. It shows where the Russians built boats, milled their flour, and cut ice for shipment to San Francisco bars during the gold-rush boom.

2 **Castle Hill** overlooks Crescent Bay, the John O'Connell Bridge to Japonski Island, and a number of other islands, isles, and rocks in the nearby waters. A path and steps beside the post office will take you to the top. For years after Sitka's founding, a succession of residences for Russian managers was located on this lofty promontory. The last one—called Baranof's Castle, though he never lived there—burned in 1894.

Atop the hill now are venerable Russian cannons and the flagpole where, on October 18, 1867, the czarist Russian standard was lowered and the Stars and Stripes of the United States raised. Each Alaska Day (October 18), citizens of Sitka in period costumes reenact the ceremony with the same pomp and ceremony that signified the official transfer of Alaska to the United States. At this same site, on January 3, 1959, jubilant

Alaskans raised the first 49-star American flag, signifying Alaskan statehood.

The large four-level, red-roofed structure with the imposing 14-foot statue in front is the **Sitka State Pioneers' Home,** built in 1934 and the first of several state-run retirement homes and medical-care facilities for Alaska's senior citizens. The statue, symbolizing Alaska's frontier sourdough spirit, was modeled by an authentic pioneer, William "Skagway Bill" Fonda. It portrays a determined prospector with pack, pick, rifle, and supplies on his back headed for the gold country.

Across the street in **Totem Square** are three anchors discovered in local waters and believed to be 19th-century British in origin. Look on the totem pole in the park for the double-headed eagle of czarist Russia carved into the cedar.

St. Michael's Cathedral, in the middle of Lincoln Street, had its origins in a log-built, frame-covered structure erected between 1844 and 1848. In 1966 the church was totally destroyed in a fire that swept through the downtown business district. As the fire engulfed the building, local townspeople risked their lives and rushed inside to rescue the cathedral's precious icons, religious objects, vestments, and other treasures brought to the church from Russia.

Using original measurements and blueprints, an almost exact replica of onion-domed St. Michael's was built and dedicated in 1976. Today, visitors can see numerous icons, among them the much-prized *Our Lady of Sitka* (also known as the *Sitka Madonna*) and the *Christ Pantocrator* (*Christ the Judge*) on either side of the doors of the interior altar screen. Among other objects to be viewed: ornate Gospel books, chalices, crucifixes, much-used silver-gilt wedding crowns dating back to 1866, and an altar cloth said to have been worked by the first Princess Maksoutoff, who lies buried in the Russian cemetery nearby (the prince's second wife left Alaska with her husband). This is an active church, so visitors should respect the services and privacy of worshipers. *A $1 donation is requested. Tel. 907/ 747–8120. Open June 1–Sept. 30, daily 11–3.*

North of the Pioneer Home on the west edge of town are the **Russian blockhouse** and the **Russian cemetery,** where Princess Maksoutoff, wife of Alaska's last Russian governor, and others are buried under old headstones and Russian Orthodox crosses.

The **Russian Bishop's House** also stands on Lincoln Street, constructed by the Russian-American Company for Bishop Innocent Veniaminov in 1842. Now restored by the National Park Service as a unit of Sitka National Historical Park, the house is one of the few remaining Russian log structures in Alaska. *Admission free. Open daily 8–5.*

Farther north and east is the **Sitka National Cemetery** on Sawmill Creek Road, where Civil War veterans and America's dead from the Aleutian Campaign of World War II are buried along with many notable Alaskans.

South on Lincoln Street lies the campus of **Sheldon Jackson College,** founded in 1878, and the **Sheldon Jackson Museum.** The octagonal museum, built in 1895 and now under the jurisdiction of the Alaska State Division of Museums, contains priceless Indian, Aleut, and Eskimo items collected by Dr. Sheldon Jackson in the remote regions of Alaska he traveled as an educator and missionary. Carved masks, Chilkat Indian blankets, dogsleds, kayaks—even the helmet worn by Chief Katlean during the 1804 battle against the Russians—are on display here. *Tel. 907/747-8981. Admission: $1 adults, free for students. Open daily 8-5.*

11 **Sitka National Historical Park**'s Visitor Center and totem park is located at the end of Metlakatla Street, about a half mile from town. Audiovisual programs and exhibits at the site, plus Indian and Russian artifacts, give an overview of Southeast Alaska Indian culture, both old and new. Often, Contemporary artists and craftsmen may be on hand to demonstrate and interpret traditional Tlingit crafts.

A self-guiding trail through the park to the actual site of the **12** **Tlingit Fort** passes by some of the most skillfully carved totems in the state. Some of the poles are quite old, dating back more than eight decades. Others are replicas, copies of those lost to time and a damp climate. *Tel. 907/747-6281. Admission free. Open June-Sept., daily 8-5; Oct.-May, weekdays 8-5.*

Juneau

Numbers in the margin correspond to points of interest on the Juneau map.

Juneau, like Haines and Skagway to the north, is located on the North American mainland. Unlike Haines and Skagway, it can't be reached by conventional highway from the rest of the United States and Canada. No matter. There are lots of easy ways to reach Alaska's capital and third largest city. For one, there's the Alaska Marine Highway ferry system, which provides near daily arrivals and departures in the summer. For another, virtually every cruise ship plying Southeast waters calls at Juneau. And two jet airlines—Alaska and Delta—have several flights daily into Juneau International Airport from other points in Alaska and the other states.

Juneau owes its origins to two colorful sourdoughs, Joe Juneau and Dick Harris, and to a Tlingit chief named Kowee. The chief led the two men to rich reserves of gold, both in the outwash of the stream that now runs through the middle of town and in quartz rock formations back in the gulches and valleys.

That was 1880, and shortly after the discovery a modest stampede resulted in the formation of first a camp, then a town, then finally the Alaska district government (such as it was) in 1906. Thus Juneau became the capital of Alaska, a title the community still retains.

For 60 years or so after Juneau's founding, gold remained the mainstay of the local economy. In its heyday, the AJ (for Alaska Juneau) gold mine was the biggest low-grade ore mine in the world. It was not until World War II, when the government decided it needed Juneau's manpower for the war effort, that the AJ and other mines in the area ceased operations. After the war, mining failed to start up again, and government—first territorial, then state—became the city's principal employer.

These days, government (state, federal, and local) remains Juneau's number-one employer. Tourism, transportation, and trading—even a belated mining revival—provide the other major components of the city's economic picture.

❶ **Marine Park** on the dock where the cruise ships tie up is a little gem of benches, shade trees, and shelter, a great place to enjoy an outdoor meal purchased from any of Juneau's several street vendors. It contains a visitor kiosk staffed from 9 AM to 6 PM ❷ daily in the summer months. The **Log Cabin Visitor Center** up Seward Street at 3rd Street operates weekdays 8:30–5 and weekends 10–5. The cabin is a replica of a 19th-century structure that served first as a Presbyterian church, then as a brewery.

Head east a block from Marine Park to S. Franklin Street. Buildings here and on Front Street are among the older and most interesting structures in the city. Many reflect the architecture of the 1920s and '30s, and some are even older.

The smallish (40 rooms) **Alaskan Hotel** at 167 S. Franklin Street was called "a pocket edition of any of the best hotels on the Pacific Coast" when it opened in 1913. Owners Mike and Bettye Adams have restored the building with period trappings, and it's worth a visit even if you're not looking for lodging. The barroom's massive mirrored oakwood back bar is accented by Tiffany lights and panels.

Also on S. Franklin Street: **The Alaska Steam Laundry Building,** a 1901 structure with a windowed turret that now houses a coffeehouse, a film processor, and other stores. Across the street, the equally venerable **Senate Building mall** contains one of the two Juneau Christmas stores, a children's shop, and a place to buy Russian icons. Close by are numerous other curio and crafts shops, snack shops, two salmon shops, and the tourist-filled **Red Dog Saloon,** a decades-old institution now housed in new but still frontierish quarters at 159 S. Franklin Street.

After a S. Franklin Street foray, head one block toward the water, then uphill on Seward Street past the Log Cabin Visitor Center. Across 4th Street you'll see an older, obviously governmental building fronted by huge marble pillars. The pillars are of native Southeast Alaska marble, and the building is the ❸ **Alaska State Capitol,** constructed in 1930 to serve the city as federal building, governor's office, post office, and meeting place for the biennial sessions of the Alaska Territorial Legislature. Today the structure still houses the governor's office and other state agencies, and the state legislature meets there four months each year. *Tel. 907/465–2479. Tours in summer, daily 8:30–5.*

Uphill one block and two blocks to the east stands quaint, on-❹ ion-domed **St. Nicholas Russian Orthodox Church,** constructed in 1894—the oldest original Russian church in Alaska. *326 5th St., tel. 907/586–1023. A donation is requested. Check the visitor center for hours.*

Directly uphill behind the Capitol Building, between 5th and ❺ 6th streets, stands the **five-story totem,** one of Juneau's finer to-❻ tems, and at the top of the hill on 7th Street stands **Wickersham House,** the former residence of pioneer judge and delegate to Congress James Wickersham. The home, constructed in 1899, is now a part of the Alaska state park system. Memorabilia from the judge's travels throughout Alaska range from rare native basketry and ivory carvings to historic photos, 47 faithful

Alaska State Capitol, **3**

Alaska State Museum, **14**

Centennial Hall, **15**

City Museum, **8**

Cremation spot of Chief Kowee, **11**

Evergreen Cemetery, **10**

Federal Building and Post Office, **12**

Five-story totem, **5**

Governor's House, **9**

Juneau-Harris Monument, **13**

Log Cabin Visitor Center, **2**

Marine Park, **1**

St. Nicholas Russian Orthodox Church, **4**

State Office Building, **7**

Wickersham House, **6**

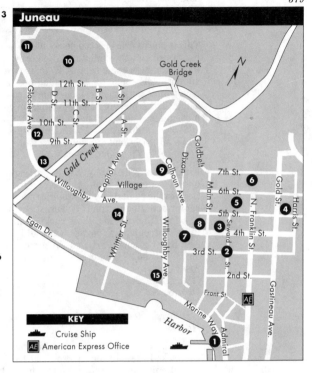

diaries (maintained even on treks through snow and blizzards), and a Chickering grand piano that came "round the horn" to Alaska while the Russians yet ruled in these parts. *Tel. 907/ 586–9001. Admission free. Tours in summer Sun.–Fri. 10–5.*

7 Back down the hill on 4th Street, you'll pass "the S.O.B."—or **State Office Building.** There on Fridays at noon you can have a picnic lunch like the state workers do and listen in the four-story atrium to organ music played on a grand old theater pipe organ, a veteran of the silent-movie era.

8 Head west from the front of the Capitol Building to the **Juneau Douglas City Museum** (4th and Main Sts., tel. 907/586–3572), which displays old mining equipment, historic photos, and pioneer artifacts, including a turn-of-thecentury store and kitchen. After passing another totem on Calhoun Avenue, you come **9** shortly to the **Governor's House,** a three-level colonial style home completed in 1912. There are no tours through the house, but the totem pole on the entrance side of the building is surely the only one of its kind to adorn the walls of a U.S. governor's mansion.

If you're still game for walking, continue on Calhoun Avenue, pass the Gold Creek bridge, and keep going until you come to **10** **Evergreen Cemetery.** A meandering gravel road leads through the graveyard where many Juneau pioneers (among them Joe Juneau and Dick Harris) lie buried. At the end of the lane you'll **11** come to a monument commemorating the **cremation spot of 12 Chief Kowee.** Turn left here, walk past the **Federal Building and 13 Post Office** at 9th St. and Glacier Ave., past the **Juneau–Harris**

Monument near Gold Creek, then walk on to Whittier Street,
⑭ where a right turn will take you to the **Alaska State Museum.**

This is one of Alaska's top museums. Whether your tastes run
to natural history exhibits (stuffed brown bears, a replica of a
two-story-high eagle nesting tree), native Alaskan exhibits (a
40-foot walrus hide umiak whaling boat constructed by Eskimos from St. Laurence Island and a re-created interior of a
Tlingit tribal house), mining exhibits, or contemporary art, the
museum is almost certain to please. *395 Whittier St., tel. 907/
465–2901. Admission: $2 adults, children and students free.
Open May 15–Sept. 15, weekdays 9–6, weekends 10–6; Sept.
16–May 14, Tues.–Fri. 10–6.*

Finally, on Willoughby Avenue at Egan Drive, there's Ju-
⑮ neau's **Centennial Hall**—the meeting place for large conventions in the capital city and the site of an excellent information
center operated by the U.S. Forest Service and the U.S. Park
Service. Movies, slide shows, and information about recreation
in the surrounding Tongass National Forest or in nearby Glacier Bay National Park and Preserve are available here. *Tel.
907/586–8806. Open daily in summer 9–6; 8–5 weekdays the
rest of the year.*

Haines

*Numbers in the margin correspond to points of interest on the
Haines map.*

Missionary S. Hall Young and John Muir, the famous naturalist, picked the site for this town in 1879 as a place to bring
Christianity and education to the native Indians. They could
hardly have picked a more beautiful spot. The town sits on a
heavily wooded peninsula with magnificent views of Portage
Cove and the Coastal Mountain Range. It lies 80 miles north of
Juneau via fjordlike Lynn Canal.

Unlike most cities in Southeast Alaska, Haines can be reached
by road (the 152-mile Haines Highway connects at Haines
Junction with the Alaska Highway). It's accessible as well by
state ferry and by scheduled light-plane service from Juneau.

The town has two distinct personalities. On the northern side of
the Haines Highway is the portion of Haines founded by Hall
and Muir. After its missionary beginnings the town served as
the trailhead for the Jack Dalton Trail to the Yukon during the
1897 gold rush to the Klondike. The following year, when gold
was discovered in nearby Porcupine (now deserted), the booming community served as a supply center and jumping-off place
for those gold fields as well. Today things are quieter; the
town's streets are orderly, its homes are well kept, and for the
most part it looks a great deal like any other Alaska seacoast
community.

South of the highway, the town looks like a military post, which
is what it was for nearly half a century.

In 1903 the U.S. Army established a post—**Ft. William Henry
Seward**—at Portage Cove just south of town. For 17 years
(1922–1939) the post (renamed Chilkoot Barracks to avoid con-
fusion with the South Central Alaska city of Seward) was the
only military base in the territory. That changed with World
War II. Following the war the post closed down.

Chilkat Center for the Arts, **8**

Halsingland Hotel, **6**

Indian tribal house, **7**

Mile 0, **5**

Mt. Ripinsky, **3**

Sheldon Museum and Cultural Center, **2**

Southeast Alaska State Fairgrounds, **4**

Visitor Center, **1**

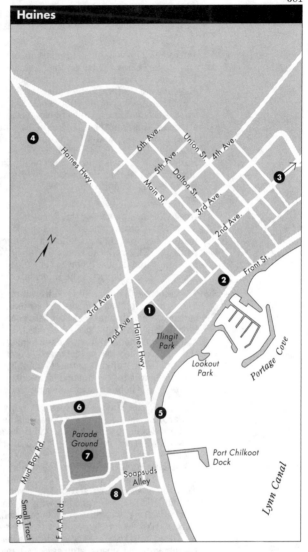

Haines

Right after the war a group of veterans purchased the property from the government. They changed its name to Port Chilkoot and created residences, businesses, and an Indian arts center out of the officers' houses and military buildings that surrounded the old fort's parade ground. Eventually Port Chilkoot merged with the city of Haines. Although the two areas are now officially one municipality, the old military post with its still-existing grass parade ground is referred to as Ft. Seward.

The Haines–Ft. Seward community today is recognized for the enormously successful Indian dance and culture center at Ft. Seward, as well as for the superb fishing, camping, and outdoor recreation to be found at Chilkoot Lake, Portage Cove, Mosquito Lake, and Chilkat State Park on the shores of Chilkat Inlet.

The latter locale, one of the small treasures of the Alaska state park system, features views of the Davidson and Rainbow glaciers across the water.

You can pick up walking-tour maps of both Haines and Ft. Seward at the **Visitor Center** on 2nd Avenue (tel. 907/766–2234). The easiest place to start your tour, however, is at the **Sheldon Museum and Cultural Center** near the foot of Main Street. This is another Alaskana collection, homegrown with personal care by an Alaskan family. Steve Sheldon began assembling Indian artifacts, Russian items, and gold-rush memorabilia, such as Jack Dalton's sawed-off shotgun, in 1924. His daughter, Elisabeth Hakkinen, carries on and is usually on hand to serve Russian tea, to recall the stories behind many of the items on display, and to reminisce about growing up in Haines before World War II. *25 Main St., tel. 907/766–2366. Small admission fee.*

One of the most rewarding hikes in the area is to the north summit of **Mt. Ripinsky,** the prominent peak that rises to 3,610 feet behind the town. Be warned: It's a strenuous trek and requires a full day. The **trailhead** lies at the top of Young Street, along a pipeline right-of-way. For other hikes, pick up a copy of "Haines Is for Hikers" at the Information Center.

The **Southeast Alaska State Fairgrounds** is probably worth a drive-through if you're a fair buff or interested in things agricultural. The fair held each August is one of several official regional fall blowouts staged around the state, and in its homegrown, homespun way it's a real winner. In addition to the usual collection of barnyard animals (chickens, goats, horses), the fair offers the finest examples of local culinary arts and the chance to see Indian dances, displays of Indian totemic crafts, lots of hobby crafts, and some fine art and photography.

As noted, the Haines Highway roughly divides Haines/Ft. Seward. At the base of the highway is **Mile 0,** the starting point of the 152-mile road to the Alaska Highway and the Canadian Yukon. Whether you plan to travel all the way or not, you should spend at least a bit of time on the scenic highway. At about Mile 6 there's a delightful picnic spot near the Chilkat River and an inflowing clear creek; at Mile 9.5 the view of the Takhinsha Mountains across the river is magnificent; and around Mile 19 there is good viewing of the **Alaska Chilkat Bald Eagle Preserve,** where, especially in late fall and early winter, as many as 4,000 of the great birds have been known to assemble. The United States–Canada border lies at Mile 40. If you're traveling on to Canada, stop at Canadian customs and be sure to set your clock ahead one hour, noon in Alaska being 1 PM in this part of Canada. (If you're headed south from Canada, check in with U.S. Customs, and of course set your timepiece back an hour.)

The Haines Highway is completely paved on the American side of the border and, except for a few remaining stretches, almost entirely paved in Canada.

Back in town, head for Ft. Seward, and wander past the huge, stately, white-columned former commanding officer's home, now a part of the **Halsingland Hotel.** Circle the flat but sloping parade ground, with its **Indian tribal house** and sourdough log cabin. In the evening, visit the **Chilkat Center for the Arts.** This building once was the army post's recreation hall, but now it's the scene of Chilkat Indian dancing (Mon. and Sat. evenings) or the outrageous "Lust for Dust" historical melodrama (Sun. performances may be at the tribal house; check posted notices.) *Both shows start at 8:30 PM and charge $5.*

Between the Chilkat Center for the Arts and the parade ground stands the former fort hospital, now being used as a workshop for the craftsmen of **Alaska Indian Arts** (tel. 907/766–2160), a nonprofit organization dedicated to the revival of Tlingit Indian art forms. You'll see Indian carvers making totems here, metalsmiths working in silver, even weavers making blankets. *Admission free. Open weekdays 9–noon and 1–5.*

The Haines ferry terminal is located 4½ miles northwest of downtown.

Skagway

Numbers in the margin correspond to points of interest on the Skagway map.

Skagway lies 13 miles north of Haines by ferry on the Alaska Marine Highway. If you go by road, the distance is 359 miles, as it's necessary to cover first the Haines Highway to Haines Junction, Yukon, then a hundred miles of Alaska Highway south to Whitehorse, and then a final hundred south to Skagway on the Klondike Highway. North country folk call this the Golden Horseshoe or Golden Circle tour, because it takes in a lot of gold-rush country in addition to lake, forest, and mountain scenery.

However you get to Skagway, you'll find the town an amazingly preserved living artifact from one of North America's biggest, most storied gold rushes. Most of the downtown district forms part of the **Klondike Gold Rush National Historical Park,** a unit of the national park system dedicated to preserving and interpreting the frenzied stampede that extended to Dawson City in Canada's Yukon. Old false-fronted stores, saloons, and brothels—built to separate gold-rush prospectors from their grubstakes going north or their gold pokes heading south—have been restored, repainted, and refurnished by the federal government and Skagway's people. When you walk down Broadway today, the scene is not appreciably different from what the prospectors saw in the days of 1898, except that the dust (or mud) of Broadway has been covered with pavement to make your meandering easier.

Skagway had only a single cabin, still standing, when the Yukon gold rush began. At first the argonauts, as they liked to be called, swarmed to Dyea and the Chilkoot Trail, 9 miles to the west of Skagway. Skagway and its White Pass trail didn't seem as attractive until a dock was built in town. Then it mushroomed overnight into the major gateway to the Klondike, supporting a wild mixture of legitimate businessmen, con artists (among the most cunning, Jefferson "Soapy" Smith), stampeders, and curiosity seekers.

Three months after the first boat landed in July 1897, Skagway numbered perhaps 20,000 persons and had well-laid-out streets, hotels, stores, saloons, gambling houses, and dance halls. By spring of 1898, the superintendent of the Northwest Royal Mounted Police in neighboring Canada would label the town "little better than a hell on earth."

A lot of the "hell" ended with a shoot-out one pleasant July evening in 1898. Good-guy Frank Reid (the surveyor who laid out Skagway's streets so wide and well) faced down bad-guy Soapy Smith on Juneau dock downtown near the present ferry terminal. After a classic exchange of gunfire, Smith lay dead and Reid lay dying. The town built a huge monument at Reid's grave. You can see it in Gold Rush Cemetery and read the inscription on it today: "He gave his life for the honor of Skagway." For Smith, whose tombstone was continually chiseled and stolen by vandals and souvenir seekers, today's grave marker is a simple wooden plank.

To begin a visit to this storied town, head first to **City Hall** on 7th Avenue. There, on the first floor of a large granite structure built in 1899 to house McCabe Methodist College, the Skagway Convention and Visitors Bureau will give you maps and lots of suggestions for seeing their town. Your first stop should be right upstairs in the City Hall building, where the ❶ **Trail of '98 Museum** is located.

Frank Reid's will is preserved under glass there, as are papers disposing of Soapy Smith's estate. Gambling paraphernalia from the old Board of Trade Saloon is on display along with native artifacts, gold scales, a red-and-black sleigh (one-horse variety), a small organ, and a blanket made from the skin of duck necks and fortified by pepper bags sewn behind the skin to afford protection from moths.

❷ After you've browsed in the museum, wander back to Broadway and 6th Avenue to the **Eagles Hall.** Here locals daily perform a show called "Skagway in the Days of '98." You'll see cancan dancers, learn a little local history, and watch desperado Soapy Smith sent to his reward. *Tel. 907/983-2545. Posted show hours depend on ship arrivals and departures. Performances are usually at 10 AM and 8 PM.*

❸ Farther south on Broadway you come to **Arctic Brotherhood Hall,** the likes of which you'll not see anywhere else in Alaska. The Arctic Brotherhood was a fraternal organization of Alaskan and Yukon pioneers. To decorate the exterior false front of their Skagway lodge building, local members created a mosaic covering out of 20,000 pieces of driftwood and flotsam gathered from local beaches.

❹ **Soapy's Parlor** is located on 2nd Avenue just west of Broadway, ❺ while the former **White Pass & Yukon Route rail depot** is located on the east side of the main thoroughfare. This building, now the headquarters and information center for the Klondike Gold Rush National Historical Park, contains exhibits, photos, and artifacts from the White Pass and Chilkoot trails. This is of special interest if you plan to take a White Pass train ride, drive the nearby Klondike Highway, or hike the Chilkoot Trail.

Lots of other stops along Broadway and its side streets merit inspection. For children, the **Sweet Tooth Saloon** with its ice cream and sodas is a special favorite. For adults, the 19th-century **Red Onion Saloon** (with its former brothel upstairs) is an interesting and thirst-quenching stop. **The Golden North Hotel,** constructed in 1898 and Alaska's oldest hotel, has been lovingly restored to its gold-rush-era milieu. It's worth a stroll through the lobby even if you're not staying there. Curio shops abound, and among the oldest—probably *the* oldest—in all of Alaska is **Kirmse's** (pronounced "KIRM-zees") on Broadway.

Arctic Brotherhood Hall, **3**

Cruise-ship dock, **8**

Eagles Hall, **2**

Ferry dock, **7**

Klondike Highway, **6**

Soapy's Parlor, **4**

Trail of '98 Museum, **1**

White Pass & Yukon Route rail depot, **5**

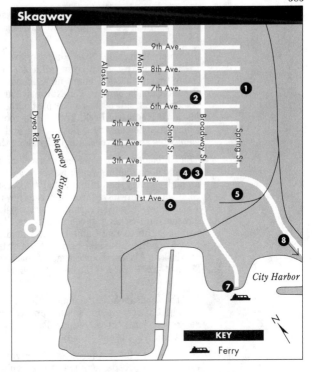

Visit the shop and see the world's largest, heaviest, and most valuable gold nugget watch chain. On display as well is a companion chain made of the world's tiniest, daintiest little nuggets.

6 At the foot of State Street is the start of the **Klondike Highway.** The Klondike often parallels the older White Pass railway route as it travels northwest to Carcross and Whitehorse in the Canadian Yukon. It merges just south of Whitehorse for a short distance with the Alaska Highway, then it heads on its own again to terminate at Dawson City on the shores of the Klondike River. From start to finish, it covers 435 miles.

Along the way the road climbs steeply through forested coastal mountains with jagged, snow-covered peaks. It passes by deep, fish-filled lakes and streams in the Canadian high country, where travelers have at least a chance of seeing mountain goat, moose, black bear, or grizzly.

If you're driving the Klondike Highway north from Skagway you must stop at **Canadian Customs,** Mile 22. If you're traveling south to Skagway, check in at **U.S. Customs,** Mile 6. And remember that when it's 1 PM in Canada at the border, it's noon in Skagway.

7
8 Just south of Broadway lies the **ferry dock,** a pleasant half-mile walk from town, and somewhat farther south is the **cruise-ship dock** where the big ships land. The mountainside cliff behind the cruise-ship dock, incidentally, is rather incredible, with its scores of advertisements and ships' names brightly painted on the exposed granite face. Most singular of all the "murals" at

the site is a large skull-like rock formation that has been painted white, given appropriate cavities, and named Soapy's Skull.

Two more excursions from Skagway are notable. The first is the **Chilkoot Trail** from Dyea to Lake Lindeman, a trek of 33 miles that includes a climb up Chilkoot Pass at the United States–Canada border. The National Park Service maintains the American side of the pass as part of the Klondike Gold Rush National Historical Park. The trail is good; the forest, mountain, and lake country is both scenic and richly historic, and campsites are located strategically along the way.

The Chilkoot is not, however, an easy walk. There are lots of ups and downs before you cross the pass and reach the Canadian high country, and rain is a distinct possibility. To return to Skagway, hikers have three choices. They can end their trek at Lake Bennett, where a rail motorcar will transport them to Fraser and further rail connections to Skagway, or they can walk a cutoff to Log Cabin on the Klondike Highway. There they can either hitchhike back to town or flag down Gray Line of Alaska's Alaskon Express motor coach (tel. 907/983–2557 or 800/544–2206; fare: $16) heading south to Skagway from Whitehorse.

For the thousands that complete the hike each year, it is the highlight of a trip to the North country. For details, maps, and references contact the National Park Service information center at 2nd Avenue and Broadway.

If you're not a hiker, there's an easier way to follow the second excursion, a prospector's trail to the gold-rush country. You can take the **White Pass & Yukon Route** (WP & YR) narrow-gauge railroad over the "Trail of '98."

The historic (started in 1898) gold-rush railroad's diesel locomotives chug and tow vintage viewing cars up the steep inclines of the route, hugging the walls of precipitous cliff sides, and providing thousands of travelers with the view of craggy peaks, plummeting waterfalls, lakes, and forests. It's a summertime operation only.

Two options are available. Twice daily the WP & YR leaves Skagway for a 3-hour round-trip excursion to the White Pass summit. Sights along the way include Bridal Veil Falls, Inspiration Point, and Dead Horse Gulch. The fare is $69. Through service to Whitehorse, Yukon, is offered daily as well—in the form of a train trip to Fraser where motor-coach connections are available on to Whitehorse. The one-way fare to Whitehorse is $89. For information call 907/983–2217 or 800/343–7373.

Glacier Bay/Gustavus

Nearly 200 years ago, Captain George Vancouver sailed by Glacier Bay and didn't even know it. The bay at that time, 1794, was hidden behind and beneath a vast glacial wall of ice. The glacier was more than 20 miles across its face and, in places, more than 4,000 feet in depth. It extended more than 100 miles to the St. Elias Mountain Range. Over the next 100 years, due to warming weather and other factors not fully understood even now, the face of the glacial ice has melted and retreated with amazing speed, exposing nearly 50 miles of fjords, islands, and inlets.

In 1879, about a century after Vancouver's sail-by, one of the earliest white visitors to what is now **Glacier Bay National Park and Preserve** came calling. He was naturalist John Muir, drawn by the flora and fauna that had followed in the wake of glacial withdrawals and fascinated by the vast ice rivers that descended from the mountains to tidewater. Today, the naturalist's namesake glacier, like others in the park, continues to retreat dramatically. Its terminus is now scores of miles farther up bay from the small cabin he built at its face during his time there. (For more on the park, *see* Chapter 4, Parks, Wildlife Refuges, and Wilderness Adventures.)

The waterways provide access to no fewer than 16 tidewater glaciers, a dozen of which actively calve icebergs into the bay. The show can be mind-boggling. With a noise that sounds like cannons firing, bergs the size of 10-story office buildings sometimes come crashing from the "snout" of a glacier. The crash sends tons of water and spray skyward, and it propels mini tidal waves outward from the point of impact. Johns Hopkins Glacier calves so often and with such volume that even the large cruise ships can seldom approach its face closer than 2 miles.

Companies that offer big-ship visits include Holland America Lines, Princess Cruises, Royal Viking Line, and World Explorer Cruises. During the several hours that the ships are in the bay, National Park Service naturalists come aboard to explain the great glaciers, to point out features of the forests and islands and mountains, and to help spot black bears, brown bears, mountain goats, whales, porpoises, and the countless species of birds that call the area home.

Smaller, more intimate, and probably more informative is the boat *Spirit of Adventure*, which operates daily from the dock at Bartlett Cove, near Glacier Bay Lodge (tel. 800/622–2042). Uniformed Park Service naturalists sail aboard these excursions, too.

At Bartlett Cove, where the glaciers stood and then receded more than two centuries ago, the shore is covered with stands of high-towering spruce and hemlock. This is a climax forest, thick and lush and abounding with the wildlife of Southeast Alaska. As you sail farther into the great bay, the conifers become noticeably smaller, and they are finally replaced by alders and other leafy species, which took root and began growing only a few decades ago. Finally, deep into the bay where the glaciers have withdrawn in very recent years, the shorelines contain only plants and primitive lichens. Given enough time, however, these lands, too, will be covered with the same towering forests that you see at the bay's entrance.

The most adventurous way to see and explore Glacier Bay is up close. Really up close—as in paddling your own kayak through the bay's icy waters and inlets. You can book one of **Alaska Discovery's** (234 Gold St., Juneau 99801, tel. 907/586–1911) four- or seven-day guided expeditions. Unless you really know what you're doing, you're better off signing on with the guided tours. Alaska Discovery provides safe, seaworthy kayaks and tents, gear, and food. Its guides are tough, knowledgeable

Alaskans, and they've spent enough time in Glacier Bay's wild country to know what's safe and what's not.

Within Glacier Bay Park and Preserve there's only one overnight facility, **Glacier Bay Lodge.** If it's booked, or too pricey for your budget, don't worry. About a half hour's drive along the 10-mile road that leads out of the park is Gustavus, where additional lodges, inns, and bed-and-breakfasts abound (*see* Lodging, *below*).

Gustavus calls itself "the way to Glacier Bay," and for airborne visitors the community is indeed the gateway to the park. The long, paved jet airport, built as a refueling strip during World War II, is one of the best and longest in Southeast Alaska, all the more impressive because facilities at the field are so limited. Alaska Airlines, which serves Gustavus daily in the summer, has a large, rustic terminal at the site, and from a free telephone on the front porch of the terminal you can call any of the local hostelries for courtesy pickup. Smaller light-aircraft companies that serve the community out of Juneau also have on-site shelters.

Gustavus also boasts no "downtown." In fact, Gustavus is not a town. The 150 or so year-round residents there are most emphatic on this point; they regularly vote down incorporation as a city. Instead, Gustavus is a scattering of homes, farmsteads, arts and crafts studios, fishing and guiding charters, and other tiny enterprises peopled by hospitable individualists. It is, in many ways, exemplary of today's version of the frontier spirit in Alaska. For a listing of the 33 firms that make up the **Gustavus Visitors Association,** write to Box 167, Gustavus 99826, tel. 907/697–2358.

What to See and Do with Children

Canoe rides in the modern equivalent of an Indian war canoe provide fun and exercise for young people and old at a woodsy lake near Ketchikan. Or try a **catamaran trip** to view seabirds near Sitka. *Alaska Travel Adventures, tel. 907/789–0052.*

Fishing is popular, and no fishing license is required in Alaska for kids under 16. For the best saltwater shoreline, lake, or stream fishing, call the local Alaska Department of Fish and Game office in the city you're visiting (in Juneau, it's 907/465–4112).

Goldpanning is fun and sometimes children actually uncover a few flecks of the precious metal in the bottom of their pans. You can buy a pan at almost any Alaska hardware or sporting-goods store, or you can look for schedules of gold-panning excursions at visitor information centers.

Indian dancing will dazzle the younger set. Masked performers wearing bearskins and brightly patterned dance blankets act out great hunts, fierce battles, and other stories. Among the best-known dance groups is the Chilkat Indian Dancers of Ft. Seward in Haines. *Performances Mon. and Sat. at 8:30 PM. Admission: $5.*

There are **totem pole parks**—featuring the sometimes fear-some countenances of bears, killer whales, great birds, and legendary hunters—at Ketchikan, Wrangell, Sitka, Juneau, and Haines/Ft. Seward (*see* Exploring Southeast Alaska, *above*). Other fine examples of the carver's art can be seen at the Indian villages of Kake, Angoon, and Hoonah (*see* Off the Beaten Track, *below*).

Kayaking in front of Mendenhall Glacier is sure to create vivid memories for youngsters as well as active adults (*see* Tours and Packages, *above*; in Chapter 1, Essential Information; and in Chapter 4, Parks, Wildlife Refuges, and Wilderness Adventures).

Summer sports are a passion in Southeast Alaska, and at Petersburg both young and old visitors are welcome to join in recreational softball or volleyball games. Call the Parks and Recreation Department for details (tel. 907/772–3392).

Off the Beaten Track

Surely one of the world's great travel bargains is the network of 150 or so **wilderness cabins** operated by the U.S. Forest Service alongside remote lakes and streams in the **Tongass National Forest** of Southeast Alaska. These cabins are equipped with bunks for six to eight occupants, tables, stoves, and outdoor privies. The cost: only $20 per night per party. Most are fly-in units, accessible by pontoon-equipped aircraft from virtually any community in the Panhandle. You provide your own sleeping bag, food, and cooking utensils. Don't be surprised if the Forest Service recommends you carry along a 30.06 or larger caliber rifle, in the unlikely event of a bear problem.

If you're a hot-springs or hot-tub enthusiast, **White Sulphur Springs** cabins, out of Sitka, or **Shakes Slough** cabins, accessible from Wrangell or Petersburg, boast these amenities. There's also a hot-springs pool of sorts, big enough for two or three to lounge in, at **Bailey Bay,** just north of Ketchikan's Revilla Island on the mainland. A 10-minute hike from a landing in a nearby lake or a 2-mile trek on an unmaintained but negotiable trail from salt water will bring you to the site. Have your pilot fly over to show you your foot route before you land. Shelter here is a three-sided Adirondack lean-to built as a public project during the Depression. *Request details and reservation information from the USFS office in each community or call or write: U.S. Forest Service, Box 1628, Juneau 99802, tel. 907/586–8806.*

Offbeat, but boasting the ultimate in catered comfort, is the **Waterfall Resort** (Box 6440, Ketchikan 99901, tel. 907/225–9461 or 800/544–5125, fax 907/225–8530) on Prince of Wales Island near Ketchikan. At this former commercial salmon cannery you sleep in Cape Cod–style cottages (former cannery workers' cabins, but they never had it so good); eat bountiful meals of salmon, halibut steak, and all the trimmings; and fish from your own private cabin cruiser under the tender loving care of your own private fishing guide.

Farther north, **Baranof Wilderness Lodge** (Box 21022, Auke Bay 99824, tel. 907/586–8110) is one of the Panhandle's newer lodge facilities, located at Warm Springs Bay on Baranof Island. Kayaking, canoeing, hiking, and exploring are all options at this facility, as well as fresh- and saltwater fishing. The most popular activity of all is probably hot tubbing, in waters supplied by the warm springs.

One of Southeast Alaska's pioneer lodges is **Thayer Lake Lodge** (in summer, Box 211614, Auke Bay 99821, tel. 907/225–4538; in winter, Box 5416, Ketchikan 99901, tel. 907/225–3343), on Admiralty Island near Juneau. This is a rustic lodge-and-cabins operation that has been playing host to Juneau folk and Alaskan visitors for decades. Bob and Edith Nelson built this resort after World War II on one of the high-country lakes in the Admiralty Island wilderness. They did it mostly with their own labor, using native timber for their buildings. Lake fishing is unexcelled for cutthroat and Dolly Varden trout (though they're not overly large). There's also canoeing, hiking, and wildlife photography.

Tenakee Springs is a tiny little fishing, vacation, and retirement community that clings to (in fact, hangs out over) the shores of Chichagof Island. The town is accessible from Juneau by air or by the smaller Alaska ferry *LeConte* on an eight-hour run. You certainly won't find any Hilton hotels here, but there is a cozy Victorian-style lodge on the beachfront, or the local general store can rent you a cabin. With either type of accommodation comes the privilege of partaking in the town's principal pastime—bathing. Tenakee Springs' bathhouse is the centerpiece of the community's lifestyle. There is no coed time. Use the baths twice in two days and you'll likely meet three fourths of the city's population who are of your gender. Use it three times and you'll meet the rest. Between baths you can fish for salmon and halibut or go crabbing; hike; pick berries; and visit with some of the friendliest townsfolk in the state. *For cabin rentals, write Snyder Mercantile, Box 505, Tenakee Springs 99841, tel. 907/736–2205.*

Tenakee Inn offers a cozy, beachfront Victorian-style lodge with kitchenettes, private bath, and family-style meals. Also provided are kayaks, bicycles, and a skiff. *Box 54, Tenakee Springs 99841, tel. 907/736–2241.*

In Sitka, Burgess Bauder rents out his hand-built **Rockwell Lighthouse** (Box 277, Sitka 99835, tel. 907/747–3056) across the sound for $125 a day for a family. The price includes the use of a motorboat to get there.

Finally, if you hanker to know how the Indian village peoples of Southeast Alaska live today, you can fly or take the state ferry *LeConte* to **Kake, Angoon,** or **Hoonah.** You won't find much organized touring in any of these communities, but small, clean hotel accommodations are available (advance reservations strongly suggested), and fishing trips can be arranged by asking around. *In Kake: contact the New Town Inn, Box 222, Kake 99830, tel. 907/785–3472. In Angoon: write or call Kootznahoo Inlet Lodge, Box 134, Angoon 99820, tel. 907/788–3501; or Whalers Cove Lodge, Box 101, Angoon 99820, tel. 788–3123. In Hoonah: contact Totem Lodge, Box 320, Hoonah 99829, tel. 907/945–3636.*

Shopping

Art Galleries   Along with the usual array of work by talented but unspectacular artists, Southeast Alaska shops and galleries carry some impressive Alaskan paintings, lithographs, and drawings. Among the best: **Scanlon Gallery,** with locations downtown in Ketchikan (308 Mission St., tel. 907/225–4730) and in the Plaza PortWest, a couple of miles north of downtown. It handles not only major Alaska artists (Byron Birdsall, Rie Munoz, John Fahringer, Nancy Stonington) and local talent but also traditional and contemporary native art, including soapstone, bronze, and ivory earrings. In Juneau, knowledgeable locals frequent the **Rie Munoz Gallery** (233 S. Franklin St., tel. 907/586–2112) near the cruise ship dock downtown. Ms. Munoz is one of Alaska's favorite artists, creator of a stylized, simple, but colorful design technique that is much copied but rarely equaled. Other artists' work is also on sale at the Munoz Gallery, including woodblock prints by nationally recognized artist Dale DeArmond. Various books illustrated by Rie Munoz and written by Alaskan children's author Jean Rogers are also available.

Crafts and Gifts Totem poles, from a few inches high to several feet tall, are among the popular Indian-made items available in the Southeast Alaska Panhandle. Other handicrafts from the Tlingit and Haida Indians include wall masks, paddles, dance rattles, baskets, and tapestries with Southeast Alaska Indian designs. You'll find these items at gift shops up and down the coast. If you want to be sure of native Alaskan authenticity, buy items tagged with the state-approved "Authentic Native Handcraft From Alaska" label.

Gold-nugget rings, bracelets, necklaces, and watchbands, though costly, are popular among Alaskans and Alaska visitors. One Juneau dealer, the Nugget Shop on Front Street, will even sell you plain gold nuggets if you've missed finding any in the streams around the region.

Salmon—smoked, canned, or packaged otherwise—is another popular take-home item, for your own consumption or for friends who had to stay behind. Virtually every community has at least one canning and/or smoking operation that packs and ships local seafood. Throughout the region, in food stores and gift shops, you'll likely run into Silver Lining Seafoods products, a Ketchikan-based company with a consistently high-quality product in attractive packaging.

Another gourmet delicacy is a product Southeasterners refer to as Petersburg shrimp. Small (they're seldom larger than half your pinky finger), tender, and succulent, they're much treasured by Alaskans and often sent "outside" by them as thank-you gifts. You'll find the little critters fresh in meat departments and canned in gift sections at food stores throughout the Panhandle. You can buy fresh vacuum-packed Petersburg shrimp in Petersburg at **Coastal Cold Storage,** downtown on Main Street, or mail order them (Box 307, Petersburg 99833, tel. 907/772–4177).

You can't take it with you because of its limited shelf life, but when you're "shopping" the bars and watering holes of Southeast Alaska, ask for Alaskan Beer, an amber beer brewed and bottled in Juneau. Visitors are welcome at the **minibrewery's plant** and can sample the product during the bottling operation on Tuesday and Thursdays 11–4. *5429 Shaune Dr., Juneau, tel. 907/780–5866.*

Up the stairs in the restored old Senate Building on S. Franklin Street in Juneau is the **Russian Shop** (tel. 907/586–2778), a depository of icons, samovars, lacquered boxes, nesting dolls, and other items that reflect Alaska's 18th- and 19th-century Russian heritage. One side of the shop is similarly, and surprisingly, devoted to Norwegian wares, including traditional Norwegian wool sweaters.

Participant Sports

Bicycling In spite of sometimes wet weather, bicycling is very popular in Southeast Alaska communities. There are plenty of flat roads to ride (and some killer hills, too, if you're game) and the cycling can be glorious beside saltwater bays or within great towering forests. Unfortunately, bike rentals in the region seem to cycle in and out of business faster than you can shift derailleurs. Best bet if you don't bring your own in the back of a car or camper is to call bike shops or the parks and recreation departments in the towns you're visiting. Ask who in town is supplying rentals at the moment. Lodgings at Tenakee and Gustavus have bikes on hand for the use of their guests. For more information on biking, *see* Participant Sports and Recreation in Chapter 1, Essential Information.

Canoeing/ Paddling has been a pleasant way for visitors to see Southeast
Kayaking Alaska since the first Russians arrived on the scene in 1741 and watched the Indians do it. **Alaska Travel Adventures** in Juneau has trips in various areas of the region (tel. 907/789–0052). The **Ketchikan Parks and Recreation Department** (tel. 907/228–6650) rents canoes. At Sitka, **Baidarka Boats** (tel. 907/747–8996) offers sea-kayak rentals and custom-guided trips. In Juneau, **Alaska Discovery** (tel. 907/586–1911) is the company to see for escorted boat excursions in Glacier Bay National Park and Preserve or Admiralty Island, or for kayaking in the lake in front of Mendenhall Glacier.

Kayak rentals for unescorted Glacier Bay exploring and camping can be arranged through **Glacier Bay Sea Kayaks** (Box 26, Gustavus 99826, tel. 907/697–2257). Twice a day, at 9 AM and 6 PM, its experienced kayakers give orientations on handling the craft plus camping and routing suggestions. The company will also make reservations aboard the regular day boat to drop kayakers off and pick them up in the most scenic country. For more information on boating, *see* Participant Sports and Recreation in Chapter 1, Essential Information. For lists of operators offering longer boating trips, *see* Tours and Packages in Chapter 1, Essential Information, and Chapter 4, Parks, Wildlife Refuges, and Wilderness Adventures.

Fishing The prospect of bringing a lunker king salmon or a leaping, diving, fighting rainbow trout to net is the reason many visitors choose an Alaska vacation. Local give-away guidebooks and the State of Alaska's "Vacation Planner" contain the names of scores of reputable charter boats and boat rental agencies in every community along the Panhandle coast. Your best bet for catching salmon in saltwater is from a boat. Similarly, the very finest angling for freshwater species (rainbows, cutthroat, lake trout) is to be found at fly-in lakes and resorts. Still, there's more than adequate fishing right from saltwater shores or in lakes and streams accessible by roads. To learn where the fish are biting at any given time, call the local office of the Alaska

Department of Fish and Game in the community you're visiting, or contact the ADFG's main office (Box 25526, Juneau 99802, tel. 907/465–4112). For more information on fishing, *see* Participant Sports and Recreation in Chapter 1, Essential Information. For a list of operators offering fishing trips, *see* Tours and Packages in Chapter 1, Essential Information.

Golf Juneau's par-three nine-hole **Mendenhall Golf course** (2101 Industrial Blvd., tel. 907/789–7323) is pretty modest. Still, its location on saltwater wetlands beside the waters of Gastineau Channel makes it one of a kind. Club rentals are available.

Hiking and Backpacking Trekking woods, mountains, and beaches is Southeast Alaska's unofficial regional sport. Many of the trails are old, abandoned mining roads. Others are natural routes—in some sections, even game trails—meandering over ridges, through forests, and alongside streams and glaciers. A few, like the backpacking Chilkoot Trail out of Skagway, rate five stars for historical significance, scenery, and hiker aids en route. There's not a community in Southeast Alaska that doesn't have easy access to at least some hiking or backpacking. The Alaska Division of Parks Southeast regional office (400 Willoughby Ave., tel. 907/465–4563) will send you a list of state-maintained trails and parks in the Panhandle; local visitors bureaus and recreation departments in the communities you're visiting can also help. Parks and Recreation/Juneau (tel. 907/586–5226) sponsors a group hike each Wednesday morning for locals and visitors. For more information on hiking and backpacking, *see* Chapter 4, Parks, Wildlife Refuges, and Wilderness Adventures. For lists of operators offering hiking and backpacking trips, *see* Guided Tours in Chapter 1, Essential Information, and Chapter 4.

Running and Jogging Hotel clerks and visitor information offices will be glad to make route suggestions if you need them. If you plan to run, bring along a light sweatsuit and rain gear as well as shorts and a T-shirt. The weather can be hot and sweaty one day, chilly and wet the next. If you plan to be in Juneau early in July, call the Parks and Recreation Department (tel. 907/586–5226) and check the date of the annual **Governor's Cup Fun Run.** Hundreds of Juneau racers, runners, joggers, race walkers, and mosey-alongers take part in this 3-mile event. Other marathons, half marathons, 5Ks, and similar events take place in various communities throughout the summer. The most grueling race in these parts is the annual September **Klondike Trail of '98 Road Relay** event, spanning 110 miles between Skagway and Whitehorse on the Klondike and Alaska highways. For details contact Carol Clark, Tourism Industry Association of the Yukon (102–302 Steele St., Whitehorse, Yukon, Canada Y1A 2C5, tel. 403/668–3331).

Scuba Considering that the visibility is not very good in most Southeast waters, there's a lot of scuba- and skin-diving activity throughout the region. Quarter-inch wet suits are a must. So is a buddy; stay close together. Local dive shops can steer you to the best places to dive for abalone, scallops, and crabs, and advise you on the delights and dangers of underwater wrecks. Shops that rent tanks and equipment to qualified divers include **Scuba Crafts, Inc.** (4485 N. Douglas Hwy., Juneau, tel. 907/586–2341), **Alaska Diving Service** (1601 Tongass Ave., Ketchikan, tel. 907/225–4667), and **Southeast Diving & Sports** (203 Lincoln Ave., Sitka, tel. 907/747–8279).

Skiing
Cross-Country Nordic skiing is a favorite winter pastime for outdoor enthusiasts, especially in the northern half of the Panhandle. Although it is promoted mostly by and for the locals, visitors are always welcome. In Petersburg, the favorite locale for Nordic skiing is the end of **Three Lakes Loop.** Old logging roads and trails are popular as well. If you arrive without your boards, call the Chamber of Commerce Visitor Center (tel. 907/772–3646). It will try to line up some loaners for you.

In Juneau, ski rentals are available along with many suggestions for touring the trails and ridges around town from **Foggy Mountain Shop** (134 S. Franklin St., tel. 907/586–6780).

From Haines, **Alaska Nature Tours** (Box 491, Haines 99827, tel. 907/766–2876) operates a winter Nordic shuttle bus to flat-tracking in the Chilkat Bald Eagle Preserve and across the Canadian border atop Chilkat Pass in British Columbia. *See also* Chapter 4, Parks, Wildlife Refuges, and Wilderness Adventures.

Downhill **Eaglecrest** (155 Seward St., Juneau 99801, tel. 907/586–5284) on Douglas Island, just 30 minutes from downtown Juneau, offers late-November to mid-April skiing on a well-groomed mountain with two double-chair lifts, a beginner's platter-pull, cross-country trails, ski school (including downhill, Nordic, and telemark), ski rental shop, cafeteria, and trilevel day lodge. Because this is Southeast Alaska, knowledgeable skiers pack rain slickers along with parkas, hats, gloves, and other gear. On weekends and holidays there are bus pickups at hotels and motels.

Tennis There are courts in Ketchikan, Wrangell, Petersburg, Juneau, and Skagway. The **Juneau Racquet Club,** about 10 miles north of downtown, adjacent to Mendenhall Mall, will accommodate out-of-towners at its first-class indoor tennis and racquetball courts. Facilities include sauna, Jacuzzi, exercise equipment, snack bar, massage tables, and sports shop. *Tel. 907/789–2181. 1-day fee for nonmembers: $8.*

Spectator Sports

With the possible exception of basketball, Southeast Alaska's spectator sports probably don't offer much excitement for visitors. There are no semi-pro or professional baseball teams in the Panhandle. The devotion of large numbers of Southeast adults to summer softball, however, borders on outright addiction.

Basketball Watching two teams of five trying to shoot balls through hoops is Southeast Alaska's major spectator sport. Each January in Juneau, the local **Lions Clubs' Golden North** tournament attracts teams from all over the Panhandle and even nearby Canada. And the University of Alaska–Southeast Whales and Lady Whales teams likewise are often in town to offer respectable court action. For schedules, contact University of Alaska–Southeast (11120 Glacier Hwy., Juneau 99801, tel. 907/789–4400).

Dining and Lodging

Highly recommended hotels and restaurants are indicated with a star ★.

Major credit cards are usually accepted, but there are exceptions. It's best to inquire in advance. Dress is casual in restaurants, except where noted.

Dining

Category	Cost*
Expensive	over $40
Moderate	$20–$40
Inexpensive	under $20

per person excluding service and drinks

Lodging Hotels, motels, lodges, and inns run the gamut in Southeast Alaska from very traditional urban hostelries—the kind you'll find almost anywhere—to charming small-town inns and rustic cabins in the boondocks.

The most rooms, and the most choices, are to be found in Ketchikan and Juneau. Accommodations in any of the Panhandle communities, however, are usually not hard to come by even in the summer, except when festivals, fishing derbies, fairs, and other special events are under way. To be on the safe side and get your first choice, you should make reservations as early as possible. In addition to the hotels and inns listed here, *see also* Off the Beaten Track, *above*, for more rustic and out-of-the-way accommodations. With the exception of bed-and-breakfasts (B&Bs), most hotels accept the major credit cards. Hotels and other lodging are listed under the following categories:

Category	Cost*
Very Expensive	over $120
Expensive	$90–$120
Moderate	$50–$90
Inexpensive	under $50

double room excluding tax (8–10%)

Glacier Bay/ Gustavus **Glacier Bay Country Inn.** It's an inn where the emphasis is on
Dining gourmet dining, with foods fresh from the sea and the inn's own
★ garden. Among guests' favorites: halibut with fresh sorrel sauce, homemade fettuccine, and rhubarb custard pie. Dinner guests not staying at the inn must make reservations in advance. The building is a large, rambling, log structure of marvelous cupolas, dormers, gables, and porches. *On the main road halfway between the airport and Bartlett Cove, tel. 907/ 697–2288. No credit cards, but personal checks are accepted. Moderate.*

★ **Gustavus Inn.** The family-style meals at this former homestead are legendary. Hosts David and Jo Ann Lesh—carrying on a tradition established decades ago by David's parents—heap bountiful servings of seafood and fresh vegetable dishes on the plates of overnight guests and walk-ins who reserve in ad-

vance. *On the main road, tel. 907/697–2254. MC, V accepted,
but cash or personal or traveler's checks preferred. Moderate.*

Glacier Bay Lodge. If it swims or crawls in the sea hereabouts,
you'll find it on the menu in the dining room at this, the only
lodge actually in Glacier Bay National Park and Preserve.
Steaks and other selections are available as well. Located on
the main floor of the massive timbered lodge, the dining room
looks out on the chill waters of Bartlett Cove. *Tel. 907/697–
2225. AE, MC, V, DC. Inexpensive–Moderate.*

Open Gate Cafe. Nothing fancy here, just good wholesome
cooking that the locals seem to like—fresh baked breads, pastries, and deli sandwiches. Monday night is pizza night; Saturdays feature prime ribs. *On the dock road, tel. 907/697–2227.
No credit cards, but personal checks are accepted. Inexpensive.*

Lodging
★ **Glacier Bay Lodge.** This consists of the only hotel accommodations actually within Glacier Bay National Park and Preserve.
The lodge is constructed of massive timbers, and in spite of its
size it blends well into the thick rain forest that surrounds it on
three sides. Room accommodations—fully modern—are accessible by boardwalk ramps from the main lodge. From the Bartlett Cove dock out front, visitors take day boats or overnight
cruises up the bay into the glacier country. *Located at Bartlett
Cove (mailing address: Box 108, Gustavus 99826 or 523 Pine
St., Seattle, WA 98101), tel. 907/697–2225 or 800/451–5952, fax
206/623–7809. 55 rooms. Facilities: lounge, gift shop,
flightseeing reservations desk. AE, MC, V, DC. Very Expensive.*

★ **Gustavus Inn.** Established in 1965 on a pioneer Gustavus homestead, the inn continues a tradition of gracious Alaska rural living and vacationing. In the original homestead building and in a
new structure completed in 1988, there are rooms with full private baths and a few that share facilities. Glacier trips, fishing
expeditions, bicycle rides around the community, or berry
picking in season are offered here. Many guests, however, prefer to do nothing but enjoy the inn's quiet, tranquillity, and notable food. *On main road (mailing address: Box 60, Gustavus
99826), tel. 907/697–2254, fax 907/697–2255; or 913/649–5220,
fax 913/649–5220, in winter. 14 rooms. Courtesy-car pickup at
the airport. MC, V accepted, but cash or personal or traveler's
checks preferred. Very Expensive.*

★ **Glacier Bay Country Inn.** It opened in 1986 with accommodations for 14 guests in a picturesque but fully modern structure
built from local hand-logged timbers. Innkeepers Al and Annie
Unrein have outfitted the inn with cozy comforters, warm flan-
nel sheets, and fluffy towels in each room for a homelike feeling.
The Unreins will arrange sightseeing and flightseeing tours.
They also operate charter-boat trips into Glacier Bay and nearby waters aboard their elegant M/V *Pacific,* a 42-foot yacht
with teak woodwork, two staterooms (sleeping four to six) and
two bathrooms. *On main road halfway between the airport and
Bartlett Cove (mailing address: Box 5, Gustavus 99826), tel.
907/697–2288 or 801/673–8480 in winter; fax 907/697–2289. No
credit cards, but personal checks are accepted. Expensive–
Very Expensive.*

The Puffin Bed & Breakfast. These are attractive cabins located in a wooded homestead. Bath and shower are in a separate building. Bikes are available for guests' use. Full
breakfast is included. The owners also operate Puffin Travel,

for fishing and sightseeing charters, and the Puffin Arts and Crafts Shop at the airport. *In central Gustavus (mailing address: Box 3, Gustavus 99826), tel. 907/697–2260, fax 907/697–2258, in summer; tel. 907/789–9787 in winter. 5 cabins. AE, MC, V. Expensive.*

Haines   **The Lighthouse Restaurant.** Located at the foot of Main Street
Dining   next to the boat harbor, the Lighthouse offers a great view of Lynn Canal, boats, and boaters, along with fine barbecued ribs, steaks, and seafoods. Its Harbor Bar is a popular watering hole for commercial fishermen. It's colorful but can get a little loud at night. *Front St. on the harbor, tel. 907/766–2442. AE, MC, V. Moderate.*

The Bamboo Room. This unassuming restaurant is popular for sandwiches, burgers, fried chicken, and seafood. *2nd Ave. near Main St., tel. 907/766–2800. No credit cards. Inexpensive.*

Chilkat Restaurant and Bakery. Family-style cooking is offered in a homelike setting. *5th Ave. near Main St., tel. 907/766–2920. AE, MC, V. Closed Sun.; winter hours vary. Inexpensive.*

Commander's Room Restaurant and Lounge. It's located in the large, white, rambling house that served as the former commanding officer's quarters at old Ft. Seward and is now the Halsingland Hotel. Seafood is the specialty here, and halibut is a consistent pleaser. The restaurant has a full salad bar and full "potato bar" of baked potatoes, boiled red potatoes, rice pilaf, and vegetables with varied toppings (cheese, chili, etc.). Nearby, at the Indian Tribal House on the parade grounds, the Halsingland also prepares a nightly salmon bake called the Port Chilkoot Potlatch, priced at $17.50 for all you can eat. *On the parade grounds, Ft. Seward, tel. 907/766–2000. AE, D, DC, MC, V. Inexpensive.*

Lodging   **Captain's Choice Motel.** This conventional motel, located in
★   downtown Haines, provides amenities such as cable TV, phones, and rooms with bath and toilet facilities. Ask for a room looking out over the waters of Portage Cove. *2nd and Dalton Sts. (mailing address: Box 392, Haines 99827), tel. 800/247–7153 or 800/478–2345 in AK. 37 rooms, 3 deluxe suites. AE, D, DC, MC, V. Moderate–Expensive.*

Halsingland Hotel. The officers of old Ft. Seward once lived in the big, white structures that today comprise the Halsingland Hotel. Most of the rooms have private baths; all are fully carpeted and have wildlife photos on the walls. The Commander's Room Restaurant (*see above*) here serves satisfying meals. *On the parade grounds, Ft. Seward (mailing address: Box 1589, Haines 99827), tel. 907/766–2000 or 800/542–6363 outside AK, fax 907/766–2445. 58 rooms. AE, D, DC, MC, V. Inexpensive–Moderate.*

There are several B&Bs in Haines, and one youth hostel. For more information call the visitor information center (2nd Ave. near Willard St., tel. 907/766–2234, fax 907/766–2404).

Juneau   **The Summit.** Unlikely as it may seem, this small, intimate, can-
Dining   dle-lit restaurant in the Inn at the Waterfront is the city's most
★   prestigious dining place. Of 30 entrées on the menu, 20 are seafood—including abalone sautéed in butter and almonds, scallops, prawns, halibut, and a tender salmon offering called Salmon Gastineau. If you like steak, its New York La Bleu features New York strip steak with blue cheese. *455 S. Franklin*

St., tel. 907/586–2050. Reservations strongly recommended. AE, DC, MC, V. No lunch. Moderate–Expensive.

Mike's. For decades, Mike's, in the former mining community of Douglas across the bridge from Juneau, has been serving up seafood, steaks, and pastas. Its treatment of tiny Petersburg shrimp is particularly noteworthy. Rivaling the food, however, is the view through the picture windows at the rear of the restaurant. Mike's looks over the waters of Gastineau Channel to Juneau and the ruins of the old AJ mine. *1102 2nd St. in Douglas, tel. 907/364–3271. AE, DC, MC, V. No lunch weekends. Moderate.*

★ **The Fiddlehead.** This is probably Juneau's favorite restaurant, a delightful place of light woods, gently patterned wallpaper, stained glass, hanging plants, and historic photos on the wall. The food is healthy, generously served, and eclectic. Offerings range from a light dinner of black beans and rice to pasta Greta Garbo (locally smoked salmon tossed with fettuccine in cream sauce) to chicken and eggplant Szechuan (chicken and eggplant sautéed with bean paste and served over rice). Homemade bread from the restaurant's bakery is likewise laudable. *429 Willoughby Ave., tel. 907/586–3150. Reservations recommended. No smoking. MC, V. Inexpensive–Moderate.*

The Silverbow Inn. Here's another place so popular with locals that you should reserve ahead for meals during normal dining hours. The decor is "early Juneau," with settings, chairs, and tables (no two are alike) of the kind you might have found in someone's parlor during the city's gold-mining era. The main structure, for years one of the town's major bakeries, was built in 1912. The wine list is limited but selective; dinner entrées change daily and might include halibut with almonds, salmon Florentine, stir-fry prawns, or red snapper. *120 2nd St., tel. 907/586–4146. AE, DC, MC, V. Hours vary Oct.–Apr. Inexpensive–Moderate.*

El Sombrero. It's tiny and a trifle crowded, but the fare in this north-of-the-border Mexican restaurant would make Pancho Villa homesick. If you eat here at noon you get more food for your dollar than if you dine in the evening. One menu favorite combines a meat or chicken taco, cheese enchilada, and rice or beans. *157 S. Franklin, tel. 907/586–6770. AE, DC, MC, V. Closed Sun. Sept.–Apr. Inexpensive–Moderate.*

★ **Gold Creek Salmon Bake.** You eat under a roofed shelter on comfortable benches and tables, but all around you are trees, mountains, and the rushing water of Gold Creek (where gold was discovered in 1880). The salmon bake itself is thought to be Alaska's oldest such outdoor offering. Fresh-caught salmon (supplemented sometimes by halibut) is cooked over an alder fire and served with a simple but succulent sauce of brown sugar, margarine, and lemon juice. With the salmon come hot baked beans, salad, Jell-O, sourdough or wheat bread, and your choice of beer, soft drink, or coffee (fixed price, $17). After dinner you can pan for gold in the stream (pans are available for your use, no charge, keep all the gold you find) or wander up the hill to the remains of AJ gold-mine buildings. *End of Basin Rd., tel. 907/789–0052. Free bus ride from in front of the Baranof Hotel in downtown Juneau. No credit cards. Closed mid-Sept.–April. Inexpensive.*

Lodging **The Baranof Hotel.** For half a century the Baranof has been— for commercial travelers, legislators, lobbyists, and tourists— the city's prestige address. That designation has been challenged in recent years by the Westmark (like the Baranof, a unit of the Westmark chain), but the nine-story hostelry continues to attract a large proportion of the city's visitors. The lobby and most rooms have been extensively refurbished in recent years in tasteful woods and a lighting style reminiscent of 1939, when the hotel first opened. Also on site are a travel agency and an Alaska Airlines ticket office. *127 N. Franklin St., 99801, tel. 907/586-2660 or 800/344-0970, fax 907/586-8315. 200 rooms. Facilities: restaurant, coffee shop, lounge with piano bar. AE, MC, V. Very Expensive.*

Country Lane Inn. This Best Western property features such amenities as a pool and Jacuzzi and a charming sitting room/lobby with couch and reading materials. Baskets of multicolored flowers hang along the entrance walk to rooms, making for a pleasant welcome. *9300 Glacier Hwy., 99801, tel. 907/789-5005 or 800/528-1234, fax 907/789-2818. 50 rooms. Facilities: pool, Jacuzzi. AE, D, DC, MC, V. Very Expensive.*

Westmark Juneau. A high rise (by Juneau standards), the seven-story Westmark is situated across Main Street from Juneau's Centennial Hall and across Egan Drive from the docks. Rooms are modern in decor, and the lobby is distinguished by a massive carved eagle figure. Extensive wood-mural carvings adorn the Woodcarver Dining Room. *51 W. Egan Dr., 99801, tel. 907/586-6900 or 800/544-0970, fax 907/225-6900. 106 rooms. AE, MC, V. Very Expensive. Facilities: restaurant, lounge.*

Airport TraveLodge. The rooms and furnishings are pretty standard fare. The structure, matching Fernando's Restaurant inside, is Mexican in design and decor. The motel is one of only two in the community with an indoor swimming pool—a plus if you want to unwind after a day of touring. *9200 Glacier Hwy., 99801, tel. 907/789-9700, fax 907/789-1969. 86 rooms. AE, D, MC, V. Expensive.*

★ **The Prospector.** A short walk west of downtown and next door to the State Museum, this smaller but fully modern hotel is what many business travelers and a number of legislators like to call home while they're in Juneau. You'll find very large rooms here, and in The Diggings dining room and lounge you can enjoy outstanding prime rib. Steaks and seafood are also popular. *375 Whittier Ave., 99801, tel. 907/586-3737 or 800/331-2711, fax 907/586-1204. 60 rooms. Facilities: restaurant, lounge. AE, MC, V. Expensive.*

★ Travelers who enjoy staying in restored historic hotels have three to choose from in downtown Juneau: the **Silverbow Inn,** in the old bakery building dating from the late 1890s (120 2nd St., tel. 907/586-4146, fax 907/586-4242, 6 rooms, and the **Alaskan Hotel,** a 1913 structure (167 S. Franklin St., tel. 907/586-1000 or 800/327-9347, fax 907/463-3775, 40 rooms, Inexpensive–Moderate); and the 1898 **Inn at the Waterfront** (455 S. Franklin St., tel. 907/586-2050, fax 907/586-2999, 21 rooms, Inexpensive–Moderate).

Ketchikan
Dining
★
Salmon Falls Resort. It's a half-hour drive from town, but the seafood and steaks served up in the huge, octagonal restaurant make the trip more than worthwhile. Seafood caught fresh from adjacent waters is especially good. Try the halibut and shellfish stew. The restaurant is built of pine logs, and at the center of the dining room, supporting the roof, rises a 40-foot section of 48-inch pipe manufactured to be part of the Alaska pipeline. The dining area overlooks the waters of Clover Pas-

sage, where sunsets can be vivid red and remarkable. *Mile 17, N. Tongass Hwy., tel. 907/225–2752 or 800/247–9059. Reservations recommended. AE, DC, MC, V. Moderate.*

Annabelle's Keg and Chowder House. Located in the Gilmore Hotel, Annabelle's is really two restaurants: the 1920s-style Keg and Chowder House, with seafood, pasta, beer, wine, and espresso bar; and Annabelle's Parlor, a more formal restaurant specializing in fine local seafoods in classic preparations. *326 Front St., tel. 907/225–6009. AE, D, DC, MC, V. Moderate–Expensive.*

Other better-than-adequate eating places in the community include the **Clover Pass Resort** (Mile 15, N. Tongass Hwy., tel. 907/247–2234, Inexpensive–Moderate) for excellent seafood and a view of sport fishermen coming, going, and bringing home their catches; **Grandeli's** (in the Plaza Portwest Mall, tel. 907/225–1414, Inexpensive); and **Kay's Kitchen** (2813 Tongass Ave., tel. 907/225–5860, Inexpensive) for homemade soups and generous sandwiches.

Lodging **Royal Executive Suites.** Nothing in the plain, square exterior of this hotel building or in its Spartan lobby hints at the deluxe accommodations within. Some of the 14 units are split-level with circular stairways; all are carpeted in steel grays or other light colors, with pastel furniture and natural wood trims. Many of the units have full kitchens and Jacuzzis, and all guests have access to an exercise room with treadmill, hot tub, and sauna. Windows are large and look out on the busy water and air traffic in Tongass Narrows. There is no restaurant on site, but meals can be brought to your room. *1471 Tongass Ave. (mailing address: Box 8331, Ketchikan 99901), tel. 907/225–1900, fax 907/225–1795. 14 rooms. AE, D, DC, MC, V. Expensive–Very Expensive.*

★ **Ingersoll Hotel.** Old-fashioned patterned wallpaper, wood wainscoting, and etched-glass windows on the oak registration desk set an old-fashioned mood for this three-story downtown hotel, built in the 1920s. Room furnishings are standard, with bright Alaskan art on the walls. Some rooms have a view of the cruise-ship dock and the waters of Tongass Narrows. *303 Mission St. (mailing address: Box 6440, Ketchikan 99901), tel. 907/225–2124, fax 907/225–8530. 60 rooms. AE, D, MC, V. Expensive.*

The Landing. This Best Western property is named for the ferry landing site in the waters of Tongass Narrows across the street. Decor is modern; all rooms were redecorated in 1989. *3434 Tongass Ave., tel. 907/225–5166 or 800/428–8304, fax 907/225–6900. 46 rooms. Facilities: cafe, lounge. AE, D, MC, V. Moderate.*

The Gilmore Hotel. With such features as a 1930s-style lobby, the Gilmore earns its place on the National Register of Historic Places, but extensive renovation in 1990 has brought welcome modern touches to the rooms here. *326 Front St., 99901, tel. 907/225–9423, fax 907/225–7442. 42 rooms. Facilities: restaurant, bar. AE, D, MC, V. No elevator. Inexpensive–Moderate.*

Petersburg **The Beachcomber Inn.** Seafood, with a distinctly Norwegian
Dining flair, is the specialty in this restored cannery building on the
★ shores of Wrangell Narrows. If you're there on a smørgåsbord night you may sample red-snapper fish cakes, salmon loaf, Norwegian (emphatically *not* Swedish) meatballs, creamed potatoes, and sugary desserts such as sandbakkelse, lefsa, or

krumkakker. Petersburg's famed beer-batter halibut is also served here, as are salmon steaks and other traditional seafoods. *Mile 4, Mitkof Hwy., tel. 907/772-3888. AE, MC, V. Inexpensive.*

Helse. Natural foods, including enormous vegetable-laden sandwiches, are a specialty here. The menu also features soups, chowders, home-baked breads, and salads. Espresso makes a nice ending to a meal. *Sing Lee Alley and Harbor Way, tel. 907/772-3444. No credit cards. Inexpensive.*

The Homestead. Nothing fancy here, just basic American steaks, local prawns and halibut, salad bar, and especially generous breakfasts. It's a popular place with the locals. *217 Main St., tel. 907/772-3900. DC, MC, V. Inexpensive.*

Pellerito's Pizza. You'll get authentic pizzas with homemade sausages here. Or try the pizza with local shrimp. *Across from the ferry terminal. Tel. 907/772-3727. No credit cards. Inexpensive.*

Lodging
★
Tides Inn. This is the largest hotel in town, a block uphill from Petersburg's main thoroughfare. All rooms are modern, with standard furnishings; some are equipped with kitchens. Rooms in the new wing have views of the boat harbor. The coffee is always on in the small, informal lobby, and in the morning you're welcome to complimentary juices, cereals, and pastries. *1st and Dolphin Sts. (mailing address: Box 1048, Petersburg 99833), tel. 907/772-4288, fax 907/772-4286. 46 rooms. AE, D, DC, MC, V. Moderate.*

Scandia House. Exuding an old-country, Norwegian atmosphere, this hotel on Petersburg's main street has been a local fixture since 1910. Here, too, the coffee is always on in a small lobby accented by etched-glass windows on the doors and large oil paintings depicting local old-timers in colorful Norwegian garb. "American" units have full toilet facilities; "European" rooms have showers and toilets down the hall. All rooms are squeaky clean. Norwegian rosemaling designs ornament the exterior. *110 Nordic Dr. (mailing address: Box 689, Petersburg 99833), tel. 907/772-4281. 24 rooms. AE, D,DC, MC, V. Inexpensive-Moderate.*

Sitka
Dining
★
Channel Club. It's a toss-up whether to order steak or seafood here, but whatever you choose will be good. Halibut cheeks are a consistent favorite; if you order steak, don't ask the chef for his steak seasoning recipe—it's a secret. Decor is ship-oriented, with fishnet floats and whalebone carvings. *Mile 3.5, Halibut Point Rd., tel. 907/747-9916. AE, DC, MC, V. Moderate-Expensive.*

Raven Room. Located in the Westmark Shee Atika Hotel, the Raven Room offers seafood, pasta, and steaks in a setting rich in Southeastern Alaska native decor. There's dancing in the evening in the Kadataan Lounge. *330 Seward St., tel. 907/747-6241. AE, D, DC, MC, V. Moderate.*

Also recommended: **Marina Restaurant,** for Mexican or Italian fare (205 Harbor Dr., tel. 907/747-8840. Inexpensive); and **Staton's Steak House** for (you guessed it) steak and seafood (Harbor Dr. and Maksutoff St., tel. 907/747-3396. Inexpensive).

Lodging
★
Westmark Shee Atika. If you stay here for a night or two, you will surely come away with an increased appreciation for Southeast Alaska Indian art and culture. Displays throughout the hotel—full wall murals in the lobby and additional artwork

in the rooms—tell of the history, legends, and exploits of the Tlingit people. Many of the hotel's nearly 100 rooms overlook Crescent Harbor and the islands in the waters beyond; others have mountain and forest views. *330 Seward St. (mailing address: Box 78, Sitka 99835), tel. 907/747–6241 or 800/544–0970, fax 907/747–5486. 98 rooms. Facilities: restaurant, bar. AE, DC, MC, V. Very Expensive.*

A number of B&Bs have sprung up in Sitka in recent years; ask the visitor center for a referral or write to the **Sitka Convention and Visitors Bureau** (Box 1226, Sitka 99835, tel. 907/747–5940, fax 907/747–3739).

Skagway **Chilkoot Dining Room.** If it's not packed with tourists (try to
Dining avoid the 6:30 PM rush hour) the Chilkoot offers some of Skagway's most gracious dining. Decor here is gold-rush style, but a lot grander and more plush than anything the stampeders ever experienced. If it's on the menu, try the family-style crab dinner. *3rd Ave., east of Broadway, tel. 907/983–2291. AE, DC, MC, V. Moderate.*

Golden North Restaurant. To eat in the dining room in the Golden North Hotel is to return to the days of gold-rush con man Soapy Smith, heroic Frank Reid, and scores of pioneers, stampeders, and dance-hall girls. The decor is *authentically* Days of '98: The hotel was actually built that year and has been tastefully restored to the era. Popular choices include sourdough pancakes for breakfasts; soups, salad-bar selections, and sandwiches for lunch; salmon or other seafood for dinner. *3rd Ave. and Broadway, tel. 907/983–2294. AE, DC, MC, V. Inexpensive–Moderate.*

Prospector's Sourdough Restaurant. You'll meet as many Skagway folk here as you will visitors, particularly at breakfast time, when the sourdough hotcakes or snow-crab omelets are on the griddle. Salmon steak is a popular favorite in the evening. Decor features the colorful works of local artists on the walls. *4th Ave. and Broadway, tel. 907/983–2865. AE, DC, MC, V. Inexpensive.*

In the inexpensive category consider the **Northern Lights Pizzeria** (4th St. and Broadway, tel. 907/983–2225).

Lodging **Westmark Inn.** Formerly called the Klondike Hotel, this is Skagway's largest inn. In keeping with the locale, the decor is gold-rush elegant, with rich red carpeting, brass trim, and historical pictures throughout. Room furnishings are first class. Ask for a room in the main structure rather than the annex: The rooms are larger and you don't have to leave the building to visit the restaurant or lounge. *3rd St., east of Broadway, tel. 907/983–2291 or 800/544–0970, fax 907/451–7478. 210 rooms. Reservations necessary. Facilities: dining room, lounge. AE, D, DC, MC, V. Closed winter. Very Expensive.*

★ **Golden North Hotel.** No question about it, this is Alaska's most historic hotel. It was built in 1898 in the heyday of the gold rush—golden dome and all—and has been lovingly restored to reflect that period. Pioneer Skagway families have contributed gold-rush furnishings to each of the hotel's rooms, and the stories of those families are printed and posted on the walls of each unit. *3rd Ave. and Broadway (mailing address: Box 343, Skagway 99840), tel. 907/983–2451 or 983–2294, fax 907/983–2755. 32 rooms. Facilities: dining room, lounge. AE, DC, MC, V. Moderate.*

★ **Skagway Inn Bed & Breakfast.** This downtown Victorian inn lies within the Klondike Gold Rush National Historical Park. Each room is named after a different gold-rush gal. The building was constructed in 1897 and is thus one of Skagway's oldest. Rooms are private, but baths are shared. *Between 6th Ave. and 7th Ave. on Broadway (mailing address: Box 500, Skagway 99840), tel. 907/983–2289, fax 907/983–2713. 12 rooms. MC, V. Moderate.*

Wind Valley Lodge. Located a long walk or a short drive from downtown, the Wind Valley Lodge is one of Skagway's newer hotels. Rooms are modern, and there's a free shuttle to downtown. *22nd Ave. and State St. (mailing address: Box 354, Skagway 99840), tel./fax 907/983–2236. 34 rooms. AE, MC, V. Moderate.*

Wrangell Dining **Dock Side Restaurant.** This is the coffee shop and dining room for the Stikine Inn, located right on the dock and offering good views of the harbor. Seafood and steaks are staples here. *1 block from ferry terminal, tel. 907/874–3388. AE, DC, MC, V. Inexpensive–Moderate.*

Roadhouse Lodge. The walls here carry practically a museum of early Alaskana. The food is wholesome, tasty, and ample. Specialties include local prawns (sautéed, deep-fried, and boiled in the shell) and deep-fried Indian frybread. A courtesy van will pick you up in town. *Mile 4, Zimovia Hwy., tel. 907/874–2335. AE, DC, MC, V. Inexpensive–Moderate.*

Lodging **Harding's Old Sourdough Lodge.** This lodge sits on the docks, in a beautifully converted construction camp. The Harding family welcomes guests in the big open dining/living room with home-baked sourdough breads and local seafood. Guest rooms have rustic paneling; the exterior is of hand-milled cedar. *Box 1062, Wrangell 99929, tel. 907/874–3613, fax 907/874–2285. DC, MC, V. 20 rooms. Facilities: conference room, charter boats, sauna, steam bath. Moderate.*

Stikine Inn. On the dock in the main part of town, the inn offers great views of Wrangell's harbor. Rooms are simply decorated, with plain, modern furnishings. Unless you're going to be among the late-night party crowd, ask the registration clerk to assign you a room away from the bar. There's no extra charge for children under 12. *Box 990, Wrangell 99929, tel. 907/874–3388, fax 907/874–3923. 34 rooms. AE, DC, MC, V. Facilities: restaurant, bar, travel agency, beauty salon. Moderate.*

Southeast Region Lodging **Alaska Bed & Breakfast Association** (369 S. Franklin, Suite 200, Juneau 99801, tel. 907/586–2959, fax 907/463–4453. Inexpensive–Moderate). Contact this association for B&B accommodations in most Southeast communities, as well as Anchorage, Fairbanks, Homer, and Soldotna.

The Arts

Theater Southeast Alaska's only professional theater company, **Perseverance Theater of Juneau** (914 3rd St., tel. 907/364–2421), presents everything from Broadway plays to Shakespeare to locally written material.

Haines hosts a statewide drama competition called ACTFEST in April of odd-numbered years. The festival is held at the **Chilkat Center for the Arts** at Ft. Seward, with entries from community theaters both large and small. For details: Mimi Gregg, ACTFEST, Box 75, Haines 99827.

Several communities stage summer musicals or melodramas for the entertainment of visitors. In Haines it's called "The Lust for Dust"; in Juneau, "The Lady Lou Revue"; in Ketchikan, "The Fish Pirate's Daughter"; and in Skagway, the "Days of '98 Show."

More cultural are the **Chilkat Indian Dancers,** who demonstrate Tlingit dancing twice weekly in Haines, and the **New Archangel Dancers of Sitka,** who perform authentic Russian Cossack-type dances whenever cruise ships are in port.

Music Festivals The annual week-long **Alaska Folk Festival** (Box 21748, Juneau 99802) is staged each April in Juneau, drawing singers, musical storytellers, banjo masters, fiddlers, and even cloggers from all over the state and Yukon Territory.

Early in summer Juneau is the scene of yet another musical gathering, this one called **Juneau Jazz 'n Classics** (Box 22152, Juneau 99802). It celebrates things musical from Brubeck to Bach.

Southeast Alaska's major classical music festival is the annual **Sitka Summer Music Festival** (Box 3333, Sitka 99835), a three-week June celebration of workshops, recitals, and concerts held in the Centennial Building, downtown.

Nightlife

Summer nightlife in Alaska doesn't just mean bar-hopping: The midnight sun makes possible activities such as late-night fishing, hikes, and strolls along the water. In Juneau, state employees pour from offices after work and head for the water. When in Alaska, do as the Alaskans do, and think of after dinner as a bonus afternoon.

Bars and   Socializing at a bar or "saloon" is an old Alaska custom, and the
Nightclubs   towns and cities of the Southeast Panhandle offer no exception. Following are some of the favorite gathering places in these parts:

Haines/Ft. Seward **The Harbor Bar** (Front St. at the Harbor, tel. 907/766–2444). Commercial fisherfolk gather here nightly at this old (1907) bar and restaurant. Sometimes there is live music.

Juneau **Alaskan Hotel Bar** (167 S. Franklin St., tel. 907/586–1000). Equally popular with locals and distinctly less touristy, here, if live music isn't playing, an old-fashioned player piano usually is.

Bubble Room (127 N. Franklin St., tel. 907/586–2660). This comfortable lounge off the lobby in the Baranof Hotel is quiet—and the site (so it is said) of more legislative lobbying and decision making than in the nearby state capitol building. The music from the piano bar is soft.

The Red Dog Saloon (278 S. Franklin St., tel. 907/463–3777) carries on in a tradition of sawdust on the floor, mounted bear and other game animal trophies on the walls, and lots of historic photos. There is live music and the crowd is lively particularly when the cruise ships are in port.

Ketchikan **Charley's** (208 Front St., tel. 907/225–5090). Located in the Ingersoll Hotel, with a 1940s tone, Charley's is popular for sipping as well as for suppering. There's usually live music.

Petersburg **The Harbor Bar** (Nordic Dr. near Dolphin St., tel. 907/772–4526). The name suggests the decor here, a place of ship's wheels, ship pictures, and a mounted red snapper.

Sitka **Kadataan Lounge** (330 Seward Ave., tel. 907/747–6241). Live soft rock music plays here in the lounge of the Westmark Shee Atika Hotel.

Skagway **Moe's Frontier Bar** (Broadway between 4th and 5th Sts., tel. 907/983–2238). A longtime fixture on the Skagway scene, Moe's is a bar much frequented by the local folk.

The Red Onion (Broadway at 2nd St., tel. 907/983–2222). You'll meet at least as many Skagway people here as you will visitors. The upstairs was a gold-rush brothel.

Wrangell **The Stikine Bar** (107 Front St., tel. 907/874–3388). This can be a louder-as-the-night-gets-later bar when a rock band is playing, but it's a friendly place to meet the locals.

Index

Abbotsford, B.C., *6*
Aberdeen, WA, *233, 245*
Acme, WA, *226*
Adams River (salmon run), *341*
Agness, OR, *121*
Air shows, *6*
Alaska, *360*
the arts, *403–404*
business hours, *31*
children, attractions for, *388–389*
emergencies, *364–365*
festivals, *7, 404*
food costs, *10*
guided tours, *362–363*
hotels, *389–390, 395–403*
native culture, *40–43*
nightlife, *404–405*
restaurants, *395–403*
scenic drives, *361–362*
shopping, *390–392*
sightseeing, *365–390*
sports, *388, 389, 392–394*
tourist information, *2, 364–365*
transportation, *29, 360–362*
Alaska Chilkat Bald Eagle Preserve, *382*
Alaska Indian Arts (workshop), *383*
Alaska Marine Highway System, *29, 337, 361*
Alaskan Hotel, *378*
Alaska State Capitol, *378*
Alaska State Museum, *43, 380*
Alaska Steam Laundry Building, *378*
Alpine Slide, *98*
Alpine Vineyards, *122*
American Advertising Museum, *69*
American Express, *9–10*
Amity Vineyards, *122*
Amusement parks
British Columbia, *343*

Portland, *73*
Vancouver, *280*
Anacortes, WA, *249*
Angoon, AK, *390*
Anne Hathaway's Cottage, *312–313*
Annie Creek Canyon, *128*
Antiques
McMinnville, *130*
Portland, *76*
Seattle, *168*
Tacoma, *244*
Vancouver, *284–285*
Victoria, *313–314*
Apartment rentals, *40*
Aquariums
Oregon, *117*
Seattle, *160*
Tacoma, *46, 229–230*
Vancouver, *276–277*
Washington, *234*
Arctic Brotherhood Hall, *384*
Arlene Schnitzer Concert Hall, *66*
Art galleries and museums
Alaska, *390–391*
British Columbia, *334*
Oregon, *125*
Portland, *66, 69, 76*
Seattle, *157, 160, 164, 165, 168*
Tacoma, *227*
Vancouver, *270, 279, 280, 282, 285*
Victoria, *319*
Art Gallery of Greater Victoria, *319*
Artist colonies, *226*
Arts and crafts fairs, *6–7*
Ashford, WA, *249*
Ashland, OR
the arts, *150*
bed-and-breakfasts, *135*
festivals, *7*
hotels, *143–144*
nightlife, *150*
restaurants, *143–144*
sightseeing, *126–127*

sports, *133*
tourist information, *107*
Astoria, OR, *107, 111, 113, 130, 135–136*
Astoria Column, *113*
Auctions, *284*
Auto racing, *78, 247*
Autumn Wind Vineyard, *122*

Baby-sitting services, *18*
Bailey Bay, *389*
Bainbridge Island Vineyard and Winery, *43, 195–197*
Ballard Locks, *167*
Ballooning, *157*
Bamfield, B.C., *333*
Bandon, OR, *120, 136–137*
Bandon Historical Museum, *120*
Bandon Lighthouse, *120*
Baranov, Alexander, *374*
Baseball, *36*
Eugene, *134*
Seattle, *171*
Tacoma, *247*
Vancouver, *288*
Basketball, *36*
Alaska, *394*
Oregon, *134*
Portland, *78*
Seattle, *171*
Bathtub races, *6*
Bay Ocean, OR, *116*
B.C. Forest Museum, *332*
Beaches, *36–37*
Alaska, *372*
British Columbia, *334*
Oregon, *99, 114, 121, 134*
Vancouver, *275, 277, 288*
Washington, *199, 206, 233, 234*
Beacon Hill Park, *311*
Beatles Museum, *283*

Beaverton, OR, *44*
Bed-and-breakfasts, *38–39*
Alaska, *396–397, 403*
Oregon, *135, 136, 138–139, 142, 146, 147, 148–149*
Bellevue, OR, *6–7, 144*
Bellingham, WA
the arts, *261*
hotels, *251*
nightlife, *261*
restaurants, *249–251*
shopping, *243*
sightseeing, *223–225, 243*
sports, *244, 245, 246, 247*
tourist information, *217*
transportation, *220*
Bend, OR, *98–99, 100–101*
Bennett Pass, *98*
Benton City, WA, *242, 243*
Bethel Heights Vineyard, *122*
Beverly Beach State Park, *134*
Bicycling, *32*
Alaska, *392*
Oregon, *99, 130–131*
Portland, *77*
Seattle, *170*
tours, *4*
Vancouver, *286*
Washington, *199, 205, 244*
Big Rock Garden, *223–224*
Big Time Brewery, *166*
Birch Bay State Park, *247*
Blackwood Canyon (winery), *243*
Blaine, WA, *251–252*
Bloedel Reserve, *197*
Blossom Bar, OR, *121*
Blue Heron French Cheese Company, *115*

Boardman State Park, *121*

Board sailing, *171*

Boating and sailing, *6, 32–33*

Seattle, *171*

Vancouver, *287*

Washington, *199, 205–206, 247*

Boat racing, *6, 171*

Boeing Field, *164*

Bonair Winery, *240*

Bonneville Dam, *95*

Bonneville Fish Hatchery, *95*

Books on Pacific North Coast, *21*

Bookstores

Portland, *76*

Seattle, *165*

Vancouver, *285*

Boulevard Park, *223*

Breweries

Alaska, *391*

Portland, *73*

Seattle, *164, 166*

Vancouver, *280*

Brew pubs, *166*

Bridal Veil Falls, *95*

Bridgeport Brewing, *73*

British Columbia, *326. See also Vancouver; Victoria; Whistler*

beaches, *36*

business hours, *31*

emergencies, *327*

festivals, *6*

guided tours, *329*

hospitals, *327*

hotels, *348–358*

native culture, *41–42*

pharmacies, *327*

restaurants, *348–358*

shopping, *344*

sightseeing, *329–344*

sports, *344–348*

tourist information, *2, 327*

transportation, *28–29, 327–329*

Brockton Point, *276*

Broken Group Islands, *334*

Brookings, OR, *107, 121, 137*

Brookings Harbor, *107*

Bruce Lee's grave

site, *167*

"Bulb Basket of the Nation," *128*

Bullards Beach State Park, *120*

Bush House, *124*

Bush's Pasture Park, *124*

Business hours, *31. See also under individual cities and areas*

Bus travel

Alaska, *361*

British Columbia, *328*

Oregon, *94, 110, 111*

within Pacific North Coast region, *27*

Portland, *62, 63*

Seattle, *153, 154*

from U.S., *25*

Vancouver, *266, 267*

Victoria, *308*

Washington, *212, 221*

Whistler, *320*

Butchart Gardens, *45, 313*

Butterfly World, *334*

Byrnes Block building, *274*

Callahan Ridge Winery, *122*

Calona Wines Ltd., *342*

Campbell River, B.C., *42, 335, 349–350*

Camping, *39*

tours, *4*

Camp Six Logging Museum, *230*

Canada Place Pier, *272*

Canadian Craft Museum, *272*

Canadian Imperial Bank of Commerce building, *273*

Canadian Pacific Station, *273*

Candy stores, *168–169*

Cannon Beach, OR, *7, 107, 114, 129, 137–138*

Canoeing

Alaska, *388, 392*

British Columbia, *344–345*

Oregon, *99, 131*

Whistler, *321–322*

Cape Arago State Park, *120*

Cape Blanco Lighthouse, *120–121*

Cape Blanco State Park, *121*

Cape Disappointment Lighthouse, *238*

Cape Foulweather, *117*

Cape Kiwanda, *116*

Cape Kiwanda State Park, *116*

Cape Lookout, *116*

Cape Meares Lighthouse, *116*

Cape Meares State Park, *116*

Cape Perpetua, *118*

Cape Scott Provincial Park, *336*

Capilano Fish Hatchery, *283*

Capitol Mall (Salem), *123*

Car rentals, *15–16*

Car travel

Alaska, *361*

British Columbia, *328*

insurance, *27*

Oregon, *94, 110*

within Pacific North Coast region, *27–28*

Portland, *62, 63*

Seattle, *153, 154*

speed limits, *27*

from U.S., *24*

Vancouver, *266, 267*

Victoria, *308*

Washington, *197, 202, 210, 212, 221*

Whistler, *320*

winter driving, *27*

Cascade Locks, OR, *95, 97, 101–102*

Cash machines, *9*

Casinos, *307*

Castle Hill, *375*

Cathedral Grove, *334*

Cathedral Provincial Park, *342*

Caverns, *118, 129, 334–335*

Cedarcreek Estate Winery, *342*

Cemeteries

Alaska, *370, 376, 379*

Seattle, *167*

Centennial Building, *374–375*

Centennial Hall, *380*

Chain-saw carvings, *117–118*

Champoeg State Park, *122*

Charles and Emma Frye Art Museum, *165*

Charles H. Scott Gallery, *279*

Charleston, OR, *120, 138*

Charlotte Martin Theatre, *165–166*

Chateau Ste. Michelle (Grandview), *242*

Chateau Ste. Michelle (Patterson), *243*

Chateau Ste. Michelle Winery, *45*

Cheese-making, *115*

Chemainus, B.C., *332*

Cheney Discovery Center, *230*

Chief Shakes gravesite, *42, 370*

Chief Shakes Island, *370*

Children

attractions for. *See under cities and areas*

stores for, *285*

traveling with, *17–18*

Children's Museum (Portland), *72*

Children's Museum Northwest (Bellingham), *243*

Children's Museum of Tacoma, *228*

Chilkat Center for the Arts, *43, 382–383*

Chilkoot Trail, *386*

Chinatown (Portland), *69*

Chinatown (Vancouver), *274–275, 284*

Chinatown (Victoria), *312*

Chinese Cultural Center, *275*

Chinese Freemasons Building, *274–275*

Chinese Times Building, *275*

Chinook, WA, *238*

Chinook Wines, *242*

Christ Church Cathedral (Vancouver), *270*

Chuckanut Bay, *224*

Churches
Alaska, *367, 373, 376, 378*
Portland, *72*
Vancouver, *270*

Clallam County Historical Museum, *234*

Clausen Museum, *372*

Cleawox Lake, *119*

Cle Elum, WA, *252*

Climate, *4–5*

Clipper, WA, *226*

Clothing for the trip, *8*

Clothing shops
Portland, *76*
Seattle, *169*
Vancouver, *285–286*

Coast Guard Station Cape Disappointment, *239*

Coast Mountain Circle (scenic drive), *344*

Coleman Glacier, *226*

Colleges and universities
Alaska, *376*
Oregon, *123, 125*
Seattle, *164, 190–191*
Vancouver, *279, 282*
Washington, *223, 261*

Columbia Gorge Sailpark, *97*

Columbia River Gorge and Oregon Cascades, *93–94*
emergencies, *95*
hotels, *101–104*
restaurants, *100–104*
scenic drives, *94*
sightseeing, *95, 97–99*
sports, *99–100*
tourist information, *94*
transportation, *94*

Columbia River Maritime Museum, *113*

Columbia River Scenic Highway, *95*

Comedy clubs

Portland, *93*

Seattle, *195*

Vancouver, *307*

Comox, B.C., *335, 350*

Computers, protection of, *113*

Cooper's Northwest Alehouse, *166*

Coos Bay, OR, *119, 132, 138–139*

Copalis Beach, *233, 252*

Cornish College of the Arts, *190–191*

Corvallis, OR, *107, 132, 144–145*

Costs of the trip, *10–11*

Coupeville, WA, *198*

Courtenay, B.C., *335, 350*

Cowboys Then & Now Museum, *73*

Crafts stores, *169*

Craigdarroch Castle, *312*

Crater Lake National Park, *128*

Credit cards, *9, 40*

Crown Point, *95*

Cruises
Alaska, *361, 365, 387*
dress codes, *8*
guided tours, *3*
in Pacific North Coast region, *29–30*

Crystal Gardens, *45, 311*

Crystal Lake State Hatchery/Blind Slough Recreation Area, *374*

Currency, U.S. and Canadian, *9, 10*

Customs, *12*

The Dalles, OR, *97, 102*

Dams, *95*

Dance
Portland, *92*
Seattle, *192, 195*
Vancouver, *306*

Dance clubs, *192*

Darlingtona Botanical Wayside, *118*

Dash Point State Park, *247*

Deadman's Island, *276*

Deception Pass State Park, *198–199*

Deepwood Estate, *124*

Deer Mountain, *369*

Deer Mountain Hatchery, *368*

Deighton, Jack, *273*

Della Falls, *335*

Delores Winningstad Theater, *66*

Deming, WA, *226*

Denman Island, *335*

Department stores
Portland, *76*
Vancouver, *284*

Depoe Bay, OR, *7, 116*

Devil's Elbow State Park, *118*

Devil's Lake, *116*

Disabled travelers, hints for, *18–20*

Dr. Sun Yat-sen Classical Chinese Garden, *45, 275*

Dog racing, *36*
Portland, *78*

Dolly's House (brothel), *369*

Douglas County Coastal Visitors Center, *119*

Douglas County Museum, *126*

D River, *116*

Duncan, B.C., *41, 332, 344*

Dundee, OR, *44, 123*

Dungeness National Wildlife Refuge, *235*

Eagles Hall, *384*

East Sooke Park, *330, 332*

Eastsound Village, WA, *203–204, 205, 206, 208*

Eaton Hill Winery, *242*

Ebey's Landing National Historic Reserve, *198*

Ecola State Park, *114*

Ed Jones Haida Museum, *340*

Ellensburg, WA, *44*

Elliott Bay Book

Company, *165*

Emergencies
Alaska, *364–365*
British Columbia, *327*
Columbia River Gorge and the Oregon Cascades, *95*
Portland, OR, *63*
Seattle, WA, *154*
Vancouver, BC, *267–268*
Victoria, *307*
Washington, *220*
Western Oregon, *110*
Whistler, *320*

Emily Carr College of Art and Design, *279*

Empress Hotel, *309*

End of the Trail Interpretive Center, OR, *74*

English Bay, *277*

Eola Hills Wine Cellars, *122*

Eugene, OR
the arts, *150*
festivals, *7*
hotels, *146*
restaurants, *145*
shopping, *130*
sightseeing, *125*
sports, *131, 132–133, 134*
tourist information, *107*
transportation, *110–111*

Evergreen Cemetery, *379*

Fable Cottage Estate, *45*

Face Rock Beach, *134*

Face Rock Wayside, *120*

Fairhaven, WA, *224*

Fairhaven Park, *224*

Fairs, *6, 7, 382*

Fall's Creek Fish Ladder, *374*

Farm tours, *226*

Father Pandosy's Mission, *342*

Feiro Marine Laboratory, *234*

Ferndale, WA, *225*

Ferry service
Alaska, *361*

British Columbia, *328,
329, 336, 337*
in Pacific North Coast
  region, *28–29*
Seattle, *154*
Vancouver, *266*
Victoria, *308*
Washington, *191–196,
198, 202–203, 221*
**Festivals and
  seasonal events,** *5–7*
Film
Portland, *66*
Seattle, *160*
Vancouver, *306*
Fire stations, *68*
Fishing, *33–34*
Alaska, *388, 392–393*
British Columbia, *345*
Oregon, *116, 120,
121, 131–132*
Portland, *77*
Seattle, *170*
Vancouver, *286*
Washington, *199, 206,
226, 245, 247*
Whistler, *322*
Fish Ladder, *167, 374*
Flavel House, *113*
Flea markets, *284*
Float-plane service,
  26
Florence, OR, *107,
118–119, 132, 139*
Football, *36*
Oregon, *134*
Seattle, *171*
Vancouver, *288*
Forest Grove, OR, *44*
Forest Park, *74*
Forks, WA, *233, 252*
**Ft. Canby State
  Park,** *238, 246*
Ft. Casey State Park,
  198
**Ft. Clatsop National
  Memorial,** *113*
**Fort Columbia State
  Park,** *236, 238*
**Ft. Dalles Surgeon's
  Quarters,** *97*
Ft. Nisqually, *230*
Forts
Alaska, *377, 382*
Oregon, *113–114*
Portland, *73–74*
Tacoma, *230*
Washington, *198, 235,
236, 238, 246*
Fort Seward, *364,*

380–381, 382, 404
Ft. Stevens, *113–114*
**Fort Vancouver
  National Historic
  Site,** *6, 73–74*
**Fort William Henry
  Seward,** *380–381*
Ft. Worden, *235*
Fountains, *68*
Fragrance Garden,
  225
**Frank Heintzleman
  Nursery,** *374*
Friday Harbor, WA,
  204, 205, 207, 209

Gabriola Island, *333*
Gaches Mansion, *227*
Gardens
British Columbia, *45,
343*
Oregon, *118, 120,
124, 128*
Portland, *70*
Seattle, *164, 167*
Tacoma, *229*
Vancouver, *275,
281–282*
Victoria, *309, 311,
313*
Washington, *45–46,
198, 223–225, 227,
232*
Garibaldi, OR, *116*
**Garibaldi Provincial
  Park,** *321*
**Geert Maas
  Sculpture Gardens,
  Gallery, and Studio,**
  344
Ghost towns, *117–118*
Gift shops
Alaska, *391–392*
Portland, *76*
Vancouver, *286*
Gig Harbor, WA, *230,
252–253*
**Girardet Wine
  Cellars,** *122*
Glacier, WA, *226*
**Glacier Bay National
  Park and Preserve,**
  *364, 386–388,
395–396*
**Glazed Terra Cotta
  National Historic
  District,** *69–70*
Gleneden Beach, OR,
  139–140
Gold Beach, OR, *121,*

132, 140
Golden Falls, *120*
Golden North Hotel,
  384
Goldpanning, *388*
Gold Rush Trail,
  343–344
Golf, *34*
Alaska, *393*
British Columbia,
  345–346
Leavenworth, *212*
Oregon, *77, 132–133*
Seattle, *170*
Vancouver, *286*
Victoria, *314*
Washington, *245*
Whistler, *322*
**Gordon Southam
  Observatory,** *283*
**Government Camp,
  OR,** *98*
**Governor's House
  (Juneau),** *379*
**Governor Tom
  McCall Waterfront
  Park,** *67*
Grandview, WA, *242*
Granger, WA, *242*
Grant's Pass, OR, *107*
**Grant Street Trestle,
  AK,** *367–368*
Granville Island,
  278–280
**Granville Island
  Brewery,** *280*
**Granville Island
  Information Centre,**
  279
**Granville Island
  Public Market,**
  279–280
Gray Monk Cellars,
  342
Great Gallery, *164*
Greenbank, WA, *198*
Gresham, OR, *7*
The Grotto (religious
  sanctuary), *72–73*
Gun control laws, *12*
Gustavus, AK, *364,
388, 392, 395–397*

Haida Indians, *280,
337, 340, 344*
Haines, AK, *380*
the arts, *404*
emergencies, *364*
festivals, *7*
guided tours, *362*

hotels, *397*
native culture, *43*
nightlife, *404*
restaurants, *397*
sightseeing, *380–383*
sports, *394*
tourist information,
  364
Haines Highway,
  361, 382, 383
**Hama Hama Oyster
  Company,** *235*
Hammer Slough, *372,
373*
Hammond, OR,
  113–114
**Harrison Hot
  Springs,** *6, 343, 355*
Hatfield Library, *123*
**Hatfield Marine
  Science Center,** *117*
Haystack Rock, *114*
Hazelton, B.C., *42,
340*
Health clubs, *287*
Health insurance,
  13–14
Heathman Hotel, *64*
Heceta Head, *118*
Hell's Gate, *342–343*
Hendrix, Jimi, *167*
Henry Art Gallery,
  164
**Henry Estate
  Winery,** *122*
**High Desert
  Museum,** *98–99*
Hiking, *34*
Alaska, *393*
British Columbia, *346*
Leavenworth,
  212–213
Vancouver, *287*
Washington, *246*
Hillsboro, OR, *44*
**Hinzerling
  Vineyards,** *242*
Hockey, *36*
Portland, *78*
Vancouver, *288*
Washington, *247*
Hogue Cellars, *242*
Hoh Rain Forest, *233*
Home exchanges,
  39–40
**Honeyman State
  Park,** *119*
Hood River, OR, *44,
97, 102*
Hoodsport, WA, *235*

Hoodsport Winery, 235–236

Hoonah, AK, 390

Hoover-Minthorne House, 122

Hoquiam, WA, 233, 245

Horizon's Edge Winery, 242

Hornby Island, 335

Horne Lake Caves Provincial Park, 334–335

Horseback riding
Leavenworth, 213
Washington, 246

Horse racing, 36
Portland, 78

Horsetail Falls, 95

Hotel Europe, 274

Hotels, 38–40. See also under cities and areas
telephone surcharge, 30

Hotel Vancouver, 270

Houseboat communities, 279

House of Mystery, 127

Houses, historic
Alaska, 369, 376, 378–379
Oregon, 113, 122, 124
Portland, 72
Victoria, 312–313
Washington, 227

Hovander Homestead Park, 225

Hoyt Arboretum, 72

Hunting, 34

Hurricane Ridge, 234–235, 246

Hyatt Vineyards Winery, 240

Ilwaco, WA, 238

Ilwaco Heritage Museum, 238

Indian Beach, 114

Indians. See Native American *headings*

Inns, 38

Inside Passage, 336

Insurance
automobile, 16
comprehensive, 14–15
flight, 14
health, 13–14
luggage, 14

trip, 14

Intermediate Theater, 66

International District, 161, 163

International Pinot Noir Celebration, 44, 123

International Rose Test Garden, 70

Island County Historical Museum, 198

Jacksonville, OR, 7, 126, 146, 150

Jacksonville Museum, 126

Japanese garden (Olympia), 232

Japanese garden (Vancouver), 281–282

Japanese Gardens (Portland), 70

Japantown, 284

Jason Lee House, 124

Jazz festivals, 6, 7

Jeff Morris Memorial Fire Museum, 68

Jewelry shops
Portland, 76
Seattle, 169

Jimi Hendrix's grave site, 167

Jogging, See Running and jogging

John D. Boon Home, 124

John McLoughlin House National Historic Site, 74

Juneau, AK, 377–378
the arts, 403–404
climate, 5
emergencies, 364
guided tours, 362–363
hotels, 398–399
native culture, 43
nightlife, 404
restaurants, 397–398
shopping, 391–392
sightseeing, 377–380
sports, 392–394
tourist information, 364

Juneau Douglas City Museum, 379

Juneau-Harris monument, 379–380

Justice Center (Portland), 67

Kakali, B.C., 280

Kake, AK, 390

Kalaloch, WA, 233

Kalamalka Lake Provincial Park, 341

Kamloops, B.C., 327, 341, 355

Kamloops Wildlife Park, 341

Kayaking
Alaska, 389, 392
British Columbia, 344–345
Seattle, 171
Vancouver, 280, 287
Whistler, B.C., 321–322

Kelowna, B.C., 327, 342, 356

Kendall, WA, 226

Ketchikan, AK, 367
arts, 404
emergencies, 364
guided tours, 363
hotels, 400
native culture, 42
nightlife, 405
restaurants, 399–400
shopping, 391
sightseeing, 367–369
sports, 392, 394
tourist information, 364, 367

Ketchikan Indian Corporation, 368

Keystone, WA, 198

Kids Only Market, 280

KikSadi Indian Park, 42, 370

Kilby General Store Museum, 343

Kingdome, 161

Kiona Vineyards, 242

Kirmse's (shop), 384–385

Kite festivals, 7

Kitimat, B.C., 340

Kitsilano Beach, 288

Klondike Gold Rush National Historical Park (Alaska), 364, 386

Klondike Gold Rush National Historical Park (Seattle), 161

Klondike Highway, 361, 385

Knox Bros. Clock, 369

Knudsen Erath (vineyard), 122

'Ksan Village, 42, 340

Kwagiulth Museum and Cultural Centre, 42

Kyan Totem Pole, 369

La Conner, WA, 226–227, 244, 253

La Conner Flats (commercial garden), 46, 227

Ladybug Theater, 73

Lafayette, OR, 44

Lake Bonneville, 95

Lake Crescent, 234

Lake Cushman, 236

Lakes District, B.C., 340

Lake Terrell Wildlife Preserve, 225

Lake Whatcom, 226

Langley, WA, 198, 200, 202

Language, 13

La Push, WA, 233

Larrabee State Park, 248

Latourell Falls, 95

Laurel Ridge Winery, 122

Leadbetter State Park, 240, 246

Leather and luggage stores, 169

Leavenworth, WA, 211–215

LeConte Glacier, 374

Lee, Bruce, 167

Legislative Building (Olympia), 231

Legislative Parliament Buildings (Victoria), 311

Lewis & Clark Interpretive Center, 238–239

Libraries
Oregon, 123
Washington, 231

Lighthouses
Alaska, 390
Oregon, 114–115, 116, 118, 119, 120

Washington, *239*
**Lime Kiln Point
State Park,** *204*
Lincoln City, OR,
*107, 116, 132,
140–141*
Linfield College, *123*
Lions Gate Bridge,
277
Lithia Park, *127*
Little Italy, *284*
Lodge facilities,
389–390
Lodging, *38–40. See
also* hotels *under
cities and areas*
Loeb State Park, *121*
Loganberry Farm, *198*
**Log Cabin Visitor
Center,** *378*
Long Beach, B.C.,
334
Long Beach, WA, *7,
239, 244, 245, 246,
253*
**Long Beach
Peninsula region**
the arts, *261*
festival, *7*
hotels, *254–255*
restaurants, *253–254*
shopping, *243–244*
sightseeing, *236–240*
sports, *244, 245, 246,
247*
tourist information,
217
transportation, *220*
Lopez Island, *203,
205, 206, 207–208*
Lost Lake, *97*
Luggage
airline rules, *8*
insurance for, *14*
Lumberman's Arch,
276
Lummi Casino, *225*
Lummi Island, *225,
244*
Lynden, WA,
225–226, 244
**Lynn Canyon
Suspension Bridge,**
283

**McKenzie Bridge,
OR,** *146*
**McLoughlin Historic
District, OR,** *74*
McMenamins on

Broadway
(brewery), *73*
McMinnville, OR, *44,
107, 123, 130, 133,
146–147*
Mail, *30–31*
Malahat, BC, *350*
Manzanita, OR, *141*
Maple Falls, WA, *226*
Maplewood Farms,
283
Marine Building, *272*
Marine Park, *273, 378*
**Marion County
Museum of History,**
123–124
**Maritime Heritage
Center** (Bellingham),
223
Maritime Museum
(Seattle), *160–161*
Maritime Museum
(Vancouver), *281*
**Maritime Museum of
British Columbia,**
312
**Maude I. Kerns Art
Center,** *125*
Medford, OR, *110,
130, 133, 147*
Medical care. *See*
emergencies *under
cities and areas*
**Meerkerk
Rhododendron
Gardens,** *198*
Merritt, B.C., *356*
Methodist Parsonage
(Salem), *124*
**Metropolitan Center
for Public Art**
(Portland), *66–67*
Mile 0, *382*
Mill Ends Park, *67*
Miniature World, *309*
Minter Gardens, *45*
Mission Mill Village,
123
Moclips, WA, *233,
255–256*
Money, *9–10*
Monrean House, *369*
Moran State Park,
204
Motels/motor inns, *38*
Motor lifeboats, *239*
Mountain climbing,
33
Washington, *245*
Mt. Angel Abbey, *44*

**Mt. Baker-
Snoqualmie
National Forest,**
226, 246, 256
Mt. Baker Theater,
261
Mt. Baker Vineyards,
226
Mt. Constitution, *204*
Mt. Golden Hinde,
335
Mt. Hood, *7, 97, 103*
**Mt. Hood National
Forest,** *97–98*
**Mt. Rainier National
Forest,** *97–98*
**Mt. Rainier National
Park,** *245, 246, 248*
Mt. Ripinsky, *382*
Mt. Shuksan, *226*
Mt. Vernon, WA, *46*
Muir, John, *380, 387*
Multnomah Falls, *95*
**Museum of
Anthropology**
(Vancouver), *41, 281,
282*
Museum of Flight
(Seattle), *164*
**Museum of History
and Industry**
(Seattle), *164*
**Museum of Natural
History**
(Bellingham), *261*
**Museum of Natural
History** (Eugene),
125
**Museum of Northern
British Columbia,**
42, 337
Museums. *See also*
Art galleries and
museums
Alaska, *367, 370–371,
372, 376–377, 379,
380, 384*
British Columbia, *332,
333, 337, 340, 343*
native culture
displays, *41–43*
Oregon, *97, 98, 113,
115, 120, 123–124,
125, 126*
Portland, *66, 67, 68,
69, 72, 73*
Seattle, *157, 160–161,
163, 164, 165*
Tacoma, *230*
Vancouver, *268, 272,*

281, 282, 283
Victoria, *309, 311,
312*
Washington, *198, 204,
223, 227, 228, 230,
232, 234, 235, 243,
261*
Music, classical
festivals, *7*
Oregon, *150*
Portland, *92, 93*
Seattle, *192–193*
Vancouver, *306*
Music, popular
Alaska, *404*
festivals, *6, 7*
Portland, *93*
Seattle, *165, 194–195*
Vancouver, *307*
Victoria, *320*
**Myrtle Edwards
Park,** *160*
Myrtlewood trees,
121

Nahcotta, WA, *239*
**Naikoon Provincial
Park,** *337, 340*
Nanaimo, B.C., *6,
41, 332–333,
350–351*
**Nanaimo Centennial
Museum,** *41, 333*
**National Exhibition
Centre and
Museum,** *340*
**National Motor Life
Boat School,** *239*
**Native American
dancing,** *388*
**Native American
sites**
Alaska, *367, 368, 369,
370, 382, 389*
British Columbia, *332,
337, 340*
Oregon, *98–99*
Seattle, *156*
Vancouver, *276*
Washington, *234*
**Native Heritage
Centre,** *41, 332*
Nature tours, *4, 329*
Naval bases, *198*
**Neahkahnie
Mountain,** *115*
Neskowin, *132*
Newberg, OR, *44,
122, 133*
Newcastle Island, *333*

New Market Theater Building, *69*

Newport, OR, *107, 117, 129, 132, 141–142*

Nike Town (factory outlet), *64, 66*

Nine O'Clock Gun, *276*

Nippon Kan Theater, *163*

Nitobe Garden, *45, 281–282*

Nooksack Falls, *226*

North Bend, OR, *107, 120, 132*

North Head Lighthouse, *239*

Northwest Trek Wildlife Park, *230*

Norwegian Independence Day celebration, *372*

Oak Harbor, WA, *198*

Oakland, OR, *147–148*

Oakridge, OR, *126*

Oaks Amusement Park, *73*

Oakwood Cellars, *242*

Ocean Park, WA, *239*

Odlin County Park, *203*

Odyssey Contemporary Maritime Museum, *160–161*

Officers' Row Historic District, *74*

Okanagan Game Farm, *342*

Okanagan Valley region

hotels, *355–358*

restaurants, *355–358*

shopping, *344*

sightseeing, *341–343*

sports, *345–346*

O'Keefe Historic Ranch, *341–342*

Old Church (Portland), *72*

Older travelers, hints for, *20–21*

Old School House Gallery and Art Centre, *334*

Olga, WA, *208*

Olympia, WA,

Olympic National Forest, *248*

Olympic National Park, *248*

Olympic Peninsula region

the arts, *261*

nightlife, *261*

shopping, *244*

sightseeing, *230–236*

sports, *245, 246*

tourist information, *220*

transportation, *220*

Omnidome Film Experience, *160*

Oneonta Falls, *95*

Oneonta Gorge, *95*

Opera

Portland, *93*

Seattle, *192, 193*

Vancouver, *306*

Orcas Island, *203–204, 205, 206, 208, 210*

Oregon, *106–107.* See *also* Columbia River Gorge and Oregon Cascades; Portland

the arts, *150*

beaches, *36–37*

business hours, *31*

children, attractions for, *127–128*

emergencies, *110*

festivals, *7*

guided tours, *111*

hotels, *135–149*

nightlife, *150*

restaurants, *119, 125, 135–149*

shopping, *129–130*

sightseeing, *111–129*

sports, *130–134*

tourist information, *2, 107, 110*

transportation, *110–111*

Oregon Caves National Monument, *129*

Oregon City, *74*

Oregon Coast Aquarium, *117*

Oregon Dunes National Recreation Area, *119, 134*

Oregon Historical Center, *66*

Oregon Maritime

Center and Museum, *68*

Oregon Museum of Science and Industry, *72*

Oregon Shakespeare Festival, *7, 126–127, 150*

Oregon Trail, *74*

Oregon Vortex, *127*

Oregon Wine Center, *111*

Oswald West State Park, *115*

Otter Crest Loop, *117*

"Our Collections" (museum), *370–371*

Outdoor equipment stores, *169*

Oyama, B.C., *341*

Oysterville, WA, *239*

Ozette Lake, *234*

Pacific Beach, WA, *233*

Pacific Center Mall, *283*

Pacific City, OR, *116*

Pacific Crest Trail, *98*

Pacific Northwest Brewing Co., *166*

Pacific Rim National Park, *334*

Pacific Spirit Park, *282*

Pacific Undersea Garden, *309, 311*

Package deals, *2–4*

Pantages Theater, *228*

Paradise, WA, *248, 256*

Parks, national

Alaska, *377, 383*

British Columbia, *334*

Oregon, *97–98, 128*

Washington, *204, 226, 247–248*

Parks, state and provincial

British Columbia, *333, 334–335, 336, 337, 340, 342*

Oregon, *97–98, 114, 115, 116, 118, 119, 120, 121, 122, 134*

Washington, *198–199, 203, 204, 236, 238, 240, 247–248*

Parksville, B.C., *334, 351*

Passports, *11*

Peachland, B.C., *341*

Penticton, B.C., *342, 356–357*

Perfume shops, *76*

Petersburg, AK, *371–372*

emergencies, *364*

festivals, *7*

guided tours, *363*

hotels, *401*

nightlife, *405*

restaurants, *400–401*

shopping, *391*

sightseeing, *371–374*

sports, *394*

tourist information, *364*

Petroglyph Beach, *42, 371*

Petroglyph Provincial Park, *41, 333*

Photographers, tips for, *12–13*

Pier 70 (shopping complex), *160*

Pike Place Market, *160*

Pioneer Museum, *115*

Pioneer Park (Ferndale), *225*

Pioneer Park (Seattle), *161*

Pittock Mansion, *72*

The Planetarium (Vancouver), *283*

Planetariums and observatories, *283*

Plane travel

airports and airlines, *21–24, 25*

Alaska, *360*

British Columbia, *327–328*

with children, *18*

discount flights, *22–24, 25*

float-plane service, *26*

luggage, *8*

Oregon, *94, 110*

in Pacific North Coast region, *25–26*

Portland, *62*

Seattle, *153*

smoking, *24*

from U.K., *25*

from U.S., *21–23*

Vancouver, *263, 266*
Victoria, *307–308*
Washington, *197, 202, 212, 220*
Point Defiance Park, *46, 229*
Point Defiance Zoo and Aquarium, *229–230*
Point Grey Beaches, *288*
Police Museum, *67*
Pontin del Rosa (winery), *242*
Port Alberni, B.C., *333*
Port Angeles, WA, *234, 257*
Port Hardy, B.C., *42, 336, 352*
Portland, OR, *61–62*
the arts, *92–93*
Chapman Square, *67*
children, attractions for, *73*
Chinatown, *69*
climate, *5*
emergencies, *63*
excursions, *93–104*
festivals, *7*
Forest Park, *74*
Glazed Terra Cotta National Historic District, *69–70*
guided tours, *63–64*
hotels, *85–92*
Japanese-American Historical Plaza, *68*
Lownsdale Square, *67*
nightlife, *93*
Officers' Row Historic District, *74*
pharmacies, *63*
Pioneer Courthouse Square, *64*
radio stations, *30*
restaurants, *69, 78–84*
Salmon Street Plaza, *67*
shopping, *64, 66, 69, 75–76*
sightseeing, *64–74*
Skidmore Old Town National Historic District, *68*
South Park Blocks, *66*
sports, *77–78*
tourist information, *63*
transportation, *62–63*
Washington Park, *68*

wineries, *44*
Yamhill National Historic District, *68*
Portland Art Museum, *66*
Portland Audubon Society, *74*
Portland Brewing, *73*
Portland Building, *66*
Portland Center for the Performing Arts, *66*
Portlandia (statue), *66*
Portland Saturday Market, *69*
Port McNeill, B.C., *42*
Port Orford, OR, *121*
Portteus Vineyards, *242*
Port Townsend, WA, *7, 235, 244, 258, 261*
Poulsbo, WA, *6*
Powell River, B.C., *335*
Powerboating, *36*
Prehistoric Gardens, *127–128*
Prince George, B.C., *327, 340*
Prince Rupert, B.C., *42, 327, 336–337, 344, 354*
Prospect Point, *277*
Prosser, WA, *242*
Puget Sound region. *See* Bainbridge Island; San Juan Islands; Whidbey Island
Puyallup, WA, *7*

Quail Run Vintners, *240, 242*
Qualicum Beach, *334*
Queen Charlotte Islands, *328, 337, 340, 344, 354–355*
Queen Charlotte Islands Museum, *340*
Queen Elizabeth Park, *45, 282*
Queets, WA, *233*
Quinault, WA, *258–259*

Radio stations, *30*
Rafting

British Columbia, *346*
Leavenworth, *213*
Oregon, *99, 131*
Vancouver, *287*
Rail passes, *16*
Railroads
Alaska, *361, 386*
Washington, *210*
Rainbow Country, *342*
Rainier Brewery, *164*
Ranches, *341–342*
Rathtrevor Provincial Park, *334*
Record shops, *76*
Recreational Equipment, Inc., *165*
Red Barn (Boeing airplane factory), *164*
Red Dog Saloon, *378*
Red Onion Saloon, *384*
Reedsport, *132*
Reid, Bill, *280*
Reid, Frank, *384*
Resorts, *39*
Restaurants, *37. See also under cities and areas*
Rex Hill Vineyards, *122*
Rialto Beach, *233*
Richmond Nature Park, *283*
Rie Munoz Gallery, *391*
Roche Harbor, WA, *204, 207*
Rock climbing, *212–213, 245*
Rock Point Oyster Company, *225*
Rockwell Lighthouse, *390*
Roderick Haig-Brown Conservation Area, *341*
Rogue River National Forest, *126*
Rollerskating, *170*
Rooster Rock State Park, *99*
Roozengaarde (commercial garden), *46, 227*
Roseburg, OR, *107, 126, 133*

Rose festival, *7*
Rose Garden at Fairhaven Park, *224–225*
Roslyn, WA, *259*
Royal Bank building, *273*
Royal British Columbia Museum, *41, 311*
Royal London Wax Museum, *309*
Running and jogging
Alaska, *393*
Seattle, *170*
Vancouver, *287*
Russian Bishop's House, *376*
Russian blockhouse and cemetery, *376*

Sailboarding, *34, 171*
Sailing. *See* Boating and sailing
Ste. Michelle Winery, *43–44, 166–167*
St. John's Church and Seaman's Center, *367*
St. Michael's Cathedral, *376*
St. Nicholas Russian Orthodox Church, *378*
Salem, OR
festivals, *7*
hotels, *148–149*
nightlife, *150*
restaurants, *148*
shopping, *129*
sightseeing, *123–124*
sports, *133*
tourist information, *107*
wineries, *44*
Salishan, OR, *116*
Salmon Falls, Fish Ladder, and Salmon Carving, *368*
Salmon Harbor, OR, *119*
Salmon Street Fountain, *67*
Sam Kee Building, *274*
Sandcastle Contest, *7, 114*
Sandy Beach, *372*

San Juan Historical Museum, 204
San Juan Island National Historic Park, 204
San Juan Islands
the arts, 210
beaches, 206
guided tours, 203
hotels, 207–210
restaurants, 206–207, 210
shopping, 205
sightseeing, 203–204
sports, 205–206
tourist information, 202
transportation, 202–203
Sappho, WA, 234
Saxman Indian Village, 42, 369
Scanlon Gallery, 391
Schreiner's Iris Gardens, 128
Science World (museum), 281
Scuba diving, 34
Alaska, 393
Sea Gulch (ghost town), 117–118
Sea Lion Caves, 118
Seal Rock (chain-saw carving), 117–118
Sea Resources Hatchery Complex, 238
Seaside, OR, 107, 114, 132
Seattle, WA, 152–153
art in public places, 156–157
the arts, 190–193
children, attractions for, 165–166
Chinatown, 156
climate, 5
downtown, 157–163
emergencies, 154
excursions, 195–215
festivals, 6, 7
free attractions, 164–165
gardens, 45–46
guided tours, 155–157
hospitals, 154
hotels, 181–190
International District, 161, 163
monorail, 154

nightlife, 193–195
pharmacies, 155
Pioneer Square, 161
radio stations, 30
restaurants, 163, 171–181
shopping, 168–169
sightseeing, 157–167
Skid Row, 161
sports, 169–171
tourist information, 154, 157
transportation, 153–154
waterfront, 155, 160
wine tour, 43–44
Seattle Aquarium, 160
Seattle Art Museum, 157, 160
Seattle Center, 163, 187–188
Seattle Children's Museum, 165
Seaview, WA, 239
Second Beach, 277
Senate Building mall (Juneau), 378
Sequim, WA, 235, 259
Sequim-Dungeness Museum, 235
Seymour Botanical Conservatory, 46, 229
Shafer Vineyard Cellars, 122
Shakes Island, 42, 370
Shakespeare Festival Exhibit Center, 127
Shakes Slough, 389
Shaw Island, 203
Sheldon Jackson College, 376
Sheldon Jackson Museum, 43, 376–377
Sheldon Museum and Cultural Center, 43, 382
Shelton, WA, 236
Shopping, 31–32. See also under cities and areas
Shore Acres State Park, 120
Sidney, B.C., 352
Silver Falls State Park, 120, 129
Silver Star Mountain, 357–358

Sinclair Centre, 273, 284
Sitka, AK, 374
the arts, 404
emergencies, 364
festivals, 7
guided tours, 363
hotels, 401–402
native culture, 42–43
nightlife, 405
restaurants, 401
sightseeing, 374–377
tourist information, 364
Sitka National Cemetery, 376
Sitka National Historical Park, 43, 377
Sitka State Pioneers' Home, 376
Siwash Rock, 277
Skagit County Historical Museum, 227
Skagway, AK, 383–384
emergencies, 364
guided tours, 363
hotels, 402–403
nightlife, 405
restaurants, 402
sightseeing, 383–386
tourist information, 364
Skating, 170
Skidmore Fountain, 68
Skidmore Fountain Building, 69
Skidmore Old Town National Historic District, 68
Skiing, 34–35
Alaska, 394
British Columbia, 346–348
Leavenworth, 212
Oregon, 98, 99–100, 133–134
Portland, 77
Seattle, 170
Vancouver, 287
Washington, 211, 226, 246
Whistler, 322
Smith, Jefferson "Soapy," 383–384
Smokehouses, 130
Snoqualmie Falls,

210–211
Snoqualmie Falls Forest Theater, 210–211
Snoqualmie Pass, 211
Snoqualmie Valley Railway, 210
Snoqualmie Winery, 44, 211
Soapy's Parlor, 384
Sol Duc Hot Springs, 234
Soleduck Hatchery, 234
Sons of Norway Hall, 373
Sooke, B.C., 41, 330, 332, 352–353
Sooke Regional Museum and Travel Infocentre, 41, 332
Southeast Alaska. See Alaska
Southeast Alaska State Fairgrounds, 7, 382
South Slough National Estuarine Reserve, 120
Space Needle, 163
Spencer Spit State Park, 203
Splashdown Park, 282–283
Sports, 32–37. See also specific sports; under cities and areas
halls of fame, 73
Spouting Horn, 116
Springfield, OR, 107, 132–133
Squalicum Harbor Marina, 223
Sri Lankan Gem Museum, 272
Stadium High School, 228
Staircase Rapids, 236
Stanley Park, 41, 275–277, 282
Stanley Park Zoo, 277, 282
State Capitol Museum (Olympia), 232
State Library (Olympia), 231
State Office Building (Juneau), 379

State of Oregon
Sports Hall of
Fame, *73*
Staton Hills Winery,
240
Steamboat, OR, *149*
Steam trains, *226,
282*
Stewart Winery, *242*
Strathcona
Provincial Park, *335*
Student and youth
travel, *16–17*
Summerland, B.C.,
341
Sunnyside, WA, *242*
Sunset Bay State
Park, *120, 134*
Sun Yat-sen, Dr., *45,
275*
Swan Lake
Christmas Hill
Nature Sanctuary,
313
Sweet Tooth Saloon,
384
Swimming, *35*

Tacoma, WA
hotels, *260–261*
restaurants, *229,
259–261*
shopping, *244*
sightseeing, *227–230*
sports, *244, 245, 246*
tourist information,
220
transportation, *220*
Tacoma Art Museum,
227
Taholah, WA, *233*
Talent, OR, *149*
Taxes, *11, 32*
Taxis
Portland, *62, 63*
Seattle, *153, 154*
Vancouver, *266*
Telephones, *30*
Tenakee Springs, AK,
390
Tenino, WA, *261*
Tennant Lake
Natural History
Interpretive Center,
225
Tennis
Alaska, *394*
Portland, *77–78*
Seattle, *170*
Terrace, B.C., *340*

Theater
Alaska, *403–404*
British Columbia, *320*
Oregon, *7, 150*
Portland, *66, 92*
Seattle, *163, 165–166,
191–192*
Vancouver, *280,
305–306*
Victoria, *320*
Washington, *191–192,
228, 261*
Theater on the
Square (Tacoma),
228
Thomas Basin, *368*
Thomas Burke
Memorial
Washington State
Museum, *164*
Thomas Creek
Bridge, *121*
Thomas Kay Woolen
Mill Museum, *123*
Three Capes Loop,
110, 116
Tillamook, OR, *110,
115, 132*
Tillamook Bay, *116*
Tillamook County
Creamery, *115*
Tillamook Head, *114*
Tillamook Rock
Light Station,
114–115
Tillicum Village, *156*
Timberline Lodge,
98, 100, 103
Tipping, *31*
Tlingit Fort, *377*
Tlingit Indians, *374,
375, 377, 383*
Tofino, B.C., *329,
333, 353*
Tongass Historical
Museum, *42, 367*
Tongass National
Forest, *389*
Toronto-Dominion
Bank building, *273*
Totem Bight State
Historical Park, *42,
369*
Totem Heritage
Center and Nature
Path, *368*
Totem poles
Alaska, *367, 368, 369,
370, 376, 377, 378,
389*

Vancouver, *276*
Totem Square, *376*
Tour groups, *2–4*
Tourist information,
*2. See also under
cities and areas*
Tour operators, *18,
19, 21*
Toy shops
Portland, *76*
Seattle, *169*
Vancouver, *285*
Trail of '98 Museum,
384
Trains, miniature,
282
Train travel. *See also
Railroads*
Alaska, *361*
British Columbia, *329*
Oregon, *94, 110, 111*
in Pacific North Coast
region, *26–27*
Portland, *62, 63*
rail passes, *16*
Seattle, *153*
from U.S., *24–25*
Vancouver, *266–267*
Washington, *221*
Whistler, *320*
Trans-Canada
Waterslides, *343*
Travel agencies,
16–17, 19
Traveler's checks, *9*
Trillium Lake, *98*
Trolleyman brew
pub, *166*
Trolleys, *154, 268*
Troutdale, OR, *95,
104*
Tualatin Vineyards,
44, 122
Tucker Cellars, *242*
Tulip festival, *6*
Tyee Wine Cellars,
122

Ucluelet, B.C., *329,
333, 353*
U'mista Cultural
Center, *42*
Umpqua Lighthouse
Park, *119*
Umpqua River
Lighthouse, *119*
United Kingdom
insurance, *15*
passports and visas,
11

plane travel from, *25*
tourist information, *2,
19*
University of British
Columbia Botanical
Garden, *282*
University of Oregon,
7, 125, 134
University of Oregon
Museum of Art, *125*
University of
Washington, *164*
Uwajimaya (Japanese
store), *163*

Vancouver, B.C., *263*
air tours, *269*
the arts, *305–306*
beaches, *37, 275, 277,
288*
Blood Alley, *274*
boat tours, *269*
business hours, *268*
Cathedral Place, *270*
children, attractions
for, *282–283*
Chinatown, *274–275,
284*
climate, *5*
consulates, *267*
downtown, *270–275*
East Indian district,
284
embassies, *267*
emergencies, *267–268*
excursions, *307–324*
festivals, *6*
free attractions, *282*
Gaoler's Mews, *274*
Gastown, *273–274*
Granville Island,
278–280
guided tours, *268–269*
Hastings Street, *272*
hotels, *270, 273, 274,
298–305*
Japantown, *284*
Little Italy, *284*
Maple Tree Square,
274
native culture, *41*
nightlife, *306–307*
parks and gardens,
45–46, 281–282
radio stations, *30*
restaurants, *277, 280,
288–298*
Robson Square, *270*
Robson Street, *270*
SeaBus, *267*

Vancouver, B.C.
(*continued*)
shopping, *268,
278–279, 280,
283–286*
sightseeing, *269–283*
sports, *286–288*
Stanley Park, *275–277*
subway, *267*
taxis, *267*
tourist information, *267*
transportation in, *263,
267*
transportation to, *263,
266–267*
travel agencies, *268*
West End, *277*
**Vancouver Art
Gallery,** *270, 282*
**Vancouver Children's
Festival,** *6*
Vancouver Club, *272*
Vancouver Island,
330. See also British
Columbia; Victoria
hotels, *349–353*
restaurants, *349–353*
shopping, *344*
sightseeing, *330–336*
sports, *346*
transportation, *328,
329*
Vancouver Museum,
41, 281, 282
**Vancouver Public
Aquarium,** *276–277*
**Van Dusen Botanical
Garden,** *45, 282*
Van Zandt, WA, *226*
Veritas Vineyard, *122*
Vernon, B.C., *341,
358*
Victoria, B.C., *309.
See also* Vancouver
Island
the arts, *319*
Bastion Square,
311–312
children, attractions
for, *312–313*
Chinatown, *312*
emergencies, *307*
festivals, *6*
gardens, *46*
guided tours, *308*
hospitals, *307*
hotels, *314–319*
Market Square, *312*
native culture, *41*
nightlife, *320*

restaurants, *314–319*
shopping, *313–314*
sightseeing, *309–313*
sports, *314*
tourist information,
307
transportation,
307–308
**Victoria Conference
Centre,** *309*
Viking festivals, *6*
Villa rentals, *40*
Visas, *11*
**Volunteer Fireman's
Museum,** *227*

**W. W. Seymour
Botanical
Conservatory,** *229*
Wahkeena Falls, *95*
Wah Mee Club, *161,
163*
Waldo Lake, *129*
Waldport, OR, *142*
**Ward Cove
Recreation Area,**
369
Warm Springs, OR,
104
**Wasco County
Courthouse,** *97*
Washington, *217. See
also* Seattle
the arts, *261*
beaches, *36–37*
business hours, *31*
children, attractions
for, *243*
emergencies, *220*
festivals, *6–7*
guided tours, *221–222*
hotels, *249–261*
nightlife, *261*
parks and forests,
247–248
restaurants, *248–261*
shopping, *243–244*
sightseeing, *222–243*
sports, *244–248*
tourist information, *2,
217, 220*
transportation, *29,
220–221*
**Washington Hills
(winery),** *242*
**Washington Park
(Portland),** *70*
**Washington Park
Arboretum** (Seattle),
45, 164

**Washington Park
Zoo,** *70*
**Washington State
Historical Society,**
229
Waterfalls
British Columbia, *335*
Oregon, *95, 120*
Washington, *210–211,
226*
Wax museums, *309*
Weather information,
4–5
Wedderburn, OR, *121*
Welches, OR, *104*
Westbank, B.C., *341*
West Coast Trail, *334*
West End Beaches,
277, 288
Western Union, *10*
**Western Washington
University,** *223, 261*
Westlake Center, *157,
168*
Whale Museum, *204*
**Whale-watching
tours**
British Columbia, *329,
333, 335*
Washington, *204, 222,
247*
**Whatcom and Skagit
Counties, WA**
sightseeing, *222–227*
sports, *244, 245, 246,
247*
tourist information,
217
transportation, *220*
**Whatcom Museum of
History and Art,**
223, 261
Whidbey Island
hotels, *201–202*
restaurants, *200–202*
shopping, *200*
sightseeing, *198, 200*
sports, *199*
tourist information,
197
transportation,
197–198
**Whidbey Island
Naval Air Station,**
198
Whistler, B.C., *321*
emergencies, *320*
festivals, *321*
guided tours, *321*
hotels, *323–324*

restaurants, *322–323*
scenic drives, *321*
sightseeing, *321*
sports, *321–322*
tourist information,
320
transportation, *320*
**White Pass and
Yukon Route,** *361,
384, 386*
**White Sulphur
Springs,** *389*
**Wickaninnish
Gallery,** *41*
Wickersham, WA, *226*
Wickersham House,
43, 378–379
Wilderness tours, *4*
Wildlife preserves
Alaska, *382*
British Columbia, *341*
Oregon, *120*
Victoria, *313*
Washington, *225,
229–230, 235*
Wildlife Safari, *128*
Wildlife viewing, *35*
**Willamette Science
and Technology
Center,** *125*
**Willamette
University,** *123*
Willamette Valley,
*44, 121–127,
129–130, 131,
132–133, 143–149*
**Willamette Valley
Wineries,** *43, 44,
107, 121–122*
Winchester Bay, *119*
Windmills, *226*
Windsurfing, *287*
Wineries
British Columbia, *342*
Oregon, *44, 107, 111,
121–122, 125–126*
Seattle, *166–167*
Washington, *43–44,
45, 196, 211, 222,
226, 235–236,
240–243*
Wine shops, *169*
Wing Luke Museum,
163
Wolfhaven, WA, *232*
Woodinville, WA, *44*
Woodland Park Zoo,
163–164
**World Forestry
Center,** *70, 72*

World Trade Center, *67*

Wrangell, AK, *357*
emergencies, *364*
guided tours, *363*
hotels, *403*
native culture, *42–43*
nightlife, *405*
restaurants, *403*
sightseeing, *369–371*
tourist information, *364, 370*

Wrangell City Museum, *42, 370*
Wright Park, *229*

Yachats, OR, *110, 118, 142–143*
Yacht races, *6*
Yakima, WA, *44*
Yakima Indian Reservation, *44*
Yakima River Winery, *242*

Yakima Valley wine country, *43, 44, 220, 240–243*
Yamhill, OR, *131, 149*
Yamhill National Historic District, *68*
Yamhill Valley Vineyards, *122*
Yaquina Head, *117*
YMCAs/YWCAs, *39, 187*
Young, S. Hall, *380*

Youth hostels, *17, 187*

Zillah, WA, *240*
Zillah Oakes Winery, *240*
Zoos
Portland, *70*
Seattle, *163–164*
Tacoma, *46, 229–230*
Vancouver, *277*

Personal Itinerary

Departure   *Date*

Time

Transportation

Arrival   *Date*   *Time*

Departure   *Date*   *Time*

Transportation

Accommodations

Arrival   *Date*   *Time*

Departure   *Date*   *Time*

Transportation

Accommodations

Arrival   *Date*   *Time*

Departure   *Date*   *Time*

Transportation

Accommodations

Addresses

Name	*Name*
Address	*Address*
Telephone	*Telephone*
Name	*Name*
Address	*Address*
Telephone	*Telephone*
Name	*Name*
Address	*Address*
Telephone	*Telephone*
Name	*Name*
Address	*Address*
Telephone	*Telephone*
Name	*Name*
Address	*Address*
Telephone	*Telephone*
Name	*Name*
Address	*Address*
Telephone	*Telephone*
Name	*Name*
Address	*Address*
Telephone	*Telephone*
Name	*Name*
Address	*Address*
Telephone	*Telephone*

Fodor's Travel Guides

Available at bookstores everywhere, or call 1–800–533–6478, 24 hours a day.

U.S. Guides

Alaska

Arizona

Boston

California

Cape Cod, Martha's Vineyard, Nantucket

The Carolinas & the Georgia Coast

Chicago

Colorado

Florida

Hawaii

Las Vegas, Reno, Tahoe

Los Angeles

Maine, Vermont, New Hampshire

Maui

Miami & the Keys

New England

New Orleans

New York City

Pacific North Coast

Philadelphia & the Pennsylvania Dutch Country

The Rockies

San Diego

San Francisco

Santa Fe, Taos, Albuquerque

Seattle & Vancouver

The South

The U.S. & British Virgin Islands

The Upper Great Lakes Region

USA

Vacations in New York State

Vacations on the Jersey Shore

Virginia & Maryland

Waikiki

Walt Disney World and the Orlando Area

Washington, D.C.

Foreign Guides

Acapulco, Ixtapa, Zihuatanejo

Australia & New Zealand

Austria

The Bahamas

Baja & Mexico's Pacific Coast Resorts

Barbados

Berlin

Bermuda

Brazil

Brittany & Normandy

Budapest

Canada

Cancun, Cozumel, Yucatan Peninsula

Caribbean

China

Costa Rica, Belize, Guatemala

The Czech Republic & Slovakia

Eastern Europe

Egypt

Euro Disney

Europe

Europe's Great Cities

Florence & Tuscany

France

Germany

Great Britain

Greece

The Himalayan Countries

Hong Kong

India

Ireland

Israel

Italy

Japan

Kenya & Tanzania

Korea

London

Madrid & Barcelona

Mexico

Montreal & Quebec City

Morocco

Moscow & St. Petersburg

The Netherlands, Belgium & Luxembourg

New Zealand

Norway

Nova Scotia, Prince Edward Island & New Brunswick

Paris

Portugal

Provence & the Riviera

Rome

Russia & the Baltic Countries

Scandinavia

Scotland

Singapore

South America

Southeast Asia

Spain

Sweden

Switzerland

Thailand

Tokyo

Toronto

Turkey

Vienna & the Danube Valley

Yugoslavia

Special Series

Fodor's Affordables

Caribbean

Europe

Florida

France

Germany

Great Britain

London

Italy

Paris

Fodor's Bed & Breakfast and Country Inns Guides

Canada's Great Country Inns

California

Cottages, B&Bs and Country Inns of England and Wales

Mid-Atlantic Region

New England

The Pacific Northwest

The South

The Southwest

The Upper Great Lakes Region

The West Coast

The Berkeley Guides

California

Central America

Eastern Europe

France

Germany

Great Britain & Ireland

Mexico

Pacific Northwest & Alaska

San Francisco

Fodor's Exploring Guides

Australia

Britain

California

The Caribbean

Florida

France

Germany

Ireland

Italy

London

New York City

Paris

Rome

Singapore & Malaysia

Spain

Thailand

Fodor's Flashmaps

New York

Washington, D.C.

Fodor's Pocket Guides

Bahamas

Barbados

Jamaica

London

New York City

Paris

Puerto Rico

San Francisco

Washington, D.C.

Fodor's Sports

Cycling

Hiking

Running

Sailing

The Insider's Guide to the Best Canadian Skiing

Skiing in the USA & Canada

Fodor's Three-In-Ones (guidebook, language cassette, and phrase book)

France

Germany

Italy

Mexico

Spain

Fodor's Special-Interest Guides

Accessible USA

Cruises and Ports of Call

Euro Disney

Halliday's New England Food Explorer

Healthy Escapes

London Companion

Shadow Traffic's New York Shortcuts and Traffic Tips

Sunday in New York

Walt Disney World and the Orlando Area

Walt Disney World for Adults

Fodor's Touring Guides

Touring Europe

Touring USA: Eastern Edition

Fodor's Vacation Planners

Great American Vacations

National Parks of the East

National Parks of the West

The Wall Street Journal Guides to Business Travel

Europe

International Cities

Pacific Rim

USA & Canada

WHEREVER YOU TRAVEL, *H*ELP IS NEVER FAR AWAY.

From planning your trip to

providing travel assistance along

the way, American Express®

Travel Service Offices* are

always there to help.

For the office nearest you, call

1-800-YES-AMEX

American Express Travel Service Offices are found in central locations throughout the Pacific Northwest.